"This terrific book provides an authoritative guide to recent philosophical work on trust, including its entanglements with justice and power. Excitingly, it also demonstrates how such work can engage deeply with urgent practical questions of trust in social institutions and emerging technologies. A major landmark for trust research within philosophy and beyond."

Katherine Hawley, St. Andrews University

"This Handbook contains insightful analyses of a variety of pressing issues about trust. There are nuanced assessments of the impact of sociopolitical biases on trust, interesting discussions about the interrelation between trust and technology, and careful reflections on people's trust – and distrust – in experts, institutions, and office-holders. All the while, the volume covers perennial problems about trust in philosophy. It's a must-read both for people who are new to this literature and for those who've long been acquainted with it."

Carolyn McLeod, Western University, Canada

"Trust is a key issue in all parts of social life, including politics, science, everyday interaction, or family life. Accordingly, there is a vast literature on the topic. Unfortunately, this literature is distributed over many disciplines. Significant advances in one field take years if not decades to reach other fields. This important anthology breaks down these barriers and allows for fruitful and efficient exchange of results across all specializations. It is timely, well done and original. It will be required reading for specialists and students for the next decade."

Martin Kusch, University of Vienna

THE ROUTLEDGE HANDBOOK OF TRUST AND PHILOSOPHY

Trust is pervasive in our lives. Both our simplest actions – like buying a coffee, or crossing the street – as well as the functions of large collective institutions – like those of corporations and nation states – would not be possible without it. Yet only in the last several decades has trust started to receive focused attention from philosophers as a specific topic of investigation. *The Routledge Handbook of Trust and Philosophy* brings together 31 never-before published chapters, accessible for both students and researchers, created to cover the most salient topics in the various theories of trust. The *Handbook* is broken up into three sections:

I. What is Trust?
II. Whom to Trust?
III. Trust in Knowledge, Science, and Technology

The *Handbook* is preceded by a foreword by Maria Baghramian, an introduction by volume editor Judith Simon, and each chapter includes a bibliography and cross-references to other entries in the volume.

Judith Simon is Full Professor for Ethics in Information Technologies at the Universität Hamburg, Germany, and member of the German Ethics Council.

ROUTLEDGE HANDBOOKS IN PHILOSOPHY

Routledge Handbooks in Philosophy are state-of-the-art surveys of emerging, newly refreshed, and important fields in philosophy, providing accessible yet thorough assessments of key problems, themes, thinkers, and recent developments in research.

All chapters for each volume are specially commissioned, and written by leading scholars in the field. Carefully edited and organized, Routledge Handbooks in Philosophy provide indispensable reference tools for students and researchers seeking a comprehensive overview of new and exciting topics in philosophy. They are also valuable teaching resources as accompaniments to textbooks, anthologies, and research-orientated publications.

Also available:

THE ROUTLEDGE HANDBOOK OF PHILOSOPHY OF THE CITY
EDITED BY SHARON M. MEAGHER, SAMANTHA NOLL, AND JOSEPH S. BIEHL

THE ROUTLEDGE HANDBOOK OF PANPSYCHISM
EDITED BY WILLIAM SEAGER

THE ROUTLEDGE HANDBOOK OF PHILOSOPHY OF RELATIVISM
EDITED BY MARTIN KUSCH

THE ROUTLEDGE HANDBOOK OF METAPHYSICAL GROUNDING
EDITED BY MICHAEL J. RAVEN

THE ROUTLEDGE HANDBOOK OF PHILOSOPHY OF COLOUR
EDITED BY DEREK H. BROWN AND FIONA MACPHERSON

THE ROUTLEDGE HANDBOOK OF COLLECTIVE RESPONSIBILITY
EDITED BY SABA BAZARGAN-FORWARD AND DEBORAH TOLLEFSEN

THE ROUTLEDGE HANDBOOK OF PHENOMENOLOGY OF EMOTION
EDITED BY THOMAS SZANTO AND HILGE LANDWEER

THE ROUTLEDGE HANDBOOK OF HELLENISTIC PHILOSOPHY
EDITED BY KELLY ARENSON

THE ROUTLEDGE HANDBOOK OF TRUST AND PHILOSOPHY
EDITED BY JUDITH SIMON

For more information about this series, please visit: https://www.routledge.com/Routledge-Handbooks-in-Philosophy/book-series/RHP

THE ROUTLEDGE HANDBOOK OF TRUST AND PHILOSOPHY

Edited by Judith Simon

Routledge
Taylor & Francis Group
NEW YORK AND LONDON

First published 2020
by Routledge
605 Third Avenue, New York, NY 10017

and by Routledge
2 Park Square, Milton Park, Abingdon, Oxon OX14 4RN

First issued in paperback 2021

Routledge is an imprint of the Taylor & Francis Group, an informa business

Publisher's Note
The publisher has gone to great lengths to ensure the quality of this reprint but points out that some imperfections in the original copies may be apparent.

Library of Congress Cataloging-in-Publication Data
A catalog record for this title has been requested

ISBN 13: 978-1-03-223570-7 (pbk)
ISBN 13: 978-1-138-68746-2 (hbk)

DOI: 10.4324/9781315542294

Typeset in Times New Roman
by Taylor & Francis Books

CONTENTS

ILLUSTRATIONS

Figures

Table

CONTRIBUTORS

Mark Alfano is Associate Professor of Philosophy at Macquarie University (Australia). His work in moral psychology encompasses subfields in both philosophy (ethics, epistemology, philosophy of science, philosophy of mind) and social science (social psychology, personality psychology). He also brings digital humanities methods to bear on both contemporary problems and the history of philosophy (especially Nietzsche), using R, Tableau and Gephi.

Cristiano Castelfranchi is Full Professor of Cognitive Science, University of Siena. The guiding aim of Castelfranchi's research is to study autonomous goal-directed behavior as the root of all social phenomena.

Fabrice Clément first trained as an anthropologist before his involvement in philosophy of mind. To check some of his theoretical hypotheses on the acquisition of beliefs, he then worked as a developmental psychologist. He is now Full Professor in Cognitive Science at the University of Neuchâtel (Switzerland).

Marc A. Cohen is Professor at Seattle University with a shared appointment in the Department of Management and the Department of Philosophy. He earned a doctorate in philosophy from the University of Pennsylvania and, prior to joining Seattle University, worked in the banking and management consulting industries.

Karen S. Cook is the Ray Lyman Wilbur Professor of Sociology at Stanford University. She has edited, co-edited, or co-authored a number of books on trust, including *Trust in Society* (Russell Sage, 2001), *Trust and Distrust in Organizations* (Russell Sage, 2004, with Roderick M. Kramer), and *Cooperation without Trust?* (Russell Sage, 2005, with Russell Hardin and Margaret Levi).

Jason D'Cruz is Associate Professor of Philosophy at the University at Albany, State University of New York. He specializes in moral psychology with a focus on trust, distrust, self-deception and rationalization.

Susan Dimock is an award-winning Professor of Philosophy and University Professor at York University in Canada. Her research interests span topics in moral and political philosophy, public sector ethics, and philosophy of law. She has authored/edited numerous books and scholarly articles.

Charles M. Ess is Professor in Media Studies, Department of Media and Communication, University of Oslo. He works across the intersections of philosophy, computing, applied ethics, comparative philosophy and religious studies, and media studies, with emphases on research ethics, Digital Religion, virtue ethics, existential media studies, AI and social robots.

Rino Falcone is Director of the CNR Institute of Cognitive Sciences and Technologies. His main scientific competences range from Multi-agent-Systems to Agent-Theory. He has published more than 200 conference, book and journal articles. Chair of "Trust in Virtual Societies" International Workshop (1998–2019). Advisor of the Italian Minister of Research (2006–2008).

Paul Faulkner is a Professor in Philosophy at the University of Sheffield. He is the author of *Knowledge on Trust* (Oxford UP, 2011), and numerous articles on testimony and trust. With Thomas Simpson, he edited *The Philosophy of Trust* (Oxford UP, 2017).

Richard Foley is Professor of Philosophy at New York University. He is the author of *The Geography of Insight* (Oxford UP, 2018); *When Is True Belief Knowledge?* (Princeton UP, 2012); *Intellectual Trust in Oneself and Others* (Cambridge UP, 2001); *Working without a Net* (Oxford UP, 1993); and *The Theory of Epistemic Rationality* (Harvard UP, 1987).

Lily Frank is Assistant Professor of Philosophy and Ethics at the Technical University of Eindhoven, in the Netherlands. Her areas of specialization are biomedical ethics, biotechnology and moral psychology. Her current research focuses on issues at the intersection of bioethics and metaethics and moral psychology.

Ori Freiman is a Ph.D. student at Bar-Ilan University. His dissertation develops the social-epistemic concepts of "trust" and "testimony" and applies them to technologies such as blockchain and digital assistants. His paper "Can Artificial Entities Assert?" (with Boaz Miller) was recently published in *The Oxford Handbook of Assertion* (2019).

Karen Frost-Arnold is Associate Professor of Philosophy at Hobart & William Smith Colleges. Her research focuses on the epistemology of trust, the epistemology of the Internet and feminist epistemology.

Triantafyllos Gkouvas is a Lecturer in Legal Theory at the University of Glasgow. His current research focuses on the jurisprudential relevance of classical pragmatism (Charles Sanders Peirce, William James, John Dewey) and the role of statutory canons as avenues for implementing constitutional and statutory rights instruments.

Sanford C. Goldberg is Professor of Philosophy at Northwestern University. He works in the areas of epistemology and philosophy of language. He is the author of *Anti-Individualism* (Cambridge UP, 2007), *Relying on Others* (Oxford UP, 2010), *Assertion* (Oxford UP,

2015), *To the Best of Our Knowledge* (Oxford UP, 2017), and *Conversational Pressure* (Oxford UP, forthcoming).

Frances Grodzinsky is Professor Emerita of Computer Science and Information Technology at Sacred Heart University in Fairfield, CT. She was co-director of the Hersher Institute of Ethics.

Edward Hinchman is Associate Professor of Philosophy at Florida State University. He works on issues pertaining to both interpersonal and intrapersonal trust, including the reason-givingness of advice, promising and shared intention, the epistemology of testimony, the diachronic rationality of intention and the role of self-trust in both practical and doxastic judgment.

Nicole Huijts is a researcher at the Human-Technology Interaction group of the Eindhoven University of Technology, and former member of the Ethics and Philosophy of Technology section of the Delft University of Technology. Her areas of specialization are the public acceptance and ethical acceptability of new, potentially risky technologies.

Klemens Kappel is Professor of Philosophy at the University of Copenhagen. His main topics of research are within social epistemology, political philosophy and bioethics.

Arnon Keren is Senior Lecturer at the Department of Philosophy, and chair of the Psyphas program in psychology and philosophy at the University of Haifa, Israel.

Bernd Lahno was a Professor of Philosophy at a leading German business school until his retirement in 2016. His research interests are in social philosophy and ethics, a prime concern being trust as a foundation of human cooperation and coordination leading to two books and numerous articles within this field.

Benjamin McMyler is an affiliate faculty member in the Department of Philosophy at the University of Minnesota. He is interested in agency, culture, and social cognition, and he has written extensively on testimony and epistemic authority. His book, *Testimony, Trust, and Authority*, was published by Oxford UP in 2011.

José Medina is Walter Dill Scott Professor of Philosophy at Northwestern University and works in critical race theory, social epistemology and political philosophy. His latest book, *The Epistemology of Resistance* (Oxford UP, 2012) received the *North-American Society for Social Philosophy Book Award.* His current projects focus on intersectional oppression and epistemic activism.

Franck L.B. Meijboom studied theology and ethics at the Universities of Utrecht (NL) and Aberdeen (UK). As Associate Professor he is affiliated to the Ethics Institute and the Faculty of Veterinary Medicine Utrecht University. Additionally, he is Head of the Centre for Sustainable Animal Stewardship (CenSAS).

Boaz Miller is Senior Lecturer at Zefat Academic College. He works in social epistemology and philosophy of science and technology, studying the relations between individual knowledge, collective knowledge, and epistemic technologies. He has recent publications in *New Media and Society* (2017) and *The Philosophical Quarterly* (2015).

Keith Miller is the Orthwein Endowed Professor for Lifelong Learning in the Sciences at the University of Missouri – St. Louis's College of Education. His research interests include computer ethics, software testing and online education.

Patricia Mindus is Professor of Practical Philosophy at Uppsala University, Sweden, and Director of Uppsala Forum for Democracy, Peace and Justice. She has an interest in legal realism, democratic theory and migration and directs research on citizenship policy in the EU, with a political and legal theory perspective.

Philip J. Nickel specializes on philosophical aspects of our reliance on others. Some of his research is in the domain of biomedical ethics, focusing on the impact of disruptive technology and the moral status of health data. He is Associate Professor in the Philosophy and Ethics group at Eindhoven University of Technology.

Onora O'Neill combines writing on political philosophy and ethics with public life. She has been a crossbench member of the House of Lords since 2000, and is an Emeritus Honorary Professor of Philosophy at Cambridge University.

Gloria Origgi is Senior Researcher at the Institut Nicod, CNRS in Paris. Her work revolves around social epistemology, philosophy of social science and philosophy of cognitive science. Among her publications: *Reputation: What it is and Why it Matters* (Princeton UP, 2018).

Nancy Nyquist Potter is Professor Emeritus of Philosophy and Adjunct with the Department of Psychiatry and Behavioral Sciences, University of Louisville. Her research interests are philosophy and psychiatry; feminist philosophy; virtue ethics; voice, silences, and giving uptake to patients/service users. Most recent publication: *The Virtue of Defiance and Psychiatric Engagement* (Oxford UP, 2016).

Kristina Rolin is Research Fellow at Helsinki Collegium for Advanced Studies and University Lecturer in Research Ethics at Tampere University. Her areas of research are philosophy of science and social science, social epistemology and feminist epistemology.

Jessica J. Santana is Assistant Professor in Technology Management at the University of California, Santa Barbara. She has published articles on computational social science methods, entrepreneurship, trust, risk, and the sharing economy in leading journals including *Social Psychology Quarterly*, *Social Networks*, and *Games*.

Naomi Scheman is an Emerita Professor of Philosophy at the University of Minnesota. Her essays in feminist epistemology are collected in two volumes: *Engenderings: Constructions of Knowledge, Authority, and Privilege* (Routledge, 1993) and *Shifting Ground: Knowledge & Reality, Transgression & Trustworthiness* (Oxford UP, 2011).

Sadjad Soltanzadeh is a Research Associate at the University of New South Wales in Canberra, Australia. His area of research is philosophy and ethics of technology. Sadjad is also an experienced mechanical engineer and a high school teacher.

John P. Sullins is Professor of Philosophy at Sonoma State University, California and co-director of the Center for Ethics, Law and Society (CELS). His research interests are computer ethics and the philosophical implications of technologies such as Robotics, AI and Artificial Life.

Andreas Tutić is a Heisenberg Fellow of the German Research Foundation and works at the Institute of Sociology at the University of Leipzig. His research focuses on interdisciplinary action theory, cognitive sociology and experimental social science.

Thomas Voss is Professor of Sociology at the University of Leipzig where he holds the chair on Social Theory. His research focuses on rational choice theory and its applications to informal institutions like norms and conventions.

John Weckert is Emeritus Professor at Charles Sturt University in Australia. He spent many years working in the ethics of information technology and the ethics of technology more generally and was the founding Editor-in-Chief of the Springer journal *NanoEthics*.

Marty J. Wolf is Professor of Computer Science at Bemidji State University in Bemidji, Minnesota, USA where he was designated a University Scholar in 2016.

ACKNOWLEDGMENTS

Trust, distributed labor, and collaboration have been central topics within this handbook, but they also characterize the process of its creation and I am thus indebted to many. First and foremost, I would like to express my sincere gratitude to the contributors for their support, geniality and patience. Not only did they contribute by writing their own chapters, they also reviewed, commented, and provided feedback on other chapters. Furthermore, I want to thank several external reviewers, who shared their expertise and provided additional feedback on many chapters and Maria Baghramian for the wonderful foreword. I am also grateful to the exceptionally professional team at Routledge, in particular Andrew Beck, Vera Lochtefeld and Marc Stratton for their assistance throughout this process. I started working on the handbook at the University of Vienna, supported by the Austrian Science Fund (Grant P23770), continued at the IT University of Copenhagen, and completed it at the Universität Hamburg. I would like to thank my colleagues at these different institutions, but particularly the members of my research group on Ethics in Information Technologies in Hamburg. In the final stages Laura Fichtner, Mattis Jacobs, Gernot Rieder, Catharina Rudschies, Ingrid Schneider and Pak-Hang Wong provided important feedback and invaluable aid. Very special thanks go to Anja Peckmann for her meticulous help. Finally, and most importantly, I would like to thank my family for their continuous support, encouragement, and patience.

FOREWORD

Western Democracies, we are told on daily basis, are facing a crisis of trust. There is not only a breakdown of trust in politicians and political institutions but also a marked loss of trust in the media, the church and even in scientific experts and their advice. The topic of trust has become central to our political and social discourse in an unprecedented fashion and yet our understanding of what is involved in trust does not seem to match the frequency and intensity of the calls for greater trustworthiness. This wonderful collection of articles will go a long way towards clearing the rough ground of the debate about trust by giving it both depth and nuance.

At one level, the need for trust and the demand for trustworthiness are basic and commonplace. Trust makes our social interactions possible. Without it we cannot conduct the simplest daily social and interpersonal transactions, learn from each other, make plans for the future, or collaborate. And yet, there is also a demandingness to trust that becomes obvious once we explore the conditions of trustworthiness. We need to trust when we are not in possession of full knowledge or of complete evidence; to trust, therefore, is to take a risk and to be susceptible to disappointment, if not outright betrayal. Trust should be placed wisely and prudently for it can have a cost. The demandingness of trust also depends on the conditions of its exercise. Not only different levels but also different varieties and conditions of trust are at issue behind the uniform sounding outcry about a crisis of trust. So, as Judith Simon, the editor of this excellent volume, observes, the right approach in the search for an in-depth understanding of trust is not to attempt to distinguishing between proper and improper uses of the term "trust," but to attend carefully to the different contexts and conditions of trust, in the hope of providing the sort of nuanced and multi-facetted perspective that this complex phenomenon deserves.

So, a notable strength of this timely book is to lay bare the complexities of the very idea of trust, the multiple forms it takes and the varied conditions of its exercise. Judith Simon has managed to bring together some of the most important thinkers on the topic in an attempt to answer what may be seen as the "hard" questions of trust; questions about the nature of trust or what trust is, questions about the conditions of trustworthiness or who is it that we should trust and, most crucially, questions about the changing aspects of trust under conditions of rapid technological and scientific transformation. Each of these sets of questions is explored in some depth in the three sections of the book and the responses make it clear that a simple account of what trust is and who we should trust cannot be given. For one thing, to understand trust, it is not enough to explore the conditions for a trusting attitude but we also need to distinguish trust from related states such as reliance and belief. We also need to calibrate it carefully against a range of contrast attitudes such as distrust and lack of trust. The finer grained analysis of the blanket term "trust" presents us with further difficult questions: Should trust be seen as a cognitive state, or a feeling, or maybe as an attitude with both cognitive and emotive dimensions? And if we were to opt for the latter response, how are we to relate the epistemic dimensions of trust to its normative and affective dimensions? Moreover, how are the above questions going to help us to distinguish between trust and mere reliance or decide if trust is voluntary or whether we have a choice in exercising or withholding it? Still further questions follow: Is trust exercised uniformly or should it be seen as falling along a spectrum where context and circumstances come to play determining roles? These foundational questions and many more are investigated with great originality and depth in the first part of the Handbook by a host of exceptional philosophers, including the doyen of philosophy of trust, Onora O'Neill.

The focus of part two is on the difficult and pressing question of "whom to trust" or, more abstractly, what the conditions of trustworthiness are. Reponses to this question largely, but not solely, depend on the theoretical and conceptual positions on trust discussed in part one. Some specific considerations, as Judith Simon rightly highlights, arise from the differences between who the subjects and objects of trust are. The headlines about "a crisis of trust" often fail to look at the important distinctions between interpersonal vs group trust and the impact of factors such as asymmetrical power relations, biases and prejudices on our judgments of trustworthiness. Other distinctions are also important, for instance does mistrust in a specific office-holder readily, or eventually, translate into mistrust in the office itself? Should we allow that the objects of trust can be abstract constructions, such as democratic systems or modes of governance in general, or should we only discuss the trustworthiness of their concrete instantiations as institutions or particular persons? Here again, the Handbook manages to throw light on important dimensions of the question of whom to trust.

Part three, I believe, makes the most urgently needed and original contribution to contemporary discussions of trust. The section deals, in particular, with scientific and technological knowledge and the trustworthiness of the testimonies that are the primary means of conveying such knowledge. Trust in experts and their policy advice has become a new political battleground of the (new) right. Populist politicians around the world have cast doubt on the advice and opinions of scientific experts on topics ranging from climate change to vaccination to economic projections, identifying claims to expertise with the arrogance of the elites. The alleged breakdown of trust in experts of course does not stop people from going to mechanics to fix their cars or to IT experts when their computers break down. Epistemic trust is also necessary for the effective division of cognitive labor which, in turn, is crucial for the smooth functioning of complex societies, so at this elemental level, trust in those who know more than we do in a particular domain is inevitable. The question of trust in experts, however, manifests itself in a striking fashion at the intersection of science and policy as well as in areas where the impact of scientific and technological developments on our lives is most radical and least tested. The book covers this important question with great success. The more general topic of trust in science and scientists, both by scientific practitioners and the general public, is discussed in an excellent article by Kristina Rolin. The article manages to bring together, very convincingly, various strands of recent discussions of the what, how, why and when of trust in science and treats the topic in an original and illuminating way. But the Handbook goes beyond the general topic of trust in science and examines some of the pressing concerns about trust in specific areas of science and technology, issues that in the long run are at least as momentous as the politically inspired recent concerns about the trustworthiness of scientific expertise. I think this editorial choice gives currency and relevance to the collection that are absent from other similar publications. Two interesting examples from quite distinct areas of breakthrough technologies – trust in nanotechnology (by John Weckert and Sadjad Soltanzadeh) and in food biotechnology (by Franck L.B. Meijboom) – illustrate the point. Food, its production and consumption, are clearly central to human life. Biotechnological innovations have created new opportunities for food production but also have led to concerns about the safety of their products. Controversies around genetically modified food is one important example of the concerns in this area. While the issue is of considerable significance to consumers and is discussed frequently in the popular media and online, philosophical discussions of the topic have been infrequent. Despite some similarities, there are different grounds for concern about the trustworthiness of nanotechnology. As in the case of biotechnologies, nanotechnology is relatively new, so its positive or negative potentials are not yet fully explored. But nanotechnology is a generalized, enabling technology used for improving other technologies, ranging from computers, to the production of more effective sunscreens, to the enhancement of weapons of war. So, the consequences of its application are even more uncertain than those of many other new technologies. The trustworthiness of nanotechnology cannot be boiled down to its effects but it should also be assessed according to the specific context of its application and the reasons for its use. Unsurprisingly then there are convergences and differences in the conditions for trust in these emerging technologies and any generalized discussion of trust in science and technology will not do justice to the complexities of the topic. It is a great strength of this book that it shows the connections, as well as the divergences, between these areas and also illuminates the discussion by cross referencing to the more abstract topics covered in part one and two, a welcome strategy that helps the reader to achieve a clearer idea of how to trace the threads connecting the core concerns of the book.

The Routledge Handbook on Trust is a unique and indispensable resource for all interested, at theoretical or practical levels, in questions of trust and trustworthiness and the editor, the contributors and the publisher should be congratulated on this timely publication.

Maria Baghramian
School of Philosophy, University College Dublin, Ireland

INTRODUCTION

Imagine a world without trust. We would never enter a taxi without trusting the driver's intention and the car's ability to bring us to our desired destination. We would never pay a bill without trusting the biller and the whole social and institutional structures that have evolved around the concept of money. We would never take a prescribed drug without any trust in the judgment of our doctor, the companies producing the drug, and all the systems of care and control that characterize our healthcare system. We would not know when and where we were born if we would distrust the testimony of our parents or the authenticity of the official records. We may even still believe that the sun rotates around the earth without trust in experts and experiments providing counter-intuitive results. Trust appears essential and unavoidable for our private and social lives, and for our pursuit of knowledge. Given the pervasiveness of trust, it may come as a surprise that trust has only rather recently started to receive considerable attention in Western philosophy.[1]

Apart from some early considerations on trust amongst friends and trust in God, and some contributions regarding the role of trust in society by Hobbes (1651/1996), Locke (1663/1988), Hume (1739–1740/1960) and Hegel (1807/1986; cf. also Brandom 2019), trust emerged as a topic of philosophical interest only in the last decades of the 20th century. This hesitance to consider trust a worthy topic of philosophical investigation may have some of its roots in the critical thrust of philosophy in the Enlightenment tradition: instead of trusting our senses, we were alerted to their fallibility; instead of being credulous, we were asked to be skeptical of others' opinions and to think for ourselves; instead of blindly trusting authorities, we were pointed to the inimical allurement of power. Senses, memory, testimony of others – all sources of knowledge, yet testimony in particular, appeared fallible, requiring vigilance and scrutiny rather than trust within the epistemological realm. In the societal and political realm, comprehensive metrics of reputation emerged and trust in authorities was gradually replaced by democratic systems based upon elections as a fundamental instrument to express distrust in the incorruptibility of those in power.

Trust seems to be a challenging concept for philosophers: prevalent and not fully avoidable, yet also risky and dangerous because it makes us vulnerable to those who let us down or even intentionally betray us. From a normative perspective then, the most pressing philosophical question is when trust rather than distrust is warranted, and the short answer is: when it is directed at those who will prove to be trustworthy. These relations between trust and distrust on the one hand, and trust and trustworthiness on the other, run as a red thread through almost all contributions to this handbook.

To provide a thorough analysis of trust while being attentive to the manifold ways in which the term is used in ordinary language, this volume is divided into three parts: (1) What is Trust? (2) Whom to Trust? (3) Trust in Knowledge, Science and Technology.

The first part of the handbook focuses on the ontology of trust, because as pervasive as trust appears as a phenomenon, as elusive it seems as a concept. Is it a belief, an expectation, an attitude or an emotion? Can trust be willed or can I merely decide to act *as if* I trusted? What is the difference between trust and mere reliance? How should we characterize the relation between trust and distrust, between trust and trustworthiness? Do the definitions of these terms depend upon each other? Trust appears to have an intrinsic value – we normally aim at being trusted and avoid being distrusted – as well as an instrumental value for cooperation and social life. This instrumental value in particular is also explored in neighboring disciplines such as sociology, psychology and cognitive science. Yet despite these values, trust always carries the risk of being unwarranted. Trusting those who are not worthy of our trust can lead to exploitation and betrayal. In turn, however, not trusting those who would have been trustworthy can also be a mistake and cause harm. Especially feminist scholars have emphasized this Janus-faced nature of trust, exploring its relation to epistemic injustice and epistemic responsibility.

The second part of the handbook asks whom we trust, thereby illuminating differences in our trust relations to various types of trustees. How does trust in ourselves differ from trust in other individuals or in institutions? One insight, which is also mirrored in many chapters of the handbook, is that the definitions and characterizations of trust depend strongly on the examples chosen. It makes a difference to our conception of trust whether we analyze trust relations between children and their parents, between humans of equal power, between friends, lovers or strangers. Trust in individuals differs from trust in groups, trust in a specific representative of the state differs from trust in more abstract entities such as governments, democracy or society. Finally, the question arises whether we can trust artificial agents and robots or whether they are merely technological artifacts upon which we can only rely. Instead of prematurely distinguishing proper and improper uses of the term trust, we should carefully attend to these different uses and meanings and their implications to provide a rich and multifaceted perspective on this complex and important phenomenon.

The third and final part of the handbook is devoted to the crucial role of trust for knowledge, science and technology. Ever since the seminal papers by John Hardwig (1985, 1991) trust has emerged as a topic of considerable interest and debate within epistemology and philosophy of science. Discussions have centered in particular around the relationship between trust and testimony, the implications of epistemic interdependence within science and beyond as well as the role and status of experts. A central tension concerns the relation between trust and evidence: how can knowledge be certain, if even scientists have to rely not only on the testimony of their peers, who may be incompetent or insincere, but also on the reliability of the instruments and technologies employed? Moreover, how can the public assess the trustworthiness of experts and decide which ones to trust, in particular in case of apparent disagreement? How do trust, trustworthiness and distrust matter within particularly contested fields of techno-scientific development, such as bio- or nanotechnology? Finally, which role do information and communication technologies play as mediators of trust relations between humans, but also as gatekeepers to knowledge and information?

Questions like these indicate that trust in general and trust in knowledge, science and technology in particular, is not only a topic of philosophical reflection but also one of increasing public concern. Trust in politics, but also in science and technological developments, is said to be in decline, the trustworthiness of scientific policy advise is being challenged, experts and expertise are considered obsolete. Without buying into hyperbolic claims regarding a contemporary *crisis of trust*, challenges to trust and trustworthiness do prevail. Understanding these concepts, their antipodes, relations and manifestations in different contexts is thus of theoretical and practical importance. The 31 chapters of this *Routledge Handbook of Trust and Philosophy* aim to further this understanding by providing answers to the questions raised above and many more. In the following, each chapter will be outlined briefly.

The volume opens with **Onora O'Neill's** chapter **"Questioning Trust,"** which emphasizes a theme that will be recurring throughout the volume, namely that from a normative standpoint trust is not valuable per se, but only in so far as it is directed at those who are trustworthy. O'Neill reminds us that trust is pointless and even risky if badly placed, and that the important task is thus to place trust well. In order to do so, we need evidence of others' trustworthiness. Such judgment of trustworthiness, however, is both epistemically and practically demanding, even more so in a world where evidence is being selected, distributed and possibly manipulated by many actors. O'Neill pays particular attention to the anonymous intermediaries that colonize the realm of the digital, thereby highlighting the relevance of information and communication technologies as mediators of trust relations, a theme to be further explored in Part III of the handbook.

The fragile yet essential normative relation between trust and trustworthiness is also at the center of **Naomi Scheman's** chapter "**Trust and Trustworthiness.**" While she agrees with O'Neill that in ideal cases trust and trustworthiness align, she focuses on instances where they come apart in different ways, pointing to questions of justice, responsibility and rationality in trusting or withholding trust. Scheman emphasizes that practices of trusting and being trusted take place within and are affected by societal contexts characterized through power asymmetries and privilege. More precisely, the likelihood of being unjustifiably distrusted as opposed to unjustifiably trusted may differ profoundly between people, placing them at unequal risk of experiencing injustices and harm. It may thus, Scheman argues, sometimes be rational for the subordinate to distrust those in power, while those with greater power and privilege ought to have more responsibility for establishing trust and repairing broken trust.

Distrust, broken trust and their relations to biases and stereotypes are also at the heart of **Jason D'Cruz's** chapter on **"Trust and Distrust."** Distrust, apart from some notable exemptions (e.g. Hardin 2004; Hawley 2014, 2017), appears to be a rather neglected topic within philosophy. Yet some have indeed argued that any solid understanding of trust must include an adequate account of distrust, not least because trust often only becomes visible when broken or questioned. Exploring the nature of distrust, D'Cruz initially analyzes the relations between trust, distrust, reliance and non-reliance, arguing that trust and distrust are contrary rather than contradictory notions: while trust and distrust rule each other out, a lack of trust does not necessarily indicate distrust. Apart from such ontological issues, D'Cruz also investigates the warrant for distrust and its interpersonal effects. People usually do not want to be distrusted, yet there are instances where distrust is rational or even morally justified, for example in cases where potential trustees are insincere or incompetent. When being unwarranted, however, distrust may come with high costs, in particular for those being distrusted. D'Cruz stresses that distrust is not only susceptible to biases and stereotypes but also has a tendency towards self-fulfillment and self-perpetuation. As a consequence, we may have reason to be distrustful of our own distrustful attitudes and a corresponding duty to monitor our attitudes of trust and distrust. These consequences are further explored in the subsequent two chapters on the relations between trust, epistemic injustice and epistemic responsibility.

Epistemic injustices occur when individuals or groups of people are being wronged as knowers. Such mistreatment can result from being unfairly distrusted, but also from being unfairly trusted as knowers. In his chapter "**Trust and Epistemic Injustice,**" **José Medina** first analyzes how unfair trust and distrust is associated to three different kinds of epistemic injustice: testimonial injustice, hermeneutical injustice (cf. Fricker 2007) and participatory injustice (Hookway 2010). By carefully unfolding how dysfunctional practices of trusting and distrusting operate on personal, collective and institutional levels and within different kinds of relations, he explores the scope and depth of epistemic injustices and draws attention to the responsibilities we have in monitoring our epistemic trust and distrust.

These responsibilities in trusting to know, but also being trusted to know, are being addressed in **Karen Frost-Arnold's** contribution on **"Trust and Epistemic Responsibility."** Stressing the active nature of knowing, epistemic responsibility places demands on knowers to act in a praiseworthy manner and to avoid blameworthy epistemic practices. Since trusting others to know makes us vulnerable, such epistemic trust requires epistemic responsibility from both the trustor and the trustee, which can be captured by the following three questions: When is trust epistemically irresponsible? When is distrust epistemically irresponsible? And what epistemic responsibilities are generated when others place trust in us?

In his chapter on **"Trust and Authority," Benjamin McMyler** focuses on the relationship between interpersonal trust and the way in which authority is exercised to influence the thought and action of others. Initially, trust and deference to authority appear similar in that they refer to instances in which we do not make up our own minds, but instead defer to reasons provided by others. There are, however, differences between trust and authority. First, while trust is often conceived as an attitude, authority is better understood as a distinctive form of social influence. Second, trust and authority can come apart: one may defer to authorities without trusting them. McMyler argues that distinguishing between practical and epistemic authority, i.e. between authority in regards to what is to be done as opposed to what is the case, may help illuminate the relation between trust and authority, and also provide insights into the nature of trust. Practical authority aims at obedient action and does neither necessarily require belief nor trust on the side of those deferring to obedience. In contrast, epistemic authority aims at being believed and trusted and is in fact only achieved if being trusted for the truth.

Focusing also on the epistemic dimension of trust, **Gloria Origgi** agrees that trusting others' testimony is one of our most common practices to make sense of the world around us. In her chapter on **"Trust and Reputation"** she argues that the perceived reputation of someone is a major factor in attributing trustworthiness and deciding whom to trust. Origgi conceives reputation as a social property that is mutually constructed by the perceiver, the perceived and the social context. Indicators of reputation are fallible as they are grounded in our existing social and informational landscape and may thus be notoriously biased by prejudices – a point stressed by many authors of this handbook – or even intentionally manipulated. Nevertheless, Origgi argues, reputation can be a valuable resource in assessing trustworthiness if we are able to pry apart epistemically sound ways of relying on others from such biases and prejudices. In analyzing different types of formal and informal reputation, Origgi develops a *second-order epistemology of reputation* which aims at providing a rational basis for using reputational cues in our practices of knowing.[2]

One of the most crucial relations pertaining to the very nature of trust concerns the distinction between trust and reliance. Whether there is a difference between trust and mere reliance and, if so, what this difference consists in has kept philosophers busy at least ever since the seminal paper by Annette Baier (1986). Following this tradition of seeing trust as a form of reliance yet requiring something more, **Sanford C. Goldberg**, in his chapter on "**Trust and Reliance,**" discusses and evaluates different approaches to characterize this special feature which distinguishes trust from reliance. One central controversy concerns the question whether this feature is epistemic or moral: is it sufficient for trust that the trustor *believes* that the trustee will act in a certain way, or does trust require a moral feature, such as the trustee's *good will* towards the trustor? Goldberg argues that these debates about the difference between trust and reliance raise important questions about the moral and epistemic dimensions of trust.

One fundamental divide among philosophers studying the nature of trust concerns the relation between trust and belief. According to so-called doxastic accounts of trust, trust entails a belief about the trustee: either the belief that she is trustworthy with respect to what she is trusted to do or that she will do what she is trusted to do. Non-doxastic accounts, in contrast, deny that trusting entails holding such a belief. In the chapter "**Trust and Belief,**" **Arnon Keren** describes and evaluates the main considerations that have been cited for and against doxastic accounts of trust. He concludes that considerations favoring a doxastic account appear to be stronger than those favoring non-doxastic accounts and defends a *preemptive reasons account of trust*, which holds that trustors respond to second-order reasons not to take precautions against being let down, arguing that such an approach neutralizes some of the key objections to doxastic accounts. The chapter also suggests that the debate about the nature of trust and the mental state required for trusting can benefit from insights regarding the value of trust.

The tension between trust and evidence is also central in **Klemens Kappel's** chapter on **"Trust and Disagreement,"** which takes its point of departure in the observation that while we all trust, we do not necessarily agree on whom we consider trustworthy or whom and what we trust. In his contribution, Kappel therefore asks how we should respond when we learn that others do not trust the ones we trust and relates his analyses to debates on peer disagreement about evidence within epistemology (e.g. Christensen and Lackey 2013). Should we decrease our trust in someone when we learn about someone else's distrust in this person? And if we persist in our trust, can we still regard the non-trusting person as reasonable or should we conclude that they have made an error in their assessment of trustworthiness? Kappel argues that these questions can only be addressed if we consider trust as rationally assessable. In critical dialogue with Keren's account, he proposes a *higher-order evidence view* according to which disagreement in trust provides evidence that we may have made mistakes in our allocation of trust which, in return, should affect our (future) allocation of trust.

Closely connected to the question of whether trust is a form of belief is the bidirectional relationship between trust and will. In the more classical direction, this concerns the question whether one can willingly trust or whether one can merely act *as if* one trusted upon will. Taking the opposite direction, however, much of **Edward S.**

Hinchman's work has focused on whether and how (self-)trust is necessary for exercising one's will. In his contribution **"Trust and Will,"** Hinchman uses this second question as a guide to answering the first, arguing that the role of trust in exercising one's will reveals how you can trust at will. The key lies in distinguishing two ways of being responsive to evidence: while trust is indeed constrained by one's responsiveness to evidence of untrustworthiness, it does not require the positive judgment that the trustee is trustworthy.

A contrasting perspective on trust contends that trust is not a form of belief, but an emotion or affective attitude. In his chapter on **"Trust and Emotion," Bernd Lahno** notes that trust is an umbrella term used to describe different phenomena in vastly different contexts. In analyses of social cooperation, which are explored in more depth in the succeeding chapters, cognitive accounts of trust tend to dominate. Such accounts, however, seem to conflate trust and reliance. Providing various examples where people appear to rely on but not to trust each other, Lahno argues that genuine trust indeed differs from mere reliance, and that accounts of trust focusing solely on the beliefs of trustor and trustee cannot explain this crucial difference. Instead, genuine trust needs to be understood as a participant *attitude towards* rather than a certain *belief about* the trusted person, entailing a feeling of connectedness grounded in shared aims, values or norms. He concludes that such an understanding of genuine trust as an emotional attitude is not just important for any theoretical understanding of trust, but also of practical relevance for our personal life and the design of social institutions.

One crucial instrumental value of trust is that it enables social cooperation, a topic which **Susan Dimock** explores in depth in the chapter "**Trust and Cooperation.**" Cooperation enables divisions of labor and specialization, allowing individuals to transcend their individual limitations and achieve collective goods. Cooperation requires trust and trust can indeed facilitate cooperation in a wide range of social situations and between diverse people, such as friends, family members, professionals and their clients and even between strangers. However, traditional rational choice theory, which understands rationality as utility maximization, condemns such trust as irrational. Arguing against this dominant view of rationality, Dimock contends, first, that cooperation is often rational, even in circumstances where this may be surprising and, second, that both trusting and being trustworthy are essential to cooperation in those same circumstances. More controversially, she also argues that even in one-shot prisoner's dilemmas trust can make cooperating not only possible but rational.

Rational choice theory is further explored in the chapter on **"Trust and Game Theory"** by **Andreas Tutić and Thomas Voss**, which describes different game-theoretic accounts of trust. Elementary game-theoretic models explicate trust as a risky investment and highlight that social situations involving trust often lead to inefficient outcomes. Extensions of such models focus on a variety of social mechanisms, such as repeated interactions or signaling, which, under certain conditions, may help to overcome problematic trust situations. Resonating with Dimock's criticism of traditional rational choice theory, Tutić and Voss conclude their chapter with a word of caution and advice for future research. The authors hold that the vast majority of game-theoretical literature on trust rests on narrow and empirically questionable action-theoretic assumptions regarding human conduct. Taking into account more recent developments in alternative decision and game theory, in particular literature on bounded rationality (Rubinstein 1998) and dual-process theories in cognitive and social psychology (Kahneman 2011), may therefore be essential to increase the external validity of game-theoretic accounts of trust.

Philosophy is not the only discipline interested in the concept of trust and insights obtained in other theoretical and empirical disciplines can serve as important inspiration and test cases for philosophical reasoning about trust. While the focus on game theory in the previous chapters already provides links to accounts of trust in other disciplines, most notably within sociology and economics, the last three chapters of Part I broaden the handbook's perspective on trust with further insights from sociology, psychology and cognitive science.

In their chapter entitled **"Trust: Perspectives in Sociology," Karen S. Cook** and **Jessica J. Santana** introduce us to sociological views on trust and explain why trust matters in society. In contrast to psychological approaches where trust is primarily viewed as a characteristic of an individual's willingness to accept vulnerability and take risks on others, they portray trust as relational, that is, as a significant aspect of social relations embedded in networks, organizations and institutions. Drawing on the works of Putnam (2000) and Fukuyama (1995), they describe recent characterizations of trust in the social science literature as an element of social capital and as an important facilitator of economic development. They conclude their analysis with a note on the value of distrust in society and how – if placed well – it can shore up democratic institutions.

Fabrice Clément opens and concludes his chapter **"Trust: Perspectives in Psychology"** by stressing a crucial difference between philosophical and psychological perspectives on trust: while philosophers traditionally ponder on normative questions, psychologists are more interested in how people actually trust or distrust in everyday life. Drawing on a number of empirical examples, Clément claims that trust manifests itself within very different scenarios, from an infant's trust in her mother to the businessman's trust in a potential partner. As a consequence, and resonating with the different perspectives on trust outlined above, conceptions on trust may depend upon the case in question and oscillate between trust as a rational choice and trust as an affective attitude. To engage with trust on a conceptual level, Clément proposes an evolutionary perspective and asks why something like trust (and distrust) would have evolved in our species. The answer he provides is that trust appears to be necessary to enable the complex forms of cooperation characterizing human social organizations, which in return provided adaptive advantages. Yet practices of trusting are fallible and blind trust would not have served humankind well. As a consequence, there was a need to distinguish reliable from unreliable trustees and Clément shows that such assessments of trustworthiness happen fast and are already present in very young children. Unfortunately, such assessments are highly biased in favor of those who we perceive as similar, and the so-called "trust hormone" oxytocin intensifies ingroup–outgroup distinctions between "us" and "them" rather than making us more trusting per se. Such empirical insights lead back to some of the normative questions addressed earlier, namely: how should we respond to such biases and which epistemic responsibilities do we have in monitoring and revising our intuitions regarding trust and trustworthiness?

Cristiano Castelfranchi and **Rino Falcone** conclude the first part of the handbook with their chapter **"Trust: Perspectives in Cognitive Science."** Cognitive Science is a cross-disciplinary research domain which draws on psychology and sociology, but also on neuroscience and artificial intelligence. In their chapter, Castelfranchi and Falcone outline the discourse around trust in cognitive science and argue for a number of controversial claims, namely that (a) trust does not involve a single and unitary mental state, (b) trust is an evaluation that implies a motivational aspect, (c) trust is a way to exploit ignorance, (d) trust is, and is used as, a signal, (e) trust cannot be reduced to reciprocity, (f) trust combines rationality and feeling, (g) trust is not only related to other persons but can be applied to instruments, technologies, etc. While the combination of rationality and feeling resonates well with debates within this part of the handbook, the possibility of trust in technologies will be explored in further detail in the next two parts.

While Part I of the handbook aims at characterizing the nature of trust through its relation to other concepts, Part II focuses on the different relations between trustors and trustees and asks: "Whom to Trust?"

Richard Foley commences this part with his chapter on **"Self-Trust,"** the peculiar case in which the subject and object of trust coincide. Focusing on intellectual self-trust, i.e. the trust in the overall reliability of one's intellectual efforts and epistemic abilities, he addresses these fundamental philosophical questions: (a) whether and for what reasons is intellectual self-trust reasonable, (b) whether and how can it be defeated and (c) how does intellectual self-trust relate to our intellectual trust in others. Acknowledging that we cannot escape the Cartesian circle of doubt (Descartes [1641] 2017), he argues that any intellectual inquiry requires at least some basic trust in our intellectual faculties. Nonetheless, given our fallibility in assessing our own capacities and those of others, we need to scrutinize our practices of trusting ourselves and others and be ready to revise them, in particular, in cases of intellectual conflicts with others. Foley concludes by arguing that despite the unavailability of non-question-begging assurances of reliability, we can have prima facie intellectual trust not only in our own cognitive faculties but also in the faculties, methods and opinions of others.

Nancy Nyquist Potter's chapter on **"Interpersonal Trust,"** further explores trust in other individuals, thereby focusing on the type of trust relation that has received most attention within both epistemology and ethics. Potter first draws attention to the vast scope of interpersonal trust relations, including relations between friends and lovers, parents and children, teachers and students, doctors and patients, to name only a few. While some of these relations persist over long periods of time, others are elusive; while some connect peers as equals, others are marked by power differences. Keeping this complexity in mind, Potter carves out some of the primary characteristics of interpersonal trust, namely that (a) it is a matter of degree, (b) it has affective as well as cognitive and epistemic aspects, (c) it involves vulnerability and thus has power dimensions, (d) it involves conversational and other norms, (e) it calls for loyalty. These characteristics indicate that even if interpersonal trust almost by definition foregrounds dyadic relations between two individuals, these do not take place in a vacuum but are affected by the social context in which they are embedded. Not only is our assessment of trustworthiness fallible and bound to systematic distortions, violent practices such as rape and assault may damage the victim's basic ability to trust others. Such instances of broken trust raise the question whether and, if so, how broken trust can be repaired, leading Potter to conclude with an emphasis on the role of repair and forgiveness in cases when interpersonal trust has gone wrong.

Not only individuals, but also institutions can be objects of both trust and distrust. In their chapter "**Trust in Institutions and Governance," Mark Alfano** and **Nicole Huijts** analyze cases of trust and distrust in technology companies and the public institutions tasked with monitoring and governing them. Acknowledging that trustors are always vulnerable to the trustee's incompetence or dishonesty, they focus on the practical and epistemic benefits of warranted trust, but also of warranted lack of trust or even outright distrust. Building upon Jones' (2012) notions of "rich trustworthiness" and "rich trustingness" and expanding it from dyadic relations to fit larger social scales, they argue that private corporations and public institutions have compelling reasons to be and to appear trustworthy. Based upon their analyses, Alfano and Huijts outline various policies that institutions can employ to signal trustworthiness reliably. In the absence of such signals, individuals or groups, in particular those who have faced or still face oppression, may indeed be warranted in distrusting the institution.

A specific type of public institution where trust plays a crucial role is the legal system. In their chapter **"Trust in Law," Triantafyllos Gkouvas** and **Patricia Mindus** address the manifold issues of trust emerging in the operations of legal systems with regard to both legal doctrine and legal practice. Following Holton (1994), they assume that trust invites the adoption of a *participant stance* from which a particular combination of reactive attitudes is deemed an appropriate response towards those we regard as responsible agents. This *responsibility-based* conception of trust is consistent with the widely accepted understanding that addressees of legal requirements are practically accountable for their fulfillment. Building upon this understanding of trust, Mindus and Gkouvas outline in four subsequent sections the legal relevance of trust in different theories of law which, more or less explicitly, associate the participant perspective on trust with one of the following four basic concepts of law: sociological, doctrinal, taxonomic and aspirational.

The role of trust in yet another important societal realm is addressed in the chapter by **Marc A. Cohen.** His chapter on **"Trust in Economy"** commences with a critique of Gambetta's (1988) influential account of trust, which takes trust to be an expectation about the trustee's likely behavior. While Gambetta's and other expectation-based accounts can explain certain highly relevant effects of trust in economics – e.g. in facilitating cooperation or reducing transaction costs – they cannot capture the possibility of betrayal. After all, if a trustee does not behave as expected, this unfulfilled expectation should merely result in surprise, but not in the feeling of betrayal. How then can we account for this common reaction to being let down? Cohen argues that explaining this reaction requires a moral account of trust based upon notions of commitment and obligation. It is from such a moral perspective that Cohen offers an alternative reading of some of the most influential accounts of trust in economics, namely the works by Fukuyama (1995), Zucker (1986), Coleman (1990) and Williamson (1993), in order to explain what trust adds to economic interactions.

Finally, we turn towards two specific types of technology as potential objects of trust: artificial agents and robots as their embodied counterparts. While many philosophers hold that we cannot trust, but merely rely upon, technologies, some have argued that our relation to artificial agents and robots, in particular to those equipped with learning capacities, may differ from reliance in other types of technology.

In **"Trust in Artificial Agents," Frances Grodzinsky, Keith Miller** and **Marty J. Wolf** outline work on trust and artificial agents over the last two decades, arguing that this research may shed some new light on philosophical accounts of trust. Trust in artificial agents can be apprehended in various ways: as trust of human agents in artificial agents, as trust relations amongst artificial agents, and finally as trust placed in human agents by artificial agents. Grodzinsky et al. first outline important features of artificial agents and highlight specific problems in regards to trust and responsibility which may occur for self-learning systems, i.e. for artificial agents which can autonomously change their programming. Assessing various philosophical accounts of trust in the digital realm, they propose an *object-oriented model of trust*. This model is based on the premise that there is an overarching notion of trust found in both face-to-face and electronic environments which entails four attributes: predictability, identity, transparency, reliability. They conclude by arguing that attending to the differences and similarities between trust in human and artificial agents may inform and advance our understanding of the very concept of trust.

In the chapter **"Trust in Robots," John P. Sullins** argues that robots are an interesting subset of the problem of trusting technologies in general, in particular because robots can be designed to exploit the deep pro-social capacities humans naturally have to trust other humans. Since some robots can move around in our shared environment and appear autonomous, we tend to treat them in similar ways to animals and other humans and learn to "trust" them. Distinguishing trust from *ethically justified trust* in robots, the chapter analyzes the ethical consequences of our usage of and trust in such technologies. Sullins concludes that carefully assessing and auditing the design, development and deployment of robots may be necessary for the possibility of an ethically justified level of trust in these technologies. Similar conclusions will be reached in regards to other types of technologies in the next part of the handbook.

Finally, Part III focuses on the role of "Trust in Knowledge, Science and Technology" and explores research of trust particularly in epistemology and philosophy of science as well as within philosophy of technology and computer ethics.

One central path to knowledge, apart from perception, memory or inference, is testimony – or learning through the words of others. That testimonial uptake can be a matter of trust seems obvious: we may believe what others say because we trust them. Yet how exactly trust engages with the epistemology of testimony is far from obvious. In his chapter on **"Trust and Testimony," Paul Faulkner** outlines the central controversies regarding the role of trust in testimony, in particular concerning the question whether trust is a doxastic attitude, thereby involving a belief in the trustworthiness of the trusted, or not. Faulkner argues that metaphysical considerations do not decide this question, but that epistemological considerations favor a non-doxastic view of trust. His conclusion is that trust can only be given a meaningful epistemic role by the *assurance theory of testimony.*

Trust in testimony, particularly trust in the testimony of scientists, is also discussed in the next chapter. In **"Trust and Distributed Epistemic Labor," Boaz Miller** and **Ori Freiman** explore the different properties that bind individuals, knowledge and communities together. Proceeding from Hardwig's (1991) seminal paper on the trust in knowledge and his arguments regarding the necessity for trust in other scientists' testimonies for the creation of advanced scientific knowledge, they ask how trust is grounded, formed and breached within and between different disciplines as well as between science and the public. Moreover, they explore who and what counts as genuine objects of trust, arguing that whether or not we consider collective entities or even artifacts objects of genuine trust may not only affect our understanding of research and collective knowledge, but is also relevant to debates about the boundaries of collective agency and extended cognition.

We have seen that trust plays an important role within research groups, scientific communities and the relations these communities have with the society. In her chapter on **"Trust in Science," Kristina Rolin** therefore addresses the question of what can ground rational epistemic trust within and in science. Trust is epistemic, she argues, when it provides epistemic justification for one's beliefs, and epistemic trust is rational when it is based on evidence of the right kind and amount. Her chapter discusses different answers to the following questions: What can ground rational epistemic trust in an individual scientist? What can ground rational trust in (or reliance on) the social practices of scientific communities and the institutions of science?

Trust is not only of vital concern for science, but also for medicine. In their chapter **"Trust in Medicine," Philip J. Nickel** and **Lily Frank** argue that trust is important to the identity of those who deliver care such as physicians, nurses and pharmacists, and has remained important through a wide range of technological and institutional changes to the practice of medicine. They consider philosophical accounts of trust in medicine at three levels: the level of physician–patient relationships, the level of professions and the level of the institutions of medicine. Nickel and Frank conclude by considering whether some anticipated future changes in the practice of medicine, in particular in regards to the increasingly mediating role of technology, might be so fundamental that they may reduce the importance of interpersonal trust in medicine.

The questions of how technologies can affect or mediate trust amongst humans and whether they can even be proper objects of trust and distrust themselves are of central concern for the remaining chapters of this handbook.

Another contested field of technology, in which a lack of public trust is sometimes lamented, especially by those promoting it, is biotechnology. Focusing on **"Trust in (Food) Biotechnology," Franck L.B. Meijboom** argues that part of the controversy surrounding food biotechnology arises from uncertainties and risks related to the technology itself, whereas other concerns arise from the ethical and socio-cultural dimensions of food. This dual source of concern has important implications on how a perceived lack of trust could potentially be addressed. Yet, instead of framing public hesitancy towards genetically modified food as a *problem of trust*, Meijboom advises that it should rather be conceived and addressed as a *problem of trustworthiness*. While being and signaling trustworthiness cannot guarantee trust, it appears to be the most ethical and, over the long-term, also the most promising path towards trust. In the context of food biotechnology, showing oneself worthy of trust implies awareness of and clear communication about one's competence and motivation.

The first question addressed by **John Weckert** and **Sadjad Soltanzadeh** in their chapter on **"Trust in Nanotechnology"** is whether we can actually talk about trust in nanotechnology or whether we then conflate trust with reliance. If we contend that yes, we can rightly talk about trust in nanotechnology, the follow-up question then is: what exactly do we trust when we trust nanotechnology? Does trust in nanotechnology refer to trusting a field of research and development, a specific product, a specific producer, protocols, oversight institutions or all of those together? Weckert and Soltanzadeh carefully unravel the question what it may mean to trust in nanotechnology and in what ways such trust may differ from mere reliance in technological artifacts. They conclude by arguing that nanotechnology can be trusted in a thin sense if we choose to trust the technology itself and in a thick sense if trust is directed to the scientists, engineers or regulators involved in nanotechnology, thereby reserving trust in a rich sense to human actors or institutions.

Finally, **Charles M. Ess** investigates the relationship between **"Trust and Information and Communication Technologies,"** i.e. technologies which increasingly mediate trust relations between humans. He begins with K.E. Løgstrup's account of trust as requiring embodied co-presence, initiating a philosophical anthropology which emphasizes human beings as both rational and affective, and as relational autonomies. Aligning this view on human beings with both virtue ethics and Kantian deontology offers a robust account of the conditions of human-to-human trust. However, several features and affordances of online environments challenge these conditions, as especially two examples illustrate: pre-emptive policing and loss of trust in (public) media. Ess concludes by arguing that virtue ethics and contemporary existentialism offer ways to overcome challenges to trust posed by digital media. These include the increasingly central role of virtue ethics in technology design, and the understanding that trust is a virtue, i.e. a capability that must be cultivated if we are to achieve good lives of flourishing and meaning.

Notes

1 For an overview please confer the entries on trust in the *Stanford Encyclopedia of Philosophy* (McLeod 2015) and the *Oxford Bibliographies in Philosophy* (Simon 2013). More recent monographs and anthologies on trust include Hawley (2012), Faulkner and Simpson (2017) and Baghramian (2019).

2 The epistemic dimension of trust focused upon in the chapters by McMyler and Origgi will be further explored in several chapters in Part III of this handbook, most notably in the chapters by Faulkner and Rolin, as well as by Miller and Freiman.

References

Baghramian, M. (2019) *From Trust to Trustworthiness.* New York: Routledge.

Baier, A. (1986) "Trust and Antitrust," *Ethics* 96: 231–260.

Brandom, R.B. (2019) *A Spirit of Trust: A Reading of Hegel's Phenomenology*, Cambridge, MA: Harvard University Press.

Christensen, D. and Lackey, J. (eds.) (2013) *The Epistemology of Disagreement New Essays*, Oxford: Oxford University Press.

Code, L. (1987) *Epistemic Responsibility*, Hanover, NH: Brown University Press.

Coleman, J.S. (1990) *The Foundations of Social Theory*, Cambridge, MA: Harvard University Press.

Descartes, R. ([1641] 2017) *Meditations on First Philosophy*, J. Cottingham (trans.), Cambridge: Cambridge University Press.

Faulkner, P. and Simpson, T. (eds.) (2017) *The Philosophy of Trust*, Oxford: Oxford University Press.

Fricker, M. (2007) *Epistemic Injustice: Power and Ethics in Knowing*, New York: Oxford University Press.

Fukuyama, F. (1995) *Trust: The Social Virtues and the Creation of Prosperity*, New York: Free Press.

Gambetta, D. (1988) "Can We Trust Trust?" in D. Gambetta (ed.), *Trust: Making and Breaking Cooperative Relations*, New York: Basil Blackwell.

Hardin, R. (2004) *Distrust*, New York: Russel Sage Foundation.

Hardwig, J. (1985) "Epistemic Dependence," *The Journal of Philosophy* 82(7): 335–349.

Hardwig, J. (1991) "The Role of Trust in Knowledge," *The Journal of Philosophy* 88(12): 693–708.

Hawley, K. (2012) *Trust: A Very Short Introduction*, Oxford: Oxford University Press.

Hawley, K. (2014) "Trust, Distrust and Commitment," *Noûs* 48(1): 1–20.

Hawley, K. (2017) "Trust, Distrust, and Epistemic Injustice," in I.J. Kidd, J. Medina and G. Pohlhaus Jr. (eds.), *The Routledge Handbook of Epistemic Injustice*, New York: Routledge.

Hegel, G.W.F. ([1807] 1986) *Phänomenologie des Geistes*, Frankfurt: Suhrkamp Verlag.

Hobbes, T. ([1651] 1996) "Leviathan," in R. Tuck (ed.), *Leviathan*, Cambridge: Cambridge University Press.

Holton, R. (1994) "Deciding to Trust, Coming to Believe," *Australasian Journal of Philosophy* 72 (1): 63–76.

Hookway, C. (2010) "Some Varieties of Epistemic Injustice: Reflections on Fricker," *Episteme* 7(2): 151–163.

Hume, D. ([1739–1740] 1960) *A Treatise of Human Nature*, L.A. Selby-Bigge (ed.), London: Oxford University Press.

Jones, K. (2012) "Trustworthiness," *Ethics* 123(1): 61–85.

Kahneman, D. (2011) *Thinking, Fast and Slow*, London: Penguin Books.

Locke, J. ([1663] 1988) *Two Treatises of Government*, Cambridge: Cambridge University Press.

Løgstrup, K.E. ([1956] 1971) *The Ethical Demand*, Philadelphia: Fortress Press. [Originally published as Den Etiske Fordring, Copenhagen: Gyldendal.]

McLeod, C. (2015) "Trust," in E.N. Zalta (ed.), *The Stanford Encyclopedia of Philosophy.* https://plato.stanford.edu/archives/fall2015/entries/trust/

Putnam, R. (2000) *Bowling Alone: The Collapse and Revival of American Community*, New York: Simon & Schuster

Rubinstein, A. (1998) *Modeling Bounded Rationality*, Cambridge: MIT Press.

Simon, J. (2013) "Trust," in D. Pritchard (ed.), *Oxford Bibliographies in Philosophy*, New York: Oxford University Press. www.oxfordbibliographies.com/view/document/obo-9780195396577/obo-9780195396577-0157.xml

Williamson, O.E. (1993) "Calculativeness, Trust, and Economic Organization," *Journal of Law and Economics* 36: 453–486

Zucker, L.G. (1986) "Production of Trust: Institutional Sources of Economic Structure, 1840–1920," *Research into Organizational Behavior* 8: 53–111.

PART I

What is Trust?

1
QUESTIONING TRUST

Onora O'Neill

It is a cliché of our times that trust has declined, and widely asserted that this is a matter for regret and concern, and that we should seek to "restore trust." Such claims need not and usually do not draw on research evidence. Insofar as they are evidence-based – quite often they are not – they are likely to reflect the findings of some of the innumerable polls and surveys of levels of trust that are commissioned by public authorities, political parties or corporations, or other organizations, are carried out by polling companies,[1] and whose findings are then published either by those who commissioned the polls, by the media or by interested parties.

Even when polls and surveys of public attitudes of trust and mistrust are technically adequate, the evidence they provide cannot show that there has been a *decline* in trust. That would also require robust comparisons with earlier evidence of public attitudes of trust and mistrust to the same issues – if available. And even when it is possible to make such comparisons, and they indicate that trust has declined, this may still not be a reason for seeking to "restore trust." A low (or reduced) level of trust can provide a reason for seeking to "restore" trust only if there is *also* evidence that those who are mistrusted, or less trusted, are in fact *trustworthy*: and this is not generally easy to establish (see Medina, this volume).

In short, polls and surveys of attitudes or opinions do not generally provide evidence of the trustworthiness or the lack of trustworthiness of those about whom attitudes or opinions are expressed. Trust may be misplaced in liars and fraudsters, in those who are incompetent or misleading, and in those who are untrustworthy in countless other ways. Equally mistrust and suspicions may be misplaced in those who are trustworthy in the matters under consideration. Judgments of trustworthiness and of lack of trustworthiness matter greatly, but attitudinal evidence is not enough to establish them. Trustworthiness needs to be evidenced by establishing that agents and institutions are likely to address tasks and situations with reliable honesty and competence.

Evidence of attitudes is therefore not usually an adequate basis for claiming that others are or are not trustworthy in some matter. Yet such evidence is much sought after, and can be useful for various other purposes, including persuasion and reputation management. Here I shall first outline some of those other uses, and then suggest what further considerations are relevant for placing and refusing trust intelligently. Broadly speaking, my conclusion will be that doing so requires a combination of epistemic and practical judgment.

1.1 The Limits of Attitudinal Evidence

Investigations of trust that are based on opinion polls and surveys can provide evidence of respondents' generic attitudes of trust or mistrust in the activity of types of institution (e.g. banks, companies, governments), or types of office-holder (e.g. teachers, scientists, journalists, politicians). Responses are taken as evidence of a *trust level*, which can be compared with trust levels accorded to other office-holders or institutions, and these comparisons can be tabulated to provide *trust rankings* for a range of types of institutions or office-holder at a given time. Repeated polling may also provide evidence of changes in trust levels or in trust rankings for types of institution or office-holder across time.

However, attitudinal evidence about trust levels and rankings has limitations. Most obviously, a decline or rise in reported levels of trust in specific types of institution or office-holder across time can be detected only by *repeated* polling, using the same or comparable methods. However, for the most, part polling was less assiduous and frequent in the past than it is today, so reliable comparisons between past and present trust levels and rankings are often not available. And where repeated and comparable polls have been conducted, and reliable comparisons are feasible, the evidence is not always that trust levels have declined, or indeed that trust rankings for specific types of institution and office-holder have changed. For example, in the UK journalists and politicians have (for the most part) received low trust rankings in attitudinal polls in the past and generally still do, while judges and nurses have received high trust rankings in polls in the past and generally still do.

Even where polling suggests that levels of trust have declined, the evidence they offer must be treated with caution. Polls and surveys collate evidence about informants' *generic attitudes* to *types* of institution or to *types* of office-holder, but cannot show whether these attitudes are well-directed. But while the evidence that polls and surveys of trust levels provide cannot show who is or who is not trustworthy, trust rankings can be useful for some other quite specific purposes. I offer two examples.

One case in which trust rankings are useful is in summarizing consumer rankings of the quality and performance of *standardized products or services*, when these rankings are based on combining or tabulating the views of *a wide range of consumers*. For example, trust rankings of hotels or restaurants, of consumer durables or retail outlets, can be usefully informative because they are *not* mere expressions of generic attitudes. Such rankings reflect the *experience* of those who have bought and used (or tried to use!) a specific standardized product or service, so can provide relevant evidence for others who are considering buying or using the same product or service.

However, it is one thing to aggregate ratings of standardized products and services provided by those who have had some experience of them, and quite another to crowd-source views of matters that are not standardized, or to rely on ratings of standardized products or services that are provided by skewed (let alone gerrymandered) samples of respondents. Reputational metrics will not be a reliable guide to trustworthiness if the respondents whose attitudes are summarized are selected to favor or exclude certain responses (see Origgi, this volume).

A second context in which the attitudinal evidence established by polling can be useful is for persuading or influencing those who hold certain attitudes. Here attitudinal evidence is used not as a guide for those who are planning like purchases or choices, but for quite different (and sometimes highly manipulative) purposes.

Some uses of polling evidence are entirely reputable. For example, marketing departments may use attitudinal evidence to avoid wasting money or time cultivating those unlikely to purchase their products. Some are more dubious. For example, political parties may use evidence about political attitudes, including evidence about attitudes of trust in mistrust in specific policies and politicians, to identify which "demographics" they can most usefully cultivate, how they might do so, and where their efforts would be wasted. In some cases this is used to manipulate certain groups by targeting them with specific messages, including misinformation and disinformation.[2] Information about generic attitudes, and in particular about generic attitudes of trust and mistrust, can be useful to marketing departments, political parties and other campaigning organizations *whether or not those attitudes are evidence-based* because the evidence is not used to provide information for others with like interests or plans, but as a basis for influence or leverage. I shall not here discuss whether or how the use of polling results to target or orchestrate campaigning of various sorts may damage trust – including trust in democracy – although I see this as a matter of urgent importance in a digital world.[3]

1.2 Judging Trustworthiness

Once we distinguish the different purposes to which attitudinal evidence about trust levels can be put, we have reason to reject any unqualified claim that where trust is low (or has declined) it should be increased (or "restored"). In some situations increasing or restoring trust may be an improvement, and in others it will not. Nothing is gained by raising levels of trust or by seeking to restore (supposed) former levels of trust unless the relevant institutions or office-holders are *actually* trustworthy. Placing trust well matters because trustworthiness is a more fundamental concern.[4]

Seeking to gain (more) trust for institutions or individuals that are not trustworthy is more likely to compound harm. The point is well illustrated by the aptly named Mr. Madoff, who made off with many people's money by running a highly successful Ponzi scheme that collapsed during the 2008 banking crisis. It would have been worse, not better, if Madoff had been more trusted, or trusted for longer – and better if he had been less trusted, by fewer people, for a shorter time, since fewer people would then have lost their money to his scam. Aiming to "restore" or increase trust will be pointless or damaging without evidence that doing so will match trust to levels of trustworthiness. By the same token, mistrust is not always damaging or irrational: it is entirely reasonable to mistrust the untrustworthy (see D'Cruz, this volume).

Aligning trust with trustworthiness, and mistrust with untrustworthiness is not simple. It requires intelligent judgment of others' trustworthiness or untrustworthiness, and the available evidence may not reveal clearly which agents and which institutions are trustworthy in which matters. Typically we look for evidence of reliable competence and honesty in the relevant activities, and typically the evidence we find underdetermines judgments of trustworthiness or lack of trustworthiness.

There are, I think, two quite distinct reasons why this is the case. The first is that available evidence about trustworthiness may be epistemically complex and inconclusive. Judging any particular case will usually require two types of epistemic judgment. Judgment will be needed both to *determine* whether a given agent or institution is trustworthy or untrustworthy in some matter, and to *interpret* evidence that could be taken in a range of ways. Both *determining* (alternatively *determinant*, or *subsumptive*) and *reflective* judgment are indispensable in judging whether some institution or office-holder is trustworthy in some matter.[5]

But determinant and reflective judgment are only part of what is needed in judging trustworthiness and lack of trustworthiness. Judgments of trustworthiness also usually require *practical* judgment. Practical judgment is needed not in order to classify particular agents and institutions as trustworthy or untrustworthy, but to guide the placing or refusal of trust where evidence is incomplete, thereby shaping the world in some small part. Practical judgment is not judgment of a particular case, but judgment that guides action and helps to shape a new or emerging feature of some case.

Decisions to place or refuse trust often have to go beyond determining or interpreting existing evidence. For example, where some agent or agency has meager powers it may make sense to place *more* trust in them than is supported by available evidence or any interpretation of the available evidence, for example because the downside of getting it wrong would be trivial or because the experience of being trusted may influence the other party for the better. In other cases there may be reason to place *less* trust than the available evidence or any interpretation of that evidence suggests is warranted, for example because the costs of misplacing trust would be acutely damaging.[6]

Making practical judgments can be risky. If trust and mistrust are badly placed, the trustworthy may be mistrusted, and the untrustworthy trusted. Both mismatches matter. When we refuse to trust others who are in fact trustworthy we may worry and lose opportunities, not to mention friends and colleagues, by expressing suspicions and by intrusive monitoring of trustworthy people. Those who find their trustworthiness wrongly doubted or challenged may feel undermined or insulted, and become less sure whether the effort of being trustworthy is worthwhile. And when we mistakenly trust those who are in fact untrustworthy we may find our trust betrayed, and be harmed in various, sometimes serious, ways. So in placing and refusing trust intelligently we have to consider not only where the evidence points and where it is lacking and where interpretation is needed but also the costs and risks of placing and misplacing trust and mistrust. Judging trustworthiness is *both* epistemically *and* practically demanding.

1.3 Aligning Trust with Trustworthiness in Daily Life

The epistemic challenges of placing and refusing trust well despite incompleteness of evidence are unavoidable in daily life. A comparison with the equally daily task of forming reliable beliefs is suggestive. Both in scientific inquiry and in daily life we constantly have to reach *beliefs* on the basis of incomplete rather than conclusive evidence, and do so by seeking *relevant* evidence for *specific* claims and by accepting that further check and challenge to those beliefs may require us to change them. Both in institutional and in daily life we constantly have to place or refuse *trust* on the basis of incomplete rather than conclusive evidence of others' trustworthiness.

However trust and mistrust can be placed intelligently by relying on *relevant* evidence about *specific* matters, by allowing for the possibility that further evidence may emerge and require reassessment, and also by addressing *practical questions* about the implications of trusting or refusing to trust in particular situations. In judging others' trustworthiness we often need to consider a fairly limited range of *specific* evidence. If I want to work out whether a school can be trusted to teach mathematics well, whether a garage can be trusted to service my car, or whether a colleague can be trusted to respect confidentiality, I need to judge the trustworthiness of that particular school, garage or colleague *in the relevant matter* – and any generic attitudes that others hold about average or typical schools, garages or colleagues will be (at most) marginally relevant. We are not lemmings, and can base our judgments of trustworthiness in particular cases on relevant evidence, rather than on others' generic attitudes.

Typically we need to consider a limited range of quite specific questions. Is A's claim about an accident that damaged his car honest? Is B's surgical competence adequate for her to undertake a certain complex procedure? Assuming that C is competent to walk home from school alone, and honestly means to cross the road carefully, can we be sure that he will *reliably* do so when walking with less diligent school friends? Is he impetuous or steady, forgetful or organized?

In these everyday contexts, judging trustworthiness and lack of trustworthiness may be demanding, but may also be feasible, quick and intuitive. Indeed, judging trustworthiness and untrustworthiness is so familiar a task that it is easy to overlook how complex and subtle the epistemic and practical capacities used in making these judgments often are. Placing and refusing trust in everyday matters often relies on complex and subtle cultural and communicative capacities, such as abilities to note and respond to discrepancies between others' tone, words and action. These capacities are not, of course, infallible but they are often sufficient for the purpose, and can sometimes be reinforced by additional and more intrusive checks and investigation if warranted.

1.4 Aligning Trust with Trustworthiness in Institutional Life

Placing trust and mistrust well can be harder in institutional settings, and particularly so in the large and complex institutions that now dominate public and corporate life (see Alfano and Huijts, this volume). Here too our central *practical* aim in placing and refusing trust is to do so *intelligently*, by aligning trust with trustworthiness, and mistrust with untrustworthiness. But since much public, professional and commercial life takes place in large and complex institutions, and involves transactions that link many office-holders and many parts of many institutions to unknown others, it can be much harder to judge trustworthiness. Indeed, the assumption that there is a general decline in trust may not reflect greater untrustworthiness, but rather the current domination of institutional over personal connections, of the *system world* over the *life world*.[7] Some standard ways of addressing the additional demands of placing and refusing trust intelligently have been well entrenched in institutional life, but they also raise problems.

Two types of approach have been widely used to improve the alignment of trust with trustworthiness in complex institutional contexts. Some approaches aim to raise levels of trustworthiness *across the board*, typically by strengthening law, regulation and accountability. If this can be done the likelihood that trust will be placed in untrustworthy institutions or office-holders can be reduced. Other approaches seek to support capacities to place and refuse trust intelligently by making evidence of others' trustworthiness – or lack of trustworthiness – more available and more public.

Approaches that aim to improve trustworthiness often combine these forward-looking and retrospective elements. Forward-looking measures include establishing clearer and stricter requirements for trustworthy action, and for demonstrating trustworthiness, as well as stronger measures to deter and penalize untrustworthy action. The rule of law, a non-corrupt court system, and enforcement of contracts and agreements and penalties for their breach are standard ways of supporting and incentivizing trustworthy action. More laws are enacted; legislation in different jurisdictions is better coordinated; primary legislation is supplemented with additional regulation and with copious guidance and (where relevant) by setting more precise technical standards (see Gkouvas and Mindus, this volume).

In parallel with these forward-looking measures for improving trustworthiness, retrospective measures for holding institutions and office-holders to account have also often been strengthened. These retrospective measures include a wide range of measures to secure accountability by monitoring and recording compliance with required standards and procedures. However, approaches to strengthening accountability have a downside. They are often time-consuming, may be counterproductive, and at worst may undermine or damage the very performance for which office-holders and institutions are supposedly being held to account.[8] Over-complex ways of holding institutions and office-holders to account are widely derided by those to whom they are applied, and sometimes undermine rather than support capacities to carry the central tasks of institutions and of professionals. At the limit they generate perverse incentives or incentives to "game" the system. Even when incentives are not actually perverse, they may offer limited evidence that is useful for placing or refusing trust intelligently.

A second range of measures that supposedly improve trustworthiness focuses neither on regulating institutions and their office-holders, nor on holding them to account for compliance, but on making information about their action and their shortcomings more *transparent*, thereby enabling others to judge their trustworthiness – or untrustworthiness – for themselves. Transparency is generally understood as a matter of placing relevant information in the public domain. This can provide incentives for (more) trustworthy action, since untrustworthy performance *may* come to light, and *may* be penalized. The approach is not new: company accounts and auditors' reports have long been placed in the public domain, and similar approaches have been taken in many other matters.

However, transparency is often not particularly helpful for those who need to place or refuse trust in specific institutions or office-holders for particular actions or transactions. Material that is placed in the public domain may in practice be *inaccessible* to many for whom it might be useful, *unintelligible* to some of those who find it, and *unassessable* for some who can understand it.[9] Transparency does not require, and often does not achieve, communication – let alone dialogue – with others. Placing information about performance in the public domain may provide (additional) incentives for compliant performance by institutions and office-holders, but its contribution to "restoring" trust is often meager. Many people will have too little time, too little knowledge and too many other commitments to find and make use of the information.

So while additional law, additional regulation, and more exacting demands for accountability and transparency can each provide *incentives* for (more) trustworthy performance, they are often less effective than their advocates hope. Where accountability requires too much of institutions and office-holders, one effect may be that excessive time is spent on compliance and on documenting compliance, sometimes to the detriment of the very matters for which they are being held to account. In some cases measures intended to improve accountability create perverse incentives, which encourage an appearance of compliance by supplying high scores on dubious metrics and by ticking all the right boxes. The idea that multiplying requirements and assembling and releasing ever more ranking and other information about what has been done or achieved will always improve performance is not always borne out, and is sometimes no more than fantasy.[10]

1.5 Trust and Mediated Discourse

Given the difficulty of measuring, monitoring and publicizing, let alone communicating, evidence of trustworthiness in institutional contexts, it is reasonable to ask whether further or different means could be used to support judgments of trustworthiness and untrustworthiness in institutionally complex contexts. What is needed is neither complete evidence nor conclusive proof, but adequate evidence of reliable honesty and competence that allows others to judge with reasonable assurance which office-holders and institutions are likely to be trustworthy in which specific matters, combined with a sufficient understanding of the practical implications of placing and refusing trust.

Often we do not need to know a great deal about the relevant institutions and office-holders, any more than we need detailed knowledge about others in everyday situations. Every day we manage with some success to place trust intelligently in drivers (whom most of us do not know) not to run us over, in retailers (whom most of us do not know) to provide the goods we purchase, in doctors to prescribe appropriate treatment (which most of us cannot identify for ourselves). However, in these everyday cases the task is feasible in large part because judgments of trustworthiness can focus on a limited range of *relevant* and *specific* matters and do not require comprehensive judgments of others' honesty and competence, or of their reliability.

However where action is mediated by complex systems it may be harder to find analogues of the cultural and communicative capacities that support the intelligent placing and refusal of trust in everyday life. Has the complexity of institutional structures perhaps now undermined capacities to judge trustworthiness? Or are there better measures which could support the intelligent placing and refusal of trust in institutional life? Although we seldom need to make across-the-board judgments of others' trustworthiness, difficulties can mount when we need to judge the trustworthiness of claims and commitments that depend on complex institutions or arcane expertise, and more so when communication and evidence pass through numerous intermediaries whose trustworthiness is not assessable.

Difficulties are seemingly compounded if there is no way of telling who originates or controls the claims that are made, or even whether content has been produced by persons or by automated microtargeting, and whether claims and commitments are evidenced or invented. The difficulty of placing and refusing trust in institutions and office-holders has recently been compounded by widespread assertions that "experts" are not to be trusted, by the easy proliferation of "fake news," by the fact that originators of claims can remain anonymous and that some content may have been produced, multiplied and targeted by artificial rather than human intelligence.

In a remarkably short time we have moved from hoping that digital technologies would support a brave new world of universal participation in discussion that would be helpful to trustworthy relations with others, and even to democracy, to something entirely different. Rather than finding ourselves in a quasi-Habermasian world, in which citizens can check and challenge one another's claims and reach reasonable views of their truth and their trustworthiness – or otherwise – we now find ourselves in a world in which these technologies are often used to undermine or limit abilities to assess the trustworthiness of others' claims. However, these problems may arise not from the technologies that now provide communications *media*, but from the fact that they allow content to travel via large numbers of unidentified and unknown *intermediaries* whose ability to modify, suppress and direct content is often unknown and undiscoverable.

It is easy to imagine that the problem lies in the *media* we use, rather than in the role of *intermediaries*. That is exactly the worry that Plato articulated in his account of Socrates' concerns about written communication. In *Phaedrus* Plato sets out the issues in these words:

> You know, Phaedrus, writing shares a strange feature with painting. The offspring of painting stand there as if they are alive, but if anyone asks them anything, they remain most solemnly silent. The same is true of written words. You'd think they were speaking as if they had some understanding, but if you question anything that has been said because you want to learn more, it continues to signify just that very same thing forever. When it has once been written down, every discourse roams about everywhere, reaching indiscriminately those with understanding no less than those who have no business with it, and it doesn't know to whom it should speak and to whom it should not. And when it is faulted and attacked unfairly, it always needs its father's [i.e. its author's] support; alone, it can neither defend itself nor come to its own support.[11]

The worry about writing that Plato ascribes to Socrates is that texts can become separated from their authors, with the result that nobody stands ready to interpret or explicate the written word, or to vouch for its meaning, its truth or its trustworthiness. The passage contrasts writing with face-to-face, spoken communication in which hearers can ask speakers what they mean, and why they hold certain views, or act in certain ways. In doing this speakers provide "fatherly" support and help hearers to understand what they mean and allow them to check and challenge claims and commitments, and to reach more intelligent judgments about speakers' honesty, competence and reliability, and so about their trustworthiness. In face-to-face communication evidence is provided by the context of speaking, by speakers' expressions and gestures, and by the testimony of eyewitnesses. Hearers can use this immediate evidence to assess speakers' honesty, competence and reliability – and to detect failings. The relation between speaker and hearer, as Plato describes it, allows us to place and refuse trust in the spoken word, but is missing when we have only the decontextualized written word and its author cannot be identified, let alone questioned.

Yet while face-to-face speech has these – and other – merits, writing has advantages for judging trustworthiness. The fact that texts can be detached from writers and the context of writing can provide lasting and transmissible records that can be used by many, over long periods, and often provides indispensable evidence for judging trustworthiness and untrustworthiness. Although readers can seldom see writers' expressions and gestures, or judge the contexts in which they wrote, they have advantages that listeners lack. Writing supports intelligent judgment of the truth and trustworthiness of past and distant claims and commitments because it can provide a lasting trace that permits back references, reconsideration, reassessment and the creation of authorized versions. This is why writing is essential for many institutional processes, including standard ways of supporting and incentivizing trustworthiness, such as the rule law, reliable administration and commercial practice. By contrast, appeals to what is now known about ancient sayings may be no more than hearsay or gossip, and may offer little support for judging others' trustworthiness or untrustworthiness. The fact that the written word can bridge space and time rather than fading with the present moment contributes hugely to possibilities for placing and refusing trust well.

Moreover, the contrast that Plato drew between spoken and written communication is obsolete. The communication technologies of the last century enable the spoken word and images to be recorded and to bridge space and time, and contemporary discussion about placing and refusing trust no longer debates the rival merits of speech and writing, or of other communications media. We live in a multimedia world in which speech, like writing, can be preserved across time and can be recorded, revisited or transmitted, rather than fading as it is spoken, so can often be checked or challenged, corroborated or undermined, including by cross-referring to written sources, images or material evidence. Although face-to face communication has distinctive and important features, these reflect the fact that speaker and listener are present to one another, rather than their reliance on oral communication. For us ancient debates about the rival merits of the spoken and the written word, of orality and literacy, are interesting but remote.[12] And yet Plato highlighted a genuine problem.

1.6 Media, Intermediaries and Cultures

While the *medium* of communication may not be the key to judging trustworthiness and untrustworthiness, the role of *intermediaries* in communication is fundamental. The new communication technologies of the last 50 years not only support a wide variety of *media* for communication (see Ess, this volume). They also make it possible – and sometimes unavoidable – to route communication through complex *intermediaries*. Some of these intermediaries are institutions and office-holders; others are components or aspects of communication systems and internal institutional processes including algorithmic processes. Not only can these intermediaries shape and reshape, redirect or suppress, communication, but they can often do so while remaining invisible, and without this being apparent or their contribution being known to or understood by the ultimate recipients of the communication that they (partly) shape. Those intermediaries that are institutions or office-holders may be honest in some respects and dishonest in others, competent for some matters but not for others; reliable in some contexts and unreliable in others: and each of these is relevant to the trustworthiness of mediated communication. Often intermediaries are shaped by the structure of communication systems, which most will find hard to assess, and which may not be open to any scrutiny.

It is this proliferation of *intermediaries*, rather than the differences between various communications *media* that shapes and modifies communicated content, and that can support or disrupt processes for checking or challenging, corroborating or undermining, mediated claims and commitments, and so also affect capacities to make judgments that bear on the placing or refusal to trust. Where intermediaries not merely transmit communicated content, but can edit or alter, suppress or embellish, insert or omit, interpolate or distort content, both the intelligibility and the assessability of claims and commitments, and capacities to judge trustworthiness and untrustworthiness, truth and falsity, may be affected and may falter or fail.

However, failure is not inevitable. Where mediated communication is entirely linear and sequential, as in the children's game of "Chinese whispers," and messages pass sequentially between numerous intermediaries, judging the truth or the trustworthiness of mediated communication may face insurmountable obstacles. Many approaches to judging others' claims and commitments would founder if we had to compare mediated messages with originals in order to judge their truth or trustworthiness.[13] However, this image of serial communication, in which trustworthiness requires those at later stages of transmission to judge claims and commitments by reference to earlier stages, indeed to originals, seems to me mistaken.

Both communication and judging trustworthiness and lack of trustworthiness can be helped where *multiple* intermediaries are linked by *multiple* pathways with *varied* capacities to originate or modify content. Where messages can travel by many paths, abilities to note and respond to evidence of discrepancies in tone, words and action, and so to judge trustworthiness and untrustworthiness, can be supported by cultural as well as by formal legal and institutional measures. Institutional culture can then supplement the evidently incomplete approach to judging trustworthiness that formal institutional and digital processes offer.

However, institutional cultures also vary. Some are trustworthy and others are not. Some provide ways of judging trustworthiness and lack of trustworthiness, others damage capacities to judge trustworthiness and lack of trustworthiness. Cultures, like institutions and their office-holders, may be corrupt or untrustworthy. Neither a corrupt culture, nor a culture of mere compliance with institutional rules and requirements (law, regulation, accountability, transparency and internal rules) is likely to provide sufficient cultural support for judging or for fostering trustworthiness.

So if we conclude that culturally mediated ways of judging trustworthiness are necessary to augment those provided by institutional systems (law, regulation, accountability, transparency), it is worth working out which sorts of cultures might best be incorporated into institutional life. Rather than inflating and expanding formal systems for securing compliance and accountability yet further, it may be more effective to build and foster cultures that support trustworthiness and capacities to judge trustworthiness. Doing so would evidently not be easy, but there may be gains to be had by rejecting cultures of fear, intimidation or corruption as well as fragmented cultures that compartmentalize institutions into silos or enclaves,[14] and by considering how good cultures can contribute robustly to institutional trustworthiness.

Notes

1 Many organizations conduct attitudinal polls and surveys. Some – such as Gallup, IpsosMori or Eurobarometer – have become household names; some are less known or more specialized; some are covertly controlled by varying interest groups.
2 Moore (2018).
3 Taplin (2017).
4 O'Neill (2018a); Hawley (2019).
5 Kant (2000), 5:180.
6 O'Neill (2018b).
7 Habermas (1981); Baxter (1987).
8 I once heard the effects of excessive demands for documenting compliance nicely illustrated by a midwife, who told an inquiry into the safety of maternity care in England and Wales that it now took longer to do the paperwork than to deliver the baby.
9 Royal Society (2012).
10 Consider for example the unending debates about the metrics used to rank schools and universities in many developed countries, such as *PISA* rankings of schools or the Times Higher Education World University Rankings.
11 Plato, *Phaedrus*, 275d-e.
12 Ong (1980).
13 Coady (1992).
14 Tett (2016).

References

Baxter, H. (1987) "System and Life-World in Habermas's 'Theory of Communicative Action,'" *Theory and Society* 16(1): 39–86.

Coady, C.A.J. (1992) *Testimony: A Philosophical Study*, Oxford: Oxford University Press.

Habermas, J. (1985) *A Theory of Communicative Action*, T.J. McCarthy (trans.), Boston, MA: Beacon Press.

Hawley, K. (2019) *How To Be Trustworthy*, Oxford: Oxford University Press.

Kant, I. ([1790] 2000) *Critique of the Power of Judgement*, P. Guyer and E. Matthews (trans.), Cambridge: Cambridge University Press.

Moore, M. (2018) *Democracy Hacked: Political Turmoil and Information Warfare in the Digital Age*, London: Oneworld.

O'Neill, O. (2018a) "Linking Trust to Trustworthiness," *International Journal of Philosophical Studies* 26(2): 1–8.

O'Neill, O. (2018b) *From Principles to Practice: Normativity and Judgement in Ethics and Politics*, Cambridge: Cambridge University Press.

Ong, W.J. ([1980] 2002) *Orality and Literacy: The Technologizing of the World*, 2nd edition, New York: Routledge.

Plato (1973) *Phaedrus*, W. Hamilton (trans.), Harmondsworth: Penguin Books.

Royal Society (2012) *Science as an Open Enterprise.* https://royalsociety.org/-/media/policy/projects/sape/2012-06-20-saoe.pdf

Taplin, J. (2017) *Move Fast and Break Things: How Facebook, Google, and Amazon Cornered Culture and Undermined Democracy*, New York: Macmillan.

Tett, G. (2016) *The Silo Effect: Why Every Organisation Needs to Disrupt Itself to Survive*, New York: Simon & Shuster.

2
TRUST AND TRUSTWORTHINESS

Naomi Scheman

2.1 Introduction

Trust and trustworthiness are normatively tied: it is generally imprudent to trust those who are not trustworthy, and it typically does an injustice to the trustworthy to fail to trust them. But not always: trustworthiness may not be necessary for being appropriately trusted, as in cases of "therapeutic trust," when trust is placed in someone in the hope that they will live up to it (McGeer 2008; Hertzberg 2010); nor is trustworthiness always sufficient for being appropriately trusted, since there can be good reasons for withholding trust even from someone who has done everything in their power to earn it. I want to explore a range of cases where trust and trustworthiness come apart, especially when their so doing indicates some sort of normative failure.

How we understand each of trust and trustworthiness shifts in synch with how we understand the other. These shifts occur in actual situations of trusting or being trusted as well as in theoretical accounts.[1] In trusting others we are taking them to be trustworthy – sometimes because we have reflectively judged them to be so, and sometimes because we just feel sufficiently confident about them; but sometimes that taking is contemporaneous with our coming to trust, as when our trusting is therapeutic, but also when we trust "correctively," deciding to trust in the face of doubts we judge to be wrongly prejudicial (Fricker 2007; Frost-Arnold 2014).[2] In both these latter cases we do not trust because we take the other to be trustworthy, but rather, through the choice to trust, we place ourselves and the other in a reciprocal relationship of trust and trustworthiness.

Especially since Annette Baier's germinal work trust has been generally understood as deeply relational, not just or primarily a matter of a rational, empirically based judgment about the trustworthiness of the one trusted but rather a more or less critically reflective placing of oneself in a relationship of vulnerability to them; it is, among other things, a matter of respect (Baier 1986). I want to explore what goes into the inclination or decision to place oneself in such a relationship, one that, as a number of theorists have noted, invokes what Strawson has called "reactive attitudes," typically a sense of betrayal when the one trusted fails to come through (Strawson 1974). We also, I want to suggest, turn reactive attitudes back on ourselves when we judge ourselves to have trusted or mistrusted not just unwisely but unjustly, as when we presumptuously place on someone the unwelcome burden of therapeutic trust, or when we find ourselves unable to trust someone for reasons having to do more with us than with them.

I want to look especially at this latter sort of case and in particular at "corrective trust," where the potential truster is suspicious of their own mistrust and endeavors to override it in the name of treating the other more justly. While I am concerned with trust in its many manifestations, an important entry into these questions is specifically epistemic, notably through Miranda Fricker's theorizing of testimonial injustice, which occurs when someone, for systemically prejudicial reasons, fails to extend appropriate credence to another's testimony, thus denying to them the full measure of human respect as contributors to what we collectively know (Fricker 2007; see also Medina, this volume).

For Fricker a commitment to recognizing and correcting for one's own inclinations toward testimonial injustice constitutes an important epistemic virtue, one needed by all those (that is, all of us) who acquire what she calls "sensibilities" shaped by social milieux permeated by such prejudice-inducing systems as racism, sexism, classism, ableism, and heterosexism. We are, she argues, responsible for acting on these prejudices, though appropriately held blameworthy only when the conceptual resources for naming them are sufficiently part of the world we inhabit. While I agree in general with Fricker's analysis, I think more needs to be said about what an individual can and ought to do to avoid committing testimonial injustice, that is, to extend epistemically and morally appropriate trust. I also want to explore the phenomenon of corrective trusting as aimed not just at countering a specific instance of testimonial injustice but more importantly at cultivating in oneself more just – in part because more accurate – attributions of trustworthiness to relevantly similar others. And, unlike Fricker, I will be concerned not just with testimonial injustice, but equally with problematic cases of extending trust when it is not truly warranted, in particular, cases of over-estimating someone's trustworthiness based on unreliable positive stereotypes.[3]

Taking seriously the relative placement in social space of the parties to a potentially trusting relationship is relevant to another set of issues, namely those that arise when less powerful or privileged groups rationally mistrust more powerful or privileged others even when those others are scrupulously obeying the norms that are intended to underwrite trustworthiness. Such situations can arise within personal relationships – as, for example, when people of color are not just understandably but rationally distrustful of white people for systemic reasons that go beyond whatever those particular people might be doing. Similarly, much (though by no means all) of the mistrust in institutional authority is not just an understandable but actually a rational response to historical (and too-often continuing) trust-eroding practices that can seem, to those inside of the authorizing institutions, to have no bearing at all on their trustworthiness. What I want to suggest is that trustworthiness needs to be more broadly understood than it tends to be by those in positions of relative privilege and institutionalized authority. Institutional reputations for trust-eroding practices not only account for the social psychological likelihood of mistrust; they also make such mistrust rational, and – insofar as various insiders bear some responsibility for those practices – make those insiders less trustworthy.

2.2 Corrective (Dis)Trust

Better trust all, and be deceived,

And weep that trust, and that deceiving;

Than doubt one heart, that, if believed,

Had blessed one's life with true believing.

"Faith," Frances Anne (Fanny) Kemble (1859)

Consideration of distrust's susceptibility to bias and stereotype, together with its tendencies toward self-fulfillment and self-perpetuation, may lead us to be distrustful of our own distrustful attitudes. Gandhi advocated in his *Delhi Diary* for a comprehensive disavowal of distrust: "we should trust even those whom we suspect as our enemies. Brave people disdain distrust" (1951/2005:203). But a natural worry about this stance is that a broad policy of disavowing distrust will have the effect of exposing vulnerable parties to hazard. What right do we have to be "brave people" on the behalf of others?

(D'Cruz, this volume)

Trusting and being trusted are ubiquitous aspects of all our lives, and we typically calibrate our attributions of trustworthiness based on what we have reason to believe about those we are trusting: because this is Boston, I – somewhat warily – trust drivers to stop when I step into a crosswalk;[4] and (at least until regulatory agencies are decimated) I trust that the food in my local grocery store is correctly labeled and safe to eat. But – I want to argue – no matter how much such calibrating we can and should do, ultimately trust is extended and trustworthiness earned on grounds that are ineliminably implicit.

I first encountered the Fanny Kemble poem above in *Bartlett's Familiar Quotations* (a popular middle-brow reference book found in many American households in the 20th century) when I was a child, and I was much taken with it: I would far rather be a dupe than a cynic. But I have long known the role that privilege plays both in my having the temperament that I do and in my being able to move through the world with that temperament in relative safety. I have not experienced (or do not recall having experienced) significant betrayals; and on occasions when I have misplaced trust, there have been safety nets in place to prevent my suffering serious harm. Some of the privilege in question has been idiosyncratic (my sister had a sufficiently different relationship with our parents to be far less temperamentally trusting than I am), but most of it is structural, a matter primarily of race and class.

I am inclined, on a gut level, to trust even many of those I rationally judge not to be trustworthy; and that inclination, if unchecked, can undermine my own trustworthiness in relation to those less privileged. One way, paradoxically, in which my trustworthiness is undermined is through my inclination to *distrust* reports of mistreatment – reports that those whom I instinctively (though, I truly believe, mistakenly) trust have behaved appallingly. I have, that is, trouble believing that the world is truly as bad as others without my privileges say that it is: my excessive instinctual trust in the justness of the social world I inhabit makes me instinctively mistrustful of those who testify even to what I rationally and reflectively believe to be the case.[5] Clearly I need to trouble the ground on which, uncomfortably, I comfortably stand.

Troubling the ground on which we stand is at the heart of a philosopher's job description, most famously exemplified by Socrates and Descartes. But, especially as articulated by Descartes, that troubling can take the form of a demand that we dig down until we have reached bedrock, prompted by nothing more specific than a universalizable commitment to intellectual integrity. I want to resist such demands – a demand, for example, for fully explicitly grounded trust – while recognizing the urgency of more specifically articulated demands both to render explicit some piece of implicit practice and also to transform that practice, often by means of explicitly formulated norms. In Wittgensteinian terms, what is called for is a new form of life; but working toward that will often need to start with a handbook filled with new rules, as maladroit as it will inevitably seem.

In 2016 the American Philosophical Association issued a code of conduct (www.apaonline.org/general/custom.asp?page=codeofconduct) with sections on a general code of ethics, legal requirements, responsibility of faculty to students, electronic communications, and bullying and harassment. Among the responses to the code was a post on the Feminist Philosophers blog by "Prof. Manners," worth quoting at length:

> … I do want to raise something I haven't seen addressed. The Code is, I think, a failure … because it exists, because it is *needed*.
>
> Early Confucianism is all over the importance of moral micropractices (i.e., manners) and one insightful result of this is their recognizing the difference between unstated, socially shared, collective norms and explicit rule or law. Flourishing social environments largely operate by the former, enjoying a shared ethos that governs interaction without ever having to be made explicit … Law and rule are seen as safeguards – the ugly stuff you have to bring in when ethos has failed. So, rules are always failures of a sort or, more precisely, they remark social failures and try to repair these. And they're always going to be disappointing and problematic, for they'll have to work by rendering explicit and into something formula-like what a shared ethos does more naturally, fluidly, and with a commendable, happy vagueness …
>
> … Consequently, even if we have strong disagreements with how the committee framed the Code, I wish any criticism were first framed by hearty, collective self-accusation: "*Look what we made them do!*" That might be – *maybe* – the first step in restoring an ethos or building one for the first time.[6]

As Prof. Manners suggests in her final phrase, the need for explicit rules might come about not because of the breakdown of the shared ethos characteristic of a "flourishing social environment," but rather because – despite what some might think – the environment had been anything but flourishing, at least from the perspective of some of its inhabitants. That is, the impetus to excavate the ground underneath our feet and attempt to rebuild it with often clumsy explicitness might arise from the recognition that what had been grounding our practices was unjust, affording comfort and ease to some at the expense of the discomfort, silencing, marginalization, or oppression of others. (Many of the arguments around affirmative action policies, campus speech codes, and explicit consent sexual policies reflect these tensions.)

The Confucian perspective Prof. Manners presents is a normative one, that is, meant to be descriptive of a well-functioning society. Wittgenstein, most notably in his discussion of rule-following (Wittgenstein 2009:§§185–243 and *passim*), makes a more general point, that any practices whatsoever inevitably rely on unspoken, taken-for-granted expectations of "what we do." The equally important complement to his anti-foundationalism is his exhortation that we not disparage the ground on which we stand when we discover that it is not – cannot be, since nothing is – bedrock.[7] While any particular component of what underlies our practices can – and often should – be made explicit, we cannot achieve – and we need to learn not to demand – explicitness all the way down. Trust, including the expectation of trustworthiness, is part of what forms the actual, albeit metaphorical, ground on which we stand; and we need to ask what – if not explicitly spelled-out warrant – makes the requisite trust rational. Whether or not we trust – ourselves or others – can be more or less rational, but it will always be the case that some of the ground we are standing on remains implicit and unexamined. Much of it is also value-laden and affective, including the implicit biases that shape the trust we extend – or fail to extend – to others.

Think about what are frequently called "gut" responses. There is emerging evidence that our guts do in fact play a significant role in our cognitive, as well as our affective, lives (Mayer et al. 2014), and it is of course literally true that our guts are teeming with micro-organisms, with which we live symbiotically. Our microbiome is both idiosyncratic and affected by the environment, and the suggestion I want to make metaphorically is that one of the effects of occupying a privileged social location is the development of what I call in my own case a "good-girl gut," in particular, a microbiome that fosters biased attributions of trustworthiness.

There is a growing literature on implicit bias and a recognition of the extent to which our evaluations of others (including of their trustworthiness), however explicit we might take the grounds of those evaluations to be, are shaped by biases – by "gut" responses – that lie beyond our conscious awareness and control. Such biases largely account for testimonial injustice, and corrective trusting is the principal way in which Fricker argues that we can exercise the responsibility to counter them. I want to explore what it means to engage in this practice, in particular, how we can and should calibrate and adjust for our problematic gut inclinations to trust or mistrust.

Unlike Fricker, I am equally concerned with problematically excessive trust as with unjust withholding of trust, in part because, as others have argued (Medina 2011 and 2013:56–70), the two are intertwined: typically overly trusting X is at least part of what leads to under-trusting Y. Certainly in my own case, it is my excessive comfort with the ground under my feet – my inclination to trust in the basic benevolence of the world I move in – that largely accounts for my reflexive mistrust of those who claim (rightly, I honestly believe) that that ground is rotten and in need of critical excavation.

Here is a true story. Some years ago, a woman student went to the university police claiming that she was being stalked. The police did not believe her and sent her away. She went to the Women's Center, where she was believed, and among their responses was organizing a rally to call out the police for not having taken her seriously. I was asked to speak at the rally. My gut response to the young woman's account was skeptical. But, knowing what I know about my gut responses, I dismissed my doubts and spoke at the rally. It turned out that my gut in this case had gotten it right: she was not in fact being stalked. Clearly, she was troubled and needed to be listened to, and the police ought to have responded more sympathetically, but my gut had not led me astray. I might have learned from this episode to re-examine my dismissive attitude toward my gut responses, but I did not. Given the uncertainties involved, and the reasons I have to be wary of my "good girl gut," it seemed to me that what I needed to do was to weigh the risks and vulnerabilities involved in my decisions about whom to regard as trustworthy. Had she been accusing a particular person, those calculations would have needed to take the risks to him into account, but she was not. And given the difficulties people – women especially – face in being taken seriously when they report things like being stalked or harassed, it seemed – and seems – to me that it is an appropriate use of my privileged position to "trust all and be deceived."

But there are problems with that maxim. One is that total credulousness is hardly an appropriate response to the realization that one is committing testimonial injustice. Uncritical acceptance of just anything someone says constitutes not respect but rather a failure to seriously engage. Calibrating the degree of extra, compensatory credence one extends is far from a simple matter, nor is it clear that the question is best thought of in quantitative terms. There will, for example, be cases when people in the identity category toward which I am called on to extend corrective trust will disagree with each other.[8] Another problem with the maxim of trusting all is that it is indiscriminate, thus especially ill-suited to dealing with the other side of my "good-girl gut": my inclination to trust when (even by my own lights) I ought not to. It is in such cases that D'Cruz's concern in the epigraph to this section is particularly apt: I may, for example, as a faculty member be inclined to trust an administrator on matters that potentially put students or non-academic employees at risk. In such cases what I mistrust is precisely my inclination to trust.

As different as these two problems – of over- and under-trusting – are, they point toward a common solution: what I need is a little help from my (sufficiently diverse and caringly critical) friends. Certainly my own rational capacities are of some use: just as I can become aware of my own tendencies to wrongly extend or withhold trust, I can come to some conclusions about how to correct for those tendencies – that is, I can extend or withhold trust based not on my gut responses but rather on my rational assessment of others' trustworthiness. This sort of explicit critical reflection can carry me some distance toward appropriate attributions of trustworthiness, but it cannot take me all the way, largely because of the ineliminably implicit nature of grounding: my rational, critical capacities are not somehow shielded from my gut, as much as they can provide some corrective to it. I cannot simply reason my way out of the web of impressions, biases, inclinations, and perceptual habits that constitute my sensibility (I take the term from Fricker 2007). But I might be able, with persistence and time, to live my way out of that web, in particular, through sharing enough of my life with others whose gut microbiomes are sufficiently different from mine, especially in ways that fit with how I think I ought to be seeing and responding. And friends are importantly useful in the interim: until I have acquired a more biodiverse, more reliable gut, I can defer to the judgment of those whose judgment I have good reason to trust over my own – in particular, those who are members of groups that typically face prejudicial trust deficits.[9] That is, I am likely to be better at identifying reliable guides than I am at discerning the proper route.

There is a strong Aristotelean echo in this approach: moral virtue, practical wisdom, for Aristotle is a matter of habit, including not just habitual action but importantly habits of perception and of feeling, helping one to move from acting as though one trusts to actually trusting.[10] One acquires these habits by emulating the responses of one who already possesses practical wisdom, the *phronemos*. The presumption is that one can identify such a person prior to possessing practical wisdom – that is, one can identify a good teacher prior to having the skills and knowledge that teacher will impart – and furthermore that for some time one will act as one's teacher does, or would, without being able to fully understand just why one ought to act that way. Over time, ideally, one's perceptions and feelings will come into alignment with those of one's teacher, making one's actions a matter of "second nature," of one's "sensibility," a transformation, we might say, at the gut level. These transformations extend beyond the individual to the milieux in which our gut microbiomes are formed: witness the enormous shifts in the social atmosphere around matters of sexuality.

2.3 Rational Distrust of the Apparently Trustworthy

> What Obama was able to offer white America is something very few African Americans could – trust. The vast majority of us are, necessarily, too crippled by our defenses to ever consider such a proposition. But Obama, through a mixture of ancestral connections and distance from the poisons of Jim Crow, can credibly and sincerely trust the majority population of this country. That trust is reinforced, not contradicted, by his blackness … He stands firm in his own cultural traditions and says to the country something virtually no black person can, but every president must: "I believe you."
>
> *(Coates 2017)*

Characterizing the gap between being trustworthy and actually being trusted by some particular other(s) tends to be conceptually straightforward when the responsibility for the gap lies with the one who mistrusts the trustworthy (or who leads others to do so). In such cases trust and trustworthiness do seem to clearly come apart: those, for example, who commit testimonial injustice do not thereby undermine the actual trustworthiness of those whose word they doubt (though over time the erosion of one's trustworthiness might well be one of the effects of one's experiences of testimonial injustice). Similarly, disinformation campaigns aimed at undermining scientific research, notably on the health effects of tobacco or on anthropogenic climate disruption, do not undermine the actual trustworthiness of that research.[11]

It is more difficult to characterize the situation when mistrust is understandable and non-culpable, when the responsibility for it either lies at least in part with the putatively trustworthy party or is more broadly systemic. Thus, while Coates can account for Obama's ability to trust white Americans and sees that ability as crucial to his electoral success, he does not dismiss the distrust of nearly all Black Americans as irrational or ungrounded. Obama's ability to trust, and in turn be trusted by, white Americans was in tension with others' justified mistrust. Obama's trust certainly flattered especially those white Americans whose self-image included being non-racist, and in some cases that trust may have been well-placed as well as being instrumentally useful. But insofar as it licensed perceptions of a "post-racial" United States and buttressed the motivated ignorance that supports the continuation of white supremacy (Mills 2007), Obama's trust served to delegitimize the pervasive mistrust of the vast majority of African-Americans, mistrust that might (especially to white people) seem not to be tracking untrustworthiness.

Onora O'Neill has attempted to give an account of situations (notably involving public institutions and agencies), where trust and trustworthiness pull apart in cases where (at least by some standards) appropriate measures have been taken to ground trustworthiness but public trust is nonetheless understandably lacking – even, in some cases, because of, rather than despite, efforts at grounding trustworthiness (O'Neill 2002a). Thus, she argues, regulatory schemes may in fact make agencies, corporations, and the like trustworthy (reliably doing their jobs of, e.g. ensuring safety), but will fail to produce public trust when the regulators are themselves mistrusted or when the efforts at grounding trustworthiness backfire, as they typically do when they are implemented through algorithmic assessment schemes that attend to measuring something that matters mainly because it is easily quantifiable or when they take transparency to call for impenetrably massive and incomprehensible data dumps.

Karen Jones addresses situations such as these – when mistrust is neither clearly wrongful nor clearly a response to untrustworthiness – in terms of what she calls "signaling," which underlies what she calls "rich trustworthiness." Unlike "basic trustworthiness," which is a three-place relation: "A trusts B to do Z," rich trustworthiness is two-place: "B is willing and able to signal to A those domains in which A can rely on B." (Jones 2013:190; see also Potter 2002:25–32). Successful signaling thus requires actual communication, and responsibility for signaling failures can be placed with A or B or with features of the world in which they move. Thinking about rich trustworthiness – and what can lie behind its failure – can help make sense of pervasive, justified mistrust that seems not to attach to any individual's specifiable transgression, but is rather, like racism, systemic.

O'Neill's work is noteworthy in part because of her attentiveness to situations in which those to be trusted are nested within institutions, a nesting that makes it impossible for outsiders to extend or withhold trust based on characteristics of particular individuals. Those individuals might be acting impeccably, might as individuals be wholly trustworthy, and it might nonetheless be rational – even advisable – for outsiders to those institutions not to trust them. Institutions as well as individuals engage in signaling – directly or indirectly, intentionally or not. Thus, for example, research universities undermine their institutional trustworthiness through exploitative treatment of non-academic employees, arrogant relationships with surrounding neighborhoods, faculty dismissiveness of the familial and traditional knowledge that students bring with them into classrooms, and condescending or uncaring attitudes toward researched communities. The legacies of such practices are long-lived and pervasive, meaning that individuals can find themselves mistrusted based on things that were done by others, perhaps long ago. Often this mistrust will be rational, however baffling to those subject to it: the internal workings of universities are opaque to most outsiders, while the sorts of practices I listed are readily apparent; and, especially for those excluded from or marginalized within universities and other sites of power and privilege, those practices properly ground a general suspicion of what such institutions are up to (Scheman 2001).

I want to suggest that the separation O'Neill draws between trustworthiness and trust does not work in cases like this. Rather, the failure of nesting institutions to properly ground the rationality of trust in what goes on within them does undermine the trustworthiness of even the most scrupulously conscientious individuals. The typical – and, as O'Neill argues, typically unsuccessful – efforts to get institutions to play their roles in grounding trustworthiness are supposed to effect the transmission of signaling, either through accountability schemes or through transparency. However, accountability schemes, as O'Neill argues, tend to be driven by what is measurable rather than by what matters, and efforts at transparency tend to treat the institution as something to see through, rather than as itself an object of scrutiny. In neither case is the institution itself – in all its manifest enmeshments in various communities – thought of as signaling its own rich trustworthiness. And this failure of the institution distorts whatever signals are being sent by those working within it. Thus, for example, the signals may successfully communicate the trustworthiness of insiders to whomever they consider to be their peers, but – in the face of problematic institutional signaling – those insiders will be unable successfully to signal trustworthiness to diverse others who are routinely institutionally disrespected. And those insiders – while quite possibly not at all blameworthy for the problematic institutional signaling – nonetheless bear some of the responsibility for remedying it, in part because their own trustworthiness is at stake.

Trustworthiness, that is, is in part a matter of responsibility, understood not as backward-looking and grounded in what one caused to happen, but rather forward-looking, a matter of what one takes responsibility for, to what and to whom one is willing and able to be responsive. One implication of this line of thought is that judgments about trustworthiness cannot be made in abstraction from politically and ethically charged matters of relative power and privilege (Potter 2002). Claims of individual white innocence, for example, are beside the point when it comes either to accounting for Black mistrust or to assigning responsibility for alleviating it. As important as it is for white people to acknowledge the ways in which we have internalized racist attitudes, it is more important to acknowledge responsibility that arises not from our individual culpability but rather from our structural positioning.

2.4 Toward Aligning Trust and Trustworthiness

Consider two sorts of cases that are, at least initially, describable as cases in which trustworthy agents fail to be trusted, but the loci of responsibility and the routes toward appropriate trust are quite different. The first sort of case, just discussed, involves the type of distorted signaling that occurs when embedding institutions are rationally taken by at least some outsiders to be untrustworthy, thereby shedding doubt on the trustworthiness of (quite possibly individually blameless and trustworthy) insiders. The second sort of case involves (either literally or something like) testimonial injustice, in which a trustworthy testifier (or other sort of agent) fails to be believed (or otherwise trusted) for prejudicial (or otherwise problematic) reasons.

Consider first the case of climate change skepticism. Using climate science as a case study, Stephen John has provocatively argued against "sincerity, openness, honesty, and transparency" as appropriate ethical norms for scientists' communications with the public (John 2018). Central to this conclusion is an argument that adherence to these norms does not facilitate the public's coming to believe what is actually scientifically most warranted and most likely to be true. And central to that argument is the claim that non-scientists tend to hold, however unreflectively, a problematic "folk" philosophy of science, so that when they are presented – typically by those with an interest in undermining a scientific consensus – with a description of actual scientific practice, that description can easily be made to seem at odds with what they take to be proper scientific practice. In his critical response to John's paper, Alfred Moore (approvingly) quotes Onora O'Neill's making a somewhat broader claim: "Plants don't flourish when we pull them up too often to check how their roots are growing: political, institutional and professional life too may not flourish if we constantly uproot it to demonstrate that everything is transparent and trustworthy." (Moore 2018:19; O'Neill 2002b:19). While Moore agrees with John's and O'Neill's cautioning about transparency, he argues that John's alternative – the adoption by scientists of practices that deviate from norms of sincerity, openness, honesty, and transparency precisely in order to communicate accurately – problematically patronizes the public, neglecting practices and institutions that can facilitate both active engagement as well as trustworthy mediation: he uses the example of ACT-UP in relation to HIV research and researchers as an example. His suggestion is that distrust can be a start, not an end, if it leads to the building of trustworthy and trusted mediating institutions and relationships.

Such mediating institutions and relationships are vitally important given the practical impossibility of our individually assessing the trustworthiness of those on whom we are dependent – not only for what we believe, but for most of the activities of our everyday lives. Importantly, the mediation goes both ways, not only rationally grounding trust in expertise but, equally importantly, serving as a conduit for critical engagement, making experts more likely to be responsive and responsible to others, but also open to learning from them – and thus becoming more trustworthy. Trustworthy mediating institutions are especially crucial when the undermining of expert authority is done intentionally and maliciously or when the institutions housing the expertise are reasonably regarded with distrust. The responsibility for aligning trust with (presumptively) trustworthy science thus falls on those in a position to build and to influence institutions and relationships that can accomplish effective signaling. Respectful engagement with non-scientists, including from distinctively vulnerable groups, is an important part of this process, but it is crucial that relative insiders recognize their role not just in doing good science but in addressing the range of factors that prevent that science from being trusted.

In the second sort of case I have in mind – that of testimonial injustice (and structurally similar non-epistemic cases) – no one is setting out to intentionally cast doubt on the trustworthy, nor are the trustworthy imbedded within unjust or otherwise problematic institutions that distort their efforts at signaling their trustworthiness. The blame lies rather with the recipients of the signaling, who for prejudicial reasons fail to correctly interpret the signals. This phenomenon is rampant and related to what I discuss above as my "good girl gut." As Karen Jones puts it, "epistemic injustice – unfair in itself – also functions to maintain substantive social injustice. For example, how credible you think a particular report of incestuous sexual abuse is depends on your understanding of male sexuality and of the role and structure of the patriarchal family and, in addition, on your beliefs about the ability of women and girls to understand their experiences … and report them truthfully. Likewise for reports of, and statistics regarding the prevalence of, sexual harassment, race-based police harassment, torture, human rights abuse, and so on" (Jones 2002:158).

In some cases the person unjustly mistrusted is in fact distinctively trustworthy – as a testifier, public official, or other individual in whom others should be expected to place their trust. In other cases the trustworthiness in question simply grounds the background presumption that one does not pose a threat to those in one's vicinity. The trust involved in taking others to be basically harmless is typically unarticulated: what is noticed is rather its absence. Thus, a significant part of the explanation for unprovoked attacks on unarmed Black men lies in their being perceived as untrustworthy – as a threat, as always "armed," given the racist perception of "black skin as a weapon" (Rankine 2015).[12] Those targeted by police or white bystanders for surveillance or violence are denied the unarticulated, default presumption of trustworthiness. Such targeting is clearly individually blameworthy, especially when it issues in violent assault, but the underlying perceptual structures are part of the racist social imaginary, and responsibility for that is shared in particular by white people, who are its beneficiaries, however unwillingly and unwittingly.

That responsibility calls for the Aristotelean cultivation of habits of perception and affect. José Medina takes this matter up in his discussion of the epistemic consequences of differentiated social locations, in particular, the ways in which occupying subordinated locations produces what he calls "epistemic friction," arising from being caught between conflicting perspectives, and consequently the "meta-lucidity" that allows one to see the one-sidedness and limitations of dominant perspectives (Medina 2013:186–249). The active ignorance that characterizes privileged social locations produces, by contrast, what he calls "meta-blindness" – an active failure to see what one does not see.[13] But there is nothing inevitable about meta-blindness, nor is meta-lucidity reserved for those in subordinated locations: it is possible for those whose perceptual repertoire is shaped by the limitations of privilege to overcome those limitations, in part by intentionally and attentively placing themselves in situations in which they will experience epistemic friction. Insofar as many of those (like me) whose "gut" attributions of trustworthiness are problematically skewed by privileged insensitivity are committed to more accurately, and justly, perceiving the world and the diverse people in it, it is reasonable to expect us to be held responsible for our failures to trust the trustworthy.

In general, I want to suggest, judgments about how to think about failures to trust the trustworthy need to track responsibility as not reducible to blame and need to be attentive to matters of power and privilege. Following Nancy Potter (2002), I would argue that those with greater power and privilege ought to bear more of the responsibility for establishing trust and repairing its breaches. Distrust on the part of subordinated people toward more powerful and privileged groups and institutions can not only be rational and epistemically wise, as Potter argues (2002:17–19); it can also be, as Krishnamurthy emphasizes, politically salutary (2015). And, as Karen Jones and José Medina argue, epistemic vices characteristic of privileged social locations lead to distrusting the trustworthy both directly as well as indirectly, through over-trusting more privileged others. In general, the tasks of calibrating when and whom to trust, as well as those of cultivating the reality and perception of one's own appropriate trustworthiness, are embedded within larger tasks of understanding and taking responsibility for one's placement in the world – in particular, the relationships of dependency and vulnerability in which one stands to diverse others.

Notes

1 See Jones (2013). My own sense is that the difference in theoretical accounts can be largely explained by the difference in paradigmatic examples and that no one theoretical account will work well for all cases: as Wittgenstein notes, we are often led astray by a "one-sided diet of examples," and I see no reason for expecting or demanding a single unified account of such a variable phenomenon as trusting.

2 On therapeutic trust, see McGeer (2008), and Hertzberg (2010). On corrective trust, see Frost-Arnold (2014), and Fricker (2007), discussed below.

3 Fricker acknowledges (2007:169) that there is an unavoidable vagueness in the notion of the appropriate level of credence, but suggests – rightly, I think – that this vagueness does not stand in the way of our recognizing clear cases where someone is denied (or is wrongly credited with more than) the credibility they are due. Fricker's bracketing of credibility excess has been disputed by, among others, Medina 2011 and 2013:58f.

4 This is one situation among many where both the fact and the rationality of my trust are inflected by my whiteness. See Goddard et al. (2015).

5 For discussion of a related phenomenon, see Manne (2018:196–205), on "himpathy," misplaced prosocial attitudes, including of trust, extended toward (in her main examples) men, with the consequence of both disbelieving and vilifying those (in her main examples women) who claim to have been victimized.

6 Prof. Manners 2016. During a discussion on the Feminist Philosophers blog about the propriety of internet anonymity, Amy Olberding outed herself as Prof. Manners, and I have received her

permission to credit her for this post. The concerns I raise are similar to ones raised in comments on the blog and are ones that Olberding herself takes seriously.

7 For connections between Wittgensteinian and Confucian thought, see Peterman (2015).

8 Melanie Bowman addresses this problem specifically in her dissertation (Bowman 2018). See also Kappel's chapter in this volume on trust and disagreement.

9 Thanks to Jason D'Cruz for emphasizing this point, and for noting that, given tendencies to form friendships with those similar to us, this is easier said than done. And thanks to Karen Frost-Arnold for pointing to additional problems: exactly the sorts of gut responses I have been discussing (and others' awareness of them) are likely to hinder my ability to form those friendships, and even friends can engage in what Kristie Dotson calls "testimonial smothering": refraining from saying things they have reason to believe I will be unable or unwilling to hear (Dotson 2011).

10 Thanks to Jason D'Cruz for urging me to distinguish between acting as though one trusts and actually trusting and for recognizing the extent to which the latter is typically beyond our control. While I agree that we cannot trust by mere force of will, I think the Aristotelean picture of the role of conscious habituation in shaping our not-directly-voluntary responses is a useful one.

11 See Oreskes and Conway (2011) for an account of how the same people who engaged in the sowing of doubt about tobacco research were hired, after those efforts collapsed, to sow doubt about the reality and anthropogenic nature of global warming.

12 See also Yancy (2008) for a discussion of the viscerally embodied structures of racialized perception that, in the example that frames his analysis, lead to a white woman's flinching at his presence in the elevator.

13 Medina is attentive to the problematic use of "blindness": he wants both to draw attention to the prevalence of the visual in how we (not just philosophers) typically think about knowledge but also to move beyond it (Medina 2013:xi–xiii).

References

American Philosophical Association (2016) "APA Code of Conduct." www.apaonline.org/page/codeofconduct

Baier, A. (1986) "Trust and Antitrust," *Ethics* 96(2): 231–260.

Bowman, M. (2018) "An Epistemology of Solidarity: Coalition in the Face of Ignorance." Ph.D. dissertation, Department of Philosophy, University of Minnesota.

Coates, T.-N. (2017) "My President Was Black," *The Atlantic*, January/February. www.theatlantic.com/magazine/archive/2017/01/my-president-was-black/508793/#III

Dotson, K. (2011) "Tracking Epistemic Violence, Tracking Patterns of Silencing," *Hypatia* 26(2): 236–257.

Fricker, M. (2007) *Epistemic Injustice: Power and the Ethics of Knowing*, Oxford: Oxford University Press.

Frost-Arnold, K. (2014) "The Cognitive Attitude of Rational Trust," *Synthese* 191(9): 1957–1974.

Gandhi, M. (1951/2005) *Gandhi, Selected Writings*, R. Duncan (ed.),New York: Dover Publications.

Goddard, T., Kahn, K.B. and Adkins, A. (2015) "Racial Bias in Driver Yielding Behavior at Crosswalks," *Transportation Research Part F: Traffic Psychology and Behaviour* 33: 1–6.

Hertzberg, L. (2010) "On Being Trusted" in A. Grøn, A.M. Pahuus and C. Welz (eds.), *Trust, Sociality, Selfhood*, Tübingen: Mohr Siebeck.

John, S. (2018) "Epistemic Trust and the Ethics of Science Communication: Against Transparency, Openness, Sincerity and Honesty," *Social Epistemology* 32(2): 75–87.

Jones, K. (1999) "Second-Hand Moral Knowledge," *The Journal of Philosophy* 96(2): 55–78.

Jones, K. (2002) "The Politics of Credibility" in L.M. Antony and C.E. Witt (eds.), *A Mind of One's Own: Feminist Essays on Reason and Objectivity*, Boulder, CO: Westview.

Jones, K. (2012) "Politics of Intellectual Self-Trust," *Social Epistemology* 26(2): 237–251.

Jones, K. (2013) "Distrusting the Trustworthy" in D. Archard, M. Deveaux, N. Manson and D. Weinstock (eds.), *Reading Onora O'Neill*, London: Routledge.

Kemble, F.A. (1859, 1997) "Faith," in J. Gray (ed.), *She Wields a Pen: American Women Poets of the Nineteenth Century*, Iowa City: University of Iowa Press.

Krishnamurthy, M. (2015) "(White) Tyranny and the Democratic Value of Distrust," *The Monist* 98: 391–406.

Manne, K. (2018) *Down Girl*, Oxford: Oxford University Press.

Mayer, E.A., Knight, R., Mazmanian, S.K., Cryan, J.F. and Tillisch, K. (2014) "Gut Microbes and the Brain: Paradigm Shift in Neuroscience," *The Journal of Neuroscience* 34(46): 15490–15496.
McGeer, V. (2008) "Trust, Hope and Empowerment," *Australasian Journal of Philosophy* 86(2): 237–254.
Medina, J. (2011) "Relevance of Credibility Excess in a Proportional View of Epistemic Injustice: Differential Epistemic Authority and the Social Imaginary," *Social Epistemology* 25(1): 15–35.
Medina, J. (2013) *The Epistemology of Resistance: Gender and Racial Oppression, Epistemic Injustice, and Resistant Imaginations*, Oxford: Oxford University Press.
Mills, C. (2007) "White Ignorance" in S. Sullivan and N. Tuana (eds.), *Race and the Epistemologies of Ignorance*, Albany NY: SUNY Press.
Moore, A. (2018) "Transparency and the Dynamics of Trust and Distrust," *Social Epistemology Review and Reply Collective* 7(4): 26–32.
Olberding, A., blogging as Prof. Manners (2016) "The APA Code and Perils of the Explicit," Feminist Philosophers blog. https://feministphilosophers.wordpress.com/2016/11/03/the-apa-code-and-perils-of-the-explicit/https://feministphilosophers.wordpress.com/2016/11/03/the-apa-code-and-perils-of-the-explicit/
O'Neill, O. (2002a) *Autonomy and Trust in Bioethics*, Cambridge: Cambridge University Press. https://feministphilosophers.wordpress.com/2016/11/03/the-apa-code-and-perils-of-the-explicit/
O'Neill, O. (2002a) *Autonomy and Trust in Bioethics*, Cambridge: Cambridge University Press.
O'Neill, O. (2002b) *A Question of Trust*, Cambridge: Cambridge University Press.
Oreskes, N. and Conway, E. (2011) *Merchants of Doubt: How a Handful of Scientists Obscured the Truth on Issues from Tobacco Smoke to Global Warming*, London: Bloomsbury Press.
Peterman, J.F. (2015) *Whose Tradition? Which Dao?: Confucius and Wittgenstein on Moral Learning and Reflection*, Albany: SUNY Press.
Pettit, P. (1995) "The Cunning of Trust," *Philosophy and Public Affairs* 24(3): 202–225.
Potter, N.N. (2002) *How Can I Be Trusted?: A Virtue Theory of Trustworthiness*, Lanham, MD: Rowman & Littlefield.
Rankine, C. (2015) "The Condition of Black Life Is One of Mourning," *New York Times*, 22 June.
Scheman, N. (2001) "Epistemology Resuscitated: Objectivity as Trustworthiness," in S. Morgen and N. Tuana (eds.), *(En)Gendering Rationalities*, Albany: SUNY Press; reprinted in Scheman, N. (2011) *Shifting Ground: Knowledge and Reality, Transgression and Trustworthiness*, Oxford: Oxford University Press.
Strawson, P. (1974) "Freedom and Resentment," in *Freedom and Resentment and Other Essays*, London: Methuen.
Wittgenstein, L. (2009) *Philosophical Investigations*, 4th edition, P.M.S. Hacker and J. Schulte (eds. and trans.), Oxford: Wiley-Blackwell.
Yancy, G. (2008) "Elevators, Social Spaces and Racism: A Philosophical Analysis," *Philosophy & Social Criticism* 34: 827–860.

3
TRUST AND DISTRUST

Jason D'Cruz

3.1 Preliminaries: Trust, Distrust and in between

Trust is commonly described using the metaphor of an invisible "social glue" that is conspicuous only when it is absent. It is initially tempting to think of distrust as the absence of the "glue" of trust. But this way of thinking oversimplifies the conceptual relationship between trust and distrust. Not trusting a person is not tantamount to distrusting a person. Distrust is typically accompanied by feelings of insecurity, cynicism, contempt or fear, which distinguishes it from the agnostic mode of "wait and see" (Hardin 2001:496). So, trust and distrust do not exhaust the relevant options: they are contraries rather than contradictories (Govier 1992b:18).

While trust and distrust are not mutually exhaustive, they do seem to be mutually exclusive. I cannot simultaneously trust and distrust you, at least not in the very same domain or with respect to the very same matter (Ullmann-Margalit 2004:60). Distrust rules out trust, and vice versa. If I do not trust you this could either mean that I positively distrust you, or that I neither trust nor distrust you (Ullmann-Margalit 2004:61). Indeed, I may decline to consider something to be a matter of trust or distrust for reasons that are orthogonal to my assessment of your trustworthiness. I may simply recognize that you prefer not to be counted on in a particular domain, and I may respect that preference. Making something a matter of trust or distrust can be an undue imposition. As Hawley (2014:7) notes, "Trust involves anticipation of action, so it's clear why someone might prefer not to be trusted to do something she would prefer not to do. But that does not mean she wants to be distrusted in that respect."

Just as distrust is not the absence of trust, so also distrust is not the absence of reliance. You may decide not to rely on someone for reasons that have nothing to do with distrust. Reliance, like trust, can sometimes be a burden, and you may have reason not to so burden someone. Moreover, a judgment that someone is untrustworthy is very different from a judgment that it is not wise to rely on them. As Hawley (2014:3) points out, a fitting response to the discovery that I have wrongly distrusted you includes remorse, apology and requests for forgiveness. Such responses need not normally accompany mistaken judgments about reliability. For example, if you are reliably gregarious but I don't pick up on this, there is no need to apologize to you for my mistake all things being equal. To apply the label "untrustworthy" is to impugn a person's moral character. But to recognize that someone is not to be relied on in a particular domain need not have any moral valence at all. For example, if I recognize that you are not to be relied on to be gregarious, no insult to your character is implied. Distrust has a normative dimension that non-reliance often lacks.

To distrust a person is to think badly of them (Domenicucci and Holton 2017:150) and for the most part people do not want to be thought of in this way. But even if a person prefers not to be distrusted, they may, quite consistently, also prefer not to be trusted in that same domain (Hawley (2014:7). For example, you might enjoy bringing snacks to faculty meetings. But just as you prefer not to be trusted to do this (since you do not want your colleagues to *count on you* to bring snacks), so also you would not want to be *distrusted* in this matter (or to be perceived as *untrustworthy*). So, not being distrusted is something that is worth wanting even in circumstances in which you prefer not to be trusted.

The view that trust and distrust are contraries rather than contradictories is widely endorsed (e.g. Govier 1992b:18; Jones 1996:15; Hardin 2001:496; Ullmann-Margalit 2004:60). But in recent work Paul Faulkner (2017) argues that this orthodoxy is premised on a problematic three-place conceptualization of trust, "X trusts Y to ø" where X and Y are people and ø is a task. According to Faulkner (2017:426), on this "contractual" view of trust, "a lack of trust need not imply distrust because there might be a lack of trust because there is a lack of reliance." On the other hand, "Where trust is the background attitude – where it is two-place [X trusts Y] or one-place [X is trusting] – if trust is lost what remains is not merely its lack but distrust." He maintains that when "it can no longer be taken for granted that [a person] will act in certain ways and will not act in others what is left is distrust" (Faulkner 2017:426). However, Faulkner's observation shows only that the *undoing* of trust results in distrust (the key phrase is *no longer*). This observation does not cast any doubt on there being a state in which we neither trust nor distrust, simply because we, for instance, lack evidence of moral integrity, of competence or of a track record in a salient domain. I neither trust nor distrust my colleagues in the domain of financial planning. In this circumstance, the absence of the attitude of trust does not indicate distrust (D'Cruz 2018).

Indeed, we can even imagine circumstances where trust is *lost*, but where the resulting attitude is agnosticism rather than distrust. Suppose you learn that your evidence of a solid track record has defeaters (maybe you learn that a person had no other feasible options but to be steadfastly reliable). You may then decide that your previous appraisal of her trustworthiness is now baseless. But this does not mean that you will or ought to adopt an attitude of distrust toward the person, or that you will or ought to stop relying on the person. So, trust and distrust remain contraries rather than contradictories even when they are conceived of independently of the act of relying on a person to perform an action.

What of Faulkner's skepticism that distrust has the three-place structure, *X distrusts Y to ø*?[1] Following Faulkner, Domenicucci and Holton (2017:150) also maintain that there is no three-place construction of distrust: "We do not say that we distrust someone to do something. We simply distrust, or mistrust, a person." I think there is something right about this. But it also seems right to say that we might bear a more specific attitude than trusting or distrusting a person *globally*. Perhaps there is a third option. Just as trust may be understood in terms of "X trusts Y in domain of interaction D" (Jones 1996, D'Cruz 2018) perhaps distrust could be analyzed in terms of "X distrusts Y in D." The plausibility of this proposal depends on whether it makes sense to distrust a person in a delimited domain of interaction, or whether distrust characteristically infects multiple, or even all, domains of interaction.

It would seem that the basis of distrust – whether it be skepticism about quality of will, integrity or competence – has a bearing on this question. Distrust based on skepticism about competence may be confined to a particular domain of expertise. I may distrust you when it comes to doing the wiring in my house but not when it comes to doing the plumbing. But even this competence-based distrust has a tendency to spread across domains. If I *distrust* you regarding the wiring (in contrast to simply not trusting you in the agnostic mode), that is likely because you have invited me to trust you and I have declined the invitation. My refusal might be based on the suspicion that you do not know the limits of your competence. So, not only do I not trust you with the plumbing, I do not trust you to reliably indicate the spheres in which you can be responsive to my trust.[2] If in addition I think that you are liable to invite my trust recklessly, then the breadth of my distrust is widened. If I think that you extend an invitation to trust recklessly because you simply do not care enough about my well-being (rather than because you are too full of bravado), then my distrust of you is broad indeed. Distrust based on skepticism about quality of will seems by its nature more general. If you think a person is indifferent to the fact of your vulnerability, or that a person is hostile to you, then you will distrust them across multiple domains of interaction.[3] Even so, such distrust may not cover *all* domains of interaction. For instance, you may think it reasonable to rely on a person to perform certain tasks related his work even while harboring profound skepticism about his good will or moral character. But the fact remains that while trust can be easily confined to a relatively narrow domain of interaction, the same is not true of distrust.

Many of the above considerations indicate that having an adequate account of trust does not straightforwardly give us an adequate account of distrust. Indeed, there is a case to be made for considering distrust *first*. Although philosophers are apt to intellectualize trust, in ordinary life we generally only scrutinize our trust explicitly when we suspect that *distrust* is called for ("Is it a mistake to trust?"), or in contexts where it becomes salient that we are wrongly distrusted by others ("How could they so misjudge me?"). We think explicitly about whether we trust when we suspect that there might be grounds for distrust, and we think explicitly about whether we are trusted when we suspect that we might be distrusted.

There is still much work to be done in giving a perspicuous characterization and taxonomy of distrust, as well as in specifying the analytical connections between trust and distrust. In what follows I describe what I take to be the state of art and I lay out some of the challenges ahead.

3.2 The Concept of Distrust

Although there are many theories of trust, few theorists of trust in the philosophical literature have elaborated explicit theories of distrust. A recent account due to Katherine Hawley (2014) is a notable exception.[4] "To understand trust," Hawley (2014:1) writes, "we must also understand distrust, yet distrust is usually treated as a mere afterthought, or mistakenly equated with an absence of trust."

As has been widely noted since Baier (1986:234), one may rely on a person's predictable habits without trusting them. Hawley (2014:2) offers as an example relying on someone who regularly brings too much lunch to work because she is bad a judging quantities. Anticipating this, you plan to eat her leftovers and so rely on her. Hawley observes that if one day she eats all her lunch herself, she would owe you no apology. Disappointment on your part would be understandable, but feelings of betrayal would be out of place. Just as trust is richer than reliance, distrust is richer than non-reliance. In another example, Hawley (2014:3) observes that even though she does not rely on her colleagues to buy her champagne next Friday, it would "wrong or even offensive, to say that [she] distrust[s her] colleagues in this respect" or to think that they are untrustworthy in this regard. If her colleagues were to surprise her with champagne, it would not be appropriate for her to feel remorse for her non-reliance on them, or to apologize for not having trusted them.

Hawley proposes that what distinguishes reliance/non-reliance from trust/distrust is that the latter attitudes are only appropriate in the context of commitment. It is only appropriate to trust or distrust your colleagues to bring your lunch if they have a commitment to bring you lunch; it is only appropriate for you to trust or distrust your colleagues to bring champagne if they have a commitment to bring champagne. In generalized form,

> To trust someone to do something is to believe that she has a commitment to doing it, and to rely upon her to meet that commitment. To distrust someone to do something is to believe that she has a commitment to doing it, and yet not rely upon her to meet that commitment.
>
> *(Hawley 2014:10)*

But what about people who rely on the commitments of others cynically, like Holton's "confidence trickster" (Holton 1994:65)? Consider the case of a person who tries to fool you into sending him a $1,000 payment to "release your million-dollar inheritance." Even though he relies on you to keep your commitment, it would be odd to say that he *trusts* you to do this. (Consider how ridiculous it would be for him to feel betrayed if you see through his scheme). Or consider a variation story involving non-reliance. The confidence trickster starts to worry that you will not follow through on your commitment, and so decides not to rely on you to send the payment. Surely it does not seem right to say that the confidence trickster *distrusts* you. The example and the variation suggest that reliance or non-reliance, even when combined with belief in commitment, do not amount to trust or distrust.

Hawley (2014:12) anticipates this challenge. She points out that the confidence trickster does not believe that you have a *genuine* commitment; rather, he relies on your mistaken belief that you are committed: "Although you don't realize it you do not have a genuine commitment, the trickster recognizes this, and this is why he does not trust you." Presumably Hawley could say the same thing about the trickster who anticipates you won't follow through: he does not believe you have a genuine commitment, and so his withdrawal from reliance does not amount to distrust.[5]

Hawley's response to the confidence trickster objection is a good one. But we may still wonder whether the commitment account is sufficiently comprehensive. What if you (correctly) believe that someone is committed, but you also think that they lack the necessary *competence* to carry through on their commitment? For example, imagine that you face a difficult court case, and your nephew who has recently earned his law degree enjoins you to let him represent you. Despite your confidence that he is fervently committed to representing you well, you decline his offer simply because you think he is too inexperienced. Does this show that you distrust your nephew despite your faith in his commitment? There is still theoretical work to be done on how we should understand withdrawal from or avoidance of reliance based on skepticism about competence as opposed to commitment. On certain ways of filling out the story, your attitude *does* seem to be one of distrust. For example, if you suspect your nephew is just using you to jump start his new practice, distrust of him certainly seems appropriate. What if your nephew invites you to rely on him without ulterior motives, but you surmise that he ought to have a better reckoning of his own capacity to carry off the work? This, too, seems grounds for distrust if you think he is flouting a professional duty to know the limits of his own expertise. In each of these cases, you may have no doubt about his commitment.[6]

Belief in commitment, even when paired with non-reliance, may not be sufficient for distrust to be an appropriate response. Suppose you decide not to rely on a person, and you *hope* that person will not meet his commitment. Here's an example: A financier buys insurance on credit defaults, positioning himself to profit when borrowers default. The financier seems to satisfy the conditions for distrust: he believes (truly) that the borrowers have a commitment, and yet he does not rely on them to meet that commitment, because he believes that they will fail. Does it seem right to say that the financier *distrusts* the loan holders even though the borrowers' lack of integrity represents for him a prospect rather than a threat? For those who are moved to say that this falls short of distrust, it is worth asking what the missing element is. Perhaps distrust is essentially a *defensive* stance that responds to another person as a threat. This practical, action-oriented aspect of distrust is explored in more depth by Meena Krishnamurthy (2015).[7]

Drawing on the work of Martin Luther King, Krishnamurthy (2015) advances an account of the political value of distrust that foregrounds distrust's practical aspect. Rather than offering a general conceptual analysis of distrust, Krishnamurthy (2015:392) aims to articulate an account of distrust that is politically valuable. Krishnamurthy focuses on Martin Luther King's distrust of moderate whites to carry out the actions required to bring about racial justice. She argues that King believed that though white moderates possessed "the right reasons" for acting as justice required, he thought that fear and inertia made them passive (2015:395). According to Krishnamurthy, King distrusted them "because he believed with a high degree of certainty or was confident in his belief that they would not, on their own, act as justice required" (2015:395). Krishnamurthy reconstructs King's conception of distrust as "the confident belief that another individual or group of individuals or an institution will not act justly or as justice requires" (2015:391). King's distrust of white moderates, Krishnamurthy maintains, was a safeguard against white tyranny. Krishnamurthy describes the relevant concept of trust as narrow and normative: "It is a narrow concept because it concerns a specific task. It is a normative concept because it concerns beliefs about what individuals ought to do" (2015:392). Schematized, Krishnamurthy's account of distrust takes the form "x distrusts y to ø" where distrust is grounded in the "confident belief" that X will not ø. On this account distrust is isomorphic to the three-place structure of trust: "x trusts y to ø" where ø is some action, and the attitude of trust is grounded in the confident belief that y will ø.

But is distrust always, or even typically, grounded in a belief that the distrusted party will fail to do something in particular? When we speak of distrusting a doctor or a politician, say, is there always, or even typically, a particular action that we anticipate they will fail to do? I find more plausible Hawley's view that "distrust does not require confident prediction of misbehaviour" (Hawley 2014:2). One's distrustful attitude toward a doctor, for example, might involve a suspicion of general inattentiveness, or of susceptibility to the emoluments of drug companies. But one need not anticipate any particular obligatory action that the doctor will fail to perform. While it is sometimes natural to talk of trust in terms of "two people and a task," it is not clear that this framework works equally well for paradigm instances of distrust.

Erich Matthes (2015) challenges Krishnamurthy's characterization of the cognitive aspect of distrust as "belief." He contends that understanding distrust in terms of belief does not capture distrust's voluntary aspect. There are contexts, Matthes maintains, where distrusting is something we *do*. A decision to distrust consists in a refusal to rely or a deliberate withdrawal from reliance. Matthes (2015:4) maintains that while Krishnamurthy is correct to highlight the political value of distrust, to understand how distrust may *constitute* a democratic value (rather than be merely instrumentally valuable) we must see how "to not rely on others to meet their commitments (in particular, when you have good reason to believe that they will not meet them) is part and parcel of the participatory nature of democratic society." Matthes (2015:4) concludes that "the *process* of cultivating a healthy distrust, particularly of elected representatives, is constitutive of a well-functioning democracy, independently of whether or not it happens, in a given instance, to guard against tyranny."

Distrust of government and of the state (as opposed to interpersonal distrust) plays a prominent role in the history of liberal thought. Russell Hardin contends that "the beginning of political and economic liberalism is distrust" (2002:73). On the assumption that the incentives of government agents are to arrange benefits for themselves, it follows that those whose interests may be sacrificed by state intervention have warrant for distrust. The idea that governments are prone to abusing citizens has led liberal thinkers such as Locke, Hume, and Smith and, in the American context, James Madison, to contrive of ways to arrange government so as to diminish the risk of abuse.

3.3 The Justification, the Signals, the Effects and the Response to Distrust

In addition to thinking about ontological and definitional questions of about what distrust *is*, philosophers have also addressed questions the rational and moral warrant for distrust as well as the interpersonal effects of distrust. Trudy Govier describes the conditions for warranted distrust as those in which people "lie or deliberately deceive, break promises, are hypocritical or insincere, seek to manipulate us, are corrupt or dishonest, cannot be counted on to follow moral norms, are incompetent, have no concern for us or deliberately seek to harm us" (1992a:53). The list may not be exhaustive, but it does seem representative. One thing to notice is that the basis of distrust can be quite variable, and so we should expect the affective character of distrust to vary widely as well. If distrust is based on suspicion of ill will, the reactive attitude of resentment will be to the fore. If distrust is based on pessimism about competence, then distrust will manifest itself more as wariness or vexation than as moral anger. If it is based on pessimism about integrity, it may be tinged with moral disgust.

It is noteworthy that even when we know distrust to be warranted and even when we 'feel it in our bones,' we often take measures to conceal its expression. There is significant social pressure to refrain from expressing distrust: we are awkward and uneasy when we must continue to interact with a person after having expressed distrust of them. This poses problems when we find ourselves in circumstances in which we have no choice but to rely on those we distrust. We seem to have two options, neither of them good. We can choose to reveal our distrust, which risks insulting and alienating. Or we can try to conceal distrust. But this is also risky, since our trust-related attitudes are often betrayed by subtle and non-voluntary aspects of our comportment (Slingerland 2014:Ch. 7). As Govier (1992a:53) puts it, "We are left, all too often, to face distrust as a practical problem."

Distrust that is revealed, whether deliberately or involuntarily, has the power to insult and to wound, sending a signal to the distrusted party and to witnesses that one regards the person one distrusts as incompetent, malevolent or lacking in integrity. As a result, we have weighty reason to be wary of the pathologies of trust and distrust, including susceptibility to distortion by dramatic but unrepresentative breaches of trust, and vulnerability to bias and stereotype (Jones 2013:187, see also Scheman, this volume). Over-ready trust is perilous, exposing us to exploitation and manipulation; but so is over-ready distrust, which leads us to forgo the benefits of trusting relationships and to incur the risk of "acting immorally towards others whom we have, through distrusting, misjudged" (McGeer 2002:25).

In article for *Ebony* entitled, "In My Next Life, I'll be White," the philosopher Laurence Thomas (1990:84) relates with bitter irony that, "At times, I have looked over my shoulder expecting to see the danger to which a White was reacting, only to have it dawn on me that I was the menace." He relates that black men rarely enjoy the "public trust" of whites in America, "no matter how much their deportment or attire conform to the traditional standards of well-off White males." To enjoy the public trust means "to have strangers regard one as a morally decent person in a variety of contexts." Thomas (1990:84) notes that distrust of black men is rooted in a fear that "goes well beyond the pale of rationality." Thomas's case illustrates that distrust, when it is irrational, and particularly when it is baseless, eats away at trustworthiness:

> Thus the sear of distrust festers and becomes the fountainhead of low self-esteem and self-hate. Indeed, to paraphrase the venerable Apostle Paul, those who would do right find that they cannot. This should come as no surprise, however. For it is rare for anyone to live morally without the right sort of moral and social affirmation. And to ask this of Blacks is to ask what is very nearly psychologically impossible.
>
> *(Thomas 1990:2)*

Thomas picks out a feature of wrongful distrust that is particularly troubling: Distrust has a tendency to be self-confirming. Just as trustworthiness is reinforced by trust, untrustworthiness is reinforced by distrust. Distrust may serve to undermine the internal motivation toward trustworthiness of those who are wrongly distrusted (Kramer 1999). If the person who is distrusted without warrant feels that there is nothing he can do to prove himself worthy of trust, he will lack incentive to seek esteem.[8] In addition, he will lack the occasion to prove *to himself* that he is worthy of trust, and thereby lack the opportunity to cultivate a self-concept as of a trustworthy person.[9] Finally, he is deprived of the galvanizing effect of hope and vicarious confidence.[10]

Just as distrust confirms itself, distrustful interpretation of others perpetuates itself. McGeer (2002:28) claims that "trusting and distrusting inhabit incommensurable worlds" insofar as "our attitudes of trust and distrust shape our understanding of various events, leading us to experience the world in ways that tend to reinforce the attitudes we already hold." This echoes Govier's (1992a:56) observation that "[w]hen we distrust a person, even evidence of positive behavior and intentions is likely to be received with suspicion, to be interpreted as misleading, and, when properly understood, as negative after all." Distrust's inertia makes it both morally and epistemically perilous. Govier describes how taken to "radical extremes, distrust can go so far as to corrode our sense of reality," risking "an unrealistic, conspiratorial, indeed virtually paranoiac view of the world" (Govier 1992a:55). Such an attitude in is sharp contrast to the strategic and defensive distrust of government described by Hardin. Paranoiac distrust is indiscriminate in finding its target, and serves to undermine rather than to bolster autonomy. As we systematically interpret the speech and behavior of others in ways that confirm our distrust, suspiciousness builds on itself and our negative evaluations become impenetrable to empirical refutation. Jones (2013:194) describes how distrust functions as a *biasing* device (de Sousa 1987, Damasio 1994), tampering evidence so as to make us insensible to signals that others are trustworthy. She takes as a paradigm the frequency with which young black men in the United States are stopped by the police: "By doing nothing at all they are taken to be signaling untrustworthiness" (Jones 2013:195).

Jones (2013) identifies two further distorting aspects of distrust understood as an affective attitude: recalcitrance and spillover. Distrust is *recalcitrant* insofar as it characteristically parts company from belief: "Even when we believe and affirm that someone is trustworthy, this belief may not be reflected in the cognitive and affective habits with which we approach the prospect of being dependent on them. We can believe they are trustworthy and yet be anxiously unwilling to rely" (Jones 2013:195). Distrust exhibits *spillover* in cases where "it loses focus on its original target and spreads to neighboring targets" (Jones 2013:195). Distrust easily falsely generalizes from one particular psychologically salient case to an entire group. It is distressingly familiar how this aspect of distrust can be leveraged by those seeking to stoke distrust of marginalized groups such as refugees and asylum seekers by fixating on dramatic but unrepresentative cases.

Consideration of distrust's susceptibility to bias and stereotype, together with its tendencies toward self-fulfillment and self-perpetuation, may lead us to be distrustful of our own distrustful attitudes.[11] Gandhi (1951/2005:203) advocated in his *Delhi Diary* for a comprehensive disavowal of distrust: "we should trust even those whom we suspect as our enemies. Brave people disdain distrust." But a natural worry about this stance is that a broad policy of disavowing distrust will have the effect of exposing vulnerable parties to hazard. What right do we have to be "brave people" on the behalf of others whose positions are more precarious than our own? How confident can we be that our trust will inspire trustworthiness?

H.J.N. Horsburgh develops Gandhi's views to formulate more precisely a notion of "therapeutic trust" whereby one relies on another person with the aim of bolstering that person's trustworthiness and giving them the opportunity to develop morally: "it is no exaggeration to say that trust is to morality what adequate living space is to self-expression: without it there is no possibility of reaching maturity" (1960:352). Horsburgh's stance is more carefully hedged than Gandhi's. But one might worry whether strategic "therapeutic trust" is merely pretense of trust.[12] If it is, therapeutic trust seems to rely on obscuring one's true attitudes, possibly providing warrant for *distrust*. This worry is particularly acute if we are skeptical about the possibility of effectively concealing doubts about trustworthiness. Hieronymi (2008) points out that whether or not the person relied-upon is inspired by such reliance would seem to depend, at least partially, on whether the person perceives the doubts about her trustworthiness as reasonable. If such doubts are perceived as reasonable, then the decision to rely may well inspire someone to act so as to earn trust. On the other hand, if feelings of distrust are perceived as unreasonable, then the attempt to build trust through reliance may well be perceived as high-handed (Hieronymi 2008:231) or even insulting.

Hieronymi (2008:214) articulates a "purist" notion of trust according to which "one person trusts another to do something only to the extent that the one trustingly believes that the other will do that thing." In contrast, McGeer (2002:29) maintains that "it irresponsible and occasionally even tragic to regard these attitudes as purely responsive to evidence." But this stance gives rise to a sticky problem: if the norms of trust and distrust are not purely evidential, how should they be rationally assessed? Can they be evaluated as they would by a bookmaker coolly seeking to maximize his advantage? According to McGeer (2002:37), the desire for this kind of affective neutrality is the mark of a narrowly self-protective and immature psyche. The alternative paradigm of rationality that she espouses foreswears this kind of calculation. Reason "is not used to dominate the other or to protect the self; it is used to continuously discover the other *and* the self, as each party evolves through the dynamics of interaction." Rather than offering fortification against disappointment and betrayal, reason provides "the means for working through and moving beyond disappointment when such moments arise."

Both Hieronymi (2008) and McGeer (2002) focus their analyses on norms relevant to the person who trusts or distrusts. It is worth noting that the moral and practical point of view of the subject who is trusted or distrusted is comparatively under-explored in the philosophical literature.[13] Relevant questions include: What is the (or an) appropriate response to being wrongfully distrusted? How do moral and practical norms interact with each other in crafting and evaluating such a response?

One strategy for responding to unmerited distrust that might immediately suggest itself is to try to offer proof one's trustworthiness. As you walk into a store, you might ostentatiously display your disinclination to shoplift by zipping up your bags before entering and keeping your hands always visible. But this strategy risks backfiring because it appears too artful. We often assume that genuine trustworthiness is spontaneous and unselfconscious. But how can the wrongly distrusted person deliberately project trustworthiness in a way that appears artless? Psychologists of emotions find that the characteristic signals of sincere emotional expressions tend to be executed by muscle systems that are very difficult, if not impossible, to bring under conscious control (Ekman 2003). Drawing both on psychology and on Daoist thought, Slingerland (2014:320) describes the paradox of *wu*-wei as the problem "of how we can consciously try to be sincere or effortless ... to get into a state that, by its very nature, seems unattainable through conscious striving." Just as trustworthiness is hard to fake, false impressions of untrustworthiness (based on, for example, one's accent, the color of one's skin) are difficult to counteract. Effortful behaviors aimed at appearing trustworthy are the stock and trade of confidence tricksters; when such strategies are recognized they backfire whether the person is honest or not.

Direct confrontation with those who distrust us is another possible strategy. Consider the case of an African-American customer who is conspicuously followed around a store. Challenging unmerited distrust might serve to raise consciousness as well as to address an insult. But distrust is often not demonstrably manifest, and it is easily denied by those who bear the attitude and who may be oblivious, self-deceived or in denial about their distrust. So, in many contexts it may not be wise to reveal knowledge or suspicion of the distrustful attitudes of others. Sometimes the best available strategy for the distrusted is to suppress any indication of awareness that they are insulted by wrongful distrust, and to make as if they take themselves to be trusted. Trying to appear as if you take yourself to be trusted could be easier to pull off than trying to appear trustworthy. It could also lead to the feeling that you are in fact trusted via the familiar pathway of "fake it till you make it." This in turn might lead to being trusted, since in feeling that you are trusted you send the signals of trustworthiness in a characteristically effortless way. Doubtless, this strategy is uncertain and requires great patience. It also relies on a kind of misdirection that depending on the individual may be personally alienating, difficult to pull off, and is perhaps also morally dubious depending on how rigorous we are about authenticity and deception.

A third avenue is to try to cultivate a kind of noble generosity in being patient with unmerited distrust. The liability of this strategy, it seems to me, is that it risks suppressing warranted indignation, stoking resentment and compromising a person's self-respect. The enjoyment of the public trust – as Thomas puts it, "to have strangers regard one as a morally decent person in a variety of contexts" (Thomas 1990:84) – is fundamental to participation in civic life and something that decent people are entitled to irrespective of race, national origin, class or gender. Surely we should be morally indignant when others are denied this entitlement. So is this indignation not also appropriate for the person who is the target of prejudicial distrust?

What constitutes an appropriate response to unmerited distrust will often depend on the basis of the distrust (e.g. – prejudicial vs merely mistaken attribution of incompetence, prejudicial vs merely mistaken attribution of criminality).[14]

The complexity and the context-dependence of such considerations makes the topic both daunting and ripe for careful and methodical exploration.

Notes

1 Krishnamurthy (2015), following Hawley (2012), adopts "x distrusts y to ø" as the explanatorily fundamental form.
2 Jones (2013:62) points out that "we want those who can be trusted to identify themselves so that we can place our trust wisely" and she labels this further dimension to trust "rich trustworthiness." There is also a distinctive kind of untrustworthiness when a person is unable or unwilling to identify the limits of their trustworthiness to signal the domains in which they lack competence or are unwilling to be responsive to trust.
3 Naomi Scheman points out to me that such distrust may not be general in other ways. For example, I might distrust a racist police officer quite generally in his interactions with me but not in his interactions with you (because you and he are of the same race).
4 Another is Krishnamurthy's (2015) account.
5 One might think that you *do* have a genuine commitment (after all you have committed yourself!), but no *obligation* to meet that commitment. Hawley (2014:18) presents independent reasons to prefer the commitment account of trust and distrust to the obligation account.
6 Hawley (2014:17) notes that "part of trustworthiness is the attempt to avoid commitments you are not competent to fulfill."
7 Karen Frost-Arnold (2012) offers an account where trust involves taking the proposition that someone will do something as a premise in one's practical reasoning.
8 Cf. Pettit (1995).
9 Cf. Alfano (2016).
10 Cf. McGeer (2008).
11 In this vein, Ryan Preston-Roedder argues that having a measure of faith in humanity is central to moral life (2013) and articulates a notion of "civic trust" that involves interacting with strangers without fear while relying on their goodwill (2015).
12 Cf. Hieronymi (2008).
13 But see Potter (2002:12).
14 Thank you to Naomi Scheman for directing my attention to these issues.

References

Alfano, M. (2016) "Friendship and the Structure of Trust," in A. Masala and J. Webber (eds.), *From Personality to Virtue*, Oxford: Oxford University Press.
Baier, A. (1986) "Trust and Anti-Trust," *Ethics* 96(2): 231–260.
Damasio, A. (1994) *Descartes Error*, New York: Putnam.

D'Cruz, J. (2018) "Trust within Limits," *International Journal of Philosophical Studies* 26(2): 240–250.
de Sousa, R. (1987) *The Rationality of Emotion*, Cambridge, MA: MIT Press.
Domenicucci, J. and Holton, R. (2017) "Trust as a Two-Place Relation," in *The Philosophy of Trust*, P. Faulkner and T. Simpson (eds.), Oxford: Oxford University Press.
Ekman, P. (2003) *Emotions Revealed*, New York: Macmillan.
Faulkner, P. (2017) "The Attitude of Trust is Basic," *Analysis* 75(3): 424–429.
Frost-Arnold, K. (2014) "The Cognitive Attitude of Rational Trust," *Synthese* 191(9), pp. 1957–1974.
Gandhi, M. (1951/2005) *Gandhi, Selected Writings*, R. Duncan (ed.), New York: Dover Publications.
Govier, T. (1992a) "Distrust as a Practical Problem," *Journal of Social Philosophy* 23(1): 52–63.
Govier, T. (1992b) "Trust, Distrust, and Feminist Theory," *Hypatia* 7(1): 15–33.
Hardin, R. (2001) "Distrust," *Boston University Law Review* 81(3): 495–522.
Hawley, K. (2014) "Trust, Distrust, and Commitment," *Nous* 48(1): 1–20.
Hieronymi, P. (2008) "The Reasons of Trust," *Australasian Journal of Philosophy* 86(2): 213–236.
Holton, R. (1994) "Deciding to Trust, Coming to Believe," *Australasian Journal of Philosophy* 72 (1): 63–76.
Horsburgh, H.J.N. (1960) "The Ethics of Trust," *Philosophical Quarterly* 10(41): 343–354.
Jones, K. (1996) "Trust as an Affective Attitude," *Ethics* 107(1): 4–25.
Jones, K. (2013) "Distrusting the Trustworthy," in D. Archard, M. Deveaux, N. Manson and D. Weinstock (eds.), *Reading Onora O'Neill*, Abingdon: Routledge.
Kramer, R. (1999) "Trust and Distrust in Organizations," *Annual Review of Psychology* 50: 569–598.
Krishnamurthy, M. (2015) "White Tyranny and the Democratic Value of Distrust," *The Monist* 98 (4): 392–406.
Matthes, E. (2015) "On the Democratic Value of Distrust," *Journal of Ethics and Social Philosophy* 3: 1–5.
McGeer, V. (2002) "Developing Trust," *Philosophical Explorations* 5(1): 21–28.
McGeer, V. (2008) "Trust, Hope and Empowerment," *Australasian Journal of Philosophy* 86(2): 237–254.
Pettit, P. (1995) "The Cunning of Trust," *Philosophy and Public Affairs* 24(3): 202–225.
Potter, N. (2002) *How Can I Be Trusted?: A Virtue Theory of Trustworthiness*, Oxford: Rowman & Littlefield.
Preston-Roedder, R. (2013) "Faith in Humanity," *Philosophy and Phenomenological Research* 87(3): 664–687.
Preston-Roedder, R. (2017) "Civic Trust," *Philosophers Imprint* 17(4): 1–23.
Slingerland, E. (2014) *Trying Not to Try: The Ancient Art of Effortlessness and the Surprising Power of Spontaneity*, New York: Crown Publishers.
Thomas, L. (1990) "In My Next Life, I'll be White," *Ebony*, December, p. 84.
Ullmann-Margalit, E. (2004). "Trust, Distrust, and In Between," in R. Hardin (ed.), *Distrust*, New York: Russell Sage Foundation.

4 TRUST AND EPISTEMIC INJUSTICE[1]

José Medina

Epistemic injustices are committed when individuals or groups are *wronged as knowers*, that is, when they are mistreated in their status, capacity and participation in meaning-making and knowledge-producing practices. There are many ways in which people can be epistemically excluded, marginalized or mistreated in those practices as a result of being distrusted or of being unfavorably trusted when compared to others in the same epistemic predicament. In the two sections of this chapter I will elucidate how trust and distrust operate in dysfunctions that are at the heart of epistemic injustices. Section 4.1 will elucidate the trust/distrust dysfunctions associated with three different kinds of epistemic injustice. Section 4.2 will explore how those dysfunctions operate at different levels (personal, collective and institutional) and in different kinds of relations ("thin" and "thick"), thus covering a wide range of cases in which trust and distrust can go wrong and derail justice in epistemic terms.

4.1 Trust/Distrust and Kinds of Epistemic Injustice

In her influential article "Trust and Antitrust" (1986), Annette Baier underscored the normative dimension of trust by drawing a contrast between trust and reliance (see also Goldberg, this volume). As Baier's analysis shows, trust and reliance involve different kinds of expectations and they trigger different kinds of reactive attitudes when frustrated: when one merely relies on someone else to do something, the frustration of such reliance involves disappointment, but it does not warrant negative moral emotions and condemnation; however, when someone trusts someone else to do something, the violation of the trust warrants moral reactive attitudes such as anger, resentment or a sense of betrayal. Trusting someone involves placing strong normative expectations on them and, therefore, it involves vulnerability to betrayal (and/or other moral reactive attitudes). Accordingly, we can add, distrusting people involves a refusal to place normative expectations on them – i.e. a refusal to enter into epistemic cooperation with them – and a readiness to feel betrayed by them in epistemic interactions (that is, if the epistemic cooperation cannot be avoided). Distrust typically leads to the exclusion or marginalization of the distrusted subject in epistemic activities (see also D'Cruz, this volume). People can be epistemically mistreated by being unfairly distrusted and, as a result, excluded from (or marginalized in) activities of epistemic cooperation: they may not be asked to speak on certain subjects, or their contributions may not be given the credibility they deserve, or they may not be properly understood. But, as we shall see, people can also be epistemically mistreated by being inappropriately trusted and unfairly burdened with normative expectations or with misplaced reactions of resentment and betrayal. Misplaced trust can lead to pernicious normative consequences, such as being unfairly condemned for not meeting unwarranted expectations. And it can result in faulty forms of inclusion in activities of epistemic cooperation: being given excessive credibility, being forced into epistemic cooperation when one should be allowed to disengage, or being overburdened by unfair epistemic demands the subject should not be expected to meet. Misplaced trust and distrust can create epistemic dysfunctions among subjects and communities and lead to epistemic injustice. In what follows I will elucidate how trust and distrust dysfunctions contribute to different kinds of epistemic injustice.

I will focus on three different kinds of epistemic injustice that have been discussed in the recent literature, leaving open whether there are other kinds of epistemic injustice that deserve separate treatment.[2] The first and third kind of epistemic injustice I will discuss – testimonial and hermeneutical – have been identified by Miranda Fricker (2007) and they have been the most heavily discussed. The second kind – participatory injustice – has been identified by Christopher Hookway (2010).

4.1.1 Testimonial Injustice

Fricker describes the phenomenon of *testimonial injustice* as those cases of unfair epistemic treatment in which a speaker is attributed *less credibility* than deserved due to an identity prejudice (Fricker 2007:28). An unfair credibility deficit means an unfair lack of trust in testimonial dynamics. For example, in Fricker's celebrated illustration, Tom Robinson in the novel *To Kill a Mockingbird* is disbelieved by an all-white jury because, as a black man, he is not trusted as a witness and his version of the events is not treated as credible. Note that, so described, the unfair treatment in testimonial dynamics in which the injustice consists concerns a very specific kind of trust dysfunction: an unfair credibility deficit. However, as some scholars in this field have argued (Medina 2011; Davis 2016), when testimonial injustice revolves around issues of credibility, the injustice may concern *not only deficits but also excesses or surpluses*, that is, not only misplaced, excessive or malfunctioning *distrust*, but also misplaced, excessive or malfunctioning *trust*. For example, to continue with Fricker's heavily discussed illustration, the testimonial injustice suffered by Tom Robinson in *To Kill a Mockingbird* involves *both* the credibility deficit that attaches to people of color in the witness stand *and* also (simultaneously and relatedly) the *credibility excess* that attaches to the white voices of other witnesses and to the district attorney and judge who reformulate and distort Tom's voice and testimony (see Medina, 2011 and 2013). Fricker has argued that credibility is not a distributive good for which the deficits of some should be correlated with the surpluses of others. This seems right, but, as I have argued (2011 and 2013) our ascriptions of credibility do have a *comparative and contrastive* quality, so that we trust people as more, less or equally credible than others; and we need to critically examine the complex dynamics of testimonial trust, tracing how relations of trust/distrust flow and fluctuate, comparatively and contrastively, among groups of people.[3] Even before the members of a group are actively distrusted (think for example of a newly established sub-community, such as a new immigrant community, or a newly visible social group such as the trans community), the fact that the voices of those who are unlike them are disproportionately trusted already creates an unfair testimonial climate in which the voices of people like them may not be well received or may encounter obstacles and resistances which others do not face. That situation requires being vigilant and on our guard even before the breach of trust is inflicted in a systematic way, and paying attention to the credibility surpluses of some can help us detect issues of epistemic privilege that are crucial to understand (and in some cases even anticipate) the emergence of unfair credibility deficits.

But it is worth noting also that a credibility excess or surplus can be part of a pattern of epistemic mistreatment in a very different way. There can be cases in which people are unfairly treated epistemically *precisely* because they are being trusted: cases in which people are selectively trusted in virtue of their identity (e.g. black people on "black matters"), and they thus become vulnerable to *epistemic exploitation*. As Davis has argued, epistemic exploitation can proceed via the credibility surplus assigned to non-dominantly situated subjects who are expected to act as "epistemic tokens," being called upon to provide "raw experience" and to "represent" for the groups to which they are perceived as belonging (Davis 2016). In this way, one can be mistreated in testimonial dynamics (one's voice can be distorted or unfairly narrowed), or one can bear unfair epistemic burdens, not only by being discredited and deemed unworthy of testimonial trust but also by being *credited* and deemed disproportionately worthy of testimonial trust by virtue of one's social location or membership in a group.[4]

Moreover, testimonial injustices can involve trust/distrust dysfunctions in different ways depending on the reasons why subjects are found credible or not credible. In particular, the assessment of a speaker's credibility typically concerns two things: the assessment of her competence and the assessment of her sincerity. But there are aspects of the overall communicative cooperation involved in trust that go beyond competence and sincerity (at least narrowly conceived).

Apportioning adequate trust to a speaker in testimonial exchanges is not simply regarding her (and the contents of her utterances) competent and sincere, but it also typically involves trusting that the speaker is being cooperative in other ways, for example, in not being opaque or in not hiding information. If a speaker is competent and sincere in what she says, but she does not disclose everything she knows; she may be misleading or deceitful in subtle ways and hence not to be trusted (at least not fully). This is captured by what Sandy Goldberg (in personal correspondence) terms *non-misleadingness*, which he illustrates with the following example: suppose that I know that p, and I also know that if I tell you that p, but neglect to tell you that q, you will be misled and will draw false inferences; then I might tell you that p, where I am perfectly credible (that is, sincere and competent) on the matter of whether p, and yet I am still misleading you in some way. Having the right cooperative attitudes,[5] along with competence and sincerity, is indeed a crucial component of testimonial trust. Members of oppressed groups are often stigmatized by being regarded as incompetent, insincere, or deceitful just by virtue of their membership in those groups; and, as a result, trust is unfairly withdrawn from them. In these different ways, stigmatized oppressed subjects become excluded from and marginalized or unfairly treated in testimonial exchanges; that is, they become the victims of testimonial injustices. In sexist and racist societies women and racial minorities have been traditionally depicted as untrustworthy because of their incompetence, insincerity or deceitfulness. These epistemic stereotypes continue to marginalize and stigmatize women and racial minorities in testimonial practices even when they are believed to possess credible information, for they may still not be *trusted* with the use and transmission of such information. And note that even when someone is considered to be a sincere and competent witness (whether in a court of law or in less formal contexts), it is still possible that the subject in question may not be fully trusted and her participation and contributions may be prejudicially undermined in various ways, as we shall see with the next two kinds of epistemic injustices, which interact with testimonial injustice and often become compounded with it. We can conclude that testimonial trust often contains a variety of heterogeneous ingredients among which competence, sincerity and non-misleadingness (or overall cooperation) figure prominently.

4.1.2 Participatory Injustice

As Christopher Hookway (2010) has suggested, being treated fairly in epistemic interactions often involves more than being treated as a credible subject of testimony. It involves being trusted in one's overall epistemic competence and participatory skills, and not just as a possessor of knowledge but also as a producer of knowledge: that is, not just trusted as someone who can answer questions about one's experiences and available information, but also trusted as someone who can formulate her own questions, evaluate evidence, consider alternative explanations or justifications, formulate and answer objections, develop counterexamples, etc. When particular kinds or groups of people are not trusted equally to participate in these diverse epistemic practices that go well beyond the merely testimonial (e.g. when male students are given more class time than female students to develop counterexamples or objections; or when female scientists are not equally trusted in the production of scientific hypotheses and explanations), we can say that they suffer a non-testimonial, epistemic injustice. This is what Hookway terms a *participatory injustice*, which he describes as unfairly excluding knowers from participating in non-testimonial epistemic practices such as those involved in querying, conjecturing and imagining. We can add to Hookway's analysis that participatory injustices result from failing to receive the *participatory trust* one deserves. Being the recipient of participatory trust involves being trusted in one's capacity to participate in epistemic interactions: having trust in one's general intelligence and in one's specific epistemic capacities; being trusted in producing, processing and assessing knowledge adequately, in speaking truthfully, in making sense, etc. Within this general domain of epistemic trust, we can highlight the trust in one's expressive capacities and in one's repertoire of meanings and interpretative resources, which I will term *hermeneutical trust*. Unfair dysfunctions in hermeneutical trust/distrust constitute a distinctive kind of epistemic injustice, which Fricker (2007) has termed *hermeneutical injustice.*

4.1.3 Hermeneutical Injustice

Hermeneutical injustice is the phenomenon that occurs when the intelligibility of communicators is unfairly constrained or undermined, when their meaning-making capacities encounter unfair obstacles (Medina 2017), or, as Fricker puts it, "when a gap in collective interpretive resources puts someone at an unfair disadvantage when it comes to making sense of their social experience" (2007:1). What would it mean to think about this phenomenon in terms of the erosion of *trust*? In the first place, we can talk about dysfunctions of hermeneutical trust/distrust at a *structural, large-scale, cultural level*, since, as Fricker emphasizes, hermeneutical injustice is a structural, large-scale phenomenon that happens at the level of an entire culture: it is the shortcomings of the available expressive and interpretative resources of a culture that produces hermeneutical marginalization, obscuring particular contents (e.g. the difficulty in expressing experiences of "sexual harassment" before such label was available to name the experience), or demeaning particular expressive styles (e.g. the perception of a way of talking as less assertive or less clear because it is non-normative or non-mainstream). At this *collective level*, we can talk about problematic relations of trust or distrust between a hermeneutical community or cultural group[6] and the individual members of that community who communicate within it. Under adverse hermeneutical climates (which make it difficult to communicate, for example, about certain sexual or racial issues), subjects can become unfairly distrusted in their meaning-making and meaning-expressing capacities, not only as they interact communicatively with other subjects but also as they address entire communities and institutions, for example, in raising a complaint about sexual harassment or racial discrimination. Such hermeneutically marginalized subjects should rightly distrust the expressive and interpretative community in question (and the individual members who support it and sustain it), at least with respect to the areas of experience that are difficult to talk about within that community. But, in the second place, we can also talk about dysfunctions of hermeneutical trust/distrust at the *personal and interpersonal level*, that is, we can also talk about how dysfunctional forms of hermeneutical trust/distrust can mediate the communicative interactions among particular individuals. Communicators can be more or less complicit with adverse hermeneutical climates, and they can more or less actively distrust themselves or others in the expression and interpretation of meanings, thus contributing to the perpetuation of the hermeneutical obstacles in question. Although hermeneutical injustices are indeed very often collective, widespread and systematic, they do not simply happen without perpetrators, without being committed by anyone in particular, as a direct result of lacunas or limitations in "the collective hermeneutical resource" (Fricker 2007:155) of a culture.[7] As I have argued elsewhere (Medina 2017), the structural elements of hermeneutical injustice should not be emphasized at the expense of disregarding its *agential* components; and, indeed, within a hermeneutically unjust culture, we can identify particular individuals and particular groups and publics as bearing different kinds of responsibility for their complicity with hermeneutical disadvantages and obstacles, for their hermeneutical neglect in certain areas, and/or for their hermeneutical resistance to certain expressive or interpretative efforts.

Fighting hermeneutical injustice involves fighting the erosion of hermeneutical trust, which often means being proactive in instilling hermeneutical trust in the expressive and interpretative capacities of disadvantaged groups. On the one hand, part of the struggle for hermeneutical justice here consists in finding spaces, opportunities and support for members of hermeneutically marginalized groups to build self-trust and to find the courage to break silences and develop new expressive and interpretative resources. This hermeneutical struggle is a crucial part of social movements of liberation. For example, as Fricker has emphasized, an important part of the women's movement was the organization of "speak-outs." There, women activists found themselves in the peculiar situation of gathering to break a silence (i.e. the silence about women's problems such as domestic abuse or sexual harassment) without yet having a language to speak, that is, "speak-outs" in which "the 'this' they were going to break the silence about had no name" (2007:150). In these "speak-outs" women trusted each other's expressive powers of articulation even before they had a language, thus developing trust in their capacity to communicate their experiences with inchoate and embryonic expressions (what Fricker terms "nascent meanings").

On the other hand, non-marginalized subjects can also contribute to fight the erosion of hermeneutical trust and to overcome hermeneutical marginalization. In communicative interactions with hermeneutically disadvantaged subjects, communicators should cultivate attitudes and policies that compensate for the lack of trust in the intelligibility and expressive powers of marginalized subjects, enhancing the trust in those subjects by overriding prevalent suspicions of defective intelligibility and applying special principles of hermeneutical charity. An epistemic policy for enhancing hermeneutical trust under adverse conditions can be found in Louise Antony's suggestion of a policy of *epistemic affirmative action*, which recommends that interpreters operate with the "*working hypothesis* that when a woman, or any member of a stereotyped group, says something anomalous, they should assume that it's *they* who don't understand, not that it is the woman who is nuts" (1995:89). While seeing merits in this proposal, Fricker has argued persuasively that "the hearer needs to be *indefinitely context sensitive* in how he applies the hypothesis," and that "a policy of affirmative action across all subject matters would not be justified" (2007:171; my emphasis). It is only with respect to those contents or expressive styles for which there are unfair hermeneutical disadvantages that we should take special measures (such as a policy of *epistemic affirmative action*) in order to ensure hermeneutical trust. In other words, it is only in adverse hermeneutical climates and for those negatively affected in particular ways that enhanced forms of hermeneutical trust should be given. This requires that we identify first how dysfunctional patterns of hermeneutical trust/distrust emerge and are maintained, so that we can then design the measures needed for disrupting our complicity with such patterns and for mitigating the hermeneutical injustices in question. We need to be critically vigilant about structural conditions and institutional designs that favor certain languages, expressive styles and interpretative resources, disproportionately empowering some groups and disempowering others (for example, when a criminal justice system exercises suspicion over languages, dialects and mannerisms that deviate from "standard" – i.e. white, middle-class – American English). And we also need to be critically vigilant about both *interpersonal* dynamics and *institutional* dynamics that obscure certain areas of human experience and social interaction, or prevent the use of certain hermeneutical resources and expressive styles. Elsewhere (Medina 2017 and forthcoming) I have discussed both hermeneutically unfair *interpersonal* dynamics (e.g. the hermeneutical intimidations in interpersonal exchanges illustrated by the literature on micro-aggressions – see Dotson 2011), and hermeneutically unfair *institutional* dynamics (e.g. when institutions refuse to accept certain categories and expressive styles to the detriment of particular publics, as for example when questionnaires force individuals to self-describe in ways they do not want to because of the limited options such as the binary male/female categories when it comes to gender identity).

In short, epistemic injustices are rooted in (and also deepen) the erosion of trust and the perpetuation of dysfunctional patterns of trust/distrust. The mitigation of epistemic injustices requires repairing trust/distrust dysfunctions and working toward ways of trusting and distrusting more fairly in epistemic interactions. Struggles for improving ways of trusting and distrusting have to be fought on different fronts and in different ways, including efforts at the personal, interpersonal and institutional levels.

4.2 Scope and Depth of Trust/Distrust Dysfunctions

In the previous sections I elucidated different kinds of epistemic injustices – testimonial, participatory and hermeneutic – and how trust/distrust was negatively impacted in relation to them, thus calling attention to dysfunctional patterns of testimonial, participatory and hermeneutic trust/distrust. But it is important to note that these dysfunctional patterns can have different scope and depth, depending on the range of subjectivities and agencies that the dysfunctional trust/distrust is directed toward and depending on the kinds of relations in which the trust/distrust in question is inscribed. Epistemic injustices can erode the trust the people have *in one another* in their epistemic interactions; but they also negatively impact the trust that people have *in themselves*, often resulting in weak or defective forms of self-trust for marginalized subjects and in excessive forms of self-trust for privileged subjects (see Medina 2013[8] and Jones 2012). Finally, they also negatively impact the trust that people have in communities and institutions with which and within which they interact. Working toward epistemic justice therefore involves learning to trust and distrust oneself, others and communities and institutions in adequate and fair ways. In this section I will briefly discuss the different *scope* that trust/distrust dysfunctions can have and also how *deep* those dysfunctions can go depending on the relations one has with the relevant subjects, communities and institutions. It is crucial to pay attention to the *kinds* of relation one has with particular others as well as with particular communities and institutions in order to properly assess the patterns of trust/distrust binding us to them: it is not the same when we trust/distrust (or are trusted/distrusted by) a friend, a peer, a partner, a collaborator, a fellow citizen, a complete stranger, etc.; or when we trust/distrust (or are trusted/distrusted by) the press, the social media, the judicial system, the police, one's own countries, other countries, etc.

As we discussed in the previous section, under conditions of epistemic injustice, it is typically the case that unfairly trusting/distrusting particular subjects and particular groups go hand in hand: it is because of identity prejudices, as Fricker argues, that particular subjects are epistemically mistreated *qua* members of particular groups – e.g. someone can be unfairly misheard, misinterpreted or disbelieved as a woman, or as a queer person, or as a disabled person, or as person of color, etc. But notice that although the mistreatment involved in epistemic injustice is typically more than incidental or a one-off case, its scope can vary and it can target individuals, groups or institutions in very different ways. Sometimes the unfair treatment of individual subjects, of groups and of institutions, although interrelated, can take different forms. Although it is probably more common to find forms of epistemic mistreatment and unfair attributions of trust/distrust happening simultaneously at various levels and without being confined exclusively to the personal, the collective or the institutional level, it is in principle possible for those dysfunctions to appear only (or primarily) at one level. For example, it is possible for subjects to hold prejudicial views and attitudes against collectives and the organizations and voices that represent those collectives, without necessarily acting prejudicially against all (or the majority of, or even any of) the individual members of those collectives. For example, a business owner may have fair epistemic attitudes with respect to his workers as he interacts with them and he may not have any particular distrust for their individual claims and concerns. However, he may have prejudicial views of his workers *as a collective*, thinking, for example, that when they speak and act as a group they are insincere or deceitful and their collective claims untrustworthy. Such a business owner may direct his class prejudices against a group – workers as a collective – without undermining his trust in the particular individuals who belong to that group; and he may systematically distrust workers' organizations (such as unions) and the representatives of the group, without exhibiting any particular kind of distrust in dealing with individual workers.

It may seem counterintuitive to claim that a prejudicial view that creates distrust may be directed at a collective without necessarily being directed at all the individual members of that collective. Let me revisit the example of the business owner with prejudicial views of workers as a collective in order to clarify this point. What is the difference between the individual claims that an individual worker can make when he speaks on his own behalf and the collective claims that he makes when he speaks as a representative of the staff? When Wally speaks to his boss about being treated unfairly as a worker, it is hard to see whether he should be heard by the boss differently than when he speaks as a representative of the staff. But there can be an important difference here: the difference between, for example, complaining about a particular work assignment because of one's personal situation – for example, complaining about being forced to work extra hours because one is a single parent – versus complaining about that assignment as a representative of the staff because they think it will take an unbearable toll in their personal lives. What is at stake is obviously quite different: in the individual case the boss retains his power to assign additional hours in general, whereas in the latter case he doesn't. But that the stakes are higher only means that the boss may have added *practical* reasons to distrust the collective claim and to be particularly skeptical about the justification of the complaint. But does the boss have *epistemic* reasons[9] to distrust workers as a collective that he does not have when he interacts with individual workers? It depends on the specifics of the boss's prejudicial view of workers as a collective: the prejudicial view may contain distributive features that apply to all the members of the collective (e.g. workers are lazy – and so is Wally if he is a worker); but the prejudicial view may also contain non-distributive features that only apply to group dynamics and not to the individuals in the group acting and speaking in isolation. These are examples of the latter (non-distributive features that the boss may ascribe to workers as a collective but not necessarily to every individual worker qua worker). The boss may think that when workers get together, they are power-hungry, always trying to undermine his power and trying to acquire collective power for themselves; or he may think that when workers get together, they tend to be greedy and unreasonable, much more so than they would otherwise be as individuals speaking on their own behalf.

Moreover, trust/distrust can function differently not only in personal relations and group relations but also in institutional relations. Dysfunctional trust/distrust with respect to institutions may, at least in some cases, operate independently of the trust/distrust given to the individual subjects who speak and act on behalf of the institution, the officers of such institution. This may seem implausible in some cases: for example, if one has a deep distrust of the police, one is likely to have a deep distrust of individual police officers (a distrust that may or may not be unfair, depending on whether or not it is warranted in the light of the relevant histories of police treatment). But think, for example, of a government agency, such as border security and immigration, whose policies and attitudes one considers to be prejudicial and to be distrusted as racist or xenophobic, without necessarily viewing particular immigration and border security officers as racist or xenophobic and to be distrusted. In this case, one may face epistemic obstacles in answering an immigration questionnaire because one distrusts how the information will be used by the agency itself, without necessarily distrusting the particular immigration officer one communicates with in face-to-face interactions. Even more clear perhaps is the case of dysfunctional excessive trust in institutions without necessarily having an excessive trust in the agents or officers of that institutions: people may have a blind trust in the police, in the justice system or in science, without blindly trusting all police officers, judges or individual scientists.

Of course, typically the scope of dysfunctional trust/distrust cannot (and should not) be narrowly circumscribed and it is important to pay attention to how the different levels at which dysfunctional trust/distrust can operate – personal, collective, and institutional – work together and reinforce each other. The point of distinguishing these levels is not to suggest that they can be understood separately or that they work independently of each other, but rather, to call attention to the fact that each of them has peculiar features and a distinctive phenomenology, so that we are vigilant to the diverse configurations that dysfunctional trust/distrust can take and we never assume that we do not have such dysfunction at one level just because it does not seem to appear at other levels (e.g. that there is no dysfunctional institutional trust just because the officers of that institution interact smoothly with the public).

If distinguishing the different kinds of scope that dysfunctional trust/distrust can have is crucial for a fine-grained analysis of the problem, just as important is to pay attention to the *depth* that the problem can take, whether in personal, collective or institutional relations. In order to identify how deep a dysfunctional trust/distrust goes, we need to interrogate our specific involvement with particular others, particular collectives and particular institutions. At the personal level, for example, it is not the same to be unfairly distrusted by a stranger, by a friend, by a partner, by a family member, etc. Focusing on testimonial injustices and a breach of testimonial trust, Jeremy Wanderer (2017) has distinguished between *thin* and *thick* cases of epistemic maltreatment: the *thin* cases are those in which the maltreatment consists in the abrogation of epistemic responsibilities that can be detected in the formal relationship between a speaker and a hearer – *any* speaker and *any* hearer – independently of the content of their relationship, that is, without recognition of the specific roles and relations that bind them together; by contrast, the *thick* cases are those in which "the maltreatment involves a rupture of, or disloyalty within [thick relations of intimacy]." Following Wanderer, I want to suggests that in the thick cases of epistemic injustice the breach of trust or *trust-betrayal* compromises relationships that we cherish and can become constitutive of who we are, shaking our social life – and in some cases our very identity – to the core.

The phenomenon of epistemic injustice acquires different qualities in the thin and thick cases, and repairing the problem takes different shapes: repairing a breach of trust in formal relations is quite different from repairing a trust-betrayal in a thick, intimate relation. And note that this applies not only to *personal* trust/distrust dysfunctions, but also to *group* trust/distrust dysfunctions and to *institutional* trust/distrust dysfunctions. One can be trust-betrayed by entire groups of people and institutions one is in thick relationships with. Tom Robinson, for example, was not only unfairly distrusted by the district attorney, the judge and the individual jury members, but also by his entire town and country. It was the criminal and judicial system that was supposed to serve him and protect him, the system as a whole, which failed him and mistreated him epistemically. When one is unfairly distrusted by collectives one is in a thick relationship with (e.g. by what one has taken to be one's own community, one's own town or one's own country), the trust-betrayal can constitute the basis for severing the tie with that collective, that is, for no longer considering those collectives as one's own (e.g. one's own community, town or country). Similarly, when one is unfairly distrusted by institutions one is in a thick relationship with – not just *any* institution, but the very institutions one is supposed to be served and protected by (e.g. by one's own government, by one's own state and local authorities, by the police, etc.), we should talk about the erosion (and in extreme cases, the dissolution) of a social relation that binds together subjects and institutions. When trust-betrayal occurs in thick relations, one is being failed by the very people, communities and institutions to whom and to which one is bound by relations of loyalty and mutual responsibility. The collapse of this kind of mutuality, the failure of mutual trust, can undermine one's status and epistemic agency, making one feel epistemically abandoned in such a radical way that one may feel lost, without epistemic partners, communities or institutional supports. In these cases, trust-betrayal involves a social isolation and abandonment that is characteristic of radical and recalcitrant forms of epistemic injustice.

Because of the potential for particularly damaging consequences of trust-betrayals in thick relations, these relations bring with them special responsibilities with respect to the trust that is owed and needs to be protected and cultivated in active ways within those relations (see also Frost-Arnold, this volume). In thick personal relationships such as friendships, partnerships or familial relations, for example, individuals owe to one another special efforts to create and maintain trust despite the particular obstacles in trusting each other that life may throw their way. In other words, thick personal relations involve a special commitment to overcome trust problems and to make every possible effort in preventing those problems from becoming dysfunctional patterns. In some thick relationships such special responsibilities with respect to trust are mutual and reciprocal (as in the cases of friendships and partnerships among adults); but in other thick relationships, they may not be (for example, in filial relations between parents and children). Similarly, thick relations between collectives and their individual members involve enhanced trust commitments and responsibilities: a collective such as a town or a country would *betray* its citizens or sub-communities by arbitrarily casting doubt in their epistemic powers, marginalizing them epistemically and forcing them to live under suspicion; but individuals can also *betray* a collective such as a town or a country by unfairly withdrawing all trust in it without having grounds for doing so (think, for example, of cases of treason grounded in a deep distrust that the individual unfairly cultivates against his own community). Finally, thick relations between institutions and individual subjects also involve enhanced trust commitments and responsibilities: an institution such as the criminal justice system that has particular responsibilities with respect to the public (responsibilities that a private corporation, for example, does not have) betrays the individuals who go through it when it does not give them the trust they deserve; and there could also be thick cases of betrayal in which individuals unfairly distrust institutions to which they owe loyalty when they are functioning properly (cases that are not hard to imagine in these days in which institutional legitimacy is in crisis and trust in institutions has become so precarious, with public officials directing agencies they do not trust and are committed to obstruct). More research needs to be done for a full analysis of trust dysfunctions in thick relationships at the personal, collective and institutional levels. This is an area of social epistemology that is particularly under-researched given the traditional emphasis on abstract and generic cases.

Building on the discussion of different kinds of epistemic injustice and their impact on trust/distrust in the previous section, this section has provided a preliminary analysis of the different scope and depth that trust/distrust dysfunctions can have, distinguishing between the personal, collective and institutional levels, and between thin and thick cases. Detailed accounts of how to repair thin and thick cases of trust-betrayal in personal, collective or institutional relations are needed. Unfortunately, this will remain beyond the scope of this chapter, but it is worth noting that it is part of the ongoing discussion in different areas of critical theory broadly conceived[10] and in liberatory approaches within social and political epistemology.[11]

Notes

1 I am grateful to Sandy Goldberg who read previous versions of this chapter and gave me critical feedback and suggestions for revisions on an earlier version of it. I am also grateful to Karen Arnold-Frost, Gloria Origgi and Judith Simon for critical comments and suggestions that have helped me to improve this chapter substantially.

2 See Medina (2017) and Pohlhaus (2017) for arguments that underscore that there is not a single, definitive and complete classification of all the kinds of epistemic injustice that we can identify. As these authors argue, our list of the variety of epistemic injustices has to be left open-ended because our classifications may not capture *all* the possible ways in which people can be mistreated as knowers and meaning-makers, and because different classifications are offered for different purposes and in different contexts, and we should not expect a single and final classification to do all the work in teaching us how to diagnose and repair epistemic injustices in *every* possible way and in *every* possible context.

3 Note that this calls into question whether the notion of *justice* underlying the notion of *epistemic injustice* is properly conceived as *distributive justice*. Which theory of justice is presupposed in discussions of epistemic justice? This is a central question that needs to be carefully addressed in discussions of epistemic injustice, but a difficult question that goes beyond the scope of this chapter.

4 This is related to a more general phenomenon that Katherine Hawley (2014) has discussed: the burdens that go along with being trusted to do something. As Hawley suggests, one might not want to inherit those burdens, and so might resist being trusted, even as in the past one has reliably done the thing for which one is about to be trusted – for example, a partner who regularly makes dinner for the other partner, and who has come to be relied upon to do so, might not want to be *trusted* to do so as this would involve a moral burden she did not previously have.

5 Note that this discussion of cooperation versus misleadingness can be fleshed out pragmatically in terms of Grice's (1975) principle of cooperation and his conversational maxims. This is an interesting domain of intersection between pragmatics and social epistemology.

6 By "hermeneutical community" or "cultural group" I refer to those social groupings whose members share expressive and interpretative resources, such as a language or dialect, the use of certain concepts, a set of interpretative frameworks, etc. Note that this notion admits heterogeneity and diversity – i.e. not all members of a hermeneutical community or cultural group will use their expressive resources in the same way or will agree on the interpretation and scope of these resources. As I have argued elsewhere, hermeneutical communities or cultural groups always contain sub-communities and subgroups (or their possibility); they can have movable and negotiable boundaries; and subjects can belong to multiple hermeneutical communities or cultural groups (see Medina 2006).

7 For Fricker (2007), hermeneutical injustice is not a harm perpetrated by an agent (159), but "the injustice of having some significant area of one's social experience obscured from collective understanding owing to a structural identity prejudice in the collective hermeneutical resource" (155).

8 I have argued that fair epistemic practices should ensure that those who participate in it can achieve a minimum of self-trust but also a minimum of self-distrust, so that they do not develop either *epistemic self-annihilation* or *epistemic arrogance* (see Medina 2013, chapter 1).

9 For the contrast between practical and epistemic reasons to trust/distrust, see Goldberg's chapter "Trust and Reliance" in this volume.

10 Exciting new discussions of epistemic injustice and how to repair them can be found in critical race theory, feminist theory, queer theory, trans theory, disability theory, decolonial and post-colonial theory, and other areas of critical studies. See the chapters in these different areas of critical theory in Kidd, Medina, and Pohlhaus (2017).

11 See the different essays in "Liberatory Epistemologies and Axes of Oppression", Section II of Kidd, Medina, and Pohlhaus (2017).

References

Antony, L. (1995) "'Sisters, Please, I'd Rather Do It Myself': A Defense of Individualism in Feminist Epistemology," *Philosophical Topics* 23(2): 59–94.

Baier, A. (1986) "Trust and Antitrust," *Ethics* 96: 231–260.

Davis, E. (2016) "Typecasts, Tokens, and Brands: Credibility Excess as Epistemic Vice," *Hypatia* 31 (3): 485–501.

Dotson, K. (2011) "Tracking Epistemic Violence, Tracking Practices of Silencing," *Hypatia* 26(2): 236–257.

Fricker, M. (2007) *Epistemic Injustice: Power and the Ethics of Knowing*, New York: Oxford.

Grice, H.P. (1975) "Logic and Conversation," in P. Cole and J. Morgan (eds.), *Syntax and Semantics*, Volume 3, New York: Academic Press.

Hawley, K. (2014) "Trust, Distrust, and Commitment," *Noûs* 48(1): 1–20.

Hookway, C. (2010) "Some Varieties of Epistemic Injustice: Reflections on Fricker," *Episteme* 7 (2):151–163.

Jones, K. (2012) "The Politics of Intellectual Self-trust," *Social Epistemology* 26(2): 237–251.

Kidd, I., Medina, J. and Pohlhaus, G. (2017) *Routledge Handbook of Epistemic Injustice*, London: Routledge.

Medina, J. (2006) *Speaking from Elsewhere: A New Contextualist Perspective on Meaning, Identity, and Discursive Agency*, Albany, NY: SUNY Press.

Medina, J. (2011) "The Relevance of Credibility Excess in a Proportional View of Epistemic Injustice: Differential Epistemic Authority and the Social Imaginary," *Social Epistemology* 25 (1): 15–35.

Medina, J. (2013) *The Epistemology of Resistance: Gender and Racial Oppression, Epistemic Injustice, and Resistant Imaginations*, New York: Oxford University Press.

Medina, J. (2017) "Varieties of Hermeneutic Injustice," in I. Kidd, J. Medina and K. Pohlhaus (eds.), *Routledge Handbook of Epistemic Injustice*, London: Routledge.

Medina, J. (2017) "Epistemic Injustice and Epistemologies of Ignorance," in P. Taylor, L. Alcoff and L. Anderson (eds.), *Routledge Companion to the Philosophy of Race*, London and New York: Routledge.

Pohlhaus, G. (2017) "Varieties of Epistemic Injustice," in I. Kidd, J. Medina and K. Pohlhaus (eds.), *Routledge Handbook of Epistemic Injustice*, London: Routledge.

Wanderer, J. (2017) "Varieties of Testimonial Injustice," in I. Kidd, J. Medina and K. Pohlhaus (eds.), *Routledge Handbook of Epistemic Injustice*, London: Routledge.

5

TRUST AND EPISTEMIC RESPONSIBILITY

Karen Frost-Arnold

5.1 Introduction

What is the role of trust in knowledge? Does trusting someone involve an epistemically blameworthy leap of faith in which we ignore evidence? When is distrust irresponsible? What kinds of knowledge and epistemic skills ought I develop in order to be a trustworthy person? These are some of the many questions raised at the intersection of trust and epistemology. This chapter investigates the philosophical literature at this intersection by focusing on the concept of epistemic responsibility. First, I begin with a brief introduction to the central concepts of trust and epistemic responsibility.

Other chapters in this handbook address the difficulties of answering the question: what is trust? For the purposes of this chapter, trust is conceived of as a three-part relation in which person *A* (the trustor) trusts person *B* (the trustee) to care for valued good *C*, or perform action ϕ (cf. Baier 1994:101; Frost-Arnold 2014). For example, when I say that I trust my cat sitter, I may mean that I trust my cat sitter to care for my cat (a valued good in my life), or I might mean that I trust my cat sitter to feed my cat while I am away from home (an action that I trust them to perform). Whether it be trust in someone to care for a good or trust to perform an action, trust is a complex suite of cognitive, affective, and conative attitudes (Baier 1994:132). In trusting, the trustor counts on the trustee, and this makes the trustor vulnerable to being betrayed (Baier 1994:99). It is how we handle this vulnerability that connects trust to questions of epistemic responsibility.

The term "epistemic responsibility" is a polysemic phrase used in debates surrounding justification, knowledge, epistemic virtue, and epistemic injustice. The term has several different but related meanings in these overlapping literatures in epistemology. One place the concept of epistemic responsibility figures is in the internalism/externalism debate. Many epistemic internalists are responsibilists who hold that "what makes a belief justified is its being appropriately related to one's good evidence for it, and … this appropriate relation … involves one's being epistemically responsible" (Hetherington 2002:398). For example, Hilary Kornblith argues that "When we ask whether an agent's beliefs are justified we are asking whether he has done all he should to bring it about that he have true beliefs. The notion of justification is thus essentially tied to that of action, and equally to the notion of responsibility" (Kornblith 1983:34). As this passage illustrates, the concept of epistemic responsibility is often used to emphasize the active nature of knowers (cf. Code 1987:51). Rather than passive recipients of beliefs, knowers are agents whose actions of gathering and weighing evidence can be epistemically praiseworthy or blameworthy. If an agent fails to take all the steps she could have taken to arrive at a true belief, then we might assess her actions as epistemically blameworthy. Assessments of epistemic praiseworthiness or blameworthiness are often seen as analogous to our practices of morally praising and blaming actions. Thus, the literature on epistemic responsibility often intersects with the literature on the ethics of belief, which examines the ethical norms governing belief formation, and the literature on epistemic injustice, which investigates the ethical and political norms governing belief formation and dissemination (see Medina, this volume).

Assessments of epistemic responsibility can also be made of an agent's character, which connects discussions of epistemic justification to the literature on virtue epistemology. For example, in Kornblith's argument for a responsibilist account of justification, he maintains that:

> [W]e may assess an agent, or an agent's character, by examining the processes responsible for the presence of his beliefs just as we may evaluate an agent, or his character, by examining the etiology of his actions. Actions which are the product of malice display a morally bad character; beliefs which are product of epistemically irresponsible action display an epistemically bad character.
>
> *(Kornblith 1983:38)*

Virtue epistemology is a normative enterprise that focuses on epistemic agents rather than isolated actions. Virtue epistemologists investigate the nature of epistemic virtue itself and attempt to identify the various epistemic virtues. Epistemic responsibility is often cited as a core epistemic virtue (cf. Code 1987:34),[1] and "epistemically responsible" is often used interchangeably with "being epistemically virtuous." For Lorraine Code, epistemically responsible agents are intellectually virtuous persons who "value knowing and understanding how things really are" (Code 1987:59). Epistemic responsibility in this sense involves cultivating epistemic virtues and just epistemic communities that enable us to know and understand.[2]

With these conceptions of trust and epistemic responsibility in mind, we can see that a plethora of questions about the beliefs, actions and characters of trustors and trustees can be investigated. This chapter focuses on three questions: (1) When is trust epistemically irresponsible? (2) When is distrust epistemically irresponsible? (3) What epistemic responsibilities are generated by others' trust in us? The first two questions center on the epistemic responsibilities of the trustor: what actions ought she take and what virtues ought she cultivate to ensure that her trust or distrust are epistemically praiseworthy? The third question pivots to examine the epistemic responsibilities of the trustee: what epistemic virtues ought she cultivate in order to avoid betraying the trust of those who count on her?

5.2 When Is Trust Epistemically Irresponsible?

Trust has often been viewed as an epistemically suspect attitude. This is because, on many accounts of trust, trust involves some lack of attention to evidence. There are two ways we might not pay attention to evidence when we trust: (1) we may discount the evidence available to us that the trustee is untrustworthy, or (2) we may fail to take steps to collect additional evidence that would tell us whether the trustee is trustworthy. Both of these approaches to evidence raise questions about whether trust is epistemically responsible.

First, consider cases in which we overlook evidence that our intimate relations are untrustworthy. Suppose that I trust my friend Tina, but someone tells me that Tina is a thief and that she has stolen money from past friends. Despite hearing evidence of Tina's theft, I nonetheless still trust her. I do not believe that Tina is a thief, and when Tina tells me that she is innocent, I reply "Don't worry. I trust you. I know that's not who you are." Since I trust Tina, I do not change any of my behaviors around her as a result of the evidence that she is a thief; I still leave my purse lying around my apartment when she comes to visit. Such scenarios are commonplace in our close relationships with friends and loved ones. As Judith Baker notes, we often demand and expect that our friends believe us (Baker 1987:6). But are such practices of overlooking evidence epistemically irresponsible? W.K. Clifford's essay "The Ethics of Belief" (1879) argues that we have duties of inquiry, and that every instance of forming a belief based on insufficient evidence is a violation of these duties. Using examples of individuals who formed a belief by ignoring doubts or failing to pay attention to countervailing evidence that was easily available, Clifford argues that many harms result when we fail to do our due diligence. Ignoring evidence against our beliefs can cause us to form beliefs that harm other people either through the consequences of those beliefs or because we pass on those beliefs to others. Additionally, by developing habits of credulity rather than diligent skepticism, we weaken our characters and the characters of others whom we encourage to take truth lightly by our example. Thus, one might be concerned that our practice of trusting our intimates and believing them even in the face of some countervailing evidence is an epistemically irresponsible habit.

Of course, there are times when it would be seriously epistemically irresponsible to maintain trust in the face of overwhelming evidence of untrustworthiness, but is it ever epistemically responsible to trust despite some such evidence? Several philosophers have argued that the phenomenon of trust-responsiveness provides an answer (James 1896; Holton 1994; Pettit 1995; Jones 2004; McGeer 2008). Sometimes our trust in someone can motivate them to become what we hope them to be. This is a point made by William James in his response to Clifford's argument that it is always a violation of our intellectual duties to believe on the basis of insufficient evidence. James says, "Do you like me or not? … Whether you do or not depends, in countless instances, on whether I meet you half-way, am willing to assume that you must like me, and show you trust and expectation" (James 1896:23). His point is that while I may initially not have evidence that you like me, my trust and expectation that you do can motivate you to respond to that trust and begin to like me. Trust can motivate people to live up to that trust. Thus, if we follow Clifford's view of our epistemic responsibilities and refrain from trusting that others like us until we have sufficient evidence that they do, then we may lose out on many fruitful relationships.[3]

Others have expanded on this idea by providing accounts of trust that draw on this phenomenon of trust-responsiveness to show that trust, despite some evidence of the trustee's untrustworthiness, may be rational. For example, Victoria McGeer (2008) argues that there is a type of trust that involves hope. When one trusts someone else in this way, one holds out to the trustee a hopeful vision of the kind of person they can be. This vision of the trustee can be motivating as a kind of role model; it moves the trustee to think, "I want to be as she sees me to be" (McGeer 2008:249). Through this motivating mechanism, one's own trust in someone can count, under the right conditions, as evidence that they will be trustworthy. To return to my trust in Tina, my trust in her, despite some evidence that she may have stolen in the past, is not necessarily an epistemically irresponsible abandonment of my duty to be responsive to evidence. In fact, my own demonstrated trust in her can provide its own reason to believe that she is likely to be motivated to become the person I hope she can be.

Another facet of trust that may seem epistemically irresponsible is that those who trust often forgo the opportunity to collect additional evidence about the trustee's trustworthiness. On some accounts of trust, trust involves an attitude of acceptance of some vulnerability and confidence that one's trust will not be violated (Baier 2007:136). With such acceptance and confidence, "one forgoes searching (at the time) for ways to reduce such vulnerability" (Jones 2004:8). And this often involves refraining from checking up on the trustee (Baier 1994; Jones 2004; Townley 2006). In fact, Baier argues that excessive checking up on the trustee is a sign of a pathological trust relationship (Baier 1994:139). Consider some examples. If I set up a webcam to watch my cat sitter while I am away to make sure she is feeding my cat, then my cat sitter might rightly say that I do not trust her. And if Sasha is constantly checking her girlfriend Tanya's phone to make sure Tanya is not texting any other women, then we might judge that Sasha does not really trust her girlfriend. So it seems that trust involves some withholding from collecting evidence, but is this epistemically responsible? One might worry that trust seems to conflict with epistemically beneficial habits, such as inquisitiveness and diligence, which motivate us to search for evidence for our beliefs. Kornblith argues that it is epistemically irresponsible to refuse to look at evidence one does not already possess (Kornblith 1983:35).[4] Thus, to the extent that we trust, are we abandoning our epistemic responsibilities? Should we be more distrustful and check up on people more?

Cynthia Townley argues that this call for more distrustful checking stems from a mistaken attitude towards knowledge, which she calls "epistemophilia – the love of knowledge to the point of myopia" (Townley 2006:38). Townley argues that focusing on acquiring knowledge can make us overlook the value of ignorance. Ignorance can be instrumentally valuable as a means to further knowledge (Townley 2006:38). For example, both researchers and participants in double-blind drug trials need to be ignorant of which subjects are receiving the drug and which are receiving the placebo. Additionally, ignorance is inherently valuable as a necessary condition to epistemically valuable relationships of trust and empathy (Townley 2006:38). In order to trust, the trustor has to be in a position of some ignorance – she must forgo checking up on the trustee.[5] Townley argues that this kind of ignorance is necessary for many relationships of trust, which are themselves epistemically valuable. We are constantly learning from others and collaborating in knowledge production. This collaboration "enables me to construct, adjust, and fine-tune my understandings. Some of them inspire (or curb) my creativity and help me reflect on and improve my epistemic standards and practices" (Townley 2006:40). Collaborative relationships are essential to our ability to learn, produce and disseminate knowledge and understanding. But distrust can poison these relationships. If I constantly check what you say to make sure that it is true, I demonstrate a lack of trust in your epistemic abilities or your sincerity. This practice can undermine everyday epistemically valuable relationships. For example, my cat sitter is an important epistemic partner to me in knowing about my cat's health and understanding his behavior; checking up on her can show distrust in her and make her feel that I do not trust her, which can harm our relationship. This is not just an everyday phenomenon; this dynamic can also damage the rarefied collaborative relationships between scientific collaborators that are a central feature of contemporary science.[6] Therefore, some acceptance of our epistemic vulnerability when we trust others as epistemic partners is not necessarily a sign of epistemic irresponsibility. In fact, Townley argues that epistemic responsibility requires us to go further by investigating how oppressive norms, stereotypes, and power relations shape whose knowledge we trust, and whose epistemic agency is routinely subject to distrust. This brings us to the next topic: epistemic injustice.

5.3 When Is Distrust Epistemically Irresponsible?

Recent work on epistemic injustice and epistemic violence has shown that our habits of epistemic trust and distrust can be shaped by prejudices and systemic oppressions. Kristie Dotson (2011), drawing on the work of Patricia Hill Collins (2000) and other black feminist thinkers, argues that black women are systemically undervalued in their status as knowers. Stereotypes and prejudices cast black women as lacking in credibility, which causes what Dotson calls 'testimonial quieting,' which happens when a speaker is not taken to be a knower (Dotson 2011:242). Similarly, Miranda Fricker argues that 'testimonial injustice' is a pervasive epistemic problem that occurs when a speaker "receives a credibility deficit owing to identity prejudice in the hearer" (Fricker 2007:28). For example, suppose I am in the grips of a stereotype of women as overly emotional and prone to overreaction. This stereotype may cause me to grant a woman's testimony of a harm she suffered less credibility than it deserves. Stereotypes can make us suspicious and distrustful of people, and as Karen Jones argues, "When we are suspicious of a testifier, we interpret her story through the lens of our distrust" (Jones 2002:159). Testimonial injustice and testimonial quieting are both ethically and epistemically damaging. These acts of epistemic injustice show disrespect to knowers in a fundamental aspect of their humanity (i.e., their capacity to know) (Fricker 2007:44), they undermine knowers' self-trust and ability to form beliefs in a trusting community (Fricker 2007:47–51), and they deprive the rest of the community of the knowledge that disrespected knowers attempt to share (Fricker 2007:43).

So what can an epistemically responsible agent do to avoid doing a speaker an epistemic injustice? According to Fricker, when a hearer is aware that one of her prejudices may affect the credibility she grants a speaker, there are a number of actions in the moment that she can take to avoid a testimonial injustice. First, she can revise her credibility assessment upwards to compensate for the unjustly deflated assessments that the prejudice will cause.[7] Second, she can make her judgment more vague and tentative. Third, she can suspend judgment about the testimony altogether. Fourth, she can take the initiative to get further evidence for the trustworthiness of the testimony (Fricker 2007:91–92).

While these actions may avoid doing harm in the moment, an epistemically responsible agent will recognize the need to develop habits to avoid epistemic injustice on an ongoing basis. Of course, one of the best ways to do this is to develop habits of getting to know people belonging to different groups so that one can unlearn incorrect stereotypes that circulate in one's culture (Fricker 2007:96). However, avoiding and unlearning stereotypes can be a difficult and long-term process. Jones argues that, in the meantime, epistemically responsible agents can cultivate habits of reflecting on their patterns of distrust (Jones 2002:166). Suppose that I notice that I have a pattern of distrusting people of a certain group, and this distrust is best explained by stereotypes and prejudices, then I ought to adopt a metastance of distrust in my distrust. In other words, I ought to distrust my tendency to distrust members of this group. Jones argues that this metastance of distrust will have epistemic consequences for my judgments about others' testimony. The more I distrust my own distrust, the less weight my judgment that the speaker is untrustworthy has and the more corroborating evidence I ought to seek of the agent's trustworthiness (Jones 2002:164–165). Thus, by developing habits of reflecting on their prejudices, epistemically responsible agents can adopt attitudes towards their own trust that put them in epistemically better positions to judge when their rejection of testimony requires more evidence (see Scheman, this volume)

Fricker and Jones' arguments that there are steps agents can take to avoid testimonial injustice rest on the assumption that agents can, to some degree, recognize when they are subject to stereotypes and prejudices. However, some authors have argued that the problem of epistemic injustice is harder to solve, since research on implicit bias[8] shows that we are often unaware of our prejudices and the extent to which they shape our credibility assessments (Alcoff 2010; Anderson 2012; Antony 2016). If I do not know when I am subject to a prejudice, how can I know when I need to correct for the distrust I show towards a speaker? And if I do not know how much my prejudice is causing me to distrust a speaker, how can I know how much to revise upwards my credibility assessment (see Scheman, this volume)? Thus it may be difficult for an individual to be epistemically responsible in the ways outlined by Fricker and Jones, i.e., it may be hard to know whether a particular bias is operating in a concrete situation and to correct for it in the moment. However, one might have good reason to suspect that one has biases in general, and one can take steps to learn about them, try to reduce them, and attempt to prevent them from shaping one's judgments. Additionally, Linda Alcoff (2010) and Elizabeth Anderson (2012) suggest that structural changes to our institutions may be necessary in order to help avoid the problems of distrust that cause testimonial injustice. For example, increased integration of schools may help marginalized groups acquire more markers of credibility (Anderson 2012:171). Therefore, epistemic responsibility may require broader institutional and social changes.[9]

5.4 What Epistemic Responsibilities Are Generated by Others' Trust in Us?

Turning from questions related to how the trustor's practices of trust and distrust can be epistemically responsible, another set of questions arise when we consider what others' trust in the trustee demands from her. There are several different areas in which these questions arise, including scientific collaboration, research ethics, and the epistemology of trustworthiness. What these discussions of epistemic responsibilities generated by trust have in common is a recognition of the vulnerability inherent in trust. When *A* trusts *B* with *C* (or trusts *B* to ϕ), *A* is vulnerable. This vulnerability often generates epistemic responsibilities for *B*.

These questions were pressed forcefully by John Hardwig in two papers about the role of trust and epistemic dependence in knowledge (Hardwig 1985; Hardwig 1991). Hardwig argues that since much of our knowledge is collaborative and based on testimony, we are extremely epistemically dependent on others. Consider scientific knowledge. Science has become increasingly collaborative in recent decades, with papers published with as many as one hundred co-authors (Hardwig 1991:695). In many of these collaborations, no one scientist could collect the data by themselves, due to differences in expertise or time and resource constraints. In order to receive evidence from their collaborators, scientists must trust their colleagues. This means that if their colleagues are untrustworthy, then scientists cannot obtain knowledge. From this, Hardwig concludes that the character of scientists is the foundation of much of our knowledge. Consider an example: scientists *A* and *B* are interdisciplinary collaborators. Neither of them has the expertise to check the other's work, but they each rely on the other's data and analysis in order for their project to proceed. When *B* gives *A* some of *B*'s experimental results that will shape the next steps *A* will take, *A* has to trust that *B* is being truthful and not giving her fabricated results. Thus, unless *B* has the moral character trait of truthfulness, *A*'s work will suffer. Additionally, a successful collaboration requires that *B* have an epistemically good character:

> *B* must, first, be competent – she must be knowledgeable about what constitutes good reasons in the domain of her expertise, and she must have kept herself up to date with those reasons. Second, *B* must be conscientious – she must have done her own work carefully and thoroughly. And third, *B* must have 'adequate epistemic self-assessment' – *B* must not have a tendency to deceive herself about the extent of her knowledge, its reliability, or its applicability …
>
> *(Hardwig 1991:700)*

Competence, Hardwig argues, rests on epistemically virtuous habits of self-discipline, focus, and persistence (Hardwig 1991:700). Thus, in order for these scientists' collaboration to produce knowledge, each of the scientists must have epistemically good characters. Why? Because they are epistemically vulnerable to each other and must trust each other to be epistemically responsible.

Hardwig's argument that much of our scientific knowledge rests on trust in scientists' characters has been objected to on the grounds that reliance on scientists' self-interest is sufficient to ground scientific knowledge (Blais 1987; Rescher 1989; Adler 1994). On this objection, scientist *A* does not need to trust *B* to have a good character, *A* simply needs to rely on the fact that the external constraints set up by the institutions of science make it in *B*'s self-interest to tell the truth and conscientiously produce reliable results. Those pressing this objection often refer to the peer review and replication process as providing mechanisms for detecting epistemically irresponsible behavior such as scientific fraud. Additionally, it is argued that the scientific community punishes irresponsible behavior harshly by shunning scientists who engage in fraud. Therefore, it is not in the self-interest of scientists to be irresponsible, and scientific collaborations and knowledge can flourish. In sum, these objectors agree with Hardwig that scientists are, considered in isolation, epistemically vulnerable and dependent on each other, but they disagree that this means that scientists must have virtuous characters. Instead, the community simply needs effective mechanisms for detection and punishment that make it in the self-interest of scientists to be epistemically responsible. Trust in character is replaced by reliance on self-interest and a system for detecting and punishing bad actors.[10]

Hardwig and others have replied to these objections by pointing out that these mechanisms proposed by their opponents are insufficient to deal with the problems of epistemic vulnerability (Hardwig 1991; Whitbeck 1995; Frost-Arnold 2013; Andersen 2014). Hardwig focuses on the limited ability of the scientific community to detect epistemically irresponsible behavior. There are significant limitations of the peer review process; for instance, it is often difficult for editors to find well-qualified peer reviewers, and reviewers often do not have access to the original data that would allow them to discover fraud (Hardwig 1991:703). And while replication is the ideal in science, very little of it actually happens, given the incentives for scientists to focus on publishing new results rather than replicating older ones (Hardwig 1991:703). While Hardwig argues that scientist *A* may not be able to rely on the scientific institutions to *detect* scientist *B*'s fraud, Frost-Arnold (2013) adds that there are reasons to doubt that *A* can rely on the community to *punish* *B*'s fraud. Not all scientists are in a position to safely call upon the community to sanction collaborators who have betrayed them. Some scientists do not report fraud for fear of retaliation, others may complain but find their reports dismissed because those they accuse have greater power or credibility, and still other scientists may find themselves let down by colleagues who commit offenses that do not rise to the level of fraud (Frost-Arnold 2013:304). Therefore, while ideally the scientific institutions function to make it in scientists' self-interest to produce reliable results, in actuality these institutions may not provide sufficient incentive. Thus, in the face of these gaps, scientific knowledge may still rest on the epistemic character of scientists. To some degree, scientists are forced to trust each other, and this trust places epistemic responsibilities on them.

Finally, moving from the narrow realm of trust in science to broader questions about trust in general, an important relationship between trust and epistemic responsibility is found in the epistemology of trustworthiness. Several authors have argued that trustworthiness is an epistemically demanding virtue, requiring trustworthy people to demonstrate epistemic responsibility (Potter 2002; Jones 2012).[11] Both Potter and Jones develop ethically rich accounts of trustworthiness, according to which epistemic skills play a crucial role. Potter argues that to be fully trustworthy, we need to have a clear vision of what it is that others are trusting us to do, what we are able to offer them, and how social relations may shape our relationship of trust (Potter 2002:27–28). This is often much more complicated than it might sound:

> Being trustworthy requires not merely a passive dependability but an active engagement with self and others in knowing and making known one's own interests, values, moral beliefs, and positionality, as well as theirs. To do so may involve engaging in considerable study: how does one's situatedness affect one's relation to social or economic privileges? How do one's particular race and gender, for example, affect relations of trust with diverse others? In what ways do one's values and interests impede trust with diverse others? In what ways do one's values and interests impede trust with some communities and foster it with others?
>
> *(Potter 2002:27)*

Many features of our social location, such as our race, class, gender, sexual orientation, religion, nationality, etc., shape our relationships of trust with others. Being trustworthy, Potter argues, requires us to be sensitive to these issues. For example, if a white woman wants to conduct research in an Australian Aboriginal community, then she will need to learn about the history of betrayals by past white researchers that makes it hard for people in Aboriginal communities to trust outside researchers.[12] Thus, becoming worthy of others' trust often requires that we learn about their history and our own social location. As Jones puts it, failing to have relevant background social knowledge can prevent us from being trustworthy (Jones 2012:72–73).

Additionally, both Potter and Jones argue that being fully virtuous requires signaling to others what they can count on us to do (Potter 2002:26; Jones 2012:74). For Potter, "It is not enough merely to be trustworthy; to be fully virtuous, one must indicate to potential trusting others that one is worthy of their trust" (Potter 2002:27). Jones argues that what she calls "rich trustworthiness" has an important social role: we all need to count on other people, and we need others to signal to us that they can be counted on so that we know where to turn (Jones 2012:74). But knowing how to signal our trustworthiness to others requires us to exercise epistemic responsibility. It requires grasping enough about the other's background knowledge and assumptions to know what they will take as a signal of our trustworthiness (Jones 2012:76).[13] Since, as Potter points out, our background assumptions are shaped by our social location, knowing how to signal properly requires understanding others' social location and histories in order to be able to send them signals that they will recognize. Finally, Potter argues that we have a responsibility to cultivate others' trust in us (Potter 2002:20). This does not mean that we ought to lead others to expect that we can be trusted to care for every good (or to perform every action). But, to be a virtuous person, we should try to become the kind of person who can be counted on in various respects and in various domains. Which respects and domains are relevant often depends on the social roles we play. For example, as a teacher, one has a role-responsibility to cultivate one's students' trust with respect to objectivity in grading and creating a class environment in which every student can participate in intellectual exchange. A teacher whose students do not trust her to grade objectively or provide an equitable classroom is, all things being equal,[14] doing something wrong. Perhaps she is not trustworthy in these domains, or she does not know how to signal her trustworthiness to her students. Additionally, there may need to be broader systemic changes to the educational institutions involved in order to create an environment in which the teacher can be fully trusted by her students. Thus, our social roles often create epistemic responsibilities for us to cultivate the competencies and epistemic skills that will allow us to both be trustworthy and signal that trustworthiness to others who need to trust us (cf. Potter 2002:20).

I conclude by using the example of the trustworthy teacher to draw together many of the threads of our discussion of trust and epistemic responsibility. The trustworthy teacher needs to cultivate her students' trust that the classroom is a space in which they are all respected and can contribute their ideas. This is often no easy task due to the problem of "testimonial smothering." Dotson argues that testimonial smothering is another form of epistemic violence; it is a kind of coerced self-silencing that occurs when a marginalized speaker decides to truncate her testimony because of perceived harmful ignorance on the part of the hearer (Dotson 2011). This may occur in the classroom when a student of color in a majority white classroom perceives that her audience (including her peers and/or her teacher) "doesn't get" issues of race, so she decides not to share her insights about how the class topics relate to racial injustice. This self-silencing is coerced by the ignorance of her audience, which may be demonstrated to her by previous comments made by the teacher or students that show that they are ill-informed about racial inequality. The audience's ignorance of the realities of race could be harmful to the speaker were she to share her insights, since it may cause them to do the speaker a testimonial injustice, or to ridicule, harass, or shun her for her comments. To avoid these risks, the marginalized student may withhold her contributions to class discussion. Withholding her ideas is an act of distrust; it stems from distrust in her teacher and peers to be a trustworthy audience on matters of race. This dynamic is a widespread problem that can create systemically inequitable and epistemically impoverished classrooms. This is due to the fact that, as the epistemologies of ignorance literature has shown, white privilege in a racially unjust society has a tendency to hide itself so that white people are often unaware of their own privileges and prejudices (Mills 2007; McIntosh 2008).

So consider the epistemic responsibilities of the white teacher. She has a role-responsibility to cultivate the trust of all of her students. This means that she needs to both be trustworthy and effectively signal her trustworthiness to her students. Being trustworthy confers epistemic responsibilities to develop competence with issues of race, to assess adequately her own competence, and to signal effectively her trustworthiness to her students so that all her students can trust her as an audience (and also as an authority figure when it comes to managing the comments of other students). As we saw earlier, this involves a host of epistemic skills and practices ranging from unlearning her implicit biases to learning about the history that shapes the distrust of her students of color, and reflecting on how her own social situatedness affects her ability to communicate her trustworthiness. Additionally, to draw a parallel to Anderson (2012) and Alcoff's (2010) arguments with respect to testimonial injustice, individual attempts may not be enough; sometimes institutional steps may be necessary. Educational institutions may need to restructure their curricular priorities and provide resources to teachers to help them unlearn their own ignorance and develop the skills to signal effectively with diverse groups of students. This is just one example of the ways in which the issues discussed in this chapter can connect in the complex relations of trust we encounter in our social relations.

Notes

1 James Montmarquet uses the term "epistemic conscientiousness" similarly, and he argues that it is the fundamental epistemic virtue (Montmarquet 1993:viii).

2 Note that there is much more that Code argues in this ground-breaking book through her articulation of the concept of epistemic responsibility, including an argument that we ought to extend our epistemic aims beyond simply truth.

3 For a useful discussion of the difference between the ethics of belief debates (between Clifford and James, among others) and the concept of epistemic responsibility, see Code (1987:77–83). Code argues that one area where these issues coincide is issues of trust in personal relationships where it is not unethical or epistemically irresponsible to maintain trust by avoiding evidence.

4 For a dissenting view on this point, see Conee and Feldman (2004:189).

5 For a discussion of related issues with regard to faith, see Buchak (2012).

6 The complex issues of trust and epistemic responsibility in science will be discussed in section 3.

7 For a discussion of the type of trust involved in revising one's credibility assessments, see Frost-Arnold (2014).

8 For some of the psychological literature on implicit bias and ways to reduce it see Devine, Forscher, Austin and Cox (2012); Lai et al. (2014).

9 For further discussion of the need for structural and systemic changes to prevent epistemic injustice, see Fricker (2017); Medina (2017).

10 For a discussion of the difference between trust and reliance, see Baier (1994:98–99).

11 Jones and Potter disagree about whether trustworthiness is properly called a virtue. I follow Potter in calling trustworthiness a virtue.

12 For an example of this history of betrayal, see Townley (2006).

13 Like Hardwig, Jones argues that trustworthiness also requires adequate self-assessment of one's own competence, another epistemic virtue (Jones 2012:76).

14 It is important to note that often all things are not equal for faculty members from groups traditionally underrepresented in the academy; they are often distrusted due to others' prejudice. For example, white students may distrust faculty of color due to their own prejudices and not because of any failure on the teacher's part.

References

Adler, J. (1994) "Testimony, Trust, Knowing," *Journal of Philosophy* 91(5): 264–275.

Alcoff, L.M. (2010) "Epistemic Identities," *Episteme* 7(2): 128–137.

Andersen, H. (2014) "Co-Author Responsibility," *EMBO Reports* 15(9): 914–918.

Anderson, E. (2012) "Epistemic Justice as a Virtue of Social Institutions," *Social Epistemology* 26 (2): 163–173.

Antony, L. (2016) "Bias: Friend or Foe? Reflections on Saulish Skepticism," in M. Brownstein and J. Saul (eds.), *Implicit Bias and Philosophy, Volume 1: Metaphysics and Epistemology*, New York: Oxford University Press.

Baier, A. (1994) *Moral Prejudices*, Cambridge, MA: Harvard University Press.

Baier, A. (2007) "Trust, Suffering, and the Aesculapian Virtues," in R.L. Walker and P.J. Ivanhoe (eds.), *Working Virtue: Virtue Ethics and Contemporary Moral Problems*, New York: Oxford University Press.

Baker, J. (1987) "Trust and Rationality," *Pacific Philosophical Quarterly* 68(10): 1–13.

Blais, M. (1987) "Epistemic Tit for Tat," *Journal of Philosophy* 84(7): 363–375.

Buchak, L. (2012) "Can It Be Rational to Have Faith?" in J. Chandler and V. Harrison (eds.), *Probability in the Philosophy of Religion*, New York: Oxford University Press.

Clifford, W.K. (1879) "The Ethics of Belief," in *Lectures and Essays*, Volume 2, London: Macmillan.

Code, L. (1987) *Epistemic Responsibility*, Hanover, NH: Brown University Press.

Collins, P.H. (2000) *Black Feminist Thought: Knowledge, Consciousness, and the Politics of Empowerment*, 2nd edition, New York: Routledge.

Conee, E. and Feldman, R. (2004) *Evidentialism: Essays in Epistemology*, New York: Clarendon Press.

Devine, P.G., Forscher, P.S., Austin, A.J. and Cox, W.T.L. (2012) "Long-Term Reduction in Implicit Race Bias: A Prejudice Habit Breaking Intervention," *Journal of Experimental Social Psychology* 48(6): 1267–1278.

Dotson, K. (2011) "Tracking Epistemic Violence, Tracking Practices of Silencing," *Hypatia* 26(2): 236–257.

Fricker, M. (2007) *Epistemic Injustice: Power and Ethics in Knowing*, New York: Oxford University Press.

Fricker, M. (2017) "Evolving Concepts of Epistemic Injustice," in I.J. Kidd, J. Medina and G. Pohlhaus Jr. (eds.), *The Routledge Handbook of Epistemic Injustice*, New York: Routledge.

Frost-Arnold, K. (2013) "Moral Trust & Scientific Collaboration," *Studies in History and Philosophy of Science Part A* 44(3): 301–310.

Frost-Arnold, K (2014) "The Cognitive Attitude of Rational Trust," *Synthese* 191(9): 1957–1974.

Hardwig, J. (1985) "Epistemic Dependence," *The Journal of Philosophy* 82(7): 335–349.

Hardwig, J (1991) "The Role of Trust in Knowledge," *The Journal of Philosophy* 88(12): 693–708.

Hetherington, S. (2002) "Epistemic Responsibility: A Dilemma," *The Monist* 85(3): 398–414.

Holton, R. (1994) "Deciding to Trust, Coming to Believe," *Australasian Journal of Philosophy* 72 (1): 63–76.

James, W. (1896) *The Will to Believe and Other Essays in Popular Philosophy*, Norwood, MA: Plimpton Press.

Jones, K. (2002) "The Politics of Credibility," in L.M. Antony and C.E. Witt (eds.), *A Mind of One's Own: Feminist Essays on Reason and Objectivity*, Boulder, CO: Westview Press.

Jones, K. (2004) "Trust and Terror," in P. DesAutels and M.U. Walker (eds.), *Moral Psychology: Feminist Ethics and Social Theory*, New York: Rowman & Littlefield.

Jones, K. (2012) "Trustworthiness," *Ethics* 123(1): 61–85.

Kornblith, H. (1983) "Justified Belief and Epistemically Responsible Action," *The Philosophical Review* 92(1): 33–48.

Lai, C.K., Marini, M., Lehr, S.A., Cerruti, C., Shin, J.E. L., Joy-Gaba, J., Ho, A.K.*et al.* (2014) "Reducing Implicit Racial Preferences: I. A Comparative Investigation of 17 Interventions," *Journal of Experimental Psychology: General* 143(4): 1765–1785.

McGeer, V. (2008) "Trust, Hope and Empowerment," *Australasian Journal of Philosophy* 86(2): 1–18.

McIntosh, P. (2008) "White Privilege and Male Privilege," in A. Bailey and C. Cuomo (eds.), *The Feminist Philosophy Reader*, New York: McGraw Hill.

Medina, J. (2017) "Varieties of Hermeneutical Injustice," in I.J. Kidd, J. Medina and G. Pohlhaus Jr. (eds.), *The Routledge Handbook of Epistemic Injustice*, New York: Routledge.

Mills, C. (2007) "White Ignorance," in S. Sullivan and N. Tuana (eds.), *Race and Epistemologies of Ignorance*, Albany, NY: SUNY Press.

Montmarquet, J.A. (1993) *Epistemic Virtue and Doxastic Responsibility*, Boston, MA: Rowman & Littlefield.

Pettit, P. (1995) "The Cunning of Trust," *Philosophy & Public Affairs* 24(3): 202–225.

Potter, N. (2002) *How Can I Be Trusted? A Virtue Theory of Trustworthiness*, New York: Rowman & Littlefield.

Rescher, N. (1989) *Cognitive Economy: an Inquiry into the Economic Dimension of the Theory of Knowledge*, Pittsburgh, PA: University of Pittsburgh Press.

Townley, C. (2006) "Toward a Revaluation of Ignorance," *Hypatia* 21(3): 37–55.

Whitbeck, C. (1995) "Truth and Trustworthiness in Research," *Science and Engineering Ethics* 1(4): 403–416.

Further Reading

Brownstein, M. and Saul, J. (eds.) (2016) *Implicit Bias and Philosophy*, Volumes 1 and 2, New York: Oxford University Press. (A key anthology on the philosophical questions raised by implicit bias.).

Kornblith, H. (ed.) (2001) *Epistemology: Internalism and Externalism*, Cambridge, MA: MIT Press. (Anthology containing classic texts in the internalism/externalism debate; includes relevant critiques of responsibilism.).

Sullivan, S. and Tuana, N. (eds.) (2007) *Race and Epistemologies of Ignorance*, Albany, NY: SUNY Press. (Founding anthology of the epistemologies of ignorance literature.).

Zagzebski, L.T. (1996) *Virtues of the Mind: An Inquiry into the Nature of Virtue and the Ethical Foundations of Knowledge*, New York: Cambridge University Press. (A classic text in virtue epistemology.).

6
TRUST AND AUTHORITY

Benjamin McMyler

> It is familiarly known, that, in our progress from childhood to manhood, during the course of our education, and afterwards in the business of life, our belief, both speculative and practical, is, owing to our inability or unwillingness to investigate the subject for ourselves, often determined by the opinion of others. That the opinions of mankind should so often be formed in this manner, has been a matter of regret to many writers: others again have enforced the duty of submitting our convictions, in certain cases, to the guidance of fit judges; but all have admitted the wide extent to which the derivation of opinions upon trust prevails, and the desirableness that the choice of guides in these matters should be regulated by a sound discretion. It is, therefore, proposed to inquire how far our opinions may be properly influenced by the mere authority of others, independently of our own conviction founded on appropriate reasoning.
>
> *(Lewis 1875:5–6)*

In this passage from *An Essay on the Influence of Authority in Matters of Opinion*, George Cornewall Lewis, a 19-century British politician and one-time Home Secretary, draws a smooth and intuitive connection between our natural human propensity to trust others and our unavoidable reliance on authority. "All have admitted the wide extent to which the derivation of opinions on trust prevails," he claims, and so he sets himself to investigate "how far our opinions may be properly influenced by the mere authority of others." Here forming a belief on the basis of trust and forming a belief on the basis of authority are all but identified, and this identification can appear quite natural. After all, if we do not trust an authority, then why should we believe what she says? Such a thought is surely behind the consternation that is sometimes expressed concerning the public's possible lack of trust in governmental, scientific and religious authorities.

More substantively, both interpersonal trust and reliance on authority appear to have a key characteristic in common, a characteristic that distinguishes these phenomena from various different ways in which we might rely on other people and from various different ways in which other people might seek to influence our thoughts and actions (see also Potter, this volume). Both interpersonal trust and social influence by authority appear to involve our coming to a conclusion or making up our mind "independently of our own conviction founded upon appropriate reasoning," as Lewis puts it. Both interpersonal trust and the upshot of social influence by authority involve an agent's *not making up her own mind* about some matter, not making up her own mind about what she is told by the person she trusts or by the authority. To the extent to which an agent is in fact making up her own mind or coming to her own conclusion about what another person tells her, then to that extent she is not genuine trusting the other or genuinely treating the other as an authority.

Recognizing this deep similarity between relations of trust and relations of authority, philosophers writing on issues relating to trust have recently begun to appeal to the political philosophy literature on authority in an attempt to elucidate the distinctive nature of interpersonal trust (Origgi 2005; McMyler 2011; Keren 2014). However, as intuitive as Lewis' aligning of trust and authority can appear, interpersonal trust and social influence by authority can also appear to be quite distinct and frequently unrelated phenomena. While trust is (arguably) a distinctive kind of attitude, authority is a distinctive form of social influence, and while philosophers disagree about how exactly to characterize what it is that distinguishes trust from other attitudes and authority from other forms of influence, it appears that there are many cases in which authority can be exercised in the absence of trust. After all, even if we do not trust someone, she might still be in charge. We can recognize another's authority without trusting her a bit, and thus widespread lack of trust in public figures, however lamentable this might be, does not inexorably lead to widespread civil disobedience. From this perspective trust and authority can seem like very different matters.

I think that we can begin to sort through these competing intuitions by distinguishing between practical and epistemic (or theoretical) authority, between the way in which authority is exercised in the context of reasoning about what to do and the way in which it is exercised in the context of reasoning about what is the case. Given a particular conception of the nature of interpersonal trust, namely that trust is an at least partially cognitive attitude, it should be no surprise that, despite the deep and important commonalities between trust and authority, one can recognize and act on another's authority without trusting her. Given that the exercise of practical authority aims at obedient action, the successful exercise of practical authority does not require trust. Obedience to practical authority is a kind of action, and this action can be performed in the absence of the attitude of trust. Deference to epistemic authority, in contrast, is a kind of belief, and this belief, I will argue, can be construed as an instance of the attitude of interpersonal trust. The attitude of interpersonal trust is the aim of the exercise of epistemic authority, vindicating Lewis's aligning of trust and authority with regard to matters of opinion.

The concepts of both trust and authority are highly promiscuous, being employed in ordinary language in a wide variety of ways. In addition to trusting another person, we can speak of trusting ourselves, trusting groups and institutions, entrusting goods to others, trusting inanimate objects and even simply trusting that something is the case. Similarly, in addition to epistemic and practical authority, we can speak of the authority of the state, of law, of morality and even of the self or of reason. While these various uses of these two concepts are loosely connected, they differ widely and there likely is not a univocal sense of trust or authority that they all have in common. Here I will focus narrowly on interpersonal trust (trusting another person to Φ or that p) and authority as a form of social influence (a person's being an authority about what to do or what is the case) by asking:[1] what is the relationship between interpersonal trust and the way in which authority is exercised in order to influence the thoughts and actions of others?

6.1 Interpersonal Trust

In attempting to explain the nature of interpersonal trust, philosophers often distinguish between trust and various forms of non-trusting reliance on people, objects and states of affairs (see also Goldberg, this volume). While I might have no choice but to rely on a rope to bear my weight, this is not to trust the rope in the way that we typically trust our friends and family members. Similarly, while I might rely on a thermometer to accurately indicate the temperature or rely on a clock to accurately tell the time, this is different from trusting a neighbor to pick up the kids or even trusting a stranger to tell the truth. If we trust another person to do something, and they fail to do it, then baring extenuating circumstances, we feel let down. If the clock fails to accurately tell the time, then we might be frustrated, but the clock has not let us down. Of course, we often do rely on people in the way that we rely on clocks and thermometers, and we are liable to be disappointed when this reliance proves to be a mistake. However, as the thought goes, such disappointment is very different from our ordinary reaction to a breach of interpersonal trust. Unlike mere reliance, interpersonal trust can be betrayed, and when it is, we often feel it appropriate to adopt reactive attitudes like resentment (Holton 1994). Interpersonal trust thus appears to involve more than mere reliance.

Philosophers impressed by this line of thought have often sought to characterize trust as a more specific or sophisticated form of reliance. Annette Baier (1986), for example, claims that interpersonal trust requires, beyond mere reliance, reliance on another's good will towards one, and Richard Holton (1994) claims that trust is reliance that is adopted from what P.F. Strawson (1962) calls "the participant stance." Such accounts accept that interpersonal trust is a form of reliance, but they seek to articulate the further features that distinguish trusting reliance from non-trusting reliance (see also Goldberg, this volume).

Related to this project of construing interpersonal trust as a distinctive form of reliance is a particular view of how it is that we exercise agency in trusting others, of how it is that we go about deciding to trust. Here the way in which we can decide to trust is often contrasted with the way in which we decide to believe. While we can "decide" to believe that p on the basis of considerations that we take to show p true, many philosophers contend that we cannot believe at will, voluntarily, in the way that we can act at will.[2] One way to motivate such non-voluntarism about belief is to note that we do not appear to be able to believe something directly for practical reasons in the way that we can act directly for practical reasons. Consider the case of inducements like threats and offers (Alston 1988; Bennett 1990). If I offer you a large sum of money to believe that there is a pink elephant in the room right now, something concerning which you do not take there to be good evidence, then no matter how much you might want the money, no matter how much you might take my inducement to be "reason to believe" that there is a pink elephant in the room, you cannot believe for this reason.[3] You can act directly for this reason, and act in ways designed to try to bring yourself to believe, but you cannot believe directly for this practical reason. The same is true for other kinds of practical reasons for belief. I might recognize that if I believe that I will get the job, then I am more likely to get the job, but I cannot believe that I will get the job simply for this reason. Considerations concerning the consequences of holding a belief do not appear to be reasons on the basis of which we can directly believe.[4] Practical reasons are, in this respect, "reasons of the wrong kind" for believing (Hieronymi 2005), and so it appears that we cannot believe at will in the way that we can act at will.

In holding that we can decide to trust in a way that we cannot decide to believe, many philosophers appear to contend that we can trust a person to Φ directly for practical reasons. Holton, for example, argues that a shopkeeper might decide for moral or prudential reasons to trust an employee not to steal from the till even if the shopkeeper cannot believe this for such practical reasons (1994:63).[5] We can place trust in others – decide to rely on them in the way that is distinctive of interpersonal trust – directly for practical reasons. Trust is in this sense action-like. Unlike belief, interpersonal trust is directly subject to the will in the same sense as are ordinary intentional actions.

This kind of voluntarism about trust, as we might call it, fits neatly with the project of characterizing interpersonal trust as a distinctive form of reliance. After all, reliance is itself naturally construed as a kind of action. To rely on a person or object is to act in a way the success of which depends on that person or object's behaving in a certain way in certain circumstances (Marušić, forthcoming). To rely on a rope to bear my weight is to act in a way the success of which depends on the rope's not breaking when I put my weight on it. I thus rely on the rope when I act in a certain way, when I climb it, and I can do this even if I do not believe that the rope will bear my weight. I might not be sure that the rope will bear my weight, and I might even positively believe that it will not, but if I have no other choice, I can decide to rely on the rope anyway.

We have already seen that such reliance differs from the kind of interpersonal trust that most philosophers are seeking to elucidate. If the rope were to break, however much of a disaster this might be, the rope would not be letting me down in the particular way that we can be let down by other persons whom we trust. I would not be inclined to feel resentment at the rope's betrayal. Nevertheless, if interpersonal trust is a distinctive kind of reliance, if it is, as Holton contends, reliance adopted from the participant stance, then as a form of reliance it should still be a kind of action, perhaps a mental action like imagining a starry sky or supposing that something is true for the sake of reasoning.[6] And like relying on the rope, we should be able to choose to trustingly rely on others to Φ directly for practical reasons, even in cases in which we cannot believe that they will Φ for such reasons.

Such a conception of interpersonal trust as an essentially practical phenomenon makes Lewis's aligning of trust and authority in matters of opinion look suspicious. Clearly the exercise of epistemic authority aims at influencing the beliefs of others, and it does so by way of providing others with epistemic reasons in the form of testimony. Perhaps the practical attitude of interpersonal trust plays a role in generating this authority-based belief (Faulkner 2011, this volume), but it remains unclear why trust *must* be involved in the generation of authority-based belief, as Lewis appears to contend. At the very least, trust should not be identified with authority-based belief. Moreover, if trust is an essentially practical phenomenon, then one would expect that it should play a more central role in the exercise of practical authority than epistemic authority, but this appears to be the opposite of the truth. I can recognize another's authority – recognize that she is in charge and in a position to influence my practical decisions by giving me practical reasons in the form of orders or commands – without trusting her to make the correct decisions. Obedience does not require trust. Trust seems to play a more central role in the exercise of epistemic authority than it does in the exercise of practical authority.

Fortunately, while the above conception of interpersonal trust as an essentially practical phenomenon has a good deal of intuitive appeal, there is reason to think that it is mistaken, and appreciating this is helpful for understanding the connection between relations of trust and relations of authority. While it is often claimed that we can exercise a kind of agency over our trusting that we cannot exercise over belief, it is far from clear that this is true. Consider again the case of practical inducements. Just as it appears that we cannot believe something directly for the reason of things like monetary offers, so it appears that we cannot trust someone to do something directly for the reason of such inducements. Modifying Holton's example, imagine that you are a store manager and that I offer you a large sum of money to trust a particular employee with the till. Imagine also that this employee has a long criminal record such that otherwise you would not trust her with the till. Even if you take the benefits of my offer to outweigh the possible costs associated with trusting the employee with the till, it does not appear that you can trust the employee simply for the reason of my offer. Of course, you can act for the reason of my offer, giving the employee the keys, etc., but this looks insufficient for trusting the employee to safeguard the money. Whatever exactly interpersonal trust involves, it appears to involve seeing the trusted person in a particular light, and such "seeing" is not something that we can do simply for the reason of monetary inducements (Jones 1996). I think that the same goes for other kinds of practical reasons for trusting. I might think that I would be happier if I trusted certain people to do certain things, and I might think that certain people would be better off if I trusted them, but I cannot directly trust them for such reasons. Interpersonal trust is more demanding than this.

In this respect, interpersonal trust looks to be non-voluntary in a way that parallels that in which belief is non-voluntary. Just as we cannot believe that p directly for practical reasons, we cannot trust someone to Φ or that p directly for practical reasons.[7] Interpersonal trust thus appears to be a member of a large class of attitudes that are not action-like, that are not directly subject to the will.[8] Arguably, one cannot intend to do something, fear something, love someone or feel pride about something, simply for the reason of things like monetary inducements.[9] Such inducements are "reasons of the wrong kind" for these attitudes (Hieronymi 2005).

I offer this argument not as a definitive refutation of the idea that interpersonal trust is action-like, but rather as a reason for entertaining a different conception of the general nature of interpersonal trust, a conception of interpersonal trust as an attitude (or perhaps a suite of attitudes) that embodies a distinctive way of representing the world or a distinctive kind of take on the world.[10] Understanding the nature of this attitude then requires understanding the distinctive kind of take on the world that this attitude embodies.

There is good reason to think that the distinctive kind of take on the world that this attitude embodies is an at least partly cognitive take, that it involves, at least in part, taking something to be true. This is most readily apparent in cases of trusting someone for the truth. If a speaker tells me that p, and I do not believe her, then I clearly do not trust her for the truth. Trusting a speaker for the truth positively requires believing what the speaker says. As I will argue below, interpersonal trust plausibly requires more than mere belief. Believing what a speaker says is insufficient for trusting her for the truth, but it is certainly necessary. And this is reason to think that distinctive kind of take on the world that the attitude of trust embodies is an at least partly cognitive take, that it involves, at least in part, taking something to be true in a particular way or for certain reasons.[11] I will argue that such a cognitive conception of interpersonal trust can help to explain the competing intuitions about the relationship between trust and authority outlined earlier, how on the one hand trust can seem integral to the exercise of authority while on the other it can seem largely unnecessary.

6.2 Practical versus Epistemic Authority

To exercise authority, as I will conceive of it here, is to exercise a particular kind of rational influence over the thoughts or actions of others. It is to get others to believe something or do something by giving them a reason for belief or action. Typically, this is accomplished by the issuing of what we might call authoritative directives, by *telling others to Φ* (orders, commands, legal decisions) or *telling others that p* (what epistemologists typically call testimony, see also Faulkner, this volume). Such authoritative directives provide others with reasons for Φ-ing or for believing that p, and these reasons appear to be of a distinctive kind. Unlike the reasons for action provided by advice, threats, or offers, and unlike the reasons for belief provided by argument, demonstration or explanation, the reasons provided by such authoritative directives are such that, when an agent does believe or act on the authority of a speaker, while the agent is genuinely believing or acting for a reason, she is not making up her own mind about what is the case or what to do.[12] Understanding the nature of social influence by authority requires understanding how this is possible. How can there be reasons for belief or action that are such that, when an agent believes or acts for these reasons, the agent does not count as making up her own mind about what is the case or what to do?

While my argument in this chapter will not rely on any particular answer to this question, it will be helpful to have at least one possible answer in view. The standard answer to this question available in the contemporary literature is due to Joseph Raz.[13] Raz contends that authoritative practical directives are a species of what he calls "preemptive" or "exclusionary" reasons, which are themselves a species of what he calls "second-order reasons for action" (1986, 1990). While first-order reasons for action are ordinary reasons for Φing, second-order reasons are reasons for Φing-for-a-reason or refraining from Φing-for-a-reason. Preemptive or exclusionary reasons are reasons for refraining from Φing-for-a-reason, for refraining from acting for certain other reasons, these other reasons being thus preempted or excluded. Preemptive reasons do not preempt an agent from considering or deliberating about these other reasons; they simply preempt the agent from acting for these reasons. They exclude these reasons from figuring into the basis upon which the agent acts. While preemptive or exclusionary reasons thus serve to defeat certain other reasons, the way in which they do so differs from what epistemologists typically call rebutting or undercutting defeaters (Pollock and Cruz 1999). Preemptive reasons do not outweigh the reasons that they preempt, but neither do they affect their strength. The preempted reasons retain their strength in the face of the preemptive reason; they are simply excluded from figuring into the basis upon which the agent acts.

Raz contends that authoritative practical directives are both first-order reasons for action and second-order preemptive reasons. A practical authority's command to Φ provides an agent with both a reason for Φ-ing and a reason for refraining from acting otherwise for certain other reasons. The second-order preemptive reason thus "protects" the first-order reason, allowing it to rationalize the agent's action despite the agent's having other reasons with which it might conflict. Authoritative practical directives thus provide what Raz calls "protected reasons for action."

This account of the kind of reason for action provided by authoritative directives is meant to explain the way in which, in obeying an authoritative directive, an agent counts as genuinely acting for a reason while not making up her own mind about what to do. The agent is acting for the first-order reason provided by the directive, but insofar as the directive also provides a second-order reason for refraining from acting otherwise for certain other reasons, such as reasons of personal preference or of one's own self-interest, the directive "removes the decision" from the agent to the authority (Raz 1990:193). The authority is, in this respect, making up the agent's mind for her.

Raz is almost entirely concerned with practical authority, with authority over action, but he does hold that his preemptive account of authority should apply equally to epistemic (or theoretical) authority.

> Just as with any practical authority, the point of a theoretical authority is to enable me to conform to reason, this time reason for belief, better than I would otherwise be able to do. This requires taking the expert advice, and allowing it to pre-empt my own assessment of the evidence. If I do not do that, I do not benefit from it.
>
> *(Raz 2009:155)*

As in the case of practical authority, authoritative theoretical directives (such as expert testimony) will not preempt agents from considering or deliberating about other reasons, but they will provide agents with second-order reasons for not believing otherwise for certain other reasons, these other reasons being excluded from the balance of reasons on which the agent's belief is based. When an epistemic authority tells me that p, this provides me with both a first-order reason for believing that p and a second-order reason for not believing otherwise for certain other reasons. The authoritative testimony thus provides me with a reason for belief that "replaces" my own assessment of the balance of reasons (Zagzebski 2012). It is in this respect that, in telling me that p, the epistemic authority is making up my mind for me.[14]

6.3 Trust and Theoretical Authority

I have claimed that what characterizes the reasons for belief or action provided by authoritative directives is that, when an agent believes or acts for these reasons, she is not making up her own mind about what is the case or what to do. The Razian preemptive account of authority attempts to explain this by contending that these reasons are both first-order epistemic or practical reasons and second-order preemptive reasons, reasons for not believing or acting on the balance of reasons. Since the authoritative reasons replace the agent's own assessment of the balance of reasons, the agent does not count as making up her own mind about what is the case or what to do, even though she genuinely counts as believing or acting for a reason.

There is an intuitive sense in which the attitude of interpersonal trust also involves refraining from making up one's own mind. Trusting someone to Φ, or trusting someone that p, seems incompatible with my determining for myself, on the basis of independent impersonal evidence, that the person will Φ or that p is true. To the extent that I determine this for myself, I appear not to trust the person.

A thought like this is likely part of what has motivated philosophers to deny that interpersonal trust is a kind of belief and to contend that trust can be willed in the absence of positive reasons for belief. As we have seen, however, there is reason to think that trust is not action-like and that it positively requires belief. We cannot trust a speaker's testimony, for example, directly for practical reasons, and trusting the speaker's testimony positively requires believing what the speaker says. Believing what a speaker says is insufficient for trusting a speaker for the truth, however, since I might believe the content of the speaker's testimony but for reasons entirely independent of her saying it. At the very least, trusting a speaker's testimony that p requires believing that p *for the reason* that the speaker told me that p. As Elizabeth Anscombe (2008) has pointed out, however, even this is insufficient for trusting someone for the truth. Imagine that you want to deceive me and so tell me the opposite of what you believe. If I know that you are trying to deceive me in this way, but also that what you believe in this case will likely be the opposite of the truth, then by calculating on this, I might believe what you say for the reason that you said it. But this would not be to trust you for the truth. Given the way in which I have calculated on your testimony, treating it in effect as impersonal inductive evidence, I seem to have made up my own mind that what you say is true.

In this respect, there appears to be a deep similarity between interpersonal trust and the upshot of the exercise of authority. Authority aims to influence agents to believe or act in such a way that they are not making up their own minds about what is the case or what to do. Interpersonal trust is an attitude that requires an agent's not making up her own mind. As such, we might suppose that interpersonal trust is the attitude at which the exercise of authority aims.

When it comes to epistemic authority, I think that this is exactly right. The exercise of epistemic authority aims at an addressee's trusting the speaker for the truth. When an epistemic authority tells an addressee that p, this provides the addressee with an epistemic reason for believing that p, a reason that is such that, when the agent believes for this reason, the agent is not making up her own mind about whether p. If one accepts the Razian preemptive account of authority, this can be explained in terms of the preemptive nature of the relevant reason. To trust a speaker for the truth is then to believe that p for a reason that is both a first-order epistemic reason and a second-order reason that preempts one from believing otherwise for certain other reasons.[15] To believe for such a reason is to believe on the authority of the speaker, which is also precisely what it is to trust the speaker for the truth. This vindicates Lewis's aligning of trust and authority in matters of opinion.

This explains why the lack of trust in epistemic authorities is so harmful. To say that a certain population does not trust certain scientific authorities, for example, is to say that the population does not believe what they say on their authority. The scientists are not in a position to make up the minds of the population for them, and so if they wish to convince the population of something, they must either convince them that they, the scientists, are in fact authorities (that they are to be trusted) or else resort to other means of influencing their beliefs such as argument, explanation, etc. When it comes to matters that are highly technical or that require a considerable amount of background knowledge, these other means of influencing a population's beliefs might be ineffective. In such cases, the lack of trust in epistemic authorities can have deleterious effects on a population's ability to acquire the information that might be necessary for action. Mechanisms aimed at cultivating and sustaining trust are thus integral to the successful functioning of epistemic authority within a society.

6.4 Trust and Practical Authority

While interpersonal trust is necessary for the exercise of epistemic authority, things are very different when it comes to practical authority. I have claimed that social influence by authority is characterized by the way in which it purports to make up others' minds for them. Moreover, I have claimed that the attitude of interpersonal trust can be understood as an attitude that involves allowing another to make up one's mind for one. Nevertheless, the exercise of practical authority does not aim at interpersonal trust on the part of those it seeks to influence, and this is because practical authority aims at a particular kind of action – obedient action – rather than a particular kind of attitude. If interpersonal trust is a kind of attitude that cannot be adopted directly for practical reasons, then it cannot be the aim of practical authority.

On the Razian preemptive account of practical authority, authoritative practical directives provide agents with first-order reasons for action that are also second-order preemptive reasons for not acting otherwise for certain other reasons. When a soldier is ordered by her commanding officer to commandeer a vehicle, the order is both a reason to commandeer the vehicle and a reason not to do otherwise for certain other reasons, such as reasons the soldier may have for thinking that commandeering the vehicle is not the best way to achieve their objective. The commanding officer's judgment about what to do thus "replaces" the soldier's; the decision about what to do is "removed" from the soldier to the officer. The officer here purports to make up the soldier's mind about what to do for her. The officer is not giving the soldier advice or trying to convince her by argument that commandeering the vehicle is in fact the thing to do in the situation. She is telling (ordering) her to so act, and in so doing she purports to settle this question for the soldier. But the question she is settling is here a practical question the settling of which is not to form a belief about what is the best thing to do but rather to act in a particular way. The officer's order is fulfilled when the soldier commandeers the vehicle. The order aims at obedient action, not trusting belief. The order can therefore succeed even if the soldier does not believe, let alone trust, that commandeering the vehicle is the thing to do.

This helps to explain why practical authority does not require trust on the part of those it aims to influence. Practical authority aims to influence action in the world, not one's beliefs about the world, and so one can recognize others as being in charge, as being in a position to determine for one what to do, without trusting them, even without trusting them to make the appropriate practical decisions. The soldier might believe that her officer's orders are wrong, that her tactical decisions are a mistake, but she might obey nonetheless.

Even though interpersonal trust is not necessary for the successful exercise of practical authority, extensive lack of trust in practical authorities can certainly serve to undermine their authority. Typically, the reason that practical authorities occupy their authoritative position is that they are presumed to be in a better position to settle practical questions for the agents over whom they have authority than are the agents themselves. As Raz's (1986) service conception of authority contends, the point of practical authority is to maximize agents' conformity with reason. Authorities provide the service of helping agents to conform to reason better than the agents would be able to if they tried to settle these questions for themselves. To the extent that a purported authority is believed by agents to be unable to provide this service, then to that extent the agents will fail to recognize the purported authority as genuine. Certain attitudes on the part of agents can thus form part of the background that needs to be in place in order for a practical authority to be recognized as such. It is not clear that trusting belief that the authority will generally make better practical decisions, as opposed to non-trusting belief that the authority will do so, must be a part of this background, but actual distrust of a purported authority's ability to make the correct decisions does seem to undermine the background that must be in place in order for the authority to be able to successfully exercise her authority. This is consistent, however, with the thought that practical authority can be successfully exercised without agents trusting that the authority's particular practical decisions are correct and even in the presence of positive belief on the part of agents that the authorities decisions are mistaken.

Moreover, there is a species of practical authority that does not even require that agents believe that the authority is generally in a better position to settle practical questions for the agents than are the agents themselves. Practical authority is often employed in order to solve coordination problems, problems with respect to which any answer will count as "correct" as long as everyone in the community agrees to it. It might not matter whether citizens drive on the right-hand side or the left-hand side of the road, as long as everyone does the same thing. A community might then appoint an authority to settle this question for everyone, to simply make a decision, and then direct everyone to act accordingly. Here the belief that the authority is generally in a better position to settle such questions than others in the community is not required to recognize the authority's ability to settle questions for the community, and so trusting the authority to do so appears irrelevant.

Distinguishing between the aims of epistemic and practical authority can thus help us to appreciate how it is that interpersonal trust on the part of agents subject to the authority can sometimes appear necessary for the successful exercise of authority and sometimes appear irrelevant. Epistemic authority plausibly aims at an agent's trusting the authority for the truth. To trust the authority for the truth is to believe what the authority says in a way that involves allowing the authority to make up one's mind for one. Authority generally aims at making up others' minds for them, but practical authority aims at settling for agents practical rather than theoretical questions. Insofar as interpersonal trust is an attitude that cannot be adopted directly for practical reasons, it cannot be the aim of practical authority. Practical authority aims at obedient action, and while obedient action has something in common with interpersonal trust in that it too involves allowing another to settle a question for one, it is not an attitude and so cannot be identified with interpersonal trust. This explains why one can obey a superior without trusting the superior to make the correct decision but cannot believe on the authority of an expert without trusting the expert for the truth. Appreciating the societal significance of interpersonal trust thus requires appreciating the differences between epistemic and practical authority.

Notes

1 A distinction is sometimes drawn between being *an authority* and being *in authority*, where being an authority is a matter of having special knowledge or expertise concerning some subject matter while being in authority, in contrast, is a matter of being placed by an established procedure in a position to solve problems of coordinating action (Friedman, 1990). Here epistemic authorities are always an authority, while practical authorities can be either in authority or an authority.

2 A classic statement of non-voluntarism about belief is Williams (1973). My presentation here is heavily indebted to Hieronymi (2006).

3 If one worries that the explanation for why one cannot believe for this reason is that one has overwhelming perceptual evidence that there is not an elephant in the room, we might imagine a case in which one is offered an inducement to believe something that is consistent with all of one's other beliefs. If I offer you a large sum of money to believe that I grew up in Wisconsin, for example, then even if this is consistent with everything else that you know about me, you cannot believe directly for this reason. You could believe if you took my inducement to be testimony or evidence that I grew up in Wisconsin ("he wouldn't make this offer if it wasn't true"),

but then my inducement would be functioning as an epistemic rather than a practical reason. This would not show that one can believe directly for practical reasons.

4 This is recognized even by Pascal who notes that one convinced by his prudential wager argument for believing in God will not thereby form the belief but rather act in ways that will hopefully bring oneself to believe. One convinced by the wager argument will attend religious services, read the Bible, and otherwise act as a believer in the hopes that in so doing one will come to believe.

5 See also Faulkner (2014), Hawley (2014), Frost-Arnold (2014).

6 Note that such mental actions can be performed directly for practical reasons like inducements. If I offer you a large sum of money to imagine that there is a pink elephant in the room, or to assume this for the sake of argument, you can easily do this.

7 For a more detailed argument against voluntarism about trust, see McMyler (2017).

8 Hieronymi calls these attitudes "commitment-constituted attitudes" (2006) or attitudes that "embody an agent's answer to a question" (2009).

9 A classic example in the case of intention is Kavka's toxin puzzle (1983).

10 It is sometimes claimed that interpersonal trust can be either an action or an attitude. See, for example, Faulkner (2011) and (this volume). However, it seems to me that while we can describe an act of Φ-ing as a trusting action, to do so is to characterize the act in terms of the attitude that motivates it or is expressed by it. In this respect, describing an action as trusting is like describing an action as fearful or prideful. Actions can be motivated by or express fear or pride, but fear and pride are attitudes, not actions. Similarly, actions can be motivated by or express trust, but trust is an attitude, not an action.

11 For recent cognitivist or doxastic accounts of trust along these lines see Hieronymi (2008), McMyler (2011), Zagzebski (2012), Keren (2014), and Marušić (2015) and (forthcoming). Keren (this volume) examines arguments for and against doxastic accounts of interpersonal trust.

12 Recall Lewis's claim that in believing an epistemic authority we believe "independently of our own conviction founded on appropriate reasoning" (1875:5–6). Similar claims pertaining to either practical or epistemic authority can be found throughout the literature on authority. See, for example, Hobbes (1996:176), Godwin (1971:22), Marcuse (1972:7), Friedman (1990:67), Hart (1990:100), Raz (1990:193), and Zagzebski (2012:102). For a general discussion of what is involved in not making up one's own mind about a theoretical or practical question, see McMyler (forthcoming).

13 For critical discussion of this Razian answer, see McMyler (forthcoming).

14 For doubts that there can be such a thing as a Razian preemptive epistemic reason, see McMyler (2014) and Jäger (2016).

15 For an account of interpersonal trust along these explicitly Razian lines, see Keren (2014). Zagzebski's (2012) account of epistemic authority, in particular her account of the authority of testimony, also parallels Raz's account of practical authority, though her account of interpersonal trust does not. For an alternative to the Razian preemptive account of what is involved in not making up one's own mind, see McMyler (forthcoming).

References

Alston, W. (1988) "The Deontological Conception of Epistemic Justification," *Philosophical Perspectives* 2: 257–299.

Anscombe, E. (2008) "What Is It To Believe Someone?" in M. Geach and L. Gormally (eds.), *Faith in a Hard Ground: Essays on Religion, Philosophy and Ethics*, Charlottesville, VA: Imprint Academic.

Baier, A. (1986) "Trust and Anti-Trust," *Ethics* 96: 231–260.

Bennett, J. (1990) "Why Is Belief Involuntary?" *Analysis* 50: 87–107.

Faulkner, P. (2011) *Knowledge on Trust*, New York: Oxford University Press.

Faulkner, P. (2014) "The Practical Rationality of Trust," *Synthese* 191: 1975–1989.

Friedman, R. (1990) "On the Concept of Authority in Political Philosophy," in J. Raz (ed.), *Authority*, New York: New York University Press.

Frost-Arnold, K. (2014) "The Cognitive Attitude of Rational Trust," *Synthese* 191: 1957–1974.

Godwin, W. (1971) *Enquiry Concerning Political Justice*, Oxford: Clarendon Press.

Hart, H. (1990) "Commands and Authoritative Legal Reasons," in J. Raz (ed.), *Authority*, New York: New York University Press.

Hawley, K. (2014) "Partiality and Prejudice in Trusting," *Synthese* 191: 2029–2045.

Hieronymi, P. (2005) "The Wrong Kind of Reason," *Journal of Philosophy* 102: 437–457.

Hieronymi, P. (2006) "Controlling Attitudes," *Pacific Philosophical Quarterly* 87: 45–74.

Hieronymi, P. (2008) "The Reasons of Trust," *Australasian Journal of Philosophy* 86: 213–236.

Hieronymi, P. (2009) "Two Kinds of Agency," in L. O'Brien and M. Soteriou (eds.), *Mental Actions*, Oxford: Oxford University Press.

Hobbes, T. (1996) *Leviathan*, Cambridge: Cambridge University Press.

Holton, R. (1994) "Deciding to Trust, Coming to Believe," *Australasian Journal of Philosophy* 72: 63–76.

Jäger, C. (2016) "Epistemic Authority, Preemptive Reasons, and Understanding," *Episteme* 13: 167–185.

Jones, K. (1996) "Trust as an Affective Attitude," *Ethics* 107: 4–25.

Kavka, G. (1983) "The Toxin Puzzle," *Analysis* 43: 33–36.

Keren, A. (2014) "Trust and Belief: A Preemptive Reasons Account," *Synthese* 191: 2593–2615.

Lewis, G. (1875) *An Essay on the Influence of Authority in Matters of Opinion*, London: Longman's, Green, and Co.

Marcuse, H. (1972) *A Study on Authority*, New York: Verso.

Marušić, B. (2015) *Evidence and Agency: Norms of Belief for Promising and Resolving*, Oxford: Oxford University Press.

Marušić, B. (forthcoming) "Trust, Reliance, and the Participant Stance," *Philosopher's Imprint*.

McMyler, B. (2011) *Testimony, Trust, and Authority*, New York: Oxford University Press.

McMyler, B. (2014) "Epistemic Authority, Preemption, and Normative Power," *European Journal for Philosophy of Religion* 6: 121–139.

McMyler B. (2017) "Deciding to Trust" in P. Faulkner and T. Simpson (eds.), *The Philosophy of Trust*, New York: Oxford University Press.

McMyler, B. (forthcoming) "On Not Making up One's Own Mind," *Synthese*. doi:10.1007/s11229-11017-1563-0

Origgi, G. (2005) "What Does It Mean to Trust in Epistemic Authority?" Columbia University Academic Commons. https://doi.org/10.7916/D80007FR

Pollock, J. and Cruz, J. (1999) *Contemporary Theories of Knowledge*, New York: Roman & Littlefield.

Raz, J. (1986) *The Morality of Freedom*, New York: Oxford University Press.

Raz, J. (1990) *Practical Reason and Norms*, New York: Oxford University Press.

Strawson, P. (1962) "Freedom and Resentment," *Proceedings of the British Academy*, 48: 1–25.

Williams, B. (1973) "Deciding to Believe" in *Problems of the Self*, Cambridge: Cambridge University Press.

Zagzebski, L. (2012) *Epistemic Authority: A Theory of Trust, Authority, and Autonomy in Belief*, New York: Oxford University Press.

7
TRUST AND REPUTATION

Gloria Origgi

7.1 Introduction

Trusting others is one of the most common epistemic practices to make sense of the world around us. Sometimes we have reasons to trust, sometimes not, and many times our main reason to trust is based on the *reputation* we attribute to our informants. The way we usually weight this reputation, how we select the "good informants,"[1] which of their properties we use as indicators of their trustworthiness and why our informants are responsive to our trustful attitude are rather complex matters that are discussed at length in this volume (see Faulkner, Goldberg, this volume). Indicators of trustworthiness may be notoriously biased by our prejudices, they may be faked or manipulated by malevolent or just interested informants and change through time and space (see also Scheman, this volume). In this chapter I will try to specify conditions of rational trust into our informants and their relations to the reputational cues that are spread throughout our cognitive environment.

Why we trust, how we trust, and when have we reasons to trust are features of our cognitive, social and emotional life that are highly dependent on how the informational landscape is organized around us through social institutions of knowledge, power relations and systems of acknowledging expertise, i.e. what Michel Foucault brilliantly defined as *The Order of Discourse* typical of every society.[2] In my contribution I will focus on *epistemic trust*, i.e. the dimension of trust that has to do with our coming to believe through reliance on other people's testimony (Origgi 2012c), yet many of the reflections on the relation between trust and reputation may be applied to the general case of interpersonal trust discussed in other chapters of this handbook. I will first introduce the debate around the notion of epistemic trust, then discuss the notion of reputation and finally list a number of mechanisms and heuristics that make us rely, more or less rationally, on the reputations of others.

7.2 Epistemic Trust

I was born in Milan on February 8, 1967. I believe this is true because the office of Vital Records in the Milan Municipal Building registered few days after that date the testimony of my father or my mother that I was indeed born on 8 February in a hospital in Milan, and delivered a birth certificate with this date on it. This fact concerns me, and of course I was present, but I can access it only through this complex, institution-mediated form of indirect testimony.

Or else: I know that smoking causes cancer, I have been told this and it was enough relevant information for me to make me quit cigarettes years ago. Moreover, information regarding the potential harm of smoking cigarettes is now mandatorily advertised on each pack of cigarettes in the European Union. I do not have the slightest idea of the physiological process that a smoker's body undergoes from inhaling smoke to developing a cellular process that ends in cancer. Nevertheless, the partial character of my understanding of what it really means that smoking causes cancer does not refrain me from stating it in conversations and to rule my behavior according to this belief. I trust the institutions that inform me on the potential harm of smoking if I have reasons to think that they are benevolent institutions that care about my health. Our cognitive life is pervaded with partially understood, poorly justified, beliefs. The greater part of our knowledge is acquired from other's people spoken or written words. The floating of other people's words in our minds is the price we pay for thinking. This epistemic dependence on other people's knowledge doesn't make us more gullible; rather it is an essential condition to be able to acquire knowledge from the external world.

Traditional epistemology warns us of the risks of uncritically relying on other people's authority in acquiring new beliefs. One could view the overall project of classical epistemology – from Plato to the contemporary rationalist perspectives on knowledge – as a normative enterprise aiming at protecting us from credulity and ill-founded opinions. The status of testimonial knowledge throughout the history of philosophy is ambivalent: sometimes it is considered as a sort of "minor" source of knowledge, linked to communication that had to be sustained by moral norms against lying in order to work among humans. In the Christian Medieval tradition, it is considered as an act of faith in the *auctoritas*, i.e. a different source of "knowledge" from that provided by a priori knowledge or by the senses.

Trust is an essential aspect of human cognitive and communicative interactions. Humans not only end up trusting one another much of the time but are also trustful and willing to believe one another to start with, and withdraw this basic trust only in circumstances where they have special reasons to be mistrustful.

There is a meager tradition in classical philosophy of testimony from the Scottish philosopher Thomas Reid that has made the claim that humans are epistemically justified in believing what other people say. Relying on other people's testimony is a necessary condition, although not a sufficient one, for epistemic trust. Epistemic trust involves a mutual relation between a trustor and a trustee, and a series of implicit and explicit mutual commitments that mere reliance does not require. The very idea of epistemic trust presupposes the acceptance of other people's testimony, although doesn't reduce to it: trusting others enriches the moral and interpersonal phenomenology of testimony by adding an emotional dimension to the relation between the trustor and the trustee and implies a mastery of the reputational cues that are distributed in the social institutions of knowledge. But let me first present the philosophical debate around the reliability of testimony.

In classical epistemology, uncritical acceptance of the claims of others was often seen as a failure to meet rationality requirements imposed on genuine knowledge. Although testimony is considered an important issue by many philosophers, such as Augustin, Aquinas, Montaigne, Locke and many others, the rise of modern philosophy puts intellectual autonomy at the center of the epistemic enterprise, thus dismissing testimony as a path to knowledge that does not present the same warrants as clear and distinct ideas or sense impressions arrived at by oneself. This individualistic stance was clearly a reaction against the pervasive role in Scholasticism of arguments from authority. It persists in contemporary epistemology, where a common view, described as "reductivist" or "reductionist," holds that true beliefs acquired through testimony qualify as knowledge only if acceptance of the testimony is itself justified by other true beliefs acquired not through testimony but through perception or inference (see Fricker 1995; Adler 2002; van Cleve 2006).

This reductionist view contrasts with an alternative 'anti-reductionist' approach, which treats trust in testimony as intrinsically justified (Hardwig 1991; Coady 1992; Foley,1994). According to Thomas Reid, who provided an early and influential articulation of this anti-reductionist view, humans not only trust what others tell them, but are also entitled to do so. They have been endowed by God with a disposition to speak the truth and a disposition to accept what other people tell them as true. Reid talks of two principles "that tally with each other," the *Principle of Veracity* and the *Principle of Credulity* (Reid, 1764, § 24). We are entitled to trust others because others are naturally disposed to tell the truth. A more contemporary version of the argument invokes language (instead of God) as a *purely preservative* vehicle of information (Burge 1993): we trust each other's words because we share a communication system that preserves the truth. Cases of misuses of the system (for example, lying) are exceptions that we can deal with through other forms of social coordination (norms, sanctions, pragmatic rules of "good use" of language).

Although the debate between reductionists and anti-reductionists is still ongoing in contemporary epistemology (Lackey 2008; Goldberg 2010), the very *fact* that *epistemic reliance*[3] on others is a fundamental ingredient of our coming to know is now widely acknowledged in philosophy (see also Goldberg, this volume). Contemporary philosophy has rehabilitated testimony as a source of knowledge and widened the debate on testimony and trust in knowledge. The affective dimension of trust as a fundamental *epistemic* need in our cognitive life, how this complex social-emotional attitude impacts our knowledge processes, the depth of interpersonal dimension of this relation are nowadays mainstream themes in social epistemology (see Faulkner 2011; Faulkner and Simpson 2017). To what extent is our trust justified? How are the justification processes of assessing the reliability of a testimonial beliefs not limited to the receiver's cognitive systems but *extend* to the producer's cognition? What is the creative role of the communication process in coming to believe the words of others? What is the role of trust and the expectations of trustworthiness it elicits? These are still open issues in contemporary epistemology in order to make sense of the apparently contradictory notion of *epistemic trust*, that is, a fundamental epistemic attitude that is based on a deep cognitive and emotional vulnerability. How can we justify an epistemic attitude on the grounds of a vulnerable attitude such as trust? Epistemic trust makes us cognitively vulnerable because we trust others not only to empower our epistemic life but to take critical decisions that are based on expertise (as for example when we go to the doctor) and to shape our political opinions that crucially involve expert knowledge we do not fully master (Origgi, 2004).

The cognitive vulnerability that epistemic trusts involves makes of it a special epistemic attitude, in a sense, richer than reliance on testimony. Our trust is pervasive; we cannot decide if we want to "jump into" an epistemic trust relation or stay out of it: we are born immersed in an ocean of beliefs, half-truths, traditions, and chunks of knowledge that float around us and influence the very structure of our knowledge acquisition processes.

Yet the fact that we navigate in an *information-dense* world in which knowledge of others is omnipresent in our making up our mind about *any* issue does not make us more gullible or lead us to a sort *mass irrationality* that inexorably drags us towards a *credulous society* of people who will believe just about anything, to use the phrase of Gérald Bronner, who, along with Cass Sunstein, depicts society in exactly these bleak and disparaging terms.[4] People develop strategies of *epistemic vigilance*[5] to assess the sincerity of their informants, the credibility of the institutions that produce the "epistemic standards" and the chains of transmission of information that sustain the *coverage* of facts.[6] Factors affecting the acceptance or rejection of a piece of communicated information may have to do with the *source* of the information (*whom* to believe), with its *content* (*what* to believe), or else with the various *institutional designs* that sustain the credibility of information. Given the impossibility of directly checking the reliability of information we receive, we rather are competent in an *indirect* epistemic vigilance, i.e. we check the reputations of those who inform us, their commitments towards us, how their reputations are constructed and maintained. In most situations, our epistemic conundrum is not about the *direct* reliability of our informants but about the reliability of the *reputations* of our informants, their true or pretended authority, their certified expertise. The project of an *indirect epistemology*, or a *second order epistemology* that I pursue in my work on reputation aims at understanding the ways in which we reduce our *cognitive deficit* towards complex information by labeling the information through a variety of *reputational devices* (Origgi 2012e). We do not trust directly our informants, we trust the reputations we are able to grasp about them, what we are told about them, or their particular status in an epistemic network. We place our trust in social information about our informants and it is at this social level of gathering information about them that we are epistemically vulnerable. Social information can be more or less reliable and depend on the reliability of the epistemic network in which it is embedded. Reputations spread around our social world, they recruit epistemic networks in order to signal the epistemic virtues of their bearers. They are not always reliable: the competences we need to acquire in order to distinguish between reliable and unreliable reputations and come to trust others through their reliable reputations are varied and depend more on our social cognition than on our analytical skills.

I will now turn to the epistemic uses of reputation and how we come to trust "the order of knowledge" that is embedded in the various epistemic networks and institutions that organize our epistemic trust through a number of complex devices that rank and rate this knowledge.

7.3 Is Reputation a Reliable Source of Epistemic Trust?

As the philosopher and economist Friedrich August von Hayek (1945) wrote: "Most of the advantages of social life, especially in its advanced forms, which we call *civilization*, rests on the fact that people benefit from knowledge they do not possess." We do not possess knowledge that is possessed by other individuals or group in our society and thanks to a division of cognitive labor we may act as we possess that knowledge by trusting those who have it. Yet, most of the time, we do not acquire *knowledge* through others. We acquire social information that allows us to use a piece of knowledge held by others, to evaluate it, without knowing it directly. If I buy a bottle of wine by reading the social information that is printed on its label, I do not acquire direct knowledge on the taste of wine, but I can act as I knew it (Origgi 2012a). I trust the social information that surrounds the bottle of wine, what is written on the label, what other people say of this wine, how experts and connoisseurs evaluate it. This form of epistemic trust is not blind trust. *Social information*, that is, reputation, is organized in various epistemic networks that go from informal gossip to formal ratings of expertise that orient us in choosing a doctor, a bottle of wine or a scientific claim published in some *peer-reviewed* journal. We can evaluate these networks in terms of their trustworthiness and put our trust in them in a reasoned way.

People, ideas and products have a *reputation*, that is, they crystallize around them a certain amount of social information that we may extract in order to evaluate them and trust them. Reputation is a cloud of opinions that circulates according to its own laws, operating independently of the individual beliefs and intentions of those who hold and communicate the opinions in question. It is part of the *social track* that all our interactions leave in the mind of others. This fundamental *collateral information* that accompanies the lives of people, of things and ideas is becoming so crucial in information-dense societies like ours that the way in which other people *value* information is more informative about any content than information itself. If I read a positive opinion about the French prime minister in a newspaper whom I value credible, my opinion *not* of the newspaper *but* the prime minister will have more chances to be positive too. The social information about the newspaper influences the reputation of the prime minister. Reputations travel through epistemic networks, become representations of the credibility of a certain agent. They are *public representations*, i.e. they spread through a population through gossips and rumors and other more controlled epistemic devices (such as rating and ranking systems). The publicity of reputations and their way of circulating in a population are an essential aspect of the epistemic use of reputation and its role in our trust in others. What makes reputations a fragile signal of the informational content they are attached to is that they circulate, are communicated and may be modified by the very process of communication.

The *essentially* communicative nature of reputation is often disregarded in studies of the phenomenon. Yet reputation, far from being a simple opinion, is a public representation of what we believe to be the opinions of others. We may find ourselves expressing and conveying this *opinion about opinions* for all sorts of reasons, out of conformism or to appear in sync with the opinions of everyone else, or because we see a potential advantage in make it circulate, or else because we want to contribute to stabilize a certain reputation of an individual. There is a fundamental difference between a mere opinion and what we believe we *should* think of someone based on the opinion of those we consider more or less authoritative. Hence, reputation is a three-place relation that may be defined as follows: a reputation is a relation between X (a person), Y (a target person, a target object) and an authority Z (the common sense, the group, another person, the institutional rankings, what I think I should think about others … The way in which the authority Z evaluates Y influences X's evaluation of Y (Origgi, 2012d; 2018).

The definition tries to capture the idea that reputation is a social property that is mutually constructed by the perceiver, the perceived and the social context. Judgments of reputation involve always a "third party": a community of peers, experts or acknowledged authorities that we defer to for our evaluations and formal rankings. Reputation is in the eyes of the others: we look at how others look at the target and defer, with complex cognitive strategies, to this social look.

Understanding the way in which this social information influences our trust may seem a hopeless intellectual enterprise. We all know how fragile reputations are, how often they are undeserved. As Iago replies to Cassio, who is desperate after having lost his reputation in the eyes of Othello, in a famous passage of Shakespeare's masterpiece tragedy: "*Reputation is an idle and most false imposition, often got without merit and lost without deserving.*"[7]

It seems impossible to make sense of our trust in information on at least reasonable grounds without paying attention to the biased heuristics we use to evaluate the social information and to the systemic distortions of the reputational systems in which the information is embedded (Origgi, 2012b). My strong epistemological point here is that reputation is not just a collateral feature that we may consider or not in our epistemic practices. Without access to other people's reputations and evaluations, without a mastery of the tools that crystallize collective evaluations, coming to know would be impossible. In societies where information grows, the role of reputational devices that filter information becomes ever more crucial. Accordingly, social uses of new technologies, such as social networks, are geared by our cognitive dispositions to look for other's reputations and care about our own image at the same time. I am able to check the signals of the credibility of others' reputation, but many times I simply accept their reputation out of a sort of "conformism"; e.g. when I trust someone only because everybody in a certain circle that I wish to belong to trust her. Thus, not only do I care about my own reputation of being a trustworthy person, I also care about being the kind of person who trusts that kind of others. The management of reputation is a complex attitude that mixes rationality, social norms and many psychological and social biases. Yet it is possible to pry apart epistemically sound ways of relying on reputations from the biases and prejudices that may influence the way in which we weight social information. Reputations may be more or less reliable and their epistemic reliability depends on many factors that we are going to explore in the following section.

7.4 How Reputations Circulate: Formal versus Informal Reputations

What are the signals of a reliable reputation? What are the reasonable heuristics? Which biases exist? I now turn to the assessment and reliability of reputations. People emit signals meant to convince others of the credibility of their reputations. Similarly, all things, objects, ideas and indeed everything that points beyond appearances to hidden qualities, emit signals that inform us more or less credibly that these qualities really exist. These signals are then transformed by the communication processes in social information, that is, public representations that circulate about a item or a person.

There are at least two broad categories of reputations:

Informal reputations, i.e. all the socio-cognitive phenomena connected to the circulation of opinions: rumors, gossip, innuendo, indiscretions, informational cascades, and so forth.

Formal reputations, i.e. all the official devices for putting reputations into an "objective" format, such as rating and ranking systems, product labels and informational hierarchies established e.g. by algorithms on the basis of Internet searches.

Informal reputations have a very bad reputation themselves as being vehicles of falsities, tendentious information and, nowadays, *fake news*. Yet, this informal circulation of reputations is not completely uncontrolled. Its spreading follows some rules and it is continuously influenced by the (good or bad) intentions of the producers of information and the aims and stakes of the receivers of information. For example, evidence shows[8] that the spreading of false information on social networks in case of *extreme events* (earthquakes, terrorist attacks) is rapidly corrected by the users. In contrast, other kinds of news, whose relevance is less crucially related to their truth and more with the opinion and values they express, can circulate and enter into *informational cascades*, i.e. informational configurations that occur when a group of people accepts an opinion – or behaves as if it did – without any even indirect assessment of the epistemic quality of the information. As Clément (2012) explains, when other individuals, who have given no thought to the matter, parrot the opinion of that group, "They become in turn the heralds of that opinion. They don't even have to believe in it. It suffices that they don't question it publicly (for instance, from fear of losing the respect of their fellow group members) for other people who have been exposed to that rumor to believe it should be given credit." That is to say that even in the case of informal reputations, we develop strategies of epistemic vigilance which are more or less reliable given the informational context. The amount of cognitive investment in a rational strategy of epistemic vigilance depends on many factors, as we will see in the next session, one of the most fundamental being a rapid assessment of the risks at stake in acquiring or neglecting a piece of information.

The case of *formal reputations* is much more complex. Why do we trust our doctor? Are we really sure that the climate is changing? What are in general the scientific theories that I should believe? Were there weapons of mass destruction in Iraq that influenced the decision to start the invasion of Iraq in 2003? Should we trust Google in its capacity of delivering the appropriate result in an information query? All these questions can be answered if we consider two kinds of possible biases in regards to the information we have to trust: cognitive/emotional/cultural biases about whom we think we *should* trust and structural/reputational biases that depend on the way in which the different formal reputational devices are designed.

7.5 How Do We Trust Reputations?

What we know about others, how we judge people and things, always depends on *traditions* that are structured by *reputational devices* more or less adequate to the transmission of these traditions. It is through these devices that we learn to navigate in the world of social information, that is, as I said, the collateral information that each person, object, ideas emits each time it enters a social interaction. Without the *imprimatur* of presumably knowledgeable others upon a corpus of knowledge, this corpus would remain silent, impossible to decipher. Competent epistemic subjects should be capable of integrating these reputational devices in their search for information. In other words, we do not need to know the world in order to evaluate it. Rather, we evaluate what other people say of the world in order to know it. Nowadays, classifications and indicators have invaded the cognitive, social and political sphere. Schools, hospitals, businesses, states, fortunes, financial products, Internet search results, academic publications (which should be the ultimate encapsulation of *objective* quality) are classified, organized, valued and set in hierarchical relations to each other, as if their intrinsic value were no longer calculable without their being compared to one another. The objectivity of these rankings is a matter of public debate, a major issue in sociology of knowledge and a crucial aspect of our responsible civic participation to social life. A contributor to this volume, Onora O'Neill, has challenged the use of formal rankings in bioethics, and proposed trust as an ideal for patient-physician relations, in contrast to that of promoting individual autonomy, arguing that efforts to achieve the latter have undermined the former (O'Neill 2002). If we are aware of a major bias that influences the way a specific rating device displays its results, we should be *epistemically responsible* and make people aware of that bias. For example, it took a political intervention to force the change from the first generation to the second generation of search engines in which paid inclusions and preferred placements had to be explicitly marked as such.[9]

Although a unified theory of the reliability of reputational devices is far from being a reality in philosophy and social sciences, there are some dimensions along which we can try to assess the way reputational devices can be constructed and influence the perception of reputations. For example, *informational asymmetries*[10] spread across different domains, from traditional domains of expertise like science, to the evaluation of some classes of products, like financial product or cultural ones. A simple law of reputation is the following: the greater the informational asymmetry the greater is the weight of reputation in evaluating information. Another dimension along which reputation may vary is the level of formalization of the reputational device: clearly, a ranking algorithm of a search engine is a more formalized ranking system than the three glasses system of rating wines of the wine guide *Gault-Millau*. The more a reputational device is formalized, the less the judgment is dependent on the weight of authorities, that is, the less is dependent on the judgments of other experts: the device becomes an authority itself.

How can we trust formal reputations given that they may be so biased on many dimensions and given our biased judgments towards them? How can we distinguish cases in which we trust a reputation based on authority (because my professor tells me to trust it) or on the basis of an objective ranking that is constructed in order to maximize the epistemic quality of the information we end up accepting? Given that there is no general epistemological theory of reputation that may answer these questions for all reputational devices, the best strategy is to "unpack" each device and see how the hierarchy of information is internally constructed. Sometimes it is easy (like for example, unpacking the devices that establish academic rankings), sometimes it is very difficult or just impossible because of proprietary information (algorithms of search engines and other reputational devices on the web, or proprietary information of rating agencies). A fair society that fosters epistemic trust should encourage practices of transparency vis-à-vis the methods by which rankings are produced and maintained. Moreover, a diversity of ranking and rating systems would provide a better distribution of the epistemic labor and a more differentiated informational landscape in which people can orient their choices.

Trusting others is a fundamental cognitive and emotional activity that is deeply embedded in our social institutions and reflects layers of practices, traditions and also prejudices. Understanding how our trust can be still reasonable through the use of reputations of others is a fundamental step towards the understanding of the interplay between the cognitive order and the social order of our societies.

Notes

1 On the concept of "good informant" see E. Craig (1990) where he argues that our very concept of knowledge originates from the basic epistemic need in the state of nature of recognizing the good informants, i.e. those who are trustworthy and bear indicator properties of their trustworthiness.
2 Cf. Foucault (1971).
3 On the notion of *epistemic reliance*, see Goldberg (2010).

4 Cf. Clément (2012); Bronner (2012).
5 The view the humans are endowed of cognitive mechanisms of *epistemic vigilance* has been defended in Sperber et al. (2010).
6 On the notion of *epistemic coverage* cf. Goldberg (2010).
7 Cf. W. Shakespeare, *Othello*, Act 2, scene 3.
8 Cf. Origgi and Bonnier (2013).
9 Cf. Rogers (2004).
10 For this expression, see Karpik (2010).

References

Adler, J. (2002) *Belief's Own Ethics*, Cambridge MA: MIT Press.

Bronner, G. (2012) *La démocratie des crédules*, Paris: PUF.

Burge, T. (1993) "Content Preservation," *Philosophical Review* 101, 457–488.

Clément, F. (2012) Preface to the French edition of C. Sunstein, *Rumors* [Princeton University Press], *Anatomie de la rumeur*, Geneva: Markus Haller.

Coady, C.A.J. (1992) *Testimony*, Oxford: Oxford University Press.

Craig, E. (1990) *Knowledge and the State of Nature*, Oxford: Clarendon Press.

Faulkner, P. (2011) *Knowledge on Trust*, Oxford: Oxford University Press.

Faulkner, P. and Simpson, T. (2017) *The Philosophy of Trust*, Oxford: Oxford University Press.

Foley, R. (1994) "Egoism in Epistemology," in F. Schmitt (ed.), *Socializing Epistemology*, Lanham, MD: Rowman & Littlefield.

Foucault, M. (1971) "The Order of Discourse," *Social Science Information* 10(2): 7–30.

Fricker, E. (1995) "Critical Notice: Telling and Trusting: Reductionism and Anti-Reductionism in the Epistemology of Testimony," *Mind* 104: 393–411.

Fricker, E. (2006) "Testimony and Epistemic Autonomy," in J. Lackey and E. Sosa (eds.), *The Epistemology of Testimony*, Oxford: Oxford University Press.

Goldberg, S. (2010) *Relying on Others*, Oxford: Oxford University Press.

Hardwig, J. (1991) "The Role of Trust in Knowledge," *The Journal of Philosophy*
88(12): 693–708.

Karpik, L. (2010) *Valuing the Unique: The Economics of Singularities*, Princeton, NJ: Princeton University Press.

Lackey, J. (2008) *Knowing from Words*, Oxford: Oxford University Press.

O'Neill, O. (2002) *A Question of Trust*, Cambridge: Cambridge University Press.

Origgi, G. (2004) "Is Trust an Epistemological Notion?" *Episteme* 1(1): 61–72.

Origgi, G. (2012a) "Designing Wisdom through the Web: Reputation and the Passion of Ranking," in H. Landermore and J. Elster (eds.), *Collective Wisdom*, Cambridge: Cambridge University Press.

Origgi, G. (2012b) "Epistemic Injustice and Epistemic Trust," *Social Epistemology* 26(2): 221–235.

Origgi, G. (2012c) "Epistemic Trust," in B. Kaldys (ed.), *SAGE Encyclopedia of Philosophy of Social Science*, New York: Sage Publications.

Origgi, G. (2012d) "Reputation," in B. Kaldys (ed.), *SAGE Encyclopedia of Philosophy of Social Science*, New York: Sage Publications.

Origgi, G. (2012e) "A Social Epistemology of Reputation," *Social Epistemology* 26 (3–4): 399–418.

Origgi, G. (2018) *Reputation: What It Is and Why It Matters*, Princeton, NJ: Princeton University Press.

Origgi, G. and Bonnier, P. (2013) "Trust, Networks and Democracy in the Age of the Social Web," Proceedings of the ACM Web Science Conference, Paris, May 2–4. www.websci13.org/program

Rogers, R. (2004) *Information Politics on the Web*, Cambridge, MA: MIT Press.

Sperber, D., Clement, F., Mercier, H., Origgi, G. and Wilson, D. (2010) "Epistemic Vigilance," *Mind & Language* 25(4): 359–393.

van Cleve, J. (2006) "Reid on the Credit of Human Testimony," in J. Lackey and E. Sosa (eds.), *The Epistemology of Testimony*, Oxford: Oxford University Press.

von Hayek, F.A. (1945) "The Use of Knowledge in Society," *American Economic Review* 35(4): 519–530.

8 TRUST AND RELIANCE[1]

Sanford C. Goldberg

Most philosophers interested in characterizing the nature of trust regard it as a species of reliance. This chapter reviews attempts to demarcate trust as a distinct species of reliance. Some of the main accounts introduce a moral dimension to trust absent from "mere" reliance; these accounts raise interesting questions about the relationship between the moral and the epistemic dimensions of trust, and this chapter concludes by discussing these.

8.1 Reliance

Examples of one person relying on another person abound: one neighbor relies on another to keep an eye on her house when her family is out of town; a student relies on her lab partner to complete his task on time. We rely on artifacts as well: you rely on your watch to tell the correct time; I rely on the bridge not to collapse under the weight of my car. And we rely on natural phenomena: you rely on the sunrise to wake you up each morning; I rely on bodily pains to let me know when I should schedule a visit to the doctor. Indeed, we might even treat other people's behaviors as akin to natural phenomena in this way: Kant was said to be so regular in the time of his daily walk that the citizens of Königsberg relied on his walks to set their watches; I rely on my neighbor's screams of joy to let me know that something good has just happened to the Cubs (as he is otherwise very reserved).

Following Richard Holton (1994), we might characterize reliance in terms of a supposition one is prepared to act on: where X is a person, artifact, or natural process, and φ is an action, behavior or process, to rely on X to φ is to act on the supposition that X will φ.

Several features of this account of reliance are noteworthy.

First, insofar as we characterize reliance in terms of preparedness to act on the supposition that X will φ, we need not treat this supposition as a *belief* that X will φ: one can act on suppositions regarding whose truth one harbors doubts. For example, if the only way to safety is to cross a very rickety bridge, you might rely on the bridge to hold you without fully believing that it will. While *dis*belief (= the belief that X *will not* φ) would appear to render reliance irrational and perhaps impossible, the mere absence of belief is compatible with reliance: one can rely on X to φ while remaining agnostic (or while harboring doubts) whether X will φ.

Second, the foregoing account makes clear that a relied-upon party need not be aware of being relied upon. This is clear in the example of Kant's daily walks, or my relying on my neighbor's screams for letting me know about the Cubs.

Third (and relatedly), the foregoing account also makes clear that one can rely on an entity *without being aware of this fact oneself.* In crossing the bridge with my car, I rely on it to hold the weight of the car. I might not have explicitly thought about the bridge holding the weight, but my reliance on its doing so comes out in my behavior. (If I thought the bridge would not hold me, I would not have driven over it.)

Fourth, the foregoing account makes clear that if one is let down when one relies on someone or something in some way, one might feel disappointed or saddened by this, but – at least in the sorts of case we have been discussing – one is not entitled to feel resentment or anger or a sense of betrayal at the thing which is relied upon. This is obvious in cases involving reliance on artifacts or natural regularities, but it is also clear where one is relying on another person. In general, unless there was some prior arrangement whereby it became accepted practice that Kant was relied upon in these ways – unless (say) Kant promised to behave in the relevant ways, or he consented to participate in a practice to this effect – Kant's fellow citizens would have no right to be resentful or angry if he decided to take the day off from walking. So, too, without the relevant prior arrangement I would have no right to be resentful or angry if my neighbor did not shout (and so I was not made aware) when something good happened to the Cubs.

8.2 Trust as a Species of Reliance

Most philosophers who write on the nature of trust regard it as a species of reliance. As a species *of reliance*, it is a matter of being prepared to act on a supposition to the effect that X will φ. What differentiates trust from what we might call "mere" reliance is a matter of some dispute.

Perhaps the simplest account holds that trust is a species of reliance *involving belief* – in particular, the belief that the trustee will do as she is being relied upon to do. Call any account on which trust involves a belief of this sort a "doxastic" account (see Keren, this volume). The simplest doxastic account holds that this is all there is to trust: it is reliance on a person to φ grounded in the belief that she *will* φ. A slightly more complicated version of this sort of position can be found in Gambetta (1988), who proposed that trust is a matter of a subject assigning a high subjective probability to the hypothesis that another person X will φ.

Such a view does not appear to capture the ordinary notion of trust. After all, one can believe (or assign a high probability to the hypothesis) that a person will φ without *trusting* her to do so – say, because one believes that the person, though highly untrustworthy, is under threat of extreme punishment if she does not φ. A proponent of the doxastic account might respond by distinguishing between (i) trusting X *simpliciter* and (ii) trusting X to φ. Still, critics have found this use of "trust" to be an attenuated one; I will return to this distinction below.

An alternative doxastic account, known as the "Encapsulated Interest" account of trust, is owed to Hardin (1992). According to this account, S trusts X to φ when and only when S relies on X to φ, and does so on the basis of the belief that *X will φ because X's incentives regarding whether to φ encapsulate S's relevant interests.* Such a view recognizes that the threat case, in which S discerns that X is under threat to φ, is not a case of trust.

Still, it can seem that doxastic accounts, including the Encapsulated Interest account, miss something important in the nature of the attitude of trust. Annette Baier (1986) famously argued that there is an important *moral* dimension to trust that doxastic accounts fail to capture. Recall cases of mere reliance, where one acts on the supposition that X will φ. If X fails to φ in such cases, then while one might be disappointed, one would not have grounds for being resentful of X or for regarding X as having betrayed one. By contrast, when one *trusts* X to φ, X's failure to φ will lead to attitudes such as anger, resentment and/or a sense of betrayal. Since these attitudes appear appropriate only when the trustee owes it (morally) to the truster to do as she was trusted to do, the presence of such attitudes in cases of the violation of trust suggests an important moral dimension to trust. None of the previous doxastic accounts – neither Gambetta's simple doxastic account, nor Hardin's Encapsulated Interest account – would lead us to expect this moral dimension.

Most of the philosophical work on trust since Baier's very influential (1986) paper has followed her in thinking that trust has a salient moral dimension, as seen in the reactions elicited by vindications or violations of trust. Baier's own account of trust, which we might call the "Good Will" account, aimed to capture that dimension by construing trust as *reliance on another's good will* to act or behave in the relevant way. In particular, Baier's view is that S's trusting X to φ is a matter of S's relying on X to φ, where this reliance reflects S's attitude of *accepted dependence on X's good will towards S* in this connection. She paraphrases this as follows:

> Trust … is accepted vulnerability to another's possible but not expected ill will (or lack of good will) towards one.
>
> *(Baier 1986:235)*

Such an account enables us to make sense of the moralized reactions in cases of trust: one is *grateful* when one's trust is vindicated, since one takes this outcome to reflect the trustee's *good will* towards one; whereas one feels *betrayed* when one's trust is violated, since one takes this outcome to reflect the trustee's *ill will* (or lack of good will) towards one.

Unfortunately, Baier's Good Will account is threatened by examples which appear to call into question the centrality of good will in the phenomenon of trust. For example, Richard Holton (1994:65) has questioned whether reliance on another's good will is *sufficient* for trust. Imagine a "confidence trickster" who gets you to commit to φing, and who (having extracted this commitment from you) proceeds to rely on you to φ. Such a trickster relies on you to φ out of your good will, but it would be wrong to describe him as *trusting* you; rather, he is *exploiting* your good will. As above, one might try to respond by distinguishing between (i) trusting a person *simpliciter* and (ii) trusting that they will φ in such-and-such circumstances. An alternative response, owed to Karen Jones (1996), modifies the original Good Will account of trust to include a reference to the trustee's motives. Jones spells out her modification, which I will call the "Optimistic Good Will" account of trust, as follows:

> … to trust someone is to have an attitude of optimism about her goodwill and to have the confident expectation that, when the need arises, the one trusted will be directly and favorably moved by the thought that you are counting on her.
>
> *(Jones 1996:5–6)*

Jones argues that this sense of optimism should not be reduced to mere belief, as she emphasizes that it amounts to an emotive element in trust – the sort of emotion typical of one who is *hopeful* with respect to another's good will (Jones 1996:15). One of the virtues of such a (non-doxastic) account is that it seems well positioned to make sense of our feelings of betrayal when our trust is violated: on this view, we feel let down by the fact that the trustee was not directly and favorably moved by her recognition of our counting on her.

A nearby variant on Jones' view is what we might call the "nested reliance" view of trust. On such a view, my trusting you to φ is a matter of my relying on you to φ, under conditions in which I *also* rely on you to treat my relying on you to φ as a (perhaps decisive) *reason* to φ. I describe this as a "nearby variant" since the proponent of the "nested reliance" view need not embrace Jones' characterization of the higher-order attitude in terms of hope.

However, both Jones' Optimistic Good Will account as well as "Nested Reliance" accounts more generally are susceptible in their turn to another sort of counterexample. Against Good Will accounts, Onora O'Neill (2002) gives examples which appear to call into question whether reliance on another's good will is *necessary* for trust: a person might trust his doctor to operate competently on him, not out of a sense that she (the doctor) has good will toward him as her patient, but because it is her job as his doctor. Similarly, enemies trust each other not to shoot one another during a ceasefire, not out of a sense of good will, but because each takes the other to do what is, in that situation, obligatory. In such cases, good will seems beside the point. Arguably, a similar point can be made against the "nested reliance" account: the patient's trust in the doctor need not reflect the patient's sense that she (the doctor) will be moved by the patient's reliance on her, but rather that she will be moved by professional duty.

Richard Holton himself has provided an influential alternative to Good Will accounts. Following Baier and others in thinking that the attitude of trust involves a salient moral dimension, he proposes that we think of the attitude of trust in terms of what he (in the spirit of Strawson 1974) describes as taking a *participant stance* towards someone. To a rough first approximation, trusting another person to φ is, on this "Participant Stance" account, a matter of relying on that person to φ, where this reliance is backed by a "readiness to feel betrayal should it be disappointed, and gratitude should it be upheld" (Holton 1994:67). It is in this readiness to feel the reactive attitudes (of disappointment, gratitude, etc.) that one manifests one's taking a participant stance towards another person, regarding her as susceptible to moral appraisal insofar as one trusts her. (According to Holton, taking such a stance towards another is "one way of treating them as a person" (Holton 1994:67).) One of the advertised virtues of the Participant Stance account is that it can make sense of the phenomenon whereby one *decides* to trust another: on this account, deciding to trust is simply a matter of deciding (not merely to rely on another to φ, but also to) to take up this sort of practical stance towards her in connection with her φing.

Still, as formulated, the Participant Stance account does not seem quite right. For one thing, it would seem that taking such a stance toward someone on whom one relies is not *sufficient* for trusting them. For example, Katherine Hawley notes that one can rely on another person on whom one has taken up the participant stance without *trusting* that person, as "some interactions lie outside the realm of trust and distrust" (Hawley 2014a:7). Hawley's example is of a couple one of whose partners, A, reliably makes dinner for the other, S, where S comes to rely on A's doing so, but where A makes clear to S that she (A) does not want to inherit the burdens of being trusted to do so. (Even so, S, coming home one night to see that dinner is ready, might well feel gratitude towards A, thereby showing that his reliance is part of his taking up of a participant stance towards A.) This is not the only worry about the Participant Stance account. Karen Jones (2004) has argued that the Participant Stance account fails to appreciate the role that the trustee's perspective has on the propriety of the reactive attitudes: if you rely on me to φ, and I succeed in φing but only by accident, then gratitude would not seem appropriate; so too, if you rely on me to φ, and I fail to φ but through no fault of my own, feelings of betrayal are not appropriate (Jones 2004:17). On these points, Good Will accounts seem to fare better than the Participant Stance account.

More recently, Jones herself has offered a theory which purports to capture what she sees as correct in the Participant Stance view, while rectifying its shortcomings. She presents the view as follows:

> Trust is accepted vulnerability to another person's power over something one cares about, where (1) the truster foregoes searching (at the time) for ways to reduce such vulnerability, and (2) the truster maintains normative expectations of the one-trusted that they not use that power to harm what is entrusted.
>
> *(Jones 2004:6)*

Jones herself is at pains to distinguish between "normative expectations" (where the "expectation" is a matter of holding the trustee accountable in the relevant way) and what she calls "predictive expectations" (where the "expectation" is merely a prediction). In a footnote she makes clear what she has in mind with the former. She writes that "normative expectations" are "multistranded dispositions, including dispositions to evaluative judgment and to reactive attitudes" (Jones 2004:17, note 8). The multistranded nature of these dispositions helps to account for cases in which the trustee (A) accidentally lets down the one who trusts her (S): while resentment is not appropriate in such cases, Jones notes, still S might think that an apology is called for. In this way, trust maintains its distinctiveness as a kind of moralized reliance.

Another recent view, developed by Katherine Hawley, holds that

> To trust someone to do something is to believe that she has a commitment to doing it, and to rely upon her to meet that commitment.
>
> *(Hawley 2014a:10)*

Hawley (2014a) argues that, in addition to being able to capture the moral dimension of trust, her "Commitment account" appears suited (in ways that its rivals are not) to provide a natural and complete account of distrust as well. Distrust is not merely the absence of trust: sometimes we rely, or choose not to rely, on others without either trusting or distrusting them. (Think of Kant's fellow citizens: their reliance on him is mere reliance without trust, and if they chose not to do so, say because they began to worry that he might become less regular in his walks, this would not be a matter of distrust.) Nor is distrust a matter of non-reliance out of doubts about the goodness another's will towards one: one might distrust another because one doubts his *competence*. So, too, distrust is not a matter of non-reliance out of a sense that the participant stance is inappropriate, since one might not rely precisely because one anticipates being betrayed. In contrast to these false starts, the Commitment account would appear to have a good characterization of distrust, according to which distrust is simply a matter of (i) believing that someone has a commitment to φ but (ii) not relying on her to follow through on that commitment. Still, Hawley herself anticipates a challenge: one might trust others to behave in a certain way, not because they have committed to so behaving, but rather because one regards them as obliged to behave in that way. Her examples include the trust you have in your friends not to steal your cutlery while over for dinner, and the trust we have that people on the street will allow us to pass unhindered (Hawley 2014a:11). While she grants that these are cases of trust, she proposes to loosen the sense of "commitment" to cover them.

Some philosophers, surveying the literature aiming to demarcate trust as a species of reliance, have come to doubt whether "trust" designates any *single* type of reliance in the first place. Thus Simpson urges us to see "trust" as covering a range of phenomena that are all related to the basic need "to rely on [another's] freely cooperative behavior" (Simpson 2012:558). He argues that this need is a natural part of the human condition, given our social nature and our complex social lives – as these lives often place us in need of relying on the behaviors of our conspecifics, under conditions in which we cannot force them to do so (or otherwise guarantee the desired behavioral outcome). Simpson then identifies and characterizes various subsidiary notions of trust that emerge from this core notion, and he goes on to argue that the various accounts in the literature are mistaken only in thinking that there is one single phenomenon to which an account of trust ought to be answerable.

8.3 Reliance and Trust: Ethics and Epistemology

As we have seen, most philosophical accounts of trust follow Baier in thinking that trust is a kind of *second-personal reliance*. The guiding idea is simply that trust is a relationship between two (or more) people that warrants the trusting subject to have certain normative expectations of the trustee – including (most saliently) the normative expectation to the effect that the trustee will do as she is being relied upon to do. Such accounts can make sense of why a trustee who disappoints one's trust (without an adequate excuse for doing so) can seem to have betrayed one, and why a trustee who has vindicated one's trust can seem to deserve gratitude. Call any account that construes trust as a distinctively second-personal sort of relation a *second-personal reliance account* of trust. The range of accounts that fall under this rubric is great: it includes the various Good Will accounts, the Participant Stance account, as well as the Commitment account.

One question arises if we assume, with second-personal reliance accounts of trust, that S's trusting A to φ introduces the prospect of having A's behaviors subject to S's normative evaluation. Following Hawley, we might wonder about the conditions under which S is *entitled* to bring A under this sort of normative scrutiny.

To appreciate the force of this question, note that there are burdens that come with being trusted: if another person trusts you then your relevant behavior becomes susceptible to her normative (second-personal) evaluation. If you let her down she will be entitled to *resent* you, or to regard you as having *betrayed* her. It would seem that she cannot simply place such burdens on you; she needs some sort of prior permission or authorization to do so. In short: as Hawley (2014a) argued, more than reliance on a reliable person is required if one is to be "permitted" or "authorized" to place the relied-upon person under this sort of second-personal normative scrutiny. Consequently, more than reliance on a reliable person is required if one is to be morally entitled to *trust* another person. The question from the previous paragraph concerns precisely this: when is it morally permissible for one person (S) to hold another person (A) responsible for φing? In other words: when does S have the moral right to trust A to φ? I will call this the *moral entitlement question*. This is a question for any second-personal account of trust.

It is worth distinguishing this question from the question concerning our *epistemic* entitlement to trust another, that is, our entitlement or permission *from an epistemic point of view* to trust another person. This question arises because trust is a kind of reliance, and one's reliance on another person to φ can be evaluated as more or less reasonable, or as based on better or worse evidence of the trusted person's reliability. For example, it would seem most reasonable to trust (and so to rely on) someone whom one has reason to believe is relevantly trustworthy, while it seems unreasonable to trust (and so to rely on) someone whom one has reason to believe is relevantly *un*trustworthy. We might ask: under what conditions is it epistemically reasonable to trust (and so to rely on) another person to φ? I will call this the *epistemic entitlement question*.

When considering the epistemological dimensions of trust, it is important to bear in mind the traditional distinction between *epistemic* reasons and *practical* reasons. To a first approximation, epistemic reasons are considerations that indicate the likely truth of a proposition (or a belief), whereas practical reasons are considerations that count in favor of the choice-worthiness of a proposed act. *That the sky is overcast* is an epistemic reason to believe that it will rain soon; and if I have this reason to believe that it will rain soon, *that I want to remain dry* is a practical reason to cancel the picnic. It is natural to think that one is epistemically entitled to trust another person only when one has adequate *epistemic* reasons to believe that she is trustworthy.

Interestingly, some proponents of second-personal reliance accounts of trust have urged that we complicate this picture.

Clearly, it sometimes happens that we have practical reasons to trust – reasons that indicate, *not* that the relied-upon person is trustworthy, but rather that *it would be a good or worthy thing to trust*. Various theorists have argued, for example, the fact that someone is your friend is itself a reason to trust him or her, independent of your (epistemic) reasons for regarding him or her as trustworthy. The idea here appears to be that trusting your friends is a good thing to do, as it will enhance the friendship (whereas distrust will undermine the friendship).

In other cases, it seems that practical reasons to trust can generate epistemic reasons to trust (Horsburgh 1960; Pettit 1995). The standard example of this (see e.g. Holton 1994) involves a shopkeeper who hires someone recently released from prison to mind the money till, trusting the ex-convict to refrain from stealing. We might then speak of the shopkeeper's *practical* reason for trusting: namely, that in doing so the shopkeeper hopes to inspire the very behavior he is trusting the ex-convict to exhibit. Insofar as the ex-convict is aware of being trusted in this way, he himself has a practical reason to behave as he is being expected to behave (i.e., the desire to avoid letting the shopkeeper down); and insofar as the shopkeeper is aware that the ex-convict has this practical reason, *the shopkeeper herself* has an epistemic reason to think that the ex-convict *will* be trustworthy in this respect (as she regards the ex-convict as likely to act on the practical reasons he, the ex-convict, has). This sort of phenomenon, whereby one person S *entrusts* another person A with something valued, hoping thereby to motivate A to regard S's act of trust as a reason to do what S trusts A to do, has been described as "therapeutic trust." (A related notion of "aspirational trust," wherein one trusts in the aim of generating the trustworthy behavior in the trustee, was developed in Jones (2004).)

The claim that the motivational aspect of therapeutic trust itself generates epistemic reasons for trusting, and so is at the heart of our epistemic entitlement to trust, has been fruitfully explored in the literature on testimony, in connection with the sort of trust that is involved in trusting others to tell us the truth. If we apply Horsburgh's and Pettit's notion of therapeutic trust to the case of trusting another for the truth, the result is a novel account of the epistemology of testimony. Paul Faulkner (2011) has developed and defended such an account. According to Faulkner's trust-based account, trusting another person to be telling the truth, together with the mutual familiarity of what Falkner calls the norm of trust itself, generates an epistemic reason to regard the trusted speaker as trustworthy – thereby rendering the trust itself (and so the belief acquired through that trust) rational.

However, Darwall (2006:287–8), Lackey (2008) and others have argued against this account of the epistemology of testimony. Lackey herself raised two objections. First, it is only if the trusted person is *trust-sensitive* – sensitive to (and motivated to act on) the normative expectations on her in virtue of being trusted – that her awareness of being trusted will motivate her to tell the truth; and it is far from clear how the act of trusting another speaker can generate epistemic reasons to think that the speaker *is* trust-sensitive. Second, even those speakers who *are* trust-sensitive, and so who *are* motivated to tell the truth when they are trusted to do so, might nevertheless fail to do so out of epistemic incompetence. As a result, if an audience's trust of a speaker is to be reasonable from an epistemic perspective, the audience must be epistemically entitled to regard the speaker (not only as trust-sensitive but also) as epistemically competent. Yet the mere act of trusting a speaker does not generate epistemic reasons to regard the speaker as epistemically competent. Lackey's conclusion is that the act in which one manifestly extends one's trust to another, even as supplemented by the norm of trust, is epistemically insignificant.

Faulkner's (2011) trust-based account of the epistemology of testimony is not the only attempt to try to trace our epistemic entitlement to trust other speakers to the normative pressures on the trustee to do as she is trusted to do. Where Faulkner's account traces this epistemic entitlement to the reasons that are generated by the audience's act of *manifestly trusting the speaker*, other accounts trace the epistemic entitlement to the reasons that are generated by the speaker's manifest act of *telling another person something*. Ted Hinchman, one of the proponents of this sort of account, highlights this aspect of the view when he describes the act of telling as an act of "inviting to trust" (Hinchman 2005). Here, to invite someone to trust one is an act of (second-personal) normative significance, and it is the normative significance of this act that generates a reason for the audience to trust the speaker (and so accept her say-so).

This sort of approach to the epistemology of testimony is inspired by a famous remark by Elizabeth Anscombe about the phenomenon of *being believed*. Anscombe noted that

> It is an insult and may be an injury not to be believed. At least it is an insult if one is oneself made aware of the refusal, and it may be an injury if others are.
>
> *(Anscombe 1979:9)*

Anscombe's idea, that not being believed is a kind of "insult" or "injury," points to a kind of normative pressure on a hearer to accept what she is told. Hinchman ascribes this normative pressure to the act of telling itself. To tell an audience that p. is (on Hinchman's view) to invite them to rely on your word: it is to offer one's *assurance* that p to the audience.[2]

According to the "assurance" view of testimony, our epistemic entitlement to trust other speakers reflects the second-personal dimension of trust. This is because the act of telling itself is governed by two distinct sorts of normative demands. The demands on *the speaker* derive from the fact that her act of assurance amounts to an invitation to another to rely on her, where it is common knowledge that it would be wrong (i.e., in violation of the norm governing acts of this kind) to let another down after having invited her reliance. In this way, a speaker who tells an audience something *takes responsibility for* the truth of what she says, and so owes it to her audience to make amends if her word is faulty. The demands on *the hearer*, by contrast, derive from the fact that one who is told something owes it to the speaker S to regard her (S) as presenting herself as worthy of the audience's trust (Hinchman 2005:568). Assurance theorists go on to argue that in the act by which a speaker S assures her audience A that p, S takes responsibility for the truth of what she says, and so takes responsibility for the audience's belief (when this belief is formed on the basis of that say-so).

The result, proponents of the assurance view contend, is that the act of telling generates for one's audience a distinctly "second-personal" reason for belief. The generated reason is *second-personal* in that it is available only to the audience that was the target of the act of assurance: in the same way that S's promise to A that S will φ entitles A (but not others) to hold S responsible for φing, so too (according to the assurance view) S's telling A that p entitles A (but not others) to hold S responsible for the truth of the proposition that p.[3] The generated second-personal reason is a *reason* insofar as it is a consideration on the basis of which the audience can reach the rational conclusion that p. Assurance theorists thus conclude that when S tells A that p, thereby "inviting" A to trust S, then, absent reasons for doubt regarding S's word, A has an epistemic entitlement to believe that p.[4]

Unfortunately, assurance views of testimony, like Faulkner's trust-based account, appear susceptible to the charge of conflating non-epistemic considerations (pertaining to the second-personal nature of testimonial transactions) for epistemic ones.[5] There is a difference between recognizing another's *purporting to be* trustworthy, and granting them the *presumption* of trustworthiness. Arguably, the speech act norms that pertain to acts of telling require that when a speaker S tells an audience A that p, A owes it to S to regard S as *purporting* to be trustworthy. But it would seem that this has no bearing on the question whether A owes it to S to regard S's telling as *presumptively* trustworthy – as trustworthy so long as A has no reasons for doubt. For to suppose this is to suppose that there is a normative demand on us – a demand deriving from the second-personal nature of testimonial transactions – to presume that a speaker who tells us something is *reliable*. While one who purports to be trustworthy is owed some sort of respect (and her word should be regarded as such), more argument is required to establish that the very act of telling another person that p generates an epistemic reason for the audience to believe that p.

The two second-personal reliance accounts of testimonial trust discussed so far –Faulkner's (2011) trust-based account, and the assurance view – both aim to show that second-personal considerations can underwrite an epistemic entitlement to trust. Interestingly, others have argued that second-personal considerations are sometimes *in tension with* epistemic reasons for trust. The standard claim in this vicinity focuses on the demands of friendship: many think that we ought to trust our friends and loved ones, and some theorists hold that these demands can require us to have a higher degree of credence in the say-so of our friends or loved ones than what the evidence itself warrants. This view is sometimes formulated as a "partiality" claim, to the effect that the very same evidence can warrant a higher credence in the say-so of a close friend than it would in the say-so of a stranger. Hence the doctrine of *epistemic partiality*, which has been defended in one form or another by Baker (1987), Jones (1996), Keller (2004), Stroud (2006) and Hazlett (2013) (see also Lahno, this volume).

However, even in such cases it is not easy to establish that there is a conflict between the normative but non-epistemic demands on trust and the epistemic standards themselves. For while it can seem that one ought to be epistemically partial to one's friends, the appearance of normative pressure to violate epistemic standards may itself be illusory. It is widely acknowledged that we tend to choose as our friends only those whom we have some antecedent reason to regard as trustworthy. Keller (2004) himself makes this very point when he writes,

> If I say, "That Steven, he certainly isn't a selfish, lying scoundrel," and you say, "You only believe that because you're his friend," then you are probably getting things the wrong way around. I am friend with Steven partially *because* I do not think that he is a selfish, lying scoundrel
>
> *(2004:337; italics in original)*

In addition, as Hawley (2014b) and others have noted, friends typically do take their duties to their friends seriously, and they know this about one another.

Indeed, this consideration suggests a more general point: when it comes to our close friends and family members, we will have some epistemic reason to believe what they tell us *whenever we have reasons to regard them as valuing our relationship with them*.[6] Part of what it is to be a friend is to value the friendship, and part of what it is to value a friendship is to do the things that promote the friendship and to avoid doing things that would harm that friendship. But now consider that a friend who speak falsely – whether through lies or through inexcusable incompetence – risks doing serious harm to the friendship. (This risk materializes if her lie or unwarranted talk is discovered.) Notice too that to disbelieve a close friend risks harming the friendship as well. (Again, the risk materializes if the speaker discovers that she was not believed.) As a result, when a speaker and audience are close friends, they both have a strong practical reason (deriving from their valuing of the friendship) to ensure that all goes well. And this explains the appearance of *added normative pressure* on an audience to believe what she is told when the speaker is a close friend. (It also explains the appearance of *added normative pressure* on a speaker to speak sincerely and competently when the audience is a close friend).[7] But all of this will be known by both sides; and so insofar as both sides are familiar with the character of their friend, they will have *epistemic* reasons to believe that their friend will act on these strong *practical* reasons. And this is just to say that the audience has epistemic reasons to think that the testimony of her close friend is trustworthy, and the speaker has epistemic reasons to think that she will be seen as trustworthy by her close friend.

It would seem, then, that even if we assume a second-personal reliance account of trust, and so even if we allow that trust differs from mere reliance in having a salient second-personal dimension (as well as an epistemic dimension), we have not yet seen a reason to think that non-epistemic but normative considerations intrude on the epistemic dimension – either by generating epistemic reasons for trust, or by conflicting with the requirements of epistemic rationality. Still, for those who endorse a second-personal reliance account of trust, a full account of the second-personal and epistemic dimensions of trust is wanted. Such an account should aim to characterize both of these dimensions and to make clear how (if at all) they interact with one another. Failing that, it will continue to seem somewhat mysterious how the second-personal dimensions of trust can be accommodated within a theory that also recognizes that reliance on A is epistemically rational only if one is epistemically entitled to regard A as reliable.

Notes

1 With thanks to Bernard Nickel, Ted Hinchman, José Medina, Philip Nickel, Judith Simon and Pak-Hang Wong for comments on an earlier draft of this paper. All errors remain mine and mine alone.
2 Versions of this sort of account, commonly characterized as "assurance views of testimony," have been developed and defended not only in Hinchman (2005) but also in Moran (2006), McMyler (2011), Fricker (2012), and elsewhere.
3 Others might well regard S's telling as evidence, but only A is entitled to hold S responsible in this way, and so only A is given this "second-personal" sort of reason.
4 See Hinchman (2005:565) and Moran (2006:301).
5 This is a central theme in my (forthcoming b).
6 In Goldberg (forthcoming a) I called these *value-reflecting* epistemic reasons.
7 We can easily imagine cases in which one has practical reasons of friendship to hide the truth, or perhaps even to lie. I would regard them as cases in which one has competing practical reasons. (With thanks to José Medina.)

References

Anscombe, E. (1979) "What is it to Believe Someone?" in C.F. Delaney (ed.), *Rationality and Religious Belief*, South Bend, IN: University of Notre Dame Press.
Baier, A. (1986) "Trust and Antitrust," *Ethics* 96: 231–260.
Baker, J. (1987) "Trust and Rationality," *Pacific Philosophical Quarterly* 68: 1–13.
Darwall, S. (2006) *The Second-Person Standpoint: Morality, Respect, and Accountability*, Cambridge, MA: Harvard University Press.
Faulkner, P. (2011) *Knowledge on Trust*, Oxford: Oxford University Press.
Fricker, M. (2012) "Group Testimony? The Making of a Collective Good Informant," *Philosophy and Phenomenological Research* 84(2): 249–276.
Gambetta, D. (1988) "Can We Trust Trust?" in D. Gambetta (ed.), *Trust: Making and Breaking Cooperative Relations*, Oxford: Basil Blackwell.
Goldberg, S. (Forthcoming a) "Against Epistemic Partiality in Friendship: Value-Reflecting Reasons," *Philosophical Studies*.
Goldberg, S. (Forthcoming b) *Conversational Pressure: Normativity in Speech Exchanges*, Oxford: Oxford University Press.
Hardin, R. (1992) "The Street-Level Epistemology of Trust," *Analyse & Kritik* 14: 152–176.
Hawley, K. (2014a) "Trust, Distrust, and Commitment," *Noûs* 48(1): 1–20.
Hawley, K. (2014b) "Partiality and Prejudice in Trusting," *Synthese* 191: 2029–2045.
Hazlett, A. (2013) *A Luxury of the Understanding: On the Value of True Belief*, Oxford: Oxford University Press.
Hinchman, T. (2005) "Telling as Inviting to Trust," *Philosophy and Phenomenological Research* 70 (3): 562–587.
Holton, R. (1994) "Deciding to Trust, Coming to Believe," *Australasian Journal of Philosophy* 72 (1): 63–76.
Horsburgh, H. (1960) "The Ethics of Trust," *Philosophical Quarterly* 10: 343–354.
Jones, K. (1996) "Trust as an Affective Attitude," *Ethics* 107: 4–25.
Jones, K. (2004) "Trust and Terror," in P. DesAutels and M. Walker (eds.), *Moral Psychology*, Lanham, MA: Rowman & Littlefield.
Keller, S. (2004) "Friendship and Belief," *Philosophical Papers* 33(3): 329–351.
Lackey, J. (2008) *Knowing from Words*, Oxford: Oxford University Press.
McMyler, B. (2011) *Testimony, Trust, and Authority*, Oxford: Oxford University Press.

Moran, R. (2006) "Getting Told and Being Believed," in J. Lackey and E. Sosa (eds.), *The Epistemology of Testimony*, Oxford: Oxford University Press.
O'Neill, O. (2002) *Autonomy and Trust in Bioethics*, Cambridge: Cambridge University Press.
Pettit, P. (1995) "The Cunning of Trust," *Philosophy and Public Affairs* 24(3): 202–225.
Simpson, T. (2012) "What is Trust?" *Pacific Philosophical Quarterly* 93: 550–569.
Strawson, P. (1974) "Freedom and Resentment," in P. Strawson, *Freedom and Resentment*, London: Methuen.
Stroud, S. (2006) "Epistemic partiality in friendship," *Ethics* 116(3): 498–524.

9
TRUST AND BELIEF

Arnon Keren[1]

9.1 Introduction

Trust, we are often told, is the bond of society.[2] Trust is not merely a pervasive phenomenon, it is one on which so much of what we value depends. On this there is widespread agreement among social scientists, historians and philosophers (Baier 1986; Hollis 1998; Simpson 2012).

But what is this thing which is so valuable? What is trust? What kind of psychological and mental attitude, if at all, is involved in trusting a person, or an institution? On this question there seems to be much less agreement.

One fundamental divide among philosophers studying the nature of trust concerns the relation between trust and belief. There is no question that trust is often a source of belief, that we often form our beliefs on trust. But is trust itself a kind of belief about the trusted person? Or does it at least entail holding a belief about her? On these questions there is little agreement within contemporary philosophy. And yet they have important implications for several fundamental questions about trust: from questions about the rationality of trust to questions about its value.

Let us make some distinctions. According to doxastic[3] accounts of trust, trust entails a belief about the object of trust (call these beliefs "trust beliefs"): either the belief that she is trustworthy with respect to what she is trusted to do, or that she will do what she is trusted to do (Adler 1994; Hardin 2002; Fricker 2006; Hieronymi 2008; McMyler 2011; Keren 2014). Pure doxastic accounts (Hardin 2002; Hieronymi 2008; McMyler 2011) claim that trust just is such a trust-belief, as Hardin seems to suggest when he writes that "the declarations 'I believe you are trustworthy' and 'I trust you' are equivalent." (2002:10). Impure doxastic accounts maintain that while belief about the trusted person is necessary for trust, it is not sufficient (Keren 2014).

Non-doxastic accounts of trust deny that trust entails a belief that the trusted person is trustworthy, or that she will do what she is trusted to do (Holton 1994; Becker 1996; Jones 1996; Faulkner 2007, 2011; Frost-Arnold 2014). While trust may often be accompanied by such a belief, such a belief is not required for trust: You can trust a person without believing that she is trustworthy, and without believing that she will do what she is trusted to do. What we ascribe to Adam, when we describe him as trusting Bertha to perform action Φ, is neither the belief that Bertha is trustworthy with respect to Φ, nor the belief that Bertha will Φ. Some non-doxasticists claim that trust entails a different psychological attitude or mental state, such as an emotion or affective attitude towards the trusted person (Jones 1996; McLeod 2015); according to others, trust involves adopting a moral stance towards her (Holton 1994); some endorse a disjunctive non-doxastic view, claiming that trust entails either believing or accepting that the person will do what she is trusted to do (Frost-Arnold 2014). Still others deny that trust involves any particular mental state, either claiming that it amounts to no more than a disposition to rely on the trusted person in certain ways (Kappel 2014) or denying that there is a single phenomenon to which "trust" refers (Simpson 2012).

In discussing the question of the nature of trust and its relation to belief, I will be considering trust, as is customary in the literature, as a three-place relation, where person A trusts person B to perform an act of type Φ. Note, however, that not all attributions of trust we encounter in everyday English have this form. In particular, one kind of trust-ascription employs the form "trust that," as in "I trust that Bertha will buy milk on the way back from work" or "I trust that there will be a resolution tomorrow."[4] Here the object of "trust" is not a person, but a proposition ("that Bertha will buy milk on the way back from work"). It is widely agreed that such locutions amount to no more than an ascription of belief (McMyler 2011). But this does not settle any question about the apparently thicker relation of trust involved in ascriptions of trust where the object of "trust" is a person rather than a proposition, as in "I trust Bertha to buy milk," or in "I trust Bertha."[5] It is important thus to note that "I trust Bertha to buy milk" is not equivalent to "I trust that Bertha will buy milk." There are possible situations where the latter would be true, but the former false, for instance, where I do not trust Bertha at all, but still believe that she will do certain things, such as buying milk (McMyler 2011). So while locutions of the form "A trusts that B will Φ" clearly ascribe to A the belief that B will Φ, this fact leaves open the question whether a similar belief is ascribed to A by locutions of the form "A trusts B to Φ." It is on the latter kind of ascriptions that I focus here.

In what follows, I describe and evaluate some of the main considerations which have been cited by philosophers arguing for or against doxastic account of trust, and explain why considerations favoring a doxastic accounts appear to be stronger. Before that, I explain why the question about the mental state involved in trusting is a significant one. I then discuss some considerations favoring doxastic accounts and considerations that have appeared to support non-doxastic accounts. In the final section I briefly discuss how this debate connects to the question of the value of trust, and highlight an underappreciated problem about the value of trust, the discussion of which could further help shed light on the nature of trust.

9.2 Trust and Belief: Why Does It Matter and How Can We Tell?

The question about the kind of mental state required for trust is a significant one, because the answer we give would have important implications for questions about the rationality of trust, about how trust can be brought about, and about the value of trust. Belief is a mental state, which, it has been argued, has a set of essential distinctive features. Thus, for example, many philosophers accept an evidentialist claim about the justification of beliefs, according to which, a person is justified in her belief if and only if the person's belief fits or is supported by the evidence available to her (Conee and Feldman 2004): Non-evidential reasons may make your actions rational or irrational, but they are irrelevant to the rationality of what you believe. Therefore, if we accept a doxastic account of trust this would make a difference to what we may need to say about what justifies trust. If trust just is a belief, then we should be able to derive the conditions for the rationality of trust from the epistemological study of rational belief. Evidential considerations would have primary place in the evaluation of the rationality of trust even if trust is not a belief, but merely entails one. In contrast, if we accept a non-doxastic account of trust, then evidence should be no more central for the justification of trust than ethical and instrumental reasons.

The special relation between belief and evidence is exhibited not only in the way in which beliefs are evaluated but also in the way in which they are motivated: what we can and do actually believe is responsive to evidence, in a way that it is not responsive to other kinds of reasons. Thus, on one side, it is difficult, and perhaps impossible, to hold a belief while simultaneously believing that one does not have evidence supporting it. On the other side, beliefs do not typically respond to non-evidential reasons, such as those provided by monetary payments. Non-evidential reasons have no place in our deliberations regarding what we ought to believe. We cannot get ourselves to believe a proposition by deliberating on non-evidential reasons (Owens 2003).

Another feature of beliefs, very possibly related to the latter, is that beliefs are not subject to direct voluntary control. There are some things we can directly do at will, but believing does not appear to be one of them. We can raise our hand at will; all that is required for that is for us to decide to do so. Similarly, we can imagine at will that the moon is made out of cheese, or that the next American president will be a Democrat. But we cannot voluntarily believe these or any other propositions (Williams 1970). The only voluntary control we have over our beliefs seems to be indirect: we can do things that tend to make us form a belief. But we cannot adopt a belief simply by deciding to do so.

A final feature of beliefs is that relations among beliefs seem to be systematically governed by logical norms (Davidson 1985). Thus, for example, while we do sometimes believe in contradictions, it seems impossible, or almost impossible, to *knowingly* believe a contradiction. And if we believe a proposition, and believe that a second proposition follows from the first, then it would be difficult for us to hold on to the first belief unless we also hold a belief in the latter.

Does trust have similar features? The answer depends, at least partially, on whether trust is or entails a belief. Conversely, we can evaluate the plausibility of doxastic accounts of trust by studying features of trust. Thus, if we can voluntarily decide to trust in ways that we cannot voluntarily decide to believe, this would be a source of challenge to doxastic accounts of trust. Accordingly, the most prominent way in the literature of trying to determine whether trust entails a belief involves studying features of trust, and asking whether trust's having these features is best explained by doxastic or non-doxastic accounts. In what follows I explore some of the central considerations for and against a doxastic account. Towards the end of this chapter, I also say something about how all this is related to the value of trust.

9.3 For Doxastic Accounts: Trust and (Other) Beliefs

Doxastic accounts of trust maintain that trusting a person to Φ requires holding a trust-belief: either the belief that she is trustworthy with respect to Φ, or that she will Φ. One type of consideration in favor of doxastic accounts emerges from considerations of systematic relations between trusting a person, and holding certain beliefs, other than trust-beliefs (beliefs which I call here "other-than-trust" beliefs). The relations between trust and various types of other-than-trust beliefs appears to be just as we would expect them to be on the assumption that trust entails belief; moreover, they would be difficult to explain otherwise.

One important class of other-than-trust beliefs is that of beliefs based upon trust. Much of what we believe, and much of what we take ourselves to know, we believe because speakers tell us things, and we trust them for the truth of what they say. Call this kind of trust "epistemic trust."[6] The case of epistemic trust provides a strong prima-facie case for doxasticism about trust. On the one hand, epistemic trust is a form of trust. On the other hand, epistemic trust systematically results in believing the speaker's testimony. If a speaker tells us that *p*, and we understand that she has told us that *p*, but nonetheless do not believe what she has told us, then we cannot be said to trust her to speak the truth. This fact would seem to be readily explained if trust entails belief, given the logical relations between beliefs.

In contrast, it is difficult to explain the systematic relations between trusting a speaker and believing her testimony if trust, quite generally, does not entail belief (Keren 2014). Why should trusting a speaker to speak knowledgeably and sincerely, without believing that she will, invariably result in believing what she says? Non-doxastic accounts might be able to explain why epistemic trust tends to give rise to belief in speaker's testimony. Thus, for instance, if epistemic trust involves an affective attitude of optimism about the speaker, then we can explain why epistemic trust tends to give rise to beliefs, given that emotions, quite generally, tend to give rise to certain beliefs, and not to others (Jones 1996). But emotions only have a tendency to give rise to corresponding beliefs, and do not invariably do so: thus, Al may fear a dog, without having the corresponding belief in its dangerousness; indeed, Al may know that the dog is not dangerous, but nonetheless fear it. Accordingly, this tendency of emotions does not explain why trusting speakers invariably gives rise to belief in their testimony. A similar point seems to apply to other non-doxastic accounts. For while the kinds of mental states or dispositions required for epistemic trust on such non-doxastic accounts may have the tendency to give rise to the certain beliefs, it is unclear on such accounts why one cannot trust a speaker for the truth of what she says without believing what she says.[7]

Moreover, even if non-doxastic accounts can meet this challenge, they would be faced with a second one, of explaining how the trusting thinker can see her own resulting belief as trust-based, without believing that the speaker is trustworthy (Hieronymi 2008; Keren 2014). The problem is that we are not able to hold onto beliefs if we find that they are not supported by any truth-conducive reasons. But if you see your belief as based upon trust, then unless you also believe that the speaker is trustworthy, it is not clear how you can see it as supported by truth-conducive reasons.

Another relevant kind of other-than-trust beliefs, which have systematic relations with trust, includes beliefs in the negation of trust-beliefs: For instance, the belief that the person will not do what she is relied upon to do, or that she is not trustworthy with respect to what she is trusted to do. Call such beliefs 'negated trust-beliefs.' Supporters of non-doxastic accounts usually join the widespread agreement that it is impossible to trust a person while holding certain negated trust-beliefs about her, such as the belief that the person will not do what she is trusted to do (Holton 1994; Faulkner 2007; Frost-Arnold 2014).[8] However, it is not clear how they can explain this impossibility. Thus, while we normally would not accept p. if we strongly believe that not-*p*, and while accepting *p* may normally be irrational when we have strong evidence for our belief that not-*p*, it is nonetheless possible to accept *p* while believing that not-*p*, and even to do so knowingly (Cohen 1992). So on a non-doxastic disjunctive account according to which trusting A to Φ entails either accepting that she will Φ or believing that she will Φ (Frost-Arnold 2014), it is difficult to explain why we cannot trust A to Φ while believing that A will not Φ. Similar points apply to other non-doxastic accounts. For while the kinds of mental states or dispositions required for trust on such non-doxastic account may be in tension with believing that she will not do what she is trusted to do, they are nonetheless compatible with such a belief. So, on such accounts, it would be unclear why we cannot trust a person while holding this kind of negated trust-beliefs about her.

Doxastic accounts seem to be in a much better position to explain why we cannot trust a person to Φ while holding negated trust-beliefs about her, such as the belief that she will not Φ. On doxastic accounts, trusting a person to Φ while holding negated trust-beliefs about her involves holding a belief and its negation. And while we are arguably able to hold a belief in a proposition alongside a belief in its negation, at least when we do not appreciate the fact that we hold both, or that they are contradictory, we arguably can neither believe a proposition of the form [p and not-p], (Davidson 2005), nor knowingly believe a proposition and its negation.[9] Accordingly, doxastic accounts can appeal to whatever explanation accounts of belief and of belief ascriptions provide for the limits on our ability to hold such inconsistent beliefs to explain the constraints on our ability to trust a person to Φ while holding negated trust-beliefs about her.

It might be objected that doxastic accounts of trust are not in a better position than non-doxastic account when it comes to explaining the systematic relations between negated trust-beliefs and our constrained ability to trust. After all, most accounts of belief and of belief ascriptions allow for the possibility of one person holding a belief in a proposition and a belief in its negation. So doxastic accounts, just like non-doxastic accounts, cannot explain why we cannot trust a person to Φ while believing that she will not Φ.

However, while it is true that leading accounts of belief ascription allow for the possibility of belief in two propositions which are inconsistent with each-other, this does not mean that doxastic accounts have no advantage over non-doxastic accounts in explaining the systematic relations between negated trust-beliefs and our constrained ability to trust. For the widespread agreement about the impossibility of trusting a person to Φ while holding the beliefs that she will not Φ, while true under most conditions, is not always true, and, as doxastic accounts would suggest, the conditions under which it is false seem to be precisely the conditions under which we in fact can hold two contradictory beliefs. So consider the fact that Al can trust Boris to lower unemployment rates if elected, but at the same time, believe that the person on TV will not lower unemployment rates if elected, when, unbeknownst to Al, the person speaking on TV is in fact Boris. Under such conditions, plausible accounts of belief ascriptions would entail that, contrary to the widely-held view, Al both trusts Boris to lower unemployment rates, and believes that he will not lower unemployment rates (Kripke 1979). But obviously, under these conditions Al can both believe that Boris is bald, and that the person speaking on TV is not bald, and the very same accounts of belief ascription would therefore ascribe to Al both the belief that Boris is bald and the belief that Boris is not bald. So the fact that doxastic account of trust entail that under such conditions it is in fact possible to believe that a person will not Φ while trusting him to Φ is, in fact, not a problem for such accounts. Indeed, it is a virtue of doxastic accounts that they not only can explain why the widely-held view is mostly true, but also why under certain conditions, it is false.

Thus, systematic relations between trust and various other-than-trust beliefs provide strong prima-facie reasons for doxasticism about trust. For while doxastic accounts are able to explain them, it is difficult to see how non-doxastic accounts can explain them.

It should be noted that some of the considerations cited here also seem to favor non-pure doxastic accounts over pure doxastic accounts of trust. We have noted that mental states required by non-doxastic account – such as having an affective attitude of optimism about a person – are compatible with beliefs that seem to be incompatible with trusting a person (such as the belief that a person is non-trustworthy with respect to Φ'ing). Similarly, trust-beliefs seem to be compatible with attitudes and behavioral tendencies that seem to be incompatible with trust. For example, S may believe that A is trustworthy, and that A will Φ, but nonetheless not rely on A to Φ, because she is overcome by fear of what might happen if A does not Φ. In such a case, it would seem that S does not trust A to Φ, in spite of her belief that A is trustworthy and will Φ. Thus, such cases suggest that even if trust-beliefs are necessary for trust, they are not sufficient. We should not identify trusting a person with having certain trust-beliefs, for one can have such beliefs, without these beliefs being reflected in one's reliance behavior or in one's disposition to rely. Accordingly, in the remainder of this chapter, when discussing doxastic accounts, I focus on non-pure doxastic accounts.

9.4 Against Doxastic Accounts: Trust and Evidence

If the relations between trust and other-than-trust beliefs provide a strong case for doxastic accounts of trust, why have several philosophers nonetheless adopted non-doxastic accounts? Two kinds of considerations have been central: considerations appealing to the relations between trust and evidence (Faulkner 2007; Jones 1996), and considerations appealing to the voluntariness of trust (Faulkner 2007, Holton 1994).

Several philosophers have observed that the relation between trust and evidence is different from that between belief and evidence. We have noted the special causal and normative relations between a person's beliefs and her evidence: beliefs are normally based on evidence, and are normally evaluated in terms of their relation to the evidence. Trusting, in contrast, often seems to be in tension with the evidence. First, trust, including commendable trust, appears to exhibit a certain resistance to counter-evidence (Baker 1987; Jones 1996; McLeod 2002, 2015; Faulkner 2007, 2011). Thus, if I trust my friend to distribute money to the needy, I will not merely tend to disbelieve accusations that she has embezzled that money, but, moreover, will have a tendency to disregard such accusations.

Second, trust can be undermined by rational reflection on its basis, even when this basis is secure. Again, in this respect trust seems to be unlike belief: If a belief is supported by the evidence, and we reflect on its basis, this will tend to strengthen, rather than undermine, our belief. In contrast, in the case of trust, an attempt to eliminate the risk involved in trusting by reflecting on the evidence for and against the trusted person's trustworthiness tends to undermine trust (Baier 1986; McLeod 2015).

Supporters of doxastic accounts might try to account for these features of trust by rejecting evidentialism about belief (Baker 1987). Even if trust involves a belief, the fact that commendable forms of trust are resistant to evidence would not appear to be problematic, if the standard for the evaluation of belief is not its relation to the evidence. But this kind of response is insufficient. The evidentialist thesis is a general claim with both a normative and explanatory function; it purports to guide our evaluation of belief, and to explain both how we tend to evaluate beliefs, and why our beliefs respond differently to various kinds of reasons. Denying evidentialism may explain how there could be a difference between trust and other beliefs in terms of their causal and normative relations to evidence, but it does not explain the nature of these differences: An explanation of this would need both to explain general features of beliefs – their general responsiveness to evidence and lack of responsiveness to non-evidential reasons such as to monetary payments – and why trust is nonetheless responsive to non-evidential reasons and supposedly not to evidence. The mere denial of a general claim about beliefs such as evidentialism, without a suggestion of an alternative general account, does not even start to explain the nature of the difference.

If denying evidentialism does not explain the nature of this difference between trust and non-trust beliefs, might the adoption of a non-doxastic account do the job? Of the various non-doxastic accounts suggested in the literature, an account of trust in terms of an affective attitude seems to be in the best position to succeed in this. It can explain why trust seems to be resistant to evidence without rejecting the evidentialist idea that beliefs should and do respond to evidence (Jones 1996). For it is a familiar mark of emotions, that they resist the evidence: They make us focus on a partial field of evidence, giving us what Jones called "blinkered vision" (Jones 1996:12), and they tend to persist even in light of what we take to be strong counter-evidence.

However, this kind of account explains only one aspect of the difference between trust's and belief's relation with evidence: It explains why trust is resistant to counter-evidence, but not why trust is undermined by reflection on the evidence supporting it. Indeed, emotions, unlike trust, tend to withstand such reflection (Keren 2014), so an account of trust in terms of an affective attitude would only make this feature of trust seem even more mysterious.[10]

Can we account for both trust's resistance to evidence, and its tendency to be undermined by reflection on the evidence? Keren (2014) suggests that these two aspects of trust are best seen as a manifestation of a single feature: That to trust someone to Φ involves responding to reasons for not taking precautions against the possibility that she will not Φ.[11] Trusting involves, in other words, responding to preemptive reasons against acting for precautionary reasons. (Preemptive reasons are second-order reasons for not acting or believing for some reasons.) Thus, the shop owner who leaves a new employee alone with the till, but operates the CCTV camera as a precaution, does not really trust the new employee. Trust requires not taking such precautions. Moreover, Keren (2014) claims, if trust involves responding to such preemptive reasons against taking precautions, then we should expect trust to be both resistant to counter-evidence and to be undermined by extensive reflection on relevant evidence. For operating the CCTV camera, like other precautionary measures, serves as precautions precisely because it can provide us with evidence about the risk of being let down. Accordingly, the kind of reasons against taking precautions we see ourselves as having when we trust a person are not only reasons against acting in ways that would provide us with such evidence, but also reasons against being attuned to such evidence, or against reflecting on evidence in an attempt to minimize the risk of being let down.[12]

The claim that trusting involves seeing yourself as having preemptive reasons against taking precaution can explain both trust's resistance to evidence, and its being undermined by excessive reflection on the evidence supporting it. Moreover, the claim also neutralizes objections to doxastic accounts of trust based on these features of trust. For not only is the idea that trust involves belief compatible with the claim that trust involves responding to such preemptive reasons against taking precautions. Moreover, it is in virtue of certain beliefs about the trusted person – for instance that she has good will towards us and would respond to our dependence on her by being particularly careful not to let us down – that we can have preemptive reasons against taking precautions. Thus, the argument from trust's relation to evidence has no force against a doxastic account of trust which accepts the idea that trusting involves seeing oneself as having such preemptive reasons.

9.5 Against Doxastic Accounts: Trust and the Will

Another argument against doxastic accounts appeals to the claim that trust, unlike belief, is subject to direct voluntary control. This claim is backed by two kinds of examples: one in which we end our initial hesitation about whether to trust by deciding to trust (Holton 1994). The second is the case of therapeutic trust, in which we seem to decide to place our trust in someone in order to promote her trustworthiness (Faulkner 2007, Simpson 2012). But if trust can be thus willed, it is claimed, we must reject doxastic accounts of trust, because belief is not subject to direct voluntary control.

How strong an argument is this? Note first, that even on the assumption that beliefs are not subject to direct voluntary control, non-pure doxastic accounts can allow for a limited ability of direct voluntary control over our trust. They can allow for the possibility that we can voluntarily decide to trust, if we already believe that a person is trustworthy.[13] For instance, in the trust circle, a person, surrounded by friends, is asked to let herself fall backwards, with hands to her sides and straight legs, and to trust her friends to catch her. Holton claims that in such situations, we seem to be able to decide to trust (1994). Non-pure doxastic accounts are consistent with his claim that we can decide to trust in such cases: Prior to the decision, I believed in the trustworthiness of my friends; but too frightened to let myself fall, my belief did not manifest itself in my behavior, and therefore, I did not trust them to catch me. I then decided to trust. My decision was a decision to overcome the fear that prevented my actions from responding to my belief in my friends' trustworthiness.[14] Non-pure doxastic accounts are therefore compatible with the idea that sometimes our hesitation about trusting ends through a voluntary decision to trust. They will suggest, however, that our ability to decide to trust will be more limited than often suggested by non-doxastic accounts. Unfortunately, there is very little agreement on the correct description of the limitations on our ability to decide to trust, and so it is difficult to judge which of the alternative accounts provides the best explanation of these limitations.

The case of therapeutic trust may appear to raise a greater challenge for doxastic accounts. Consider the case of the parents who trust their teenage daughter to look after the house despite her past record of carelessness, hoping by their trust to promote her trustworthiness. Such cases seem to suggest that we can trust a person to Φ without believing that she is trustworthy. Because the point of therapeutic trust is precisely to promote the trusted person's trustworthiness, they seem to involve trust accompanied by the belief that the trusted person is not fully trustworthy.

If it was clear that we are intuitively committed to the idea that we can decide to therapeutically trust someone while lacking the belief that she is trustworthy, this would indeed present a serious challenge to doxastic accounts. However, it is far from clear that this is the correct interpretation of our intuitions. Doxasticists about trust have suggested at least two ways in which this can be denied: The first is to note that trust, belief and trustworthiness come in degrees. Accordingly, what happens in cases of therapeutic trust is that we believe, to some degree, that the trusted person has a degree of trustworthiness, and we also believe, or hope, that our trusting her, to some degree, will help her become more trustworthy. The second is to claim that in cases of therapeutic trust, the decision made is not actually a decision to trust, but rather, a decision to *act as if* one trusted.

For an example of therapeutic trust to serve as the basis for a strong argument against doxastic accounts of trust, it should be relatively clear that the decision made in the example is indeed one involving a decision to trust, rather than to act as if one trusted; and where the trusting person did not believe, even to a degree, that the trusted person's is trustworthy. Such an example has still not been produced. Accordingly, as it stands, there is no strong argument against doxastic accounts of trust from the voluntariness of trust.

9.6 Trust and Mere Reliance: Belief and the Value of Trust

I conclude, therefore, that considerations of the conditions under which we can trust, and under which we can rationally trust, offer a pretty strong case for (non-pure) doxastic accounts of trust. Such accounts provide the best explanation of key features of trust, namely, the systematic relations between trust and different kinds of other-than-trust beliefs; they can explain why trust has a different relation to evidence than most other beliefs; and the strongest argument against such accounts, the argument from the voluntariness of trust, turns out on closer scrutiny not to be a strong one.[15]

However, the question of the nature of trust is far from being settled. Literature about the nature of trust and of the mental state involved in trusting has so far largely focused on the ability of doxastic and non-doxastic accounts to explain the phenomenology of trust and our intuitions about our ability to trust, and to trust rationally, under various conditions. However, there may be other ways of furthering our understanding of these questions, by connecting the debate about the nature of trust with other discourses about trust within the rich and varied literature on the subject. In particular, one way of evaluating accounts of the nature of trust and of the mental state involved in trusting would appeal to the ability of such accounts to fit in within plausible accounts of the value of trust.

As noted above, it is widely agreed that trust is not merely valuable, but, moreover, that it is indispensable for the existence of a thriving society and thriving social institutions. Arguably, an account of the nature of trust should allow us to account for these kinds of intuitions, and should allow us to explain why trust is so valuable. Accordingly, considerations relating to the value of trust may provide us with another way of evaluating accounts of trust. However, philosophers have so far made little effort to draw on claims about the indispensable value of trust within the debate about the nature of trust.[16]

One reason for thinking that considerations relating to the value of trust might be helpful in shedding further light on the nature of trust is that lurking in the background is an unappreciated challenge to the consensus about the indispensable value of trust. Because different accounts of the nature of trust would have to face different versions of this challenge, and would have different resources available to them in responding to the challenge, considering the challenge may provide another way of evaluating such accounts.

The challenge emerges from the conjunction of two widely accepted claims: that trust has distinct and indispensable value; and that trust is not to be equated with mere reliance. If it is claimed that trust is indispensable for the existence of a thriving society and for the thriving of much of what we value, then an account of the value of trust must explain why this is so. But philosophical discussions of the value of trust, which have mostly focused on the instrumental value of trust (McLeod 2015), usually do not provide an adequate answer to this question. For to understand why trust is indispensably valuable, we must explain not merely why trust is valuable, but, moreover, why trust is more valuable than what falls short of trust. The common explanation, that unless we relied on others in ways characteristic of trust, various things we value would not thrive (Baier 1986), fails to meet this challenge, because we can rely on others in ways characteristic of trust without trusting them. Accordingly, what we need to explain is why trust is more valuable than such forms of reliance that fall short of trusting. The challenge is somewhat analogous to one raised by Plato's (1976) in the *Meno*: the challenge of explaining why knowledge is more valuable than something that arguably falls short of knowledge, namely, mere true belief. Accordingly, we can call this problem *Trust's Meno Problem*).[17]

This is, in particular, a challenge for doxastic accounts of trust. Thus, as we have seen, supporters of doxastic accounts respond to the challenge from voluntary trust by arguing that we can decide to act as if we trusted, and that doing so is easily confused with, but does not amount to, deciding to trust. On the doxastic account, acting as if one trusts is not to be equated with trusting, because the belief essential for trust may be lacking. Trust's Meno Problem for such a view is that of explaining why this difference should at all matter to us: What is the additional value of relations involving trust when compared with those involving merely *acting as if* one trusted without believing that the person is trustworthy? Why should we be interested in the very distinction? Is a relation in which I act trustingly because I believe that you are trustworthy more valuable than a relation in which I act in exactly the same way, without having such a belief? If it is indeed more valuable, why is this so? If not, then does not mere reliance, without trust, allow us to enjoy the very same goods that trust allows us to enjoy? In that case, it would seem difficult to maintain that trust is indispensably valuable.

I am not suggesting that this is an insurmountable challenge for doxastic accounts of trust. But it is a challenge that has so far not been properly addressed, neither by supporters of doxastic accounts, nor by supporters of alternative accounts. Accordingly, there are reasons to think that the debate about the nature of trust, and in particular, about the claim that trust entails belief, could benefit if more attention is paid to considerations relating to the value of trust.

Notes

1 For helpful comments, I am grateful to participants at a workshop on Trust and Disagreement in Institutions at the University of Copenhagen. Work on this paper was generously funded by the Israel Science Foundation (Grants No. 714/12 and 650/18).

2 The original metaphor appears in Locke (1954 / 1663), but is echoed and used in numerous more contemporary writings. See, e.g. Hollis (1998).

3 From "doxa," the Greek word for "belief". In the literature, doxastic accounts are sometimes also referred to as "cognitivist" accounts (McMyler 2011), and non-doxastic account are sometime called "non-cognitivists".

4 The latter example is from McMyler (2011:118).

5 The latter is of course another example of a form of trust ascription that does not employ the three-place trust predicate. However, unlike "trust that" locutions, this two-place ascription of trust does seem to involve the same kind of thick, interpersonal relation of trust attributed by the kind of three-place ascriptions that are the focus of our discussion. There is some debate in the literature as to whether the three-place or the two-place trust ascription is more fundamental (Faulkner 2015; Hawley 2014), but I will not go into this debate here.

6 From "episteme," the Greek word for "knowledge". In the literature, epistemic trust is sometimes also called "speaker trust" (Keren 2014) and "intellectual trust" (McCraw 2015).

7 In some of his earlier writings, Faulkner (2007) suggests that one actually can trust a speaker without believing what she says; but in more recent writings (2011) he seems to have revised his view. For a discussion of some reasons which may require such a revision, particularly within Faulkner's account of trust, see Keren (2012).

8 We should be careful here: different doxastic accounts maintain that trust requires different kinds of trust-beliefs, and therefore do not agree on what counts as a negated trust-belief. Moreover, whether it is possible to trust a person to Φ while holding a negated trust-belief about her depends on the content of the belief. Take for instance Hardin's claim that trust is identical with a very general trust-belief: that the person is trustworthy. On this view, the belief that the person is not generally trustworthy might count as a negated trust-belief, but it is not obvious that one cannot trust a person to Φ while believing that she is not generally trustworthy.

In contrast, there is widespread agreement that one cannot trust a person to Φ while holding other more specific negated trust-beliefs about her, such as the belief that she will not Φ, or, at least, that one cannot do so knowingly. It is on this kind of belief that we focus here.

9 Note that the claim is not merely that such beliefs are irrational, but moreover, that while it is metaphysically possible to unknowingly hold a belief in a proposition and its negation, it is metaphysically impossible to believe a proposition of the form [p and not p], or to knowingly believe two propositions known to be inconsistent with each other.

10 Emotions tend to survive reflection not only when our judgment, upon reflection, conforms to the emotion, but also when our considered judgment is in tension with the emotion. For a discussion of the latter kind of case, of what is known as a recalcitrant emotion, see Benbaji (2013). This is not to deny that in some cases excessive reflection on the appropriateness of an emotion might undermine it; but as this is not a general characteristic of emotions, categorizing trust as an emotion would not explain why trust tends not to survive reflection.

11 See McMyler (2011) for a somewhat similar claim about the nature of reasons for trust.

12 See Kappel (this volume) for a critical discussion of Keren (2014).

13 This would mean, of course, that our ability to voluntarily decide to trust is limited. But even those who argue for non-doxastic accounts of trust because trust is subject to voluntary control admit that there are important limitations on our ability to trust at will.

14 Hieronymi (2008:217) deals with cases of the kind discussed by Holton in a similar way; but because she accepts a pure doxastic account of trust, it is not entirely clear how this kind of analysis of the case would fit within her account.

15 For discussion of some further considerations in favor of a doxastic account of trust, see McMyler (this volume).

16 Simpson (2012) is a notable exception. For relevant suggestions, see also Faulkner (2016).

17 The analogy with the Plato's original Meno problem should not be overdrawn. Thus, several contemporary writers have suggested that Plato's Meno challenge about the value of knowledge can be met by appealing to the intrinsic value of knowledge (Pritchard 2007); matters might be different in the case of trust. Nonetheless, the analogy between the two problems is apt, given that in the Meno, the problem of accounting for the distinct value of knowledge is presented as a challenge to an account of its instrumental value.

References

Adler, J. (1994) "Testimony, Trust, Knowing," *Journal of Philosophy* 91(5): 264–275.

Adler, J. (2002) *Belief's Own Ethics*, Cambridge, MA: MIT Press.

Baier, A. (1986) "Trust and Antitrust," *Ethics* 96(2): 231–260.

Baker, J. (1987) "Trust and Rationality," *Pacific Philosophical Quarterly* 68(10): 1–13.

Becker, L.C. (1996) "Trust as Noncognitive Security about Motives," *Ethics* 107(1): 43–61.

Benbaji, H. (2013) "How Is Recalcitrant Emotion Possible?" *Australasian Journal of Philosophy* 91 (3): 577–599.

Cohen, L.J. (1992) *An Essay on Belief and Acceptance*, Oxford: Clarendon Press.

Conee, E. and Feldman, R. (2004) *Evidentialism: Essays in Epistemology*, New York: Clarendon Press.

Davidson, D. (1985) "Incoherence and Irrationality," *Dialectica* 39(4): 345–354.

Davidson, D. (2005) "Method and Metaphysics," in *Truth, Language, and History*, Oxford: Clarendon Press.
Faulkner, P. (2007) "On Telling and Trusting," *Mind* 116(464): 875–902.
Faulkner, P. (2011) *Knowledge on Trust*, Oxford: Oxford University Press.
Faulkner, P. (2015) "The Attitude of Trust Is Basic," *Analysis* 75(3): 424–429.
Faulkner, P. (2016) "The Problem of Trust," in P. Faulkner and T. Simpson (eds.), *The Philosophy of Trust*, Oxford: Oxford University Press.
Fricker, E. (2006) "Second-Hand Knowledge," *Philosophy and Phenomenological Research* 73(3): 592–618.
Frost-Arnold, K. (2014) "The Cognitive Attitude of Rational Trust," *Synthese* 191(9): 1957–1974.
Hardin, R. (2002) *Trust and Trustworthiness*, New York: Russell Sage Foundation.
Hawley, K. (2014) "Trust, Distrust and Commitment," *Nous* 48: 1–20.
Hieronymi, P. (2008) "The Reasons of Trust," *Australasian Journal of Philosophy* 86(2): 213–236.
Hollis, M. (1998) *Trust within Reason*, Cambridge: Cambridge University Press.
Holton, R. (1994) "Deciding to Trust, Coming to Believe," *Australasian Journal of Philosophy* 72 (1): 63–76.
Jones, K. (1996) "Trust as an Affective Attitude," *Ethics* 107(1): 4–25.
Kappel, K. (2014) "Believing on Trust," *Synthese* 191: 2009–2028.
Keren, A. (2012) "Knowledge on Affective Trust," *Abstracta* 6: 33–46.
Keren, A. (2014) "Trust and Belief: A Preemptive Reasons Account," *Synthese* 191(12): 2593–2615.
Kripke, S.A. (1979) "A Puzzle about Belief," in A. Margalit (ed.) *Meaning and Use*, Dordrecht: Springer.
Locke, J. ([1663] 1954) *Essays on the Laws of Nature*, W. von Leyden (ed.), Oxford: Clarendon Press.
McCraw, B.W. (2015) "The Nature of Epistemic Trust," *Social Epistemology* 29(4), 413–430.
McLeod, C. (2002) *Self-Trust and Reproductive Autonomy*, Cambridge, MA: MIT Press.
McLeod, C. (2015) "Trust," in E.N. Zalta (ed.), *The Stanford Encyclopedia of Philosophy*. https://plato.stanford.edu/archives/fall2015/entries/trust/
McMyler, B. (2011) *Testimony, Trust, and Authority*, Oxford: Oxford University Press.
Owens, D.J. (2003) "Does Belief Have an Aim?" *Philosophical Studies* 115(3): 283–305.
Plato (1976) *Meno*, G.M.A. Grube (trans.),Indianapolis, IN: Hackett Publishing.
Pritchard, D. (2007) "Recent Work on Epistemic Value," *American Philosophical Quarterly* 44(2): 85–110.
Simpson, T.W. (2012) "What is Trust?" *Pacific Philosophical Quarterly* 93(4): 550–569.
Williams, B. (1970) "Deciding to Believe," in *Problems of the Self*, Cambridge: Cambridge University Press.

10

TRUST AND DISAGREEMENT

Klemens Kappel[1]

10.1 Introduction

We trust individuals and we trust institutions. We trust them for what they say, and for what we hope or expect them to do. Trust is a practically important attitude as our distribution of trust in part determines what we believe and how we act. But we disagree about whom or what we trust, sometimes sharply. In the 2016 U.S. presidential race many American voters trusted Hillary Clinton for what she said, and promised to do, and distrusted Donald Trump, but many had the reverse attitudes. For both groups, apparently their allocation of trust and distrust strongly affected their beliefs and actions, and for some, it will influence whom they voted for.

As this case illustrates, it is often perfectly clear to us that we disagree about whom to trust. This raises an obvious question. How should we respond when we learn that others do not trust the ones we trust? The question is analogous to the now familiar question in the epistemology of disagreement. Upon inspecting some body of evidence I believe some proposition *p*. However, I then learn that you, whom I consider about as competent in this area as I am, have come to the conclusion *not-p* after having considered the same body of evidence. How should this affect my confidence in my belief that *p*? Should I conciliate, that is, revise my view to move closer to yours? Or can I at least sometimes remain steadfast, that is, be rationally unmoved in my confidence that *p*? (Feldman 2007; Feldman 2006; Feldman and Warfield 2011; Christensen and Lackey 2013).

This chapter seeks to address the similar question about disagreement in trust. Suppose I trust Fred to Φ, but then I learn that you distrust Fred to Φ. What should I do? Should I diminish the degree to which I trust? Or should I ignore your distrust, and remain unabated in my trust? Can I fully trust Fred and still regard you as reasonable even if you distrust Fred? Is my trust in Fred even compatible with these sorts of reflections?

10.2 Disagreement in Trust

Disagreement in trust is a practically and theoretically important problem, though it has received almost no attention. It is not even clear how one should conceptualize the very topic of this chapter, disagreement in trust. Therefore, as a first step, I offer some stipulations which will allow us to conceptualize disagreement in trust, and the question it raises.

First, I suggest that we should think of trust as a matter of degree. Assuming that our degree of trust in an individual or an institution is displayed or constituted by the actions we are willing to undertake, or the risks we will expose ourselves to, we may suggest the following:

> *Degree of trust.* A has a higher degree of trust in B's Φ-ing, when A is willing to perform a wider set of actions, or more risky actions, where performing these actions embed the assumption of B's Φ-ing.

We may represent the degree of trust as a scale, where full trust is one extreme end, and full distrust is the other. While trust involves some sort of expectation or reliance that some agent will act in a certain way, distrust in Hawley's words "involves an expectation of unfulfilled commitment" (Hawley 2014:1). So, both trust and distrust evolve around an expectation of commitments of some sort, but are different attitudes to that expectation. Of course, we sometimes we have no expectations of commitments whatsoever from other people, and in that case we neither trust nor distrust people. However, throughout my discussion, I will assume that disagreement in trust concerns cases where trust and distrust are contrasted, not cases where some trust and others neither trust nor distrusts.

Accepting this rough notion of degree of trust, we can define disagreement in trust as follows:

> *Disagreement in trust.* A_1 and A_2 disagree in trust regarding B's Φ-ing if they trust B to Φ to different degrees.

I here presuppose that A_1 and A_2 care equally about B's Φ-ing, so that their different attitude to B is due to difference in trust, not due to, say, differences in how much they care about B's Φ-ing. This gives some sense of what disagreement in trust is. To conceive of the question of how to respond rationally to disagreement in trust more is needed, however. Fundamentally, we need to assume some sense in which trust can go wrong, either because we trust too much or trust to little. The obvious guiding idea is that A's trust in B is appropriate if B is in fact trustworthy. To explicate this, we need a notion of trustworthiness. As a first approximation, we can say the following:

> *Trustworthiness.* B is trustworthy with regard to Φ if B is capable of Φ-ing and B will Φ for the right reasons.

There are different views about what is required by 'right reasons' here, but for present purposes, we can set aside these further questions (for an overview, see (McLeod 2015)). Trustworthiness also seems to be a matter of degree. Just as we can trust someone to a greater or lesser extent, a trustee can be more or less trustworthy. We can again loosely capture degrees of trustworthiness in modal terms: the wider the set of obstacles you can and will overcome when doing what you are trusted to do, the more trustworthy you are. So, if Bob will make sure to turn up at the café, as I trust him to do, even when this means that he skips going to the movies with his friends, then he is more trustworthy than Charlie, who would let me down in favor of his friends. We can specify this idea as follows:

Degree of trustworthiness. B is more trustworthy in regard Φ-ing the wider the set of circumstances in which B is capable and willing to Φ (for the right reasons).

Having now sketched what we might mean by degrees of trust and degrees of trustworthiness, we can state a graded version of the idea that A's trust in B is appropriate just when B is trustworthy:

Fitting trust. A's trust in B is fitting if A's degree of trust in B's Φ-ing corresponds to B's degree of trustworthiness in regard to Φ.

Essentially the idea is that degrees trust and trustworthiness are measured on each their scale, and that trust is fitting in a given instance when the degree of trust fits the degree of trustworthiness. As trust and trustworthiness may fit more or less, fit is itself really a matter of degree, though this is not reflected in the definition above.[2]

Clearly, people differ in gullibility and guardedness. Some people are vigilant observers of cues warranting suspicion or distrust, and some find themselves unable to trust even when they should. Others are less attentive to signals of untrustworthiness and more disposed to trust, and maybe they sometimes trust too readily. So, consider the idea that for an individual S and a type of situation C, there is something like *S's capacity to allocate trust in a fitting way*, where this is S's capacity to adjust degrees of trust in agents in C in accordance with how trustworthy these agents actually are. With this in mind we can now define peerhood about trusting, the equivalent to the much employed notion of epistemic peers:

Peerhood in trusting. A_1 and A_2 are peers with respect to trusting in a type of circumstances C iff they are equally competent in allocating degrees of trust in accordance with degree of trustworthiness in C, given that A_1 and A_2 have access to the same set of evidence and have considered it with equal care and attention.

The question raised by disagreement in trust concerns the rationality of maintaining one's degree of trust after learning that others do not trust to the same degree. Now, stating the problem in this way presupposes that trusting can be evaluated not only for degrees of fittingness but also for epistemic rationality. You can trust someone in a completely random way, but your trust may happen by to be fitting. In such a case, there is a sense in which you should not have trusted as much as you did, though you were fortunate that things did go well. While your trust is fitting, it is still epistemically irrational. Similarly, if you fully trust Charlie to do a certain thing, and then learn that everyone else distrusts him, the question is whether it is epistemically rational to remain unmoved in your trust. So, trust, it seems, can be evaluated for fittingness as well as for epistemic rationality. This, of course, is analogous to the way that beliefs can be evaluated both for their truth and for their epistemic rationality. Views about epistemically rational trusting seem to be less developed in the literature, but to keep the presentation less abstract it may be helpful to state at least one possible view that might seem attractive:

Evidentialism about rational trusting. A's trusting B to Φ is epistemically rational in so far as A's trusting is a proper response to A's evidence regarding B's trustworthiness with respect to Φ.[3]

Note finally a potential complication that may arise when we talk about epistemically rational trusting. There are two main classes of theories about the nature of trust attitudes: doxastic and non-doxastic accounts. On doxastic accounts, trust is basically a belief, the content of which is that someone is trustworthy to a certain degree and in a certain respect. In early work on trust, many authors took doxastic accounts of trust for granted (see e.g. Baier 1986; Hardin 1996). On doxastic accounts of trust, the idea that trust can be evaluated for epistemic rationality is not problematic, as trust is just a species of beliefs. However, many later authors have proposed non-doxastic accounts according to which my trust is not a belief, but a complex emotional attitude. Roughly, my trust in you is an emotion that inclines me to perform actions embedding the assumption that you do certain things that I depend upon, and you will do so out of concern for me or the trust I place in you (see e.g. (Holton 1994; Jones 1996; Faulkner 2007)). Now, one might worry that non-doxastic accounts of trust do not support the assumption that trust can be evaluated epistemically. This does not seem correct to me, though a full discussion of this question is beyond the scope of this chapter. Compare to emotional attitudes. Emotional attitudes can, it seems be epistemically irrational in a certain sense. My emotion of fear, for example, seems epistemically irrational if it does not respond to evidence about the fearfulness of the objects I fear. Suppose that I, based on sound evidence, believe that a particular dog does no harm and yet I persist in my uncontrollable emotion of fear of the dog. There is a clear sense in which my fear is epistemically irrational. If this is right, we might reasonably say that trust, even on the non-doxastic account can be epistemically rational or irrational depending on whether it sensitive to relevant evidence (for recent discussions of rational assessments of emotions and further references see Brady (2009)).

We are now finally in a position to conceptualize disagreements in trust, and the questions that this raises. Suppose that I, under certain circumstances, have a high degree of trust in Fred to do something. George and I have approximately the same history and previous experiences with Fred, and other evidential sources are also comparable, and we have exercised the same care and attentiveness. So, assume that George and I are at least approximate peers as regards trusting in this case. I then learn that George's degree of trust in Fred is much lower than mine; indeed George even distrusts Fred.

One question is whether I would be epistemically obliged to decrease my degree of trust in Fred, upon learning of my disagreement with George. As in the general disagreement debate, we might distinguish two general positions here. On the one hand there is conciliationism, which holds that in cases of disagreement in trust with a peer one should always adjust one's degree of trust towards one's peer. On the other hand, some might favor the position called steadfastness, according to which one should sometimes keep one's degree of trust unaltered in peer disagreement cases.

Another question is whether reasonable disagreement in trust is possible (Feldman 2006, 2007). Can two individuals both regard one another as peers with respect to trust, and yet disagree in whom to trust, once they are fully aware of the disagreement? Consider again the American presidential race in 2016. Many voters distrusted Trump to deliver on certain issues but other trusted him. Consider those who distrusted Trump. What were they rationally committed to think about their fellow citizens who evidently did trust Trump on those same issues? Can they view them as peers on the above definition? Can they see them as reasonable fellow citizens who just happen to trust differently? Or are they rationally compelled to think of them as gullible, misled or ignorant?

10.3 The Higher-Order Evidence View of Trust and Disagreement

To begin answering these questions, let me start by stating a view about disagreement in trust I regard as plausible, namely what I will call the *higher-order evidence view of disagreement in trust*, before contrasting it with certain other views. Consider first two sorts of evidence about trustworthiness we may come across. Suppose first I trust Albert, whom I recently met, on a certain matter of great importance to me. I then discover evidence that on a number of similar occasions, Albert has simply let down people like me who trusted him. This is *first-order evidence* that Albert is not trustworthy. Consider now a different situation. I trust Albert on a certain matter of great importance to me. I am then told that I have been given a trust-inducing pill that makes me fully trust random people, even in matters that are very important for me, despite having no grounds for doing so. This is clearly not evidence that Albert is not trustworthy. Rather, it is higher-order evidence that I have no reliable capacity to judge trustworthiness in other people.

Surely, it intuitively seems that my first-order evidence regarding Albert's trustworthiness and my higher-order evidence concerning my capacity to detect trustworthiness should both rationally make me reduce my trust in Albert. It also seems that the higher-order evidence that my ability to discern trustworthiness is unreliable can have a very profound impact on my rational trusting. When I learn that I am under the spell of a trust-inducing pill this should make me change my degree of trust in Albert quite substantially.

The higher-order evidence view of disagreement in trust applies these ideas to disagreement in trust. It roughly says that when A trusts B to Φ and C distrusts B to Φ, this provides first-order evidence for A that B might not be trustworthy, and higher-order evidence that A might not be as good at allocating trust as she assumed. Both first-order evidence and higher-order evidence should rationally compel A to revise her trust in B (and the same for C). So, when I have a high degree of trust in Albert, and learn that you distrust Albert, this constitutes first-order evidence that Albert might not be as trustworthy as I take him to be. It also constitutes higher-order evidence that I may not be as good as allocating trust as I tacitly assumed. This is why disagreement in trust rationally compels me to revise my trust. For discussions of related views about disagreement in belief, see Christensen 2007, 2011; Bergmann 2009; Kelly 2010, 2013; Kappel 2017, 2018, 2019.

Of course, the strength of first-order and higher-order evidence generated by a disagreement in trust depends on the details of the case. Suppose I know you care immensely about whether Albert does the thing he is entrusted to do, but I do not care too much. Because more is at stake for you than for me, you are less inclined to trust Albert than I am. Or suppose that I know you are pathologically suspicious about any individual with blond hair, and Albert is blond. Then I can fully explain your lack of trust without invoking the assumption that Albert might not be trustworthy despite impressions, or by suspecting that my capacity for judging trustworthiness might be impaired. We can say that the evidence provided by the disagreement in trust has been defeated.

The disagreement debate has often focused on epistemic peers, but it worth remarking that it is a mistake to think that disagreement only concerns peers. What matters is what evidence a disagreement constitutes, in particular whether our disagreement provides higher-order evidence that I am not a reliable trustor. Whether someone is a peer or not is not itself decisive. Suppose, for example, that I know that I am somewhat better than you at detecting trustworthy individuals in a certain context. Let us say that I get it right 80% of the time, whereas your success rate is only 60%. Should I then be unmoved by our disagreements? It seems not; the fact that you disagree with me is some indication that I may have made a mistake (though see (Zagzebski 2012:114) for a dissenting view and (Keren 2014b) for a discussion). Numbers matters for similar reasons. Suppose I trust some individual, but I realize many other people do not, and that they have formed their distrust independently of one another. This might be significant evidence that I have made a mistake, even if I am better at allocating trust than any of those individuals I disagree with.

Turn then to the question of *reasonable disagreement*. Suppose I trust Albert, and I then I realize that you distrust Albert, even though we both have had access to the same evidence and experiences regarding Albert, and we both care equally about what Albert has committed to do. Can we now agree to disagree? Can I still regard you as my peer in trusting, but as someone who simply trusts in a way different from mine? Or should I see you as excessively suspicious, or erroneous in your distrust, if I remain firm in my own trust?

The answer to this question in part depends on whether we should accept the equivalent of what is known as the uniqueness principle in the epistemology of disagreement (cf. White 2005). Roughly, the uniqueness principle asserts that for a given body of evidence there is just one most rational doxastic attitude which one can have. The uniqueness principle suggests that reasonable disagreement in belief between two individuals possessing the same evidence is not possible. Two individuals assessing the same body of evidence differently cannot both be accurate. The uniqueness principle is controversial, however, and currently subject to a complicated discussion.

It might be objected that while the higher-order evidence view may be plausible for doxastic accounts of trust, it is not plausible for non-doxastic accounts according to which trusting is more like an emotional attitude. In response, consider again an emotional attitude like fear. Suppose I fear the dog, but then become convinced that the dog presents no danger at all, or convinced that my tendency to react with fear does not track the dangers or aggressiveness of dogs. There is a sense in which my fear is irrational if it persists. Rationally, I should revise the emotion, though of course it is far from certain that I can. I should revise my emotion even if the state of fear is a non-doxastic attitude which itself has no propositional content, the truth of which can be evaluated. Similarly, non-doxastic accounts of trust attitudes can agree that when I get evidence that my capacity for allocating trust in a fitting way is not as good as I thought, then I should trust less, and agree that when I learn about disagreement in trust, I may get exactly this kind of evidence.

Like any other view in the disagreement debate, the higher-order evidence account of disagreement and trust will be controversial. Though I cannot defend the higher-order evidence view here, it is worth briefly pointing to what is most controversial about it. What is contested is whether higher-order evidence can have such a profound rational import on what we should rationally believe at the expense of first-order evidence, as is asserted by the higher-order evidence view (see discussions in Titelbaum 2013; Horowitz 2014; Aarnio 2014; Sliwa and Horowitz 2015).

The higher-order evidence view tends to disregard the asymmetries that may exist in disagreements. Suppose that upon assessing the same body of evidence e A believes p, and B believes not-p. While A and B both receive the same higher-order evidence indicating they have made a mistake in assessing e, their evidential situations may otherwise be quite asymmetrical. Suppose, for example, that A is right about p, and that B is wrong. Or suppose that A actually makes a correct appreciation of the evidential force of e, whereas B misjudges e (Kelly 2010; Weatherson 2019). Or suppose (similarly) that A's process of belief formation is reliable and not subject to performance errors or the like, whereas something is wrong with B's processes (Lackey 2010). Or suppose that there is the following asymmetry between A and B: by considering e, A comes to know that p, whereas B, who believes not-p, by implication does not know that not-p (Hawthorne and Srinivasan 2013). A class of views in the disagreement debate argues asymmetries at the object level implies that A and B should not react in the same way to the disagreement. Rather, the rationally proper response to disagreement is determined in significant part by the asymmetries at the object level: when A gets it right at the object level in one or more of the above ways, then A is rationally obliged not to revise her belief about p, or not revise as much, despite the higher-order evidence arising from her disagreement with B. B, on the other hand, should revise her belief that not-p to make it fit better to the evidence.

None of the above views have, as far as I can tell, been applied to the problem of disagreement in trust, but they suggest the general structure of views that reject the higher-order evidence view of disagreement in trust. According to this class of views, the rational response to disagreement in trust is, in significant part at least, determined by the first-order level. Suppose I trust Albert while you distrust Albert. Suppose further that my degree of trust in Albert is fitting and arises from a proper appreciation of evidence for Albert's trustworthiness, or from a process that reliably allocates fitting degrees of trust in the relevant contexts, whereas your distrust does not have this fortunate legacy. A class of views holds that my rational response to disagreement in trust is determined by the facts on the ground, so to speak. Since I get it right at the first-order level, and you do not, I am not under a rational obligation to change my degree of trust in Albert, but you are. Unfortunately, space does not permit a detailed discussion of these important views.

10.4 Trust and Preemption of Evidence

I now turn to a potential worry about the higher-order evidence view of disagreement in trust which turns on features that are specific to the nature of trust. It may seem that on the doxastic account of trust, the disagreement in trust is just a special case of disagreement in belief. This is true for some doxastic views of trust, for example Hardin's view on trust (Hardin 1996), which can be rendered as follows:

> A trusts B to Φ: A believes that B commits to Φ, and A believes that B's incentive structure will provide an overriding motivation for B to carry out her commitment to Φ.

However, more recent doxastic theories of trust present a more complicated picture. Keren (2014a) argues that trust, though itself a doxastic state, is not just an ordinary belief, but rather a doxastic state that is in certain ways related to preemptive reasons. As we shall shortly see, this is directly relevant for what we should think about disagreement and trust. Keren writes:

> … if I genuinely trust my friend to distribute money to the needy, I will tend to disbelieve accusations that she has embezzled that money. Moreover, I will not

> arrive at such disbelief by weighing evidence for her honesty against counter-evidence (Baker 1987:3). This insensitivity to evidence supporting accusations against trusted friends appears different from that exhibited by confident beliefs that are immune from doubt because they are supported by an extensive body of evidence. For our disbelief in such accusations is often not based on extensive evidence against the veracity of the accusations.
>
> *(Keren 2014a:2597)*

So, on this view, trust is somehow related to a distinctive resistance to evidence, along with sensitivity to excessive reflection. In Keren's view, these "appear to be manifestations of a single underlying feature of trust: that in trusting someone to Φ I must respond to preemptive reasons against my taking precautions against her not Φ'ing" (Keren 2014a:2606).

Before considering how this relates to the higher-order evidence view, consider a case to illustrate the idea. I trust my babysitter Clara to look after my child. The idea is that trusting Clara is (in part at least) a response to preemptive reasons not to take (certain) precautions to guard against the eventuality that Clara is not doing her job, or not to respond in the otherwise normal ways to evidence that Clara is not trustworthy. So, reasons for trusting are grounded in preemptive reasons that licenses dismissing counter-evidence and "not basing my belief on my own weighing of the evidence" (Keren 2014a:2609). According to Keren, this makes best sense on the following doxastic account of trust:

> A trusts B to Φ only if A believes that B is trustworthy, such that in virtue of A's belief about B's trustworthiness, A sees herself as having reason to rely on B's Φ'ing without taking precautions against the possibility that B will not Φ, and only if A indeed acts on, or is responsive to, reasons against taking precautions
>
> *(Keren 2014a:2609)*

Though Keren does not use this label, I will call this *the preemptive reason view of trust*. Consider how the preemptive reason view of trust may affect what we should think about disagreement in trust. Suppose I trust Albert to Φ, but I then learn that you distrust Albert. Should this affect my degree of trust? On the preemptive reason view it should not, or at least to a lesser extent. The reason is that when I trust Albert, I see myself as having reasons to dismiss evidence that Albert is not trustworthy. In so far as our disagreement in trust is evidence that Albert is not trustworthy, my reasons for trusting Albert entitle me to ignore this evidence. So, our disagreement in trust should not rationally affect my degree of trust in Albert, or it should at least do so to a lesser extent.

While illuminating, I want to question the plausibility of the preemptive reason view of trust, and I do so on grounds having to do with the nature of preemptive reasons. Consider first a paradigmatic case of a preemptive reason, hopefully providing a clear illustration of how one can have a sort of epistemic reason for preempting certain evidential considerations. Suppose I receive compelling evidence that Cal's beliefs about astrophysics reflect the available evidence much more accurately than my own beliefs about astrophysics and that Cal is far superior to me in weighing the evidence for and against various claims in astrophysics. Surely, I should then defer to Cal in astrophysical matters (given that I take her to be honest and responsible). If Cal firmly holds a particular belief in astrophysics, I should hold this belief as well, even if it otherwise seems to me that the evidence suggests the belief is false. There is a natural way to understand how preemptive epistemic reasons work in this case: What happens is that I acquire an epistemically justified higher-order belief about my own capacity to assess first-order evidence in a certain domain, as well as a belief about how this capacity compares to Cal's similar capacity. So, what does the preempting here is my epistemically justified higher-order belief that I am unable to assess the relevant evidence as well as Cal is.

Now, the problem is that while this is a perfectly intelligible case of a preemptive epistemic reason, it is difficult to see how it carries over to ordinary cases of trust. Suppose I trust my babysitter Clara to do her job. No matter how much I trust Clara, this does not seem to relate to a justified higher-order belief that I will be unable to assess evidence about the trustworthiness of Clara. Consider what would ordinarily seem to make my trust in Clara epistemically rational. I might, for example, trust Clara because she has an outstanding track record and I accept this as evidence for her trustworthiness. Or I may trust her because she simply strikes me as a trustworthy person and I believe to have a fairly reliable capacity to detect trustworthy babysitters. But neither of these grounds of my trust in Clara has anything to do with a higher-order belief that I am unable to assess evidence regarding her trustworthiness. My evidence for Clara's trustworthiness speaks to her character, and not to my ability to assess certain forms of evidence. So, whatever preemptive reasons that may relate to my trust in Clara, they do not follow the model of Cal. My trust in Clara does not somehow give me a reason to believe that I cannot reliably assess evidence pertaining to the trustworthiness of Clara.

Moreover, it is instructive to compare epistemic preemptive reasons to moral preemptive reasons. Suppose I am morally obligated to Φ because I made a promise to you, because of my loyalty to you, or because of some other special relation that I bear to you, such as family, marriage or friendship. It is plausible that this, too, generates preemptive reasons not to consider reasons that I might have for or against Φ-ing. When my wife is ill, I should visit her in the hospital and my concerns about the slight discomfort this may involve, or gains in my reputation, or even concerns about maximizing overall utility, should not affect me. It is not that these reasons do not exist or that I cannot cognitively assess them. It is rather that a constitutive part of what is to be a loyal husband is that one is blind to certain reasons for actions in certain contexts.

I suggest that rather than saying that trust involves preemptive reasons that annul evidence, we should think of trust as similar in certain respects to promises, friendship and loyalty. Trust is an attitude that constitutively involves bracketing certain evidential and pragmatic considerations, just like friendship or loyalty constitutively involve the inclination to disregard certain type of evidence. To keep this view distinct from Keren's view, call it the *bracketing view of trust*. According to this view, part of what it is for A to trust B to Φ is to be inclined to dismiss or ignore certain types of evidence that B will not Φ after all, and to be disinclined to taking certain forms of precaution that B will not Φ. It is not that when A trusts B to Φ then A has an epistemic reason to dismiss evidence that B might not do what she is entrusted to. Rather, to trust just is to be inclined to dismiss such evidence. The bracketing view explains why trust and evidence have a strained relation. If A considers evidence for or against the belief that B will Φ, and let her belief about this matter be decided by this evidence, then A no longer has a trusting attitude to B.

10.5 Bracketing Evidence, Rationality, Disagreement

I have proposed that we might think of trust as constitutively involving a disposition to ignore certain types of evidence or evidential considerations, including certain types of evidence that the trustee is not trustworthy. By implication, trusting is to some extent and in certain ways resistant to evidence stemming from disagreement in trust. There is, it seems to me, something intuitively right about this. When you trust someone, you should not easily be swayed by learning that others do not – otherwise you did not really trust in the first place. In this final section, I will consider an objection the bracketing view of trust.

Suppose I trust you, and then come across first-order evidence that you are not trustworthy. Since I trust you, I am inclined to disregard this evidence. Am I rationally permitted or even rationally required to disregard this evidence? I suggest that the answer to this question is 'No.' My trusting you makes me inclined to dismiss evidence of this kind, but my trusting you does not thereby make it rationally permitted or rationally required for me do so. Compare again to friendship. Friendship may sometimes morally require that one disregards evidence, but it does not make it epistemically rational to disregard this evidence.

Consider then higher-order evidence. When I trust my babysitter Clara, my trust in her disposes me to ignore certain suggestions that she is not trustworthy. But it is more difficult to see why my trust in Clara would also incline me to disregard higher-order evidence that I am not a reliable trustor in the first place. After all, this higher-order evidence does not concern Clara or her trustworthiness, but my own capacity for assessing certain sorts of evidence. If this is right, then trust makes us disposed to disregard one form of evidence generated by disagreement in trust, but not another, though we are epistemically irrational when we ignore either kind of evidence.

One implication seems to be that on the bracketing view, trusting commits to epistemic irrationality. Is this implausible? Note first that the view does not imply that placing trust in some agent is irrational. My trust in Albert can be entirely rational if it comes about as a response to evidence of Albert's trustworthiness, or is the result of a reliable process. Trusting Albert can be a rational response, even if the attitude itself constitutively involves a commitment to irrationally disregard certain sorts of evidence about Albert's trustworthiness. Note next that while trusting constitutively involves a commitment to irrationality, trusting need not actually make me epistemically irrational. I may simply be fortunate enough that the sort of evidence that I would be inclined to irrationally disregard never comes up. If I am lucky in this way, then my trusting will not implicate that my epistemic irrationality materializes. Another form of luck could be that the disregarded evidence turns out to be misleading (i.e. it suggests that the person I trust is not trustworthy, while in fact he or she is). If my trust makes me ignore misleading evidence, then I am blessed by a kind of epistemic luck, though I may still be epistemically irrational. Note thirdly that trust may be a good thing, even if it involves manifests epistemic irrationality, just as may be the case for friendship or loyalty.

Curious as this may sound, these features of the bracketing view of trust actually fits perfectly well with what seems a natural view about the *value* of trust. One way in which trust seems valuable is that once it is established it allows for a cognitively cheap and yet successful modes of interpersonal interaction in environments where those you tend to trust are in fact generally trustworthy, and where evidence that they are not is absent or misleading. In such *trust-friendly environments* we have a great benefit by relating to one another by bonds of trust, because trusting is cheaper than constantly assessing evidence for or against the trustworthiness of others, and safeguarding oneself against being let down. It is interesting to note that environments featuring significant disagreements in trust are typically not such trust-friendly environments (see also Cohen as well as Scheman, this volume). When disagreements in trust abound, then either your potential trustees are not trustworthy, or they are trustworthy, but you are exposed to misleading evidence that they are not, or to misleading evidence that you are not a reliable trustor. In such environments trusting is more difficult. Even when we try to trust people and institutions that are in fact trustworthy, we may not succeed. In this way, disagreement in trust may prevent us from realizing the value of trust. This is one important reason why intentionally engendering disagreement in trust may inflict a serious harm.

Notes

1 This chapter has benefited greatly from Arnon Keren's work on related issues, and from insightful comments from him and Judith Simon, and Boaz Miller and John Weckert, who commented for this volume. Also, I would like to thank Giacomo Melis, Fernando Broncano-Berrocal, Bjørn Hallsson, Josefine Palvicini, Einar Thomasen, Frederik Andersen, Alex France. An earlier version was presented at a workshop in Copenhagen in November 2016.

2 While this notion of fitting trust seems intuitively adequate, I suspect that it may slide over a serious complication worth mentioning. What is it for a given measure on the degree of trust scale to fit a particular measure on the trustworthiness scale? How are the two scales to be calibrated? I am not sure there is an easy solution to this problem, but I will set it aside for now. The basic idea that one can trust too much or too little depends on how trustworthy a trustee seems right, even if it raises further unresolved questions.

3 Evidentialism as a general view is defended by many epistemologists, including Conee and Feldman (2004).

References

Aarnio, M.L. (2014) "Higher-Order Evidence and the Limits of Defeat," *Philosophy and Phenomenological Research* 88(2): 314–345.

Audi, R. (2007) "Belief, Faith, and Acceptance," *International Journal for Philosophy of Religion* 63 (1–3): 87–102.

Baier, A. (1986) "Trust and Antitrust," *Ethics* 96(2): 231–260.

Baker, J. (1987) "Trust and Rationality," *Pacific Philosophical Quarterly* 68: 1–13.

Bergmann, M. (2009) "Rational Disagreement after Full Disclosure," *Episteme* (6): 336–353.

Brady, M.S. (2009) "The Irrationality of Recalcitrant Emotions," *Philosophical Studies* 145(3): 413–430.

Buchak, L. (2014) "Buchak Rational Faith and Justified Belief," in T. O'Connor and L.F. Callahan (eds.), *Religious Faith and Intellectual Virtue*, Oxford: Oxford University Press.

Christensen, D. (2007) "Epistemology of Disagreement: The Good News," *Philosophical Review* 116(2): 187–217.

Christensen, D. (2011) "Disagreement, Question-Begging and Epistemic Self-Criticism," *Philosophers Imprint* 11(6): 1–22.

Christensen, D. and Lackey, J. (eds.) (2013) *The Epistemology of Disagreement: New Essays*, Oxford: Oxford University Press.

Conee, E. and Feldman, R. (2004) *Evidentialism*, Oxford: Oxford University Press.

Faulkner, P. (2007) "A Genealogy of Trust," *Episteme* 4(3): 305–321.

Feldman, R. (2006) "Epistemological Puzzles about Disagreement," in S. Hetherington (ed.), *Epistemology Futures*, Oxford: Clarendon Press.

Feldman, R. (2007) "Reasonable Religious Disagreements," in L. Antony (ed.), *Philosophers without Gods*, Oxford: Oxford University Press.

Feldman, R. and Warfield, T. (eds.) (2011) *Disagreement*, Oxford: Oxford University Press.

Goldman, A. (2001) "Experts: Which Ones Should You trust?" *Philosophy and Phenomenological Research* 63(1): 85–110.
Goldman, A. and Beddor, R. (2016) "Reliabilist Epistemology," in E.N. Zalta (ed.), *Stanford Encyclopedia of Philosophy*, Stanford, CA: Stanford University Press.
Hardin, R. (1996) "Trustworthiness," *Ethics* 107(1): 26–42.
Hawley, K. (2014) "Trust, Distrust and Commitment," *Noûs*, 48(1): 1–20.
Hawthorne, J. and Srinivasan, A. (2013) "Disagreement without Transparency, Some Bleak Thoughts," in D. Christensen and J. Lackey (eds.), *The Epistemology of Disagreement: New Essays*, Oxford: Oxford University Press.
Holton, R. (1994) "Deciding to Trust, Coming to Believe," *Australasian Journal of Philosophy* 72 (1): 63–76.
Horowitz, S. (2014) "Epistemic Akrasia," *Nous*, 48(4): 718–744.
Jones, K. (1996) "Trust as an Affective Attitude," *Ethics* 107(1): 4–25.
Kappel, K. (2017) "Bottom Up Justification, Asymmetric Epistemic Push, and the Fragility of Higher-Order Justification," *Episteme* 16(2): 119–138.
Kappel, K. (2018) "Higher-Order Evidence and Deep Disagreement," *Topoi*, First Online.
Kappel, K. (2019) "Escaping the Akratic Trilemma," in A. Steghlich-Petersen and M.S. Rasmussen (eds.), *Higher-Order Evidence*, Oxford: Oxford University Press.
Kelly, T. (2010) "Peer Disagreement and Higher-Order Evidence," in R. Feldman and T.A. Warfield (eds), *Disagreement*, Oxford: Oxford University Press.
Kelly, T. (2013) "Disagreement and the Burdens of Judgment," in D. Christensen and J. Lackey (eds.), *The Epistemology of Disagreement: New Essays*, Oxford: Oxford University Press.
Keren, A. (2014a) "Trust and Belief: A Preemptive Reasons Account," *Synthese* 191(12): 2593–2615.
Keren, A. (2014b) "Zagzebski on Authority and Pre-emption in the Domain of Belief," *European Journal for Philosophy of Religion* 4: 61–76.
Lackey, J. (2010) "A Justificationist View of Disagreement's Epistemic Significance," in A. Haddock, A. Millar and D. Pritchard (eds.), *Social Epistemology*, Oxford: Oxford University Press.
McCraw, B.W. (2015) "Faith and Trust," *Int J Philos Relig* 77: 141–158.
McLeod, C. (2015) "Trust," in E.N. Zalta (ed.), *Standford Encyclopedia of Philosophy*, Stanford, CA: Stanford University Press
Oppy, G. (2010) "Disagreement," *International Journal for Philosophy of Religion* 68(1–3): 183–199.
Sliwa, P. and Horowitz, S. (2015) "Respecting All the Evidence," *Philosophical Studies* 172(11): 2835–2858.
Titelbaum, M.G. (2015) "Rationality's Fixed Point (or: In Defense of Right Reason)," *Oxford Studies in Epistemology*, 5. doi:10.1093/acprof:oso/9780198722762.003.0009
Weatherson, B. (2019) *Normative Externalism*, Oxford: Oxford University Press.
White, R. (2005) "Epistemic Permissiveness," *Philosophical Perspectives* 19: 445–459.
Zagzebski, L.T. (2012) *Epistemic Authority: A Theory of Trust, Authority, and Autonomy in Belief*, Oxford: Oxford University Press.

11
TRUST AND WILL

Edward Hinchman

We might ask two questions about the relation between trust and the will. One question, about trust, is whether you can trust "at will." Say there is someone whom you would like to trust but whose worthiness of your trust is not supported by available evidence. Can you trust despite acknowledging that you lack evidence of the trustee's worthiness of your trust? Another question, about the will, is whether you can exercise your will at all without trusting at least yourself. In practical agency, you act by choosing or intending in accordance with your practical judgment. Self-trust may seem trivial in a split-second case, but when the case unfolds through time – you judge that you ought to φ, retain your intention to φ through an interval, and only at the end of that interval act on the intention – your self-trust spans a shift in perspectives that mimics a relation between different people. Here too we may ask whether you can trust "at will." Can you enter "at will" into the self-relation that shapes this diachronic exercise of your will? What if your earlier self does not appear to be worthy of your trust? If you cannot trust at will, does that entail – perhaps paradoxically – that you cannot exercise your will "at will"?[1]

In this chapter, I explore the role of the will in trust by exploring the role of trust in the will. You can trust at will, I argue, because the role of trust in the will assigns an important role to trusting at will. Trust plays its role in the will through a contrast between trust in your practical judgment and a self-alienated stance wherein you rely on your judgment only through an appreciation of evidence that it is reliable. When you have such evidence, as you often do, you can choose to trust yourself as an alternative to being thus self-alienated. When you lack such evidence, as you sometimes do, you can likewise choose to trust, provided you also lack significant evidence that your judgment is not reliable. In each case, you exercise your will by trusting at will. You regulate your trust, not through responsiveness to positive evidence of your judgment's reliability, but through responsiveness to possible evidence of your judgment's unreliability: if you come to have significant evidence that your judgment is not reliable, you will cease to trust, and (counterfactually) if you had had such evidence you would not have trusted.[2]

The key to my approach lies in distinguishing these two ways of being responsive to evidence. On the one hand, you cannot trust someone – whether another person or your own earlier self – whom you judge unworthy of your trust. Though you can for other reasons rely on a person whom you judge untrustworthy, it would be a mistake to describe such reliance as "trust." On the other hand, trust does not require a positive assessment of trustworthiness. When you trust, you are responsive to possible evidence that the trustee is unworthy of your trust, and that responsiveness – your disposition to withhold trust when you encounter what you assess as good evidence that the trustee is unworthy of it – makes trust importantly different from a "leap of faith." You may lack sufficient evidence for the judgment that your trustee is worthy of your trust, but that evidential deficit need not constrain your ability to trust. Even if you have such evidence, that evidence should not form the basis of your trust.

I thus take issue with Pamela Hieronymi's influential analysis of trust as a "commitment-constituted attitude."[3] Your trust is indeed constrained by your responsiveness to evidence of untrustworthiness. But you need not undertake an attitudinal commitment to the trustee's worthiness of your trust: you need undertake no commitment akin to or involving a judgment that the trustee is trustworthy. An attitudinal commitment to a person's worthiness of your trust creates normative tension with your simply trusting her. If you judge that she is worthy of your trust, you need not trust her; you can rely, not directly on her in the way of trust, but on your own judgment that she will prove reliable. That sounds paradoxical. Are you thereby prevented from trusting those whom you deem most worthy of your trust? There is no paradox; there is merely a need to understand how we trust at will. A volitional element in trust enables you to enforce this distinction, trusting instead of merely relying on your judgment that the trustee is reliable.

Since the contrast between these two possibilities is clearest in intrapersonal trust, I make that my focus, thereby treating the question of "trust and will" as probing both the role of the will in trust and the role of trust in the will. We can see why trust is not a commitment-constituted attitude by seeing how trust itself plays a key role in the constitution of a commitment. In order to commit yourself to φing at *t*, you have to expect that your future self will at *t* have a rational basis for following through on the commitment not merely in a spirit of self-reliance but also, and crucially, in the spirit of self-trust.

11.1 Why Care about Trusting at Will?

What then is it to form a commitment? And how might it matter that the self-trust at the core of a commitment be voluntary? We can see how it might matter by considering the alternative. Say you intend to φ at *t* but just before *t* learn that context makes it imperative that you either assess your intending self as trustworthy before you act on the intention or redeliberate whether to φ from scratch. Imagine that it is too complicated to redeliberate from scratch but that materials for assessing your trustworthiness are available in the form of evidence that you were indeed reliable in making the judgment that informs your intention. If you proceed to act on that judgment, having made this assessment, you do not simply trust your judgment. Without that trust, your judgment that you ought to φ does not inform your intention to φ in the normal way.

You are not simply trusting your judgment if you require evidence that it is reliable. To say that you simply trust your judgment that you ought to φ is to say that you reason from it by, e.g. forming an intention to φ, or act on it by φing, without explicitly redeliberating. When you follow through on your intention to φ without redeliberating, your follow-through is not mediated by an assessment or reassessment of the self that judged that you ought to φ. There is, of course, the problem that you cannot keep assessing yourself – assessing your judgment that you ought to φ, assessing *that* judgment, then *that* judgment, ad infinitum (or however high in this hierarchy you are able to formulate a thought). But my present point is different: there is an important contrast between (i) the common case in which you trust your judgment that you ought to φ by forming an intention to φ and then following through on that intention and (ii) the less common but perfectly possible case in which you feel a need to assess your judging or intending self for trustworthiness before feeling rationally entitled to follow through on it.

That distinction, between trusting yourself and relying on yourself through an assessment of your reliability, marks an important difference between two species of self-relation. The difference is functional, a matter of how the two stances ramify more broadly through your life. Do you second-guess yourself – forming a practical judgment or intention but then wondering how trustworthy that judgment or intention really is? In some regions of your life such self-mistrust may be perfectly appropriate – when you are learning a new skill or when a lot is at stake. But in the normal course of life you must exercise this virtue of temperance: to intend in a way that is worthy of your trust, and to act on that intention unless there is good evidence that you are not worthy of that trust. When there is no significant evidence of your untrustworthiness in intending, or any good reason to believe that circumstances have changed in relevant ways since you formed the intention, then you should trust yourself and follow through. Evidence of your own untrustworthiness constrains your capacity to trust yourself. But in the absence of such evidence you may avoid self-alienation by exercising your discretion to trust yourself at will.

In what respects is it "self-alienating" to rely on your responsiveness to evidence of your reliability instead of trusting yourself? One respect is simply that doing so does not amount to making a decision or choice, or to forming an intention. But why care about those concepts? What would you lose if you governed yourself without "making choices" or "forming intentions" but instead simply by monitoring the reliability of your beliefs about your practical reasons? One problem is that your beliefs about your reasons may pull you in incompatible directions, so you need the capacity to settle what to do by forming the "practical judgment" that you have conclusive or sufficient reason to do A, even though you may also believe you have good reasons to do incompatible B.[4] Another problem is that, because you have limited evidence about the reliability of your practical judgments, you will be unable to govern your reactions to novel issues. But what does either problem have to do with "self-alienation"? The threat of self-alienation marks the more general datum that our concepts of choice and intention enable us to govern ourselves even when we lack evidence that our beliefs about our reasons are reliable. Instead of responding to evidence of your reliability, your choice or intention manifests responsiveness to the normative dynamic of a self-trust relation.

What is that normative dynamic? And how does your responsiveness to it ensure that you are not self-alienated? We can grasp the distinctive element in self-trust by grasping how the distinctive element in trust lies in what it adds to mere self-reliance. In any form of reliance, including trust, you risk disappointment: the trustee may not do what you are relying on her to do.[5] But in trust, beyond mere reliance, you also risk betrayal – in the intrapersonal instance, self-betrayal.[6] We can understand the precise respect in which self-trust embodies the antidote to self-alienation by grasping how the risk of betrayal shapes the normative dynamic of a trust relation.

How exactly does trust risk betrayal? Annette Baier set terms for subsequent debate when she argued that the risk of betrayed trust is distinctively moral. What is most fundamentally at stake in a trust relation, Baier argued (1994:137), is not simply whether the trustee will do what you trust her to do – on pain of disappointing your trust – but whether she thereby manifests proper concern for your welfare. I agree with Baier's critics that her approach over-moralizes trust.[7] But these critics link their worry about moralism with a claim that I reject: that the risk of betrayal adds nothing, as such, to the risk of disappointment. Baier is right to characterize the distinctive risk of trust as a form of betrayal, but the assurance that invites trust targets the trustor's rationality, not the trustor's welfare or any other distinctively moral status. I do not emphasize rationality to the exclusion of morality; I claim merely that the rational obligation is more fundamental: while it does not follow from how trust risks betrayal that trust is a moral relation, it does follow from how trust risks betrayal that trust is a rational relation.

I elsewhere defend that claim about interpersonal trust (see also Potter, this volume), arguing that the assurance at the core of testimony, advice or a promise trades on the risk of betrayal (Hinchman 2017; see also Faulkner, this volume). I review that argument briefly in section 11.4 below. In the next two sections I extend my argument to intrapersonal trust. To the objection that an emphasis on self-betrayal over-moralizes our self-relations, I reply that this species of betrayal is rational – not, as such, moral. To put my thesis in a single complex sentence: you betray yourself when, in undertaking a practical commitment, you represent yourself as a source of rational authority for your own future self without manifesting the species of concern for your future self's needs that would provide a rational basis for that authority. Such betrayed self-trust shapes the self-relations at the core of diachronic agency – of your forming and then later following through on an intention – by serving as a criterion of normative failure. The prospect of self-betrayal reveals how trust informs your will: when you exercise your will by forming an intention, you aim not to influence yourself in a self-alienated manner, through evidence of your reliability, as if your later self were a different person, but to guide yourself through trust, by putting yourself in position to treat your worthiness of that trust as itself the rational basis of that guidance. Trust could not thus inform your will if you could not trust at will, thereby willing a risk of self-betrayal.

11.2 How Betrayed Self-Trust Differs from Disappointed Self-Trust

How then does betraying your own trust differ from disappointing it? And how does the possibility of self-betrayal figure in the exercise of your will? When you form an intention, you institute a complex self-relation: you aim that you will follow through on the intention through trust in the earlier self that formed it. Such projected self-trust rests on a rational capacity at the core of trust: your counterfactual sensitivity to evidence of untrustworthiness in the trustee. Within this projection, if there is evidence that your earlier self is unworthy of your trust, you will not trust it, and if there had been such evidence, you would not have trusted it. Our question is what that sensitivity is a sensitivity *to*: what is it to be thus unworthy of trust? My thesis is that you are on guard against the prospect of betrayed, not of disappointed, self-trust. In a typical case of self-trust, as in a typical case of trust, you run both risks at once and interrelatedly. But we can learn something about the nature of each by seeing how they might come apart – in particular, how you might betray your self-trust without disappointing it.

First consider a general question about the relation between disappointed trust and betrayed trust. If A trusts B to φ, can B betray A's trust in her to φ without thereby disappointing that trust? If A's trust in B to φ amounts to something more than her merely relying on B to φ, then we can see how B might betray A's trust even though she φs and so does not disappoint it. Perhaps B φs only because someone – perhaps A himself – coerces her into φing. Or perhaps B φs with no memory of A's trust in her and with a firm disposition not to φ were she to remember it. In either case, B betrays A's trust in her to φ, though she does φ and in that respect does not disappoint A's trust – even if A finds it "disappointing" (in a broader sense) that his trust has been betrayed. We are investigating the distinction specifically in intrapersonal or "self"-trust. Our challenge is to explain how there are analogues of these interpersonal relations in the relations that you bear to yourself as a single diachronically extended agent.

The first step toward meeting the challenge concedes a complexity in how you would count as "betraying" your own trust. In an interpersonal case, the trustee can simply betray the trustor's trust – end of story. But it is unclear how there could be a comparably simple story in which an individual betrays his own trust. Can we say that the individual is both the active "victimizer" and the passive "victim" of betrayed self-trust? If he worries that he is being "victimized," there is something he can do about that – stop the "victimizing"! As we will see, this is precisely where the concept of betrayed self-trust does its work: the subject worries that she is betraying her own self-trust and responds by abandoning the judgment that invites the trust. When she abandons the judgment, her worry about betrayal is thereby resolved. But the resolution reveals something important about intrapersonal trust: that the subject resolves this question of trust by responding to a worry, not about disappointed self-trust, but about betrayed self-trust. The following series of cases reveals how it is in the context of such a worry – and of such a resolution – that intrapersonal trust may figure as undisappointed yet betrayed.

Consider first a standard case of akrasia:

> *Tempted voter.* Ally is a firm supporter of political candidate X based on an impartial assessment of X's policies. She thereby judges that she has conclusive reason to vote for X, rather than for X's rival Y, and forms an intention to vote accordingly. While waiting in line to vote, however, she overhears a conversation that reminds her how X's policies will harm her personally, which in turn creates a temptation to vote for Y. Despite still judging that she has conclusive reason to vote for X, the temptation "gets the better of her" and she votes for Y. She almost immediately regrets her vote.

How should Ally have resolved this moment of akratic temptation? Her regret reveals that she ought to have resolved the akrasia in a "downstream" direction: by letting the judgment that she retains, even while tempted, guide her follow-through.[8] Does she betray her trust? We might think there is no intrapersonal trust here, since Ally fails to act on her intention, but that would overlook how she has trusted her intention to vote for X for weeks before election day. Imagine that she has campaigned for X, partly on the basis of her intention to vote for X. She thereby treats her trustworthiness in intending to vote for X as a reason to campaign for X – not as a sufficient reason unto itself, but as one element in a set of reasons that, she judges, suffices for campaigning. Simply put, if she had not intended to vote for X, she would not have regarded herself as having sufficient reason to campaign for X. And she does betray her trust in herself in that respect; she betrays her self-trust while also disappointing it.

We get one key contrast with a case that lacks this akratic element:

> *Change of Mind.* Amy arrives at the voting place judging that she has conclusive reason to vote for candidate X rather than the opposing candidate Y. But while in line to vote, she overhears a discussion that re-opens her deliberation whether to vote for X. After confirming the accuracy of these new considerations via a quick Internet search on her phone, Amy concludes that she has conclusive reason to vote for Y instead of X and marks her ballot accordingly.

Unlike Ally's worry, Amy's worry targets the deliberation informing her judgment. Ally does not worry about her deliberation whether to vote for X; she remains confident that she has decided the matter correctly – despite the fear of personal harm that generates her temptation to rebel against that judgment. But Amy does worry about her deliberation: specifically, she worries that she may have made a misstep as she conducted that deliberation, misassessing the considerations that she did assess (including evidence, practical principles, or anything else that served as input to her deliberation), or ignoring considerations available to her that she ought to have assessed. If, like Ally, Amy has campaigned for X partly on the basis of her intention to vote for X, then she disappoints her trust – but, unlike Ally, without betraying it. It is no betrayal if you fail to execute an intention that you come to see you ought to abandon.

Consider now a case with this different normative structure:

> *Change of Heart.* Annie, like Ally and Amy, arrives at the voting place judging that she has conclusive reason to vote for X rather than Y. But while in line she overhears a heartfelt tale of political conversion, wherein the speaker recounts her struggles to overcome the preconceptions that led her earlier to support candidates from X's party. Annie recognizes herself in the speaker's struggles; she was likewise raised to support that party uncritically. She wonders how this political allegiance might lead to similar regret – but, even so, the preconceptions are *her* preconceptions, and she finds it difficult to shake them. Though shaken by the felt plausibility of the hypothesis that she is untrustworthy, she continues to judge that she has conclusive reason to vote for X. When her turn to vote arrives, she stares long and hard at the ballot, unsure how to mark it.

Unlike Ally's worry in Tempted Voter, Annie's worry targets her judgment that she has conclusive reason to vote for X. But unlike Amy's worry in Change of Mind, Annie's worry does not target the deliberation informing her judgment – or, at least, not in the way that Amy's does. Annie does not worry that she has made a misstep as she conducted that deliberation. She is perfectly willing to take at face value her confidence that she has correctly assessed all the considerations that she did assess, and that she did not ignore any consideration available to her that she ought to have assessed within that deliberation. Her worry instead targets the "sense of" or "feeling for" what is at stake for her in the deliberative context that informs how she is guided by this confidence, her broader confidence not merely that she has correctly assessed everything she did assess, among those considerations available to her, but that she has considered matters well and fully enough to permit drawing a conclusion. She worries that her feeling of conclusiveness – her sense that she has considered matters long enough and well enough to justify this conclusion – may not be reliably responsive to what is really at stake for her. Though she cannot shake this sense of the stakes, she worries that she ought to try harder to shake it. As long as she thereby retains the judgment without letting it guide her, Annie counts as akratic. But her akrasia is crucially unlike Ally's in Tempted Voter. Whereas Ally betrays her trust while also disappointing it, Annie fears she will betray her trust by failing to disappoint it. If the metaphor for Ally's predicament is *weakness*, the metaphor for Annie's predicament is *rigidity*.

We might thus describe the phenomenological difference between the three cases. But what are the core normative differences? The first difference is straightforward: Change of Heart generates a second-order deliberation, whereas Change of Mind generates a first-order deliberation. Here are two possible bases for the second-order deliberation in Change of Heart: Annie may worry that impatience makes her hasty, or she may worry that laziness makes her parochial. Whichever way we imagine it, the fundamental target of Annie's worry is her feeling for what is at stake: specifically, her sense of how much time or energy she should devote to the deliberation informing her judgment. Each addresses not her truth-conducive reliability but, to coin a term, her *closure-conducive* reliability. She does not re-open her first-order deliberation as Amy does, by suspending her earlier presumption that she is truth-conducively reliable about her reasons. Unlike Amy, she continues to judge that she has conclusive reason to vote for X. What Annie questions is *whether* to suspend her presumption of truth-conducive reliability – that is, whether to re-open her first-order deliberation. In asking this question, she suspends the presumption that she is closure-conducively reliable, the presumption that informs her sense that she is entitled to treat that first-order deliberation as closed.

How does Annie undertake this higher-order species of reflection? What is it to question one's own closure-conducive reliability? This leads us to the second normative difference between Change of Heart and Change of Mind. How could Annie adopt a mistrustful higher-order perspective on whether to trust her own first-order deliberative perspective?

11.3 How the Prospect of Betrayed Self-Trust Plays Its Normative Role

Annie's higher-order perspective on her first-order judgment projects a broader future for her, insofar as it crucially involves an attitude toward her own future regret. Unlike reflection on her truth-conducive reliability, reflection on her closure-conducive reliability represents her agency as extending not merely to the time of action but out to the horizon that Michael Bratman calls *plan's end*, the point beyond which she will no longer think about the action.[9]

We can codify this forward-looking reflection as follows. When Annie judges that she has conclusive reason to vote for X, she projects a future, out beyond election day, in which:

(Down) (a) she will not regret having voted for X, and
(b) she will regret not having voted for X.

But when Annie worries about the trustworthiness of this judgment, thereby deliberating whether to redeliberate, she projects a future, out beyond election day, in which:

(Up) (a) she will regret having voted for X, and
(b) she will not regret not having voted for X.

I have labeled the projection that emerges from the perspective of judgment "Down" because it points downstream: Annie will have nothing to regret if she trustingly commits herself to this judgment and then acts on the commitment. This is how Ally struggles with temptation: her viewing it as "temptation" rather than an occasion to change her mind derives from the downstream-pointing projection of her judgment. She believes that she will regret giving in to the "temptation" because she expects that it will amount to a merely transient preference reversal. By contrast, I have labeled the projection that emerges from Annie's mistrust in her judgment 'Up' because it points upstream: she will regret it if she lets herself be thus influenced by her judgment, and she will not regret it if she does not let herself be thus influenced. This regret does not mark a merely transient preference reversal within the projection but expresses her settled attitude toward the self-relation that she manifests in thus following her judgment.

Why should the concept of regret play this role in structuring the two projections? Here is my hypothesis: regret plays this normative role as the intrapsychic manifestation of betrayed self-trust. As others have emphasized,[10] betrayal finds its natural expression in reactive attitudes, engendering contempt or resentment in the betrayed toward the betrayer. If regret functions as an intrapersonal reactive attitude, that enables the concept of betrayed trust to shape self-governance in prospect, as referring not to something actual but to something to be kept non-actual – on pain of regret. It could not play this role if it – that is, betrayed self-trust experienced as regret that you trusted your judgment – were not something with which we are familiar in ordinary experience. Such regret is common in two sorts of case, in each of which the subject is concerned for her intrapersonal rational coherence, not merely for her welfare.[11]

First, we do sometimes make bad choices that we regret in this way. "What could I have been thinking?" you ask yourself at plan's end, appalled that you trusted a judgment that now seems manifestly unworthy of your trust. This experience is crucially unlike merely being displeased by the results of following through on a judgment. You may well be displeased with the results of trusting your judgment yet not regret the self-influence as such. You may think you did your best to avoid error yet fell into error anyway. Or you may temper your self-criticism with the thought that no evidence of your own untrustworthiness – including your closure-conducive unreliability – was then available to you. If there was no evidence of untrustworthiness available to you when you trusted, then your trust was not unreasonable, however displeased you may be with the results. In an alternative case, however, you may think that there was evidence of your own untrustworthiness available, and that you trustingly followed through on your judgment through incompetence in weighing that evidence. That case motivates a deeper form of regret that targets your self-relations more directly.

Here then is the second source of everyday familiarity with betrayed self-trust. As we mature, we do much that we wind up regretting in this way: you judge that you have conclusive reason to φ, trust that judgment because you are too immature to weigh available evidence of your untrustworthiness, then later realize your mistake. Your question is not: "What could I have been thinking?" It is all too clear how immaturity led you to deliberative error. One of our developmental aims is to learn to make judgments that will prove genuinely authoritative for us.

How might Annie's judgment fail to be authoritative? Here, again, is my answer: she fears that her judgment will, looking back, appear to have betrayed her own trust. The answer presents the case in all its diachronic complexity, wherein the subject looks ahead not merely to the time of action but all the way out to "plan's end."

Annie fears that the deliberative perspective informing her judgment does not manifest the right responsiveness to her ongoing – and possibly changing – needs. When she reasons "upstream," she aims to feel the force of these needs from plan's end, by projecting a retrospect from which she would feel relevant regret.[12] We thus return to the idea from which we began: though reactive attitudes are the key to distinguishing trust from mere reliance, they need not be moral. Our focus on reactive attitudes reveals not their moral but their rational force: they target the subject's rational authority and coherence. Annie's projection out to plan's end serves as a reactive-attitudinal retrospect on her planning agency, not because it represents her as planning through that entire interval, but because it represents her as having settled the question of her needs in more local planning. The local planning that informs her voting behavior, with its implications for broader planning, requires that she view her judgments as rationally adequate to that exercise of self-governance. And her reactive-attitudinal stance from plan's end settles whether her judgments were indeed thus adequate insofar as they avoided self-betrayal in the way they presumed. Her self-mistrustful attitude in the voting booth both projects this verdict and uses the verdict as a basis for assessing the presumption.

When you reason "upstream" – abandoning your judgment because you mistrust it – you show responsiveness to the possibility of betrayed self-trust. Such self-mistrust does not entail betrayed self-trust, since it is possible that you do care appropriately about what is at stake for you in your deliberative context and therefore that your self-mistrust is mistaken. But it is possible that your self-mistrust is not mistaken: perhaps you really have betrayed the invited self-trust relation. The responsiveness at the core of trust is a rational responsiveness because it targets the possibility that your trust in this would-be source of rationality has been betrayed.

11.4 Inviting Others to Trust at Will

How does this intrapersonal normative dynamic run in parallel with an interpersonal dynamic? The intrapersonal dynamic unfolds between perspectives within the agency of a single person, as the person acts on an aim to bring those perspectives into rational coherence. The interpersonal dynamic, by contrast, engages two people with entirely separate perspectives that cannot, without pathology, enter into anything like that coherence relation. Interpersonal trust must therefore engage an alternative rational norm – but what norm? It helps to reflect on a parallel between intending and promising: just as you invite your own trust when you form an intention to φ, so you invite the trust of a promisee when you promise him that you will φ. In neither case does the invitation merely prompt the invitee to respond to evidence of your reliability in undertaking the intention or promise. In each case, you aim that the recipient of your invitation should trust you and feel rationally entitled to express that trust through action – following through on your intention in the first case, performing acts that depend on your keeping your promise in the second – even in the absence of sufficient evidence that you are worthy of the trust, as long as there is no good evidence that you are unworthy of it. And we can make similar remarks about other forms of interpersonal assurance – say, testimony and advice. The parallel reveals something important about the value of a capacity to trust at will. Both intrapersonally and interpersonally, a capacity for voluntary trust makes us susceptible to rational intervention – whether to preserve our rational coherence or to give us reasons we would not otherwise have.

As in the intrapersonal case, the rational influence unfolds through two importantly different perspectives. Take first the perspective of the addressee, and consider the value in trusting others, beyond merely relying on your own judgment that another is relevantly reliable. If someone invites your trust by offering you testimony, advice, or a promise, and evidence is available that the person is relevantly reliable, you can judge that she is reliable on the basis of that evidence and on that basis believe what she testifies, or do what she advises, or count on her to keep her promise – on the basis, that is, of *your* evidentially grounded judgment that she will prove to be or have been relevantly reliable. But what if no such evidence is available? Or what if, though the evidence is available, there is insufficient time to assess it? Or what if she would regard your seeking and assessing evidence of her worthiness of your trust as a slight – as a sheer refusal of her invitation to trust? You might on one of these bases deem it preferable to trust without seeking evidence of her worthiness of your trust – as long as you can count on your capacity to withhold trust should evidence of her unworthiness of your trust become available. Here again we see why it might prove a source of value to be capable of trusting at will. Though you could not trust if there were evidence that the would-be trustee is unworthy of your trust, if there is no such evidence you can decide to trust merely by disposing yourself to do so.

Is this a moral value inhering in the value of the trust relation? As in the intrapersonal case, that over-moralizes trust. Say, after asking directions, you trust the testimony or advice of a stranger on the street. Or say you trust your neighbor's promise to "save your spot" in a queue. Do you thereby create moral value? Moral value seems principally to arise on the trustee's side, through whatever it takes to vindicate your trust. Setting morality aside, a different species of value can arise on your side of the relation. Assuming the trustee relevantly reliable, you can acquire a reason that you might not otherwise have – a reason to believe her testimony, the follow her advice or to perform actions that depend on her keeping her promise. This reason is grounded partly in the trustee's reliability and partly in the (counterfactual) sensitivity to evidence of the trustee's unreliability that informs your trust: if you have (or had) such evidence you would cease trusting (or would not have trusted). The latter ground marks the difference between a reason acquired through trust and a reason acquired through mere reliance. Sometimes you cannot trust a person on whom you rely, because evidence of her unreliability forces you to rely, not directly on her, but on your own judgment that relying on her is nonetheless reasonable. But when you lack such evidence you can get the reason by choosing to trust her – even if you have evidence that would justify relying on her without trust.

How could a reason be grounded even partly in your trusting sensitivity to evidence of the trustee's unworthiness of your trust? The key lies in understanding how the illocutionary norms informing testimony, advice and promising codify your risk of betrayal. The normative basis of your risk of disappointment lies in your own judgment: you judge that the evidence supports reliance that would incur this risk, so the responsibility for the risk itself lies narrowly on your side – whatever else we may say about responsibility for the harms of disappointing your reliance. When you trust, however, responsibility for the risk of betrayal you thereby undergo is normatively distributed across the invited trust relation. What explains this distribution? In the cases of assurance at issue, you trust by accepting the invitation that informs the trustee's assurance, which is informed by the trustee's understanding of how that response risks betrayal. You thus respond to the trustee's normative acceptance of responsibility for that risk – something that has no parallel in mere reliance. You can trust "at will" because you can choose to let yourself be governed by the trustee's normative acceptance of responsibility for how you are governed, an exercise of will that may give you access to reasons to do or believe things that you would not otherwise have reason to do or believe, but at the cost of undergoing the risk that this trustee will betray you, When I say that the trustee accepts "normative" responsibility, I mean that she thereby commits herself to abiding by the norms that codify that responsibility. If she is insincere, she flouts those norms and in that respect does not even attempt to live up to the responsibility she thereby incurs. This is one principal respect in which your trust risks betrayal.

The normative nature of this exchange emerges more fully from the other side. When you offer testimony, advice or a promise, do you merely "put your speech act out there," aiming to get hearers to rely on you for whatever reasons the evidence available to those hearers can support? If that were your aim, your testimony would not differ from a mere assertion, your advice would not differ from a mere assertion about your hearer's reasons, and your promise would not differ from a mere assertion of intention. What is missing in these alternative acts is the distinctive way in which you address your testimony, advice or promise: you invite your addressee's trust. In inviting his trust, you engage your addressee's responsiveness to evidence of your unworthiness of his trust, and thereby to the possibility that his trust might be betrayed. But you more fundamentally engage your addressee's capability to draw this distinction in his will: to trust you *instead* of merely relying on you through an appreciation of positive evidence that you are reliable. If he can do the first, then he can also do the second – perhaps irrationally (if there is insufficient evidence that you are reliable). Why should he trust? The simplest answer is that that is what you have invited him to do. In issuing that invitation, you aim at this very exercise of will – that he should trust you at will. You take responsibility for the reason you thereby give him (assuming you reliable) by inviting him to rely on your normative acceptance of responsibility for the wrongfulness of betraying the trust you thereby invite.

What if you do not believe that you *can* engage your addressee's capacity for trust, because you believe that there is good evidence available to this addressee that you are not worthy of it?[13] You thereby confront an issue that you can attempt to resolve in either of two ways. You can attempt to counter the appearance that this evidence of your untrustworthiness is good evidence, thereby defusing its power over your addressee's capacity to trust you. Or you can shift to the alternative act, attempting instead to get your addressee to rely on you for reasons of his own – including perhaps a reason grounded in evidence that you are, on balance, relevantly reliable. On this second strategy, you now longer invite the addressee's trust. The only way to invite his trust – without insincerity or some other normative failure – is to counter the appearance that you are unworthy of it. You must counter this appearance because without doing so you cannot believe that your addressee will enter freely – "at will" – into this trust relation, by accepting your invitation, not by responding to positive evidence of your reliability but by relying on you in the way distinctive of trust. In inviting trust, you aim at willed trust.

By this different route we again contrast the intimacy of trust with a form of alienation. In intrapersonal and intrapersonal cases alike, governance through trust contrasts with an alienated relation mediated by evidence. To the worry that an emphasis on betrayal over-moralizes trust, I reply that the norms informing each relation are rational, not moral. Appreciating the rational force of the trustee's invitation to trust helps us grasp the parallel species of intimacy at stake in the intrapersonal relation. As a self-governing agent, each of us sometimes encounters Annie's predicament in Change of Heart: she fears that follow-through on her voting intention may amount to self-betrayal. In that worst-case scenario for her rational agency, as she followed through she would manifest trust in her intending self but betray that trust by not having adequately served, in the judgment that informs her intention, the needs of her acting self – as she will learn when she regrets from plan's end. You run that risk whenever you follow through on an intention: you risk betrayal by your own practical judgment. Like Annie, you can address the risk by being open to a change of heart. But every time you form an intention you are already like Annie in this respect: you are responsive to the possibility that you ought to undergo such a change of heart, and you aim to avoid that possibility. Your aim as you commit yourself looking downstream thus acknowledges not merely the psychological but also the normative force of upstream-looking self-mistrust. As you judge or intend, you thereby acknowledge the normative bearing of your capacity to trust at will.[14]

Notes

1 Self-trust has been a topic in recent epistemology (e.g. Foley 2001 and Zagzebski 2012) and in discussion of the moral value of autonomy (e.g. McLeod 2002). My angle on self-trust is different: I am interested in its role in action through time, without any specifically moral emphasis.

2 Nothing in what follows turns on any difference between trustworthiness and reliability: by "reliability" I mean the core of what would make you worthy of trust.

3 For the view that trust is constituted by a commitment (by a commitment-constituting answer to a question), see Hieronymi (2008) and McMyler (2017). For more general treatments of "commitment-constituted attitudes," see Hieronymi (2005, 2009).

4 For more on this, see Watson (2003).

5 To cover trust in testimony or advice, we can modify this to include the trustee's not being as you trust her to be (viz. reliable in relevant respects).

6 Many philosophers join me in holding that trust distinctively risks not mere disappointment but betrayal. See, e.g. Baier (1994: chapters 6–9); Holton (1994); Jones (1996, 2004); Walker (2006: chapter 3); Hieronymi (2008); McGeer (2008); McMyler (2011: chapter 4); and Hawley (2014).

7 For example, Hardin (2002: chapter 3); Nickel (2007: section 6); and Rose (2011: chapter 9).

8 I take the "stream" metaphor from Kolodny (2005: e.g. 529).

9 Bratman (1998, 2014). Though I am indebted to Bratman for the idea that projected regret is crucial to the stability of intention, in Hinchman (2010, 2015, 2016) I dissent from some details in how he develops it.

10 See note 3 above, especially Holton (1994).

11 One background issue: does your capacity to serve as a source of rationality for your future self license illicit bootstrapping, whereby you get bumped into a rational status "for free" merely by forming an intention? For developments of this worry, see Bratman (1987:23–27, 86–87); and Broome (2001). Smith (2016) offers a dissenting perspective. I treat the issue in Hinchman (2003, 2009, 2010, 2013, 2017: sections II and IV). For present purposes, it does not strictly matter how I reply to the bootstrapping challenge, both because my present argument could work in conjunction with the weaker view that we operate under an ("error-theoretic") fiction that we can give ourselves the rational status (following Kolodny 2005: section 5) and because my core claim is not that a trustworthy intention to φ gives you a reason to φ (which does look like bootstrapping) but that it (a) gives you "planning reasons" to do other things – things that you would not have sufficient reason to do if you were not trustworthy in intending to φ – and (b) more generally serves as a source of rational coherence.

12 I offer a much fuller defense of upstream reasoning (replying to the objections in Kolodny (2005), 528–539) in Hinchman (2013: section 3). The most fundamental challenge lies in explaining how it is possible for you to judge that you ought to φ while also mistrusting that judgment. If this is impossible, then reasoning must always point "downstream," since mistrusting a judgment would simply amount to abandoning it.

13 This is not precisely the question of "therapeutic trust" (see e.g. Horsburgh 1960; Holton 1994; Jones 2004; McGeer 2008). But it raises a question about whether you can *invite* therapeutic trust.

14 Thanks to Ben McMyler, Philip Nickel, and Judith Simon for stimulating comments on an earlier draft. I develop this view of intrapersonal trust more fully in Hinchman (2003, 2009, 2010, 2016). And I develop this view of interpersonal trust more fully in Hinchman (2005, 2014, 2017 and forthcoming).

References

Baier, A. (1994) *Moral Prejudices*, Cambridge, MA: Harvard University Press.

Bratman, M. (1987) *Intention, Plans, and Practical Reason*, Cambridge, MA: Harvard University Press.

Bratman, M. (1998) "Toxin, Temptation, and the Stability of Intention," reprinted in his *Faces of Intention*, Cambridge: Cambridge University Press, 1999.

Bratman, M. (2014) "Temptation and the Agent's Standpoint," *Inquiry* 57(3): 293–310.

Broome, J. (2001) "Are Intentions Reasons? And How Should We Cope with Incommensurable Values?" in C. Morris and A. Ripstein (eds.), *Practical Rationality and Preference*, Cambridge: Cambridge University Press, 98–120.

Faulkner, P. and Simpson, T. (eds.) (2017) *The Philosophy of Trust*, Oxford: Oxford University Press.

Foley, R. (2001) *Intellectual Trust in Oneself and Others*, Cambridge: Cambridge University Press.

Hardin, R. (2002) *Trust and Trustworthiness*, New York: Russell Sage Foundation.

Hawley, K. (2014) "Trust, Distrust, and Commitment," *Noûs* 48(1): 1–20.

Hieronymi, P. (2005) "The Wrong Kind of Reason," *Journal of Philosophy* 102(9): 437–457.

Hieronymi, P. (2008) "The Reasons of Trust," *Australasian Journal of Philosophy* 86(2): 213–236.

Hieronymi, P. (2009) "Controlling Attitudes," *Pacific Philosophical Quarterly* 87(1): 45–74.

Hinchman, E. (2003) "Trust and Diachronic Agency," *Noûs* 37(1): 25–51.

Hinchman, E. (2005) "Advising as Inviting to Trust," *Canadian Journal of Philosophy* 35(3): 355–386.

Hinchman, E. (2009) "Receptivity and the Will," *Noûs* 43(3): 395–427.

Hinchman, E. (2010) "Conspiracy, Commitment, and the Self," *Ethics* 120(3): 526–556.

Hinchman, E. (2013) "Rational Requirements and 'Rational' Akrasia," *Philosophical Studies* 166 (3): 529–552.

Hinchman, E. (2014) "Assurance and Warrant," *Philosophers' Imprint* 14, 1–58.

Hinchman, E. (2015) "Narrative and the Stability of Intention," *European Journal of Philosophy* 23 (1): 111–140.

Hinchman, E. (2016) "'What on Earth Was I Thinking?' How Anticipating Plan's End Places an Intention in Time," in R. Altshuler and M. Sigrist (eds), *Time and the Philosophy of Action*, New York: Routledge, 87–107.

Hinchman, E. (2017) "On the Risks of Resting Assured: An Assurance Theory of Trust," in P. Faulkner and T. Simpson (eds.), *The Philosophy of Trust*, Oxford: Oxford University Press.

Hinchman, E. (forthcoming) "Disappointed yet Unbetrayed: A New Three-Place Analysis of Trust," in K. Vallier and M. Weber (eds), *Social Trust*, New York: Routledge.

Holton, R. (1994) "Deciding to Trust, Coming to Believe," *Australasian Journal of Philosophy* 72 (1): 63–76.

Horsburgh, H.J.N. (1960) "The Ethics of Trust," *Philosophical Quarterly* 10(41): 343–354.

Jones, K. (1996) "Trust as an Affective Attitude," *Ethics* 107(1): 4–25.

Jones, K. (2004) "Trust and Terror," in P. DesAutels and M. Walker (eds), *Moral Psychology*, Lanham: Rowman & Littlefield, 3–18.

Kolodny, N. (2005) "Why Be Rational," *Mind* 114(455): 509–563.

McGeer, V. (2008) "Trust, Hope, and Empowerment," *Australasian Journal of Philosophy*, 86(2): 237–254.

McLeod, C. (2002) *Self-Trust and Reproductive Autonomy*, Cambridge: MIT Press.

McMyler, B. (2011) *Testimony, Trust, and Authority*, Oxford: Oxford University Press.

McMyler, B. (2017) "Deciding to Trust," in P. Faulkner and T. Simpson (eds.), *The Philosophy of Trust*, Oxford: Oxford University Press.

Nickel, P. (2007) "Trust and Obligation-Ascription," *Ethical Theory and Moral Practice* 10(3): 309–319.
Rose, D. (2011) *The Moral Foundation of Economic Behavior*, Oxford: Oxford University Press.
Smith, M. (2016) "One Dogma of Philosophy of Action," *Philosophical Studies* 73(8): 2249–2266.
Walker, M.U. (2006) *Moral Repair*, Cambridge: Cambridge University Press.
Watson, G.(2003) "The Work of the Will," in S. Stroud and C. Tappolet (eds.), *Weakness of Will and Practical Irrationality*, Oxford: Oxford University Press.
Zagzebski, L. (2012) *Epistemic Authority*, Oxford: Oxford University Press.

12
TRUST AND EMOTION

Bernd Lahno

"Trust" is an umbrella term (Simpson 2012:551). It refers to different phenomena in different contexts. Sometimes it simply designates an act, sometimes a reason for such an act (e.g. a belief), and sometimes a specific state of mind that is regularly associated with such acts or reasons to act. In some contexts it is used as a three place relation – "A trusts B to Φ" – in others a two place relation. For some meanings of the term, "trust" is necessarily directed at a person, whilst for others groups, institutions or even inanimate objects may be the objects of trust.

However, I am not interested in language issues here. In this chapter I will concentrate on a specific phenomenon that we refer to as trust and sometimes mark as "real" or "genuine" to emphasize its contrast to mere reliance (see Goldberg, this volume). This form of trust is – in some specifiable sense – emotional in character. I will refer to it as "genuine trust" or "trust as an emotional attitude." My reason for concentrating on this specific form of interpersonal trust is that it plays an important role in social interaction, a role which is frequently neglected (see Potter, this volume).

My argument will start with a short presentation of the opposing idea that somebody who is interested in understanding social cooperation will concentrate on a notion of trust as essentially a cognitive belief (section 12.1). From this point of view there is no significant difference between trust and mere reliance. Based on a critical discussion of this claim (section 12.2), I will then introduce a notion of *genuine trust* that clearly marks the difference (section 12.3) and specify its emotional character (section 12.4). Finally, I will argue that genuine trust in this sense is in fact crucial for our understanding of social cooperation (section 12.5).

12.1 Trust as Belief

A number of prominent scholars from all quarters of the social sciences and philosophy met at King's College, Cambridge, in the 1980s to discuss the notion of trust; the debate was shaped and motivated by the insight that social cooperation is often precarious even though individuals are well aware of its advantages (see Dimock, this volume). Thus, in the foreword to the seminal collection of essays stemming from these seminars, Diego Gambetta identifies the exploration of "... the causality of cooperation from the perspective of the belief, on which cooperation is predicated, namely *trust*" (Gambetta 1988a:ix) as a central and unifying target of the common project. Trust appears here as essentially cognitive. It is a belief that may motivate a cooperative move in a situation where this move is somehow problematic.

Contemporary studies into the problem of cooperation were strongly influenced by the analysis of dilemma games which typify situations in which individually rational decision-making mismatches with individual advantage and collective welfare (see, e.g. prominently Axelrod 1984). So it is not by coincidence that scholars with a game-theoretical background (as represented in the Gambetta Collection by Partha Dasgupta) gave a particularly sharp and clear account of trust as belief (see Tutić and Voss, this volume).

A dilemma game displays typical features of a situation in which trust may matter: At least one of the actors faces a choice that bears some risk. One of his options – the "*trusting act*" – offers some (mutually) positive prospect if others respond suitably ("cooperate") but may also result in a particular loss if they do not. However, there is another option that reduces the potential loss by foregoing some of the potential gains. Let us call a situation that displays such a characteristic a "*trust problem*." By choosing the trusting act in a trust problem an agent makes himself vulnerable to the actions of others. He may do so *because* he trusts those others.[1]

The key assumption of rational choice theory upon which game theory is grounded is: every human action is guided by specifiable aims; the human agent will choose his actions rationally in the light of these aims. In any particular choice situation, an actor may be characterized by his beliefs about the potential consequences of action and his subjective evaluation of these consequences. His choices, then, are to be understood as an attempt to maximize the expected utility representing his subjective evaluation in the light of his beliefs.

From a rational choice point of view the problem of trusting another person, thus, reduces to the problem of assessing the probability that the other will act in desired ways. This assessment may even be identified with trust. This central idea is neatly captured in the definition of trust that Gambetta formulates at the end of his volume as a purported summary of the volume's accounts (1988b:217):[2]

> [Trust] is a particular level of the subjective probability with which an agent assesses that another agent or group of agents will perform a particular action both *before* he can monitor such action (or independently of his capacity ever to be able to monitor it) *and* in a context in which it affects *his own* action.

If we keep in mind that – within rational choice theory – beliefs are generally conceptualized as probability distributions of consequences of actions or potential states of the world, this amounts to the more general thesis:

> (C) Trust is (or may be totally understood in terms of) the trustor's belief that the trusted person will respond positively to the choice of a trusting act in a trust problem.

The trouble with such an account of trust is that it seems to neglect a very familiar difference, easily recognized in common parlance, namely the difference between trust and mere reliance (see Goldberg, this volume). To rely on somebody is generally understood as acting on the expectation that the other will act in some preferred ways. If (C) is correct, trust simply coincides with reliance. But there are cases in which this does not seem to be true. A may rely on B doing Φ after threatening to hurt B severely if B fails to Φ. Burglar F may rely on policeman E not to prevent F from robbing the local bank at time t after calculating as sufficiently low the risk that E, who is the only policeman in town, will be around and ready to intervene. Both cases are clear cases of reliance and, thus, of trust in the sense of (C). But, in both cases, most people would hesitate to affirm genuine trust. Of course, the word "trust" is occasionally used in a very wide sense which hardly expresses anything more than reliance. Thus we sometimes use the word to express reliance on things: we trust a pullover to keep us warm or our car to bring us home safely. In this sense of the word, one may also say that A trusts B to Φ and that F trusts E not to interfere with his plans. However, most people would add that, despite this use of the word, these are not cases of "real" or "genuine" trust.

Standard examples may suggest that the difference is due to the demand that trusting expectations in the sense of genuine trust must be grounded in a belief that the trusted person is (in some sense) trustworthy.[3] But what does "trustworthy" mean in this context? If it simply means that the trusted person is disposed to act in a desired way, the difference vanishes again. Annette Baier argues that the motivation ascribed to the trusted person is decisive (1986:234):

> … trusting others … seems to be reliance on their good will toward one, as distinct from their dependable habits, or only on their dependably exhibited fear, anger, or other motives compatible with ill will toward one, or on other motives not directed at one at all.

The rational choice theorist may respond that this does not *really* make a difference. Thus Russell Hardin (1991:193f.) argues:

> Is there really a difference here? I rely on *you*, not just on anyone, because the experience that justifies reliance is my experience of you, not of everyone … Trust does not depend on any particular reason for the trusted's intentions, merely on credible reasons.

The general reaction is: if it is possible at all to define the difference between mere reliance and genuine trust clearly, this difference will turn out to be irrelevant. Accordingly, Phillip Nickel (2017) recently argued that discrimination between mere reliance and genuine trust is of no explanatory value. Knowing that people cooperate on genuine trust does not add anything important to our understanding of the respective cooperative endeavors. The distinction is simply irrelevant, if we are out to "explain the emergence and sustenance of cooperative practices and social institutions" (Nickel 2017:197).

I think Nickel and Hardin are mistaken. But before I argue that it does make a difference whether cooperation is based on genuine trust or mere reliance, I will first make an attempt to substantiate the alleged difference in sufficiently clear terms.

12.2 Trust and Reliance

Baier (1986:235) remarks that her definition of trust cited above is to be understood merely as a "first approximation." There are, in fact, good reasons to be cautious here. Standard cases of reliance on goodwill towards the relying person certainly exemplify genuine trust. But, as Richard Holton (1994:65) argues, reliance on goodwill towards one is neither necessary nor sufficient for trust. It is not necessary as there are clear cases of genuine trust without the trustor believing that the trusted person is motivated by goodwill towards him. A mother may entrust her baby to the neighbor for an afternoon without expecting any goodwill for the mother yet knowing that the neighbor loves her baby. Neither is it sufficient: a marriage trickster may rely on the goodwill of his victim towards him when telling her that he is temporarily in financial distress. He is relying on her naivety but one would certainly hesitate to speak of trust in this case.

Confronted with such counterexamples, one may still stick to the general idea that the difference between genuine trust and mere reliance is essentially grounded in the specific kind of motive that a trustor ascribes to the trusted person. One may simply try to adjust the relevant kind. The babysitter example suggests, for instance, that it is not goodwill towards the trustor but goodwill to any person or any person whose welfare is of some value to the trustor which is the crucial kind of motive. But there are cases of genuine trust where no goodwill or belief in goodwill is involved. I may trust in your promise because I think that you are an honest person who keeps his word. This is genuine trust even if I know that my welfare does not touch you at all.

Following an idea of Karen Jones (1996), Paul Faulkner (2007a:313) suggests that genuine (or what he calls "affective") trust is defined by the trustor's expectation that the trusted person will be motivated by the fact that the trustor is relying on him. But again this seems to be unduly restrictive. It excludes particularly all cases in which the trusted person is obviously not aware of being trusted. Assume that my 15-year-old daughter asks me to let her attend a party at night. I know it is going to be fairly wild, but I also know that her friend is a decent person who loves my daughter. He will thoroughly look after her. So I let her go. This is a simple and clear case of trust in the daughter's friend. This also remains true, if I know that my daughter will tell the friend that she secretly left home without asking for permission, or if I simply know that the friend is solely motivated by his love and care for my daughter, whether I rely on him or not.

There is a more promising candidate for the class of motives that can be the object of genuine trust. A minimal unifying element in all examples and counterexamples seems to be: the trustor expects the trusted person to act on motives that the trustor in some way or other confirms as valuable and binding. Such motives may stem from common interests or goals (e.g. in business cooperation), from shared values (as in the babysitter case) or from norms, which are understood as commonly binding (as in the case of promises). The attribution of such motives seems to be present in all cases of genuine trust, whereas one can rely on another person whatever motive one hypothesizes regarding the expected behavior.

So we seem to have a class of motives here, at least one of which is necessarily ascribed to the trusted person in every case of genuine trust while mere reliance does not require such an ascription. However, it is doubtful whether this could also serve as a sufficient condition for genuine trust. We can produce a counterexample in much the same way as in the marriage trickster example.

Assume a scientist holds the belief that people will under certain circumstances cooperate on some specific honest motive. Further assume that he considers it to be the only adequate motive under these circumstances and that a decent person should be motivated in this way. The scientist now tests his hypothesis that people will actually behave in this way on the specific motive by designing a suitable experiment. In conducting the experiment, he is relying on people acting as expected on the assumed motive; if they do not, he cannot reject his null hypothesis and his investment in the experiment will be void. It seems odd to say in such a case that he trusts in his subjects.

It is very plausible that counterexamples of the same kind can be constructed for all attempts to establish the ascription of a motive of some specific kind as a sufficient condition for genuine trust. These examples may appear as somewhat artificial. Still, they convey an important general lesson on the difference between trust and mere reliance. What goes wrong in these examples? Obviously, the problem is not grounded in the specific kind of motive ascribed. It could be any kind proposed as characteristic for genuine trust. The problem arises from how the person relied on is being treated. The marriage trickster uses his victim as a means of achieving his (wicked) aims. The scientist looks at his subject from an objective point of view just as a physicist would look at the particles in his atom smasher. Both do not really interact with their counterpart and both do not really treat them as persons in their respective specific situations. The way of treating another person observed in these examples is simply incompatible with genuine trust. If this is the core of the problem, then it is impossible to give a general characterization of genuine trust by sole reference to the beliefs of trustor and trusted. Any comprehensive and general attempt to define genuine trust as a special sort of reliance must at least in part refer to the way people treat each other when trusting, how they relate to each other, how they perceive each other when choosing how to act.

A further argument points in the same direction. Assume a good friend is suspected of having committed some crime. There is, for instance, substantial evidence that he embezzled a considerable amount of money. You know all the evidence against your friend just as well as everybody else does. The friend affirms his innocence to you. Of course, the others know that he denies the offense, too. But, in contrast to them, you trust him. Why?

First, you know him better than all the others do. So you may have specific information not available to others which absolves your friend. As far as this is the case, your trust is due to your specific cognitive state. But assume further that the evidence against your friend is truly overwhelming. What will you do? Most likely you will ask yourself how this strong evidence against your friend came about. You will try somehow to overcome the dissonances between the character of your friend as you know him and the picture that the evidence seems to suggest. You will be looking for explanations of the evidence that are consistent with your friend's innocence. You do not just evaluate the given evidence in some objective and indifferent way. The special relationship that connects you and your friend will rather motivate you to see the given information in a certain light and question it critically. This particular form of genuine trust cannot be understood as the result of a purely cognitive process. It is not based on an uninvolved evaluation of information by calculating what will most probably happen or actually did most probably happen. It is rather a particular way of asking questions as well as thinking about and evaluating information (Govier 1993; 1994). Your expectations are a consequence of your trust rather than vice versa.[4] Trust presents itself as something deeper than belief. It appears as a mechanism that transforms information into belief.

12.3 Trust as an Attitude

If the argument in the last section is sound, genuine trust is best understood as a complex attitude rather than a certain belief about the trusted person. Discussion in the previous section also indicates what the essential elements of this attitude are.

The first essential element of genuine trust is that we treat the trustee as a person. The marriage trickster and the scientist above are not said to trust genuinely because this condition is violated. Referring to a distinction by Peter Strawson (1974),[5] Richard Holton (1994:66f.) specifies this condition by pointing to the particular emotional dispositions that a trusting person exhibits:

> In cases where we trust and are let down, we do not just feel disappointed, as we would if a machine let us down ... We feel betrayed ... betrayal is one of those attitudes that Strawson calls reactive attitudes ... I think that the difference between trust and reliance is that trust involves something like a participant stance towards the person you are trusting.

In adopting a participant attitude or, as Holton calls it, a "participant stance" towards another person we perceive ourselves and the other as mutually involved in *inter*action. Individual acts are perceived as essentially interrelated. A participant attitude is characterized by the disposition to react to the actions of another person with "reactive attitudes," emotions that are directed at the other person, such as hate, resentment or gratitude. In having such emotional dispositions the other is treated as the author of his acts, as somebody who is responsible and can, therefore, be held responsible. This points to another peculiarity of genuine trust. Trusting expectations based on genuine trust are as a rule normative; we do not just expect the trusted person to behave in a certain favored way; we also feel that he *should* act in this particular way.[6]

In contrast, adopting an "objective attitude" in the sense of Strawson means perceiving another person from a more distanced point of view, as an observer rather than as directly involved, just as we perceive a mechanism governed by natural laws. Nevertheless, guided by an objective attitude, we may make predictions about the behavior of others. It seems inappropriate, however, to make normative demands.

Normative expectations require a normative base. Discussion in the last section suggests that common interests, shared aims, values or norms form such a normative base. This is the second essential element of an attitude of genuine trust, which I will refer to as '*connectedness*': when trusting, the trustor perceives the trusted person as somebody whose actions in the given context are guided by common interests, by shared aims or by values and norms which the trustor himself takes to be authoritative.

This definition of the potential normative ground of trust covers cases of trust in close relationships. But it is wide enough also to cover cases of trust between people that are not connected by personal bonds as, for instance, in business when one partner trusts the word of another because there is a shared understanding that contracts should be kept. In any case, connectedness adds an element of person-specificity[7] to trust. A participant stance implies relating to the other as a person. Connectedness adds that the trusted person is perceived as someone specifically related to oneself by a common normative ground of action.

Because of examples such as that with the scientist above (Section 12.2: 150f), I take it that connectedness is best construed as an attitude toward – a way to perceive – the trusted person, and not as a mere cognitive belief about the person's motivation. However, as I will discuss in more detail below, connectedness and trusting beliefs are causally related. My perception of another person will be affected by my beliefs about that person and, conversely, my beliefs about a person will, at least in part, be formed by my perception of that person. Because the normative base is perceived as a common ground of interaction, it motivates typical normative expectations and rationalizes reactive attitudes connected with trust.

To conclude, I think that genuine trust can be characterized as follows:

> Genuine trust toward a person includes a participant attitude and a feeling of connectedness to him or her grounded in shared aims, values or norms. This attitude typically generates normative expectations. It allows the trusting person to incur risks concerning the actions of the trusted person, because this person is perceived as being guided by the shared goals, values or norms which are assumed to connect the two.

12.4 The Emotional Character of Trust

Considerable disagreement exists among scholars about what an emotion actually is.[8] It seems wise, therefore, to be cautious about the general claim that trust *is* an emotion. My modest aim here is to argue that genuine trust is essentially identified by features that we generally find characteristic of emotions. These characteristic properties of genuine trust form the "emotional character of trust"; combined they justify calling trust an "emotional attitude."

The structure of my argument owes much to Karen Jones' account of "Trust as an Affective Attitude" (1996). Although I disagree with Jones about the substantial question of what the characteristic features of trust are, I think she is perfectly right in the way she determines their emotional (or, as she says, "affective") character. Referring to an account of emotion she ascribes to Amélie Rorty, Cheshire Calhoun and Ronald de Sousa, Jones argues (1996:11):

> … emotions are partly constituted by patterns of salience and tendencies of interpretation. An emotion suggests a particular line of inquiry and makes some beliefs seem compelling and others not, on account of the way the emotion gets us to focus on a partial field of evidence. Emotions are thus not primarily beliefs, although they do tend to give rise to beliefs; instead they are distinctive ways of seeing a situation.

The idea that a characteristic feature of emotions is that they determine how we perceive the world or some part of it has a prominent history. In his Rhetoric, Aristotle defines emotions in the following way (Rhetoric 1378a):

> Emotions are all those feelings that so change men as to affect their judgments and that are also attended by pain and pleasure.

According to this definition emotions are not characterized as a specific kind of mental state or episode. Their crucial characteristic is rather their specific function in organizing and structuring conscious life. Lovers, it is said, see the world through rose-tinted glasses. This illustrates the point quite well: Emotions are like glasses through which we perceive the world. Three different ways in which an emotional state of mind may shape our thought may be discriminated (see Lahno 2001:175):

1 Emotions determine how we perceive the world in a direct manner. They do so by giving us a certain perspective on the world. They guide our attention by making some things appear more salient than others.
2 Emotions determine how we think and what judgments we make on matters of fact. That is not to say that an emotion necessarily annuls reason. Instead, it directs reason by stimulating certain associations and suggesting certain patterns of interpretation.
3 Emotions help us to evaluate some aspects of the world and motivate our actions.

Obviously connectedness, as defined above, together with a participant attitude determine how we perceive a trusted person, the interaction with this person, and most of those aspects of the world which form the significant determinants of this interaction. Thus, genuine trust guides our thought just like emotions characteristically do. This is the core of the emotional character of trust and justifies its being called an "emotional attitude."

That genuine trust is an emotional attitude in this sense, determines its relation to belief and judgment. On the one hand, the way we perceive the world is to some extent a consequence of our cognitive state: our antecedent beliefs, judgments and prejudices which make us ask certain questions will, just as the general framework of our understanding, inevitably pre-structure our perceptions. On the other hand, we find that the picture of the world which we immediately perceive is a major source of our beliefs. Because of this causal interdependence between emotional attitude and cognitive state, genuine trust is regularly associated with certain beliefs. But trust should not be identified with these beliefs. Compared with belief and judgment genuine trust appears as relatively independent of reflection and rational argument. A perception delivers some content of thought quite directly and unmediated by reflection. In as far as trust immediately determines how the world is represented in thought and in as far as it invokes certain thought patterns, it takes precedence over thought. It forms a frame for rational considerations and is a base of reasoning rather than its result.

The sense perception analogy is instructive here. Most processes of perception are, in fact, closely associated with judgments. We see an object usually "as real" without becoming consciously aware of it; a sense perception is usually tied to a spontaneous judgment that there actually is such a thing as the object perceived. But the act of assent which is crucial to the judgment can – at least conceptually – be held apart from the mere "passive" perception. Something similar applies to trust according to the argument above. Trust makes the trusted person and a potential interaction with this person appear in a certain light. This happens to the trustor, it is not something he intentionally provokes. The picture presented to the trustor demands and actually elicits assent to corresponding claims about the world under normal circumstances. But it does not already contain the assent. There is certainly a logical relation between the picture presented by trust and the trusting beliefs usually associated with trust: The picture is to be such that it evokes the corresponding beliefs *under normal circumstances.*

If this argument is sound, then it is at least in principle possible that a trustor may perceive the trusted person as connected to himself by the relevant normative ground for the situation at hand while not actually believing that the other will be guided to act in the appropriate way. One may perceive a spider as threatening while knowing very well that it is not dangerous at all. Just like irrational fear, trust is conceivable without the typical cognitive trusting expectations. I do in fact think that this is not just a logical possibility. But I will not argue for this further-going claim here.[9]

12.5 Does It Matter?

Proponents of a cognitive account of trust as represented by Nickel and Hardin do not claim that trust is never associated with typical emotions. The claim is that emotional aspects of trust – if they exist – are inessential for our understanding of trustful cooperation. All we need to know to understand why person A is willing to make himself vulnerable to the actions of person B, is what A thinks about the relevant options and motives of B. The example of the accused friend above indicates what is wrong with this argument. The argument presupposes that the relevant beliefs of the trustor can be determined independently of his emotional states. But the friend example shows that this is not true. What the trustor believes is crucially dependent on how he perceives the trusted person and the situation at hand: it is to do with how he filters, structures and processes the information given to him. To understand why the trustor considers the trusted person trustworthy, we have to know what the world looks like through the eyes of the trustor, i.e. we have to know his emotional attitude.

That trustful interaction depends on the emotional makeup and states of the interacting individuals is well reflected in the social and behavioral sciences literature on trust (see Cook and Santana as well as Clément, both this volume). There is, for instance, an extensive body of studies showing how emotional states crucially influence trusting decisions.[10] Empirical research in management and organizational science proves that the extent and quality of cooperative relations within and between organizations depend on the existence of a suitable normative basis.[11] I cannot adequately discuss even a small representative part of all relevant research here. Instead I will point to some very common phenomena that illustrate the relevance of genuine trust for our understanding of social cooperation.

Consider market exchange (see Cohen, this volume). Many things that we buy are complex products, the technical details of which are hardly comprehensible for the ordinary consumer. They are produced in extremely complex processes comprising contributions from numerous firms many of which remain unknown to us. The amount of substantial information that we possess on the products we buy and the people who sell these products is often extremely small as compared with the information that the sellers possess. Our information will, in particular, not suffice to substantiate a rational assessment of risks involved in buying the product. A complex world inevitably produces such serious information asymmetries. In contrast to what Hardin and Nickel may suggest, there is no unique, simple and straight route along which to proceed to a person's beliefs following from the information he is given. Thus, it becomes crucial to know how people actually proceed if confronted with certain risks. Knowledge on trust as an emotional attitude is of this kind and successful actors in the market obviously have such knowledge.

Professional product promotion indicates this convincingly. Commercial advertising aims at creating an image that motivates consumers to identify with the product and/or producer. If banks or insurance companies seek trust, they do not extensively inform on their successes or virtues. They may instead – accentuated by calm and relaxing music – show a man standing on a rock in the stormy sea serenely facing the strong swell. Or they show friendly advisers who care for all the concerns of their customers, including private ones, and who are likable people like you and me. Cars are seldom promoted by announcing bare technical information. As a rule, a particular attitude to life is conveyed, often picking up the childlike (or even childish) dreams of a standard male customer. Such advertising hardly conveys substantial information on the product or producer that may help in the estimation of risks; it is rather an attempt to take up the interests and values of the potential customer within an invitation to see product and producer in a certain light.

Similar considerations apply to politics in representative democracies – another complex context in which the information available is for most of us utterly insufficient to assess the risks involved (Becker 1996).[12] The consequences are as familiar as they might seem questionable. Politicians present themselves as caring parents and good spouses. We learn on television how they approach their fellow citizens with a friendly smile on their face, how they rock innocent babies in their arms with loving care, or how they become enthusiastic about their soccer team. All this is carefully arranged for us. The message is clear: here is a person who can be trusted, someone like you, leading a good life based on principles that are worthy to be shared.

Many aspects of trusting interaction are very familiar to us but would seem pretty strange if trust was just the trustor's cognitive state. One such aspect is that often neither a thought about risk nor any explicit thought about trust comes to the mind of the trustor. If I put my money on the counter of the bakery, I am hardly aware of any risk, although my payment is often provided in advance and there is no guarantee that my performance be responded in the way I desire. Will I actually receive the baked goods? Will all the rolls that I paid for be in the paper bag? Will they be of high quality as promised? Will the change be correct? Is the price of the rolls fair? No customer will actually consider such questions. Of course, in the background, it is in the well-considered self-interest of a prudent baker to be fair and honest with his customers. But the customer will not consciously consider this either. In fact, the smoothness of the transaction indicates its emotional basis. The emotional character of this transaction appears not in some more or less intense feeling of the individuals involved, but in their view of the situation being structured by certain normative patterns. If these patterns are sufficiently strong and attuned to one another, a smooth course of interaction is ensured. Perception of the situation, then, is already sufficient and there is no need for further cognitive processing to respond adequately.

Another well-known peculiarity of trust is its characteristic tendency to resist conflicting evidence (Baker 1987; Jones 1996; Faulkner 2007b), resulting in its relative stability. The theory of trust as an emotional attitude easily explains this quality that obviously conflicts with the idea that trust is nothing but belief based on the information given to the trustor. As the example of the indicted friend again illustrates, trust is a biased mechanism for the transformation of information into belief: it works as a filter which hides certain information from the attention of a trustor, it suggests certain favorable interpretation strategies and it guides the mind in integrating new pieces of information into a consistent positive outlook onto the interaction with the trusted partner. The same considerations show why trust, once destroyed, is so hard to recover. Disrupting the mechanism of information processing characteristic for trust will inevitably result in the search for new ways of orientation. The former trustor will see the world through a different pair of glasses; he will sort, structure and process information in a different way. What was perceived as consistent with or evidence of a positive outlook onto the potential interaction may now appear as pointing to the opposite. Moreover, the general fabric of our emotional constitution and the character of the reactive attitudes associated with trust suggest that in many cases the new pair of glasses will be one of mistrust (see D'Cruz, this volume). This pair of glasses will produce the same kind of relative stability and resistance against conflicting evidence that the trust glasses produce for the same kind of reasons.

The notion of genuine trust as an emotional attitude is not just important for our theoretical understanding of trust. It is of direct practical relevance for personal life as well as for the design of our social institutions (see Alfano and Huijts, this volume). Consider institutional design. If we want to encourage social cooperation based on trust, we should take care that those who take the risk are neither too often nor too severely hurt. Some amount of control will almost always be necessary. Suitable sanctioning mechanisms may directly shape the incentives to act in trustworthy ways. Moreover, if the relevant information about others is made available this will encourage appropriate trusting decisions and simultaneously indirectly produce incentives for trustworthy behavior by enhancing the value of a good reputation (see Origgi, this volume).

Note that such measures of control by positive or negative sanctions and by making information on others' conduct accessible are perfectly consistent with understanding trust as a rational belief. Their target is essentially the objective reduction of risk. But the ability to reduce or even eliminate risk is often substantially limited. Genuine trust is a mechanism for coping with uncertainty in those cases where a pure cognitive management of uncertainty is impossible or exceedingly costly. As I argued, an essential precondition for such genuine trust is that individuals share a normative understanding of the demands they face in their cooperative endeavors. Social institutions that build on trust should, therefore, be designed to foster the experience of a common normative ground and the emergence of connectedness.

In the ideal case measures of control and measures that promote a common normative ground of trustful cooperation will complement each other. But it is important to see, that they may also conflict. An inappropriately designed sanctioning mechanism may well tend to destroy the normative basis of trust. Consider a working team which is collectively devoted to optimally accomplishing the team's goal. Every team member is doing her best and she is doing so in part, because she trusts that others will proceed in the same way. Imagine, now, that the management – for reasons that the team members do not know – announces henceforth to control the compliance of each team member meticulously and to sanction severely all behavior which they find defective. It is easy to imagine how the management's initiative may thwart their very intention. There is, in fact, a rich body of empirical evidence that inadequate control may well "crowd out" desired behavior.[13]

The theory of trust as an emotional attitude explains how and when control may crowd out trust. Control may signal that individuals cannot without reserve count on intrinsically motivated trustworthiness. And so it may tend to destroy the idea that cooperation is motivated by a shared normative basis.

Not all social cooperation is desirable. The world would, for instance, be better without cooperation between officials in charge of awarding public contracts and those who apply for these contracts. But, after all, human society is a cooperative endeavor that cannot exist without some genuine trust among its members. Whoever wants to encourage genuine trust is facing a difficult task. On the one side he must give room for the emergence and maintenance of individual virtue, whilst on the other he must set constraints against human action to protect virtue from exploitation. But the latter measure may cast doubt on the effectiveness of virtue. There are obviously no simple general rules to solve this problem. But a solid understanding of genuine trust's role in social cooperation seems indispensable to approach a solution in the individual case.

Related Topics

In this volume:

Trust and Belief
Trust and Cooperation
Trust and Distrust in Institutions and Governance
Trust and Game Theory
Trust and Leap of Faith
Trust and Mistrust
Trust and Reliance
Trust and Trustworthiness
Trust in Economy
Trustworthiness, Accountability and Intelligent Trust

Notes

1 Note that "trusting act" was introduced here as a technical term representing any option with the defining risk characteristic. It is perfectly consistent with the definition, that a trusting act is chosen on other grounds than trust or without any trust at all. Thus, a trust problem may, in principle, be "solved" without any trust being involved.
2 It is doubtful that all authors of the collection would in fact support such a radical cognitive account.
3 See also Naomi Scheman, this volume, and Onora O'Neill, this volume.
4 See Hertzberg (1988:313ff.) for a radical version of this insight.
5 Strawson introduced the distinction in a different context. He was trying to make sense of the concept of free will.
6 This is obviously the motive behind the "obligation-ascription" account of trust in Nickel (2007).
7 Paul Faulkner drew my attention to the fact that interpersonal trust is essentially person specific.
8 See de Sousa (2014) for a recent overview.
9 See Lahno (2002:214) for an example.
10 A seminal paper in this field is Dunn and Schweitzer (2005); a recent publication that also gives a short overview on the debate is Myers and Tingley (2016).
11 Some references can be found in Lahno (2002:186).
12 In some cases it is not only difficult or contingently impossible (given the cognitive limitations of human actors) but impossible to assess a risk of being let down on the basis of the available information. A common characteristic of such cases is that there is some demand for mutual trust as, e.g. when I must trust you to trust me and vice versa in a common enterprise. The risk of trust being betrayed then depends on the extent to which actors trust each other. As a consequence there may be no information independent of trust to rationalize trust. Paradigmatic cases are simple coordination problems. For a simple example and a deeper theoretical analysis see Lahno (2004:41f.)
13 See Frey and Jegen (2001) for a general overview.

References

Aristotle (1984) "Rhetoric," in J. Barnes (ed.), *The Complete Works of Aristotle*, Vol. 2, Princeton, NJ: Princeton University Press.

Axelrod, R. (1984) *The Evolution of Cooperation*, New York: Basic Books.

Baker, J. (1987) "Trust and Rationality," *Pacific Philosophical Quarterly* 68: 1–13.

Baier, A. (1986) "Trust and Antitrust," *Ethics* 96: 231–260.

Becker, L.C. (1996) "Trust as Noncognitive Security about Motives," *Ethics* 107: 43–61.

Dasgupta, P. (1988) "Trust as a Commodity," in D. Gambetta (ed.), *Trust: Making and Breaking Cooperative Relations*, Oxford: Basil Blackwell.
de Sousa, R. (2014) "Emotion," in E.Z. Zalta (ed.), *Stanford Encyclopedia of Philosophy*, Stanford, CA: Stanford University Press. http://plato.stanford.edu/archives/spr2014/entries/emotion/
Dunn, J.R. and Schweitzer, M.E. (2005) "Feeling and Believing: The Influence of Emotion on Trust," *Journal of Personality and Social Psychology* 88(5): 736–748.
Faulkner, P. (2007a) "A Genealogy of Trust," *Episteme* 4(3): 305–321.
Faulkner, P. (2007b) "On Telling and Trusting," *Mind* 116: 875–902.
Faulkner, P. and Simpson, T. (eds.) (2017) *The Philosophy of Trust*, Oxford: Oxford University Press.
Frey, B.S. and Jegen, R. (2001) "Motivation Crowding Theory," *Journal of Economic Surveys* 15(5): 589–611.
Gambetta, D. (ed.) (1988a) *Trust: Making and Breaking Cooperative Relations*, Oxford: Basil Blackwell.
Gambetta, D. (1988b) "Can We Trust Trust?" in D. Gambetta (ed.), *Trust: Making and Breaking Cooperative Relations*, Oxford: Basil Blackwell.
Govier, T. (1993) "An Epistemology of Trust," *International Journal of Moral and Social Studies* 8 (2): 155–174.
Govier, T. (1994) "Is it a Jungle Out There? Trust, Distrust and the Construction of Social Reality," *Dialogue* 33(2): 237–252.
Hardin, R. (1991) "Trusting Persons, Trusting Institutions," in R. Zeckhauser (ed.), *The Strategy of Choice*, Cambridge, MA: MIT Press.
Hertzberg, L. (1988) "On the Attitude of Trust," *Inquiry* 31: 307–322.
Holton, R. (1994) "Deciding to Trust, Coming to Believe," *Australasian Journal of Philosophy* 72 (1): 63–76.
Jones, K. (1996) "Trust as an Affective Attitude," *Ethics* 107: 4–25.
Lahno, B. (2001) "On the Emotional Character of Trust," *Ethical Theory and Moral Practice* 4: 171–189.
Lahno, B. (2002) *Der Begriff des Vertrauens*, München: mentis.
Lahno, B. (2004) "Three Aspects of Interpersonal Trust," *Analyse & Kritik* 26: 30–47.
Myers, C.D. and Tingley, D. (2016) "The Influence of Emotion on Trust," *Political Analysis* 24: 492–500.
Nickel, P.J. (2007) "Trust and Obligation-Ascription," *Ethical Theory and Moral Practice* 10: 309–319.
Nickel, P.J. (2017) "Being Pragmatic about Trust," in F. Faulkner and T. Simpson (eds.), *The Philosophy of Trust*, Oxford: Oxford University Press.
Simpson, T. (2012) "What is Trust?" *Pacific Philosophical Quarterly* 93: 550–569.
Strawson, P.F. (1974) *Freedom and Resentment*, London: Methuen.

Further Reading

Hardin, R. (1992) "The Street-Level Epistemology of Trust," *Analyse und Kritik* 14: 152–176. www.degruyter.com/downloadpdf/j/auk.1992.14.issue-2/auk-1992-0204/auk-1992-0204.pdf (A very clear, accessible and informal Rational Choice account of trust.)
Lahno, B. (2017) "Trust and Collective Agency," in F. Faulkner and T. Simpson (eds.), *The Philosophy of Trust*, Oxford: Oxford University Press. (An application of the theory of trust as an emotional attitude to joint action. Includes an analysis of coordination problems, in which no information to assess the risk of being left alone is in principle accessible; see FN10.)

13
TRUST AND COOPERATION

Susan Dimock

13.1 Introduction

My topic is one on which I have wanted to write for some time: the role of trust in social cooperation. I hope to establish, first, that cooperation is often rational (even in some surprising circumstances) and, second, that trust (trusting and being trustworthy) is essential to cooperation in those same circumstances. The reasons for these connections are not coincidental. Given that the degree to which I trust you influences my willingness to cooperate with you in various circumstances, one way to increase opportunities for cooperation is to increase trust in society. Given the innumerable rewards of cooperation (see, for example, the chapters by Cook and Santana, and Tutić and Voss), that something is conducive to or supportive of cooperation seems prima facie a good thing; the converse is true for anything that makes cooperation less likely or more difficult to achieve. If trust is a cooperation-enabling resource, it is an important kind of social capital in communities. We have reason to want trust to flourish generally as well as to be members in good standing of many trust networks and relationships. Yet we should not want to increase trust *simpliciter*, since trust can be irrational, imprudent and immoral; we surely want to encourage only sensible trust (see O'Neill, this volume). Of course, the same can be said about cooperation.

Although I do not offer a complete theory of trust, my account of trust includes a number of familiar elements. First, trust is a five-place predicate: a complete theory of trust will analyze all five variables in "P trusts Q with *x* in circumstances C for reason (s) R."[1] I will hereafter refer to the person who trusts (the trustor) as P and the person who is trusted (the trustee) as Q. Second, trusting Q involves confidence that Q will do as he ought or is expected to do. Confidence can be interpreted cognitively (P must *believe* Q will do as trusted, at least to some degree) or non-cognitively (P has some optimistic *feeling* or *disposition* towards Q). Third, trust is typically limited in scope, ranging over a more or less determinate range of things. Fourth, trust has these features because it operates as a second-order reason. Fifth, we can trust only entities with wills (e.g., most natural persons and some animals) or the capacity to act intentionally (e.g., legal persons and collectives like Walmart, Congress and Major League Baseball). We cannot literally trust infants, natural forces or inanimate objects. I trust my dog not to eat my laptop while I am away but I do not trust (or distrust) my laptop with anything at all. Sixth, relatedly, P must believe Q can influence or affect what happens to *x*. Trusting involves risking that the trust will not be fulfilled. Seventh, thus trusting always and necessarily leaves us vulnerable to a certain kind of harm – the betrayal of our trusting expectations – in addition to any vulnerability to P that might have been contingently created by the trust (like P's being stranded in an unsafe environment because Q forgot to pick her up as agreed). Eighth, to be trustworthy, Q must be competent to execute the trust in various circumstances and to trust, P must believe in Q's competence. Finally, we appropriately feel a range of attitudes, emotions and dispositions towards those we trust or distrust (e.g., confidence, optimism, wariness, suspicion), and Strawsonian reactive emotions to violations of trust (e.g. resentment,

You			
Me		You Cooperate	You Defects
	I Cooperate	2,2 Second best for both	4,1 Worst for Me, Best for You
	I Defect	1,4 Best for Me, Worst for You	3,3 Third best for both

betrayal, feeling wronged and not merely harmed or disappointed).[2]

Such trust is necessary to support valuable cooperative activities in many common social circumstances. Cooperation enables divisions of labor, specialization and an infinite range of productive and recreational activities. Cooperation enables the preservation and dissemination of the accumulated knowledge of past generations and the creation of new knowledge (see Miller and Freiman as well as Rolin, this volume). It is only through cooperative activities that human beings are able to transcend their substantial individual limitations and create the conditions under which their needs are met and desires satisfied. Conversely, Hobbes was surely correct in saying that, in a world without cooperation, the lives of all would be "solitary, poor, nasty, brutish, and short."[3] Cooperation requires trust, however, which the dominant theory of rationality condemns as irrational. Vindicating trust and the cooperation it enables against traditional rational choice theory (TRCT), i.e. the theory of rationality as utility maximization, is thus a major objective in this chapter.

13.2 Rational Deliberation

Should we cooperate, on this specific occasion? Should we be generally cooperative? Should we trust, on this specific occasion? Should we be generally trusting or trustworthy? These are questions directed to our practical reason, questions we can answer only because we are creatures capable of temporally extended rational deliberation. Rational deliberation is the process by which individuals consider what they should do, what they have most reason to do. It can be agent relative (what should I do?) or general (what should be done?). In deciding what to do, persons are guided by their valuations of the options they face. Such valuations and deliberation on them are inescapably first personal, though they need not be egoistic or self-interested in any substantive sense. I assume with David Gauthier that in a free society individuals' valuations will vary, with value plurality resulting (Gauthier 2016). Constructivists like Gauthier and I do not presume that individuals share any substantive values or agree on a conception of the common good.

Practical deliberation about what to do involves comparing possible alternatives and ends with the decision to choose one of them. Rationality enjoins us to choose in ways that are sensible, given our values, commitments, goals, plans, relationships and circumstances. What makes sense to do is what will help agents advance their interests, achieve their goals, realize their values, honor their commitments, etc. Rational deliberation will recommend courses of action that are expected to lead to the deliberator's life going as well as possible, given her valuations. "That one's life goes as well as possible" is a purely formal end, not a substantive goal or value that everyone shares. It is nonetheless important because we should surely insist that acting rationally is expected to be better for us than would be acting irrationally. Why else should we be rational (I ask, non-rhetorically)? If being rational was expected to makes our lives go less well than they might otherwise have gone we would be hard pressed to explain why rationality is authoritative (something to which we ought to conform).

Cooperation and trust both require that we accept specific limits on our deliberative autonomy because we must consider as live options only those things that are compatible with the cooperative or trust relations in which we stand. We impose these limits by exercising our capacity for temporally extended deliberation: planning complex courses of action over time and making commitments and decisions now that are reasons giving in the future. Any acceptable theory of rational deliberation must render sensible advice concerning when to cooperate and when to trust or act in trustworthy ways.

Two thought experiments are important in contemporary thinking about rationality: the single-play simultaneous-choice Prisoner's Dilemma (PD) and its temporally extended variant called Farmers. Although when technically presented the PD seems quite artificial, the situations modeled by various PDs are actually very common.[4] They reveal a recurring problem facing individuals and groups who want to interact in cooperative ways in "the circumstances of justice."[5]

13.2.1 The Prisoner's Dilemma

Imagine that you and I are partners in crime. We committed a serious crime (say, breaking and entering a dwelling place intending to maim its owner) and are now detained by police. Before committing the crime, we mutually promised to keep quiet, not to confess to anything or inform on the other, should we be arrested. We so agreed, not because we care about each other, our relationship or reputation; all either of us cares about is minimizing our own jail time. Now imagine the prosecutor comes to you and says:

> We have enough evidence that I'm pretty sure I will be able to convict you and your partner of crime C (break and enter of a dwelling place). I believe you committed the much more serious crime C+ (break and enter of a dwelling place with the intent to commit an indictable offence/felony therein), but intent's hard to prove and I'm not sure I'd win on the more serious charge. If I could prove C+ you would both serve six years, but I'm not sure I can. So here's what I'll do: if you confess and 'rat out' your partner (give evidence that your partner committed the more serious crime C+), and he keeps quiet, then

> he will bear full responsibility for the crime and be sentenced to eight years in prison, while your cooperation will be rewarded. Your reward is that I will prosecute you only for C, and seek a penalty of just one year in jail. (One year of imprisonment is a real deal, since the standard penalty for simple break and enter imposed against non-cooperative accused at trial is three years). Of course, if your partner confesses and rats you out and you keep quiet then you will suffer the full penalty for C+ and do eight years, while he will be rewarded with the one-year sentence.

The prosecutor has made the same offer to me and is giving us a few minutes to think it over.

Here the one-play PD is represented as a *preference* matrix, in which the possible outcomes are ranked from most preferred or best (1) to least preferred or worst (4).[6] We each must decide whether to cooperate or defect, where "cooperating" means keeping one's agreement while "defecting" means violating it.

Cooperate-cooperate (2,2) is available and second best for both of us, but if we each follow the advice of Traditional Rational Choice Theory (TRCT) we will both defect, thereby realizing (3,3) which is worse for both of us. The cells (4,1) and (1,4) represent outcomes where one of us cooperates and the other defects from our agreement, known colloquially as the "sucker" and "be suckered" outcomes; one of us suckering the other is the only way either of us can achieve our highest ranked outcome, but doing so condemns the other to their worst outcome.

13.2.2 Farmers

Imagine now that we own adjoining farms, and the only thing either of us cares about in this interaction is our crop: the more we harvest the better. Further suppose that, by happenstance, we planted different crops with harvest times a week apart. Good news! We both have bumper crops, producing significantly greater yields than expected or typical. Indeed, there's so much that neither of us will be able to harvest all of our own crops before they rot in our fields, their value lost. But if we work together, we can harvest all of both crops. Suppose, finally, that the cost to me in terms of helping you harvest your crop is less than the benefit I derive from your help harvesting mine, and the same is true for you. In these conditions, I prefer {your assistance with my crop even at the expense of having to help you with yours} to the outcome {no help is given, I harvest alone and value is lost}. Of course I prefer even more {I get your assistance with my crop but then do not return it by helping you}; this is the outcome (1,4) that results if you help me but I then do not help you. In such circumstances it seemingly makes sense for us to commit to providing mutual assistance and to keep that commitment. Yet TRCT says we cannot rationally agree to provide such aid, and that we are condemned to harvest alone, with the resulting loss of crops to each.

Cooperation is both possible and necessary if we are to realize all the benefits available. Yet TRCT denies that we can cooperate because the person who performs second must act counter-preferentially. Even if I help you this week, you will not want to help me next week; after all, you have already secured the benefit of agreeing to provide mutual aid (you got my help). You will have no reason to help me later. But if that is true then you cannot sincerely *commit* to helping me or *agree* to help because you cannot commit to doing something you believe you will have no reason to do. And I (the first farmer) know all of this; I know that if I help you first, you will have no reason to reciprocate (despite having agreed to do so). TRCT says it is never rational to choose counter-preferentially, and one's preferences are determined at the time of choice. Next week when you must choose whether to return my help you will have no reason to reciprocate. If I believe you will be rational next week, I cannot expect you will then help me and so I do not help you this week. We bring about the no-assistance outcome even though the mutual assistance option was available and preferred by both of us. For this reason the PD and Farmers are characterized by TRCT as "non-cooperative" games, games in which cooperation is never rational.[7]

13.3 Traditional Rational Choice Theory

TRCT advises agents to choose so as to bring about the most preferred outcome available to them at the time of choice. Utility is a measure of preference over those outcomes realizable in choice. TRCT says that rational agents will choose so as to maximize their utility. Utility maximization is the dominant theory of rationality in many fields. It is used to evaluate not only individual ("parametric") choices, in which the environment is treated as fixed and the only thing that determines which outcome results is the individual's choice, but also "strategic" choices made when interacting with at least one other intentional agent and in which the outcome that results is determined by the combined choices of all. Choosing between an apple and a banana from a bowl of fruit is a parametric choice: you should choose whichever fruit you most prefer, thus realizing an outcome (you eat an apple) that you prefer to the other options you faced (eating a banana or nothing). Choice in the PD or Farmers is strategic, because which outcome results (how much time we each spend in jail, whether we harvest all of our crops or only some of them) is the product of our combined choices.

Despite its dominance, TRCT's advice – maximize your utility as the measure of your preferences over outcomes at the time of choice – is inadequate for both parametric and strategic choice. TRCT is too restrictive to give acceptable recommendations. First, it confines preferences to ranking only *outcomes of possible choices*, states of affairs realizable by the choice of the individual. But we value significantly more than just outcomes immediately open to us – including possible strategies for choice, dispositions, character traits and virtues, as well as future-oriented plans and commitments – and those valuations should play a role in our subsequent deliberation and choices. The fact that we are planning creatures also drives us irresistibly toward a broader understanding of rational deliberation, one that asks not only "what to choose now" but also "what to intend now" and "what to do in the future and over time." We need a temporally extended understanding of rational deliberation.

Consider, for example, the importance of plans in our practical lives.[8] Plans are temporally extended commitments requiring the adoption of intentions to make future choices as required by the plan. Imagine I have accepted an invitation to present a paper at a conference on practical rationality in Ireland next spring. I am thereafter *required* to adopt other intentions and make other choices that support that plan: I must intend to register for the conference, book a hotel room and flights to and from Ireland, arrange to have my cat fed while I am away, renew my passport, and much else. I must also avoid making other plans, commitments or choices that are incompatible with me attending the conference. Executing plans requires that one does certain things, often in a certain order, and does not do others. Such plan-based requirements must be given weight in one's practical deliberations.

When executing a plan, one takes one's reasons for action from the plan rather than reasoning *de novo* at every choice point by evaluating the outcomes available at that time (as TRCT recommends). What might have been highly valued options prior to adopting one's plan can no longer be treated as eligible for choice. Suppose I would have preferred going to Rio de Janeiro over Dublin if I had had that choice and that, after I accepted the invitation to Ireland, I was invited to Brazil. That I would have accepted this invitation had it been issued prior to my agreeing to go to Ireland does not settle the question of whether I should accept it when it is offered (i.e., after I have accepted the Ireland invitation). Because I am now embarked on a plan to present work in Ireland, which is incompatible with accepting the invitation to Rio, I should (with suppressed caveats) take my reasons from my plan (i.e., my commitment) and send regrets to my Brazilian colleagues. Refusing the invitation to Brazil is contrary to my preferences between Dublin and Rio (it is counter-preferential at the time of choice considered in isolation) but it is nonetheless the choice I should make so long as the commitment to go to Ireland (which I make when I accept their invitation and make plans to fulfill it) was rational.

Commitments to future actions operate through plans and so pose parallel problems for TRCT. TRCT is inadequate because it cannot accommodate the role played by *commitments, promises* and *agreements* in rational deliberation. TRCT is too a-temporal for beings like us, who make commitments and promises for the very purpose of having them influence our future deliberations and actions. Once we have made a promise or committed to doing something in the future, those facts must be given proper weight in our subsequent deliberations: we must then take our reasons for action from our promise or commitment. Traditional marriage vows allow individuals to commit now to rejecting certain options in the future, indeed, to give such options no deliberative weight at all. Suppose an attractive colleague at the conference is clearly signaling their desire for sex with me. That is an outcome I might much prefer to grading essays alone in my hotel room, if I were to consider the matter at only the moment of choice and in isolation (when I must choose between inviting them to my room or saying goodnight). But if in marrying I committed to being sexually monogamous, I do not consider sleeping with someone else to be an open option. I do not deliberate about what to do as though I had made no such commitment; instead, I take my reasons directly from my commitment and say *oiche mhaith.*[9]

At any given time, individuals in ongoing societies have many such commitments and are executing multiple plans which should constrain rational deliberation. If TRCT says fulfilling our commitments, keeping our promises, executing our plans and the like are irrational whenever they require counter-preferential choices then it is inadequate both descriptively (it cannot explain the role commitments, plans, etc. have in actual deliberation and behavior) and normatively (it cannot explain why we should treat TRCT-rationality as authoritative).

The problems facing us in the PD and Farmers are instances of what Gauthier calls the "interaction problem" (Gauthier 2016). The interaction problem illustrates the shortcomings of TRCT. If persons in such strategic choice situations act to maximize their utility via TRCT, the results will be worse than they could have been had they deliberated and chosen in a different way. Our choices – to rat each other out, to refuse to offer harvesting assistance – were our best (i.e., maximizing) replies to what we expected the other to do. Do not Cooperate, Do not Cooperate (Rat, Rat or 3,3) is in *equilibrium* because it is the result of each of us making our best reply to the anticipated choices of the other. Such equilibrium is the standard of rational success under

TRCT. Yet "achieving" equilibrium in the PD leaves us both worse off than we could have been. At the most general level, the interaction problem arises whenever each agent correctly anticipates the actions of her fellows and chooses her best response to those expectations (thus realizing an outcome that is in equilibrium and so acting TRCT-rationally) but the result is worse for all than another that is available.

Situations modeled by the interaction problem stand as counter-examples to TRCT: following its advice – specifically, seeking equilibrium through best replies – is not sensible. Contractarians believe morality and/or politics are solutions to the various interaction problems we face. The unique Gauthierian position I defend is that solving the interaction problem requires that we seek *optimal* rather than *equilibrium* outcomes whenever (as in the PD itself) the two come apart. An optimizing theory of rationality will direct individuals to choose so as to bring about optimal outcomes that are dispreferred by none of the agents and which realize all the benefits available on terms that each can accept.[10] If we are optimizers facing the interaction problem we will cooperate, thus securing outcome 2,2, and thus do better than can maximizers seeking equilibrium. Optimizing Rational Choice Theorists, as we might call those who accept Gauthier's basic insight, think spending six years in prison when we could have spent three, and watching our rotting crops feed crows rather than our customers, are unsatisfying "success stories" of practical reason. Being able to say, from my cell, "At least I was rational!" rings a discordant note of consolation.

Freed from the limits of TRCT, theories of rational deliberation can take useful account of the many things that, properly, constrain such deliberation. As previously noted, cooperating over time involves planning, committing and intending, which impose deliberative burdens on us, for once we commit to being loyal criminal co-conspirators or to providing mutual assistance we must use those commitments or plans to determine what thereafter we should do. And they should continue to exert their influence on deliberation until the commitment is satisfied or fulfilled, the plan executed, or the optimal outcome realized.[11] That is the very point of committing and planning: to affirm that you will take your reasons for choice and action from your commitment or plan. In significant part we define ourselves by our major commitments and plans; they then should play essential normative roles in our deliberation, making some previously open options ineligible for choice and making others that were optional now mandatory. Autonomous agents define themselves as much by which options they treat as ineligible or unthinkable as by what they endorse and commit to.[12] Rational agents take their reasons for action only from the set that is eligible given their commitments, plans and cooperative activities. If we believe we are interacting with agents who are willing and able to restrict their deliberations to just those options that are compatible with our cooperating then we can achieve optimal outcomes acceptable to all. In cooperating we identify an acceptable optimal outcome and then choose so as to realize it, trusting that our fellows will do the same.

13.4 Trust?

That trust is involved in the interaction problem seems intuitively obvious. If you can trust me to help you later and if I can trust you not to rat then we can solve our problems, right? Alas things are not quite so simple because trusting and being trustworthy are not always rational. My project is to explain when and why trust (and trustworthiness) is rational, including between persons not related by more particular ties. Such trust is rational when it enables us to achieve optimal outcomes.

It seems natural to say that agents in a PD have a trust problem. What they need to solve their problem is trust. If only we could trust each other to honor our agreements (to keep quiet or help harvest) we could do much better than we do. Yet TRCT says that trusting your partner in either situation is irrational. Thus we need an alternative theory of rational choice, deployment of which can show when trust is warranted. My core argument is that trust will be warranted whenever keeping trusts allows us to achieve optimal results that would not otherwise be attainable.

If I have succeeded in showing that cooperating in PDs is rational, however, two related worries arise. One might think rational cooperation can motivate *reliance* but not genuine *trust*, because trust requires certain "trust-compatible" motives, and the prospect of one's own advantage is not among them. Many theorists of trust insist that if we are relying upon Q to do as he should *because* doing so is practically rational for him (i.e. to his benefit), then we are not in fact trusting Q. Trusting, they suppose, requires that the person trusted be motivated to do what he should for a specific subset of reasons or motives: goodwill, love or affection toward P, recognition of and response to the fact that P is trusting him, optimistic orientations, the desire to maintain a good reputation, etc.[13] (see Lahno; Potter; and Goldberg, this volume). All have been thought compatible with genuine trust. You can trust me if I am motivated by any of these trust-compatible motives. But if I cooperate because doing so allows me to better realize my concerns, advance my interests or expand my opportunities for leading a life I find fulfilling, they deny that my action is trusting. If it is instrumentally rational then it is not trust. Alternatively, if I can be counted on to do what I should just because I am rational then trust is an explanatory fifth wheel: we do not need it to explain why people cooperate in PDs. This second objection suggests that we do not need trust to solve the interaction problem; rationality suffices.

We have then two possible challenges to my view. The first alleges that rational cooperation does not exemplify genuine trust because it is not motivated by the right kind of reasons. The second suggests that trust is explanatorily otiose because if rationality can motivate Q to do as he should (act cooperatively) then there's no need for trustworthiness. The second is more quickly disposed of so I consider it first.

13.4.1 The Explanatory Power of Trust

Trust is not explanatorily empty, contrary to the challenge being considered. Trust plays an essential role in motivating rational cooperation in PDs because cooperating requires that we forgo the opportunity to maximize our utility when doing so would be at the expense of our cooperative partners. Cooperating requires that we reject "suckering" our partner (seeking outcome 1,4) as a viable option. That is what we trust our cooperative partners to do. Thus trust is not otiose; it is necessary to explain and justify cooperation in PDs.

I return then to the first of the possible objections to my view: that trust requires a specific motive or subset of motives, which excludes considerations of rationality.

13.4.2 Trust Relations, Goodwill and Reasons for Trust

If P trusts Q then P must have some confidence that Q will do as trusted to do. That belief may fall well short of virtual certainty, but it cannot be wholly absent. This is the doxastic core of any plausible theory of trust.[14] But if we are to distinguish between trust and mere reliance or confidence, we must attend to *why* P is confident that Q will do as expected. It matters what reasons we ascribe to Q in explaining Q's reliability. Here we frequently encounter claims that an interaction is one of trust only if Q is motivated to act reliably by a specific subset of motives: goodwill toward P, a desire to maintain a good reputation among her peers (see Origgi, this volume), valuing the relationship with P, recognition that P is counting on her, etc. Some reasons for Q's reliability, including her incapacity to do other than as trusted or her narrow self-interest, may give us good grounds for confidence that she will act as expected even though she is not actually trustworthy or trusted.

Individuals' motives are, accordingly, central in some of the best-known theories of trust. Annette Baier (1986 and 1991), for example, insists on specific motives in her seminal articles on trust. On Baier's view, I can trust you only if I believe you have goodwill towards me and I expect that goodwill to motivate action in line with my expectations; P must expect Q to act as trusted to *because of Q's goodwill toward P.* More generally, meeting expectations must be motivated by a restricted set of "trust-related" reasons (goodwill being an example) if they are to count as trustworthy. Karen Jones' well-known affective theory of trust is another requiring that trust-related reasons motivate Q to act as expected. Jones suggests that trust is primarily "an affective attitude of optimism that the goodwill and competence of another will extend to cover the domain of our interaction with her, together with the expectation that the one trusted will be *directly and favorably moved by the thought that we are counting on her*" (Jones 1996:4 emphasis added).

Others deny that goodwill or its ilk is necessary for trust. A few of examples reveal why I think this is the winning side in the debate. Consider a divorced couple who share custody of their children after their divorce. The mother trusts the father to care properly for the children when the father has them. The mother may not expect her ex-husband to act with goodwill towards her, yet she can trust him not to abuse the children when in his care. The father will be motivated to fulfill the mother's trust by his love and concern for his children, while he may lack any motive to meet the expectations of his ex-wife as such and be utterly unmoved by the thought that she is counting on him. This seems an instance of trust without goodwill. Likewise, I might trust another person to do [is] what is morally right because I believe he is a person who cares greatly about his moral integrity, even if he doesn't much care about me or our relationship. Or consider the situation of two warring armies, between which there is no goodwill but actual hostility and ill will. Despite the lack of goodwill, each can nonetheless trust the other not to shoot if one of them raises a white flag (Wright 2010:619, referring to Holton 1994:65). Finally, trust in professionals is based much more often on beliefs about their competence, professional integrity and desire to maintain good professional reputations than it is on any felt goodwill the professionals have for their clients or even any desires to maintain specific professional relationships. Thus, I can believe you are trustworthy and so sensibly trust you even if I do not believe you bear me goodwill or care about my well-being or our trust relationship as such. Theories relying on goodwill and the like might model some forms of interpersonal trust but do not fit many others.

13.4.2.1 Reasons for Confidence

We started on this path in an attempt to distinguish between cases in which I trust another person to do as I expect and those in which I merely expect he will do so. The role played by expectations or confidence in trust needs careful analysis, however.

Trust typically increases with confidence that Q will do as trusted to do and decreases as confidence that Q will do as expected declines. Yet in some cases even complete confidence does not reveal or support trust. Imagine a range of possible cases involving someone I call Bully.[15] Bully punches me in the stomach every time he sees me. Thus I believe that at our next encounter the likelihood of his punching me is very high and my trust in him to refrain is virtually nonexistent. But now consider these variations.

Religious Bully: I learn that Bully has had a religious conversion that includes renouncing violence. Thus I judge that the risk of being punched next time is now much lower and so my trust that he will not punch me is correspondingly higher. Religious Bully's reason for refraining from punching me is compatible with my trusting him to do as he should.

Quadriplegic Bully: I learn that Bully has been rendered a quadriplegic and is no longer physically capable of punching me in the stomach. I now have complete confidence that he will not punch me. But it seems wrong to say that I now trust Bully not to punch me because there is no need to trust. Doran Smolkin concludes that, because there is no vulnerability to trusting Quadriplegic Bully, my confidence that he will not punch me is not trust but mere reliance (Smolkin 2008:436). Since I agree that vulnerability is always an element in trusting, I agree this is not trust. But that conclusion is actually overdetermined; I add, for completeness, that Quadriplegic Bully also lacks the capacity to affect x, which is a necessary condition of trusting him with x. Assuming his motivations remain unchanged after the disabling event, moreover, I am also inclined to say that Quadriplegic Bully does not actually "refrain" from punching me, any more than I am currently refraining from flying to the moon or writing a revolutionary book on physics. There are thus multiple explanations of why my expectation that Quadriplegic Bully will not punch me does not amount to trust.

Coerced Bully: I learn that Bully is being monitored by the police and that he will be under active surveillance the next time we meet. Punching people as he usually does is criminal assault and so he runs a substantial risk of being arrested and punished for assaulting me if he punches me as I normally expect him to. Thus I am very confident that he will not punch me. Smolkin thinks I do not trust him nonetheless; his intuition is that if my confidence that Coerced Bully will do as trusted to is based on factors like force or threats then I do not really trust him. "Threats or compulsion seem to replace the need for trust, rather than enhance trust" (Smolkin 2008:437). This again suggests that the *reasons* for my confidence that Q will act appropriately are important. The puzzle is that trust is a kind of confidence, but some reasons for being confident (notably incapacity, threats, and force) preclude trust, while other reasons for confidence increase trust.

Constrained Bully: I learn that Bully has assumed legally enforceable duties to refrain from punching people. He has signed a legally binding contract committing himself henceforth to non-violence. Many scholars think that trust is diluted or debased to the extent that it employs such external inducements to act as one should. Constrained Bully can comply with my expectation that he will not punch me, thereby proving reliable, but when done to avoid a penalty attached to doing otherwise the situation again ceases to be primarily trust based (Cf. Wright 2010:625). And yet there are many other situations in which trust relationships are compatible with and can even be enhanced by the use of external devices designed to support the honoring of trusts. I think Constrained Bully is trustworthy despite the presence of legal elements in our relationship.[16]

Many external inducements and constraints can enhance the reliability of others and so make trusting them more reasonable. Making a commitment in legally enforceable form may be trust enhancing even when made between long-time friends or lovers. Compare two undertakings of traditional wedding vows, one made in a legally binding way and the other by persons who take the same vows (utter the same words, perform the same actions, with the same intentions) but decline to perform them in a legally recognizable way. When Beyoncé sings "Put a ring on it!" she is surely talking about legally binding commitments. Anthony Bellia Jr. similarly asks: "Which of the following promises is more likely to generate trust: I promise to employ you, friend, for three years, though I will not give you a contract; or, I promise to employ you, friend, for three years, and here is your three-year contract?" (Bellia Jr. 2002:35) Surely it would be more reasonable to trust those willing to provide legally enforceable promises than those who are unwilling, other things being equal. Such examples show that "the legal enforcement of promises cannot be said to detract categorically or even typically from their ability to enhance interpersonal relationships" (Bellia Jr. 2002:28; cf. Smolkin 2008). Claims that using contract law or other external devices necessarily degrades trust or is inconsistent with genuine trust are simply too strong. This is compatible with recognizing that external political devices like law are always costly, however, and so inferior to internal moral incentives when available.

In some trust relationships external devices like legal contracts, regulations, professional codes, licensing boards and law generally can be deployed to enable and enhance trust, whereas their use in other contexts would undermine it or signal its absence. Trust in government officials and countless professionals, and amongst parties to various commercial and productive ventures, is enhanced by broadly legal regulatory means. Why do such social controls build trust in some kinds of relationships but not in others? (Smolkin 2008:438)

That (even coercive) external devices enable or enhance trust in some contexts is problematic for motive-based views of trust. Such contexts are very common and host important cases of trust (see Cohen; Alfano and Huijts, this volume). They include virtually every interaction we have with strangers in modern urban societies (see Hosking 2014). Assuming anything as robust as goodwill between me and the vast majority of people with whom I interact on a daily basis is too strong though I almost certainly bear them no ill will either. We participate in various trust networks that are not properly characterized as personal relationships of the kind constituted by caring motives. We do not trust other motorists on the highway or the pilot who flies our plane because they care about us or our relationship. We trust our pilot because we think she is competent to fly safely, she has good reasons to fly safely (including her own well-being) and so she is disposed to fly safely, as well as having confidence in the competence of the engineers who built the plane, the mechanics who maintained it, the regulators who inspected it, etc. (Smolkin 2008:441). Many social institutions and practices, including important knowledge-creating institutions and professional regulatory bodies, serve to support trust even without caring motives. We can have good reasons for trust even in the absence of ongoing relationships with the individuals involved and without supposing that the trusted parties are motivated by robust concern or affection for us.

13.4.2.2 Relativized Trust

Expectations (confidence) and motives are clearly both important. We need an account that recognizes that not just any kind of confidence counts as trust, without insisting on a narrow caring motivational requirement as required in extant motive-based views. Smolkin proposes a "relativized" account of trust as fitting the bill. "On this account, what counts as trust is a certain kind of confidence that one will do as expected or as one ought; however, the kind of confidence that will count as trust will vary depending on the *kind* of relationship that it is" (Smolkin 2008:441). We should begin with how our various relationships with others – friends, lovers, family members, business partners, professionals, neighbors, colleagues, students, co-nationals, fellow citizens, government agents, etc. – ought to be understood. Any specific limitations on the reasons for action that can motivate trust-fulfilling conduct will then be determined by (and so be relative to) the kind of relationship it is.

Some relationships, e.g. friendships, will typically be incompatible with the use of external controls like legal contracts or threats of penalty for trust violations; that is because true friendships involve reciprocal care, concern and affection. We interact with our friends in trustworthy ways by our care for them and desire to see them fulfilled. When we are engaged in commercial activities, by contrast, the relationships we have with others might be much more instrumental. I am interested simply in acquiring something you have for an acceptable price. Having reached a mutually acceptable agreement, we may each be moved to honor it by nothing nobler than covetousness. Being so motivated is compatible with being in good commercial relations with you, and so would not undermine trust. Commercial relationships can often be maintained, even enhanced, by the increased confidence that legally binding agreements provide. Trust in various professionals can likewise be enhanced by external systems of control, including licensing boards, professional associations and enforceable guarantees and warrantees, all of which are designed to enable trust when the interests at stake are significant in the absence of ongoing caring relationships. Trust so relativized explains why the use of external devices reflects an absence of trust in some relationships but not in others. Trust relationships will be those in which P is confident that Q will do as trusted to do, and the reasons for that confidence are compatible with it continuing to be a good relationship of its kind. If P lacks confidence that Q will do as trusted to do, or has such confidence but based on reasons (e.g. incapacity or coercion) that are incompatible with its being a good relationship of its kind, then it is not a trusting relationship (Smolkin 2008:444).[17]

When P trusts Q in cooperative practices, P's trust is incompatible with taking certain kinds of precautions against being disappointment by Q. Jon Elster suggests that trusting invites one "to lower one's guard, to refrain from taking precautions against an interaction partner, even when the other, because of *opportunism or incompetence*, could act in a way that might seem to justify precautions" (Elster 2007:344). If trust excludes taking precautions that might otherwise be appropriate (in the absence of trust) then trust generates second-order peremptory reasons to reject acting for precautionary reasons. Reasons for trust must rationalize forgoing opportunities to guard against one's trust being violated. Reasons for trust are preemptive reasons: they preempt precautionary reasons specifically (see Keren 2014 and in this volume for further elaboration of this view).

Elster is right to identify incompetence and opportunism as the central threats to trust. *Incompetence* of any relevant kind can make a person (or institution) untrustworthy. The success of every trust depends upon Q's competence (with respect to x); incompetence can render even the best intended, most cooperative agent untrustworthy. And *opportunism* is precisely the risk inherent to trusting in PDs: that you will act opportunistically, seizing the opportunity to benefit yourself though knowing it is at my expense. Even when cooperating is rational, there is a role for trust to play in suppressing opportunism. For recall that in every PD there is an outcome that individuals prefer (1,4) even to the optimal cooperative outcome (2,2) that ORCT rationality recommends. In outcome (1,4) I exploit your trust/cooperation; to secure this result, I must be willing to exploit your anticipated cooperation and to act in a way that benefits me by harming you. In trusting, one necessarily opens oneself up to such exploitation; when another takes advantage of one's willingness to cooperate the exploiter acts opportunistically. Trustworthy people do not make that choice. To be trustworthy is to willingly forgo opportunities to exploit the cooperation of one's fellows, to eschew acting in ways that secure one's benefit but only at the expense of others.

13.5 Conclusion

We need a theory that captures the important differences between various kinds of trust: between intimates, colleagues, friends and family members, between individuals related in joint activities or united by common cause, between professionals and their clients, between government officials and citizens, etc. Each gives rise to distinct reasons for action, and trusting involves expectations about how others will respond to those reasons. We trust strangers to not harm us, to be law abiding, and to understand and willingly comply with the norms for interaction between strangers. We trust professionals' technical competences and assume they are motivated to meet their professional responsibilities. We trust friends because we believe they have the moral competencies that friendship requires, such as loyalty, kindness and generosity (Jones 1996:7). My relativist theory of trust recognizes that different kinds of relationships are characterized by different normative expectations, and being trustworthy involves fulfilling them, whatever they are. Individuals are trustworthy with respect to any specific relationship just so long as they are motivated to do what they are expected to do for reasons that are compatible with the relationship being a good token of its type.

Almost everything we value depends upon cooperation, and cooperation requires trust. Trustworthy people are cooperators who seek optimal solutions to the interaction problems they face. Committing to deliberate and choose in ways that are compatible with our trust commitments enables us to better realize what matters to us, but only if we really do reject "suckering" our cooperative partners as viable options.

Notes

1 Karen Frost-Arnold also identifies all five elements involved in trust: "who is being trusted, by whom, to do what, for what reasons, and in what environment" in Frost-Arnold (2014:791). What she calls "environment" and Karen Jones calls "climate" in Jones (1996), I call "circumstances." We are each identifying a range of external conditions that can affect the rational or moral status of trusting or being trustworthy.

2 Strawson (1962). This is a common way of distinguishing between mere *reliance* or *expectation* and genuine *trust* – if a mere reliance is unmet P should feel disappointed, whereas if trusts are violated P should feel the reactive emotions – betrayal, resentment – in response.

3 Hobbes (1651, chapter 13).

4 "PDs" plural because there are one-shot PDs, iterated PDs (played over time with the same parties meeting each other an indeterminate number of times), a-temporal or temporally extended PDs, and more. Cf. Peterson (2015).

5 The term "the circumstances of justice" refers to David Hume's description of the conditions that make justice both possible and necessary. Justice arises whenever individuals live in

conditions of limited scarcity, where the natural supply of goods is insufficient to meet the needs and desires of people, but where that supply can be increased by productive activities and cooperation. It also includes limited benevolence: we care most about ourselves and those closest to us, though we bear strangers and distant others no ill will. In these conditions, justice enables individuals to cooperate in ways that are mutually beneficial (with "beneficial" interpreted broadly to include not just material rewards but rather the whole set of things in which people find fulfillment). Hume, (1739–40, 1751).

6 Sometimes games are represented according to their payoffs or outcomes. The possible outcomes are (6 years, 6 years), (1 year, 8 years), (3 years, 3 years) and (8 years, 1 year).

7 Ken Binmore represents TRCT in this debate. Binmore defends rationality as equilibrium seeking against Gauthier in numerous works. Binmore accepts dominance reasoning demonstrating that defect, defect (or 3,3) is the unique solution to the PD. He thinks Gauthier's is a "hopeless," "impossible" task. See Binmore (2015).

8 My views about planning and its role in rational choice have been most influenced by the work of Michael E. Bratman. Cf. Bratman (2014, 1999, 1987).

9 "Good night" in Gaelic. Of course even plans it was rational to make and commitments it was rational to accept may have to be revisited, and perhaps even abandoned, should the circumstances change in relevant ways. Nothing said so far indicates how resolute we should be in fulfilling our commitments or which changes license or require reevaluation of the commitments we made in the past. See note 11.

10 An outcome will be (strongly) optimal if everyone prefers it to the others available, and (weakly) optimal if at least one person prefers it to the others and no one dis-prefers it. Weak optimality suffices for rational choice.

11 One may have good reason to reconsider, perhaps even abandon, a plan it was sensible to adopt or to renounce a commitment one had good reason to make. It is not rational to be so inflexible that one is incapable of reconsidering one's commitments or changing course, but a healthy level of resoluteness is needed. Cf. McClennen (1990).

12 Among Harry Frankfurt's many insights on autonomous agency.

13 Bibliographical details for all of these positions appear in other papers in this collection, where they are discussed in more detail.

14 It follows that so-called "therapeutic trust" – extended to someone you believe will violate it – for instrumental reasons or as moral education, is not genuine trust on my view.

15 Inspired by but going beyond Smolkin's use of a similar example.

16 Bellia Jr. (2002) is informative on the relationship between trust and alternative reasons for confidence.

17 This provides one way of articulating Baier's insight that *what* specifically I count on about you matters to the moral quality of the trust that results. If we are lovers and I believe you will do as expected toward me only because you hope to benefit from a sizable inheritance I'm likely to receive then the situation is not one of trust. Cf. Baier (1994).

References

Baier, A. (1986) "Trust and Anti-Trust," *Ethics* 96: 231–260.

Baier, A. (1991) "Trust and Its Vulnerabilities" and "Sustaining Trust," in *Tanner Lectures on Human Values*, Volume 13, Salt Lake City, UT: University of Utah Press.

Baier, A. (1994) *Moral Prejudices: Essays on Ethics*, Cambridge, MA: Harvard University Press.

Bellia Jr., A. (2002) "Promises, Trust, and Contract Law," *The American Journal of Jurisprudence* 47: 25–40.

Binmore, K. (2015) "Why All the Fuss? The Many Aspects of the Prisoner's Dilemma," in M. Peterson (ed.), *The Prisoner's Dilemma*, Cambridge: Cambridge University Press.

Bratman, M. (2014) *Shared Agency: A Planning Theory of Acting Together*, Oxford: Oxford University Press.

Bratman, M. (1999) *Faces of Intention: Selected Essays on Intention and Agency*, Oxford: Oxford University Press.

Bratman, M. (1987) *Intention, Plans, and Practical Reason*, Cambridge, MA: Harvard University Press.

Elster, J. (2007) *Explaining Social Behavior: More Nuts and Bolts for the Social Sciences*, Cambridge: Cambridge University Press.

Frankfurt, H. (1999) *Necessity, Volition, and Love*, Cambridge: Cambridge University Press.
Frost-Arnold, K. (2014) "Imposters, Tricksters, and Trustworthiness as an Epistemic Virtue," *Hypatia* 29: 790–807.
Gauthier, D. (2016) "A Society of Individuals," *Dialogue: Canadian Philosophical Review* 55: 601–619.
Gauthier, D. (2015) "How I Learned to Stop Worrying and Love the Prisoner's Dilemma," in M. Peterson (ed.), *The Prisoner's Dilemma*, Cambridge: Cambridge University Press.
Gauthier, D. (2008) "Friends, Reasons and Morals" in B. Verbeek (ed.), *Reasons and Intentions*, Aldershot: Ashgate Publishing.
Gauthier, D. (1998) "Political Contractarianism," *Journal of Political Philosophy* 5: 132–148.
Hobbes, T. (1651) *Leviathan*, London.
Hosking, G. (2014) *Trust: A History*, Oxford: Oxford University Press.
Hume, D. (1751) *An Enquiry Concerning the Principles of Morals*, Edinburgh.
Hume, D. (1739–40) *A Treatise of Human Nature*, Edinburgh.
Jones, K. (1996) "Trust as an Affective Attitude," *Ethics* 107: 4–25.
Keren, A. (2014) "Trust and Belief: A Preemptive Reasons Account," *Synthese* 191: 2593–2615.
McClennen, E. (1990) *Rationality and Dynamic Choice: Foundational Explorations*, Cambridge: Cambridge University Press.
Peterson, M. (2015) *The Prisoner's Dilemma*, Cambridge: Cambridge University Press.
Raz, J. (1990) *The Authority of Law*, Oxford: Oxford University Press.
Raz, J. (1975) *Practical Reason and Norms*, Oxford: Oxford University Press.
Smolkin, D. (2008) "Puzzles about Trust," *The Southern Journal of Philosophy* 46: 431–449.
Strawson, P. (1962) "Freedom and Resentment," *Proceedings of the British Academy* 48: 1–25.
Wright, S. (2010) "Trust and Trustworthiness," *Philosophia* 38: 615–627.

Further Reading

Gauthier, D. (1986) *Morals by Agreement*, Oxford: Clarendon Press. (Defending cooperation in PDs, based on the pragmatic value of "constrained maximization.")
Gauthier, D. (2013) "Twnety-Five On," *Ethics* 123: 601–624. (Providing an overview of his theory of optimizing rationality and its relation to cooperation, 25 years after the publication of *Morals by Agreement*.)
Peterson, M. (ed.) (2015) *The Prisoner's Dilemma*, Cambridge: Cambridge University Press. (The Prisoner's Dilemma is examined by a variety of philosophers and economists, including a debate between Gauthier and Binmore.)

14
TRUST AND GAME THEORY

Andreas Tutić and Thomas Voss

14.1 Introduction

Trust is a necessary ingredient of many kinds of social relations. Exchange relations like social exchange or economic transactions require that one or both parties place trust (Blau 1964). Consider online markets such as eBay as a case in point: a seller and a buyer interact and may agree to transfer a certain item in exchange for a payment of a specified price. The buyer may trust the seller that an item with the promised quality will in fact be delivered after the money has been sent. If there is no advance payment, the seller must place trust in the buyer's willingness and ability to pay the price after the item has been delivered. The auction platform eBay has invested considerable effort to design institutional rules which aim to mitigate trust problems involved in an anonymous auction market by reducing incentives to behave opportunistically on both sides of the market.

Trust problems not only arise within market contexts but also in many other elementary social interactions (see also Potter, this volume), for instance, in intimate relationships, marriages and families. Another class of trust problems comprises employment relations where an employer places trust in an employee who promises to put in labor effort in exchange for a material or immaterial compensation (wage, fair treatment and acceptable labor conditions). Still other trust problems can be found in relations between landlords and tenants, banks and borrowers, and so on. However, most if not all trust problems share a number of features (see Coleman 1990: chapter 5) which make them perfectly suitable for a theoretical treatment with game theoretic models.

First, trust is a component of *social relations* between at least two types of actors: a *trustor* who places trust and a *trustee* who decides to honor or abuse the received trust. Of course, more than two actors and actors other than natural persons may be involved in more complex trust relations or systems of trust (see Coleman 1990: chapter 8). In particular, the trustee can be a corporate actor like a firm (see also Cohen, this volume), a public organization, the political system as such (see also Alfano and Huijts, this volume) or the functioning of the set of interrelated societal institutions (see also Gkouvas and Mindus, this volume). A citizen who votes for a political party in a democratic election might place trust in the sense that her expectations with regard to the realization of certain political programs will be fulfilled in the future.

Secondly, trust relations are *asymmetric* in the sense that the trustor has to decide whether or not to choose the risky option of placing trust. Trust relations generally require *sequences* of decisions. After trust has been placed (e.g. the trustor has transferred a credit to the trustee), the trustee will have a "second mover" advantage and may honor the received trust or not. In the case that the trustee rejects to honor the trust she will be able to increase her own outcome (e.g. keep the received credit without paying it back). The trustor, on the other hand, will receive an inferior payoff if the trustee chooses to behave dishonestly.

Thirdly, trust involves the transfer of material or immaterial resources (e.g. a financial credit, the right to use an apartment, or, in general, rights to perform certain actions) which create opportunities for the trustee that are unavailable without the trustor's placement of trust. A trustee may, for example, use the credit to run her own business and generate profits which may be considerably larger than the financial value of the received credit. *Honored* trust will also enable the trustor to enlarge her set of opportunities. An employer may increase the viability of her firm if her employees direct considerable effort into the firm's everyday operations in exchange for the payment of wages. In this sense, the placement of trust can be an investment that will generate future payoff streams to the trustor. Thus, trust relations potentially generate *gains* for both parties, trustor and trustee. On a market such as an online auction the parties agree to perform a certain transaction on the condition that trust will be reciprocated. Since both parties agree to transact with each other, they expect to be better off in comparison to the situation where no transaction will take place. In other words, trust will enable *efficiency gains* in the Pareto sense (see Osborne 2004:483), that is, all parties involved will be better off or at least not be worse off if trust is placed and honored.

In this chapter we describe game theoretic accounts of trust. Due to spatial restrictions and for the sake of a concise treatment, we focus on the dominant and most influential strand of the game-theoretical literature on trust, which explicates the placement of trust as a risky investment, and leave aside other game-theoretical contributions towards the study of trust such as trust as a rational expectation (e.g. Dasgupta 1988), trust in evolutionary game theory (e.g. Skyrms 2008), and trust in team reasoning (e.g. Sugden 1993; Bacharach 1999). We start with a very brief primer on game theory and then turn to elementary reconstructions of trust. These elementary models show that trust situations are often problematic social situations in the sense that they are prone to inefficiencies from a collective point of view. Subsequently some extensions of the elementary accounts of trust are presented that allow a study of social mechanisms which help to overcome the problematic character of trust situations.

14.2 Game Theory

Game theory provides a set of formal models which are used to analyze social interactions in various academic disciplines. Apart from social and moral philosophy, game theoretic modelling is common in economics, sociology, political science and legal scholarship. Game theory focuses on interactions which are "strategic" in the sense that every agent knows or acts as if she knew that the consequences (outcomes, payoffs) of her decisions will be determined not only by the choices taken by herself but also by the decisions taken by other actors.

Classical game theory rests on the assumption that agents behave rationally.[1] *Rationality* means that an agent chooses among alternative strategies in accordance with certain rationality axioms. Like any theory of rational choice game theory assumes that each agent's preferences are consistent (transitive and complete).[2] In addition to consistency assumptions about desires (preferences) modern game theory postulates that expectations (beliefs) are rational in the sense of objective or of Bayesian (subjective) probabilities (Osborne 2004:278ff.). This way, one can analyze games with complete information and also games with incomplete information. Incomplete information implies that at least some participants do not acquire information with respect to certain features of the game (e.g. the preferences of other agents) as the game starts. Most versions of standard game theory require that the actors have common knowledge of rationality, that is, every agent knows that everyone knows ... (and so on) ... that every agent behaves rationally. It is important to notice that in game theory rationality assumptions do not imply that agents are self-interested. Altruism, fairness, envy or other kinds of other-regarding "social preferences" may well be represented by consistent preferences. In empirical research game theorists, in particular behavioral game theorists, distinguish between objective (material) *outcomes* which are expected to be received by the players (e.g. because they are provided in an experiment) and effective *payoffs* which reflect the "true" preferences of the agents. Theoretical models of games argue about effective preferences which may or may not correspond to material incentives (e.g. monetary units) as outcomes. In some but not all cases it is warranted to assume that effective payoffs are proportional to material outcomes.

Given the rationality postulates certain solution concepts can be justified from a normative point of view. In empirical applications these concepts are often useful components of empirical predictions about the expected behavior – at least as a first approximation. The most important concept is the *Nash equilibrium* or equilibrium for short. Roughly, an equilibrium is a combination or "profile" of strategies such that no agent has a positive incentive to unilaterally deviate from the equilibrium (Osborne 2004:22). Any *unilateral* deviation (that is, given that all other agents stick to their equilibrium strategies) to a different strategy does not yield a payoff which is superior in the strict sense (deviations can only generate payoffs which are at most equal to the equilibrium payoff).

Game theory not only analyzes static social situations such that every participant chooses her strategy simultaneously – the classic prisoner's dilemma[3] being a case in point. There are also dynamic games which require a sequence of actions taken by the participants. These sequential games can graphically be represented by a so-called extensive game form (in contrast to the so-called normal game) which depicts the sequences of actions in a more intuitive manner. Due to their richer structure, games in extensive form call for more involved solution concepts. For extensive form games with perfect information, the most important solution concept is *subgame perfectness*, which, loosely speaking, demands rationality even in counterfactual situations, thereby ruling out that incredible threats and promises can be part of an equilibrium. Equilibria in dynamic games can often be discovered via "backward induction," i.e. solving the game from behind, starting with the smallest subgames. Let us illustrate these concepts with reference to the so-called mini-ultimatum game (Figure 14.1).

In this game there are two players. The sender gets endowed with \$10 and has to decide whether she allocates this fairly between herself and a recipient (keep \$5 and

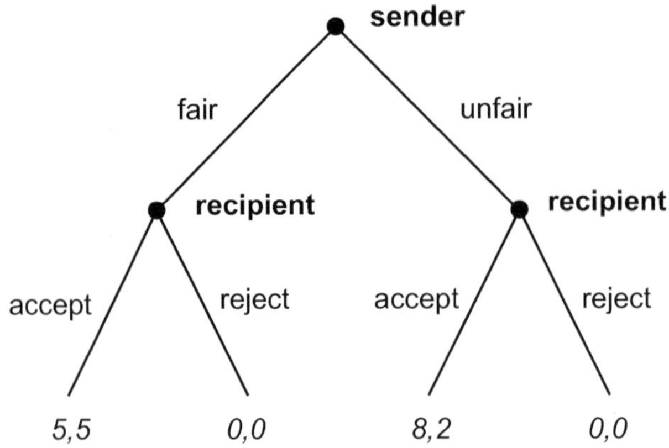

Figure 14.1 Mini-ultimatum Game

send \$5) or she distributes the endowment in an unfair manner (keep \$8 and send \$2). The recipient learns the proposed allocation by the sender and can either accept this allocation, in which case both players obtain the respective dollar amounts, or reject it, in which case both players obtain a payoff of \$0. (In the following, it is assumed for convenience that these material outcomes correspond to the subjective payoffs.)

First, note that the sender has one decision node and hence two strategies, while the recipient has two decision nodes and hence 2x2=4 strategies, i.e. the recipient has to make plans regarding both the fair and the unfair proposal. A strategy profile in the mini-ultimatum game takes the form of a triple (x,y,z), in which x denotes the strategy of the sender, y denotes the action of the recipient at her left decision node (fair proposal), and z denotes the action of the recipient at her right decision node (unfair proposal). It is easy to see that there are three Nash equilibria in this game: (fair, accept, reject), (unfair, reject, accept) and (unfair, accept, accept). However, two of these Nash equilibria involve incredible threats and hence are not subgame perfect. For instance, consider (fair, accept, reject). In this strategy profile the recipient threatens to reject the proposal if the sender chooses the unfair allocation. However, in the counterfactual event of the unfair proposal it would be in the recipient's best interest to actually deviate from this plan and secure a payoff of 2 instead of 0 by accepting the unfair allocation. In fact, there is a unique subgame perfect equilibrium in the mini-ultimatum game, which can be identified by backward induction. There are two proper subgames in this game which start at the two decision nodes of the recipient, respectively. In both subgames the recipient has a unique rational action, i.e. she should accept the fair as well as the unfair allocation to obtain a strictly positive payoff. Anticipating this, the sender has a unique rational action in proposing the unfair allocation. Hence, in contrast to the concept of Nash equilibrium, subgame perfectness is more demanding by insisting on rationality in counterfactual situations thereby ruling out incredible threats and promises by the players.

The basic idea of subgame perfectness is conserved in solution concepts for more involved games, in particular in the *sequential equilibrium*, which applies to extensive form games with imperfect information.[4]

14.3 The Basic Trust Game

Elementary trust relations can be described by a "trust game" which covers all the above mentioned features. The basic trust game is depicted in Figure 14.2 (Dasgupta 1988; Kreps 1990:66–67). First, the trustor decides on whether to trust or not to trust the trustee. In case the trustor refuses to trust the trustee, the game ends immediately. If she puts her trust in the trustee, the latter has the options to honor or abuse trust.

The payoff functions satisfy the inequalities R>P>S and t>r>p, where the first inequality refers to the payoffs of the trustor and the second inequality refers to the payoffs of the trustee. These inequalities constitute the essential incentive structure of the basic trust game. The first set of inequalities signifies that, from the perspective of the trustor, putting trust in the trustee is a *risky investment*. If the trustee honors her trust, the trustor is better off, but if the trustee abuses trust, the trustor is worse off compared to not trusting the trustee in the first place. The second set of inequalities implies that the trustee is opportunistic and prefers to abuse over honoring trust. At the same time, she would prefer to be trusted by the trustor and honor this trust over not being trusted at all.

In the basic trust game, basically all game theoretic solution concepts, which can be applied to this kind of game (in technical terms: extensive form games with perfect information and without chance moves), figure out a single strategy profile: (no trust, abuse trust). Let us check that this profile is indeed the unique subgame perfect equilibrium of this game. In the only proper subgame, which starts at the decision node of the trustee, she has a unique rational action, i.e. she abuses trust and obtains a payoff of t instead of r. Anticipating this, the trustor's best response is to place no trust in the trustee, thereby securing a payoff of P instead of S. Hence (no trust, abuse trust) is the sole subgame perfect equilibrium.

Notably, the basic trust game is a so-called *social dilemma*, a problematic social situation in which individual rational actions imply outcomes which are inefficient from a collective point of view (e.g. Raub and Voss 1986). While there is some disagreement regarding the exact definition of the term "social dilemma," the general idea is to denote games in which the set of equilibria under one or the other solution concept is not identical to the set of Pareto-efficient strategy profiles. A strategy

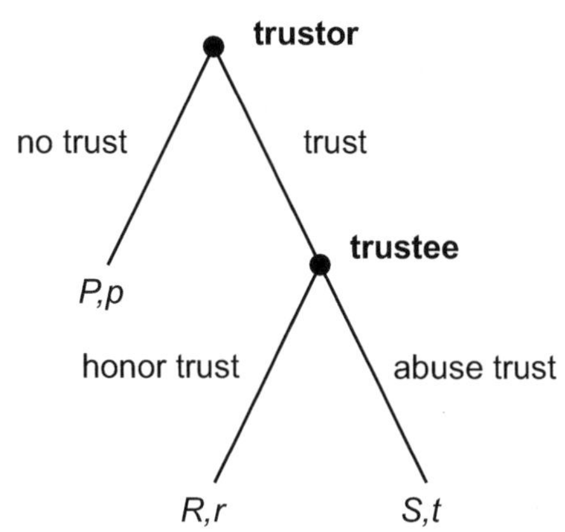

Figure 14.2 Basic Trust Game

profile is Pareto-efficient if there does not exist another strategy profile which makes a player better off without making any player worse off. Clearly, from a collective point of view, social welfare is lost if the players settle on a strategy profile which is not Pareto-efficient. In the basic trust game there are two Pareto-efficient strategy profile, i.e. (trust, honor trust) and (trust, abuse trust). So, the only strategy profile which is an equilibrium is not Pareto-efficient, i.e. the basic trust game is a social dilemma.

In the economic literature a continuous variant of the basic trust game, the so-called investment game, is popular (cf. Berg et al. 1995). In this game, both actors are endowed with resources $m>0$. The trustor decides how much of her endowment she hands over to the trustee, i.e. she puts the amount of $\tau\varepsilon[0,m]$ "trust" in the trustee. The trustee uses this trust to generate a surplus $\alpha\tau$ with $\alpha>1$ and decides how much of her overall resources she hands (back) to the trustor, i.e. she honors trust in the magnitude $h\varepsilon[0,m+\alpha\tau]$. The payoffs of the players simply equal the amount of resources controlled at the end of the game, i.e. $m-\tau+h$ for the trustor and $m+\alpha\tau-h$ for the trustee. This game inherits the essential properties of the basic trust game. In the unique subgame perfect equilibrium of this game, the trustor does not trust the trustee at all, $\tau=0$, and the trustee would completely abuse any trust of the trustor, $h(\tau')=0$ for all $\tau'\varepsilon[0,m]$. Obviously, this outcome is not Pareto-efficient, i.e. the investment game is a social dilemma as well. In regards to understanding trust, not much is gained substantially by studying the continuous variant, hence we will focus on extensions of the binary basic trust game in the remainder of this chapter.

14.4 The Concept of Trust

Given that elementary trust relations are represented by trust games it is tempting to ask how the concept of trust can be explicated. Against the background of the game-theoretical literature on the trust game, we suggest the following definition of trust (which is in the spirit of Coleman 1990; see also Snijders 1996 and Fehr 2009):

> Trust is the disposition or the act of a trustor to transfer a valuable resource to a trustee without knowing whether the trustee will honor this placement by reciprocating. The trustor's motivation to place trust is the expectation that honored trust will pay off in terms of the trustee's interests or goals. In this sense game theory explicates the act of trusting as a risky investment.

Note that the resource does not have to be "material" like money or some other economic "good," but may as well be the control over one's body (Coleman 1990:94, 97). Similarly, the expectation that honored trust will pay off must not be related to the trustor's material interests but can also depend on non-material or ideal goals ("ideelle Interessen" in Max Weber's (1988:252) sense). Trust should be distinguished from "confidence" (see e.g. Luhmann 1988). *Confidence* is relevant in a social relation where the trustee does not have an incentive to act opportunistically but may choose actions which reduce the trustor's payoffs due to lack of competence, chance or for other reasons ("dangers" which are out of the trustee's control). In situations of confidence, the trustor may not consider alternatives. If you use an airplane to travel you expect that the plane is in a good shape and that the pilot is competent; it is in general not in the pilot's interest to generate a crash. In other words, to place confidence does not involve a risky investment but the expectation that there may be a (small) positive probability that an unfavorable event happens due to results which are unintended from the perspectives of both parties. Confidence in this sense may be conceptualized and analyzed using a rational actor approach but is less suitable to a game theoretic analysis because strategic elements are less important in this kind of relation.

14.5 The Trust Game with Incomplete Information

The crux of the basic trust game is to conceptualize the act of putting trust in someone as a risky investment. The fact that all solution concepts "predict" that the trustor does not trust the trustee is a consequence of mere assumptions regarding the incentive structure of the basic trust game. That is, the assumption that the trustee is opportunistic and would abuse trust given the option is critical. Since the preferences of the players are common knowledge (i.e. everybody knows that everybody knows that everybody knows … (and so on) … that the trustee is opportunistic), the trustor anticipates this and hence does not place trust.

The basic trust game is just a baseline model that serves as a background and often explicitly as an "ingredient" of more complex game theoretic accounts of trust, which capture more nuanced aspects of social situations that involve trust. Most importantly, Figure 14.3 depicts a situation in which the trustor does not know whether the trustee is opportunistic. In this game, there are two types of trustees. Honorable trustees H prefer to honor trust over abusing trust, r'>t. Abusive trustees A prefer to abuse trust over honoring trust, t>r.

The dotted line connecting the two decision nodes of the trustor indicates that both nodes are part of the same information set. The concept of information sets allows to model incomplete information in extensive form games. To put this intuitively: a player just knows that one of the nodes in the information set is reached, once it is her time to act. She does not know which one of the nodes in the information set is reached.

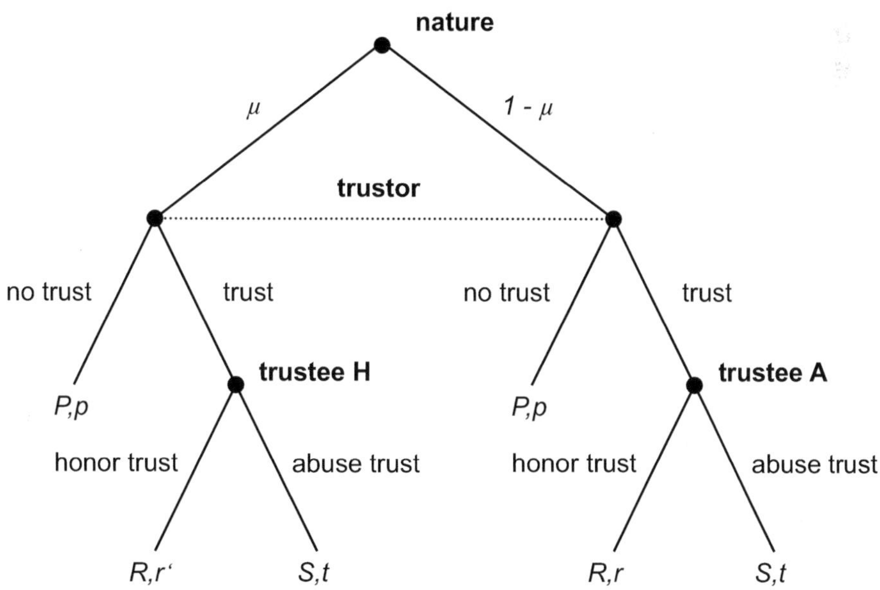

Figure 14.3 Trust Game with Incomplete Information

Since a decision node in an extensive game can be identified with the sequence of actions that leads to this node, this means that information sets allow to model that a player does not exactly know what has happened in the game so far.

In the case of the trust game with incomplete information, matters are simple. There is just one action that the trustor is uncertain of. That is, nature (also called chance) decided upon whether she plays the basic trust game with trustee H or trustee A. The parameter $\mu \varepsilon (0,1)$ measures the trustor's subjective belief regarding the two actions of nature.

Perhaps the most appealing solution concept for this kind of games is the sequential equilibrium. Speaking (very) loosely, this concept extends the backward induction logic of the subgame perfect equilibrium to games with incomplete information. Applying this logic, we find that in equilibrium trustee H will honor trust and trustee A will abuse trust. The trustor will anticipate this and since she believes to deal with trustee H with probability μ, she will put trust in the trustee if and only if $\mu R+(1-\mu)S \geq P$. The *comparative statics* of this inequality are highly plausible: Trust gets more likely, the higher the potential gains of the investment, the lower the risk of losing the investment, and the lower the opportunity costs of investing. Put differently, this inequality gives a critical value for the subjective belief of the trustor. That is, if and only if she beliefs that the trustee is honorable with a probability of at least $\mu^*=(P-S)/(R-S)$ she puts trust in the trustee. Cum grano salis, the inequality is also the backbone of James Coleman's intuitive discussion of trust in his landmark *Foundations of Social Theory* where albeit a decision theoretic framework but not game theory in the proper sense is used (Coleman 1990).

Note that if μ exceeds this critical value, the game at hand does not amount to a social dilemma. This holds, because with probability μ the payoff vector (R,r') comes about and with probability $1-\mu$ the payoff vector (S,t) is realized, both of which are Pareto-efficient. However, if the subjective belief of the trustor is too low and she refuses to trust, the inefficient payoff vector (P,p) is realized, and hence the game constitutes a dilemma.

14.6 Mechanisms Favoring Trust

Given the fact that in an one-shot anonymous trust game there is an unique equilibrium of not placing trust and of abusing trust, one is tempted to ask how this can be reconciled with the fact that there exists empirical evidence which demonstrates that trust in fact is placed (see e.g. Snijders 1996; Camerer 2003; Fehr 2009). Game theoretic reasoning indeed offers insights into social mechanisms which are prone to foster trust (and therefore also trustworthiness).

14.6.1 Social Preferences

Consider first one-shot situations. Experimental research indicates that even in one-shot situations a considerable amount of trust is placed. One mechanism which can explain this is the existence of other-regarding *social* preferences (Pelligra 2006). In experimental work, outcomes are usually supplied by experimenters to subjects in the laboratory by material incentives (money units). However, since game theory does not argue about effects of monetary incentives but about preferences which may be related to commodities different from one's own material well-being, game situations which are trust games in terms of material outcomes can effectively or psychologically be quite different games with distinct equilibria. For instance, if the trustor were an altruist who is not interested in increasing her own material outcomes but only in the trustee's material well-being, she would be disposed to transfer resources to the trustee irrespective of whether the trustee is expected to honor trust or not. (In fact, an extreme altruist may even wish that the trustee will abuse trust and not reciprocate because keeping the resource without reciprocating would make the trustee better off materially. However, in this case the situation should not be framed as a trust relation anymore but would be similar to a dictator game.)[5]

One of the most prominent and simplest models of social preferences which have been used in behavioral game theory is a fairness or inequity aversion model (Fehr and Schmidt 1999). The idea is that actors prefer situations of equity (which means equality of material outcomes) to situations of inequality. Inequity occurs under two circumstances. One is the situation that an agent receives a larger outcome than her counterpart (which may be called "guilt" and which is called "relative gratification" in sociology); the other case is "relative deprivation" where the counterpart receives a larger outcome than the agent. In a trust game relative gratification from the point of view of the trustee takes place if trust is abused. In this case the trustee's outcome is t whereas the trustor receives S (see Figure 14.2). It can be demonstrated that the trustee's likelihood to honor trust decreases with (t-r)/(t-S) – provided that the trustee is disposed to prefer fairness and dislike guilt (see Snijders 1996:53–54). There is some experimental evidence which corroborates this hypothesis (Snijders 1996; Camerer 2003).

14.6.2 Repeated Interactions

Many if not most trust relations are not one-shot anonymous interactions but embedded into repeated interactions. In this case standard results from the theory of repeated games (see Osborne 2004: Chapters 14, 15 for an introduction and overview) can be usefully applied to trust games. Infinitely repeated trust games are iterated for an indefinite number of periods among the same partners. Both agents choose their strategies for the entire repeated game and receive payoffs which are weighted sums of each period's payoff. The payoffs are weighted by a so-called "shadow of the future" (Axelrod 1984) or discount factor δ ($1>\delta>0$) which reflects the (conditional) probability that another repetition will take place. It is assumed that this probability is constant for every period. The first period will take place with certainty, the second with probability δ, the third with δ – given a second repetition; therefore, the probability that the payoff from a third period will be collected is δ^2, and so forth. To illustrate, consider the situation that trust is placed and honored in every period of the repeated game the trustee will receive as her payoff from the repeated game $r + \delta r + \delta^2 r + \ldots = r/(1-\delta)$. (The infinite geometric series of the sum of payoffs converges to a finite value because $1>\delta>0$.) Furthermore, it will be assumed that the agents are informed about each participant's choices of the previous period. This opens the opportunity to condition one's action which is selected in period k upon the choices observed after period k-1. The trustor can thus consider strategies which condition the placement of trust in k on the trustee's honorable action in period k-1. A simple strategy which is conditional in this sense is the *Trigger strategy*. The Trigger strategy demands that the trustor places trust in the very first period (k=1) and continues to choose the placement of trust as long as in every previous period trust has been placed and honored. It can be shown that a profile of strategies such that the trustor uses Trigger and the trustee always honors trust (*Trigger, Always honor*) is an equilibrium of the repeated trust game if and only if the shadow of the future δ is large enough. In particular δ must at least equal the critical value $\delta^* = (t-r)/(t-p)$.[6]

The repeated games approach can be extended to situations where the trust relation is embedded in a structure of social relations. Consider social networks of information transmission among trustors such that third parties will easily access information about (potential) trustees' past behavior. In this case, it may be in trustees' best interest to invest into a good reputation, i.e. a reputation of being trustworthy (see also Origgi, this volume). This is so because trustees who were dishonest in past interactions will not be able to find new partners who would trust them. It can be demonstrated that in a group or social network of trustors with such information diffusion to allow for *multilateral reputation* effects trust can under certain conditions be enhanced and may be somewhat "easier" to achieve than in situations with bilateral reputation effects due to repeated interactions within stable partnerships (see Raub and Weesie 1990 for a seminal analysis of this mechanism with respect to the repeated prisoner's dilemma and Buskens 2002, 2003; Raub et al. 2013 for analyses of embedded trust games).

14.6.3 Signaling

Let us now explore an extension of the trust game with incomplete information which introduces additional actions of the trustee. Under certain contingencies, the option to "burn money" will allow honorable trustees to credibly signal their trustworthiness to the trustor. This *signaling model* does not only provide subtle and perhaps even counterintuitive insights on social situations involving trust, but it also captures one of the most important mechanisms invoked by the theory of rational action to explain seemingly inefficient, irrational and even foolish social practices (cf. Posner 1998 for some anecdotal evidence and examples on signaling norms; see Osborne 2004: Chapter 10 for an introduction to signaling games).

Figure 14.4 depicts the extended trust game with signaling. As was the case in the simple trust game with incomplete information, initially nature determines whether the trustee is opportunistic or not. Both types of trustees then decide on whether to signal their trustworthiness to the trustor at a cost $c>0$. Note that the costs are simply subtracted from the payoff of the trustee in case she signals, while nothing is added to the payoffs of the trustor. Hence, signaling trustworthiness in this model really amounts to a waste of resources, i.e. "burning money." After the trustor has observed whether the signal was sent, the game plays out as in the standard trust game with incomplete information. Note that the dotted lines indicate that the trustor can only observe whether a trustee has sent the signal, but not the type of the trustee.

The concept of a strategy in extensive games is a bit odd. That is, a strategy of a player describes what action the player chooses at each of her information sets. Since the trustee has two types which have three information sets respectively, we need to specify six actions to describe a strategy of the trustee. Fortunately, backward induction logic immediately delivers the insight that opportunistic trustees A always abuse trust and honorable trustees H always honor trust, regardless of whether a signal was sent. This restricts the range of possible strategies of the trustee which can be part of a sequential equilibrium considerably.

Let us check under what conditions there exists an equilibrium, in which the honorable trustee sends a signal, the opportunistic type sends no signal, and the trustor trusts if and only if she observes a signal of trustworthiness. This action profile is called

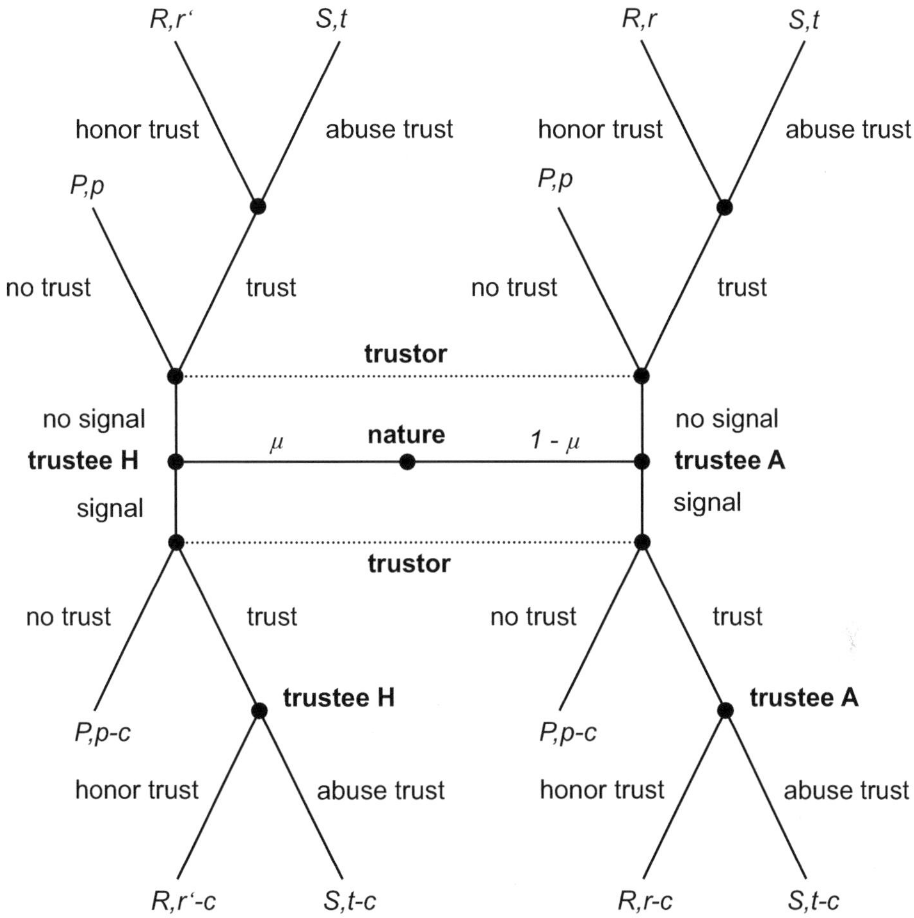

Figure 14.4 Signaling in the Trust Game

a *separating equilibrium*. Obviously, the trustor cannot improve her payoff by deviating from her strategy. Since the signal perfectly discriminates between the two types of trustees, changing her strategy amounts to either trusting an opportunistic or not trusting an honorable trustee, and hence does not pay off. Matters are more complicated regarding the incentives of the trustee. Consider the honorable trustee H. Her payoff in the separating strategy profile amounts to r'-c. If she switches her strategy and refuses to signal her trustworthiness, the trustor will not trust her, and she will obtain the payoff p. Hence, the separating equilibrium only exists if r'-c>p. Similarly, the opportunistic trustee A obtains the payoff p in the separating strategy profile. Deviating from her strategy means sending a signal of trustworthiness and leads to a payoff of t-c, because she would abuse the trust of the trustor who would fall prey to the fake signal of trustworthiness. Consequently, p>t-c is another necessary condition for the existence of a separating equilibrium. Since we considered all possible deviations by all agents, taken together these two inequalities are necessary and sufficient. By rearranging the inequalities, we find the neat characterization c∈[t-p,r'-p] for the existence of the separating equilibrium. Hence, the option of "burning money" helps to overcome problematic trust situations, provided that the costs of signaling are not too high to deter honorable trustees from signaling, but high enough to prevent fake signaling by opportunistic trustees.

Recall from our discussion of the simple trust game with perfect information that if the subjective belief μ of the trustor regarding the probability of encountering a trustworthy trustee is too low, the trustor will not put trust in the trustee and a deficient outcome in terms of Pareto-efficiency results. Now we have learned that signaling might overcome this dilemma, because in the separating equilibrium both the trustor and the honorable type of trustee are strictly better off than in the no trust outcome, while the opportunistic trustee maintains her payoff p.

Besides the separating equilibrium, other equilibria might exist in which either both or neither type of trustee send a signal of trustworthiness. Most importantly, if μ exceeds the critical value μ^*, there is an equilibrium in which the trustor always puts trust in the trustee, regardless of whether the trustee sends a signal, and no type of trustee invests in the signal. Note that it is possible that the conditions for the existence of this *pooling equilibrium* and the conditions for the existence of the separating equilibrium are satisfied at the same time. However, the trustor is strictly worse off in the pooling equilibrium. Hence, in a sense our game theoretic analysis of credible signals of trustworthiness backs Ronald Reagan's dictum: "Trust, but verify!"

Przepiorka and Diekmann (2013) conducted experiments on a variant of the signaling model. While many implications of the model were confirmed in this study, the central tenet of the model – the possibility of signaling enhances trust and hence efficiency – was not corroborated. Interestingly, this failure appears to be related to another social mechanism enhancing trust, which we already encountered. That is, the presence of trustees with prosocial preferences leads to relatively high levels of trust, even in experimental conditions under which the model predicts that no trust is put in the trustee.

14.7 Conclusion

This chapter has shown how game theoretic models explicate trust as a risky investment. Elementary models implicate that social situations involving trust tend to be problematic, i.e. inefficiencies due to a lack of trust are, from a theoretical point of view, likely to occur. Against this background, the game-theoretical literature tries to identify and study social mechanisms such as repeated interaction and signaling, which help to overcome trust problems by transforming the underlying incentive structure. Empirical tests of these models point to the necessity of studying the interaction of various social mechanisms promoting trust in both theoretical as well as in empirical terms.

Finally, we want to point out two important limitations of the game-theoretical account of trust and in particular our exposition. First, while the delineated perspective of trust as a risky investment is dominant in the game-theoretical literature, alternative approaches such as evolutionary game theory (Skyrms 2008) and team reasoning (Sugden 1993; Bacharach 1999) work with different conceptions of trust. Moreover, in the social sciences there are alternative notions of trust such as "generalized trust" (Putnam 1993; Fukuyama 1995), which are hardly captured by the risky-investment-perspective but refer to situations in which "confidence" and "trust" are merged. Secondly, the great bulk of the game-theoretical literature on trust rests on orthodox decision theory with its rather narrow and empirically questionable action-theoretic assumptions regarding human conduct. Since putting trust, honoring trust, as well as abusing trust have both emotional as well as moral connotations it seems questionable how much empirical validity analyses based on the assumption of pure rationality can achieve. Against this background, it seems worthwhile to relate the game-theoretical literature on trust with recent accounts in alternative decision and game theory, in particular with the literature on bounded rationality (Rubinstein 1998) and dual-process theories in cognitive and social psychology (Kahneman 2011).

Notes

1 There are many different branches of game theory modeling which cannot be discussed in this context: evolutionary game theory and models based on boundedly rational behavior do not depend on assumptions of unlimited rationality or information processing capacities.
2 A binary relation R on a set X is complete if it relates any two members of X, i.e. for all x and y in X it holds true that xRy or yRx. R is transitive if xRy and yRz implies xRz for all elements x, y,z in X. A preference relation is by definition always complete and transitive. Only sufficiently consistent choice behavior can be modeled by a preference relation.
3 The prisoner's dilemma is a canonical game in game theory. There are two players both having to choose simultaneously between two strategies, i.e. cooperation and defection. Payoff functions in this game are such that it is always better to defect, no matter what the other player does. However, the resulting unique Nash equilibrium of mutual defection gives rise to inefficiency in Pareto's sense, since both players would be better off if both players cooperated.
4 For more extensive and detailed treatments of these concepts see e.g. Osborne (2004) or some other textbook on game theory.
5 In the dictator game, the dictator receives a certain amount of money and simply has to allocate this money between herself and a recipient. The recipient simply is informed about the dictator's decision and gets the payoff, but has no say in the outcome.
6 The main idea is as follows: The profile (Trigger, Always honor) yields a payoff of $r/(1-\delta)$ for the trustee. If the trustee deviates from Always honor she receives (given the trustor consistently plays Trigger) $t + \delta p/(1-\delta)$ which is not larger than or equal to $r/(1-\delta)$ if and only if $\delta \geq \delta^* = (t-r)/(t-p)$.

References

Aumann, R. and Brandenburger, A. (1995) "Epistemic Conditions for Nash Equilibrium," *Econometrica* 63(5): 1161–1180.

Axelrod, R. (1984) *The Evolution of Cooperation*, New York: Basic Books.

Bacharach, M. (1999) *Interactive Team Reasoning: A Contribution to the Theory of Cooperation*, Princeton, NJ: Princeton University Press.

Berg, J., Dickhaut, J. and McCabe, K. (1995) "Trust, Reciprocity and Social History," *Games and Economic Behavior* 10(1): 122–142.

Blau, P.M. (1964) *Exchange and Power in Social Life*, New York: Wiley.

Buskens, V. (2002) *Social Networks and Trust*, Boston, MA: Kluwer.

Buskens, V. (2003) "Trust in Triads: Effect of Exit, Control, and Learning," *Games and Economic Behavior* 42(2): 235–252.

Camerer, C.F. (2003) *Behavioral Game Theory: Experiments in Strategic Interaction*, New York: Russell Sage.

Coleman, J.S. (1990) *Foundations of Social Theory*, Cambridge, MA: The Belknap Press of Harvard University Press.

Dasgupta, P. (1988) "Trust as a Commodity," in D. Gambetta (ed.), *Trust: Making and Breaking Cooperative Relations*, Oxford: Blackwell.

Fehr, E. (2009) "On the Economics and Biology of Trust," *Journal of the European Economic Association* 7(2–3): 235–266.

Fehr, E. and Schmidt, K.M. (1999) "A Theory of Fairness, Competition, and Cooperation," *Quarterly Journal of Economics* 114(3): 817–868.

Fukuyama, F. (1995) *Trust: The Social Virtues and Creation of Prosperity*, New York: The Free Press.

Kahneman, D. (2011) *Thinking, Fast and Slow*, London: Penguin Books.

Kreps, D. (1990) *Game Theory and Economic Modelling*, Oxford: Oxford University Press.

Luhmann, N. (1988) "Familiarity, Confidence, Trust: Problems and Alternatives," in D. Gambetta (ed.), *Trust: Making and Breaking Cooperative Relations*, Oxford: Blackwell.
Osborne, M.J. (2004) *An Introduction to Game Theory*, New York: Oxford University Press.
Pelligra, V. (2006) "Trust, Reciprocity and Institutional Design: Lessons from Behavioural Economics," AICCON Working Papers 37, Associazione Italiana per la Cultura della Cooperazione e del Non Profit.
Posner, E.A. (1998) "Symbols, Signals and Social Norms in Politics and the Law," *Journal of Legal Studies* 27(52): 765–798.
Przepiorka, W. and Diekmann, A. (2013) "Temporal Embeddedness and Signals of Trustworthiness: Experimental Tests of a Game Theoretic Model in the United Kingdom, Russia, and Switzerland," *European Sociological Review* 29(5): 1010–1023.
Putnam, R. (1993) *Making Democracy Work*, Princeton: Princeton University Press.
Raub, W. and Voss, T. (1986) "Conditions for Cooperation in Problematic Social Situations," in A. Diekmann and P. Mitter (eds.), *Paradoxical Effects of Social Behavior: Essays in Honor of Anatol Rapoport*, Heidelberg: Physica.
Raub, W. and Weesie, J. (1990) "Reputation and Efficiency in Social Interactions: An Example of Network Effects," *American Journal of Sociology* 96(3): 626–654.
Raub, W., Buskens, V. and Frey, V. (2013) "The Rationality of Social Structure: Cooperation in Social Dilemmas through Investments in and Returns on Social Capital," *Social Networks* 35(4): 720–732.
Rubinstein, A. (1998) *Modeling Bounded Rationality*, Cambridge, MA: MIT Press.
Skyrms, B. (2008) "Trust, Risk, and the Social Contract," *Synthese* 160(1): 21–25.
Snijders, C. (1996) *Trust and Commitments*, Amsterdam: Thesis Publishers.
Sugden, R. (1993) "Thinking as a Team: Towards an Explanation of Nonselfish Behavior," *Social Philosophy & Policy* 10(1): 69–89.
Weber, M. (1988) "Einleitung in die Wirtschaftsethik der Weltreligionen," in M. Weber (ed.), *Gesammelte Aufsätze zur Religionssoziologie I*, Tübingen: Mohr.

15
TRUST: PERSPECTIVES IN SOCIOLOGY

Karen S. Cook and Jessica J. Santana

15.1 Introduction

The role of trust in society has been the focus of intense study in the social sciences over the last two decades, to some extent fueled by the publication of Fukuyama's 1995 book entitled *Trust: The Social Virtues and the Creation of Prosperity*, which circulated widely both inside and outside of academia. In this book Fukuyama addresses the question of why societies vary in their levels of general social trust (or the perception of most people as trustworthy) and what difference it makes that they do. To support his general argument, he analyzed differences among a wide range of countries including the United States, Russia, Germany, Italy, Great Britain, France, South Korea, China and Japan. His primary thesis was that economic development was affected in various ways, often deleteriously, by the lack of general social trust in a society. He linked these effects primarily to differences within each culture in the role that family and kin play in constraining economic activity outside socially determined boundaries. In a discussion of the "paradox of family values," Fukuyama (1995) argues that cultures with large and strong families tend to be cultures with lower general social trust and prosperity.

A key assumption in Fukuyama's book is that general social trust, when it exists, provides the conditions under which competitive economic enterprises flourish because it facilitates the emergence of specific forms of organization and networks that support economic success. While this oversimplifies the nature of the determinants of economic prosperity, it does suggest that social and cultural factors may play a much larger role than often conveyed in the standard social science literature on development economics. If the ability of companies to shift from hierarchical forms of organization to more flexible networks of smaller firms relies on social capital, or social networks and the norms of reciprocity and trustworthiness that arise from them (Putnam 2000), then understanding the conditions that foster or inhibit trust is critical to an analysis of economic development and growth.

Long before Fukuyama developed his general thesis about the significance of general social trust in economic development, Arrow (1974) argued that economic productivity is hampered when distrust requires monitoring and sanctioning. Fukuyama identifies a lack of trust as the reason that organizations adopt a more hierarchical form (including large networks of organizations created by contracting). Flexible exchange within networks of smaller firms requires trust. In Fukuyama's words (1995:25):

> A 'virtual' firm can have abundant information coming through network wires about its suppliers and contractors. But if they are all crooks or frauds, dealing with them will remain a costly process involving complex contracts and time-consuming enforcement. Without trust, there will be strong incentive to bring these activities in-house and restore old hierarchies.

Susan Shapiro views trust as the foundation of capitalism in her book, *Wayward Capitalists* (1984). She argues that financial transactions could not easily occur without trust because most contracts are incomplete. In significant ways then trust can be said to provide the social foundations for economic relations of exchange and production. As Arrow (1974) argued, monitoring is often ineffective. Sanctioning can be costly. Transaction costs can be high. To the extent that actors are trustworthy with respect to their commitments, such costs can be reduced within organizations and in the economy more broadly. Institutional backing, however, is often key to facilitating relations of trust given that recourse to legal interventions is available when trust fails (see Gkouvas and Mindus, this volume). What is central to the functioning of economies is not only institutional stability, but also the capacity for general social trust that encourages engagement across cultural boundaries and national borders. A more sociological conception of trust as fundamentally relational is useful in analyzing the role of trust in such contexts.

At the same time that Fukuyama's work was gaining recognition, Robert Putnam was conducting research and writing about social capital and its role in society, especially in promoting a more civil society. For Putnam (1995:665), *social capital* refers to "social connections and the attendant norms and trust" that enable people to accomplish social objectives. This work led to an industry of research focused on defining and explaining the hypothesized societal level effects of declining social capital (e.g. Paxton 1999) and the mechanisms behind these effects. These social scientists, among others, raised important questions at the macro-level about the role of general trust and social capital (i.e. networks, norms and trust) in economic development, the maintenance of social order, and the emergence of a more civil society. In addition, they began to examine the function of social divides (e.g. by race or ethnicity) in the creation and maintenance of social cohesion and the consequences of the lack of it (e.g. Ahmadi 2018; Bentley 2016, etc.).

The broad-gauged interest in trust has continued to grow over the past several decades. Social interactions are increasingly mediated through the Internet and other forms of online communication, connecting individuals who, in the distant past, might never have had any form of connection or even knowledge of one another's existence. This globalization of social interaction has had far reaching consequences beyond business and economic transactions to include social organization on a much broader scale than previously imagined through social movement sites (e.g. moveon.org or occupywallstreet.org), as well as crowdfunding sites (e.g. Kickstarter) and many varied associational sites (e.g. Facebook) connecting people in common causes or affiliation networks. In all of these interactions, trust matters.

In the remainder of this chapter, we demonstrate the role of trust in the functioning of society. We begin by defining trust. We situate trust in social networks, where trust is viewed as an element of social capital. We then describe how trust operates in and modifies organizations and how this may evolve as some modern organizational forms change to become online platforms. We also explore the role of trust in relations between organizations as we examine the impact of trust on markets. We take a more macro view of trust in institutions in the final section to demonstrate how institutional trust sometimes enables the functioning of complex societies. We close with a comment on the value of distrust in democratic societies.

15.2 Trust Defined

The social science disciplines vary in how they define trust. In particular, psychologists tend to define trust in cognitive terms as a characteristic of a person's attitude toward others or simply the disposition to be trusting. For example, Rotter (1967) defined trust in terms of one's willingness to be vulnerable to another. Subsequently, one of the most widely used definitions of trust in the literature, especially in the field of organizations, is the one developed by Rousseau et al. (1998:395): "Trust is a psychological state comprising the intention to accept vulnerability based on positive expectations of the intentions or the behavior of another."

A more sociological approach such as that provided in Cook, Hardin and Levi (2005) takes a *relational* perspective on trust, importantly viewing trust not as a characteristic of an individual, but as an attribute of a social relationship between two or more actors. "Trust exists when one party to the relation believes the other party has incentive to act in his or her interest or to take his or her interest to heart" (Cook, Hardin and Levi 2005:2). This view is referred to as the "encapsulated interest" account of trust (as defined initially by Hardin 2002) that focuses on the incentives the parties in the mutual relationship have to be trustworthy with respect to one another based primarily on two factors: 1) their commitment to maintaining the relationship into the future and 2) their concern for securing a reputation as one who is trustworthy, an important characteristic in relations with other actors, especially in a closed network or small community. Reputations of trustworthiness are also important in the case of social entities such as groups, organizations, networks or institutions, if they are to sustain cooperation and engagement.

In the encapsulated interest view of trust articulated in Hardin's (2002) book, "Trust and Trustworthiness," A *trusts* B with respect to x when A believes that her interests are included in B's utility function, so that B values what A desires *because* B wants to maintain good relations with A. The typical trust relation from this perspective is represented as: *Actor A trusts actor B with respect to x* (a particular domain of activity), presuming that in most cases there are limits to the trust relation. A might trust B with respect to money, but not with the care of an infant, for example. Or, A might trust B with respect to one specific type of organizational task (i.e. accounting), but not another task (i.e. marketing). These judgments are, of course, often made on at least two grounds: competence and integrity (or the commitment to "do no harm"). In the end, the main distinguishing feature of a more sociological account of trust is that it is a relational account and not purely psychological. It characterizes the state of a relationship, not just the actors involved. It also allows us to extend the account to deal with groups, organizations, networks of social relations, and institutions.

Sociologists and political scientists are primarily interested in the extent to which trust contributes to the production of social order in society (Cook and Cook 2011). Economists often focus on the role of general social trust in economic development (see also Cohen, this volume). Arrow (1974), as we have noted, argued that the economy relies on relations of trust. One of the central reasons for studying trust is to understand its role in the production of cooperation not only at the interpersonal level but also at the organizational and institutional levels (Cook, Hardin and Levi 2005). Is trust central to the functioning of groups, organizations and institutions and what role does it play in relation to other mechanisms that exist to secure cooperation and facilitate the maintenance of social order? We address these issues at varying levels of analysis in the sections that follow.

Much of the published social science work on trust, not to mention literature more broadly, addresses trust in interpersonal relationships highlighting the consequences of failures of trust or betrayals. This is particularly true in applied and clinical psychology. However, trust between individuals is of interest not only to those who study personal relationships, but is also important in other domains such as work and community settings. Since it is often argued that trust fosters cooperation, it is implicated in prosocial behavior, in the production of public goods, in collective action and in intergroup relations (e.g. Cook and Cooper 2003; Cook and State 2017).

While trust cannot bear the full weight of providing social order writ large (Cook, Hardin and Levi 2005), it is significant at the micro-level in a variety of ways. In the section below on organizations we discuss the role of interpersonal trust between coworkers, employees and their supervisors, and the impact of a culture of trust versus distrust within organizations. Interpersonal trust in the workplace often leads to higher levels of "organizational citizenship behaviors," for example altruism toward co-workers or working after hours (Dirks and Ferrin 2001). It is also critical to the smooth functioning of network-based projects and enterprises which depend on the trustworthiness of those involved, especially in the absence of traditional forms of supervision and hierarchical authority (see Blomqvist and Cook 2018).

15.3 Trust in Networks

Trust, when it exists as we have noted above, can reduce various kinds of costs, including, but not limited to, transaction costs and the costs of monitoring and sanctioning. Granovetter (1985, 2017), for example, views economic relations as one class of social relations. In his view, economic transactions are frequently embedded in social structures formed by social ties among actors. A network of social relations thus represents a kind of "market" in which goods are bought and sold or bartered. In addition, they set the terms of exchange sometimes altering the mode of exchange as well as the content of the negotiations. Trust discourages malfeasance and opportunism in part because when transactions are embedded in social relations reputations come into play (see also Origgi, this volume). Individuals, he argues, have an incentive to be trustworthy to secure the possibility of future transactions. Continuing social relations characterized by trust have the property that they constrain opportunistic behavior because of the value of the association. Hardin's (2002) encapsulated interest theory of trust is based on this logic.

The relational view of trust assumes that trust involves at least two people or social units. Network dynamics can be evaluated on a dyadic level – i.e. focusing on the traits and actions of two people or social units. Tie "strength" can describe the frequency of interaction between two nodes, the "age" of the interaction, the degree of intimacy involved in the interaction, the multidimensionality of the relationship, and/or the extent of the dependence (or power) of one node on (or over) another. Encapsulated interest-based trust, the term used by Hardin and his collaborators, describes the dependence of a trustee on a trustor when the trustee's interests are "encapsulated" in those of the trustor, increasing their trustworthiness. Similarly, Guanxi networks are ties in which trustworthiness is based primarily on reciprocity (Lin 2001).

Tie strength is dynamic. It can decay, for example, as the frequency of interaction decreases or anticipated interactions come to an end (Burt 2000). This reduction in tie strength alters the "shadow of the future" influencing both trust and assumed trustworthiness. If the relationship is coming to an end, the trustee is less likely to be trustworthy (Hardin 2002). Tie intimacy can vary from deep passion and diffuse obligations at one end of a continuum to highly specific contractual relations entailing little emotion at the other end. Williamson (1993) argues that trust between lovers is the only real trust *because* it is based on passion, and that trust between business partners is not trust, but rather a rational calculation of risk moderated by contractual obligations. In our view this perspective narrows the boundaries of trust relations too much, leaving very important trust-based relationships, that do not involve love, aside. Trust does exist between friends, business partners, and employers and their employees, among others, and these are significant social connections that facilitate everyday life, especially if they are trusted connections.

The introduction of passion or contract via "multiplex," or multidimensional, ties (Smith-Lovin 2003) may alter the dynamics of trust in mixed relationships (that is, those that may entail both passion in one domain and contractual relations in another). The Medici family in Renaissance Italy, for example, were known to keep family and business relations separate within their political party (Padgett and Ansell 1993), despite the common use at the time of such multiplex ties as a form of business organization (Padgett and McLean 2006). The determinants of trust are often complex in various exchange relationships. In addition, tie strength is not necessarily positively related to trust. Mario Small (2017), for example, found that graduate students shared intimate details and sought help from those with whom they had weak ties (e.g. a colleague or acquaintance) rather than strong ties. In part, this was because the students did *not* want to share certain information with those they trusted the most in other domains and with whom they had deeper relationships (i.e. spouses, parents, close friends).

Node, rather than edge or network, attributes can also play a significant role in the emergence of trust in networks. For example, homophily, or the preference for similar others, can cause people to trust others who are like them more than those who are not (Abrahao, Parigi, Gupta and Cook 2017). This form of "bias" can create system-wide inequalities between groups. Minorities, for example, are given lower quality loan terms because banks generally distrust their ability to repay the loans (Smith 2010), they are less likely to be chosen as business partners as well as hosts or guests on certain websites (c.f. Edelman and Luca 2014 on the case of Airbnb.com).

But networks can have particularly pronounced effects on trust because they are composed of more than two people or social units and information as well as influence travels across network paths. Networks of more than two people present special conditions for trust. Social capital, reputation, and status cause people to behave in different ways when relations are connected within networks than if the trust relations occur in isolation (i.e. in isolated dyads). Studying network-based trust is challenging. As a network grows in complexity, for example, the influence the network has on trust behavior evolves and may be hard to detect let alone measure (see Abrahao, Parigi, Gupta and Cook 2017; Buskens 2002, for recent attempts to do so).

Networks are typically defined based on the types of relationships or characteristics of the edges among the nodes which compose the network. These relationships determine important network features such as the exchange structure or directionality of the relationships (or resource flows). A generalized exchange network, for example, in which all nodes are expected to play the role of trustor at some point, as manifested in many sharing economy platforms, will exhibit different trust behavior from reciprocal exchange networks in which actors trust only after trustees demonstrate their trustworthiness (c.f. Molm 2010). Chain networks of generalized exchange may break down if a single trustor does not trust or a single trustee proves untrustworthy. In non-chain generalized exchanges, participants may free-ride on the trustworthiness of others in the network, producing a collective action problem similar to that often represented in the standard "prisoner's dilemma" (see also chapters by Dimock and by Tutić and Voss, this volume).[1] Reciprocal exchanges may also break down if one exchange partner fails to reciprocate, but trust can intervene to rectify such failures (Ostrom and Walker 2003). Relational directionality (or resource flow) in a network is critical in trust relationships, since a lack of trust in one direction can influence the level of trust in the other (Berg et al. 1995). Trust relations are typically mutual and thus entail reciprocal resource flows.

Position in the network has important implications. A person or social unit's position in the network is often measured by their "centrality" in the network. There are many types of network centrality that reflect different forms of connectedness and disconnectedness. Those who are peripheral, for example, may have low *closeness centrality* to other members of the network. In other words, they have fewer contacts that can influence their capacity for trust and trustworthiness. If a trustor is on the periphery of the network – i.e. not connected to highly connected others – they may be more likely to trust less trustworthy members of the network out of desperation and dependence (Cook et al. 2006). Conversely, peripheral trustors may be less trusting of core members for the same reasons they are marginalized – e.g. minorities in an organization may rely on other minorities to share riskier information (Smith 2010). When the network is directed, as is (generally) the case with trust (except perhaps for generalized trust), trustors and trustees have a certain number of trusting relationships (out-degree) and trusted relationships (in-degree). The higher their out-degree, the more trusting they are in general. The higher their in-degree, the more others trust them. Online platforms that rely on reputation mechanisms to overcome anonymity or partner heterogeneity use out-degree and in-degree to demonstrate a person's reputation as trusting or as worthy of trust.

Betweenness centrality can indicate that a person or social unit plays a role as a trust *broker* between two parties who would not otherwise directly trust each other (Shapiro 2005). Two departments in an organization, for example, may be less trusting of each other if they have contradictory incentives or values. In this case, a cross-functional manager or executive can serve as a surrogate trustor and trustee. Institutions, such as the Securities and Exchange Commission (SEC), which regulates federal securities and investment law, can also serve as trust brokers, especially when interpersonal trust is low. Betweenness centrality matters more when networks are densely clustered or diffuse, in which few people interact directly with each other. Networks can also be variously clustered into cliques. Cohesive units are less likely to trust units outside of their clique. Brokers play an important role in bridging otherwise untrusting units (Burt 2005). The concept of triadic closure implies that trust is more likely when trust already exists between two shared contacts (Simmel 1971; Granovetter 1973). For this reason, negotiators strive to develop trust between strained parties (Lewicki and Stevenson 1998; Druckman and Olekalns 2013).

Networks are important because they are reflexive, prismatic structures rather than static containers (Podolny 2001). Members of a network have characteristics or assumed properties as a result of their connections in the network. When a person has high *eigenvector centrality*, that is, is connected to high status individuals in the network, they may be treated as having higher status, for example. In the context of trust, when a person is connected to highly trustworthy individuals, they may be viewed as more trustworthy. Conversely, when a person (or organization) is deemed untrustworthy, that reputation reflects on others connected to them so that their trustworthiness may be called into question. For this reason, being part of a network is a strong incentive, and thus catalyst, for being trustworthy.

15.4 Trust in Organizations

One defining feature of organizations is their inherent separation of office from the individual (Weber 2013). This separation transfers accountability from the individual to the organization, which is expected to outlast the individuals that pass through it, but does not eliminate the reliance on trust for coordination and cooperation (see also chapter by Dimock, this volume). The degree of trust between individuals and organizations depends on the role of the individual and the organization in a specific context. Consumers, for example, may trust a "brand" in that they expect the company to be consistent and accountable (Chaudhuri and Holbrook 2001). Employees may indicate that they trust their employer to treat them fairly, or that they distrust union membership (Ferguson 2016), by choosing not to unionize (Cornfield and Kim 1994). Members of the local community may trust a nuclear energy provider to uphold environmental safety regulations (De Roeck and Delobbe 2012). In many of these cases, trust in the organization is indicated by engaging directly with the organization rather than seeking a more trustworthy intermediary, such as a labor union.

Within organizations, trust can be built piecemeal between supervisors and subordinates, or fostered collectively across the organizational culture. Organizational culture is a powerful mechanism for promoting trust within an organization. Trust among employees, including between superiors and subordinates, can increase the pace of productivity, decrease administrative overhead such as monitoring worker engagement, and increase worker retention (Kramer and Cook 2004). Dirks and Ferrin (2001), for example, found that trust in organizational leadership resulted in increased "organizational citizenship behaviors," including altruism, civic virtue, conscientiousness, courtesy and sportsmanship, as well as increased job performance, job satisfaction and organizational commitment. Dirks and Skarlicki (2004) further unpack this relationship noting that perceptions of a leader's integrity or benevolence (two important dimensions of trustworthiness) determine whether followers engage in these organizational citizenship behaviors.

The interface through which individuals engage with organizations can influence trust. For example, people increasingly interact with organizations online instead of visiting a physical office. Online organizations entail new implications for analyzing the antecedents and consequences of trust because they are platforms, or ecosystems of individuals, communities, networks, and organizations that are not as accessible in offline contexts (Parigi, Santana and Cook 2017). While people may have greater access to the organizational ecosystem online, the Internet, as the medium of interaction, also creates a screen between people, producing a variety of new issues and concerns. While it may increase access and efficiency, not to mention result in some transaction cost savings, people can choose to remain anonymous online. Anonymity generally decreases trust (Nissenbaum 2004). Through anonymization and decentralization, online platforms further abstract trust from the individuals interacting via the platform. This diffusion of accountability weakens trust not only between individuals, but also in the platform itself. (see also chapter by Ess, this volume).

To rebuild trust in platforms, organizations rely on reputational mechanisms, including ratings and reviews, that temper anonymization (c.f. Diekmann, Jann, Przepiorka and Wehrli 2014). Reputational systems can promote generalized trust and trustworthiness in online platforms (Kuwabara 2015), even overcoming strong social biases such as homophily (Abrahao, Parigi, Gupta and Cook 2017), or the tendency to choose to interact with those who are similar, under certain conditions (e.g. risk and uncertainty). Drug markets in the "Dark Web" promote illegal exchange under high risk of incarceration using vendor reputation systems (Duxbury and Haynie 2017). Reputational tools, however, do not provide a panacea, as they are subject to biases such as those created by power dependence differentials (State, Abrahao and Cook 2016) or status-based cumulative advantage (Keijzer and Corten 2016). Moreover, providing a holistic view of reputation – i.e. one based on the historical interaction context – may be more effective than that entailed in the common dyadic reputation model (Corten, Rosenkranz, Buskens and Cook 2016).

The "sharing economy" is a special organizational form that is growing among online platforms, in which people may share or sell various products and services ranging from car rides and overnight stays in spare bedrooms to week-long rentals or trades of vacation homes (Parigi and Cook 2015; Sundararajan 2016). To some extent, this organizational form tends to replace the locus of trust from the organization to trust between individual participants. Because sharing economy participants, however, are typically strangers, trust between them cannot be based solely on dyadic tie strength. Instead, trust in the sharing economy platform is important, and trust is built between participants via reputational tools such as systems of ratings and reviews (Ter Hurrne, Corten, Ronteltap and Buskens 2017). On sharing economy platforms, buyers and sellers often alternate roles, sometimes buying and sometimes selling. Reputational tools must therefore reflect this duality. Airbnb, for example, rates both hosts and guests. OpenTable, a restaurant reservation platform, penalizes guests who do not show up for their reservation. These incentives strengthen the dual-sided nature of reputation systems as mechanisms for securing trust in the sharing economy.

15.5 Trust between Organizations

At the time of Fukuyama's (1995) book release, Powell (1996) identified a number of types of business networks in which trust plays a role in the organization of economic activity. For example, in research and development networks such as those in Silicon Valley, trust is often formed and maintained through professional memberships in relevant associations, a high degree of information flow across the network and by frequent shifting of employees across organizational boundaries. In another example, Powell explored the role of trust in business groups such as the Japanese keiretsu and the Korean chaebol. In these business groups trust emerges out of a mixture of common membership in the group, perceived obligation, and vigilance. Initially reputations matter, but long-term repeat interactions are key to the establishment of trust relations in this context as well. Repeated interactions provide the opportunity for learning, monitoring, dyadic sanctioning and increasing mutual dependence which reinforces the basis for trust. They also provide more accurate information about trustworthiness (i.e. competence, integrity and benevolence).

Trust between organizational partners in an alliance reduces the need for hierarchical controls (Gulati and Singh 1998). Higher levels of trust among partners to an alliance results in fewer concerns over opportunism or exploitation because the firms have greater confidence in the predictability and reliability of one another. Alliances between firms that view each other as trustworthy lower coordination costs improving efficiency in part because the firms are more likely to be willing to learn each other's rules and standard operating procedures. Without such trust, hierarchical controls and systems of monitoring and sanctioning are more often put into place to implement the alliance and to ensure success, though frequently increasing the overall cost of the enterprise.

In the *Limits of Organization*, Kenneth Arrow (1974) clearly recognized the economic or pragmatic value of trust. Arrow (like Luhmann 1980) viewed trust as an important lubricant of a social system: "It is extremely efficient; it saves a lot of trouble to have a fair degree of reliance on other people's word" (Arrow 1974:23). Trust not only saves on transaction costs but it also increases the efficiency of a system enabling the production of more goods (or more of what a group values) with less cost. However, trust cannot be bought and sold on the open market and is highly unlikely to be simply produced on demand. Arrow argued that a lack of mutual trust is one of the properties of many of the societies that are less developed economically, reflecting the key theme picked up two decades later by Frances Fukuyama (1995). The lack of mutual trust, Arrow notes, represents a distinct loss economically as well as a loss in the smooth running of the political system which requires the success of collective undertakings.

The economic value of trust in Arrow's view has mainly to do with its role in the production of public goods. Individuals have to occasionally respond to the demands of society even when such demands conflict with their own individual interests. According to Fukuyama (1995), more traditional hierarchical forms of governance hinder the formation of global networks and international economic activity. These factors are correlated with lower economic performance in general. Flexibility and the capacity to form these networks of small companies that can be responsive to change is key to economic growth, he argues, and cultures that support this form of organization foster success.

15.6 Trust in Institutions

Sociological perspectives on trust not only focus on the relational aspect of trust at the micro-level, they also view trust in societal institutions as relevant to the production of social order. Institutions are persistent norms and systems for maintaining norms, such as governmental structures, marriages, markets or religions. Without the cooperation produced by institutions, societies cannot function well, unless it is enforced by coercive rule.

Lynne Zucker (1986) identifies three basic modes of trust production in society. First, there is the process-based trust tied to a history of past or expected exchange (e.g. gift exchange). Reputations work to support trust-based exchange because past exchange behavior provides accurate information that can easily be disseminated in a network of relations. This form of trust is important in the relatively recent surge of online interactions and transactions. Process-based trust has high information requirements and works best in small societies or organizations. However, it is becoming significant again as a basis for online commerce and information sharing. The second type of trust she identifies is characteristic-based trust in which trust is tied to a particular person depending on characteristics such as family background or ethnicity. The third type of trust is institutional-based trust, which ties trustworthiness to formal societal structures that function to support cooperation. Such structures include third-party intermediaries and professional associations or other forms of certification that reduce risk. Government regulation and legislation also provide the institutional background for cooperation lowering the risk of default or opportunism. High rates of immigration, internal migration and the instability of business enterprises from the mid 1800s to the early 1900s, Zucker argues, disrupted process-based trust relations. The move to institutional bases for securing trustworthiness was historically inevitable.

As societies grow more complex, order is more difficult to maintain organically. Subcommunities, for example, develop distinct cultures that can make exchange across communities difficult especially when values conflict. Such communities can transfer trust from individuals who may be distrusted to a common institution that can be trusted. Trust in institutions can replace weakened trust in individuals. Individuals can distrust each other for a variety of reasons. Criminal partners can betray their loyalty when their freedom is at stake (i.e. the classic Prisoner's Dilemma). Competitors can cheat and steal from each other in the name of opportunism, or collude together to weight the market scale in their favor. Employers can take advantage of their power to coerce employees against their will. In cases such as these, an institution can replace trust among individuals in order to maintain social order and to mitigate the worst consequences of the lack of trust between individuals. A legal system advocates for fair working conditions, for example, and helps to secure better working environments even when organizations do not provide them. Government agencies regulate market forces to prevent intellectual property theft and collusion. A common moral code, or "honor among thieves," can discourage "snitching."

Trust in institutions, when it exists, is a powerful replacement for interpersonal trust, and it can promote high levels of cooperation that function to maintain order in a society despite low interpersonal trust (Cook 2009). People and organizations engage in transactions with untrusted others when they trust institutions regulating those transactions. Institutions can also invoke generalized trust, or an increase in trust of others in general. Small, isolated or cohesive populations, for example, promote internal norms of trust and cooperation. Violating these norms can result in expulsion from the community. While recognition of norm violations requires institutional monitoring, paradoxically, explicit monitoring by institutions may reduce trust in institutions (and can also be symptomatic of weak institutional trust). The most influential institutions are those that delegate monitoring to community members organically (Durkheim 1997). This is why companies and other organizations strive to foster strong organizational cultures in which their employees self-monitor (see also the recent use of civic platforms for trustworthiness ratings in China).

High trust in institutions can lead to high general social trust (Uslaner 2002), i.e. trust in strangers, under certain conditions. When people can rely on a legal system, for example, they expect others to obey laws and to be more reliable and trustworthy as a result. Low trust in the general population, on the other hand, may be correlated with higher trust in institutions (Furstenberg et al. 1999). For example, rather than rely on unfamiliar neighbors, residents in a densely populated city may turn to government services for their general welfare. But when there is low trust in institutions people have to rely on those they know or on individual reputations for trustworthiness since there is no institutional recourse. In post-communist Russia, for example, the collapse of governmental institutions led to increased reliance on familiar, reliable exchange partners (Radaev 2004a,b). In Belize, black market traders relied on trusted East Indian ethnic enclaves to circumvent legal regulation (Wiegand 1994). Although, an increase in the reliance on informal institutions such as black markets and corruption in some settings often signals low interpersonal trust interacting with low (formal) institutional trust (Puffer et al. 2010), a hard situation to rectify.

Trust in institutions also fluctuates, with one institution often replacing another as the choice trustee. This fluctuation may reflect a shift in the balance of power. As organizations gain power, for example, governments attempt to regulate their reach and diffuse their dependence on them. One way that governments do this is by providing fail-safe measures to protect the public from betrayal of their trust. The Federal Deposit Insurance Corporation (FDIC), for example, was created in response to the inability of banks to abide by their contracts with their customers in the early 20th century. Such institutions, serving as trust brokers, increase the distance between trustors and trustees. Betrayal of trust can also cause an abrupt shift in institutional trust. Following the 2008 Financial Crisis, for example, American consumers increasingly trust technology companies, such as PayPal, more than traditional banks, such as Wells Fargo (#### GrahamLet's Talk Payments 2015).

When distrust of formal institutions is high – as occurs in the case of illegal markets – people must learn whom to trust in order to successfully engage in exchanges. In such cases, reputational systems play an increasingly important role in the market (Przepiorka, Norbutas and Corten 2017). Another way those engaged in exchange can identify trustworthy individuals under such risky conditions is via identity signals, such as those provided by experiences or information that would be difficult to fake (Gambetta 2009). Network embeddedness or centralization in a social network also provide a proxy for reputation. People can gain reputational information about a potential exchange partner via networks. Networks also serve to replace reputational mechanisms, since norms of network embeddedness temper the betrayal of trust. In other words, betraying trust in a network context ripples throughout the network, harming the social capital that the individual has amassed. When those networks are composed of family or other types of special relationships, the consequences of betrayal are even more dire than the simple loss of social capital.

15.7 Distrust and Its Functions

The heavy emphasis on trust in society is often misplaced in the sense that even if general social trust is high in a society, community or place of work, not everyone is consistently trustworthy and acts of betrayal, corruption, secrecy and distrust may occur that challenge the status quo (see also chapters by D'Cruz as well as Alfano and Huijts, this volume). Acts that lead to distrust may undermine social order and lead to civil unrest, conflict or even the breakdown of social norms. Group conflict theory, for example, describes how stronger identification with one group in society is often affiliated with stronger distrust of "outsiders" (Hardin 1995; Becker 1963). Calls for increased investment in national security or harsher penal system policies play on this distrust between groups. Despite these facts, it is also important to recognize the more positive role of distrust, especially in the context of institutions (see Hardin 2002, Cook et al. 2005). Distrust, for example, can be useful for power attainment and maintenance.

Distrust can also be used to moderate power. Checks and balances in democratic institutions and other regulatory tools can increase transparency and decrease biases inherent in trust, such as those produced by homophily and by various forms of corruption. Such transparency can even empower underrepresented populations and dampen inequality. Affirmative action policies, for example, reduce the subjectivity of hiring and other selection processes (Harper and Reskin 2005). Transparency may also reduce reliance on trust. As one example, the creators of the Bitcoin blockchain, a distributed registry of every transaction using Bitcoin currency, claim that it reduces the vulnerability of international currency exchanges and dependence on trustworthiness (Nakamoto 2008). Blundell-Wignall (2014) describes the growing popularity of cryptocurrencies like Bitcoin as a shift in trust away from formal financial institutions following the global financial crises of the early 21st century.

Transparency, however, may be gained at the expense of other social values such as privacy. As more people trust government and corporations with their private data, for example, they have less control over how their data are used to the degree that personal data can be used against people in order to price discriminate, restrict access to goods and services, or target populations for discriminatory regulation. Trust of the institutions provides more access to information. This access to information shifts the balance of power. Whistleblowers are thus an important fallback when checks and balances do not function properly. The necessity of legal protections for whistleblowers implies distrust of the organizations on which they blow the whistle (Sawyer et al. 2010). A healthy democracy fosters such forms of distrust to balance the power rendered by trust. Wright (2002) argued that the American Constitution was created to check the power of the newly formed infant government during a state of high information asymmetry between government officials and U.S. citizens.

In some circumstances, trust can signal security and routine. However, innovation and improvisation, necessary under conditions of high uncertainty, may require distrust of routine process and information. Studies of entrepreneurs, for example, have noted that those who distrust tend to perform better. This may be because entrepreneurs act in a high uncertainty, high risk environment that requires "nonroutine action" (Schul, Mayo and Burnstein 2008; Gudmundsson and Lechner 2013; Kets de Vries 2003; Lewicki, McAllister and Bies 1998). When risk is particularly high, distrust can be especially critical. Perrow (2005) notes that risk scales with complexity. Complex systems are also likely to increase the distance between trustor and trustee via trust brokers. This distance can obscure the amount of risk involved until the system has already begun to collapse (Kroeger 2015). Robust complex systems thus must rely on distrust to anticipate failure and rebound from it (Perrow 2005).

15.8 Concluding Remarks

In this chapter, we have defined and illustrated the sociological, or relational, view of trust. We discussed the relationship between trust and economic development, as well as cooperation and social order. We described how organizations, groups, networks and societies rely on trust, and how trust, under some circumstances, can be harmful in these contexts. We reviewed the conditions under which trust can be jeopardized or fostered, as well as the nature of alternative mechanisms that overcome the loss of trust or replace it. Trust behavior and attitudes are both essential and influential in various contexts, even if reliance on trust alone cannot provide for the production of social order at the macro-level, especially when trust in institutions is weak or non-existent.

Note

1 The "prisoner's dilemma" (cf. Axelrod and Ambrosio 1994) describes the situation in a game where two actors who are unable to know each other's actions (e.g. suspects in separate interrogation rooms) gain the highest utility if only one betrays the other, lose the largest penalty if they are the only one betrayed, and collectively optimize their penalty by neither betraying the other.

References

Abrahao, B., Parigi, P., Gupta, A. and Cook, K. (2017) "Reputation Offsets Trust Judgements Based on Social Biases among AirBnB Users," *Proceedings of the National Academy of Sciences* 113(37): 9848–9853.

Ahmadi, D. (2018) "Diversity and Social Cohesion: The Case of Jane-Finch, a Highly Diverse Lower-Income Toronto Neighborhood," *Urban Research & Practice* 11(2): 139–158.

Arrow, K.J. (1974) *The Limits of Organization*, New York: W.W. Norton and Company.

Axelrod, R. and D'Ambrosio, L. (1994) *The Emergence of Co-operation: Annotated Bibliography*, Ann Arbor: University of Michigan Press.

Becker, H.S. (1963) *Outsiders: Studies in the Sociology of Deviance*. New York: Free Press.

Bentley, J.L.L. (2016) "Does Ethnic Diversity have a Negative Effect on Attitudes towards the Community? A Longitudinal Analysis of the Causal Claims within the Ethnic Diversity and Social Cohesion Debate," *European Sociological Review* 32(1): 54–67.

Berg, J., Dickhaut, J. and McCabe, K. (1995) "Trust, Reciprocity, and Social History," *Games and Economic Behavior* 10(1): 122–142.

Blomqvist, K. and Cook, K.S. (2018) "Swift Trust: State-of-the-Art and Future Research Directions," in R.H. Searle, A.I. Nienaber and S.B. Sitkin (eds.), *The Routledge Companion to Trust*, Abingdon: Routledge Press.

Blundell-Wignall, A. (2014) "The Bitcoin Question: Currency versus Trust-Less Transfer Technology," OECD Working Papers on Finance, Insurance and Private Pensions 37, OECD Publishing.

Burt, R.S. (2000) "Decay Functions," *Social Networks* 22: 1–28.

Burt, R.S. (2005) *Brokerage and Closure*, Oxford: Oxford University Press.

Buskens, V. (2002) *Social Networks and Trust*, Boston/Dordrecht/London: Kluwer Academic Publishers.

Chaudhuri, A. and Holbrook, M.B. (2001) "The Chain Effects from Brand Trust and Brand Affect to Brand Performance: The Role of Brand Loyalty," *Journal of Marketing* 65(2): 81–93.

Cook, K.S. (ed.) (2000) *Trust in Society*, New York: Russell Sage Foundation.

Cook, K.S. (2009) "Institutions, Trust, and Social Order," in E. Lawler, S. Thye and Y. Yoon (eds.), *Order on the Edge of Chaos*, New York: Russell Sage Foundation.

Cook, K.S. and Cook, B.D. (2011) "Social and Political Trust," in G. Delanty and S. Turner (eds.), *Routledge Handbook of Contemporary Social and Political Theory*, New York: Routledge.

Cook, K.S. and Cooper, R.M. (2003) "Experimental Studies of Cooperation, Trust and Social Exchange," in E. Ostrom and J.W. Walker (eds.), *Trust and Reciprocity: Interdisciplinary Lessons for Experimental Research*, New York: Russell Sage Foundation.

Cook, K.S. and State, B. (2017) "Trust and Social Dilemmas: Selected Evidence and Applications," in P.A.M. Van Lange, B. Rockenbach and T. Yamagishi (eds.), *Trust in Social Dilemmas*, Oxford: Oxford University Press.

Cook, K.S., Cheshire, C. and Gerbasi, A. (2006) "Power, Dependence, and Social Exchange," in P.J. Burke (ed.), *Contemporary Social Psychological Theories*, Stanford, CA: Stanford University Press.

Cook, K.S., Hardin, R. and Levi, M. (2005) *Cooperation without Trust?*New York: Russell Sage Foundation.

Cook, K.S., Yamagishi, T., Cheshire, C., Cooper, R., Matsuda, M. and Mashima, R. (2005) "Trust Building via Risk Taking: A Cross-Societal Experiment," *Social Psychology Quarterly* 68(2): 2005.

Cornfield, D.B. and Kim, H. (1994) "Socioeconomic Status and Unionization Attitudes in the United States," *Social Forces* 73(2): 521–531.
Corten, R., Rosenkranz, S., Buskens, V. and Cook, K.S. (2016) "Reputation Effects in Social Networks Do Not Promote Cooperation: An Experimental Test of the Raub and Weesie Model," *PLoS One* (July).
De Roeck, K. and Delobbe, N. (2012) "Do Environmental CSR Initiatives Serve Organizations' Legitimacy in the Oil Industry? Exploring Employees' Reactions through Organizational Identification Theory," *Journal of Business Ethics* 110(4): 397–412.
Diekmann, A., Jann, B., Przepiorka, W. and Wehrli, S. (2014) "Reputation Formation and the Evolution of Cooperation in Anonymous Online Markets," *American Sociological Review* 79(1): 65–85.
Dirks, K. and Ferrin, D.L. (2001) "The Role of Trust in Organizational Settings," *Organization Science* 12(4): 450–467.
Dirks, K.T. and Ferrin, D.L. (2002) "Trust in Leadership: Meta-Analytic Findings and Implications for Research and Practice," *Journal of Applied Psychology* 87(4): 611–628.
Dirks, K.T. and Skarlicki, D.P. (2004) "Trust in Leaders: Existing Research and Emerging Issues," in R.M. Kramer and K.S. Cook (eds.), *Trust and Distrust in Organizations*, New York: Russell Sage Foundation.
Druckman, D. and Olekalns, M. (2013) "Motivational Primes, Trust, and Negotiators' Reaction to a Crisis," *Journal of Conflict Resolution* 57(6): 966–990.
Durkheim, E. (1997) *The Division of Labor in Society*, W.D. Halls (ed.), New York: Free Press.
Duxbury, S.W. and Haynie, D.L. (2017) "The Network Structure of Opioid Distribution on a Darknet Cryptomarket," *Journal of Quantitative Criminology* 34(4): 921–941.
Edelman, B. and Luca, M. (2014) "Digital Discrimination: The Case of Airbnb.com." HBS Working Paper Series.
Ferguson, J.P. (2016) "Racial Diversity and Union Organizing in the United States, 1999–2008." SocArXiv.
Fukuyama, F. (1995) *Trust: The Social Virtues and the Creation of Prosperity*, New York: Free Press.
Furstenberg, F., Thomas, F., Cook, D., Eccles, J. and Elder, Jr., G.H. (1999) *Managing to Make It*, Chicago, IL: University of Chicago Press.
Gambetta, D. (2009) *Codes of the Underworld: How Criminals Communicate*, Princeton, NJ: Princeton University Press.
Granovetter, M. (1985) "Economic Action and Social Structure: The Problem of Embeddedness," *American Journal of Sociology*, 91(3): 481–510.
Granovetter, M. (2017) *Society and Economy*, Cambridge: Harvard University Press.
Gudmundsson, S.V. and Lechner, C. (2013) "Cognitive Biases, Organization, and Entrepreneurial Firm Survival," *European Management Journal* 31(3): 278–294.
Gulati, R. and Singh, H. (1998) "The Architecture of Cooperation: Managing Coordination Costs and Appropriation Concerns in Strategic Alliances," *Administrative Science Quarterly* 43: 781–814.
Hardin, R. (1995) *One for All: The Logic of Group Conflict*, Princeton, NJ: Princeton University Press.
Hardin, R. (2002) *Trust and Trustworthiness*, New York: Russell Sage Foundation.
Harper, S. and Reskin, B. (2005) "Affirmative Action in School and on the Job," *Annual Review of Sociology* 31: 357–379.
Hurrne, T., Ronteltap, A., Corten, R. and Buskens, V. (2017) "Antecedents of Trust in the Sharing Economy: A Systematic Review," *Journal of Consumer Behavior* 16(6): 485–498.
Keijzer, M. and Corten, R. (2016) "In Status We Trust: Vignette Experiment on Socioeconomic Status and Reputation Explaining Interpersonal Trust in Peer-to-Peer Markets," SocArXiv.
Kets de Vries, M. (2003) "The Entrepreneur on the Couch," *INSEAD Quarterly* 5: 17–19.
Kramer, R.M. and Cook, K.S. (eds.) (2004) *Trust and Distrust in Organizations*, New York: Russell Sage Foundation.
Kroeger, F. (2015) "The Development, Escalation and Collapse of System Trust: From the Financial Crisis to Society at Large," *European Management Journal* 33(6): 431–437.
Kuwabara, K. (2015) "Do Reputation Systems Undermine Trust? Divergent Effects of Enforcement Type on Generalized Trust and Trustworthiness," *American Journal of Sociology* 120(5): 1390–1428.

Let's Talk Payments (2015, June 25) "Survey Shows Americans Trust Technology Firms More than Banks and Retailers." https://letstalkpayments.com/survey-shows-americans-trust-technology-firms-more-than-banks-and-retailers/
Lewicki, R.J. and Stevenson, M. (1998) "Trust Development in Negotiation: Proposed Actions and a Research Agenda," *Journal of Business and Professional Ethics* 16(1–3): 99–132.
Lewicki, R., McAllister, D. and Bies, R. (1998) "Trust and Distrust: New Relationships and Realities," *Academy of Management Review* 23: 438–458.
Lin, N. (2001) "Guanxi: A Conceptual Analysis," in A.Y. So, N. Lin and D. Poston (eds.), *The Chinese Triangle of Mainland China, Taiwan, and Hong Kong*, Westport, CT: Greenwood Press.
Luhmann, N. (1980) "Trust: A Mechanism for the Reduction of Social Complexity," in *Trust and Power*, New York: Wiley.
Macaulay, S. (1963) "Non-Contractual Relations in Business: A Preliminary Study," *American Sociological Review* 28: 55–67.
Molm, L.D. (2010) "The Structure of Reciprocity," *Social Pyschology Quarterly* 73(2): 119–131.
Nakamoto, S. (2008) "Bitcoin: A Peer-to-Peer Electronic Cash System." Email posted to listserv. https://bitcoin.org/bitcoin.pdf
Nissenbaum, H. (2004) "Will Security Enhance Trust Online or Supplant It?" in R.M. Kramer and K.S. Cook (eds.), *Trust and Distrust in Organizations*, New York: Russell Sage Foundation.
Ostrom, E. and Walker, J. (eds.) (2003) *Trust and Reciprocity: Interdisciplinary Lessons for Experimental Research*, New York: Russell Sage Foundation.
Padgett, J.F. and Ansell, C.K. (1993) "Robust Action and the Rise of the Medici, 1400-1434," *American journal of sociology*, 98(6): 1259–1319.
Padgett, J.F. and McLean, P.D. (2006) "Organizational Invention and Elite Transformation: The Birth of Partnership Systems in Renaissance Florence," *American Journal of Sociology*, 111(5): 1463–1568.
Parigi, P. and Cook, K.S. (2015) "On the Sharing Economy," *Contexts* 14(1): 12–19.
Parigi, P., Santana, J.J. and Cook, K.S. (2017) "Online Field Experiments: Studying Social Interactions in Context," *Social Psychology Quarterly* 80(1): 1–19.
Paxton, P. (1999) "Is Social Capital Declining in the United States? A Multiple Indicator Assessment," *American Journal of Sociology* 105(1): 88–127.
Perrow, C. (2005) *Normal Accidents*, Princeton, NJ: Princeton University Press.
Piscini, E., Hyman, G. and Henry, W. (2017, February 7) "Blockchain: Trust Economy," *Deloitte Insights.*
Podolny, J.M. (2001) "Networks as the Pipes and Prisms of the Market," *American Journal of Sociology* 107(1): 33–60.
Powell, W.W. (1996) "Trust-Based Forms of Governance," in R. Kramer and T. Tyler (eds.), *Trust in Organizations: Frontiers of Theory and Research*, Thousand Oaks, CA: Sage Publications.
Przepiorka, W., Norbutas, L. andCorten, R. (2017) "Order without Law: Reputation Promotes Cooperation in a Cryptomarket for Illegal Drugs," *European Sociological Review* 33(6): 752–764.
Puffer, S.M., McCarthy, D.J. and Boisot M. (2010) "Entrepreneurship in Russia and China: The Impact of Formal Institutional Voids," *Entrepreneurship Theory and Practice* 34(3): 441–467.
Putnam, R. (1995) "Bowling Alone: American's Declining Social Capital," *Journal of Democracy* 6 (1): 65–78.
Putnam, R. (2000) *Bowling Alone: The Collapse and Revival of American Community*, New York: Simon & Schuster.
Radaev, V. (2004a) "Coping with Distrust in the Emerging Russian Markets," in R. Hardin (ed.), *Distrust*, New York: Russell Sage Foundation.
Radaev, V. (2004b) "How Trust is Established in Economic Relationships when Institutions and Individuals are not Trustworthy: The Case of Russia," in J. Kornai and S. Rose-Ackerman (eds.), *Building a Trustworthy State in Post-Socialist Transitions*, New York: Palgrave Macmillan.
Rotter, J.B.(1967) "A New Scale for the Measurement of Interpersonal Trust," *Journal of Personality* 35(4):1–7.
Rousseau, D.M., Sitkin, S.B., Burt, R.S. and Camerer, C.F. (1998) "Introduction to Special Topic Forum: Not So Different after All: A Cross-Discipline View of Trust," *Academy of Management Review* 23(3): 393–404.
Sawyer, K.R., Johnson, J. and Holub, M. (2010) "The Necessary Illegitimacy of the Whistleblower," *Business and Professional Ethics Journal* 29(1): 85–107.
Schilke, O., Reimann, M. and Cook, K.S. (2015) "Power Decreases Trust in Social Exchange," *Proceedings of the National Academy of Science (PNAS)* 112(42): 12950–12955.

Schilke, O., Riemann, M. and Cook, K.S. (2016) "Reply to Wu and Wilkes: Power, Whether Situational or Durable, Decreases both Relational and Generalized Trust," *Proceedings of the National Academy of Science (PNAS)* 113(11): E1418.

Schul, Y., Mayo, R. and Burnstein, E. (2008) "The Value of Distrust," *Journal of Experimental Social Psychology* 44(5): 1293–1302.

Schyns, P. and Koop, C. (2009) "Political Distrust and Social Capital in Europe and the USA," *Social Indicators Research* 96(1): 145–167.

Shapiro, S.P. (2005) "Agency Theory," *Annual Review of Sociology* 31: 263–284.

Simmel, G. (1971) *On Individuality and Social Forms*, D.N. Levine (ed.), Chicago, IL: Chicago University Press.

Small, M. (2017) *Someone to Talk To*, New York: Oxford University Press.

Smith-Lovin, L. (2003) "Self, Identity, and Interaction in an Ecology of Identities," in P.J. Burke, T. J. Owens, R.T. Serpe and P.A. Thoits (eds.), *Advances in Identity Theory and Research*, Boston, MA: Springer.

Smith, S.S. (2010) "Race and Trust," *Annual Review of Sociology* 36: 453–475.

State, B., Abrahao, B. and Cook, K.S. (2016) "Power Imbalance and Rating Systems," Proceedings of ICWSM. https://nyuscholars.nyu.edu/en/publications/power-imbalance-and-rating-systems

Sundararajan, A. (2016) *The Sharing Economy*. Cambridge, MA: MIT Press.

Uslaner, E.M. (2002) *The Moral Foundations of Trust*, Cambridge: Cambridge University Press.

Weber, M. (2013) *Economy and Society*, G. Roth and C. Wittich (eds.), Oakland, CA: University of California Press.

Wiegand, B. (1994) "Black Money in Belize: The Ethnicity and Social Structure of Black-Market Crime," *Social Forces* 73(1): 135–154.

Williamson, O.E. (1993) "Calculativeness, Trust, and Economic Organization," *Journal of Law and Economics* 36(1): 453–486.

Wright, R.E. (2002) *Hamilton Unbound: Finance and the Creation of the American Republic*, Westport, CT: Greenwood Publishing Group.

Zucker, L.G. (1986) "Production of Trust: Institutional Sources of Economic Structure, 1840–1920," in B.M. Staw and L.L. Cummings (eds.), *Research in Organizational Behavior*, Greenwich, CT: JAI Press.

16

TRUST: PERSPECTIVES IN PSYCHOLOGY

Fabrice Clément

Psychologists and philosophers, even when studying the same object, do not see things through the same epistemic glasses. Philosophy is traditionally invested in normative issues and, in the case of trust, the goal is to find some formal criteria to determine when it is justified to trust someone. Psychologists do not focus on how things *should* be, but rather on how information *is* processed in everyday life; this division of cognitive labor is something worth keeping in mind when involved in interdisciplinary work. But philosophers have obviously played an important role in the history of science: thanks to their conceptual work, they cleared the ground for empirical research by specifying the frontiers of the phenomenon to study. This is notably the case with trust, a "phenomenon we are so familiar with that we scarcely notice its presence and its variety" (Baier 1986:233). In order to determine the content of a concept, philosophers essentially question the way it is used in everyday speeches. The problem with the notion of trust is that different uses of the word can orient scientific research to different directions. Some favored cases, like contracts, where people decide if the amount of risk involved in cooperating with someone (usually unfamiliar), who will then reciprocate, is tolerable (Hardin 2002). These models are strongly inspired by dilemma games, where rational individuals make their decisions by counterbalancing personal and collective interests. In such contexts, the psychological processes involved are essentially conscious and, supposedly, rational – even if many empirical studies have shown that individuals do not often behave as egoistically as the economic model would suggest (Fehr and Schmidt 1999). At the other end of the spectrum, philosophers consider cases where trust seems to be of a different nature, like the trust infants have toward their parents. In such common cases, it would be odd to speak of a contract-based kind of trust; what is at stake is clearly not the result of a rational calculation, but a relationship characterized by a peaceful state of mind. As Baier (1986:234) put it, trust in such contexts can be seen as analogous to air: we inhabit a climate of trust and "notice it as we notice air, only when it becomes scarce or polluted." Seen from that perspective, trust is therefore understood as a basic attitude (Faulkner 2015), most likely of an affective nature (Jones 1996). In a nutshell, when it comes to defining the nature of trust, philosophers seem to oscillate between characterizing trust as a state of mind that could be compared either to a belief (for instance Gambetta 1988; see also Keren, this volume). or that could be compared to an emotion (see Lahno, this volume).

An evolutionary perspective is often useful to disentangle the nature of complex human phenomena; why would something like trust (and distrust) have evolved in our species? The answer has probably to be sought in the complex forms of cooperation that characterize human social organizations. Humans are said to be highly cooperative (Tomasello 2009), in the sense that they can constitute coalitions that are not related to kinship. Without the guarantee of being reciprocated in the future, an act of altruism such as helping others can be costly (Trivers 1971). As evolutionary simulations have demonstrated (Axelrod and Hamilton 1981), a strategy can only be adaptive in repeated social interactions (like a prisoner's dilemma) when participants can eliminate those who do not reciprocate. In other words, it is advantageous to cooperate, even with a certain time delay, but only when the partner will reciprocate in a not too distant future. However, it is generally held that the benefit of cooperation (and of being part of a group where individuals can help each other when needed) is so great, that it is in the interest of the trustee to satisfy the expectations of the trustor so that he can benefit in the future when more goods are exchanged. But, notably when the trustee is not engaged in a long-term relationship, the temptation to defect can be powerful, for example, to get a greater reward, or to avoid some extra cost to fulfill one's obligation. Any exchange therefore involves a certain risk for the trustor. For some, this risk is even embedded in the etymology of the word: according to Hardin (2002), the word "trust" in English comes from the way villagers organized hunting during the Middle Ages. Most of them played the role of beaters to frighten smaller game like rabbits or birds out of the bushes and trees. On the other side of the wood, the hunters waited for the fleeing animals to come out to shoot them: they stand *tryst*. Trust was therefore a role whose success depended on the actions of other members of the group.

The lesson of this evolutionary story is that trusting others by favoring cooperation had such an adaptive advantage, that trust is hardly avoidable. At the same time, given the clear risk of being let down or even betrayed by those we trust unquestioningly, it seems unlikely that something like blind trust could have evolved. Indeed, several studies seem to indicate that fast and frugal processes are in place as soon as a potential cooperator enters the perceptual field. In other words, it is probable that some psychological processes had evolved to filter our potential cooperators. Such mechanisms work implicitly, in the background of our conscious mind, and trigger some affective alarm when detecting a potential risk of manipulation. Such automaticity has been illustrated by Todorov and his colleagues, who have shown in different experiments that individuals screen others' faces extremely quickly and evaluate whether someone is trustworthy or not within a few milliseconds. For instance, Willis and Todorov (2006) asked participants to judge faces on different personality traits (trustworthiness, competence, likeability, aggressiveness and attractiveness) after 100ms, 500ms or 1,000ms. Interestingly, the scores obtained after 100ms or 1,000ms were highly correlated, especially in the case of trustworthiness. In other words, detecting the amount of trustworthiness you can attribute to another person seems to be processed extremely fast by our brains. In another experiment, the effects of face trustworthiness were even detectable when the stimuli were presented for 33ms, i.e. below the threshold of objective awareness (Todorov and Duchaine 2008). Moreover, a study conducted with participants suffering from prosopagnosia, i.e. being unable to memorize faces or to perceive facial identity, showed that, in spite of their condition, the participants could make normal and fast judgments of trustworthiness (Todorov and Duchaine 2008), suggesting the existence of a specific mechanism for forming impressions about people. From a neurological perspective, this "fast and frugal" heuristic seems to principally involve the amygdala (Engell, Haxby and Todorov 2007). Thanks to 2D computer simulations based on multiple judgments of emotionally neutral faces, Oosterhof and Todorov (2008) managed to show that the cues used for trustworthiness heuristics are related to positive or negative valence, indicating that valence may be a good proxy of trustworthiness. In a nutshell, faces of people that are evaluated as trustworthy tend to look happier, even when they display an emotionally neutral face; on the contrary, people judged as less trustworthy, look angrier (see also Clément, Bernard, Grandjean and Sander 2013). Such attention to expressed emotions for the assessment of trustworthiness may be linked to the fact that different valences elicit approach versus avoidance behavior.

The automaticity of trustworthiness assessment is further supported by the discovery that even young children are sensitive to the valence displayed by people around them who could potentially be trusted. Cogsdill and her colleagues showed that 3- and 4-year-old children generated basic "mean"/ "nice" judgments to facial characteristics in a similar way to adults. This precocity could indicate that the ability to infer traits from faces might not result from "slow social-learning mechanisms that develop through the gradual detection and internalization of environmental regularities" (Cogsdill, Todorov, Spelke and Banaji 2014:7), but instead through cognitive mechanisms whose nature is still under-determined.

Besides the propensity to detect trustworthiness in others' faces – a heuristic that is, incidentally, not always reliable (Bond, Berry and Omar 1994) – another adaptive solution could be to provide a mechanism for selectively attending to those who do not follow the rules of the game. This is precisely the hypothesis defended by the evolutionary psychologist Leda Cosmides (1989). Her starting point was the classic Wason selection task designed to test deductive reasoning abilities: a set of four cards was placed on a table, each of which had a number on one side and a colored patch on the other side. The visible faces of the cards showed 3, 8, red and brown. Participants were asked about the cards they should turn over in order to test the truth of the following proposition: "if a card shows an even number, then its opposite face shows a primary color." The right deductive rule is to turn the 8 card (if it is not red, it violates the rule), and the brown card (if it is even, it violates the rule). However, most participants chose the 8 card and the *red* card, trying to confirm the rule. Cosmides introduced a variation of the game by asking participants to verify the following rule: "if a person is drinking beer, then he must be over 20 years old." The four cards had information about four people sat a table: "drinking beer," "drinking coke," "25 years old," and "16 years old." This time, most participants responded correctly by choosing "drinking beer" and "16 years old." Cosmides explains such differences based on the *content* of the problem instead of their *intrinsic difficulty*, by arguing that the human mind includes specific inferential procedures to detect cheating on social contracts (see also Sugiyama, Tooby and Cosmides 2002; for a critique, see Sperber and Girotto, 2002). Similarly, to avoid the risk of being manipulated, one can expect that cheaters are not only rapidly detected but also punished by the other players. This idea has been developed by behavioral economists under the "strong reciprocity" hypothesis. Indeed, there are many experiments that show that participants are actually willing to punish those who fail to cooperate, even if this "altruistic" punishment is costly for them (e.g. Fehr and Gächter 2002). Moreover, it has been demonstrated that punishing cheaters activates the dorsal striatum, an area of the brain that has been implicated in the processing of reward (de Quervain et al. 2004). In other words, our brains seem motivated to detect cheaters and to punish them. In such a world, trusting is a slightly less risky endeavor. Moreover, given the fact that humans are endowed with language, cheaters are at risk not only of being discovered, but also of being publicly denounced. By having their reputation tarnished, they run the risk of being excluded from future cooperation (Fehr 2004, see also Origgi, this volume). It has, indeed, been shown that many of our conversations are about others' behaviors and that the role of gossip can be seen as detecting others' deviations from what is socially expected (Dunbar 2004).

Detecting the potential cooperators is often associated with a positive bias for people belonging to the same group (in-group) and a negative bias for those belonging to another group (out-group). While being fallible and thus potentially harmful to both trustors and trustees (see Scheman as well as Medina, this volume), the evolutionary explanation for such preferences would be that people belonging to the same group are subject to the same norms and values and tend therefore to be more cooperative, notably because they fear the social repercussions of an unfair behavior (Gil-White 2005). Social psychologists have shown how people are inclined to judge in-group members to be more helpful than out-group members and participants choose preferentially in-group members (for instance, students from the same university) as cooperators in economic games (Foddy, Platow and Yamagishi 2009). Interestingly, in-group categorization is itself a very basic mechanism that can be triggered by apparently uninformative details, like shared taste for a given artist used by Tajfel in his minimal group paradigm (Tajfel 1970). This automaticity is also demonstrated by its very early presence in infants' mind: 10-month-old infants, for instance, preferentially selected a toy offered by a person who previously spoke in their native language over a person who spoke in a different language (Kinzler, Dupoux and Spelke 2007). Similarly, the simple observation of characters showing either the same or a different taste than their own choice triggers specific preferences by 9- and 14-month-olds: they prefer individuals who treat similar others well and treat dissimilar others poorly (Hamlin, Mahajan, Liberman and Wynn 2013). In-group and out-group categorizations are therefore fallible, but very powerful shortcuts when it comes to deciphering whom to trust.

Thanks to language, humans can benefit from another kind of cooperation: the exchange of information facilitated by verbal statements, and trust plays a crucial role here. As Quine and Ullian (1978:30) stated, language affords us "more eyes to see with." Others' testimonies can be compared as vicarious observation and increasing knowledge about our environment confer major benefits, notably in terms of reducing uncertainty (see Faulkner, this volume). However, this kind of "epistemic trust" is subject to the same potential issues as other forms of social cooperation: it is possible for an informer to omit a piece of relevant information, or even to intentionally transmit a piece of information that he knows to be erroneous. Such Machiavellian manipulation can be beneficial for the informant, who can "transfer" wrong information into others' minds (Byrne and Whiten 1988). If the others were to believe such "testimony," they could adopt behaviors that are favorable for the informant, but not for themselves. With Sperber and colleagues, we proposed that the risk of manipulation is so high in human communication that something like an "epistemic vigilance" had to evolve in our species (Sperber et al. 2010). According to this hypothesis, selective pressure favored cost-effective procedures to evaluate each piece of information that was provided by someone else. Given that the relevance of the testimony depends on the source's competence (since they could be wrong by ignorance) and honesty (since they could be lying), one could expect that these two dimensions depend upon a relatively automatic evaluation. A good way to test these initial checks is to look at child development: if humans are endowed with epistemic vigilance, one would expect children to exhibit it quite early (Clément 2010). Of course, honesty is hard to perceive but a good proxy is *benevolence*: when wishing somebody well, a source is, in principle, not trying to manipulate her. Indeed, an early sensitivity to benevolence has been shown by young children: participants as young as 3 years old prefer the testimony of a benevolent informant rather than a malevolent informant – a character who behaved aggressively towards the experimenter (Mascaro and Sperber 2009). Similarly, several studies have shown that children do not blindly trust what is said to them. For instance, even a source that has been reliable in the past loses her credibility when she says something that contradicts the child's own perception (Clément, Koenig and Harris 2004). Moreover, children use past accounts of a source's reliability when deciding whom to trust (Koenig, Clément and Harris 2004; Harris et al. 2012). It has even been shown that preschoolers use different social cues to evaluate others' statements. For instance, they are more ready to trust familiar people than unfamiliar ones (Harris and Koenig 2009) and prefer informants who also have their native accent (Kinzler, Corriveau and Harris 2011). Another line of research shows that preschoolers take the number of sources into account when listening to contradictory statements; without other specifications, the testimony of a majority is selected over a minority (Haun, van Leeuwen and Edelson 2013) and this propensity can even overcome reliability until 5 or 6 years of age (Bernard, Proust and Clément 2015): children at this age are able to "resist" the majority point of view when this latter had been wrong in the past. An evaluation of the content of the information transmitted also seems to take place quite early. At 16 months, for instance, infants are surprised when someone uses a familiar name inappropriately (Koenig and Echols 2003). Three-year-olds and 4-year-olds can distinguish good from bad reasons when they are evaluating testimony (Koenig 2012). Recently, it has been shown that preschoolers evaluate the "logical quality" of explanations, preferring, for instance, non-circular over circular statements (Corriveau and Kurkul 2014; Mercier, Bernard and Clément 2014).

In summary, research in psychology leads us to believe that our ability to evaluate others' testimony before deciding whether to trust them is already present, even very early in our ontogenesis. While there is no definitive proof that something like some vigilance is "built" into our cognitive system, existing evidence seems to indicate that it is "natural" for our species to evaluate different aspects of potential partners before deciding to trust them and, for instance, to follow their advice. Moreover, the fact that very young children are able to perform at least some of these evaluative operations indicates that different cues of our social environment are automatically and implicitly processed in situations where trust is at play. Based on the psychology literature, it is therefore difficult to limit trust to its strategic dimension. This option, often taken in economics, implicitly leads to a concept of trust based solely on the premise that it is the product of explicit thinking, as a calculation of the probability that a potential cooperator is reliable. Although such conscious deliberation may sometimes happen (for instance when deciding whom to contact to decorate your house), trusting someone is most often the result of an unconscious process that will determine a certain attitude. To conclude: trust manifests itself within a large continuum starting from the infant's trust in her mother to the businessman's trust in a potential partner.

Two important questions remain unanswered. The first question is of a "rousseauist" nature: does everyone start with unquestioned faith towards others' good will and then learn to be more selective? Or has trust to be won, overcoming mistrust? A line of research has recently brought interesting insight into this issue by studying the influence of a hormone that acts as an important neurotransmitter: *oxytocin*. This hormone is involved in key social contexts when the binding between two individuals is vital, like during sex, birth and breastfeeding. Its release is notably associated with a warm and positive state of mind that favors the ongoing social relationship. The influence of this hormone most likely exists since the beginning of life. This has been shown for instance by newborn macaques which, after inhaling oxytocin, where more prompt to initiate affiliative pro-social behavior to a human caregiver (Simpson et al. 2014). With human adults, experimental economists have shown that intranasal administration of oxytocin during a trust game increase the readiness to bear risks (Kosfeld, Heinrichs, Zak, Fischbacher and Fehr 2005). Recently, we have shown that even the endogenous level of oxytocin, checked before an "egg-hunting" game, predicted the level of cooperation, but *only as long as participants belonged to the same group* (McClung et al. 2018). This last specification is important because it highlights the fact that oxytocin cannot simply be considered as a "trust hormone." Indeed, other researchers have shown that oxytocin not only enhances trust and cooperation between in-groups but also promotes aggression toward potential out-groups (De Dreu et al. 2010; De Dreu and Kret 2016). The secretion of oxytocin plays an important role therefore in establishing a psychological state where the absence of anxiety in the presence of another person will facilitate collaboration. But such warm peacefulness, that could remain unnoticed until broken, is preceded by an evaluation of the nature of the ongoing relationship (Kaufmann and Clément 2014) and, in the case of potential competition, the same hormone can have radically different behavioral consequences.

The second remaining question is about the dynamic of trust: how do we move on the "scale of trust," from an unselfconscious sense of security to a more explicit awareness of the risk, so often inherent to cooperation (Baier 1986:236)? To answer this question, we can imagine a scenario starting with the initial and implicit trust that a baby experiences, at least when the relationship develops harmoniously with her caregivers. It would be possible to imagine a widening circle to illustrate levees of trust. At the center of the circle one can expect trust to be largely unnoticed, like the air we breathe. However, things get more complex with the widening of the circle. Notably, a phenomenon well known to parents appears between 6 and 8 months of age: *Stranger Fear* (Sroufe 1977; Brooker et al. 2013). It is probably only when this anxiety can be – partially – overcome that the different implicit evaluation processes we have described can kick in. But, it is still not necessary at that point to presuppose explicit processes, as alternatives have been shown in recent research on metacognition. For a long time indeed, metacognition was thought of as a reflective process, a "cognition that reflects on, monitors, or regulates first-order cognition" (Kuhn 2000); in other words, metacognition would essentially be *metarepresentational*, involving representations that are about other representations (Sperber 2000). The problem with this conception is that it is cognitively demanding and it does not fit with young children's executive abilities (Clément 2016). However, we have seen that preschoolers are able to "decide" whom to trust based on cues about various phenomena (reliability, benevolence, consensus, familiarity, etc.). To explain these precocious monitoring abilities, the philosopher Joelle Proust proposes that metacognition can indeed be differentiated from metarepresentations (Proust 2007). To monitor one's cognition, we rely on different kinds of cues that are correlated with *feelings* (Proust 2013). The typical example, proposed by Asher Koriat, is the case of 'the feeling of knowing' (tip-of-the-tongue): even if access to a specific content is momentary impossible, we can feel that it is within "cognitive reach" (Koriat 1993). Within this perspective, trust can be understood as the intimate resonance of an evaluation process that is most often left opaque to us. With time and the development of a theory of mind, i.e. the ability to reflexively represent one's mental states and those of others, more reflexive evaluations can take place. The economists' version of trust can take its place at the other end of the spectrum: after a strategic weighting of the situation, you can consciously decide to trust a potential cooperator, with a reasonable doubt based on a rough estimation of the probability that s/he will reciprocate.

The psychological epistemic lenses adopted here highlight the unconscious processes that underlie social exchanges when the participants trust each other, i.e. accept the risk inherent of the cooperative situation with a degree of confidence. Many of these evaluations are not accessible to consciousness but the feelings they trigger can be re-evaluated and, eventually, put into question. As natural selection aims at efficient mechanisms, in terms of time and energy, the evaluation processes leading to trust are approximations which have worked sufficiently well in the past to ensure the success of our species. Therefore, it is possible that they lead us to trust – or distrust – someone, based on some unreliable cues. In some cases, these mechanisms can even have deleterious consequences, notably when decisions are based solely on group membership. The normative dimension of philosophy then becomes essential, specifying when it is justified to trust or to be skeptical, enabling us to consciously revise impressions that are too readily available. Such critical abilities are probably more desirable than ever.

References

Axelrod, R. and Hamilton, W. (1981) "The Evolution of Cooperation," *Science* 211: 1390–1396.

Baier, A. (1986) "Trust and Antitrust," *Ethics*, 96(2): 231–260.

Bernard, S., Proust, J. and Clément, F. (2015) "Four- to Six-Year-Old Children's Sensitivity to Reliability Versus Consensus in the Endorsement of Object Labels," *Child Development* 86(4): 1112–1124.

Bond, C., Berry, D.S. and Omar, A. (1994) "The Kernel of Truth in Judgments of Deceptiveness," *Basic and Applied Social Psychology* 15(4): 523–534.

Brooker, R.J., Buss, K.A., Lemery-Chalfant, K., Aksan, N., Davidson, R.J. and Goldsmith, H. H. (2013) "The Development of Stranger Fear in Infancy and Toddlerhood: Normative Development, Individual Differences, Antecedents, and Outcomes," *Developmental Science* 16 (6): 864–878.

Byrne, R.W. and Whiten, A. (1988) *Machiavellian Intelligence: Social Expertise and the Evolution of Intellect*, Oxford: Oxford University Press.

Clément, F. (2010) "To Trust or not to Trust? Children's Social Epistemology," *Review of Philosophy and Psychology* 1:531–549.

Clément, F. (2016) "The Multiple Meanings of Social Cognition," in J.A. Green, W.A. Sandoval and I. Bråten (Eds.), *Handbook of Epistemic Cognition*, Oxford: Routledge.

Clément, F., Bernard, S., Grandjean, D. and Sander, D. (2013) "Emotional Expression and Vocabulary Learning in Adults and Children," *Cognition and Emotion* 27: 539–548.

Clément, F., Koenig, M. and Harris, P. (2004) "The Ontogenesis of Trust," *Mind & Language* 19: 360–379.

Cogsdill, E.J., Todorov, A.T., Spelke, E.S. and Banaji, M.R. (2014) "Inferring Character from Faces: A Developmental Study," *Psychological Science* 25(5): 1132–1139.

Corriveau, K.H. and Kurkul, K.E. (2014) "'Why Does Rain Fall?': Children Prefer to Learn from an Informant Who Uses Noncircular Explanations," *Child Development* 85: 1827–1835.

Cosmides, L. (1989) "The Logic of Social Exchange: Has Natural Selection Shaped How Humans Reason? Studies with the Wason Selection Task," *Cognition* 31(3): 187–276.

De Dreu, C.K.W. and Kret, M.E. (2016) "Oxytocin Conditions Intergroup Relations through Upregulated In-Group Empathy, Cooperation, Conformity, and Defense," *Biological Psychiatry* 79(3): 165–173.

De Dreu, C.K.W., Greer, L.L., Handgraaf, M.J.J., Shalvi, S., Kleef, G.A.V., Baas, M. … Feith, S.W. W. (2010) "The Neuropeptide Oxytocin Regulates Parochial Altruism in Intergroup Conflict among Humans," *Science* 328(5984): 1408–1411.

de Quervain, D.J.-F., Fischbacher, U., Treyer, V., Schellhammer, M., Schnyder, U., Buck, A. and Fehr, E. (2004) "The Neural Basis of Altruistic Punishment," *Science* 305 (5688): 1254–1258.

Dunbar, R.I.M. (2004) "Gossip in Evolutionary Perspective," *Review of General Psychology* 8: 100–110.

Engell, A.D., Haxby, J.V. and Todorov, A. (2007) "Implicit Trustworthiness Decisions: Automatic Coding of Face Properties in the Human Amygdala," *Journal of Cognitive Neuroscience* 19: 1508–1519.

Faulkner, P. (2015) "The Attitude of Trust is Basic," *Analysis* 75(3): 424–429.

Fehr, E. (2004) "Don't Lose Your Reputation," *Nature* 432: 2–3.

Fehr, E. and Gächter, S. (2002) "Altruistic Punishment in Humans," *Nature* 415: 137–140.

Fehr, E. and Schmidt, K.M. (1999) "A Theory of Fairness, Competition, and Cooperation," *The Quarterly Journal of Economics* 114(3): 817–868.

Foddy, M., Platow, M.J. and Yamagishi, T. (2009) "Group-Based Trust in Strangers: The Role of Stereotypes and Expectations," *Psychological Science* 20(4): 419–422.

Gambetta, D. (ed.) (1988) *Trust : Making and Breaking Cooperative Relations*, Oxford: Blackwell.

Gil-White, F. (2005) "How Conformism Creates Ethnicity Creates Conformism (and Why this Matters to Lots of Things)," *The Monist* 88: 189–237.

Hamlin, J.K., Mahajan, N., Liberman, Z. and Wynn, K. (2013) "Not Like Me = Bad: Infants Prefer Those Who Harm Dissimilar Others," *Psychological Science* 24: 589–594.

Hardin, R. (2002) *Trust and Trustworthiness*, New York: Russell Sage Foundation. www.russellsage.org/publications/trust-and-trustworthiness-1

Harris, P.L. and Koenig, M. (2009) "Choosing Your Informants: Weighing Familiarity and Recent Accuracy," *Developmental Science* 12(3): 426–437

Harris, P.L., Corriveau, K.H., Pasquini, E.S., Koenig, M., Fusaro, M. and Clément, F. (2012) "Credulity and the Development of Selective Trust in Early Childhood," in M.J. Beran, J. Brandl, J. Perner and J. Proust (Eds.), *Foundations of Metacognition*, Oxford: Oxford University Press.

Haun, D.B., van Leeuwen, E.J. and Edelson, M.G. (2013) "Majority Influence in Children and Other Animals," *Developmental Cognitive Neuroscience* 3: 61–71.

Jones, K. (1996) "Trust as an Affective Attitude," *Ethics* 107(1): 4–25.

Kaufmann, L. and Clément, F. (2014) "Wired for Society: Cognizing Pathways to Society and Culture," *Topoi* 33(2): 20–45.

Kinzler, K.D., Corriveau, K.H. and Harris, P.L. (2011) "Children's Selective Trust in Native-Accented Speakers," *Developmental Science 14*: 106–111.

Kinzler, K.D., Dupoux, E. and Spelke, E.S. (2007) "The Native Language of Social Cognition," *Proc Natl Acad Sci USA* 104: 12577–12580.

Koenig, M.A. (2012) "Beyond Semantic Accuracy: Preschoolers Evaluate a Speaker's Reasons," *Child Development* 83: 1051–1063.

Koenig, M.A. and Echols, C.H. (2003) "Infants' Understanding of False Labeling Events: The Referential Roles of Words and the Speakers Who Use Them," *Cognition* 87: 179–208.

Koenig, M.A., Clément, F. and Harris, P.L. (2004) "Trust in Testimony. Children's Use of True and False Statements," *Psychological Science* 15: 694–698.

Koriat, A. (1993) "How Do We Know That We Know? The Accessibility Model of the Feeling of Knowing," *Psychological Review* 100(4): 609–637.

Kosfeld, M., Heinrichs, M., Zak, P.J., Fischbacher, U. and Fehr, E. (2005) "Oxytocin Increases Trust in Humans," *Nature* 435: 673–676.

Kuhn, D. (2000) "Metacognitive Development," *Current Directions in Psychological Science* 9: 178–181.

McClung, J.S., Triki, Z., Clément, F., Bangerter, A. and Bshary, R. (2018) "Endogenous Oxytocin Predicts Helping and Conversation as a Function of Group Membership," *Proc. R. Soc. B* 285 (1882): 20180939.

Mascaro, O. and Sperber, D. (2009) "The Moral, Epistemic, and Mindreading Components of Children's Vigilance towards Deception," *Cognition* 112: 367–380.
Mercier, H., Bernard, S. and Clément, F. (2014) "Early Sensitivity to Arguments: How Preschoolers Weight Circular Arguments," *Journal of Experimental Child Psychology* 125: 102–109.
Oosterhof, N.N. and Todorov, A. (2008) "The Functional Basis of Face Evaluation," *Proceedings of the National Academy of Sciences* 105: 11087.
Proust, J. (2007) "Metacognition and Metarepresentation: Is a Self-Directed Theory of Mind a Precondition for Metacognition?" *Synthese* 159: 271–295.
Proust, J. (2013) *The Philosophy of Metacognition: Mental Agency and Self-Awareness*, Oxford: Oxford University Press.
Quine, W.V.O. and Ullian, J.S. (1978) *The Web of Belief*, Vol. 2, New York: Random House.
Simpson, E.A., Sclafani, V., Paukner, A., Hamel, A.F., Novak, M.A., Meyer, J.S. ... Ferrari, P.F. (2014) "Inhaled Oxytocin Increases Positive Social Behaviors in Newborn Macaques," *Proceedings of the National Academy of Sciences* 111(19): 6922–6927.
Sperber, D. (2000). "Metarepresentations in an Evolutionary Perspective," in D. Sperber (ed.), *Metarepresentations: A Multidisciplinary Perspective*, Oxford: Oxford University Press.
Sperber, D. and Girotto, V. (2002) "Use or Misuse of the Selection Task?" *Cognition* 85(3): 277–290.
Sperber, D., Clément, F., Heintz, C., Mascaro, O., Mercier, H., Origgi, G. and Wilson, D. (2010) "Epistemic Vigilance," *Mind and Language* 24: 359–393.
Sroufe, L.A. (1977) "Wariness of Strangers and the Study of Infant Development," *Child Development* 48(3): 731–746.
Sugiyama, L.S., Tooby, J. and Cosmides, L. (2002) "Cross-Cultural Evidence of Cognitive Adaptations for Social Exchange among the Shiwiar of Ecuadorian Amazonia," *Proc Natl Acad Sci USA* 99: 11537–11542.
Tajfel, H. (1970) "Experiments in Intergroup Discrimination," *Scientific American* 223(5), 96–103.
Todorov, A. and Duchaine, B. (2008) "Reading Trustworthiness in Faces without Recognizing Faces," *Cognitive Neuropsychology* 25: 395–410.
Tomasello, M. (2009) *Why We Cooperate*, Cambridge, MA: MIT Press.
Trivers, R. (1971) "The Evolution of Reciprocal Altruism," *The Quarterly Review of Biology* 46: 35–57.
Willis, J. and Todorov, A. (2006) "First Impressions: Making up Your Mind after a 100-Ms Exposure to a Face," *Psychological Science* 17: 592–598.

17

TRUST: PERSPECTIVES IN COGNITIVE SCIENCE

Cristiano Castelfranchi and Rino Falcone

17.1 Premise: Controversial Issues in Trust Theory

Cognitive Science is not a unitary discipline, but a cross-disciplinary research domain. Accordingly, there is no single accepted definition of trust in cognitive science and we will refer to quite distinct literature from neuroscience to philosophy, from Artificial Intelligence (AI) and agent theories to psychology and sociology, etc. Our paradigm is Socio-Cognitive AI, in particular Agents and Multi-Agents modeling. On the one side we use formal modeling of AI architectures for a clear scientific characterization of cognitive representations and their processing, and we endow AI Agents with cognitive and social minds. On the other side we use Multi-Agent Systems (MAS) for the experimental simulation of interaction and social emergent phenomena.

By arguing for the following claims, we focus on *some of the most controversial issues in this domain*: (a) trust does not involve a single and unitary mental state, (b) trust is an evaluation that implies a motivational aspect, (c) trust is a way to exploit ignorance, (d) trust is, and is used as, a signal, (e) trust cannot be reduced to reciprocity, (f) trust combines rationality and feeling, (g) trust is not only related to other persons but can be applied to instruments, technologies, etc.

The basic message of this chapter is that "trust" is a complex object of inquiry and must be treated as such. It thus deserves a *non-reductive* definition and modeling. Moreover, our account of trust aims to cover not only interpersonal trust but also trust in organizations, institutions, etc.

We thus suggest that trust is:

(A) *dispositional*: an "attitude" by the trustor (X) towards the world or other agents (Y), and such an attitude is

(A1) Hybrid, with affective and cognitive components;
(A2) Composite: because it a) consists of *beliefs* (doxastic representations) but also *goals* (motivational representations), combined in *expectations* about the future, *evaluations* of trustees and the possible risks; and b) because it is about different *dimensions* of trustee Y's "qualities," as well as about external conditions, the context of Y's action.

(B) *a mental and pragmatic process*, implying several steps and a multilayered product:

the "decision" to rely on Y, the consequent formulation of such an "intention," and the performance of the "act" of trusting Y and exploiting it. This implies the establishment of a "social relation" (if Y is a cognitive agent). Thus, trust has at least three levels: the decision is grounded on X's beliefs on Y, and the act of trusting Y and the resulting social relation are based on the decision.

(C) *multilayered* also because it is *recursive*: if X trusts Y on the basis of given data, signs, messages, beliefs, X has to trust the sources of such information (signs, perception, etc.), and (the sources of) the beliefs about those sources (and so on).

(D) *dynamic*:

(D1) trust evaluations, decisions and relations can change on the basis of interactions, events and thoughts.
(D2) we can *derive trust from trust*, in several ways: we derive our degree of trust in Y from trust in our beliefs; we derive our trust on Y's performance from our trust in Y's skills, means, honesty, disposition; we can derive our trust in Y from the fact that Z trusts Y and from our trust in Z; we can derive our trust in Y from the group or category Y belongs to; moreover our trust in Y is affected by Y trusting us, and vice versa; etc.[1]

Let us start with the cognitive components: beliefs and goals.

17.2 Trust and Beliefs

In our definition and model[2] *trust* is essentially based on beliefs:[3] beliefs about the future and its possibilities; beliefs about the past, on which is based trustee's evaluations; beliefs about the contextual conditions, etc. Indeed, beliefs are so evident in trust that many scholars consider *trust* coincident with a set of beliefs (for example, in computer science).[4]

- The first basic level concerns the mere belief and attitude towards the trustee Y: is Y able and reliable, willing, not dangerous?
- the second level concerns the reasoning/feeling about the decision to trust: this is based on the beliefs of the first level as well as on other beliefs about costs, risks, opportunities, comparative entities, etc., of this decision;
- the third level concerns the act of trusting/relying Y about the defined task (τ). We call this aspect of trust: reliance. The act of trusting determines a dependence relation between X and Y, by X counting on Y, that influences the X's mental state. This level is based on the cognitive states of the first and second level.

Analyzing the necessary beliefs in *trust*:

1 *Beliefs about the future*: Trust is a positive expectation, where an expectation is a combination of a motivational mental state (a goal) together with a set of beliefs

about the future. This expectation is factual in trust as decision and action, while is just hypothetical in evaluations of Y (would Y be trustworthy and reliable?)

2 Beliefs about Y: i.e. beliefs about Y's abilities, qualities, willingness, self-confidence, etc. To trust a cognitive agent implies a sort of mind reading, in that it is necessary to ascribe mental states to the trustee and count on these states.[5]

3 Beliefs about the context in which Y has to realize the delegated task: these beliefs are about resources, supports, external events and other elements which may affect Y's realization of the delegated task while not being directly attributable to Y.

4 Beliefs about risks: trust enables to deal with uncertainty and risks.[6] Uncertainty could derive both from lack of evidence or from ambiguity due to conflicting evidence. In any case, the trustor has to have (more or less defined) beliefs about the severity and probability of risks, the goal/interest they could damage, etc. Note that we consider risks not as objective, but as subjective, i.e. as perceived by the trustor.

5 Beliefs about oneself: the trustor's beliefs are also based on evaluations of one's own competency of evaluating relevant characteristics of the trustee's and the trust context.[7]

All the above beliefs can be inferred in different ways: from signs (*krypta* vs. *manifesta*),[8] direct or indirect experiences, analogies, reputation, categories, etc.[9]

A separate issue regards the strength of these beliefs and their relationship with the degree of trust.[10]

However, we cannot reduce or identify the trust in Y with the strength of the evaluative beliefs about Y. Trust does not coincide with X's "*confidence*" in his beliefs about Y, as it seems simplified in some formal models.[11]

On the one side, the degree of subjective certainty of the belief/evaluation is only one component and determinant of the degree of *trust in* Y.[12]

On the other side, it is important to make clear that we are discussing two levels of trust:

a trust in the content of the evaluation, in the object (or event) the belief is "about" (Y or that G);

b trust in the belief itself, as cognitive object and resource.

Level (b) is a form of meta-trust, about the reliability of a given mental state. Can we rely on that assumption? Can we bet on its truth? Is it well-grounded and supported; can we believe it?

Trust in the belief – frequently cold confidence – should not be identified with trust in its object (what we are thinking about, what we have beliefs about, what we are evaluating).

17.3 Trust and Goals

Most definitions of trust[13] underestimate or do not deal *explicitly* with the important motivational aspects of trust. Trust is not just a feeling, a set of beliefs or an estimation of probability or data about Y's skills and dispositions but also entails X's goals.

i X's beliefs are in fact "evaluations," that is, judgments about "positive" or "negative" features of Y in relation to our *goals.*

ii *trust* is not a mere prediction but an "expectation": not only does X foresee that Y will do something, but X desires that something, bets on it for realizing his *goal*.

For this reason, it is crucial to specify in relation to which *goal* X is trusting Y. Not just to say "X trusts Y" (as in the majority of formal treatments of trust)[14] but "X trusts Y (as) for ..." Only an agent endowed with *goals* (desires, needs, projects) can "trust" something or somebody. No *goal*, no trust.[15]

Sometimes it can happen that the perceived availability of a tool or agent owning specific features activates a potential goal in X and the relative trust relationship.

Trust is crucial for *goal* processing, both (a) in case of delegating to others and relying on them for the goal realization; and (b) in case of the formulation of an "intention" and execution of an "intentional" action, which are strictly based on self-efficacy beliefs, on positive expectation on our own choice, persistence, skills and competence, i.e. *self-trust* (see chapter by Foley, this volume).[16]

17.4 Trust and Probability

Some influential scholars consider trust as a form of subjective probability.[17] For example, Gambetta (2000) says: "Trust is the subjective probability by which an individual X expects that another individual Y performs a given action on which its welfare depends." While such a simplification may indeed be necessary to arrive at a specific degree of trust, we argue that it is rather a *set of parameters* that needs to be considered to calculate such as degree of trust. We have outlined these different parameters as different types of belief in our definition of trust, namely beliefs about the Y's willingness, competence, persistence, engagement, etc., as well as beliefs about the context C (opportunities, favorable conditions, obstacles, etc.).[18]

17.4.1 Trust and Ignorance

Trust is fundamental for dealing with uncertainty.[19] In particular, it helps us deal with and even exploit ignorance, i.e. a lack of information for two reasons.

First, searching for and processing information for decision-making are very costly activities. Given our "bounded rationality,"[20] when we accept our own ignorance and instead rely on others, we thus save costs. Second, *trust* makes ignorance productive because, it (a) creates trustworthiness in Y (*trust* is a self-fulfilling prophecy), (b) is reciprocated (I become trustworthy for others, and an accepted member of the community), and (c) allows to preserve and use information asymmetry, privacy and secrets that are essential in social interaction, at interpersonal, economic, political levels.

17.5 Trust and Distrust

What is the relation between trust and distrust? (See also D'Cruz, this volume). We could say that each time there is a room for trust, at the same time there is some room also for lack of trust.

Psychologically speaking it does not necessarily happen that the trustor evaluates the logical complement of its trust: that if it has a positive expectation then it also considers, imagines, represents to itself the negative consequences.

In practice, we can say that while the formal logic is based on a closure principle, the psychological approach does not consider that a cognitive agent should infer all the consequences of its decision.[21]

Assessing the existing literature on distrust,[22] it becomes evident that while distrust is not simply the direct opposite of trust,[23] its exact nature is still up for debate.

If, according to our definition, trust is not just a number (like a probability),[24] or a simple linear dimension (for example, between 0 and 100), distrust is also not simply a "low trust" (a low value in a numerical range). Instead, we have to distinguish between cases of mere *weak trust* or *lack of trust* from *true distrust*, which is a kind of *negative trust*. In practice, we have to think of "*true distrust*" as a negative *evaluation* of the trustee and of its ability, intentions, possibilities that produces as a consequence a negative expectation.[25]

Negative trust implies a tendency of avoidance, a sense of the possibility of damage and harm; while *distrust* can be interpreted either as *negative trust* or as simple *weak trust*. In the first case the trustee is to be avoided, or to shun; and, in the second case the trustor simply does not choose to rely on the trustee.

In other words, the common usage of "distrust" may refer to two different mental dispositions: *insufficient trust* (or *weak trust* or *lack of trust*) and *negative trust* (*true distrust*, in which we have specific beliefs against the trustworthiness of the trustee).

Both for trusting and for distrusting Y, the trustor has to evaluate the set of beliefs that he has about Y, relative to Y's competence and motivational attitudes.

If we evaluate separately the main factors (competence and motivations), it is possible to consider that each of them could play a different role in what we have defined *weak trust*, in comparison to what we have defined *negative trust* (*true distrust*).

Trust is fundamental for acting and for the correct functioning of social relationships.[26] Without exchange and cooperation, societies will fail in the multiplication of powers; and trust is the basis of exchange and cooperation. However, distrust is also very useful precisely because non-cooperation and defense are useful. It would be a disaster to distrust everybody, but to trust everybody (not necessarily trustworthy) would be equally disastrous. The right thing is well-addressed trust and distrust (see also O'Neill, this volume): in this sense it is fundamental the concept of trustworthiness.

17.6 Trust as Action and Signal

Apart from understanding trust as an expectation or a "relation,"[27] one cannot deny the relevance of trust as an "action."[28] It is in fact the action (or the "inaction" due to our decision to rely on Y for realizing our goal) that *exposes* us to the "risk" of failure or harm. Since we take this risk by our decision and intentional (in)action, we are also *responsible* for our mistakes and wrong bets on Y.

Not only is trust an action, but usually it is a double action: a practical action and a communicative action. This communicative action is highly important. If we trust Y, we communicate to Y our positive evaluations of her through our delegation to and reliance on her. Moreover, this action also signals to others our appreciation of Y.

As a result, our act of trusting can reinforce Y's trustworthiness, e.g. for reciprocity reasons. Moreover, it towards witnesses, it may improve Y's reputation as being trustworthy (see also Origgi, this volume). Please note that the opposite holds as well: distrusting someone may affect someone's trustworthiness and self-esteem and may negatively affect his reputation. Of course, not all trust acts imply such a message. Sometimes our trust acts may be fully hidden, others or even Y herself may be unaware that we are relying on her behavior for achieving our goals.

17.7 Trust and Norms

What is the relation between trust and norms? First, norms, like trust, provide us with uncertainty reduction, predictability and reliability, and they can be the ground for trusting somebody or something (like food for not being toxic). However, not all our trust evaluations, feelings and decisions are based on some form of "norm" predicting or prescribing a certain behavior in a given context.[29]

To elucidate the relation between trust and norms, please first note that there is some ambiguity in regards to the notion of norms in several languages. In a *descriptive sense*, "norm" may refer merely to "regularity" (from Latin: "regula," rule/norm), whereas in a *normative or prescriptive* sense, norms are not merely describing a regularity but aim at inducing a given compliant behavior in self-regulated systems. As a result, the compliant behavior may indeed become the norm and thus regular. Nonetheless, to understand the relation between norms and trust, these two understandings of norms, i. e. as referring merely to regularity in contrast to stipulating compliant behavior, must be distinguished.

If it was true that any possible expectation, for its "prediction" part, is based on some "inference" and that an "inference" is based on some "rule" (about "what can be derived from what"), it would be true that any trust is based on some "rule" (but a cognitive one). However, even this is too strong; some activated expectations are not based on "inferences" and "rules" but just on associative reinforced links: I see *q* and this just activates, evocates the idea of *p*. This is not seriously a "rule of inference" (like: "*If (A is greater than B) and (B is greater than C), then (A is greater than C)*"). Thus, we would not agree that every expectation (and trust) is rule-based.

Moreover, bad events can also be regular and we thus can have negative expectations (based on the same rules, "norms" of any kind). For instance, on the basis of the laws of a given state, and the practices of the government, one may have the expectation that a murderer will be convicted and sentenced to death, irrespective of whether he/she is in principle in favor or against the death sentence. Yet, only if we are in favor of the death sentence, we may actually be said to "trust" the authorities for this.

Regularity-based beliefs/predictions are neither necessary nor sufficient for trust. They are not *necessary* because predictions are not necessarily regularity/rule-based. Even when there is regularity or rule, I can expect and trust an exceptional behavior or event, like winning my first election or the lottery. They are not sufficient, because the goal component (some wish, concern, practical reliance) is implied for us in any "expectation" and a fortiori in any form of "trust" which contains positive expectation.

As for "norms" in a stronger sense, not as regularities or mental rules but as shared expectations and prescriptions about the agent behavior in a given culture or community, it is not true that the existence of a given norm is *necessarily* the basis of "trust." In fact, X can trust Y for a behavior in the absence of any norm prescribing that behavior; and X can trust Y for some desired violation of a norm.

17.8 Trust and Reciprocity

According to a certain understanding of trust based upon game theory and prevalent in economics, psychology and some social sciences, trust has necessarily to do with contexts which require "reciprocation"; or is even defined as trust in the other's reciprocation[30] (see also Tutić and Voss, this volume). To our mind, this is an overly simplistic notion of trust.

The grounds of trust (and what trust is primarily "for") is reliance on the other's action, delegating our goals and depending on others. It is important to realize, though, that this basic pro-social structure (the nucleus of cooperation, of exchange, etc.) is *bilateral but not symmetrical*: X depends on Y, and Y has "power over" X, but not (necessarily) the other way around. Thus, sociality as pro-social bilateral relations does not start with "reciprocation" (which entails some symmetry) and trust also does not presuppose any equality. There can be asymmetric power relationships between the trustor and the trustee: Y can have much more power over X, than X over Y (like in a father-son relation). Analogously, goal-adoption can be fully asymmetrical; where Y does something for X, but not vice versa.

When there is a bilateral, symmetrical, and possibly "reciprocal" goal-adoption (where the "help" of Y towards X is (also) due to the help of X towards Y, and vice versa), there is trust and then reliance on the other from both sides.

Moreover, trust is not the feeling/disposition of the "helper" but of the expecting receiver. Trust is the feeling of the helper only if the help (goal-adoption) is *instrumental* to some action by the other (for example, some reciprocation). In this case, Y is "cooperating" with X and trusting X, but because she is expecting something from X. More precisely (this is the claim that interest the economists) *Y is "cooperating" because she is trusting* (in view of some reciprocation); she would not cooperate without such a trust in X. However, this is a very peculiar and certainly not the most common case of trust.

While it is perfectly legitimate and acceptable to be interested only in a sub-domain of the broad domain of trust (say "trust in exchange relations"), and to propose and use a (sub-) notion of trust limited to those contexts and cases (possibly coherent or at least compatible with a more general notion of trust), it is much less acceptable is to propose a restricted notion of something – fitting with a peculiar frame and specific issues – as the only, generally valid notion. Consider, by way of example, one of these limited definitions, clearly inspired by game theory, and proposed by (Kurzban 2003:85): trust is "*the willingness to enter exchanges in which one incurs a cost without the other already having done so.*"

There are two problems with such a simplification. First, as said we do not only trust in contexts of reciprocity.

Secondly, in game-theoretic accounts of trust, "being vulnerable" is often considered as strictly connected with "anticipating costs." This widespread view is quite coarse: it mixes up the fact that trust – as decision and action – *implies a bet, taking some risk, being vulnerable*[31] with the reductive idea of *an anticipated cost, a unilateral contribution*. But in fact, to contribute, to "pay" something in anticipation while betting on some "reciprocation," is just one case of taking risks. The expected beneficial action ("on which our welfare depends")[32] is not necessary "in exchange."

The risk we are exposed to and accept when we decide to trust somebody, to rely and depend on her, is not always the risk of wasting our invested resources, our "anticipated costs." The main risk is the risk of not achieving our goal, of being disappointed as for the entrusted action, although perhaps our costs are very limited or even non-existent. Sometimes, there is the risk of frustrating forever our goal since our choice of Y makes inaccessible other alternatives that were present at the moment of our decision. We may also risk the possible frustration of other goals: for example, our self-esteem as a good and prudent evaluator; or our social image; or other goods that we did not protect from Y's access. Thus, it is very reductive to identify the risks of trust with the lack of reciprocation and thus a waste of investment.

To conclude: *trust is not necessarily an expectation of reciprocation; and does not apply only to reciprocation.* In general, we can say that X can trust Y, and trust that Y will do as expected, *for any kind of reason.* Moreover, the fact that Y will adopt X's goal does not necessarily mean that she is benevolent, good-willing or altruistic towards X, Y can be self-motivated or even egoistic. What matters is that the intention to adopt X's goal (and thus the adopted goal and the consequent intention to α) will prevail on other non-adoptive, private (and perhaps selfish) goals of Y. As long as Y's (selfish) motives for adopting X's goal will prevail on Y's (selfish) motives for not doing α, X can count on Y doing as expected, in X's interest (and perhaps for Y's interest). Trustworthiness is a social "virtue" but not necessarily an altruistic one, even if help can also be based on altruistic motivations. This makes also clear that not all "genuine" trust[33] is "normative" (based on moral norms).[34]

17.9 Immoral Trust

In many accounts of trust, trust has a moral component. On such accounts to trust a trustee Y and to expose oneself to risk is centered on our beliefs about the trustee's morality, her benevolence, honesty and reliability. One the other hand, trusting is also a pro-social act, leading to possible cooperation and further good for the community of trustors. To our mind, this is a limited view of trust, just like the idea that trust is just "for cooperation." Cooperation (which presupposes a common goal) for sure needs trust among the participants, and for sure this is a relevant function (both evolutionarily and culturally) of trust (see also Dimock, this volume). However, also commercial "exchange," which are strictly based on selfishness,[35] definitely require trust. With such a moral framing, trust is usually restricted to interpersonal trust (see also Potter, this volume), whereas other trust relations are put aside.

Moreover, the by focusing on the morality of trust, possible immoral uses of trust may be neglected. Basically, trust is an evaluation and decision we make, which is useful for *our* plans. By relying on Y, by "delegating" a task to Y, we may exploit her for our goals whether these are moral or immoral. Thus, trust is necessarily present in lies and deceptions: how could I act in order to deceive Y if I would not believe that Y trusts me, if I would not rely on her credulity and confidence? The same holds in any kind of fraud, corruption or amongst gang or mafia members.[36] Trust, therefore does not depend upon morality and can even be exploited for immoral purposes.[37]

17.10 Affective Trust and Rational Trust

Finally, we need to distinguish between *affective trust* and *rational trust.* Please note that "rational" does not mean that this reasoning is necessarily a correct way of trusting. It merely means that it is *reason-based.* As with any reasoning, it can, however, fail: maybe it is irrational (based on wrong deductions) or based on ungrounded and inconclusive arguments.

So far, we have mainly focused on reasoning-based trust. Now we have to say something about *affective trust*, which is the emotional counterpart of a cold and reasoning-based decision (see also Lahno, this volume). It is true that trust can also be of the affective type, or be limited to it in some particular aspects of interaction: no judgments, no reasons, but simply intuition, attraction/repulsion, sympathy/antipathy, activated affective responses or evoked somatic markers.[38]

There is an abundance of literature on the influence of affect (moods, feelings and emotions) on trust.[39] While these studies show that not all individuals are equally influenced by affects, they all consider affects as mediators for trust.[40]

We would like to consider a different perspective in which, without neglecting the interferences between affective trust and rational trust, we also evaluate the possibility of a less unilateral dependence of one system on the other. In particular, our claim is that in many cases these two aspects of trust coexist, and they can converge or diverge. The interaction between affective and rational trust is very relevant and can have several modes: sometimes starting from an emerging *feeling of trust* the trustor can recall and develop some *reasoning* on that trust; alternatively, sometimes *rational trust* promotes the *feeling of trust*. To our knowledge, these relationships and interactions, have not been extensively studied but would be of great relevance for furthering our understanding of trust, e.g. through simulations or experiments.[41]

In the last few years, a set of studies have been developed on the neurobiological evidence of trust.[42] On the basis of these studies[43] (see also Clemént, this volume), there is an important and significant distinction between the perceived risk due to social factors and that based on interpersonal interactions. As Fehr writes: "the rationale for the experiment originates in evidence indicating that oxytocin plays a key role in certain pro-social approach behaviors in non-human mammals … Based on the animal literature, hypothesized that oxytocin might cause humans to exhibit more behavioral trust as measured in the trust game." In these experiments, they also show how oxytocin has a specific effect on social behavior because it differently impacts on the trustor and the trustee (only in the former there is a positive influence). In addition, it is also shown that the trustor is not reducing the general sensitivity to risk but specifically depending on the partner nature (human versus not-human).

Following this paradigm, we could say that when some social frameworks are given and perceived by the subject, oxytocin is released in a certain quantity, so modifying the activity of precise regions of the brain and consequently producing a more or less trusting behavior.

But, what are the features of the social framework? Is this framework just based on the presence of other humans? And what is the role played by past experiences (for modulating the oxytocin release)? What is the relation between the unconscious and spontaneous bias (characterizing the emotional, hot, not rationale trust) and the conscious deliberative reasoning (characterizing the rational and planned trust)? Is a not diffident attitude and feeling sufficient for a real trust?

The results of this discovery are no doubt quite relevant. But they must be complemented and interlinked with a general *cognitive* theory of trust. Without this link, without a mediation of more complex structures and functions, we risk to trivially translate an articulated concept into a chemical activation of a specific brain area, cutting out all the real complexity of the phenomenon (unable to explain for example why before making a very difficult decision we reflect on the problem for hours, sometimes for days. And how the contribution of the different beliefs impacts on that choice). The fact of individuating and establishing some precise and well-defined basic neuro-mechanisms can be considered an important advancement for the brain studies and also for founding the cognitive models of the behavior. In any case, in our view, they cannot be considered as the only description of the trusting behavior, and cannot really play a role in a detailed and "usable" prediction and description of the phenomenon. *Without this mediation (psychological interpretation), localization or biochemistry say nothing*. Also, because this *social confident disposition* specifically towards humans is clearly too broad and *vague* to capture precisely what "trust" is; we saw how many specific contents and dimensions true trust has, like its "aboutness" (goal) or different features of the trustee.

17.11 Non-Social Trust: Trust in Technology

Several authors (especially in philosophy and psychology) consider *trust* as an attitude (and possibly a feeling) towards other humans, or at least other agents endowed with some intelligence and autonomy only. However, on our account, trust is not just a *social* attitude; it can be also applied to instruments, technologies, functional objects, etc. Trust can be addressed towards some process, mechanisms, or technology: how effective and good is it as for its service; how reliable and predictable; how accessible and friendly?

Since Y's "operation" or "performance" is useful to X (trust disposition), and X has decided to rely on it (decision to trust), this means that X might delegate (act of trusting) some action/goal in his own plan to Y. Somebody would call that just "reliance." Yet this is contrary to the common use of the words trust. Moreover, we consider this restriction wrongheaded, because such a reliance towards a technology too is based on an evaluation of the "qualities" of the trustee Y as well as on feelings and dispositions of the trustor X, requiring X's decision and intention to count on Y and to act accordingly. Of course, some dimensions we evaluate humans on (like willingness or honesty) are absent, because they are not necessary for Y's reliable performance.

A naive attempt to cover this kind of trust (and common use of the word "trust") is to see trust in an object or technology Y as trust in its designer or producer, not in the working device and in its correct functioning. In our view this is neither true nor necessary; we can just rely on a drug, chair or machine in that we know that it is able and in condition to do what it has to do for us.[44]

Please note that this form of trust also applies to complex and dynamic interactions of many actors, like traffic in a given journey or city, or performance of the markets, etc.

Another misleading view about trust in the "functioning" of technology or of complex dynamics is the claim that we trust it if and only if it is "transparent," i.e. if we understand "how" it works. This position is naive, and, paradoxically, the opposite is frequently true and necessary. People use cash machines or cards because they trust the system enough, and they are not aware of how they work and the serious risks they are exposed to. In order to use them we need to *not* really know and understand their functioning. We need some ignorance, not full "transparency" in order to trust. We have to understand how to "use" them, and to have some approximate schema of how they work; just their basic macro-functions and operations: what they are doing, not really "how" they are doing what they do. What matters is the feeling, the impression to understand "how" they work. Trust is not due to deep or technical understanding but to a perceived dependability, usability, safety, a friendly interface, etc.

As for technology and their systems usually (especially in AI) the problem of trust is wrongly identified with or reduced to a problem of "security," which is just one component of *trust*.

One cannot reduce trust to *safety* and *security*, because: on the one side, what matters is first of all the "*perceived*" *safety*. On the other side, building a trust environment and atmosphere and trustworthy agents is one basis for safety, and vice versa.

Perceived unreliability elicits cheating and bad actions; collective distrust creates dangers (ex. panic).

Finally, as for technology, the majority of people worry about "trustworthy" systems more than about "trust," but these are not the same and there is a non-trivial and *bi-directional* relationship between "trust" and "trustworthiness": On the one side, what matters is not only trustworthiness, but the *perceived* trustworthiness. Objective trustworthiness is neither enough for technology, nor for organizations, interactions, political systems, or markets (that is in fact why we have "marketing"). Moreover, objective trustworthiness is not sufficient to create *perceived* trustworthiness and conversely we can perceive trustworthiness – and trust – even in the absence of objective trustworthiness. On the other side, the members' or users' trust in the "system" is a crucial component of its trustworthiness, and of its correct working. This is especially true for hybrid systems where the global result is due to the information processing and the actions of both humans and artificial agents.

Notes

1 Castelfranchi and Falcone (2010).
2 Castelfranchi and Falcone (1998).
3 See also Baier (1986), Hardin (2004a), Origgi (2004), Josang (2002), McKnight and Chervany (1996).
4 Marsh (1994), Jøsang (1999), Efsandiari and Chandrasekaran (2001), Jøsang and Presti (2004), Sabater and Sierra (2002).
5 In some cases, the trustor also has beliefs about the trustee's beliefs about the trustor's mind/behavior. Mind reading also means to be capable of inquiring into the reasons for the trustee's benevolence/malevolence: it is a matter of internal attribution not only of external attribution (Falcone and Castelfranchi (2001)).
6 Luhmann (1979).
7 The choice between delegating a task to Y or doing it personally is not based only on X's comparison with Y as regards the respective skills in accomplishing the task. It is mainly based on other parameters such as the costs of delegating the task to Y and exploiting him versus doing it X himself, and the social consequences – becoming dependent on Y.
8 Following the work of Bacharach and Gambetta (2000), we call "krypta" the internal features of an agent, determining its behavior, while we call "manifesta" the external features of an agent, hence as the information which is observable by other agents.
9 This opens a new chapter about *belief sources*, trust in them, their differences, their multiform nature (see Castelfranchi et al. (2003), Demolombe (2001)).
10 We analyzed this issue in Castelfranchi and Falcone (2010). Let us underline just a specific aspect. The higher the degree of certainty of X's beliefs about Y, the stronger the epistemic component of X's "expectation" and trust about Y's behavior. Of course, a positive expectation also has another quantitative dimension (degree): the one relative to the value of the goal (desire, need), and not only to the strength of the prediction or possibility. The expected outcome can be very important for me or not so desirable. Trust is not more or less strong on the basis of the degree of desirability; possibly even the other way around.
11 Jøsang (1999).
12 In fact, the evaluation is about some "quality" of Y (competence, ability, willingness, loyalty and so on) and the trustworthiness of Y (for that task) and X's trust in Y depends also on the estimated degree of such quality: X can be pretty sure that Y is not so strong in that domain; thus his trust in Y is not so high although the belief is very strong/sure. The degree of trust is a function of both the level of the ascribed quality and the certainty of the beliefs about it.
13 Gambetta (2000), Mayer et al. (1995), Zaheer et al. (1998).
14 See for example Cho et al. (2015).
15 *Generalized* forms of trust are also possible: X can trust Y for "any" goal or trust a set of agents for a given goal or for a family of goals.

16 Finally, trust *per se* can be a goal. We can have the goal (desire or need) to trust Y (our friend, parent, son, and so on) in general, or to trust that guy here and now, since we do not see any alternative; or the goal to trust somebody, to be in a trustworthy community; or the goal to be trusted by somebody, in order to receive good evaluations (esteem) and/or for being a partner in some exchange or cooperation, or for an affective relation, or for membership ("trust capital" (Castelfranchi et al. 2006).
17 Gambetta (2000), Coleman (1994).
18 In more formal terms, we may thus state: X the trustor; Y the trustee; τ= (α,g) the task, with α the action realized by Y for achieving goal g (the goal X wants to achieve in the trust action); C the environmental context in which Y realizes the action α $B_1,\ldots, B_n$ the reasons believed by X about Y and the context C; we can say: $Trust(X, Y,\tau, C) = f(B_1, B_2, \ldots, B_n)$ X's trust in Y for achieving task τ in context C is a function *f* of a set of X's beliefs: $B_1, B_2, \ldots, B_n$.
19 Luhmann (1979).
20 Simon (1955).
21 Kahneman and Tversky (1979).
22 Hardin (2004a), Hardin (2004b), Cofta (2006), Pereira (2009).
23 Pereira (2009).
24 This is exactly because trust cannot be simply formalized as an estimated probability.
25 Castelfranchi and Falcone (2010).
26 Luhmann (1979).
27 Castelfranchi and Falcone (2010), O'Neill (2002).
28 Taddeo (2010).
29 This is a quite diffused thesis (especially in sociology; for example Garfinkel (1963), Giddens (1984), Jones (2002).
30 Castelfranchi and Falcone (2010), Falcone et al. (2012), Ostrom and Walker (2003), Pelligra (2005). To be true Pelligra (2006:3) recognizes and criticizes the fact that "*most studies* [in economics and Game Theory] *consider trust merely as an expectation of reciprocal behavior*" while this is "a very specific definition of trust."
31 Barber (1983), Fukuyama (1995), Yamagishi (2003), Rousseau et al. (1998).
32 Barber (1983), Fukuyama (1995), Yamagishi (2003), Rousseau et al. (1998).
33 Some authors try to identify some sort of "genuine" trust (Hardin (2004a), Baier (1986)) it is focused on "value" and morality; or more in general it seems excluding any kind of reason external to the interpersonal relationship (no authorities, no third parties, no contracts, etc.).
34 Jones (2002), Baier (1986).
35 A. Smith (1776): "*It is not from the benevolence of the butcher, the brewer, or the baker that we expect our dinner, but from their regard to their own interest. We address ourselves, not to their humanity but to their self-love, and never talk to them of our own necessities but of their advantages*"; however, when I order the brewer to send me a box of beer and I send the money, I "trust" him as for giving me the beer. We may have a form of "cooperation," exchange, and collaboration among selfish actors for their private interests. The message of Smith however is more deep and complex: people with their selfish preferences and conduct do in fact play a social positive function.
36 Gambetta (1993).
37 Floridi (2013).
38 Damasio (1994).
39 Erdem and Ozen (2003), Johnson and Grayson (2005), Webber (2008).
40 This view is also justified by the established difference between system1 and system2, where system1 is the *automatic emotional processing system*, and system2 is the *controlled and deliberate thinking process* (Mischel and Ayduk (2004); Smith and Kirby (2001); Price and Norman (2008)). System1 is quick while system2 is relatively slow. So system2 has to work on the results of system1.
41 For example, in the field of computer-mediated interaction and trust-based ICT, the possibility of integrating affective and rational aspects of trust could lead to more realistic interactions.
42 Kosfeld et al. (2005), Fehr (2008).
43 Kosfeld et al. (2005).
44 We agree on that also with Söllner et al. (2013:121): "Separately investigating trust in the provider of the IT artifact and trust in the IT artifact itself, will allow researchers to gather a deeper understanding of the nature of trust in IT artifacts and how it can be built."

References.

Bacharach, M. and Gambetta, D. (2000) "Trust in Signs," in K. Cook (ed.), *Trust and Social Structure*, New York: Russel Sage Foundation.

Baier, A. (1986) "Trust and Antitrust," *Ethics* 96(2): 231–260. www.jstor.org/stable/2381376

Barber, B. (1983) *The Logic and Limits of Trust*, New Brunswick, NJ: Rutgers University Press.

Castelfranchi, C. and Falcone, R. (1998) "Principles of Trust for MAS: Cognitive Anatomy, Social Importance, and Quantification," in Proceedings of the International Conference on Multi-Agent Systems (ICMAS '98), Paris, July, pp. 72–79.

Castelfranchi, C. and Falcone, R. (2010) *Trust Theory: A Socio-Cognitive and Computational Model*, Chichester: John Wiley & Sons.

Castelfranchi, C. and Falcone, R. (2016) "Trust & Self-Organising Socio-Technical Systems," in W. Reif, G. Anders, H. Seebach, J.-P. Steghöfer, E. André, J. Hähner, C. Müller-Schloer and T. Ungerer (eds.), *Trustworthy Open Self-Organising Systems*, Berlin: Springer.

Castelfranchi, C., Falcone, R. and Marzo, F. (2006) "Being Trusted in a Social Network: Trust as Relational Capital," in K. Stølen, W.H. Winsborough, F. Martinelli and F. Massacci (eds.), *Lecture Notes in Computer Science*, 3986, Heidelberg: Springer.

Castelfranchi, C., Falcone, R. and Pezzulo, G. (2003) "Trust in Information Sources as a Source for Trust: A Fuzzy Approach," in *Proceedings of the Second International Joint Conference on Autonomous Agents and Multiagent Systems (AAMAS-03) Melbourne, (Australia), 14–18 July*, ACM Press.

Cho, J.-H., Chan, K. and Adali, S. (2015) "A Survey on Trust Modeling," *ACM Computing Surveys* 48(2). https://dl.acm.org/doi/10.1145/2815595

Cofta, P. (2006) "Distrust," in Proceedings of the 8th International Conference on Electronic Commerce: The new e-commerce – Innovations for Conquering Current Barriers, Obstacles and Limitations to Conducting Successful Business on the Internet, Fredericton, New Brunswick, Canada, August 13–16.

Coleman, J.S. (1994) *Foundation of Social Theory*, Cambridge, MA: Harvard University Press.

Damasio, A.R. (1994) *Descartes'Error: Emotion, Reason, and the Human Brain*, New York: Gosset/Putnam Press.

Demolombe, R. (2001) "To Trust Information Sources: A Proposal for a Modal Logical Framework," in C. Castelfranchi and T. Yao-Hua (eds.), *Trust and Deception in Virtual Societies*, Dordrecht: Kluwer.

Efsandiari, B. and Chandrasekharan, S. (2001) "On How Agents Make Friends: Mechanisms for Trust Acquisition," in Proceedings of the Fourth Workshop on Deception, Fraud and Trust in Agent Societies, Montreal, Canada.

Erdem, F. and Ozen, J. (2003) "Cognitive and Affective Dimensions of Trust in Development," *Team Performance Management: An International Journal 9* (5/6): 131–135.

Falcone, R. and Castelfranchi, C. (2001a) "Social Trust: A Cognitive Approach," in C. Castelfranchi and T. Yao-Hua (eds.), *Trust and Deception in Virtual Societies*, Dordrecht: Kluwer.

Falcone, R. and Castelfranchi, C. (2001b) "The Human in the Loop of a Delegated Agent: The Theory of Adjustable Social Autonomy," *IEEE Transactions on Systems, Man, and Cybernetics, Part A: Systems and Humans*, 31(5): 406–418.

Falcone, R., Castelfranchi, C., Lopes Cardoso, H., Jones, A. and Oliveira, E. (2012) "Norms and Trust," in S. Ossowsky (ed.), *Agreement Technologies*, Dordrecht: Springer.

Fehr, E., (2008) *On the Economics and Biology of Trust*. Technical Report of the Institute for the Study of Labor, no. 3895. Bonn.

Floridi, L. (2013) "Infraethics," *The Philosophers' Magazine* 60: 26–27.

Fukuyama, F. (1995) *Trust: The Social Virtues and the Creation of Prosperity*, New York: The Free Press.

Gambetta, D. (1993) *The Sicilian Mafia: The Business of Private Protection*, Cambridge, MA: Harvard University Press.

Gambetta, D. (2000) "Can We Trust Trust?" in D. Gambetta (ed.), *Trust: Making and Breaking Cooperative Relations*, New York: Basil Blackwell.

Garfinkel, H. (1963) "A Conception of an Experiment with Trust as a Condition of Stable Concerned Actions," in O.J. Harvey (ed.), *Motivation and Social Interaction*, New York: Ronald Press.

Giddens, A. (1984) *The Constitution of Society: Outline of the Theory of Structuration*, Cambridge: Cambridge University Press.

Hardin, R. (2004a) *Trust and Trustworthiness*, New York: Russel Sage Foundation.

Hardin, R. (2004b) "Distrust: Manifestation and Management," in R. Hardin (ed.), *Distrust*, New York: Russel Sage Foundation.
Johnson, D. and Grayson, K. (2005) "Cognitive and Affective Trust in Service Relationships," *Journal of Business Research* 58: 500–507.
Jones, A.J. (2002) "On the Concept of Trust," *Decision Support Systems* 33(3): 225–232.
Jøsang, A. (1999) "An Algebra for Assessing Trust in Certification Chains," in Proceedings of the Network and Distributed Systems Security Symposium (NDSS '99). http://citeseerx.ist.psu.edu/viewdoc/summary?doi=10.1.1.25.1233
Jøsang, A. (2002) "The Consensus Operator for Combining Beliefs," *Artificial Intelligence* 142(1–2): 157–170.
Jøsang, A. and Presti, S.L. (2004) "Analyzing the Relationship between Risk and Trust," in *Proceedings of the 2nd International Conference on Trust Management (iTrust '04)*, 2995. Dordrecht: Springer, 135–145.
Kahneman, D. and Tversky, A. (1979) "Prospect Theory: An Analysis of Decision under Risk," *Econometrica* 47(2), 1979, 263–291.
Kosfeld, M., Heinrichs, M., Zak, P.J., Fischbacher, U. and Fehr, E. (2005) "Oxytocin Increases Trust in Humans," *Nature* 435: 673–676.
Kurzban, R. (2003) "Biological Foundation of Reciprocity," in E. Ostrom and J. Walker (eds.), *Trust, Reciprocity: Interdisciplinary Lessons from Experimental Research*, New York: Sage.
Luhmann, N. (1979) *Trust and Power*, New York: John Wiley & Sons.
Marsh, S.P. (1994) "Formalizing Trust as a Computational Concept." Ph.D. dissertation, University of Stirling.
Mayer, R.C., Davis, H. and Schoorman, F.D. (1995) "An Integrative Model of Organizational Trust," *Academy of Management Review* 20(3): 709–734.
McKnight, D.H. and Chervany, N.L. (1996) "The Meanings of Trust." Technical Report 96–04, University of Minnesota, Management Informations Systems Research Center (MISRC).
Miceli, M. and Castelfranchi, C. (2000) "The Role of Evaluation in Cognition and Social Interaction," in K. Dautenhahn (ed.), *Human Cognition and Agent Technology*, Amsterdam: Benjamins.
Mischel, W. and Ayduk, O. (2004) "Willpower in a Cognitive-Affective Processing System," in R.F. Baumeister and K.D. Vohs (eds.), *Handbook of Self-Regulation: Research, Theory, and Applications*, New York: Guildford Press.
O'Neill, O. (2002) *Autonomy and Trust in Bioethics*, Cambridge: Cambridge University Press.
Origgi, G. (2004) "Is Trust an Epistemological Notion?" *Episteme* 1(1): 61–72.
Ostrom, E. and Walker, J. (eds.) (2003) *Trust and Reciprocity: Interdisciplinary Lessons from Experimental Research*, New York: Russell Sage Foundation.
Pelligra, V. (2005) "Under Trusting Eyes: The Responsive Nature of Trust," in R. Sugden and B. Gui (eds.), *Economics and Sociality: Accounting for the Interpersonal Relations*, Cambridge: Cambridge University Press.
Pelligra, V. (2006) "Trust Responsiveness: On the Dynamics of Fiduciary Interactions." Working Paper CRENoS, 15/2006.
Pereira, C. (2009) "Distrust is not always the Complement of Trust" (position paper), in G. Boella, P. Noriega, G. Pigozzi and H. Verhagen (eds.), *Normative Multi-Agent Systems*, Dagstuhl, Germany: Dagstuhl Seminar Proceedings.
Price, M.C. and Norman, E. (2008) "Intuitive Decisions on the Fringes of Consciousness: Are They Conscious and Does It Matter?" *Judgment and Decision Making* 3(1): 28–41.
Rousseau, D.M., Burt, R.S. and Camerer, C. (1998) "Not So Different after All: A Cross-Discipline View of Trust," *Journal of Academy Management Review* 23(3), 393–404.
Sabater, J. and Sierra, C. (2002) "Reputation and Social Network Analysis in Multi-Agent Systems," in *ACM Proceedings of International Joint Conference on Autonomous Agents and Multi-Agent Systems*, ACM.
Simon, H. (1955) "A Behavioral Model of Rational Choice," *Quarterly Journal of Economics* 69: 99–118.
Smith, A. ([1776] 2008) *An Inquiry into the Nature and Causes of the Wealth of Nations: A Selected Edition*, K. Sutherland (ed.), Oxford: Oxford University Press.
Smith, C.A. and Kirby, L.D. (2001) "Towards Delivering on the Promise of Appraisal Theory," in K. Scherer, A. Schorr and T. Johnstone (eds.), *Appraisal Processes in Emotion: Theory, Methods, Research*, New York: Oxford University Press.

Söllner, M., Pavlou, P. and Leimeister, J.M. (2013) "Understanding Trust in IT Artifacts – A New Conceptual Approach," in Academy of Management Annual Meeting, Orlando, Florida, USA. http://pubs.wi-kassel.de/wp-content/uploads/2014/07/JML_474.pdf

Taddeo, M. (2010) "Modelling Trust in Artificial Agents: A First Step toward the Analysis of e-Trust," *Minds and Machines* 20(2): 243–257.

Trivers, R.L. (1971) "The Evolution of Reciprocal Altruism," *Quarterly Review of Biology* 46: 35–57.

Webber, S.S. (2008) "Development of Cognitive and Affective Trust in Teams: A Longitudinal Study," *Small Group Research* 36(6): 746–769.

Yamagishi, T. (2003) "Cross-Societal Experimentation on Trust: A Comparison of the United States and Japan," in E. Omstrom and J. Walker (eds.) *Trust, Reciprocity: Interdisciplinary Lessons from Experimental Research*, New York: Sage.

Zaheer, A., McEvily, B. and Perrone, V. (1998) "Does Trust Matter? Exploring the Effects of Interorganizational and Interpersonal Trust on Performance," *Organization Science* 9(2): 141–159.

PART II

Whom to Trust?

18
SELF-TRUST

Richard Foley

18.1 Introduction

Self-trust comes in different sizes and shapes. One can have trust in one's physical abilities, social skills, technical know-how, mathematical competencies, and so on.

The most fundamental and encompassing kind of self-trust, however, is intellectual – an attitude of confidence in one's ability to acquire information about the world, process it and arrive at accurate judgments on the basis of it. It is trust in the overall reliability of one's intellectual efforts.

We all have some degree of such trust in ourselves. We would not be able to get through a day without it. Nor would inquiry be possible, whether into small private matters (the best route for an upcoming car trip) or large public ones (the causes of Alzheimer's disease).

The core philosophical questions about intellectual self-trust are, is it reasonable, and if so, what makes it so? And there are related questions waiting in the wings. If intellectual self-trust is reasonable, can it sometimes be defeated? If so, by what? And, how does intellectual trust in ourselves affect the extent to which we should rely on the opinions of others?

This chapter is organized as follows: section 18.2 uses the problem of the Cartesian Circle to illustrate the difficulty of providing non-circular defenses of our most basic intellectual faculties and methods and the opinions they generate; section 18.3 examines attempts to provide non-circular refutations of skepticism; section 18.4 discusses ways in which empirical evidence can place limits on self-trust; and section 18.5 addresses the degree to which intellectual conflicts with others should affect self-trust.

18.2 The Problem of the Cartesian Circle

Much of the history of epistemology has been devoted to searching for grounds for intellectual self-trust, ones particularly that could dispatch skeptical worries that our ways of acquiring beliefs about the world might not be reliable.

A traditional way of surfacing these worries is through thought experiments, one of the most well-known of which is the brain-in-a-vat story, which imagines a world in which, unbeknownst to me, my brain is hooked up to equipment programmed to provide it with precisely the same visual, auditory, tactile and other sensory inputs that I have in this world (Harman 1973). Consequently, my opinions about my life and environment are also the same. I have the same beliefs about my physical properties, my surroundings, my recent activities, and so on, but in fact I have no bodily parts except for my brain, which is tucked away in a vat in a corner of a laboratory. So, my beliefs about the world around me are not just mistaken about a detail here and there but deeply mistaken. The troubling skeptical question that then arises is, how can I be sure that this imagined brain-in-a-vat world is not the real world, the one I actually inhabit?

Descartes famously thought he was able to answer this question. He set out to find a method that avoided all possibilities of error and was convinced he had found it. He maintained that one could be completely assured of not making mistakes provided that one assented only to that which one finds utterly impossible to doubt (Descartes 2017).

He himself raised an obvious question about this recommendation. Might not we be psychologically constituted such that what is indubitable for us is nonetheless mistaken? His response was that an omnipotent and perfectly benevolent god would not permit this, but once again, anticipating his critics, he recognized that this pushes the questions back to ones about the existence and purposes of God. To deal with these, Descartes mounted what he claimed were indubitable arguments not only that God exists but also that God, being all good and all powerful, would not permit us to be deceived about that which we cannot doubt.

Not many have agreed that his arguments, for these conclusions are in fact impossible to doubt, but an even more intractable problem is that even if they had been, this still would not have been enough to provide non-question-begging guarantees of truth. If the claim one is trying to refute is that indubitable claims might be false, it does not help to invoke indubitable considerations in the refutation. This is the notorious problem of the Cartesian circle noted by many commentators.

What is less frequently noted is that Descartes' problem is also ours. We may not be as obsessed with eliminating all chance of error, but we too would like to be assured that our core faculties and methods are at least generally reliable. If, however, we make use of these same faculties and methods in trying to provide the assurances, we will not have secured the non-circular defense we seek, whereas if we try to rely on other faculties and methods to provide the defense, we can then ask about their reliability, and all the same problems arise again. This is a generalization of the problem of the Cartesian circle, and it is a circle from which we can no more escape than could Descartes.

The right response to this predicament is not to be overly defensive about it. It is to acknowledge that skeptical anxieties are inescapable, and the appropriate reaction is to live with them, as opposed to denying them or thinking that they can be argued away. Our lack of non-question-begging guarantees is not a failing that needs to be corrected on pains of irrationality, but a reality to be acknowledged. We must accept that inquiry, from the simple to the sophisticated, requires an element of basic trust in our intellectual faculties and the opinions they generate, the need for which cannot be eliminated by further inquiry. Inquiry requires if not a leap of intellectual faith, at least a first hop.

"Hop" because the trust should not be unlimited. That is the path to dogmatism, but there does need to be trust. The most pressing questions for epistemologists are ones about its degrees and limits. How much trust is it appropriate for us to have in our faculties, especially our most fundamental ones? And, are there conditions under which this trust can be undermined? If so, what are they?

18.3 Strategies for Refuting Skeptical Worries

It can be difficult to accept the lesson of the Cartesian circle. We would like there to be assurances that our ways of trying to understand the world are not deeply mistaken. And so, it has been tempting to continue to look for arguments capable of providing non-circular grounds for intellectual self-trust. If the arguments of Descartes and the other classical foundationalists who followed him do not succeed, there must be others that do.

One strategy is to argue that those raising skeptical worries inevitably undermine themselves, since they have to rely on their faculties and methods in mounting their concerns. But then, it is incoherent for them later to turn around and entertain the idea that these same faculties and methods are unreliable (Cavell 1979; Malcolm 1963; Williams 1995).

The problem with this strategy is that it fails to appreciate that the aims of those raising skeptical worries can be wholly negative. They need not be trying to establish any positive thesis to the effect that our faculties and methods are unreliable. They need only maintain that there is no non-question-begging way of defending their reliability, and hence no non-question-begging way of grounding intellectual self-trust. The point, when expressed in this way, is simply an extension of the Cartesian circle.

Another strategy is to look to the theory of natural selection to provide grounds for self-trust, the idea being that if the faculties of humans regularly misled them about their surroundings, the species would not have survived. But it has not just survived, it has prospered, at least in terms of sheer population size. This reproductive success provides assurances that human cognitive faculties must be for the most part reliable (Quine 1979).

It is a bit startling how similar this argument from natural selection is in structure to older views that tried to deploy theological arguments to ground self-trust. As mentioned above, Descartes did so, but he was not alone. John Locke, to cite but one additional example, located the basis for intellectual self-trust in the fact that God created us with faculties well designed to generate accurate opinions. Indeed, appeals to theology had a double purpose in Locke's epistemology. Not only did they provide assurances of reliability, they also explained why it was so important for us to have reliable opinions. We need accurate beliefs, especially in matters of religion and morality, because the salvation of our souls is at stake (Locke 1975).

The contemporary analogue would have natural design playing a comparable double role. It is to provide guarantees of reliability while also explaining why reliability is important, namely, the species would not have survived without it. It is perhaps not unexpected, then, that arguments for self-trust based on natural selection are flawed for reasons closely analogous to those that afflicted the older arguments based on natural theology.

The first and most obvious problem is the familiar one. A variety of intellectual faculties, methods and assumptions are employed in generating and defending the theory of natural selection, and doubts can be raised about them. The theory itself cannot be used to completely expunge such worries, given that the theory is to be trusted only if these faculties, methods and assumptions are.

The second shared problem is that in order to get the assurances of reliability they sought, it was not enough for Descartes and Locke to establish that God exists. They also needed a specific theology, one that provided assurances that there are no divine purposes that might be served by God's allowing our basic intellectual faculties to be unreliable. Even granting the existence of God, it is no simple matter for a theology to establish this.

Similarly, it is not easy for the theory of natural selection to have all the specific characteristics it would need to serve as a ground for intellectual self-trust. Most importantly, even if it is granted that our basic intellectual procedures and dispositions are the effects of biological evolution as opposed to being cultural products, and granted as well they were well designed for survival in the last Pleistocene when humans evolved, it is a further step to establish that they were also well designed to generate reliable (as opposed to survival enhancing) opinions in that environment,[1] and yet another step to establish that they continue to be well designed to do so in our contemporary environment.

A third class of strategies to ground self-trust maintains that a sophisticated enough metaphysics of belief, reference or truth precludes the possibility of radical error. So, contrary to first untutored impressions, it is simply not possible for our belief systems to be extensively mistaken. An overarching trust in their reliability is thus justified.

One of the most ambitious attempts to mount this kind of argument is due to Donald Davidson. Relying on situations of so-called "radical interpretation," where it is not clear that the creatures being interpreted have beliefs at all, he argued that at least in the simplest of cases, the objects of one's beliefs must be taken to be the causes of them. As a result, the nature of belief is such that it leaves no room for the possibility of the world being dramatically different from what a belief system represents to be (Davidson 1986).

The qualifier "the simplest of cases" is revealing, however. It highlights that even on the most generous assessment of the argument, it rules out only the most extreme errors, and as such still leaves plenty of room for extensive skeptical concerns. An even more basic problem is the usual one, however. Intricate and highly controversial philosophical arguments are used to defend this view about the nature of belief, and doubts can be raised about them. Moreover, any attempt to deploy the nature of belief to purge all such doubts is bound to fail, given that the plausibility of the view is supposed to be established by means of these arguments.

We are, thus, driven back yet again to the lesson of the Cartesian circle, which is that the need for some degree self-trust is inescapable. Having confidence in our most basic intellectual faculties and methods is part of our human inheritance. It is not something we could give up even we wanted to do so. This is not to say that our faculties and intellectual practices have to be relied on uncritically (more on this in a moment), but it is to say that what some have sought, namely, a non-question-begging validation of them, is not in the offing.

18.4 Limits of Intellectual Self-Trust

Any remotely normal intellectual life requires self-trust, but there are dangers from the opposite direction, that of having too much confidence in one's faculties, methods and the opinions they generate. Self-trust ought to be presumptive. It should be capable of being overridden when information generated by the very faculties and methods in which one has presumptive trust indicates they may not be operating reliably.

This is the flip side of the Cartesian circle. One's core faculties and methods cannot provide non-question guarantees of their own reliability, but they can surface evidence of unreliability. Indeed, this is not even unusual. We all have had the experience of discovering that our way of thinking about some issue or another has been off the mark. Moreover, mistakes can occur even when we have been careful in acquiring and evaluating the relevant evidence, which means that a measure of intellectual humility is an appropriate virtue for all.[2]

Potentially more disturbing, however, is evidence of systematic unreliability. "Systematic" in the sense of there being tendencies for people in general to make mistakes in the ways they collect and process certain kinds of information. It has become a bit of cottage industry for psychologists to search for such tendencies, and they have been successful. So much so that there is now a large, somewhat depressing inventory of the mistakes people regularly make.

Of course, no one should be surprised that we are prone to error. When we are tired, emotionally distressed, inebriated or just too much in a hurry, we tend to make mistakes. The recent findings are eye opening for another reason. They document our susceptibilities to making certain errors even when we are not disadvantaged in any of the familiar ways. We regularly neglect base rates when evaluating statistical claims; we are subject to anchoring effects and overconfidence biases; and short personal interviews with candidates for schools, jobs, parole, etc. tend to worsen rather than improve the accuracy of predictions about the future performance of the candidates.[3] There is also extensive documentation of the extent to which socially pervasive negative stereotypes influence judgments about members of the stereotyped class (Fricker 2007; see also Medina, this volume).

The pressing personal question raised by such studies is, how should this information about the ways in which people in general are unreliable affect one's trust in one's own intellectual reliability?

The first and most important thing to say about this question is pretty simple, namely, one should not dismiss the information as being relevant for others but not for oneself. More precisely, one should not do so unless there are indications that one is not as vulnerable as the general population to making these mistakes. And occasionally, there are such indications. Professional economists have been shown to be less likely than others to commit sunk cost fallacies.

But even without such indications, one does not necessarily have to be paralyzed by the pessimistic findings of these studies. Becoming aware and keeping in mind that people have tendencies to make mistakes of the documented sort can be helpful in avoiding them. To be forewarned is sometimes enough to be forearmed.

Moreover, the empirical studies themselves at times generate advice about how to do so. Follow-up studies to the ones documenting the mistakes that people regularly make in dealing with statistical problems have shown that the errors largely disappear when subjects approach the problems in terms of frequencies instead of probabilities.[4] The lesson, then, is that when dealing with statistical issues, one is better off framing them in terms of frequencies.

There is a similar arc to findings about the poor performance of subjects in dealing with various logic puzzles. The initial research revealed high error rates but subsequent investigations demonstrated that performance improves markedly when the puzzles are framed in terms of social rules and prohibitions.[5] So, if one is confronted with a question that has a structure similar to these puzzles and if the question is not already framed in term of prohibitions and rules, one can take the time to do so.

Then again, for other problems documented in the literature, for example, the ways in which biases and cultural stereotypes can adversely affect one's judgments, there do not seem to be obvious remedies (see also Scheman, this volume). Even in these cases, however, effective self-monitoring remains a possibility, only it is important to recognize that the best self-monitoring should not be limited to introspection. One can also observe oneself from the outside, as it were.

In particular, we can construct interpretations of ourselves from our own behavior and other people's reactions to it, in much the same way as we do for others. Indeed, sometimes there is no effective substitute. Consider an analogy. Usually the best way to convince people they are jealous is not to ask them to introspect but rather to get them to see themselves and their behavior as others do. So too it is with intellectual biases. Others may point out to me that although I was not aware of doing so, I was looking at my watch frequently during the interview, or that the tone and substance of my questions were more negative than for other candidates, or that my negative reaction to the way the interviewee handled questions is just the kind of reaction that is disproportionately frequent, given cultural stereotypes about the interviewee's gender, ethnicity, etc. These are warning signs that give me reasons to consider anew the inferences I have made from the available evidence, and reasons as well to seek out additional evidence.

On the other hand, philosophers have had no trouble swapping out real-world worries and real-world strategies for dealing with them with hypothetical cases in which opportunities for self-correction are minimum or even non-existent. Here is one such case. Imagine that 25th century neuroscience has progressed to the point where there are accurate detectors of brain states and also accurate detectors of what subjects believe. In using the detectors on subjects, neuroscientists have confirmed the following surprising generalization: subjects believe that they are in brain state P if and only if they are not in brain state P. Now consider a layperson in this 25th century society who believes that she is not in brain state P but who is then told about these studies. What should she now believe? (Christensen 2010)?

The first thing to notice about this hypothetical scenario is how thinly described it is, so much so that there can be questions about whether it remains a realistic possibility once additional details are filled in. For example, given the nature of belief, is it realistic to think that even a highly advanced neuroscience could develop completely trustworthy belief detectors? And what sort of data would such detectors have to generate to be in a position to confirm a generalization as surprising as the one above? In trying to establish the generalization, how would the detectors go about distinguishing between what subjects believe about their being in brain P and what they believe they believe about this? And so on with other questions.

Still, even if this particular what-if story at the end of the day is not realistic, it nonetheless does serve to illustrate an important point, namely, if there are situations, even if only ones far removed from everyday life, in which I have concrete evidence of my lack of reliability about an issue but no resources, pathways or methods for correcting or moderating the problem, it would no longer be reasonable for me to have trust in my ability to arrive at accurate views about the matter in question. Accordingly, it would not be possible for me to have any rational beliefs about its truth or falsity. Suspending inquiry, deliberation and judgment would be the only reasonable option.

In some respects, the scenario being imagined here may look analogous to the evil demon and brain-in-a-vat scenarios, which have long been a familiar part of epistemology,[6] but in other ways it is quite different and potentially even more distressing. For in evil demon and brain-in-a-vat stories, the hypothesis is that I am radically deceived without having any indication that this is so. As a result, I am deprived of knowledge about my immediate environment, but I am not thereby also deprived of the opportunity of having all sorts of reasonable beliefs. Since I do not have any concrete information that I am in fact being deceived in the ways imagined, my beliefs about my immediate surroundings can still be reasonable ones for me to have. I can reasonably believe that I am now sitting in a chair and holding a book in front of me even though I am a brain-in-a-vat. And more generally, I can still reasonably engage in inquiry and deliberation about my surroundings (Foley 1992).

By contrast, in the case now being imagined, there is said to be concrete information available to me about both my unreliability about the issues in question and my lack of remedies. This information undermines self-trust, and hence blocks me from having any reasonable way to conduct inquiry or deliberation about the issues, and any reasonable way to have opinions, positive or negative, about them.

18.5 Self-Trust and Disagreements with Others

Intellectual conflicts with others raise issues of self-trust analogous to those raised by empirical evidence about mistakes that people in general make. For responsible inquirers, both are warnings from the outside. Unsurprisingly then, there are also parallels in the responses that are appropriate in the two kinds of cases.

Whenever I discover that my opinions conflict with those of others, I face the question of whether or not to revise my views in light of theirs (see also Kappel, this volume). There are different rationales for doing so, however. One is by way of persuasion. Others may provide me with information or a way of approaching the issue that I come to see as compelling. As a result, I now understand what they understand and hence believe what they believe.

Other times I revise my opinions out of deference (see also Rolin as well as Miller and Freiman, this volume). I may not be in a position to acquire or perhaps even understand the information that led others to their view, but I nonetheless recognize that they are in a better position than I to make reliable judgments about the issue. The reverse is also possible, of course. I may be one who is in the superior position, or at least so I may have reasons to think, in which case it is reasonable for me to conclude that it is they, not I, who should defer. What I cannot reasonably do in either case is simply dismiss the opinions of others out of hand as having no relevance whatsoever for what I should believe. For, insofar as I trust myself, I am pressured to grant some measure of credibility to others as well.

Why is this? Part of the explanation is that none of us are intellectually isolated from others. We are all, as the historian Marc Bloch (2004) once memorably observed, "permanently floating in a soup of deference." It begins in infancy, accelerates throughout childhood, and continues through adulthood until the very end of life. The opinions of others envelop us: family, friends, acquaintances, colleagues, strangers, books, articles, newspapers, media, and now websites, blogs and tweets. Much of what we believe invariably comes from what others have said or written. There is no escape, and this has implications for issues of trust. If I have intellectual trust in myself, I am pressured, on threat of incoherence, to have some degree of intellectual trust in others as well, for I would not be largely reliable unless others were. Trust in myself radiates outward.

The extent to which my opinions are intertwined with those of others is not the full story, however. Our similarities also compel me to have a degree of trust in others. Our perceptual and cognitive faculties are roughly the same; the intellectual methods we employ, especially the most basic, are largely similar; and the environments in which we deploy these faculties and methods are not greatly different. These broad commonalities again pressure me, given that I have intellectual trust in myself, to have a presumptive degree of trust in others as well, even if they are strangers with whom I have not previously interacted and about whom I know little.

To be sure, there are significant intellectual differences among people, and these differences fascinate us. A mark of our preoccupation is that we make far finer distinctions about one another than we do about anything else, and among the most intricate of these distinctions are ones about intellectual features – not only our different opinions but also our different capacities, skills and tendencies. The availability of so many distinctions, and the enthusiasm with which we employ them, may sometimes make it appear as if individuals often have beliefs that have little in common with one another, but any careful look reveals this to be an exaggeration.

There are broad similarities in what people everywhere believe, even those who are distant from one another in time, place and culture. All, or at least virtually all, believe that some things are larger than others, some things are heavier than others, some events occurred before others, some things are dangerous and others are not, and some things are edible while others are not. The list goes on and on, almost without end. So, although our fascination with our differences may at times make it seem as if the belief systems of people in one society have little overlap with those in another, this impression is unsupported by evidence. It ignores the enormous backdrop of shared beliefs.

The views of Donald Davidson are again relevant. He argued that it is not even possible to have compelling evidence of radical cognitive diversity. He argued that in situations where it is initially an open question whether the creatures being interpreted have beliefs, it is only by assuming wide agreement on the basics with those whom we are interpreting that we can get the interpretative process started. Unless we assume that the creatures have perceptual equipment that provide them with information about their environment and this information is largely in agreement with what we take to be the features of their environment, we will not be in a position to establish the kinds of correlations between their behavior and their surroundings that would give us reasons to infer that they have beliefs at all, much less what the content of those beliefs are (Davidson 1986).

As mentioned earlier, Davidson attempted to move from this epistemological point about how we form views about the opinions of others to a more controversial metaphysical position that it is not conceivable for anyone's beliefs, our own or those of others, to be largely in error. The epistemological point, however, is important on its own. It is an effective antidote to the notion that it is easy to have evidence that the beliefs of people in other cultures and times have few commonalities with one's own.

Then again, such an antidote should not be necessary. For, given the broad similarities in intellectual equipment and environments of people across times and cultures, it is to be expected that there are also correspondingly broad similarities in their beliefs and concepts. These similarities, in turn, pressure us, on threat of inconsistency, to have a modicum of intellectual trust even in strangers, given that we have presumptive trust in ourselves.

The trust, it bears repeating, should be only presumptive. It can be and often is defeated by our having information that the people in question have a history of errors with respect to issues of the sort in question, or they lack important evidence, or they do not have the necessary abilities or training, or they simply not have not taken enough time to think about the issues.

What about situations in which there are no obvious defeaters and the individual with the conflicting opinions is a peer, "peer" in the sense of having the same evidence and background knowledge, the same training and same degree of skills, and the same track record of reliability about issues of the kind in question. What then?

Recent epistemologists have been divided about this kind of case (see also Kappel, this volume). Some say that both parties should withhold judgment or at least move their degrees of confidence in the direction of one another (much as two equally reliable thermometers that have recorded different temperatures should each be given equal weight), while others say that at least in some such cases, it can be reasonable for both to hold on to their current opinions (since reasonable people can disagree) (Kelly 2010; Christensen 2010; Feldman and Warfield 2010).

The very first reaction here, however, should be to note once again that these are very sparely described scenarios, and how best to treat them may well depend on how the details are filled in. It may hinge, for one, on whether the issues in question are ones about which there is a commonly accepted way of determining the truth. For if not, there will be questions about how to go about deciding who is epistemic peer and who is not. On the other hand, assuming there is in principle some way of determining the truth, how much expertise does each of us have in the matter at hand? And assuming that we both have a high degree of expertise, do we have access not only to the same evidence but also the detailed reasoning that led the other to a conflicting opinion? And if we are both fully familiar with the other's reasoning and still remain fully convinced by our prior opinions, do we think we understand where the other has gone wrong in thinking about the issue?

Even from the drift of these few questions, it is possible to tease out a few preliminary lessons for dealing with such cases. One is that to the extent that I have a high degree of expertise and access to all the relevant information, I myself am in a position to determine the truth about the matter in question. Hence, there is less of a rationale for me to defer to the judgment of others, even if I view them as also being experts. Once again, this is not to say I am free to ignore their opinions when they conflict with mine. On the contrary, insofar as the issue is important enough, I will need to examine the considerations they think support their position. When I do so, it may well turn out that I begin to think about the issues as they do, but if so, the mode of influence is persuasion, not deference.

The opposite may also occur. I may come to see, or at least have reasonable grounds for thinking that I see, where they have gone wrong, in which case I now have grounds for thinking with respect to this issue that they are not as reliable as I am. So, at least with respect this particular issue, they are not really my peers.

Yet a third possibility is that on examination of their grounds, I may be puzzled. I cannot see what is wrong with their thinking but neither can I see what is wrong with mine. The responsible response under these conditions, again assuming that the issue important enough to warrant additional effort, is to suspend judgment and re-engage inquiry until more clarity is possible.

The correct if unexciting moral here is that life is complicated, and dealing with intellectual disagreements, being a part of life, is also complicated. This being said, the same broad, first person guidelines appropriate for dealing with empirical evidence about the unreliabilities of humans in general are also appropriate for dealing with intellectual disagreements. The most important of these is that I should not ignore the conflict, given that I am pressured to regard the opinions of others as having some initial credibility. But, neither need I be completely immobilized by it. Further self-monitoring in light of the disagreement and adjusting my opinions (or not) in accordance with the details of the situation can also be a responsible response (see also Frost-Arnold, this volume).

Among these details is that for many issues, there will be a range of conflicting opinions for me to consider, in which case I will need to assess which to take most seriously. A further complexity is that a general presumption of intellectual trust in others is compatible with different degrees of trust being appropriate for different kinds of issues. Indeed, the structure of the above argument for trusting the opinions of others suggests that presumptive trust (as opposed to trust that derives from special information about the reliability of others) should be strongest with respect to opinions that are most directly the products of those basic intellectual faculties and methods that humans share, since it is these similarities that create the default pressure to trust others in the first place.

In particular, there is a case to be made for what can be thought of as a kind of interpersonal foundationalism, which gives special deference to the opinions of others when they are based on first-hand introspection, first-hand perception, and recent memories of such introspection and perception. In our actual practice, testimony about such matters is normally regarded as the least problematic sort of testimony, and with good reason (see also Faulkner, this volume). Just as we often rely on the opinions of experts in scientific, medical and other technical fields, because we think they are in a better position than we to have reliable opinions about issues in their fields (see also Rolin, this volume), so too for analogous reasons in our everyday lives we normally accept the reports of those who tell us, say, that they have a splitting headache or are feeling queasy. We do so because we think that they are better placed than we to know whether they are in these states. After all, they have introspective access to them whereas we do not. Likewise, we normally take the word of others about whether it is snowing in the hills and how heavy the traffic is on the freeway when they but not we are in a location to directly observe these things. By extension, we also regularly accede to their memories about what they have recently introspected or observed, for once again, we assume that under normal conditions they are in best situated to know the truth about these matters.

Of course, there is nothing that prevents others from reporting to us what they are observing even when we are in the same location and looking in the same direction. In most such cases, provided the light and our eyesight are good and the object being looked at is near at hand, we agree on what we see. But if the unusual happens and we disagree, we are then less likely to defer to their reports, and once again for the obvious reason. Unlike cases where others are reporting their observations about a time and place where we are not present, in this situation we are apt to think, absent some special reasons, that they are no better position than we to determine the truth about the matter at hand.

An interpersonal foundationalism of this sort is an intriguing possibility, but for purposes here the more fundamental point is that the materials for an adequate account of trust in the opinions of others are to be found in intellectual self-trust. This is an approach to the issues that is contrary to that of Locke, who insisted unrealistically that in the process of regulating opinion, reliance on the beliefs of others is to be avoided to the extent possible. We ought always to strive to make up our minds about issues as opposed to deferring to others (Locke 1975). Nor does the approach rely on a thin, Hume-like induction to support the general reliability of other people's opinions. Hume thought it possible to use one's observations of the track records of people with whom one has had direct contact to construct an inductive argument in favor of the reliability of human testimony in general (Hume 1975). Nor does the approach invoke a Reid-like stipulation to the effect that God or natural selection implanted in humans an ability to determine the truth, a propensity to speak the truth, and a corresponding propensity to believe what others tell us (Reid 1983).

Instead, the basic insights are, first, it can be reasonable to trust in one's basic faculties and methods even if it is not possible to provide non-question-begging assurances of their reliability, and second, given the intellectual similarities and interdependence of humans, self-trust pressures one on threat of inconsistency also to have prima facie intellectual trust in the faculties, methods and opinions of others.

Intellectual self-trust in this way radiates outward and creates an atmosphere of presumptive trust within which our mutually dependent intellectual lives take place.

Related Topics

In this volume:

Trust and Testimony
Trust and Epistemic Responsibility
Trust and Epistemic Injustice
Trust and Distributed Epistemic Labor
Trust in Science
Trust and Belief
Trust and Disagreement

Notes

1 "... the selection pressures felt by organisms are dependent on the costs and benefits of various consequences. We think of hominids on the savannah as requiring an accurate way to discriminate leopards and conclude that parts of ancestral schemes of representation, having evolved under strong selection, must accurately depict the environment. Yet, where selection is intense the way it is here, the penalties are only severe for failures to recognize present predators. The hominid representation can be quite at odds with natural regularities, lumping together all kinds of harmless things with potential dangers, provided that the false positives are evolutionarily inconsequential and provided that the representation always cues the dangers" (Kitcher 1993:300). See also Stich (1990:55–74).
2 For discussions on the importance of intellectual humility, see Roberts and Wood (2007) and Zabzebski (1996).
3 For pioneering work on these issues, see Nisbett and Ross (1980), Kahneman, Slovic and Tversky (1982) and Kahneman (2011).
4 See Cosmides and Tooby (1996) and Gigerenza 1(994).
5 See Wason (1968) and Cosmides (1989).
6 Evil demon and brain-in-a-vat scenarios are dramatic ways to illustrate how it might be the case that most of our beliefs are in error. See Descartes (2017) and Harman (1973).

References

Audi, R. (2013) "Testimony as a Social Foundation of Knowledge," *Philosophy and Phenomenological Research* 87(3): 507–531.

Baier, A. (1986) "Trust and Antitrust," *Ethics* 96(2): 23–260.

Bloch, M. (2004) "Rituals and Deference," in H. Whitehouse and J. Laidlaw (eds.), *Rituals and Memory: Towards a Comparative Anthropology of Religion*, London: Altamira Press.

Cavell, S. (1979) *The Claim of Reason*, New York: Oxford University Press.

Christensen, D. (2007) "Epistemology of Disagreement: The Good News," *The Philosophical Review* 116(2): 187–217.

Christensen, D. (2010) "Higher Order Evidence," *Philosophy and Phenomenological Research* 81 (1):185–215.

Coady, A.J. (1992) *Testimony*, Oxford: Oxford University Press.

Cosmides, L. (1989) "The Logic of Social Exchange: Has Natural Selection Shaped How Humans Reason? Studies with Wason Selection Task," *Cognition* 3: 187–276.
Cosmides, L. and Tooby, J. (1996) "Are Humans Good Intuitive Statisticians after All? Rethinking Some Conclusions from the Literature on Judgement under Uncertainty," *Cognition* 58: 1–73.
Davidson, D. (1986) "A Coherence Theory of Knowledge and Belief," in E. Lepore (ed.), *The Philosophy of Donald Davidson: Perspectives on Truth and Interpretation*, London: Basil Blackwell, 307–319.
Descartes, R. (2017) *Meditations on First Philosophy*, J. Cottingham (trans.), Cambridge: Cambridge University Press.
Egan, A. and Elga, A. (2005) "I Can't Believe I'm Stupid," *Philosophical Perspectives* 9: 77–93.
Elgin, C. (1986) *Considered Judgment*, Princeton, NJ: Princeton University Press.
Feldman, R. (2010) "Epistemological Puzzles about Disagreement" in S. Hetherington (ed.), *Epistemology Futures*, Oxford: Oxford University Press, 216–236.
Feldman, R. and Warfield, T. (2010) *Disagreement*, Oxford: Oxford University Press.
Foley, R. (1992) *Working without a Net*, Oxford: Oxford University Press.
Foley, R. (2001) *Intellectual Trust in Oneself and Others*, Cambridge: Cambridge University Press.
Fricker, M. (2007) *Epistemic Injustice: Power and the Ethics of Knowing*, Oxford: Oxford University Press.
Gigerenza, G. (1994) "How to Make Cognitive Illusions Disappear beyond Heuristics and Biases," *European Review of Social Psychology* 2: 83–115.
Hardin, R. (2002) *Trust*, New York: Russell Sage Foundation.
Harman, G. (1973) *Thought*, Princeton, NJ: Princeton University Press.
Harman, G. (1986) *Change in View*, Cambridge, MA: MIT Press.
Hume, D. (1975) "An Enquiry Concerning Human Understanding," in P.H. Nidditch and L.A. Selby-Bigge (eds.), Oxford: Oxford University Press.
Kahneman, D. (2011) *Thinking, Fast and Slow*, New York: Farrar, Straus and Giroux.
Kahneman, D., Slovic P. and Tversky, A. (eds.) (1982) *Judgement under Uncertainty: Heuristics and Biases*, Cambridge: Cambridge University Press.
Kelly, T. (2005) "The Epistemic Significance of Disagreement," in T. Szabo-Gendler and J. Hawthorne (eds.), *Oxford Studies in Epistemology*, volume 1, Oxford: Oxford University Press, 167–196.
Kelly, T. (2010) "Peer Disagreement and Higher Order Evidence," in R. Feldman and T. Warfield (eds.), *Disagreement*, Oxford: Oxford University Press.
Kitcher, P. (1993) *The Advancement of Science*, Oxford: Oxford University Press.
Lehrer, K. (1975) *Self-Trust*, Oxford: Clarendon Press.
Locke, J. (1975) *An Essay Concerning Human Understanding*, P. Nidditch (ed.), Oxford: Clarendon Press.
Malcolm, N. (1963) *Knowledge and Certainty*, Ithaca, NY: Cornell University Press.
Nisbett, R.E. and Ross, L. (1980) *Human Inference: Strategies and Shortcomings of Social Judgement*, Englewood Cliffs, NJ: Prentice-Hall.
Origgi, G. (2004) "Is Trust an Epistemological Notion?" *Episteme* 1(1): 1–12.
Quine, W.V.O. (1979) "Natural Kinds," in *Ontological Relativity and Other Essays*, New York: Columbia University Press.
Reid, T. (1983) "Essays on the Intellectual Powers of Man," in R. Beanblossom and K. Lehrer (eds.), *Thomas Reid's Inquiry and Essays*, Indianapolis, IN: Hackett.
Roberts, R. and Wood, W.J. (2007) *Intellectual Virtues: An Essay in Regulative Epistemology*, Oxford: Oxford University Press.
Shapin, S. (1994) *A Social History of Trust*, Chicago, IL: University of Chicago Press.
Sosa, E. (2010) "The Epistemology of Disagreement," in A. Haddock, A. Millar and D. Pritchard (eds.), *Social Epistemology*, Oxford: Oxford University Press.
Stich, S. (1990) *The Fragmentation of Reason*, Cambridge, MA: MIT Press.
Wason, P.C. (1968) "Reasoning about a Rule," *Quarterly Journal of Experimental Psychology* 20: 273–281.
Williams, M. (1995) *Unnatural Doubts*, Princeton, NJ: Princeton University Press.
Williams, B. (2001) *Truth and Truthfulness*, Princeton, NJ: Princeton University Press.
Zabzebski, L. (1996) *Virtues of the Mind: An Inquiry into the Nature of Virtue and the Ethical Foundations of Knowledge*, New York: Cambridge University Press.

19
INTERPERSONAL TRUST

Nancy Nyquist Potter

19.1 Introduction

Sissela Bok writes that "*Whatever* matters to human beings, trust is the atmosphere in which it thrives" (Bok 2011:69; emphasis in original). For most of us, interpersonal trust matters greatly. This chapter sets out the domain and scope of interpersonal trust, some of the primary elements of interpersonal trust, the interlinking between interpersonal trust and the social, and the role of repair and forgiveness when interpersonal trust goes wrong.

19.2 Domain and Scope

It is difficult to pin down the domain of interpersonal trust. "Interpersonal" can mean dyadic relationships such as friendships and intimate partners, but interpersonal trust can also occur between strangers when there are moments of trust (Jones 1996:6). The more intimate and personal sort might be called "thick trust" and the sort between strangers can be called "thin trust." Yet even here, the distinction is not hard and fast. Not only is interpersonal trust found between friends and lovers, but also in psychiatrist-patient relations, sometimes in teacher-student relations, in customer-service provider relations, and amongst users of social media (see also Ess, this volume). People and their animal companions may enjoy a level of interpersonal trust; siblings, or allies, too. Interpersonal trust can also include relations between a person and his ancestors (cf. Norton-Smith 2010). Moreover, parents and their grown children can be friends. Friends and lovers can be of similar or different ages, of same or different or fluid genders, of similar or different racial, ethnic or religious groups. Many interpersonal relationships are infused with power differences, an issue that is of fundamental concern to our ability to trust and also to decide whether trusting another in a particular circumstance is wise to do. Interpersonal trust seems to be a pre-condition to many of our most valued and closest relationships, yet there is no one formula or set of characteristics that constitute interpersonal trust.

Moreover, some forms of interpersonal trust extend over long periods of time while others may be more momentary. A range of depth and complexity should be expected. Yet when we talk about interpersonal trust, we typically do take it to characterize a thicker sort of relation than just a one-off trust relation; in many of its forms, interpersonal trust relations are partly constituted by reciprocal beliefs, intentions and attitudes of mutual care and concern for the other (Wanderer 2013). Jeremy Wanderer distinguishes between two sorts of interpersonal relationships: those that involve a degree of reciprocal affective regard – which include strangers on his account because, when you stand in "a philial relationship with someone, you cease to be strangers to each other" – and those that involve a reciprocal transaction such as promising or other illocutionary acts (Wanderer 2013:93–94). Wanderer recognizes that there is overlap between these two types (what he calls transactional and non-transactional) but thinks the structure of each is different due to the way certain illocutionary acts like promising change the normative orientation of the relationships. I am not convinced that the structure is that different, for reasons that will become clear below, and will just note that some transactional relationships are the domain of contracts and fiduciary relationships and, as such, are juridical; the contractual nature of them is precisely there to preclude a requirement of trust, as Annette Baier argues in her seminal work on trust (Baier 1986). Even then, though, we sometimes trust the other beyond what the contractual arrangement covers, as in therapist/client or doctor/patient relations. Trudy Govier (1992) would seem to agree. Interpersonal relationships call for equitable and fair standards, and we try to keep our practices in line with such standards – but we still need trust, and laws and regulations cannot substitute for absent trust or trust gone wrong (Govier 1992:24–25).

Regarding both the domain and scope of trust, one must be cautious about generalizations. Social locations substantively alter our material experiences, our perceptions, our phenomenological sense of our embodiment, our affect, our cosmology, our language and our sense of ourselves as knowers, agents, subjects, and so on. Structural inequalities and systemic entrenched patterns of privilege and subordination shape our lives and, hence, our trust practices. With respect to scope, then, interpersonal trust is an affective, embodied, epistemic and material relation.

19.3 Characteristics of Interpersonal Trust

In this section, I will outline some of the primary elements or characteristics of interpersonal trust – namely, that (1) it is a matter of degree; (2) it is affective as well as cognitive and epistemic (3) it involves vulnerability and thus has power dimensions; (4) it involves conversational and other norms; (5) it calls for loyalty; (6) it always exists in a social context; and (7) it often calls for repair and forgiveness.

19.3.1 Interpersonal Trust is a Matter of Degree

Friends and lovers come in so many different shapes, forms and contexts; our conception and performance of gender is changing rapidly, and meanings of race and ethnic groupings are in flux to such a degree that it would be a mistake to claim "such-and-such are the ingredients of a good interpersonal trust relationship" without many qualifications and without taking into account contextual norms. Trust is a matter of degree; it is not an all-or-nothing affair. We can have moments of trust, as when we trust strangers, and we can also have times of trust in mostly trust-conflicted relationships (Jones 1996:6, 13). In other words, interpersonal trust is dimensional rather than categorical.

19.3.2 Interpersonal Trust Has Affective, Cognitive and Epistemic Elements

Bernd Lahno argues that any adequate theory of trust must include behavioral, cognitive and affective dimensions or aspects, but he argues for a central place for affective trust aspects (Lahno 2004). Behavioral trust is when we make ourselves vulnerable to others, and cognitive trust is when we expect others not to take advantage of our vulnerability as a result of our trusting them (Lahno 2004:32, 38). By emphasizing cognitive trust, he calls attention to mental states of the truster; trusting another involves expectations of another, such as their good will or their desire to follow a normative social or role order. But, Lahno argues, neither expectations of the other's good will nor of their desire to follow norms provides a complete explanation of how we form beliefs about another's trustworthiness. "It is *because* he trusts her that his beliefs are different. So, trust seems to be part of the psychological mechanism that transforms the information given to individuals into beliefs" (Lahno 2004:38). On Lahno's account, then, affective trust, which we show when we have an emotional bond of trust among those in a relationship, is more fundamental than cognitive trust. This emotional aspect or dimension of trust provides a feeling of connection to one another through shared aims, values or norms (see also Lahno, this volume).

Lawrence Becker offers a noncognitive account of trust that involves "a sense of security about other people's benevolence, conscientiousness, and reciprocity" (Becker 1996:43). Cognitive trust concerns beliefs about others" trustworthiness, while non-cognitive trust concerns attitudes, affect, emotions and motivational structures (Becker 1996:44). Cognitive accounts of trust view trust as "a way of managing uncertainty in our dealings with others by representing those situations as risks" … "a disposition to have confidence about other people's motives, to banish suspicious thoughts about them" (Becker 1996:45–46). Becker suggests that interpersonal trust is concrete in the sense that we trust particular others, where what he means by "particular" is that the other is an identified, but uncategorized, individual.[1]

According to Karen Jones (1996) trust involves an affective optimistic attitude that others" goodwill and competence will include our interactions with them. That optimism is gradated from strangers to intimates when it comes to norms. Strangers are expected to show competence in following norms on how to interact between strangers; professionals are expected to have technical competence; and friends expect moral competence in qualities such as loyalty, kindness and generosity (Jones 1996:7). Jones includes the idea that, when we trust others, we expect that those we trust will be motivated by the thought that we trust them; this can move the trusted to come through for us, because they want to be as trustworthy as they see us (Jones 1996:5). Jones argues that trust is not primarily a belief but an affective attitude of optimism toward another, plus "the expectation that the one trusted will be directly and favorably *moved* by the thought that someone is counting on her" (Jones 1996:8; emphasis added). The reason is that we hope that the sort of care and concern that others give us when we trust in them is, in part, shaped by our particular needs and not based in more abstract, general principles (see also Potter 2002). The point is that part of reciprocal interpersonal trust relations is that we aim to help those we care about and hopeful trust can help them become the people they want to be.

The idea of the relation between interpersonal trust and the central importance that the other matters to us implicates not only cognition and affect, but *epistemic* norms as well (see also Frost-Arnold, this volume). An epistemology of knowing another person well would seem necessary for intimate trust relationships, but even this is complex. As

Lorraine Code says, "The crucial and intriguing fact about knowing people – and the reason it affords insights into problems of knowledge – is that even if one could know all the facts about someone, one would not know her as the person she is" (Code 1991:40). Knowing another person well, then, is more than epistemic (or, perhaps we should conceive epistemology more broadly.) We get a sense of others, a feeling for them; we come to experience them in their joy and anxieties and disappointments; we see, over time, what moves them (and what does not) and how they interpret their and our lives together.

Sometimes being supportive of our friend's endeavors places us in an awkward epistemic and moral position. Hawley (2014b) discusses an example from Keller (2004) about Eric's friend Rebecca's poetry reading. Though Eric knows nothing about Rebecca's poetry yet, his view is that the venue at which this reading will take place usually has pretty bad poetry, so on purely evidentiary grounds, Eric should expect Rebecca's poetry to be bad. The issue Hawley queries is what the appropriate epistemic stance is to take regarding Rebecca's poetry. Does Eric need to believe Rebecca's poetry is good? Should he not give Rebecca's poetry a more charitable assessment, because he is her friend? Hawley suggests that some of our relationships place special obligations on us and that friendship is one that permits a degree of partiality, and that such obligations are "usually discussed in connection with behaviour rather than belief" (Hawley 2014b:2032).[2] What if Eric does think Rebecca's poetry is terrible – is he then a terrible friend? What if he tells her poetry is great, even though he believes it is terrible? What does he owe her? There is no one epistemic or moral answer to these questions; the answers depend on the way their relationship is configured and the patterns they have established about addressing one another's needs in other times. A key consideration is what Rebecca wants from Eric in the way of support, and this may not be communicated directly but in different forms at different times. Rebecca may say, for instance, that she always wants Eric to be totally honest with her about herself, but then she may also have made it clear that she hopes he will not zero in on her most vulnerable areas and hurt her. Or, Rebecca may not quite know what she wants and needs from Eric in terms of support for her ventures. Eric, then, needs to get a feeling for what she "truly" needs from him after the poetry reading – something that, because trust is not contractual, and because we often place our trust in others in a variety of specific ways, leaves it open to the trustee one how to weigh their responsibilities at a given time.

The questions that arise when we probe the example of what Rebecca trusts Eric to say about her poetry are difficult to answer. Additionally, they remind us of other, just as interesting and difficult questions about interpersonal trust: the interplay between epistemic and affective knowing of others, what needs to be known about another in order to trust and be trusting, and how we go about knowing others well.

19.3.3 Interpersonal Trust Involves Vulnerability to the Other and, with this, Power Dimensions

Because trusting others involves placing something we value into their hands, without the certainty or mechanisms of contractual or formal protection, we allow ourselves to be vulnerable to them. This vulnerability can be compounded by another feature of the structure of trust: that it gives the trusted one(s) some degree of discretionary power to care for that which we place in their hands in the way that they believe is best, and hopefully, how we would want that thing cared for (Baier 1986; Potter 2002). In a "thick" trust relationship, people want the best for one another and facilitate the growth of each other – on their terms, and not merely one's own (Potter 2002). Thin trust, too, should aim at least at not hindering or standing in the way of another's betterment, even though there is less opportunity either to harm or help strangers in thin trust relationships. In both sorts of relationships, trusting others calls upon the trustee to fulfill that trust in a non-dominating and non-exploitative manner (Potter 2002), even though fulfilling trust will be a matter of degree and opportunity depending on the depth and duration of the relationship.

19.3.4 Interpersonal Trust Implicates Conversational Norms

Trust seems to call for steadfastness in keeping confidences and promises – but also in letting others know that, about *this* thing, we cannot make a promise. A central difficulty in interpersonal trust is that trust is often (usually?) unstated and implicit, and that can apply to elements of trust as well. For example, we may ask others "not to tell," but listeners may not explicitly promise. They may reply, "Of course not," yet we still have to hope and trust that that request is taken seriously. In interpersonal trust, keeping promises and confidences is not a matter merely of observing a formal rule or giving uptake to an illocutionary act. In these kinds of relationships, trust thrives when promises and confidences are kept because of the relationship – because the confiders and their personal lives matter to us.

It is not always easy to know – or to know what to do with – secrets, and secrets sometimes may need to be handled differently from confidences that honor others' privacy. Here, I cannot offer a definition of each that would provide a clear distinction, so let me give an example. When Mia asks her older sibling Claudell not to tell mom that she's "not really going to be at a church event" that night, the confidence is less problematic than if Mia tells Claudell not to tell their other three siblings that mom buys her "special presents." While Mia may indeed trust Claudell to keep the confidence, the secret gifting affects the material, emotional and psychological dynamics of the whole group; it suggests unfairness, and calls for an explanation for the special treatment. Secrets can be burdensome and, if eventually revealed, exacerbate likely resentments. If Mia asks Claudell not to tell other family members she was raped, though, Claudell's honoring that does not seem like a sign of family dysfunction. Mia should be able to keep that private – unless, perhaps, the rapist is the family uncle, or brother or religious leader. In other interpersonal relationships, too, we sometimes feel resentful, or even betrayed, when we find out that one or two people in our group were told a "secret" that others were excluded from knowing. We may take it as a sign that the secret-holder did not trust us, and that wounds us – or we may feel entitled to be told certain things. For example, in an episode of the Danish series *Dicta*, three women who are close friends are sitting in Dicta's home in the evening when it comes up that Dicta had had a son she had given up for adoption when she was 16. Anne had known for a long time, but Ida just learned of this and is quite put out for being kept from this vital piece of information. Ida feels excluded even though she knows that Anne and Dicta had been friends all those years ago and Ida had more recently come to be part of the group. "Why wasn't I told?" she asks. She feels that she *ought* to have been told (*Dicta* 2012). Note, however, that feeling betrayed does not necessarily mean we have been betrayed. We need to be able to control the flow of some of the private matters in our lives, and to decide who knows what about us – yet that control is often illusory and can hurt others who trust us to be open with them and to not practice exclusionary communicating.

In each of the above examples, communication is a key to whether or not trust is sustained or threatened. Earlier, I claimed that interpersonal trust involves knowing other persons. But just how central is this to our ability to trust them? To answer this question, let me connect communicative norms with knowing and trusting one another. Bonnie Talbert (2015) places significant emphasis on disclosure as a means to know others well (and presumably, to trust some of them appropriately.) She argues that, for us to know other people well, we typically interact with them regularly. These interactions allow others to disclose or reveal aspects of themselves. Thus, the other person has to be willing to be known and to waive a degree of privacy for the sake of being known. Typically, these interactions facilitate in each of us a shift in how we see ourselves and our own beliefs and values as well as shifts in how deeply we understand the other. Similarly, Govier (1998:25) argues that a special feature of friendship is "intimate talk." For one to trust another in an intimate and deep way, Govier says that

> I have to be able to communicate with him. I have to be able to tell him how I feel, what I have experienced, what I think should be done and how I would go about doing it; and when I tell him this, I have to feel confident that he will listen to me, that he can understand and appreciate what I have to say, even if he is not initially disposed to agree with it, that he will not willfully distort what I say or use it against me, to manipulate me or betray me to others. Just to talk meaningfully with him, I have to trust him. When he talks to me, I have to listen attentively and respectfully, and if I am to gain any information about either his feelings and beliefs or exterior reality from our interchange, I have to credit him with competence, sincerity, honesty, and integrity-despite our differences; I can't think that he is trying to deceive me, lie to me, suppress relevant information, leave things out. I must think of him as open, sincere and honest. All this requires trust; I have to trust him to listen to him, to receive what he has to say. And the same thing holds in the other direction.
>
> *(Govier 1992:30)*

Govier's description of communicative trust is very important, especially when we consider the ways that power relations can influence patterns of trust and distrust, and listening well or badly. We don't know the outcome of Eric's attendance at Rebecca's poetry reading, but we can identify some considerations: How Eric and Rebecca navigate the process of getting to know one another, and to what extent they can sense and perceive each other's needs and hopes accurately, will affect the outcome of Eric's response to Rebecca's poetry reading, and her feelings about Eric's comments. Can Rebecca say, "Don't tell me if I suck!"? Will Eric take her at face value if Rebecca asks him to give her an honest assessment of her poetry? The answers do not only depend on how well they communicate and know each other but also what each brings to the relationship of their own needs and values. We need to avoid projecting our own fears, needs and values onto those we care about (and those we should, but do not care about) but even realizing that we are doing such projection may take others pointing it out to us – which, in turn, requires a degree of trust. As Govier points out, "distrust impedes the communication which could overcome it" (Govier, 1991:56). Furthermore, we can do epistemic violence to others by violating the conversational norms that Govier suggests (see below).

Yet all this talk about "talk" is largely centered on speech acts and the idea that we cannot know others well (and hence cannot trust and be trustworthy appropriately) without revealing ourselves through spoken language. This is not always the case. We can reveal things to others – even deliberately – without talking. I can allow my anxiety, or my sadness, or my excitement, to be felt and discerned by another without using words. Lovers and friends may reveal feelings and attitudes through tactile communication – as well as through a rebuff of touching and stroking. Friends use conventional signs such as gift-giving to convey feelings of affection, appreciation or knowledge of a loved one's needs and delights.

Conversational norms, including what should be revealed, and what is necessary to reveal, vary from group to group and culture to culture, and so building interpersonal trust will feel and look different depending on context and culture.

For example, Havis (2014) makes the point that many dialects developed from ancestral African roots. The example of Mamma Ola illustrates the subtlety with which the family communicates with one another. However, many African-Americans are not "understood" by white folk – meaning that the communicative norm is that of white-speak – so when African-Americans are around them, they are expected to change their speech patterns. When interracial relationships exist, communication can be strained by similar expectations, and sorting out how to establish fair communicative norms may challenge reciprocal trust.

19.3.5 Interpersonal Trust Calls for Loyalty

Trust in interpersonal relationships also seems to call for loyalty, for example, in standing up for one another. We expect trustworthy friends, lovers and allies to defend us against salacious rumors or cruel accusations, even to the extent that we do not readily believe that such things could be true of us. This is, I think, because part of a good trusting relationship is that we think warmly and positively of each other. It is not that we hold an idealistic image of one another, but rather that we have a feeling and an experiential sense of one another such that we have a very difficult time believing the trusted other would be capable of doing terrible things. We find ways to make sense of others that preserves the trust relationship and, as part of that, we defend against others' rumors and attacks. As Jones explains, trusting others restricts the interpretations we consider both when it comes to the behavior of those we trust but also to others' rumors about them. When we can, we give those we trust a favorable interpretation of events and rumors (Jones 1996:12). Suppose you are told that your left-leaning activist friend, who does volunteer work to educate the local population on racism, prejudice and privilege, was "being racist" at a recent social gathering that you were not attending. Hawley argues that a good friend would go to some lengths to think of other ways to understand the report and would look for better evidence than just someone's word for it. A good friend might need to be wary of the motives behind the testifier in this case. In close trust relationships, we ought to be unusually hesitant to believe the worst of those we care for (Hawley 2014b:2032). Friendship gives us reasons to (continue to) see our friends as trustworthy that sometimes goes beyond strict epistemic reasons. While I agree, I also believe that such rumors may be providing important information about how trustworthy an ally our friend is. Is she a hypocrite, putting on one face for me and another for her circle of privileged friends? Have I misread her degree of commitment to anti-racist work? Friendship may provide non-epistemic reasons to trust friends in the face of odd stories, but the sorts of rumors we should defend them against and the ones we should take seriously will depend on the context of the friendship, where the friends stand in relation to one another and to social location, and to the kind of rumor being circulated. Sometimes we will need to determine what to believe about our trusted friends.

19.4 Interpersonal Trust and the Social

In section 19.3, I reviewed some of the characteristics of interpersonal trust, pointing out along the way some of the problems we can encounter in trusting relations. Here, I emphasize the social context in which not only interpersonal trusting relations can thrive but in which distrust and suspicion can also arise. I argue that trusting relations are always set in the social, material and embodied world and, as such, need to be navigated through a kind of "soup" that shapes our experiences and interpretations of ourselves and one another. Following the work of Lorraine Code, I will call this background the "social imaginary." The social imaginary circulates and maintains implicit systems of images, meanings, metaphors and interlocking explanations-expectations within which people enact their knowledge and subjectivities and develop self-understandings (Code 2006:30–36). This is not to say that agency is determined by the social imaginary but rather that its insistence on the "rightness" of explanations, norms, and so on, it can – or can seem to – limit agency. These images and schemas are distributed primarily through school, media and other social institutions, such as medicine and law (Cegarra 2012).

The social imaginary is *social* in the broadest sense. It supplies and claims salience about principles of conduct and knowledge, and we maintain those principles through our experiences of "success" that affirm its correctness – including who counts as knowers and what can be known. Yet the social imaginary

> … should absolutely not be taken in a "mentalistic" sense. Social imaginary significations create a proper world for the society considered – in fact, they *are* this world; and they shape the psyche of individuals. They create thus a "representation" of the world, including the society itself and its place in this world; but this is far from being an intellectual construct. It goes together with the creation of a *drive* for the society considered (so to speak, a global intention) and of a specific *Stimmung* or mood (so to speak, of an affect, or a cluster of affects, permeating the whole of the social life).
>
> *(Castoriadis 1994:152; emphasis in original)*

Patricia Hill Collins calls these representations in the social imaginary "controlling images" and argues that they serve to naturalize racism, sexism and poverty, making them appear to be an inevitable part of everyday life (Collins 2000: 69). Thus, one effect of the social imaginary is that it circulates representations and perceptions of groups that tend toward stereotyping and bias. Most people hold implicit, or unconscious, biases against people of color, immigrants of color, nonconforming genders and working class people, even those who explicitly hold anti-racist, feminist and egalitarian views (cf. Freeman 2014; Gendler 2011). Implicit biases, i.e. subconscious negative prejudicial associations, are grounded in stereotypes that are constituted and reinforced by the social imaginary.

Our interpersonal relationships often are complicated by the constitutive forces of the social imaginary – to the extent that even what we believe is possible and desirable in trusting relationships is given articulation through the social imaginary. For example, we may experience trust across differences to be especially difficult, given our perceptions of one another's social location and the material effects of stratified society, yet even what we take to be relevant differences is embodied and enacted through the social imaginary.

First, I will comment on systemic distrust, especially with respect to the role of emotions. The social imaginary circulates a powerful disvalue of emotions as subjective, unreliable and untrustworthy, and the perception of excessive and inappropriate emotions largely is associated with subordinate genders, races and colonized groups. Both mainstream Western/Northern epistemology and social knowledge hold fast to the notion that knowledge must be objective in order to be justified. One implication of this is that trust based on unsettled affect, or a sense of distrust, is expected to be discounted until evidence can be identified that will provide the warrant for such distrust. This view of knowledge has been widely challenged in feminist work but still prevails in the social imaginary. One implication of this is the recognition that a naïve trusting attitude toward others without using our sense can be risky; an attitude of distrust is sometimes warranted (Potter 2002). So we ought not write off our affective states when we experience distrust: it is important to pay attention to our sense of wariness when it arises. On the other hand, whether or not suspicion tracks untrustworthiness depends on who the suspicious are, and who are regarded as untrustworthy. That is, distrust may be systemic. White people, for example, have a long history of distrusting American Indians and African-Americans – usually just in virtue of group membership. This distrust is frequently mutual. Even our affective states – and which affective states are legitimated – are given meaning within a social imaginary (cf. Jaggar 1988). The point is that the social imaginary produces expectations and assumptions of distrust and untrustworthiness that may impede interpersonal trust.

One way that violence can hinder the development or sustaining of interpersonal trust is through what Kristie Dotson calls "epistemic violence" (2011). This kind of violence also is constituted through and by the social imaginary. These real-world material experiences may assail (or creep into) our interpersonal trust relations as well. Stereotypes, cognitive biases, assumptions about normalcy, and in-group/out-group categorizing get in the way of accurate perception and interpretation of others' mental states and material existence. Without an understanding of how the social imaginary constitutes knowers and not-knowers, we overlook some insidious ways that those patterns and assumptions are played out in our interpersonal trust relationships. The point is that epistemic violence and other systemic threats to trust are far-reaching and may profoundly affect our ability to make and sustain trusting interpersonal relationships (see also Medina; Frost-Arnold and Scheman, this volume).

Apart from these systemic forms of distrust resulting from the social imaginary, there are specific practices that can infect reciprocal interpersonal trust relationships and even with whom we form interpersonal relationships. Sources of damaged trust are found, for example, in social practices like rape, sexual assault, and criminalization of people of color. Rape and sexual assault often damage the survivor-victim's ability to trust a whole class of people based on the group membership of the perpetrator. This generalized distrust impedes both the development and sustaining ability of trusting interpersonal relationships. Early childhood abuse and neglect can deprive people of developmental trust and then they can have a distrustful disposition. The prison-industrial complex, together with the militarization of the police force, shape the expectations of some Black males and other men of color such that they do not trust the juridical, custodial, correctional and punitive world made by mostly white people, all the while growing up seeing the only viable option for themselves to be a life of crime (Alexander 2012; Ferguson 2001; Western 2006).

Crimes such as most sexual assaults, rape crimes, hate crimes and ongoing discrimination, disadvantage and marginalization, damage trust in the world: they call into question whether it ever makes any sense to trust in others, or in the functioning (or, dysfunctioning) world. Sexual violence and other forms of traumatic violence shake us to our core: they call into question some of the most fundamental assumptions about the world we live in and how it functions. Even when the perpetrators are male and hence some survivors feel that they cannot trust males again, survivors nevertheless must engage in the world and with at least some others with a hope that they are trustworthy people in some respects. When the targets are victims of genderqueer hate crimes, distrust might be even more all-encompassing. As Martin Endreβ and Andrea Pabst argue, violence harms basic trust in ways that raise questions about the extent to which victim-survivors can recover it (2013). Basic trust is shattered when violence occurs. "As an impairment of personal integrity, violence is closely linked to basic trust or to be more precise to the shattering of basic trust" (Endreβ and Pabst 2013:102). When basic trust is shattered – or has never had the opportunity to develop – it can make interpersonal trust much more difficult. For example, hatred toward genderqueer people and the possibility of hate crimes against them is reproduced and even celebrated in the social imaginary of many societies. When people live in a climate of hatred, they internalize fearfulness and hypervigilance, and even close friends may be subjected to distrust as a protective stance.

19.5 Broken Trust, Repair and Forgiveness

Maintaining interpersonal trust takes moral effort. One reason is that, frequently, we need to repair damaged trust and hurt or anguished feelings toward one another. Elizabeth Spelman writes that "at the core of morality is a response to the fact of fragility" (Spelman 2004:55). Interpersonal relationships themselves are fragile and will need more than just maintenance of trust; they frequently require repair work. Spelman is right to note that a crucial question is where our reparative efforts ought to go and, I would add, when it is worth trying to repair broken trust or diminish distrust. How and when can we move from distrust to trust? What conditions make it more or less possible to move on together in friendship and love after trust has been broken?

I begin by considering the ways that structural oppressions and our social situatedness can do damage to interpersonal relationships. Centuries of colonialism and enslavement make interpersonal trust across social and material differences difficult. In some cases, friendship and love can seem so strained that we wonder if repair work on such a deep level can be done. Can trust be restored, or developed, when the kind of damage done through systemic power imbalances seem so historically thorough?

Carolyn Ureña (2017) argues that the Western social imaginary of interpersonal relationships posits the mature, healthy self as one treats love as an either/or. Colonial love, she explains, only allows for interracial interpersonal love: that fetishizes the socially subordinate other. One way to challenge the colonial and dichotomous forms of love as many people know it is to engage in decolonial love. Decoloniality, Ureña argues, requires people to identify the structures and the social imaginary that maintain and support oppression and to affirm devalued systems of knowledge and power. Decolonial love is an "ethical interrelation that is premised on imagining a 'third way' of engaging otherness that is beyond that of traditional Western and colonial binary thinking." Such love, Ureña argues, is central to the process of healing from colonizing relationships. Drawing on the work of Chela Sandoval, Ureña explains that decolonial love offers a "third option," another approach to loving. This other course of action occurs when the loving subject instead tries to "slip between the two members" of the either/or alternative by saying, "I have no hope, but all the same …" or "I stubbornly choose not to choose; I choose drifting; I continue" (Sandoval 2000:143, as quoted in Ureña 2017:90). This kind of loving heals wounds and unleashes the transformative power of love (Ureña 2017).

A certain kind of loving, then, has the potential to do the repair work of broken – or barely-begun – trust. We need to do ongoing repair work in our interpersonal relationships in order to develop or maintain trust. We need forgiveness, too; inadvertently hurting our loved ones is an everyday occurrence for which we need to offer apologies and accept them (Norlock and Rumsey 2009). And sometimes the harm we do others is significant, sometimes done knowingly. Forgiveness allows us as wrongdoers to recover from harmful actions so that we do not remain caught in the consequences of our actions (Norlock and Rumsey 2009:102). Yet forgiveness should not be too broadly construed; there are some wrongs that do such deep and lasting damage to us or others that forgiveness is not appropriate (Norlock and Rumsey 2009; Card 2002; Potter 2001). To forgive, Jeffrie Murphy argues, is to change your attitude toward someone who has wronged you; an overcoming of resentment for their moral wrong to you (Murphy 1982). Murphy is careful to point out that forgiveness does not involve forgetting. Nor does it necessarily involve reconciliation. As Norlock and Rumsey state, "women who live in contexts in which women are particularly unsafe require recognition more than reconciliation" (2009:101). By this, they mean "behaving in morally responsive ways to victims' choices to forgive, or to resist forgiveness" (2009:118).

Kim Atkins also argues that, since part of what it is to be human is that we are flawed and fallible, we need not only trust but also forgiveness in our relationships (Atkins 2002). However, she emphasizes the mutual responsibility for healing damaged trust in interpersonal relationships. Trust and forgiveness are counterparts, on her account. Yet forgiveness, too, is a contested moral concept: some people argue that it is always right to forgive others, even when the wrongdoer is unapologetic; others, like Atkins, argue that there are important constraints on when it is appropriate to forgive. When trust in an intimate other is damaged or one feels a sense of betrayal,

> forgiveness cannot go ahead unless both parties are responsive to mutual drawing, direction and interpretation on the matter of the harm. It is precisely the injured and the agent's willingness to be drawn on the issue of the harm that establishes a genuine mutuality from which forgiveness and trust can emerge … Genuine regret and repentance involve a ready responsiveness to a harmed friend's interpretation of one's attitudes and actions (a preparedness to be drawn, in other words), and this is why regret and repentance provide reasons for considering forgiveness … Repentance must involve, not simply feeling sorry, but *feeling* that one was wrong …
>
> *(Atkins 2002:126; emphasis in original)*

I am inclined to agree with Atkins (see Potter 2001). However, it could be that my ideas about forgiveness, trust, friendship, and love are too tightly bound up in the instituted social imaginary and not adequately engaging in an instituting one. This distinction comes from Castoriadis, who argues that the social imaginary is both institut*ed* and institut*ing* (Castoriadis 1994). As instituted, it seems given; yet, as instituting, it is contestable. One of the central things we need to contest, in many of our interpersonal trust relationships, is our practices and assumptions about privilege and subordination. This especially calls for the need for the privileged to critically examine their own and others' complicity in white supremacy. But it will also involve rethinking love and forgiveness, not to mention the norms, expectations and metaphors that are interwoven into our institutions and practices.

19.6 Conclusion

As I stated at the outset, norms for trust and other moral concepts should not be declared as universal claims about what constituted them. In Spelman's words, "moral direction is something to be figured out by the moral travelers in the thicket of their relations with others, not something they can determine by reference to a sure and steady compass" (Spelman 2004:53). This is as true for interpersonal trust as it is for any other aspects of our moral lives: sometimes we have to figure this out as we go.

Notes

1 The notion that we cannot categorize others strikes me as part of the social imaginary, like colorblindness, or gender-neutrality – myths that nevertheless do important work for some of us to the detriment of others. I discuss the relationship of the social imaginary to trust in section 4.

2 Stroud (2006) and Hawley (2014a) are considering the question of whether or not the norms of friendship conflict with epistemic norms. Hawley's answer is that they do not, ultimately.

References

Alexander, M. (2012) *The New Jim Crow: Mass Incarceration in the Age of Colorblindness*, New York: The New Press.

Atkins, K. (2002) "Friendship, Trust, and Forgiveness," *Philosophia* 29(1–4): 111–132.

Baier, A. (1986) "Trust and Antitrust," *Ethics* 96(2): 231–260.

Becker, L. (1996) "Trust as Noncognitive Security about Motives," *Ethics* 107(1):43–61.

Bok, S. (2011) *Lying: Moral Choice in Public and Private Life*, New York: Vintage.

Brison, S. (2002) *Aftermath: Violence and the Remaking of a Self*, Princeton, NJ: Princeton University Press.

Card, C. (2002) *The Atrocity Paradigm: A Theory of Evil*, New York: Oxford University Press.

Castoriadis, C. (1994) "Radical Imagination and the Social Instituting Imaginary," in G. Robinson and J. Rundell (eds.), *Rethinking Imagination: Culture and Creativity*, London: Routledge.

Cegarra, J. (2012) "Social Imaginary: Theoretical-Epistemological Basis," *Cinta de Moebio* 43(43): 1–13.

Code, L. (1991) *What Can She Know? Feminist Theory and the Construction of Knowledge*, Ithaca, NY: Cornell University Press.

Code, L. (2006) *Ecological Thinking: The Politics of Epistemic Location*, Oxford: Oxford University Press.

Collins, P.H. (2000) *Black Feminist Thought: Knowledge, Consciousness, and the Politics of Empowerment*, 2nd edition, New York and London: Routledge.

Dotson, K. (2011) "Tracking Epistemic Violence, Tracking Practices of Silencing," *Hypatia* 26(2): 236–257.

Endreβ, M. and Pabst, A. (2013) "Violence and Shattered Trust: Sociological Considerations," *Hum Stud* 36:89–106.

Ferguson, A. (2001) *Bad Boys: Public Schools in the Making of Black Masculinity*, Ann Arbor: University of Michigan Press.

Freeman, L. (2014) "Creating Safe Spaces: Strategies for Confronting Implicit and Explicit Bias and Stereotype Threat in the Classroom," *American Philosophical Association Feminism and Philosophy Newsletter*, 13(2): 3–12.
Gendler, T. (2011) "On the Epistemic costs of Implicit Bias," *Philos Stud* 156: 33–63.
Govier, T. (1991) "Distrust as a Practical Problem," *Journal of Social Philosophy* 23: 52–63.
Govier, T. (1992) "Trust, Distrust, and Feminist Theory," *Hypatia* 7(1): 16–33.
Govier, T. (1998) *Dilemmas of Trust*, Montreal: McGill-Queens Press.
Havis, D. (2014) "'Now, How You Sound': Considering Different Philosophical Praxis," *Hypatia* 29 (1): 237–252.
Hawley, K. (2014a) "Trust, Distrust, and Commitment," *Nous* 48: 1–20.
Hawley, K. (2014b) "Partiality and Prejudice in Trusting," *Synthese* 191: 2029–2045.
Holland, S. and Stocks, D. (2015) "Trust and Its Role in the Medical Encounter," *Health Care Anal.* doi:10.1007/s10728-10015-0293-z
Jaggar, A. (1988) "Love and Knowledge: Emotion in Feminist Epistemology," *Inquiry: An Interdisciplinary Journal of Philosophy* 32(2): 151–176.
Jones, K. (1996) "Trust as an Affective Attitude," *Ethics* 107(1): 4–25.
Keller, S. (2004) "Friendship and Belief," *Philosophical Papers* 33(3): 329–351.
Lahno, B. (2004) "Three Aspects of Interpersonal Trust," *Analyse and Kritik* 26: 30–47.
Lugones, M. (1987) "Playfulness, 'World'-Traveling, and Loving Perception," *Hypatia* 2(2): 3–19.
Lugones, M. and Spelman, E. (1983) "Have We Got a Theory for You! Feminist Theory, Cultural Imperialism, and the Demand for 'The Woman's Voice,'" *Women's Studies Int Forum* 6(6): 573–581.
Murphy, J. (1982) "Forgiveness and Resentment," *Midwest Studies in Philosophy* 7(1): 503–516.
Norlock, K. and Rumsey, J. (2009) "The Limits of Forgiveness," *Hypatia* 24(1): 100–122.
Norton-Smith, T. (2010) *The Dance of Person and Place: One Interpretation of American Indian Philosophy*, Albany, NY: SUNY Press.
Potter, N.N. (2000) "Giving Uptake," *Social Theory and Practice* 26(3): 479–508.
Potter, N.N. (2001) "Is Refusing to Forgive a Vice?" in P. DesAutels and J. Waugh (eds.), *Feminists Doing Ethics*, Oxford: Rowman & Littlefield Press.
Potter, N.N. (2002) *How Can I Be Trusted? A Virtue Theory of Trustworthiness*, Lanham, MD: Rowman & Littlefield.
Potter, N.N. (2016) *The Virtue of Defiance and Psychiatric Engagement*, Oxford: Oxford University Press.
Potter, N.N. (2017) "Voice, Silencing, and Listening Well: Socially Located Patients, Oppressive Structures, and an Invitation to Shift the Epistemic Terrain," in S. Tekin and R. Bluhm (eds.), *Bloomsbury Companion to Philosophy of Psychiatry*, London: Bloomsbury.
Sandoval, C. (2000) *Methodology of the Oppressed*, Minneapolis: University of Minneapolis Press.
Spelman, E. (2004) "The Household as Repair Shop," in C. Calhoun (ed.), *Setting the Moral Compass: Essays by Women Philosophers*, Oxford: Oxford University Press.
Stroud, S. (2006) "Epistemic Partiality in Friendship," *Ethics*, 116(3): 498–524.
Talbert, B. (2015) "Knowing Other People: A Second-Person Framework," *Ratio* 28(2): 190–206.
Ureña, C. (2017) "Loving from Below: Of (De)colonial Love and Other Demons" *Hypatia* 32(1): 86–102.
Wanderer, J. (2013) "Testimony and the Interpersonal," *International Journal of Philosophical Studies* 21(1): 92–110.
Western, B. (2006) *Punishment and Inequality in America*, New York: Russell Sage Foundation.

20

TRUST IN INSTITUTIONS AND GOVERNANCE

Mark Alfano and and Nicole Huijts

20.1 Introduction

Elaborating on themes from Hobbes (1668/1994), Alfano (2016a) has argued that warranted trust fosters multiple practical, epistemic, cultural and mental health goods. In this paper, we focus on the practical and epistemic benefits made possible or more likely by warranted trust. In addition, we bear in mind throughout that trusting makes the trustor vulnerable: the trustee may prove to be unlucky, incompetent or an outright betrayer. With this in mind, we also focus on warranted lack of trust and outright distrust, the benefits they make possible, and the harms that the untrusting agent is protected against and may protect others against (see also D'Cruz, this volume). We use cases of (dis)trust in technology corporations and the public institutions that monitor and govern them as examples throughout this chapter.

In so doing, we build on the accounts of Jones (2012) and Alfano (2016a, 2016b) to develop definitions of various dispositions related to trusting and being trusted. Our goal is then to argue that private corporations and public institutions have compelling reasons both to appear trustworthy and to actually be trustworthy. From this it follows that corporations and institutions have strong instrumental and moral reasons to adopt a suite of policies that promote their appearing trustworthy and being trustworthy.

Here is the plan for this chapter: first, we explain the conception of trustworthiness that we employ. We model trustworthiness as a relation among a trustor, a trustee and a field of trust defined and delimited by its scope. In addition, both potential trustors and potential trustees are modeled as being more or less reliable in signaling either their willingness to trust or their willingness to prove trustworthy in various fields in relation to various other agents. Second, following Alfano (2016a) we argue that the social scale of a potential trust relationship partly constrains both explanatory and normative aspects of the relation. Most of the philosophical literature focuses on dyadic trust between a pair of agents (Baier 1986, Jones 2012, McGeer 2008, Pettit 1995), but there are also small communities of trust (Alfano 2016a) as well as trust in large institutions (Potter 2002; Govier 1993; Townley and Garfield 2013, Hardin 2002). The mechanisms that induce people to (reasonably) extend their trust vary depending on the size and structure of the community in question. Mechanisms that work in dyads and small communities are often unavailable in the context of trusting an institution or branch of government. Establishing trust on this larger social scale therefore requires new or modified mechanisms. In the third section, we recommend several policies that tend to make institutions more trustworthy and to reliably signal that trustworthiness to the public; we also recommend some ways to be intelligently trusting (see also O'Neill, this volume). We conclude by discussing the warrant for distrust in institutions that do not adopt the sorts of policies we recommend; warranted distrust is especially pertinent for people who belong to groups that have historically faced (and in many cases still do face) oppression (see also Medina as well as Potter, this volume).

20.2 A Framework for Global, Rich Trust

To trust someone is to rely on them to treat your dependency on them as a compelling if not universally-overriding reason to act as expected. As Jones (2012) and Alfano (2016b) emphasize, trusting and being trusted are conceptually and developmentally interlocking concepts and phenomena (see also Scheman, this volume). Jones and Alfano also agree that trusting and being trusted are always relative to a domain. Alfano (2016a) glosses the domain as a field of valued practical concern and activity that is defined and delimited by its scope. To move from the descriptive phenomena of trusting and being trusted to the normative phenomena of being trustworthy and trusting (i.e., situations in which evaluations of appropriateness or warrant play a part), we need a theory of when trust is warranted. This would allow us to say, schematically, that B is trustworthy in domain D to the extent that she possesses a disposition that warrants trust, and that A is trusting in domain D to the extent that he possesses a disposition to extend trust when it is warranted.

We begin with Jones's (2012) partner-relative definition:

> B is trustworthy with respect to A in domain of interaction D, if and only if she is *competent* with respect to that domain, and she *would* take the fact that A is counting on her, *were* A to do so in this domain, to be a *compelling* reason for acting as counted on.

Next, we extend Jones's account of partner-relative *rich trustworthiness* by articulating congruent concepts of *global rich trustworthiness, partner-relative rich trustingness* and *global rich trustingness*. Jones points out that one agent's being trustworthy without anyone being able to tell that she is trustworthy is inefficient. Such a person may end up being trusted haphazardly, but her dependency-responsiveness will go almost largely unnoticed, unappreciated and unused.

This leads to a pair of unfortunate consequences. First, people who would benefit from depending on a trustworthy person in the relevant domain will be left at sea, forced either to guess whom to trust or to try to go it alone. Second, the trustworthy person will not receive the credit, esteem, resources and respect that come with being trusted. Things would go better for both potential trustors and trustworthy people if the latter could be systematically distinguished from the untrustworthy. This leads Jones (2012:74) to articulate a conception of partner-relative rich trustworthiness as follows:

> B is richly trustworthy with respect to A just in case (i) B is willing and able reliably to signal to A those domains in which B is competent and willing to take the fact that A is counting on her, were A to do so, to be a compelling

> reason for acting as counted on and (ii) there are at least some domains in which she will be responsive to the fact of A's dependency.

Building on this definition, we can further define *global* (i.e. non-partner-relative) *rich trustworthiness* as follows:

> For all agents, B is globally richly trustworthy to the extent that (i) B is willing and able reliably to signal to others those domains in which B is competent and willing to take the fact that others are counting on her, were they to do so, to be a compelling reason for acting as counted on and (ii) there are some domains in which she will be responsive to others' dependency.

Global rich trustworthiness is a generalization of rich trustworthiness. It can be construed as the aggregate signature of rich trustworthiness that B embodies. Global rich trustworthiness measures not just how B is disposed towards some particular person but how B is disposed towards other people more broadly. It is defined using "to the extent that" rather than the biconditional because it is impossible for anyone to be globally richly trustworthy towards the entire universe of potential partners. Global rich trustworthiness therefore comes in degrees on three dimensions: partner (whom she is trustworthy towards), field (in what domains she is trustworthy), and extent (how compelling she finds the dependency of particular others in given fields).

Congruent to partner-relative rich trustworthiness, we can also define *partner-relative rich trustingness*:

> A is richly trusting with respect to B just in case (i) A is willing and able reliably to signal to B those domains in which A is willing to count on B to take A's counting on him to be a compelling reason for him to act as counted on and (ii) there are some domains in which A is willing to be dependent on B in this way.

Partner-relative rich trustingness is indexed to a particular agent. I might be richly trusting towards you but not towards your skeezy uncle. Just as it is important for potential trustors to be able reliably to identify trustworthy partners, so it is important for trustworthy partners to be able reliably to identify people who are willing to extend trust. Not only does this save the trustworthy time and effort but also it may empower them to accomplish things they could not accomplish without being trusted. For instance, an entrepreneur needs to find trusting investors to get her new venture off the ground, which she can do more effectively if trusting investors signal that they are willing to be dependent on the entrepreneur to use their money wisely and repay it on time and in full.

Aggregating rich trusting dispositions allows us to define *global rich trustingness*:

> For all agents, A is globally richly trusting to the extent that (i) A is willing and able reliably to signal to others those domains in which A is willing to count on them to take A's counting on them to be a compelling reason for acting as counted on and (ii) there are some domains in which A is willing to be dependent in this way.

Like global rich trustworthiness, global rich trustingness is a generalization of its partner-relativized cousin. It measures not just how A is disposed towards some particular person but how A is disposed towards other people more broadly. And like global rich trustworthiness, it is defined using "to the extent that" rather than the biconditional because it is impossible for anyone to be globally richly trusting towards the entire universe of potential partners. Global rich trustingness is therefore parameterized on the dimensions of partner (whom she is willing to be trusting towards), field (in what domains she is willing to be trusting), and extent (how compelling she expects her dependency to be for others).

20.3 The Social Scale of Trust

With these definitions in hand, we now turn to the social scale of trust. As Alfano (2016a) points out, restricting discussions of trust to the two extremes of the social scale (dyadic trust vs. trust in large, faceless institutions and governments) ignores all communities of intermediate size. As work on the psychological and neurological limits of direct sociality shows (Dunbar 1992), there are distinctive phenomena associated with trust at intermediate scales, which can sometimes be modulated to apply at the largest scales. Attending to the full spectrum enables us to see elements of continuity as well as breaks in continuity. Our discussion in this section is framed by the following questions:

(trustworthiness-1) How can people become responsive to the dependency of others?
(trustingness-1) How can people become willing to rely on the dependency-responsiveness of others?
(trustworthiness-2) How can people reliably signal their dependency-responsiveness?
(trustingness-2) How can people reliably signal their willingness to rely on the dependency-responsiveness of others?

Answering these questions points us in the direction of policies and practices that people and institutions can adopt to better approximate partner-relative and global rich trustworthiness and trustingness.

We will follow Alfano (2016a) by conceptualizing humans and their relations as a directed network, in which nodes represent agents and edges represent channels for both actions (e.g. communication, aid, harm) and attitudes (e.g. belief, knowledge, desire, aversion, trust, distrust). In this framework, X can become responsive to the dependency of Y only if there is one or more *short epistemic geodesic* (shortest path of communicative and epistemic edges) from X (through other nodes) to Y, giving X first-, second- … or nth-hand knowledge of Y's beliefs, desires, aversions, and so on. The longer the epistemic geodesic, the more opportunities for noise or bias to creep into the chain of transmission and thus the higher the likelihood that X will not reliably come to understand Y's epistemic and emotional perspective.

Even if X does reliably come to understand Y's epistemic and emotional perspective, this does not, on its own, guarantee that X will be responsive to Y's dependency. Recall that responsiveness is defined in this context in terms of treating someone's dependency as a compelling reason to act as counted on. X could know full well about Y's needs, preferences, dependencies and fears without treating these as a reason to act, let alone a compelling reason to act. This is similar to the insufficiency of empathy to motivate compassionate action (Bloom 2016): knowing is half the battle, but it is only half the battle. Motivation is needed as well.

One source of the needed motivation is *goodwill*, as Baier (1986) has pointed out. Goodwill is established and maintained through activities like social grooming (Dunbar 1993), laughing together (Dezecache and Dunbar 2012), singing and dancing together (Dunbar 2012), or enduring traumatic loss together (Elder and Clipp 1988). Jones (2012) persuasively argues, however, that there can be motivational sources other than goodwill. One important additional motivator is concern for *reputation*, which is especially pertinent when one is embedded in a social structure that makes it likely that others will achieve mutual knowledge of how one has acted and for what reasons one has acted (Dunbar 2005; see also Origgi, this volume). One-off defection or betrayal in an interaction exposes one to loss of reputation and thereby to exclusion from the benefits of further cooperation and coordination (see also Dimock, this volume). In a community with short epistemic geodesics, reputation-relevant information is likely to travel quickly. Dunbar (1993) estimates that at least 60% of human conversational time comprises gossip about relationships and personal experiences. As Alfano and Robinson (2017) argue, these phenomena make the disposition to gossip well (to the right people, about the right people, at the right time, for the right reason, etc.) a sort of virtue: a disposition that protects both oneself and other members of one's community from betrayal while punishing or ostracizing systematic defectors.

This brings us to an epistemic benefit of small-world communities (Milgram 1967), which are characterized by sparse interconnections but short geodesics (due to the presence of hubs within local sub-communities). Such communities are highly effective ways of disseminating knowledge. In the case of gossip and related forms of communication, the information in question concerns the actions, intentions and dispositions of another person. In computer science, it has been shown that, depending on the topology of a communicative network, almost everyone gets the message even when the probability of any particular agent gossiping is only between 0.6 and 0.8 (Haas et al. 2006).

There are two main reasons that such communities foster knowledge. First, because they effectively facilitate testimonial knowledge-transfer, they make it likely that any important information in the community eventually makes the rounds. Second, to the extent that the members of the community have at least an implicit understanding of the effectiveness of their own testimonial network, they are in a position to achieve second- and even higher-order levels of mutual knowledge. They can reasonably make inferences like, "If that were true, I would have heard it by now" (Goldberg 2010). They might also go further by making judgments like, "Because that's true, everyone in my community must have heard it by now."

In addition to goodwill and reputation, *solidarity* – understood here in terms of individuals sharing interests or needs and taking a second-order interest in each other's interests (Feinberg 1968), typically accompanied by self-identification with their group's accomplishments and failures – can motivate someone to respond to the dependency of another. Such self-identification with a group informs our self-conceptions. It gives us a sense of belonging, home and history (Nietzsche 1874 / 1997). It provides us with heroes and villains on whom to model our behavior and practice moral judgments. It helps to cement bonds within a community.

If this is on the right track, then a partial answer to **(trustworthiness-1)** is that people become responsive to dependency of others by being connected by short epistemic geodesics along with some combination of goodwill (fostered by in-person interaction), desire to maintain a good reputation (fostered by a small-world epistemic network), and solidarity between those in a dependent position and those with more power. The discussion so far also gives us a partial answer to **(trustingness-1)**. It makes sense to rely on the dependency-responsiveness of another person to the extent that one is connected by a short epistemic geodesic, one has interacted positively with them in the past, one has received positive and reliable reputational information about them, and one expects them to feel a sense of solidarity.

What about **(trustworthiness-2)** and **(trustingness-2)**? These questions relate not to being trustworthy and trusting, but to being richly trustworthy and trusting. We contend that people come to reliably signal their dependency-responsiveness in two main ways. First, they can be transparent about their reasoning processes (not just the outcomes of these processes), which will showcase which reasons they are sensitive to in the first place (and where they have moral blindspots – see DesAutels 2004) and which among the reasons they are sensitive to they typically find compelling. Second, they can solicit other agents who are already trusted by third parties to vouch for them. Such vouching can lead third parties to extend their trust. In the first instance, they enable X to trust Y through some mediator M. More generally, transitive chains of trust may help X to trust Y through M_1, M_2 … M_n, and shorter chains can in general be expected to be more robust.

Small-scale groups in which everyone knows everyone can sustain the transitivity of trust among all their members. As the size of community increases, however, the need for vicarious or mediated trust increases. X vicariously trusts Y through M with respect to field of trust F just in case X trusts M with respect to F, M trusts Y with respect to F, and X trusts M's judgment about who is trustworthy with respect to F. Vicarious trust has a distinctive counterfactual signature in the sense that, if X vicariously trusts Y through M, then were X to become directly acquainted with Y, X would continue to trust Y non-vicariously. We can think of this in terms of *delegation* (empowering someone to extend your trust vicariously) and *ratification* (explicitly confirming an instance of delegation). In cases where acquaintance with Y leads X to withdraw rather than ratify her vicarious trust in Y, she may also begin to doubt M. To illustrate, suppose my boss trusts me to complete a task, and that I sub-contract out a part of that task to someone she distrusts. If she finds out that I have done this, she will most likely withdraw her trust from me – at least regarding this task and perhaps more generally.

Shy of such a highly demanding approach to transitivity, we might ask about extending one's trust one or two steps out into a community (Figure 20.1). What reasons are there for C to trust D, who is trusted by someone she trusts (B)?

In addition to *delegation*, we might focus on the phenomenon of *vouching*. B vouches for D to C if B makes himself accountable for any failure on D's part to prove trustworthy.

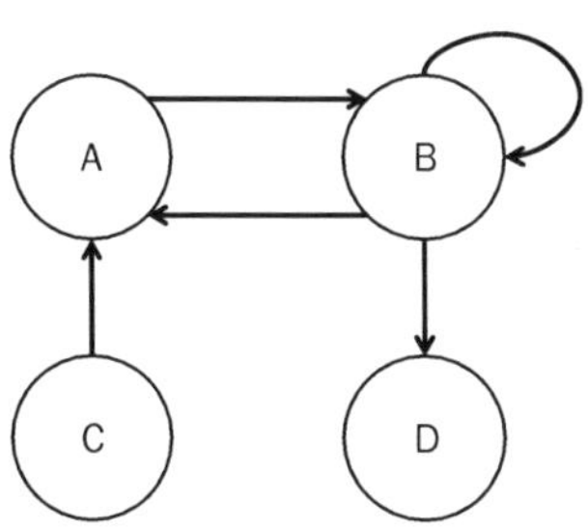

Figure 20.1 Trust Networks

How is such vouching meant to work? It relies on the rationality of extending trust transitively, at least in some cases. In other words, it relies on the idea that, at least sometimes, if C trusts B and B trusts D, then C has a reason to trust D. This reason need not be compelling. C can withhold her trust from D even as she gives it to B. Our hypothesis is that transitivity provides a *pro tanto* reason to extend trust, not an all-things-considered reason. There are two arguments for this hypothesis. First, competence in a domain is highly associated with meta-competence in making judgments about competence in that domain (Collins and Evans 2007: chapter 2). If C trusts B, that means C deems B competent with respect to their shared field of trust. It stands to reason, then, that C should expect B to be better than the average person at judging the competence of others in that field. So if B gives his trust to D, C has a reason to think that D is competent (see also Miller and Freiman, this volume).

Second, it is psychologically difficult and practically irrational to consciously engage in efforts to undermine your own values in the very process of pursuing and promoting those values. Imagine someone locking a door while they are trying to walk through the doorway. Someone could perhaps do this as a parapraxis. Someone could do it as a gag, or in pretense, but it is hard to envision a case in which someone does this consciously. Likewise, it is hard to envision a case in which someone is genuinely dependency-responsive, and consciously expresses that responsiveness by recommending that you put your fate in the hands of someone they expect to betray your trust. They might do so by mistake, as a gag or in pretense, but a straightforward case is difficult to imagine. If C trusts B, that means C judges that B is responsive to C's dependency. It stands to reason, then, that C should expect B to act on that responsiveness in a practically rational way. So if B gives his trust to D, C has a reason to think that D would act consistently with B's responsiveness to C's dependency.

Putting these together, if C trusts B and B trusts D (with respect to the same field of trust), then C has a reason to think that D is competent and responsive to the dependency of people like C. In other words, C has *pro tanto* reasons to trust D.

On the question of rich trustingness, we see two main ways to signal it. First, the agent could establish a track-record of trusting particular types of people in particular domains to particular extents. This track-record would then be the basis of a reputation for having a signature of trusting dispositions (relativized to partners, domains and extent of trust). This leaves open, however, how the first step is to be taken. How can people with no reputation – good or bad – go about establishing their rich trustingness? This brings us to our second method of signaling. Someone can begin to establish a record of trustingness by engaging in small "test" dependencies: extending her trust just a little bit even when she lacks compelling reasons to do so. Such tests simultaneously enable the trustor to establish her reputation and provide her with feedback about the trustworthiness of others. Doing so might seem reckless, but if it is viewed from the point of view of information-gathering (I trust you in order to find out what kind of person you are rather than to reap the direct benefits of trust) this strategy is sensible for people who have enough resources to take small risks.

20.4 Rich Trustworthiness for Institutions: Policy Recommendations

Some of the mechanisms that (reasonably) induce people to extend their trust vary depending on the size of the community envisioned; the ways in which (rich) trustworthiness and trustingness can be established vary with these mechanisms. Shaming, shunning, laughing together, building and maintaining a good reputation over the long run through networks of gossip, bonding over shared enjoyment and suffering, sharing a communal identity: such phenomena can warrant trust in a dyad or small community. However, with a few exceptions such as reputation-management, they are typically unavailable in the context of trusting an institution or branch of government. In addition, it may be possible for such institutions to reliably signal their trustworthiness only to some stakeholders – namely, those with whom they have already established a good-enough reputation as opposed to those who have experienced a history of neglect and betrayal. Establishing global rich trustworthiness in institutions and governance may require new mechanisms or policies.

Reputation is one mechanism that applies at both the individual/small-group level and the institutional level. As institutions have a long lifespan, it is possible that, in new trust-requiring situations, past actions or omissions have seriously damaged trust. This situation is not easy to repair, and reliable signaling might not be possible in the face of distrust. Furthermore, the public – and especially groups that have suffered from oppression or discrimination – can be reasonable in distrusting actors that have proven untrustworthy in the past (Krishnamurthy 2015). The case of opposition of the Standing Rock Sioux to the Dakota Access Pipeline (Plumer 2016) is a good example, as are various nuclear siting controversies in the United States (Kyne and Bolin 2016; Wigley and Shrader-Frechette 1996). We thus do not advocate maximizing trust, but fine-tuning it.

When a distrusted institution has, however, changed its ways and has become trustworthy, it can help to include other more trusted actors in decision-making or information provision to signal this trustworthiness. More trusted partners could potentially vouch for less trusted partners which might then lead to higher trust in the whole consortium. The fact that often parties risk their own reputations by vouching for a former offender means that they have an incentive to do so only when they have very good reason. Huijts et al. (2007) showed with a survey study about a hypothetical carbon capture and storage (CCS) project that trust in involved actors together to make the right decisions and to store CO_2 safely and responsibly was predicted by trust in three different actors: government, industry and environmental NGOs. Trust in government was rated higher than trust in the industry, and had a much larger effect on overall trust than trust in industry. This suggests that in some cases considerable involvement of and transparent oversight by the government (assuming, of course, that the government itself is trusted) can help to overcome low levels of trust in other institutions.

In this section, we describe mechanisms that can build or undermine trust (and the reliable signaling thereof) in the context of institutions and governance, using large, potentially risky, energy technology projects as an exemplary case. Energy technology projects are regularly proposed to increase energy security or reduce environmental problems such as air pollution and climate change. Examples are windmill parks, CCS, high-voltage power lines, shale gas mining, geothermal energy and nuclear power plants. Although these energy projects can offer important benefits for society and the environment, they also introduce potential risks and drawbacks (e.g., visual intrusion, increased traffic and risks of oil spills and nuclear meltdowns). Trust in institutions involved with the implementation of energy technologies, such as energy companies and governmental regulatory bodies, is an important predictor for citizens' evaluation of and responses to implementations of such technologies (Huijts et al. 2012; L'Orange Seigo et al. 2014). Higher trust in those responsible for the technology is generally associated with higher perceived benefits, lower perceived risks and more positive overall evaluations of a technology. By contrast, when people do not trust governmental institutions and private companies to manage these risks and drawbacks responsibly, the projects are likely to be contested (Huijts et al. 2014), as we have seen recently in the opposition of the Standing Rock Sioux to the Dakota Access Pipeline (Plumer 2016).

Institutions and the governmental agencies that oversee them thus have a need not only to be trustworthy but to reliably signal to affected populations that they are trustworthy. They need to approximate as closely as possible global rich trustworthiness. However, they cannot easily rely on the processes that build trust in dyads and small communities. Governmental regulators and representatives of the industries they regulate cannot be expected to bond through laughing and crying together with all stakeholders. Personally identified ambassadors can give a face to the institutions they represent, but this is typically more a matter of marketing than reliable signaling. Empirical research suggests that trust in parties responsible for a technology is based on their perceived competences and intentions (Huijts et al. 2007). Knowing this, companies could insist that they have good intentions and competence, but such a direct approach is liable to fail or backfire. "Would I lie to you?" is not an effective retort to someone who has just questioned whether you are lying to them. Indeed, Terwel et al. (2009) showed that trust in an institution is lower when it provides communication about CCS that is incongruent with the motives it is presumed to have (e.g. involving environmental arguments for companies and economic arguments for environmental NGOs) than when it gives arguments that are congruent with inferred motives. Perceived honesty was found to explain the effect of perceived congruence on trust. Directly insisting on one's own good intentions when one is not already perceived as honest is thus not suitable for building and gaining trust.

We now turn to three more indirect ways for public and private institutions to reliably signal trustworthiness to a diverse group of stakeholders (i.e. to approximate rich global trustworthiness), which we label *voice, response* and *diversity*. The first way is to give stakeholders a meaningful voice in the decision-making process. Allowing voice by different parties is epistemically valuable. As standpoint epistemologists have argued, different parties bring different values and background knowledge, and victims of oppression often have distinct epistemic advantages when it comes to the vulnerabilities of those in dependent situations (Harding 1986; Wylie 2003). Since responsiveness to dependency and vulnerability is an essential component of trustworthiness, including such people in the decision process is likely to improve decision-making.

Empirical research has shown that allowing voice can indeed increase trust. Terwel et al. (2010; study 3) showed that respondents reported more trust in the decision-makers and more willingness to accept the decision about implementing a CCS project when the public was also allowed a voice in the decision-making procedure as compared to when only the industry and environmental NGOs were allowed a voice. Not only voice by citizens but also voice by other parties can affect trust and acceptance. Study 1 in the same paper showed that allowing voice by industry and environmental NGOs led to higher trust in the decision-makers and higher acceptance of the decision outcome than when no voice was allowed. Furthermore, when only one other party was allowed to voice a view, even when this was a trusted one (e.g. environmental NGOs), this did not lead to higher trust. Only allowing voice to all of the dissimilar parties (industry and environmental NGOs) was found to lead to higher trust in the decision-makers and higher acceptance of the decision outcome (study 2). The authors argue that allowing different parties to voice their opinion speaks of procedural fairness, which increases trust.

Of course, there is a danger that allowing voice is done in a purely instrumental way, as "window dressing." However, if that becomes apparent it could substantially undermine trust by signaling that those with the power to make decisions are not actually responsive to the dependency of those who have been asked to trust them. There are thus pragmatic as well as ethical and epistemic reasons to genuinely involve stakeholders in decision-making. This provides for short epistemic geodesics and hence knowledge of people's particular dependencies, and means that decision-makers genuinely engage in an exchange between equal peers (Habermas 1990) rather than broadcasting a message without engaging in substantive dialogue.

In order to be able to judge a socio-technical proposal and to take part in decision-making, citizens need to be able to gather relevant information. Open, timely and respectfully provided information is important for how citizens perceive a decision-making process. Industry managers and policy makers should not only communicate what they think citizens should know about the technology but also provide information that citizens are particularly concerned about and interested in. Short geodesics are needed to create awareness of what citizens are concerned about and interested in and to design matching information. Response – the provision of information that is open, honest, timely, respectfully provided, and suited to the concerns and interests of the public is therefore the second way for public and private institutions to signal trustworthiness. In so doing, they establish not only their trustworthiness but also their rich and (to the extent that they signal successfully to all affected stakeholders) global trustworthiness.

The third way for public and private institutions to signal trustworthiness, thus establishing their rich global trustworthiness, is by creating diversity within the institution at all levels but especially the top levels where the most important decisions are made. Empirical studies suggest that higher perceived similarity in goals and values between oneself and those responsible for a technology leads to higher levels of trust. For example, Siegrist et al. (2000) showed for nuclear power that a higher perceived similarity between oneself and company managers with respect to values, goals, behaviors, thoughts and opinions goes together with higher trust in those responsible for the technology. Huijts et al. (2007) similarly showed that higher perceived similarity in important goals and in the way of thinking between representatives of the actor and oneself correlates with higher trust in actors involved with a new technology (CCS in this case). Having more diversity in institutions is likely to create a situation in which citizens and other stakeholders can point to an empowered individual who is relevantly similar to them, thereby fostering a sense of solidarity.

The effect of perceived similarity is not just a bias. As feminist epistemologists argue, people who are similar to you are likely to have better epistemic familiarity with your problems, concerns and values (Daukas 2006; Grasswick 2017) and are also likely to share more of your values. Embracing diversity can thus serve as a source of epistemic improvement.

In addition, the involvement of diverse parties in information provision can be helpful in creating trust in another way. When different institutions independently provide information, this may increase the likelihood that each citizen trusts at least one source of information, which can help them form an opinion. However, this can easily lead to polarization. When institutions formulate common information texts, this may be even more helpful, as then one piece of information is available that is checked and approved by parties with different value-bases and different interests. Indeed, such a process approximates the best-known way to harness the wisdom of crowds by aggregating the information and values of independent, diverse sources (Surowiecki 2005; see also Ter Mors et al. 2010).

The benefits of the diversity of decision-makers can only be reliably signaled, however, when citizens and other stakeholders are aware of this diversity and see at least some of the decision-makers as standing in solidarity with them. To increase awareness of diversity, it is necessary to make it visible. Meijnders et al. (2009) showed that trust in information provided by a journalist about genetically modified apples became higher when the journalist was expressing an attitude about something that was congruent with the attitude of the respondent, independent of whether this congruent attitude was about a similar technology (genetically modified oranges), or about a different technology (a cash machine with voice control). Judgments of similarity between oneself and the journalist were found to mediate this effect. This shows that an awareness of some kind of similarity (of a particular opinion in this case) can indeed increase trust.

Of course, these are not the only ways that institutions can signal trustworthiness. We are not offering an exhaustive list in this short chapter, but we believe that the policies suggested here do not enjoy sufficient appreciation. Attending to the phenomena we have canvassed in this section is part of what an agent needs in order to extend their trust intelligently. Moreover, by demonstrating their appreciating of *voice, response* and *diversity*, potential trustors can signal their willingness to trust (in certain conditions) and thus become richly trusting.

20.5 Trust and Distrust in Other Institutions

Thus far, we have focused on trust and distrust in corporations and governmental agencies that regulate and oversee them. Naturally, there are other relevant institutions when it comes to warranted trust and distrust, such as the military, universities, hospitals, courts and churches and other religious institutions. As we lack the space to address all the differences among these institutions in this chapter, we here make just a few remarks about them.

First, these other institutions face the same challenges in establishing trust that corporations and government agencies do. They are too large to rely on practices like social grooming, laughing together, crying together, and so on. Second, like the institutions we have focused on, they can (and should) rely on reputation-building and reputation-management mechanisms. Third, the mechanisms of *voice, response* and *diversity* should in general work just as well for these institutions as they do for corporations and governmental regulators. There may, however, be some exceptions. For example, it may not be appropriate to give equal voice in decision-making about policing to criminals and law-abiding citizens. In addition, sometimes fully embodying the ideal of *response* is impossible because doing so would violate privacy rights or other rights (e.g. in a hierarchical command structure such as the military). Finally, if our assumption of parity is on the right track, then lack of *voice, response* and *diversity* indicates that it is reasonable for many stakeholders to respond to many contemporary institutions (e.g. the Catholic Church and its all-male priesthood, along with racially segregated police forces) with distrust rather than trust. This leads us to our final section.

20.6 Warranted Distrust

While this chapter has focused primarily on the ways in which warranted trust can be established and trustworthiness reliably signaled, we want to end with a note of warning: citizens and other stakeholders (especially those who have suffered neglect or betrayal by institutions) may become reasonably distrusting of government and industry in several ways. Recognizing this fact and the difficulty of reliably signaling trustworthiness to such potential trustors is an important and under-explored responsibility of institutions. We will discuss a number of examples.

First, people may become (reasonably) distrustful when authorities have a preset agenda and at most do public consultation as a form of window dressing, if at all. In the case of a wind farm in Australia, citizens reported that they felt they were not heard in the decision-making process, which sparked opposition to the project (Gross 2007). Some residents living near a newly built powerline in the Netherlands reported that they were given a false sense of influence. The interviewed citizens thought they were heard to avoid civil unrest, but that they did not have an actual influence on the decision-making (Porsius et al., 2016). Also in a CCS case in the Netherlands, local parties and citizens protested to influence a situation in which they were not given formal influence (Brunsting et al. 2011; Feenstra et al.2010:27). Brunsting et al. (2011:6382) concluded that, "The timing of public involvement reinforced the impression that Shell would be the only beneficiary which was therefore not a highly trusted source of information about safety or costs and benefits."

Second, people may become justifiably distrustful when authorities select their experts in a way that appears to be biased to support the view of the authority. In the Dutch CCS case, it was claimed that a critical report by a university professor had been held back from the decision-making process, which generated negative media attention and questions in parliament (Feenstra et al.2010:25).

Third, people may become distrustful when important values are ignored because there is no room for genuine exchange of emotions, values and concerns. In the Dutch CCS case, fear about genuine risks had been labeled emotional and irrational, meaning that such fears were silenced (Brunsting et al. 2011). This hampers respectful exchange of values and concerns. In the case of the wind farm project in Australia, interviewed citizens complained of greed and jealousy related to the fact that the person who owns the land on which a windmill is placed gains substantial income from it, while those living nearby suffer from drawbacks such as visual intrusion and noise annoyance but receive inadequate compensation (Gross 2007). If these fairness considerations had been taken into account earlier on in the project, the outcomes of the project would have likely been more acceptable.

Fourth, improper information provision can hamper opportunities to come to a genuine exchange of emotions, values and concerns and may lead to distrust in those responsible for the technology. In several cases, information was provided too late or was not targeted to the audience's interests. For example, in the Dutch CCS case, at the start of the project no information was available that was tailored to the public, that sought information about local costs and benefits, and that was endorsed by multiple parties (Brunsting et al. 2011). This happened only later in the project when it is was likely too late to make a difference. Also around the implementation of the high-voltage powerline in the Netherlands, citizens perceived a lack of transparency; they lacked personally relevant, timely and respectful information provision, which was associated with a lack of trust in the information provision (Porsius et al. 2016). For the Australian wind farm project, a lack of clear notification of and information about the project at the start of the project was reported to spark opposition (Gross 2007).

Fifth, people may also become distrusting and take opposing actions when only arguments framed in technical language are allowed in the arena, thereby favoring experts at the expense of stakeholder involvement (cf. Cuppen et al. 2015) and when the boundaries of a debate are set in such a way that important alternatives are already excluded at the outset. Both these problems were reported to be the case in the heavily contested CCS case in the Netherlands (Cuppen et al. 2015; Brunsting et al. 2011).

So, while trust may often be a good thing, it needs to be earned. When corporations, institutions and governments do not make serious and public efforts both to be and to appear trustworthy, it is reasonable for citizens to react with distrust and take action to prevent the implementation of risky new technologies.

References

Alfano, M. (2016a) "The Topology of Communities of Trust," *Russian Sociological Review* 15(4): 30–56.

Alfano, M. (2016b) "Friendship and the Structure of Trust," in A. Masala and J. Webber (eds.), *From Personality to Virtue: Essays in the Psychology and Ethics of Character*, Oxford: Oxford University Press.

Alfano, M. and Robinson, B. (2017) "Gossip as a Burdened Virtue," *Ethical Theory and Moral Practice* 20: 473–482.

Baier, A. (1986) "Trust and Antitrust," *Ethics* 96: 231–260.

Bloom, P. (2016) *Against Empathy: The Case for Rational Compassion*, New York: HarperCollins.

Brunsting, S., De Best-Waldhober, M., Feenstra, C.F.J. and Mikunda, T. (2011) "Stakeholder Participation Practices and Onshore CCS: Lessons from the Dutch CCS Case Barendrecht," *Energy Procedia*, 4: 6376–6383.

Collins, H. and Evans, R. (2007) *Rethinking Expertise*, Chicago, IL: University of Chicago Press.

Cuppen, E., Brunsting, S., Pesch, U. and Feenstra, C.F.J. (2015) "How Stakeholder Interactions Can Reduce Space for Moral Considerations in Decision Making: A Contested CCS Project in the Netherlands," *Environment and Planning A* 47: 1963–1978.

Daukas, N. (2006) "Epistemic Trust and Social Location," *Episteme* 3(1–2): 109–124.

DesAutels, P. (2004) "Moral Mindfulness," in P. DesAutels and M. Urban Walker (eds.), *Moral Psychology: Feminist Ethics and Social Theory*, Lanham, MD: Rowman & Littlefield.

Dezecache, G. and Dunbar, R. (2012) "Sharing the Joke: The Size of Natural Language Groups," *Evolution & Human Behavior* 33(6): 775–779.

Dunbar, R. (1992) "Neocortex Size as a Constraint on Group Size in Primates," *Journal of Human Evolution* 22(6): 469–493.

Dunbar, R. (1993) "Coevolution of Neocortical Size, Group Size and Language in Humans," *Behavioral and Brain Sciences* 16(4): 681–735.

Dunbar, R. (2005) "Gossip in Evolutionary Perspective," *Review of General Psychology* 8: 100–110.

Dunbar, R. (2012) "On the Evolutionary Function of Song and Dance," in N. Bannan (ed.), *Music, Language and Human Evolution*, Oxford: Oxford University Press.

Elder, G. and Clipp, E. (1988) "Wartime Losses and Social Bonding: Influences across 40 Years in Men's Lives," *Psychiatry* 51(2): 177–198.

Feenstra, C.F.J., Mikunda, T. and Brunsting, S. (2010) "What Happened in Barendrecht?! Case Study on the Planned Onshore Carbon Dioxide Storage in Barendrecht, the Netherlands." www.osti.gov/etdeweb/biblio/21360732

Feinberg, J. (1968) "Collective Responsibility," *Journal of Philosophy* 65: 674–688.

Goldberg, S.(2010) *Relying on Others: An Essay in Epistemology*, Oxford:Oxford University Press.

Govier, T. (1993) "Self-Trust, Autonomy, and Self-Esteem," *Hypatia* 8(1): 99–120.

Grasswick, H. (2017) "Feminist Responsibilism, Situationism, and the Complexities of the Virtue of Trustworthiness," in A. Fairweather and M. Alfano (eds.), *Epistemic Situationism*, Oxford: Oxford University Press.

Gross, C. (2007) "Community Perspectives of Wind Energy in Australia: The Application of a Justice and Community Fairness Framework to Increase Social Acceptance," *Energy Policy* 35: 2727–2736.

Haas, Z., Halpern, J. and Li, L. (2006) "Gossip-Based ad hoc Routing," *IEEE/ACM Transactions on Networking (TON)* 14(3): 479–491.

Habermas, J. (1990) *Moral Consciousness and Communicative Action*, C. Lenhardt and S.W. Nicholsen (trans.), Cambridge, MA: MIT Press.

Hardin, R. (2002) *Trust and Trustworthiness*, New York: Russell Sage Foundation.

Harding, S. (1986) *The Science Question in Feminism*, Ithaca, NY: Cornell University Press.

Hobbes, T. ([1668] 1994) *Leviathan*, E. Curley (ed.), Indianapolis, IN: Hackett.

Huijts, N.M.A., Midden, C. and Meijnders, A.L. (2007) "Social Acceptance of Carbon Dioxide Storage," *Energy Policy* 35: 2780–2789.

Huijts, N.M.A., Molin, E.J.E. and Steg, L. (2012) "Psychological Factors Influencing Sustainable Energy Technology Acceptance: A Review-based Comprehensive Framework," *Renewable and Sustainable Energy Reviews* 16(1), 525–531.

Huijts, N.M.A., Molin, E.J.E. and Van Wee, B. (2014) "Hydrogen Fuel Station Acceptance: A Structural Equation Model Based on the Technology Acceptance Framework," *Journal of Environmental Psychology* 38, 153–166.

Jones, K. (1999) "Second-Hand Moral Knowledge," *Journal of Philosophy* 96(2): 55–78.

Jones, K. (2012) "Trustworthiness," *Ethics* 123(1): 61–85.

Krishnamurthy, M. (2015) "(White) Tyranny and the Democratic Value of Distrust," *The Monist* 98 (4): 391–406.

Kyne, D. and Bolin, B. (2016) "Emerging Environmental Justice Issues in Nuclear Power and Radioactive Contamination," *International Journal of Environmental Research and Public Health* 13(7): 700.

L'Orange Seigo, S., Dohle, S. and Siegrist, M. (2014) "Public Perception of Carbon Capture and Storage (CCS): A Review," *Renewable and Sustainable Energy Reviews* 38: 848–863.

McGeer, V. (2008) "Trust, Hope, and Empowerment," *Australasian Journal of Philosophy* 86(2): 237–254.

Meijnders, A., Midden, C., Olofsson, A., Öhman, S., Matthes, J., Bondarenko, O., Gutteling, J. and Rusanen, M. (2009) "The Role of Similarity Cues in the Development of Trust in Sources of Information about GM Food," *Risk Analysis*, 29(8): 1116–1128.

Milgram, S. (1967) "The Small World Problem," *Psychology Today* 1(1): 60–67.

Nietzsche, F. (1874 / 1997) *Untimely Meditations*, R.J. Hollingdale (trans.), D. Breazeale (ed.), Cambridge: Cambridge University Press.

Pettit, P. (1995) "The Cunning of Trust," *Philosophy and Public Affairs* 24(3): 202–225.

Plumer, B. (2016, November 29) "The Battle over the Dakota Access Pipeline, Explained." Vox. www.vox.com/2016/9/9/12862958/dakota-access-pipeline-fight

Porsius, J.T., Claassen, L., Weijland, P.E. and Timmermands, D.R.T. (2016) "'They Give You Lots of Information, but Ignore What It's Really About': Residents Experiences with the Planned Introduction of a New High-Voltage Power Line," *Journal of Environmental Planning and Management* 59(8): 1495–1512.

Potter, N. (2002) *How Can I be Trusted? A Virtue Theory of Trustworthiness*, Lanham, MD: Rowman & Littlefield.

Siegrist, M., Cvetkovich, G. and Roth, C. (2000) "Salient Value Similarity, Social Trust, and Risk/Benefit Perception," *Risk Analysis* 20(3), 353–362.

Surowiecki, J. (2005) *The Wisdom of Crowds*, New York: Anchor.

Ter Mors, E., Weenig, M.W.H., Ellemers, N. and Daamen, D.D.L. (2010) "Effective Communication about Complex Environmental Issues: Perceived Quality of Information about Carbon Dioxide Capture and Storage (CCS) Depends on Stakeholder Collaboration," *Journal of Environmental Psychology* 30: 347–357.

Terwel, B.W., Harinck, F., Ellemers, N. and Daamen, D.D.L. (2009) "How Organizational Motives and Communications Affect Public Trust in Organizations: The Case of Carbon Dioxide Capture and Storage," *Journal of Environmental Psychology* 29(2): 290–299.

Terwel, B.W., Harinck, F., Ellemers, N., and Daamen, D.D.L. (2010) "Voice in Political Decision-Making: The Effect of Group Voice on Perceived Trustworthiness of Decision Makers and Subsequent Acceptance of Decisions," *Journal of Experimental Psychology: Applied* 16(2): 173–186.

Townley, C. and Garfield, J. (2013) "Public Trust," in P. Makela and C. Townley (eds.), *Trust: Analytic and Applied Perspectives*, Amsterdam: Rodopi Press.
Wigley, D. and Shrader-Frechette, K. (1996) "Environmental Justice: A Louisiana Case Study," *Journal of Agricultural and Environmental Ethics* 9(1): 61–82.
Wylie, A. (2003) "Why Standpoint Matters," in R. Figueroa and S. Harding (eds.), *Science and Other Cultures: Issues in Philosophies of Science and Technology*, London: Routledge.

Further Reading

Alfano, M. (2016a) "The Topology of Communities of Trust," *Russian Sociological Review* 15(4): 30–56.
Baier, A. (1986) "Trust and Antitrust," *Ethics* 96: 231–160.
Bergmans, A. (2008) "Meaningful Communication among Experts and Affected Citizens on Risk: Challenge or Impossibility?" *Journal of Risk Research* 11(1–2): 175–193.
Dunbar, R. (2005) "Gossip in Evolutionary Perspective," *Review of General Psychology*8: 100–110.
Grasswick, H. (2017) "Feminist Responsibilism, Situationism, and the Complexities of the Virtue of Trustworthiness," in A. Fairweather and M. Alfano (eds.), *Epistemic Situationism*, Oxford: Oxford University Press.
Habermas, J. (1990) *Moral Consciousness and Communicative Action*, C. Lenhardt and S.W. Nicholsen (trans.), Cambridge, MA: MIT Press.
Jones, K. (2012) "Trustworthiness," *Ethics* 123(1): 61–85.
Krishnamurthy, M. (2015) "(White) Tyranny and the Democratic Value of Distrust," *The Monist*, 98(4): 391–406.

21
TRUST IN LAW

Triantafyllos Gkouvas and Patricia Mindus

Trust can be relevant for law under a variety of conceptual guises. Some basic empirical acquaintance with the operations of legal systems is sufficient to render visible the presence of issues of trust across the entire spectrum of legally relevant events. We might picture this spectrum as a continuum flanked by legal doctrine on one side and legal practice on the other side. Legal doctrine is a framework of rules and standards developed by courts and legal scholars which sets the terms for future resolution of cases in an area of law such as criminal or property law.[1] Legal practice, on the other hand, is the set of institutional roles (legislatures, courts, public administration), activities (procedures for the creation, application and enforcement of legal norms) and the products of those activities (constitutions, statutes, judicial precedents) which shape what we might call the "actuality" or "reality" of law as a perpetual activity.[2]

These two edges demarcate the space within which law in itself and in its relation to other concepts like trust can be theorized from a variety of viewpoints (doctrinal, philosophical, sociological, political, anthropological, historical, literary, etc.). The more a theory approximates the doctrinal edge of the legal spectrum the more committed it is to the theoretical viewpoint of a class of legal actors (judges, lawyers, legislators, etc.), whereas the closer it comes to the institutional side of legal practice the more receptive it is to extraneous methods and viewpoints.

An entry-type overview of the philosophically relevant dimensions of the relationship between trust and law should be answerable to two constraints introduced by this spectrum. First off, an important constraint regards the methodology of this chapter. Whereas the taxonomy of views on the legal relevance of trust should somehow reflect the spectral variety of theorizing about law it cannot be presented in a philosophically instructive way without registering the fact that there are competing conceptual guises under which law becomes subject to philosophical scrutiny. Different doctrinal and philosophical theories of law have incommensurable visions about the proper methodology of theorizing about law either as a distinct domain or in relation to other domains (e.g. ethics, politics, economics, literature, artificial intelligence) or concepts (e.g. justice, trust, coercion, responsibility, collective action).

A second constraint regards the theoretical commitments of this chapter with respect to the notion of trust. As will become evident in the ensuing exposition, theoretical accounts of the legal relevance of trust cannot emulate the definitional precision and metaphysical parsimony we encounter in contemporary refinements of the notions of trust and trustworthiness in moral philosophy, philosophical psychology and epistemology.[3] The legal doctrine-practice continuum is so wide that it is practically impossible to track a minimal common ground in the way in which legal theorists choose to *describe* trust as a topic of legal regulation, scrutiny or interest.

For reasons of expository clarity and reflective detachment, we shall, nonetheless, preface this chapter with a "framework" refinement of the notion of trust that invites competing depictions of its legal *relevance* without necessitating participation in more specific definitional disputes. We shall assume that in its core trust invites the adoption of a "participant" stance from which a particular combination of reactive attitudes[4] is deemed an appropriate response towards those we regard as responsible agents. This stance has two basic components: (a) a readiness on the part of the trustor to feel *betrayal* if let down,[5] and (b) the *normative expectation* of the trustor that the trustee will act not simply as the trustor assumes the trustee will act, but as the latter should act.[6] This *responsibility-based* conception of trust dovetails with a widely accepted understanding of the addressees of legal requirements as practically accountable for their satisfaction.

The chapter will be divided in four subsequent sections each outlining the most lucid elaborations of the legal relevance of trust by theories of law which, for a host of different reasons, associate, more or less explicitly, the participant perspective on trust with either one of the following four basic concepts of law: *sociological, doctrinal, taxonomic* and *aspirational*.[7] Each section will begin with a short exposition of each one of the four concepts of law followed by an analysis of the most informative samples of jurisprudential and doctrinal scholarship showcasing the legal relevance of trust.

21.1 Trust in the Sociological Concept of Law

The *sociological* concept of law is used by theories of law which purport to capture the identity criteria for classifying a social structure as a legal system. Traditionally, questions about whether Nazi law was really law or whether there can exist non-coercive legal systems fall in this conceptual domain. Disagreements featuring the use of this concept traditionally revolve around the descriptive or moral nature of the criteria that individuate a social structure as a legal system.[8] In other words, the emphasis in scholarship studying law as a sociological concept is placed on legal institutions as a metaphysically distinct subset of political institutions rather than on legal norms as the product of those institutions or on the application of these norms to particular cases.

For the sake of providing an instructive contrast this section samples out two sharply distinct jurisprudential responses to the question of whether and how trust interacts with law in its sociological conceptual guise. The first response is derived from Niklas Luhmann's systems-theoretic account of *law as an autopoietic system* which takes the common risk-mitigating role of trust and law to license the reduction of the modalities used by the former to the modalities of the latter in highly institutionalized contexts. The source of the second response is Scott Shapiro's *planning theory of law* which preserves a robust role for attitudes of trust and distrust in the context of interaction between legal institutional actors.

Niklas Luhmann's sociological understanding of law (Luhmann 2004) is an influential source of jurisprudential insights but also a major advancement of general social systems theory insofar as it marks a transition from an understanding of social structures as permeable by their environment to a theorization of social structures as cognitively open but normatively closed (namely, autopoietic) systems of communication. Law is such an autopoietic system alongside other equally autopoietic subsystems like economy, politics, science, education, the mass media, medical care, religion, art and family.[9] Legal systems are portrayed by Luhmann as self-describing in two important respects: (i) they are self-produced, namely, they generate their own operations and structures by virtue, again, of their own operations, and (ii) they are paradoxically[10] self-applying or normatively closed, namely, they cannot determine whether the disjunction between attributions of the properties of legality and illegality to communicative acts is itself legal or illegal.

For Luhmann one of the basic autopoietic functions of a legal system consists in "usurping" a central role that trust performs in extra-legal contexts, namely, that of mitigating the risks associated with failure to live up to voluntarily undertaken commitments and responsibilities. It does so by producing and stabilizing normative expectations[11] about the conduct of others as well as reflexive normative expectations *about* the normative expectations of others.[12] By formally typifying the communicative acts through which trust-based responsibility is undertaken, law operates as a more sophisticated medium of risk-mitigation rather than merely as a supplement of interpersonal trust. In Luhmann's words, "trust and law can remain closely congruent with one another only in very simple social systems" (Luhmann 2017:76) and, consequently, "[in] more complex social orders … it is inevitable for law and trust to become separate" (Luhmann 2017:77). Crucially, the differentiation between trust and law that Luhmann brings to the fore is a form of evolutionary, so to speak, succession between modalities of risk-mitigation occurring whenever a social structure acquires the shell of a proper legal system. At this point "[l]aw no longer gives any indication of the extent to which it developed out of conditions of trust" (ibid.) which means that it takes over a large portion of the responsibility-upholding task originally or primitively assumed by trust-based, pre-legal social structures.

Whereas legal autopoiesis presents itself as a substitute of trust in legally regulated contexts of upholding commitments to other persons, Scott Shapiro's positivist understanding of legal institutions as planning organizations vindicates the legal relevance of trust between the occupants of different legal offices as a ruling standard for adjudicating disputes between rival interpretive methodologies applied and defended by judges, lawyers and law professors. Adopting a critical stance towards the practical relevance of legal theory Shapiro deplores the fact that "in contrast to the important role that practicing lawyers attribute to trust relations when assessing interpretive method, the concept of trust almost never figures in philosophical discussions of legal interpretation" (Shapiro 2011:33).

In the context of operation of a legal system where exercises of supreme authority to enforce shared plans enjoy a general, irrebuttable presumption of validity the stakes of misusing and abusing power are extremely high. For this reason, the distribution of planning authority takes itself the form of a plan which, depending on where the designers of the system decide to repose their trust, reflects a decision about how to compensate for their lack of trust in the capacity of some legal officials to carry out certain tasks, as well as about how to capitalize on their trust towards other officials. For instance, it is possible that in the context of a particular political community constitutional lawmakers are distrustful of the judiciary's ability to engage in discretionary judgment about the common good or the trumping effect of individual rights on considerations of public interest. At the same time, the creators of that system's founding instrument may be positively disposed towards the competence of elected members of parliament to collectively specify policies aimed at promoting the common good or to determine permissible limitations on the exercise of individual rights.

In this regard, the norms produced in the context of constitutional and/or ordinary lawmaking will be plans aimed at solidifying an actual, historically embedded distribution of the benefits of institutional trust and the burdens of institutional distrust towards different official participants in the legal system. To this effect the system's institutional design will reflect this distribution in a variety of ways. As Shapiro notes, in such systems "authority is widely dispersed throughout the system, executive and judicial officers are forbidden from legislating, lengthy waiting times are set up before legislation can be passed, there are severe sanctions for abuse of discretion, statutes are set out in detailed codes with few open-ended standards, and so on" (ibid.).

Shapiro chooses to articulate this functional correlation between the background distribution of institutional trust and the content of legal norms in epistemic terms. *Because* the best theory of legal interpretation will be the one that manages to track the actual distribution of trust and distrust, "the more trustworthy a person is judged to be, the more interpretive discretion he or she is accorded; conversely, the less trusted one is in other parts of legal life, the less discretion one is allowed" (ibid.). It is precisely in the context of this understanding of the content of legal plans as structurally reflective of actual, historically embedded distributions of institutional trust and distrust that Shapiro chooses to label this distribution as a plan's and, concomitantly, a legal system's "economy of trust." Every legal plan presupposes an investment in the allocation of trust and distrust among institutional actors involved in different stages of the plan's "institutional life," namely, its formulation, adoption, modification, application and enforcement. The institutional constraints informing the use of legal plans become jurisprudentially visible in the context of arguing about the interpretive methodology that properly reflects a legal system's actual institutional arrangements.

21.2 Trust in the Doctrinal Concept of Law

The *doctrinal* concept of law is used by theories of law which purport to identify the facts in virtue of which propositions about the content of the law of a particular legal system are true. For Ronald Dworkin, who is credited with the coinage and substantive elaboration of this concept, the grounds of law include both normative facts about the justification of state coercion, as well as descriptive facts about legally relevant utterances, texts and mental states attributable to the activities of legal officials.

In the context of tracking the interaction between law and trust the appeal to the doctrinal concept of law can make intelligible a major aspect of this interaction, namely, those cases where trust itself becomes the *object* of legal regulation and, eventually, legal interpretation. This section will comprise a brief analysis of the philosophical foundations of fiduciary law as the main doctrinal area of law where trust is itself doctrinally elaborated. The "participant" understanding of trust as featured in doctrinal elaborations of fiduciary duties is philosophically relevant precisely because its legal regulation and interpretation is ultimately premised on concerns of trust-based responsibility.

Fiduciary law regulates relationships that are based on warranted trust whose breach operates as a source of legal responsibility. Examples of such relationships include relationships between partners, trustees and beneficiaries, agents and principals, directors and corporations, lawyers and clients, parents and children. As these typical cases indicate, the situations and contexts which give rise to fiduciary duties are so many that rarely do courts or legislation choose to provide a handbook definition of fiduciary relationships. In very general terms, such relationships may extend to every possible case in which reposing trust in one party results in an expansion of the normative powers or property of another party. For example, the fiduciary relationship of agency is a relationship resulting from the joint manifestation of consent by one person that another is entrusted to act on his behalf and subject to his control and of consent by the other person to act as entrusted.

Fiduciary relationships are marked by asymmetries of power which render the legal entrustment of action inherently risky. As Tamar Frankel notes,

> [the fiduciaries] may misappropriate the entrusted property or misuse the entrusted power or they will not perform the promised services adequately … In such situations, it is likely that the parties will not interact, unless the law intervenes to protect the interests of society in the provision of these services by meeting the needs of both parties or … by reducing the costs of the relationship to both parties.
>
> *(Frankel 2011:6)*

The normative standard by which such deviations are measured is a distinctly legal duty of loyalty whose breach operates as the ground for attributions of fiduciary liability. The legal duty of loyalty is the basic concept through which considerations of trustworthiness become doctrinally relevant.

Despite the fact that the duty of loyalty to a beneficiary is considered as a hallmark of fiduciary law there is little agreement about its core content. A leading conception of fiduciary loyalty (Miller 2011) holds that loyalty requires the avoidance of conflicts either between the pursuit of the fiduciary's self-interest and his duty to act for the benefit of the beneficiary or between the fiduciary's duty and the interest of third parties. A more demanding variant of the same approach treats the duty of loyalty as a duty of affirmative devotion of the fiduciary to the promotion of the beneficiary's best interests. A radical departure from the goodwill-based model of fiduciary duties is marked by the idea that, as Andrew Gold notes "it is possible to avoid any conflicts of interest or duty, and also to act with affirmative devotion toward another individual, and simultaneously to be disloyal because of a failure to be true" (Gold 2014:181).[13] To the extent that fiduciary loyalty is governed by the norm of being true to one's trust-based relationship with another person it would appear disloyal to lie to the beneficiary of that relationship, even if doing so would avoid a conflict of interest or amount to an affirmative promotion of the beneficiary's best interests.

Finally, the spectrum of doctrinal elaborations of fiduciary loyalty is wide enough to import interdisciplinary insights from comparative areas of legal theory, such as law and economics as well as from moral philosophy. Research in the former domain has suggested that forming a legally relevant trusting relationship amounts to concluding a bargain that purports to maximize the gain which the contracting parties (the fiduciary and the beneficiary) can divide (Easterbrook and Fischel 1993).[14] By sharp contrast, deontological ethics has also inspired the doctrinal elaboration of fiduciary loyalty in pretty much the opposite way by likening the duty of loyalty to a justice-based virtue, namely, a disposition to subordinate one's interests in favor of giving what is owed – in the morally relevant sense – to the addressee of fiduciary loyalty (Samet 2014). In the latter sense, a fiduciary duty of loyalty is in essence a moral duty whose legal relevance consists in the fact that it may be legitimately enforced by the state.

21.3 Trust in the Taxonomic Concept of Law

The *taxonomic* concept of law is used by theories of law which purport, among other things, to contrast the nature or essence of the legality of institutions and the norms they produce and enforce with the nature and the norms produced by other normative systems (e.g. religion or social morality). For instance, taxonomic positivists argue that moral principles or facts about value cannot be legally relevant in virtue of their content or status as moral entities. Taxonomic antipositivists, on the other hand, reject this claim mainly by way of advancing arguments about the essential normative function of law. Given the essentialist, so to speak, flavor of taxonomic jurisprudential disagreements, taxonomic accounts of the legal relevance of trust make the notion of trust part of the conditions for assessing or diagnosing the legality of norms.

This section will feature two representative variants of a taxonomic approach to the legal relevance of trust. The first variant belongs to Hans Lindahl's *phenomenological account of legality* (Lindahl 2013). On this account ascriptions of legality amount to ascriptions of a first-personal plural experience of the legal order as a collective self which is constituted by mutual normative expectations about who ought to do what, where and when. This phenomenological identification of the essence of being legal makes trust a basic condition of the possibility of joint action under the guise of a plurally experienced sense of selfhood. The second variant belongs to Mark Greenberg's *moral impact theory of law* (Greenberg 2014) which is grounded in a sharply different, analytic approach to lawmaking as a mode of changing, among other things, the morally relevant expectations about the conduct of members of a political community. Greenberg's analytic account of legality as moral impact reserves an important role for trust insofar as it closely associates changes in a legal system's norms with legislatively induced changes in public expectations about which courses of action will improve the moral situation of a political community.

Crucial to Lindahl's theory is the idea that law reveals itself to us in the process of our recognizing the spatiotemporal boundaries of a legal order as *our* boundaries, or equivalently, the boundaries of a jointly expressed normative order. Law as a jointly experienced normative order presupposes a sphere of legal validity within which the normative positions of different agents can be tracked only first-personally as coordinates in a system that operates on the basis of a distinction between "us" and "others" or "aliens." It is precisely in this phenomenally demarcated normative space where Lindahl locates the experience of "legality" as a commitment-upholding system of reciprocal normative expectations about what we ought to do together. This system operates on the basis of assuming a legally qualified variant of the participant stance that an ordinary trustor assumes vis-à-vis the trustee. Crucially, this stance is necessary to legitimate legally enforceable claims of responsibility. As members of such an order "[w]e are deemed to have reciprocal expectations as to what our joint action ought to be about, and we reciprocate in our behavior to the extent that each of our actions meets those expectations" (Lindahl 2013:228). Accordingly, illegal behavior can be rationalized as a temporary failure to meet those expectations and, for this reason, "rebuking or otherwise sanctioning whoever breaches normative expectations remains within the circle of reciprocity" (ibid.).

Whereas expectations in Lindahl's phenomenological account matter because the *subjective experience* of a collective self presupposes a set of shared expectations concerning what we jointly ought to do, Mark Greenberg's moral impact theory of law locates the jurisprudential relevance of responsibility-tracking expectations in their capacity to alter the requirements of morality conceived as an *objective normative reality*. Mark Greenberg's theory of law is a recent but rigorously debated critical response to available treatments of the normative relevance of the actions of legal institutions. Greenberg challenges the idea that the actions of legal institutions are the target of descriptive explanations or moral justification. Instead, he suggests that they are the source or, more accurately, the trigger of changes in what morality requires all things considered.

According to the moral impact theory of law, the actions of legal institutions are supposed to make the moral situation better by ensuring that the legal obligations they create provide morally compelling reasons for action. A major way of achieving this result is by changing public expectations as to which conduct will improve the moral situation of a political community. Greenberg refers to examples of how legislatures harness democratic considerations such that collectively reached agreements or decisions – even when they are seriously morally flawed – produce legal obligations to abide by their content.[15] The democratic process from which they have resulted *merits* the expectation that everyone will act conformably *because* it was reached in a procedurally fair way. Granted that properly induced public expectations about what others should do should not be betrayed, lawmakers and citizens alike assume the responsibility of seeing to it that these expectations will be upheld. Crucially, on Greenberg's account, the actions of legal institutions induce expectations worthy of validation not because the *authority*[16] of those institutions to perform these actions is worthy of our trust, but rather because their chosen way of trying to improve the moral situation is independently warranted by what morality requires all things considered.

Despite their sharply distinct methodologies, Lindahl's phenomenological account of legality and Greenberg's moral impact theory of law converge in their taxonomic approach to what makes governance by law worthy of our taking a participant stance towards the expectations it generates. In both cases trust bears the guise of a network of normative expectations which are taxonomically relevant[17] in the sense that they serve either as conditions of the possibility of a distinctly legal type of joint commitment (Lindahl's legal collective self) or as grounds of distinctly legal responsibilities of government towards its citizens and of citizens towards each other (Greenberg's expectationalist account of lawmaking).

21.4 Trust in the Aspirational Concept of Law

The *aspirational* concept of law is used by theories of law which either premise their analysis of legal rules or focus entirely on the rule of law as an ideal conception of governance by legal institutions. The rule of law is properly speaking a cluster of other formal principles and procedural values that bear upon the question of how a political community ought to be governed. The formal principles are usually encoded as properties of legal norms expressed by predicates like generality, clarity, publicity, stability and prospectivity. The procedural values govern the processes by which those norms are produced, applied and enforced as well as the design and function of the institutions tasked with these activities (i.e. legislatures, the judiciary and administrative agencies). On some contested accounts the rule of law also comprises certain substantive values such as the presumption of liberty and the protection of private property.

In this last section we shall forgo an otherwise illuminating exposition of the heritage of the idea of the rule of law as it has been built by the contributions of political philosophers spanning from the Greek and Roman antiquity and the early modern period to the European Enlightenment and the Federalist Papers.[18] Besides the lack of adequate space for an exegetical digression of this length the main reason for choosing to focus on the modern era is that the jurisprudential as opposed to the political and moral refinement of the concept of the rule of law is an achievement of the modern era. Partly as a result of the growing maturity of democratic legal systems in the 20th century and the global entrenchment of different variants of constitutionalism, the idea of the rule of law attracts the attention of contemporary legal philosophers mainly because it evokes a jurisprudentially and doctrinally challenging contrast with the idea of the rule *by* law, namely, the instrumental use of law as a means for achieving political ends.

The remainder of this last section will feature two partly complementary yet often conflated conceptions of the rule of law, one focusing on the proper degree of formality of legal norms and another focusing on adherence to fair procedures. Besides its obvious relevance for debates on the legitimacy of government, the distinction between the formal and procedural aspects of the rule of law lays bare a structural difference in the way we place trust in legal institutions.

The most lucidly analytic advocacy for the formal variant of the rule of law is owed to Lon Fuller's theory of law. In *The Morality of Law* (Fuller 1969) Fuller defends the idea that the rule of law does not directly require anything substantive such as the conferral of a particular type of liberty. Fuller advances the claim that the principles composing the rule of law make guidance by legal rules morally and rationally intelligible. The rule of law construed as constitutive of the intelligibility of legally compliant action requires that the state organize its activities in a properly predictable way, providing prior notice through the promulgation of general norms which will serve as the basis of their enforcement and will be applied even when departure from the public meaning of legal norms seems politically or morally beneficial. On the other hand, the procedural understanding of the rule of law requires not only that officials apply general rules to particular cases but, as Jeremy Waldron notes, "it requires application of the rules with all the care and attention to fairness that is signaled by ideals such as 'natural justice' and 'procedural due process'" (Waldron 2008:7–8). This variant of the rule of law has become associated with political ideals such as the separation of powers and the independence of the judiciary precisely because it focuses on obstructions of the work of institutions tasked with the application and enforcement of legal norms.

An instructive way to appreciate the value of keeping the two variants of the rule of law distinct is to track the precise way in which the placing of trust becomes legally relevant in each case. When legal institutions violate the rule of law in its formal guise their officials end up applying norms that do not correspond to the norms that have been made public to the citizens. In this case what is betrayed is the trust citizens are entitled to place in what will be reasonably expected of them. In this regard, trust in the formal aspect of the rule of law is *reflexive* in the sense that its subject matter is the participant stance of legal officials as exemplified by their expectation that citizens will act in a certain way because they are legally *obligated* to do so. When general legal rules are rendered immaterial (they are not applied and enforced), citizens are unable to effectively object to the use of state coercion on the basis of what they are warranted to expect with respect to the legal system's own expectations of them.

By sharp contrast, when legal institutions violate the rule of law in its procedural guise, official misconduct lies in the lack of impartial administration of general rules rather than in the non-existence or non-enforcement of general legal norms. In the latter case what is betrayed is the trust citizens are entitled to place with respect to their reasonably expected treatment by legal officials. When legal process is systematically violated citizens are unable to assume a participant perspective on the outcome of legal procedures precisely because they are prevented from having their voice properly heard in the courtroom or any other public hearing or proceeding. The distinct disvalue of violations of legal process becomes particularly visible in the operation of courts or quasi-adjudicative institutions where litigants are supposed to be given the opportunity to present their arguments and effectively object to transgressions of procedure by judges, public prosecutors and executive officers.

Whereas most of the time violations of formality are partly the result of violations of procedure, there is ample historical evidence for how the latter can occur apart from the former. Such incidents have been documented across glaringly different legal systems with varying records of adherence to rule of law principles (Tashima 2008). Failures to administer the law in an impartial, independent and non-arbitrary way are *ipso facto* breaches of trust in the capacity of legal institutions to act in a way that respects distinctly procedural rights such as the right to a hearing by an impartial and independent tribunal, the right to representation by a legal counsel, the right to advance legal argument about the weight of evidence and question witnesses as well as the right to a properly justified judicial ruling on the basis of the evidence adduced, the arguments presented and the legal rules applied.

21.5 Summary

We began with an exposition of how trust issues occur across a broad spectrum of legal incidences ranging from doctrinal concerns about the interpretation and application of legal norms to the performance of institutional roles within a legal system. We then distanced ourselves from this exposition, in search for a more committing view. Keeping track of the depth of disagreement about which *legal description* of trust ticks the majority of boxes associated with the theoretical standards by which we measure the doctrinal or philosophical rigor of a theory of law, we decided to treat the question of the *legal relevance* of trust as amenable to a minimal framework of common understanding: legally relevant trust, we assumed, necessitates the adoption of two "participant," reactive attitudes, namely, a sense of betrayal and normative expectation, precisely because, to use a well-known phrase by the famous American jurist Oliver Wendell Holmes, law is "a system for adjusting interpersonal relations, rather than a system for effectuating individual exercises of will" (Holmes 1899:419). By taking on board this responsibility-centered perspective we explored the reception of the notion of trust by theories of law that exemplify four alternative ways (sociological, doctrinal, taxonomic, aspirational) of conceptualizing law as a system of norms and institutions.

The "take-away," so to speak, message that we would like to impart is that, regardless of the degree of normative (political and/or moral) commitment evoked by conceptually irreconcilable theories of law, all theories remain uniformly answerable to the question of whether they adequately accommodate in their premises a representation of the addressees of legal requirements as responsible agents to whom interpersonal or official claims, demands or sanctions may be addressed. Taking this minimal assumption on board is sufficient to reveal the profound legal relevance of trust-conditional or trust-engendering relationships between institutional actors, between institutions and citizens as well as between private agents standing in legally consequential relations (contract, property, tort, etc.).

Notes

1 For an Anglo-American perspective see Tiller and Cross (2006); for a legal continental perspective see Peczenik (2001).

2 For a philosophical account of legal practices see MacCormick and Weinberger (1986) and Hart (1994).

3 For a dispositional account of trust see Potter (2002); for variants of the view that trustworthiness is a function of the attitudes of the trustor see Hardin (2002), Dasgupta (1988) and Jones (2012). Finally, for the view that the grounds of trustworthiness reside in the trustor's stance towards the trustee see Holton (1994) and Hieronymi (2008).

4 The term "reactive attitudes" was introduced by P.F. Strawson in an attempt to dissolve the so-called problem of determinism and responsibility. His argument is that our "reactive attitudes" towards others and ourselves, such as gratitude, anger, sympathy, resentment and betrayal are natural and not dependent on general metaphysical principles. Their presence, therefore, needs no philosophical corroboration, which is simply irrelevant to their existence or justification. His ensuing verdict is that between determinism and responsibility there can be no intelligible conflict (see Strawson 1962).

5 In this regard, trust should be distinguished from mere reliance that does not intrinsically entail vulnerability to betrayal. Richard Holton is the primary proponent of the trustor's "participant stance" (Holton 1994). This view has recently been adopted by Pamela Hieronymi as a template for testing her own theory about what tracks the wrong kind of reasons for trusting (Hieronymi 2008).

6 The second component is elaborated in greater detail by Margaret Urban Walker and Karen Jones (Walker 2006:79ff.; Jones 2012).

7 This segmentation is based on the more general division articulated by Ronald Dworkin (Dworkin 2006:223–240). A point of caution is that the conceptual vocabulary introduced here is not meant to cast Dworkin's theory in a favorable light for two distinct reasons; firstly, we do not aim to present one concept of law as more pivotal than the rest and, secondly, our illustrative use of Dworkin's suggested concepts does not strictly correspond to how Dworkin himself would prefer to allocate these concepts across the spectrum of jurisprudential disagreement about the proper philosophical status of law.

8 The spectrum of disagreement about the application of the sociological concept of law is long enough to feature views ranging from a wholehearted espousal of a naturalistic epistemology that severely limits the role of *a priori* conceptual analysis in law to indirectly evaluative theories that aspire to make a case for a morally neutral legal theory that is nonetheless informed by non-moral, evaluative considerations.

9 Different autopoietic systems are bound to interact through the interpenetration of their respective operations; see Luhmann (1992).

10 All autopoietic systems apply their own respective codes, namely, a disjunction between two opposed values, such as true/false for scientific systems and legal/illegal for legal systems, on which all meaningful communication within a system is based. Disjunctions of this sort cannot determine their own scientific, political, religious or, in our case, legal relevance thus rendering decision-making within such systems inherently inconclusive or subject to external contestation. For a critical overview of Luhmann's autopoietic account of legal systems; see Baxter (2013).

11 While commenting on the role of contract in law Luhmann notes that "[t]he legal institution of the contract formed purely through the concurrence of the parties' declared wills entails a technical reformulation of the principle of trust in terms of law which makes it too independent for trust to play a role either as factual condition or as a ground for the validity of contracts" (Luhmann 2017:77).

12 Specific doctrinal areas of law may be also conducive to the generation of normative expectations about the due future conduct of state officials. A typical example is administrative law where the doctrine of legitimate expectations offers a systematic elaboration of the conditions under which a public body promising to exercise its discretion in some way, or its having a policy or engaging in a practice of doing so generates public expectations that merit legal protection. For an overview of the doctrine, see Ahmed and Perry (2014) and Brown (2017).

13 Gold partly associates this conception of the legal duty of loyalty as being true to a trust-based relationship with Joseph Raz's perfectionist take on the value of autonomy for political morality; see Raz (1986:354ff.).

14 For a recent reassessment, see Sitkoff (2011).

15 See Greenberg (2014:1312–1313).

16 The authority of legal institutions could be the direct object of our trust only if it were a variant of *epistemic* authority, namely, an authority to provide reasons for belief or other cognitive attitudes. In this case the exercise of legal authority is not practical, in the sense that it itself produces legal duties but only provides evidence as to the existence of rights and obligations that obtain not because legislative enactments make any normative difference to what we owe to one another or to the state, but because the actions of legal institutions reflect what practical normativity requires quite independently of what legal institutions do and say. For an epistemic account of legal authority see Hurd (1990, 1991).

17 Reasons of space prevent a longer digression into other taxonomic approaches to the legal relevance of trust. For instance, another promising perspective that takes trusting expectations to be constitutive of governance by law is discourse-theoretic focusing on the practice-based rationality of legal classifications of legitimate expectations. For an overview of such an argument, see Arnold (2017).

18 Bracketing important nuances in the elaboration of the concept of the rule of law by classical thinkers it is worth mentioning that traditional references to the legal-aspirational relevance of trust are directly reflective of the actual political concerns of the era. For instance, in *The Spirit of the Laws* Montesqieu regards as a failure of the rule of law any attempt to merge the doctrine of private law (mainly property) with the doctrine of public law (the State) on the grounds that such conflation is likely to result in the economically devastating betrayal of expectations regarding the rightful treatment of private property; see (Montesqieu 1989:61). In a work called *Principles of the Civil Code* Jeremy Bentham associates the goodness of laws with "their conformity to the general expectation". In this regard he cautions that a legal system that allows a systematic disappointment of the expectations it has power over becomes tyrannical (Bentham 1931:88).

References

Ahmed, F. and Perry, A. (2014) "The Coherence of the Doctrine of Legitimate Expectations," *Cambridge Law Journal* 73(1): 61–85.

Arnold, S. (2017) "Legitimate Expectations in the Realm of Law: Mutual Recognition, Justice as a Virtue and the Legitimacy of Expectations," *Moral Philosophy and Politics* 4(2): 257–281.

Baxter, H. (2013) "Niklas Luhmann's Theory of Autopoietic Legal Systems," *Annual Review of Law and Social Science* 9: 167–184.

Bentham, J. (1840/1931) *The Theory of Legislation*, C.K. Ogden (ed.), London: Kegan Paul, Trench, Trubner & Co.

Brown, A. (2017) "A Theory of Legitimate Expectations," *Journal of Political Philosophy* 25(4): 435–460.

Dasgupta, P. (1988) "Trust as a Commodity," in D. Gambetta (ed.), *Trust: Making and Breaking Cooperative Relations*, New York: Basil Blackwell.

Dworkin, R. (2006) *Justice in Robes*, Cambridge, MA: Belknap Press.

Easterbrook, F. and Fischel, D. (1993) "Contract and Fiduciary Duty," *Journal of Law & Economics* 36(2): 425–446.

Frankel, T. (2011) *Fiduciary Law*, New York: Oxford University Press.

Fuller, L. (1969) *The Morality of Law*, rev. ed, New Haven, CT: Yale University Press.

Gold, A. (2014) "The Loyalties of Fiduciary Law," in A. Gold and P. Miller (eds.), *Philosophical Foundations of Fiduciary Law*, Oxford: Oxford University Press.

Greenberg, M. (2014) "The Moral Impact Theory of Law," *Yale Law Journal* 123(5): 1288–1342.

Hardin, R. (2002) *Trust and Trustworthiness*, New York: Russell Sage Foundation.

Hart, H.L.A. (1994) *The Concept of Law*, 2nd edition, Oxford: Oxford University Press.

Hieronymi, P. (2008) "The Reasons of Trust," *Australasian Journal of Philosophy* 86(2): 213–236.

Holmes, O. (1899) "The Theory of Legal Interpretation," *Harvard Law Review* 12(1): 407–420.

Holton, R. (1994) "Deciding to Trust, Coming to Believe," *Australasian Journal of Philosophy* 72 (1): 63–76.

Hurd, H. (1990) "Sovereignty in Silence," *Yale Law Journal* 99(5): 945–1028.

Hurd, H. (1991) "Challenging Authority," *Yale Law Journal* 100(6): 1611–1677.

Jones, K. (2012) "Trustworthiness," *Ethics* 123(1): 61–85.

Lindahl, H. (2013) *Fault Lines of Globalization: Legal Order and the Politics of A-Legality*, Oxford: Oxford University Press.
Luhmann, N. (1992) "Operational Closure and Structural Coupling: The Differentiation of the Legal System," *Cardozo Law Review* 13:1419–1440.
Luhmann, N. (2004) *Law as a Social System*, K. Ziegert (trans.), F. Kastner and R. Nobles (eds.), Oxford: Oxford University Press.
Luhmann, N. (2017) *Trust and Power*, H. Davies, J. Raffan, K. Rooney (trans.), M. King and C. Morgner (eds.), Cambridge: Polity Press.
MacCormick, N. and Weinberger, O. (1986) *An Institutional Theory of Law: New Approaches to Legal Positivism*, Dordrecht: D. Reidel.
Miller, P. (2011) "A Theory of Fiduciary Liability," *McGill Law Journal* 56(2): 235–288.
Montesqieu, C. (1748/1989) *The Spirit of the Laws*, A. Cohler, C. Miller, and H. Stone (eds.), Cambridge: Cambridge University Press.
Peczenik, A. (2001) "A Theory of Legal Doctrine," *Ratio Juris* 14(1): 75–105.
Potter, N. (2002) *How Can I be Trusted? A Virtue Theory of Trustworthiness*, Lanham, MD: Rowman & Littlefield.
Raz, J. (1986) *The Morality of Freedom*, Oxford: Oxford University Press.
Samet, I. (2014) "Fiduciary Loyalty as Kantian Virtue," in A. Gold and P. Miller (eds.), *Philosophical Foundations of Fiduciary Law*, Oxford: Oxford University Press.
Shapiro, S. (2011) *Legality*, Cambridge: Belknap Press.
Sitkoff, R. (2011) "The Economic Structure of Fiduciary Law," *Boston University Law Review* 91: 1039–1049.
Strawson, P. (1962) *Freedom and Resentment and Other Essays*, London: Methuen.
Tashima, W. (2008) "The War on Terror and the Rule of Law," *Asian American Law Journal* 15: 245–265.
Tiller, E. and Cross, F. (2006) "What Is Legal Doctrine?" *Northwestern University Law Review* 100 (1): 517–534.
Waldron, J. (2008) "The Concept and Rule of Law," *Georgia Law Review* 43(1): 1–61.
Walker, M. (2006) *Moral Repair: Reconstructing Moral Relations after Wrongdoing*, Cambridge: Cambridge University Press.

22
TRUST IN ECONOMY

Marc A. Cohen

Diego Gambetta edited an early, often cited collection of essays, *Trust: Making and Breaking Cooperative Relations* (1988). In the foreword, Gambetta noted that trust is fundamental to our social relationships but it is not widely studied or well understood:

> The importance of trust pervades the most diverse situations where cooperation is at one and the same time a vital and fragile commodity: from marriage to economic development, from buying a second-hand car to international affairs, from the minutiae of social life to the continuation of life on earth. But … in the social sciences the importance of trust is often acknowledged but seldom examined, and scholars tend to mention it in passing, to allude to it as a fundamental ingredient or lubricant, an unavoidable dimension of social interaction, only to move on to deal with less intractable matters.
>
> *(Gambetta 1988:ix–x)*

Gambetta's volume, with chapters by sociologists and economists (and one chapter by philosopher Bernard Williams), was intended to fill that gap. And, in the almost 30 years since the book was published, research on trust has become something of an industry in the social sciences.

The present chapter outlines this social science literature on the role of trust in the economic system, focusing on four foundational works that have framed the discussion – Francis Fukuyama's book, *Trust: The Social Virtues and the Creation of Prosperity* (1995); Lynn G. Zucker's paper, "Production of Trust: Institutional Sources of Economic Structure, 1840–1920" (1986); the chapter "Relations of Trust" in James S. Coleman's book, *The Foundations of Social Theory* (1990); and Oliver Williamson's criticism of Coleman in his paper "Calculativeness, Trust, and Economic Organization" (1993). Two additional works – Karen S. Cook, Russel Hardin, and Margaret Levi's (2005) *Cooperation without Trust*? and Robert Axelrod's (2006 [1984]) *The Evolution of Cooperation* – are discussed briefly. And, connections with game theoretic (or experimental) approaches to trust are outlined in a note.

The material that follows emphasizes conceptual (philosophical) questions about what it means to trust and – given these conceptualizations – this material focuses on *how* trust between persons functions in the economic system.

As a starting point, note that Gambetta (1988:217) conceptualizes trust in terms of holding certain expectations:

> When we say we trust someone or say that someone is trustworthy, we implicitly mean that the probability that he will perform an action that is beneficial or at least not detrimental to us is high enough for us to consider engaging in some form of cooperation with him.

Trust so-conceived serves a certain function: individuals must interact with others to secure their own interests; interaction of this sort depends on having clear expectations about the others' behavior; we trust when we have positive expectations about that behavior (meaning, to trust is just to hold positive expectations, where "positive" means that the behavior will be beneficial, and where "positive" is not a reference to the other party's character) – and we can choose how to act depending on our level of trust in a given context.

This characterization of trust – as expectations about the trusted party's likely behavior – treats trust as a psychological attitude. I refer to it as the expectations-conception of trust. Others in the social science literature conceptualize trust as *a willingness to act* given positive expectations; schematically, when A trusts B to do x, A makes him- or herself vulnerable, or is willing to make him- or herself vulnerable, given expectations that the risks of this trusting action will not materialize, or on the basis of expectations that the risks are justified by the potential benefit (see, e.g. Mayer, Davis and Schoorman 1995; Kramer and Lewicki 2010). This willingness to act serves the same function and is also an expectations-conception of trust.

The literature in sociology tends to emphasize this function (or effect) of trust – facilitating cooperation. The economics literature sometimes emphasizes a different function of trust, that of reducing transaction costs (in that trust reduces or even eliminates the need for monitoring, contractual safeguards, etc.). The two lines of thought are very much compatible: trust can reduce transaction costs (with the economists) because trust amounts to holding positive expectations about future behavior (with the sociologists), making monitoring and contractual safeguards unnecessary. Across the two lines of thought, trust is a form of rational economic decision-making, or trust makes possible such decision-making, in situations that involve risk and vulnerability; it is economically and/or socially rational to trust when the potential benefit justifies the risk.

The material that follows outlines the four works mentioned above – Fukuyama, Zucker, Coleman and Williams – on their own terms, with their own respective conceptualizations of trust. But those conceptualizations are problematic (for the reason discussed in a moment), and so the material that follows also offers alternative readings – with reference to an alternative, moral account of trust – in order to make clear how trust changes (or what trust adds to) economic interaction.

The problem with the expectations-conception of trust is the following. When A trusts B to do x, and B doesn't do x, A will claim to be wronged, A is betrayed. This possibility of betrayal is an essential aspect of what it means to trust, a conceptual point first advanced in the academic literature by Annette Baier (1986).[1] And this conceptual point tracks our actual trust practices; when A trusts B to do x and B fails, A will say, "but I trusted you!" This protest rebukes B because B does something wrong in violating A's trust. But, if we apply Gambetta's definition, when A expects B to do x and B does not do x, B's actions are inconsistent with A's expectations. As a result A would be surprised. But A cannot claim to be wronged, there is no conceptual space to talk of betrayal. The problem is that A's holding expectations about B's actions does not give A any sort of right with respect to B's behavior, so on Gambetta's account (and on any account that identifies trust with expectations) there is no conceptual space for identifying a trust violation as involving betrayal. B does not do anything wrong in not acting as A expects. But, the critical argument is narrow. Trust relationships involve expectations, but expectations alone cannot account for the possibility of betrayal, hence A trusting B must involve more than A holding expectations about B's behavior. This problem extends to other conceptions of trust formulated in terms of beliefs, confidence and other epistemological states.

My own work has suggested an alternative account: when A trusts B to do x, A relies on B to do x because of a *commitment* on B's part to do x. For example, if A trusts B to pick up A's mail during a trip abroad (do x), that trust relationship is given structure by the commitment on B's part to do x – that commitment creates the obligation – one we cannot derive from general moral obligations on B's part to be honest, act with goodwill, or the like. We might think of a prototypical case in which B makes a promise to A and A relies on that explicit commitment, but in many cases the commitments involved could be implicit. Either way, because there is a commitment in place, B owes that action to A in the trust relationship, and this gives A standing to rebuke B if B fails (to use Margaret Gilbert's 2013 language) – and we can make sense of the possibility of betrayal in these terms. So, there is a moral dimension to trust on this conception, even though (as just mentioned) the obligations are not derived from or explained in terms of general moral ones. And, on this conception, to say that social interaction depends on trust is to say that social interaction relies on a network of commitments and obligations binding the persons involved.[2] The critical point here and this commitment conception of trust are defended in Cohen (2015) and in Cohen and Dienhart (2013), though note that the latter uses different terminology, referring to an "invitation conception of trust" to emphasize the *process* of one party inviting the other to participate in a trust relationship. The trust relationship itself is still given conceptual and moral structure by a commitment. Also note that the conceptual point here is agnostic as to the antecedents of trust; we will return to questions of antecedents in the material below.[3]

The preceding paragraph provides a conception of *particularized trust*, a trust relationship between two parties that concerns some specific action. We can conceptualize what is called *generalized trust* (typically between strangers) in analogous terms: A trusts B when A relies on B to fulfill some background moral obligation – where these background moral obligations could include the obligation to not deliberately or knowingly do harm to others, or an obligation to respect others' property and not steal, or a general obligation to be honest. These background moral obligations can be presupposed or assumed, they represent the terms of the social order, and so they do not have to be put into place by explicit, particular commitments. So, A could trust in this generalized sense by relying on B's commitment to be honest because that background moral obligation is in place (though we must note that talk of commitment in this sense is different from commitment in the sense of really-meaning-to-do-it, B might be committed to being honest in the first sense even though B is a persistent liar).

Again, then, the material that follows will use these alternative, moral accounts of particularized and generalized trust to offer alternative readings of the four works mentioned above – in order to make clear how trust changes (or what trust adds to) economic interaction.

22.1 Fukuyama and the Need for Trust

Fukuyama's book claims that, "a nation's [economic] well-being, as well as its ability to compete, is conditioned by a single, pervasive cultural characteristic: the level of trust inherent in the society" (1995:7). The claim is strong; Fukuyama suggests that an economic system depends on – *requires* – trust because the presence of trust allows for more and deeper cooperation, fosters better outcomes across participants, and fulfills a human need for social connection with others.

Fukuyama compares the economic systems of China and Japan, noting – writing in 1995 – that the Japanese form large, inter-connected business networks called *keiretsu*; member corporations share technology and they trade with one another on preferential terms given shared interests (and cross-ownership of member corporation stock) – all of which is spontaneous (or bottom-up in the sense of not instituted by the government), and all of which depends on trust. In contrast, economic development in China was limited by the Chinese (cultural) difficulty in trusting persons outside of the family; because outside employees are not trusted, Chinese businesses have great difficulty making the transition to professional management (they are reluctant to hire outsiders), and Chinese businesses struggle to accumulate capital and grow.[4] As a result, Fukuyama observes, the Chinese could only create large firms, themselves able to make significant investments in capital and technology, with government support (30). Even with this government involvement in China, the difference in trust practices explains the difference in prosperity across the two countries. He makes a similar set of points comparing Germany (a high trust country) with Italy (another low trust country).[5] His observations about those four economic systems are part of his wider and very thought-provoking discussion.

Fukuyama's observation, that government involvement could sustain economic growth, seems to be evidence against his own hypothesis: despite the lack of trust in Chinese society, economic growth and development are possible; extraordinary growth and development have occurred in China since Fukuyama's book was published in 1995 – relying on effective institutional support despite low levels of trust. We will return to this point, about institutional support for economic systems in the absence of trust, in the discussion of Zucker's work in the next section.

Fukuyama's book is often cited (with approval) in the social science literature as documenting the importance of trust in the economic context. And, as mentioned, Fukuyama argues that he can explain differences in prosperity across countries on the basis of the level of trust present. But the empirical data is ambiguous, in part because the U.S. economy has grown in the last 30 years despite declining levels of trust (see Nannested 2008:429).

Separate from Fukuyama's claim about the economic and social consequences of trust, Fukuyama is operating with a conceptualization of trust that differs from the expectations-conception outlined above. In particular, for Fukuyama trust is a moral relationship between persons, or at least a moral phenomenon – so the claim that the economic system depends on trust is at the same time, for Fukuyama, the assertion that the economic order depends on some moral foundation or on virtue. This assertion is made clear in Fukuyama's text and even in the reference to virtue in the subtitle of his book, i.e. "*The social* virtues *and the creation of prosperity.*" But this moral dimension of Fukuyama's project, and also his particular conceptualization of trust, are largely ignored in the social science literature – the literature that accepts and cites Fukuyama's claims about the role of trust in the economic system.

Fukuyama defines trust as follows: "the expectation that arises within a community of regular, honest and cooperative behavior, based on commonly shared norms, on the part of other members of that community" (1995:26). This way of thinking about trust seems close to Gambetta, above, because Fukuyama is making reference to expectations. But, for Fukuyama, trust concerns expectations about background moral obligations, such as a commitment to be honest, where, for Gambetta, trust concerns particular actions, e.g. a corporation expecting and therefore trusting another to deliver a product on a certain day at a certain price. So, we could take Fukuyama to be referring to generalized trust as characterized above, when A relies on B to fulfill background moral obligations. And, we could take Fukuyama to claim this: commitment to certain background moral obligations makes it possible for persons to rely on one another with less risk, and in that way trust supports economic exchange. While Fukuyama's focus is only on the economic system, we could extend the point to all social interactions. On this reading, trust is a *product* of shared norms about reciprocity, moral obligation and duty toward community. Trust is the mechanism by which those norms come to play a role in economic exchange – norms "including honesty, reliability, cooperativeness, and a sense of duty to others" (1995:43, 46).

The last of these norms, a sense of duty toward others, runs through all of Fukuyama's examples. Consider the following one:

> In the Toyota Motor Company's Takaoka assembly plant, any of the thousands of assembly line workers who work there can bring the entire plant to a halt by pulling on a cord at his or her workstation. They seldom do. By contrast, workers at the great Ford auto plants like Highland Park or River Rouge – plants that virtually defined the nature of modern industrial production for three generations – were never trusted with this kind of power. Today, Ford workers, having adopted Japanese techniques, are trusted with similar powers, and have greater control over their workplace.
>
> *(Fukuyama 1995:8)*

According to Fukuyama, this shows that "economic actors supported one another because they believed that they formed a community based on mutual trust" (8). Here, when workers trust one another and when management trusts factory workers, they all rely on others' shared commitment to economic outcomes measured at the level of the overall community, even where that comes at the expense of self-interest. This shared commitment shapes their behavior, it is this sense of duty to one another that supports economic growth and prosperity. As Fukuyama puts it:

> Solidarity within the economic community in question may have had beneficial consequences over the long run for the bottom line ... But the reason that these economic actors [factory workers and management in his examples] behaved as they did was not necessarily because they had calculated these economic consequences in advance; rather, solidarity within their economic community had become an end in itself. Each was motivated, in other words, by something broader than individual self-interest.
>
> *(Fukuyama 1995:9)*

(See also Shook 2010 for confirmation of the positive effects of a trusting organizational culture in a manufacturing setting.)

The same line of thought applies to the other virtues Fukuyama mentions, honesty and reliability. Fukuyama notes,

> In many preindustrial societies, one cannot take for granted that businessmen will show up for meetings on time, that earnings will not immediately be siphoned off and spent by family and friends, rather than reinvested, or that state funds for infrastructure development will not be pocketed by the officials distributing it.
>
> *(Fukuyama 1995:45–46)*

And concerning "cooperativeness" – or what F.A. Hayek (1973) called "spontaneous sociability" – Fukuyama writes, "a distinct portion of human capital has to do with people's ability to associate with each other, that is critical not only to economic life but to virtually every other aspect of social existence as well" (Fukuyama 1995:10).

This way of understanding Fukuyama – in terms of generalized trust, conceptualized as reliance on background moral commitments – captures his point about there being a moral foundation underlying the economic order. But this way of understanding Fukuyama's project shifts the focus somewhat, away from trust and towards the underlying moral commitments, the "virtues" in Fukuyama's terms, which support and stabilize economic exchanges.[6]

22.2 Zucker's Macro Perspective: Sources of Trust in the Economic System

Zucker's (1986) paper is concerned with the foundations of (or the grounds for) one individual trusting another; so her goal is to explain the sources of trust, to explain how trust comes to exist, rather than using trust to explain other phenomena (Zucker 1986:59–60).

She suggests that trust can be "produced" (i) by *personal characteristics* (such as family, group, or ethnic identity), (ii) by *process* (meaning that the relevant expectations can be based on reputation or *past experience* with the transaction partner), or (iii) by *institutional structures* (such as the legal system, other such structures are discussed below).[7] In the pre-modern economic system (prior to 1840 in the United States), trust was grounded on the first two, on personal characteristics or process. So, for example, A might trust B because they are neighbors or because they are members of the same organization (shared personal characteristics), or A might trust B because A has worked with B a number of times in the past (process).

But, according to Zucker, as the economy industrialized and became more complex, trust could no longer be produced by personal characteristics or process. In particular, economic exchange crossed group boundaries (including boundaries with considerable social distance), crossed geographic boundaries (so exchange partners do not otherwise encounter one another), and exchange became part of a more complex system of interdependencies (with integrated supply chains, so that disruptions at one point would have cascading effects). As a result, transaction partners no longer share personal characteristics (so we cannot rely on those characteristics to form positive expectations), and they also lack personal experience with each other (so process cannot support positive expectations); across both categories, we may not even be able to identify our transaction partners. For this reason, the economic order was "reconstructed" or, put another way, the economic order had to be reconstructed, and specific institutions were created to provide an alternative source of trust. In particular,

- "rational bureaucratic structures were adopted to provide written rules and a formal hierarchy that produced trust between employers and employees";
- "professional certification became widespread, with credentialing replacing informal 'reputation'";
- "a distinctive economic sector … arose to bridge transactions between firms and between individuals and firms. This sector includes banking, insurance, government, real estate, and legal services"; and
- "regulation and legislation established a common framework, including general expectations and specific rules governing transactions" (Zucker 1986:55).

These institutions could provide grounds for forming positive expectations and – on that basis – these institutions make trust relationships possible.

Zucker's project explains the development of new and different trust practices as the American economic system evolved (meaning, trust on the basis of a new and different kind of antecedent). And her distinction between modes of trust production provides a framework for addressing further questions: What institutions are needed to sustain trust across national borders in the (now) more global economic system? What institutions support trust in the digital economy? How do the relevant institutions vary across cultures?

Two further points are important in the present context. *First*, Zucker defines trust as "a set of expectations shared by all those involved in an exchange" (Zucker 1986:54) and her project concerns the grounds for holding such expectations. This definition is consistent with the social science conceptualizations of trust. Yet, as noted before, defining trust merely with reference to expectations cannot explain the phenomenon of betrayal. Moreover, on Zucker's definition, trust actually does no work in the economic system. If "trust" is merely a label for expectations, we can reformulate her account in terms of the factors that give transaction partners *confidence* that they will not be exploited in transactions, *confidence* that their vulnerabilities will not be taken advantage of in transactions, and/or *confidence* that those vulnerabilities can be managed. To emphasize, Zucker is not saying that we trust because we are confident about the actions of the trusted party, she reduces trust to confidence – she identifies the two.

Reformulating Zucker's point in terms of confidence – which offers the most accurate reading of her paper on her terms, using her own conceptualization of trust – Zucker's point is that a new set of social factors, institutional factors, were needed to sustain confidence among persons as the economy became more complex. Confidence could no longer be based on personal characteristics or past history with a transaction partner.

There is no loss in content in making this reformulation of Zucker, because there is no sense in which a transaction that depends on trust (as she defines it) is any different from a transaction that doesn't depend on trust: all economic exchange depends on the transaction parties' expectations about their partners, and when those parties are confident that the potential benefits justify the likely risks, they will interact. Talk of trust is therefore, for Zucker, only an indirect way to refer to confidence in the sense just described. Further, in the context of Zucker's work, talk of trust as expectations *should* be replaced by talk of confidence, because using the term "trust" in this context is misleading: talk of trust suggests that moral factors (or at least non-economic factors) play some role in the economic order, or at least that there is some moral dimension in the market, which is why trust is such an interesting concept. But these moral connotations play no role on the explicit definitions offered, and the expectations-conception of trust cannot accommodate our intuitions about the moral dimension of trust. We will return to this line of thought in the context of Williamson's paper in the next section.

Second, alternatively, we could reformulate Zucker's project and take her to address the foundations for trust on the commitment conception outlined above. This would avoid the criticism just presented (that talk of trust adds nothing, trust so-conceived is just an indirect reference to the economic behavior or economic considerations already present in economic exchange). Accordingly, we could take Zucker to suggest that – in the pre-modern economy – individuals relied on personal characteristics and/or past experience with transaction partners in order to determine when to rely on those transaction partners' commitments and, in doing so, to determine when to trust. But as the economic order became more complex, transactions became impersonal, and in that context we cannot make sense of personal trust – because we cannot talk of specific commitments and obligations binding persons who are not in a relationship with one another. Instead, then, transaction partners came to rely on institutions to define and/or enforce the terms of transactions; this made it possible for transaction partners to interact but it eliminated the role of trust. One important qualification: there could be personal relationships among some transaction partners in the modern, industrialized economic system, and so there could be trust relationships (on the commitment conception) between economic agents, and trust could offer benefits for economic agents and organizations. The point here (on this re-casting of Zucker) is that personal trust relationships could not be widespread enough for trust to provide a *systematic* foundation (across transactions) for stable economic system.[8]

Cook, Hardin and Levi (2005) very much follow Zucker understood in this second way; they argue that the modern economy is both too complex and too impersonal for trust to play a central role.[9]

This point, with Zucker and also with Cook, Hardin and Levi – the possibility of widespread cooperation in the economic system without trust – might be surprising, but as Peter Nannested notes (2008:428), and as mentioned earlier, there is little and conflicting data supporting the claim that trust is essential. And the negative conclusion drawn here (on the basis of conceptual argument), that trust is not essential, could explain why there is conflicting data on the need for trust to sustain cooperation and economic growth.

To make this idea less abstract, consider the following schematic example. In the pre-modern order, one might lend money to another knowing the borrower and/or knowing about the borrower's work history; given those foundations one could trust, meaning that one could lend money relying on the borrower's commitment to repay. But banks now lend money to strangers on the basis of credit reports (data about the borrower's credit history), with contracts and a legal system that provide clear legal remedies for default. Bank loans so-conceived have nothing to do with trust; trust is unnecessary within an economic system supported by social institutions that enforce contracts. A further example: we buy prescription medicine at pharmacies from employees we do not know, manufactured in factories we cannot identify, using raw materials we cannot trace, that were approved though a set of clinical trials conducted by strangers, etc. This whole process depends on our having confidence in the institutional framework within which this very complex transaction takes place. There is no reason to talk of trust here.[10]

In short, then, given Zucker's own conception of trust as expectations, talk of trust adds nothing to the mechanics of economic transactions. Given that conception, Zucker is merely documenting the changing social factors that support economic decision-making. If, however, we re-cast her paper using the moral conception of trust outlined above, we can take her to be presenting a different social history: pre-modern economic interaction depended on trust but then, as the economy modernized, transactions came to depend on institutional support rather than trust. Understood in this second way, Zucker is not arguing that trust can play no role in the modern economic system, but she is suggesting that trust is not essential.

Axelrod (2006 [1984]) adds an important dimension here, showing that a society of the sort just described – an economic system that does not rely on trust – makes conceptual sense. In particular, using repeated prisoner's dilemma games, Axelrod showed that persons who pursue their own interest can cooperate without some central authority regulating the process or outcome. And in particular, one important factor discourages individuals from acting opportunistically (and defecting): doing so would bring sanctions in future interactions: the threat of punishment maintains communal norms of cooperativeness. As Axelrod puts it, "The foundation of cooperation is not really trust, but the durability of the relationship" (182). This comment could come as a surprise, because Axelrod is sometimes cited in support of the view that the social order or economic interaction depends on trust – but Axelrod claims nothing of the sort. So, where Zucker's account concerns the evidence that persons need to interact with some level of confidence, Axelrod suggests that other factors – social sanction in particular – could protect transaction partners by discouraging behavior that exploits vulnerability, and in that way help sustain an economic order that depends on confident interactions without trust.

To make the point from Axelrod more concrete, consider the following (true) story: Before working full-time as a professor, I managed a commercial middle-market loan portfolio for an American superregional bank. Over lunch I suggested (though not seriously), to the bank's senior credit/risk officer and also to another senior lender, that the bank make 20 loans without documentation as a philosophical experiment: we could determine whether the bank's clients repay their loans because it is the right thing to do (borrowers make a commitment to repay and the bank lends funds relying on that commitment), or because loan documents give the bank access to collateral – including (sometimes) personal collateral tied to business loans – which essentially forces clients to repay. The experiment offered, I suggested, a rare opportunity to settle a philosophical question about the role of trust and moral obligation empirically, an opportunity we should not pass up. But the senior lender rejected the experiment: he suggested that clients repay the bank because they will need to borrow again, and defaulting would close off access to bank capital in the future. Here the senior lender (essentially) defended Robert Axelrod's position, quoted immediately above: "The foundation of cooperation is not really trust [or moral considerations], but the durability of the relationship."

22.3 The Micro Perspective: Trust and Individual Economic Behavior, according to Coleman and Williamson

James Coleman's (1990) discussion of trust revolves around a set of examples, one of which is the following (which Coleman takes from Wechsberg 1966): a ship-owner needed repairs made at an Amsterdam shipyard; he needed funds to pay for these repairs; and a merchant banker in London agreed to lend the money without a contract and without paper documentation. According to Coleman (1990:92),

> The case clearly involves trust. The manager of the Norwegian department at Hambros [the London merchant bank] placed trust in the Norwegian shipowner who telephoned him – trust to the extent of £200,000 of Hambros's money. There was no contract signed, no paper involved in the transaction, nothing more substantial than the shipowner's intention to repay the money and the Hambros man's belief in both the shipowner's honesty and his ability to repay.

Here Coleman follows Gambetta's line of thought, though without referencing him, and offers a purely economic account. Coleman argues that the merchant banker provided the funds because the potential benefit to the banker justified the risk (the possible loss). According to Coleman,

> If the *chance of winning*, relative to the *chance of losing*, is greater than the *amount that would be lost* (if he loses), relative to the *amount that would be won* (if he wins), then by placing the bet he [the trustor] has an expected gain; and if he is rational, he should place it. This simple expression is based on the postulate of maximization of utility under risk.
>
> *(1990:99)*

So, where Gambetta defines trust in terms of subjective probabilities, Coleman defines trust as an action – as a "bet" made on the basis of those probabilities.[11]

Oliver Williamson (1993) accepts Coleman's calculative explanation of the transaction in this example: the loan was made because the London bank "had the most knowledge of the shipowner and the best prospect for future business" (Williamson 1993:470). Williamson thinks there are two ways to *explain* why the banker lent money to the ship-owner: the banker determined that the potential benefit justified the risks and made an economic decision, or the banker trusted the ship-owner. Trust and calculation are competing explanations for the banker's action. So, given that the bank made a calculative/economic decision, Williamson argues that Coleman's talk of trust is redundant: the banker's rationale was purely economic, "calculativeness [economic reasoning] is determinative throughout and ... invoking trust merely muddies the waters" (Williamson 1993:471).[12]

But we must distinguish two distinct points that run together in Williamson's paper.[13]

First, Williamson notes that across the social science literature, trust is defined "as a subclass of [situations] involving risk," "trust" refers to "situations in which the risk one takes depends on the performance of another actor" (Williamson 1993:463; Williamson is quoting Gambetta 1988). Trust on this social science account is a calculative or economic relationship and, for this reason, using these definitions, references to trust add nothing to the calculative considerations that are already present. It is not even an alternative explanation. Moreover, talk of trust is misleading because it suggests that something other than calculative considerations are at work (given that our intuitive way of understanding trust is in non-calculative terms). This is the same critical point as made above in the context of Zucker's work regarding confidence.

Second, Williamson himself thinks that trust is, by definition, a non-calculative relationship, and as a result he considers "[c]alculative trust … a contradiction in terms" (Williamson 1993:463). Indeed, Williamson even argues that "calculativeness is inimical to personal [genuine] trust" (Williamson 1993:483). I argue that we should reject these two claims. The introductory material above outlined a commitment conception of trust distinct from the social science conceptions, which reduce trust to expectations, and also distinct from Coleman's account of trust as a bet. One could trust – on the commitment conception – on the basis of different kinds of antecedents: A might trust B because B is A's sister, or because A thinks we have a social obligation to trust others, or for emotional reasons, etc. And, against Williamson, one could trust (in a genuine sense, here understood in commitment terms) on the basis of calculative antecedents, meaning that trust is compatible with calculative considerations! Consider a schematic example: one business [A] could rely on another's [B's] commitment to deliver a product on a certain date on the basis of past experience (B's meeting deadlines in past transactions), anecdotal evidence (B's behavior in another context, such as B meeting deadlines with other customers), and/or B's identity (if, for example, B is owned by the same corporate parent). These antecedents are thoroughly calculative and, nevertheless, A could accept B's commitment – and thereby trust – on the basis of them. So, my view is that, *against Williamson*, calculative considerations can be compatible with trust as antecedents or grounds, but *with Williamson* trust is not a calculative relationship.

As mentioned, Williamson explains the Hambros banker's decision to lend money, and all economic activity, in terms of the "relentless application of calculative economic reasoning" (Williamson 1993:453). Talk of trust (in non-calculative terms) is not necessary. But note: here Williamson has only argued that he *could* model economic behavior in purely economic terms. Or, we might say that Williamson asserts a methodological premise, that the "relentless application of calculative economic reasoning" best accounts for the behavior of economic agents. The merchant banker example could plausibly be explained on his methodological assumption. But nothing Williamson says closes off the possibility of a banker trusting a customer, with trust characterized in commitment terms, with or without calculative antecedents. To be sure, we should (probably) be skeptical when bankers talk of trust, and maybe some transactions that look like trust are actually bets – this is a question of the trusting parties actual psychological states. My point here is that the economic context does not rule out the possibility of genuine trust (on the commitment conception).

Finally, Williamson explains his underlying concern in surprising terms. He writes,

> The world of commerce is reorganized in favor of the cynics when social scientists employ user-friendly language that is not descriptively accurate – since only the innocents are taken in. Commercial contracting will be better served [meaning that individual interests will be better protected] if parties are cognizant of the embeddedness conditions of which they are part and recognize, mitigate, and price out contractual hazards in a discriminating way.
>
> *(Williamson 1993:485)*

Restated, Williams worries that "innocents" will be misled by businesses' use of the term trust, these "innocents" will think they are in trust relationships in the economic context – and as a result they will be exploited. To prevent this, Williamson wants us to be clear: talk of personal trust – "if it obtains at all" (484) – should be restricted to close relationships between family members, friends and lovers.

Williamson expresses a further, related worry: some will not be able to "shed calculativeness in personal relationships because calculativeness (or fear) is so deeply etched by their (economic) experience" (Williamson 1993:484). Richard Craswell, in his (1993) response to Williamson, calls this sort of effect "spillover": "if we become so thoroughly calculative in most areas of life, calculative habits may become so "deeply etched" in our souls that we are unable to set those habits aside, even when we would like to do so in order to sustain a loving relationship" (Williamson 1993:497). So Craswell and Williamson worry that using "trust" as a label for calculative relationships could confuse us about what it means to trust, and this confusion could damage our close personal relationships – by encouraging us to think about those relationships in calculative terms. My own concern is the reverse: paraphrasing Craswell, if we think that we can only have calculative relationships in the economic context, and not genuine trust relationships, then calculative thinking will become too deeply etched in our souls, and we lose the possibility of trust relationships – we lose the moral dimension – in the economic context.

22.4 Conclusion, and Further Application

This chapter has outlined three central lines of thought about trust in economic systems and economic behavior: Francis Fukuyama's argument that economic systems depend on trust in a fundamental way; Lynn C. Zucker's account of the changing foundations (antecedents) for trust as the American economic system industrialized in the late 18th and early 19th centuries; and the dispute between James S. Coleman and Oliver Williamson about the nature of trust relationships. Underlying these lines of thought is the more fundamental question of how to conceptualize trust.

There is a separate – and now extensive – literature on the role of trust within and between business organizations (see, for example, the papers in Bachman and Zaheer's (2008) collection, *Landmark Papers on Trust*). Much of that work is written by academics in business schools and as a result it is very tactical, in the sense that it addresses questions about how to build and repair trust relationships in managerial contexts. But, in the present context it is worth outlining one deeper, intuitive point at stake.[14]

The dominant economic model of business organizations (the transaction cost theory of the firm) assumes that persons are self-interested and also that some persons are opportunistic (meaning that they would take advantage of opportunities to exploit others for their own benefit; think of employees who would avoid work when they can, or steal property from their own organizations). Given these assumptions, managers use incentives and sanctions to align individual employees' interests with those of the organization, e.g. – meaning that managers pay employees to do what they, the managers, want and punish those employees for doing otherwise. Moreover, managers monitor employees to prevent opportunistic behavior. Paraphrasing a prominent account, managers' goal is to attenuate human opportunism using hierarchical controls. This model of business organizations is ultimately rooted in Frederick Winslow Taylor's foundational work, *The Principles of Scientific Management*, which documented Taylor's success at improving productivity by offering higher pay for more work.

Many have criticized this way of understanding business organizations – on empirical, conceptual and ethical grounds. The alternative is to build organizations on the basis of trust. This alternative is not widely theorized but, relying on the commitment conception of trust described above, the goal of management is to build a network of interpersonal commitments and obligations binding employees, where these commitments and obligations can serve as the grounds for genuinely cooperative behavior. The advantages of an organization built on cooperative relationships are direct and have been confirmed in the management literature – such organizations, or even just parts of organizations managed in this way, are more productive, more innovative, and more satisfying for employees (again, see Shook 2010 for an example). None of that should come as a surprise, but much of management education and management practice follow the dominant line (about control) instead.

Much more remains to be said to draw out these intuitions. My goal here is only to provide a starting point for thinking about the role of trust within organizations, which is material that affects our working lives on a daily basis.

Notes

1 Note that Baier's account fails to meet her own requirement; see Cohen (2015:477–478). The critical point outlined in this paragraph in the main text applies to much of the philosophical literature as well – which widely conflates trust and expectations.
2 One important clarification about the meaning of "commitment" in the account of trust suggested in the main text: on that account, when A relies on B's commitment, A is not relying on B because of contractual protections that can coerce/compel B to act – including protections/remedies built into organizational structures, such as incentives that promote some behavior(s), and sanctions that punish other behavior(s). So the reference to commitment here is *not* a reference to contracts and is, indeed, antithetical to contracts.
3 Katherine Hawley (2014) later offered a parallel account of trust in terms of commitments.
4 See Fukuyama (1995:69–95); other social factors play a role as well, see (1995:89).
5 This claim about the Chinese in particular, and Confucian cultures in general, not trusting outside of the family has been controversial, in part because data from the World Values Survey shows that the Chinese trust at very high levels. China is considered to be a "collectivist" culture because of this survey-based data. In a recent paper, however, Delhey, Newton and Welzel (2011) address this conflict with additional survey questions and defend Fukuyama's claims about limited trust practices in China. For further discussion of trust in the Chinese context see Cohen (2020).
6 In this volume, see the chapter by Cook and Sanatana for further, though different, discussion of Fukuyama's project.
7 In this volume, see the chapter by Origgi on reputation; the chapter by Alfano and Huijts on trust in institutions; and also the chapter by Gkouvas and Mindus on trust in law – a key institution.
8 Alternatively, we could re-cast Zucker in a third way, arguing that the pre-modern economy depended on personal trust while the modern, impersonal economy came to depend on generalized trust (which is impersonal). This would align Zucker's project with Fukuyama's work.
9 Cook, Hardin and Levi (2005) rely on Hardin's own idiosyncratic definition of trust, what Hardin calls an "encapsulated model." Detailed discussion is outside the scope of this chapter, but that conception reduces trust to confidence; see the discussion of Williamson in the main text.
10 Some might object: even if we can make sense of social interaction in the way just described, with persons relying on social institutions to provide protection in markets and to enforce contracts (when necessary), that requires that persons trust the underlying institutions. But the reduction of trust to confidence applies at the level of systems as well: persons can interact with others with some level of confidence if they also have confidence that social and economic institutions will enforce contracts.
11 This view is consistent with Mayer, Davis and Schoorman (1995), though it emphasizes the action involved beyond the mere willingness to act.
12 Williamson's point raises a question for Tutić and Voss's chapter (in this volume) on game theoretic approaches to trust. That chapter – summarizing experimental approaches to trust – aims

to "explicate trust as a risky investment" (p. 186), grounded in Coleman's account of trust as a bet. Williamson, however, argues that *A trusting B to do x* is different from *A betting on B to do x*. If we accept Williamson's point – and we should – then Tutić and Voss must show that their subjects do trust as opposed to make bets. The critical point is especially pressing in light of experimental papers showing that other kinds of considerations are present in such experiments, considerations besides trust. For example, Pillutla et al. (2003) conducted a series of experiments like those described by Tutić and Voss; they found that trustees were concerned with making outcomes equal. Trustees, in their experiments, were not responding to having been trusted. If this is correct, then there is an alternative explanation in the experiments Tutić and Voss describe: when Tutić and Voss say that their first subject "trusts," that subject might – instead – be betting that the second subject will equalize outcomes. Their experiments might not be about trust.

13 The following section is taken from Cohen (2014); see also Moellering (2014) for further background.

14 The material that follows is taken from the last section of Cohen and Dienhart (2013), see the further references there.

References

Axelrod, R. (2006 [1984]) *The Evolution of Cooperation*, revised edition, Cambridge, MA: Basic Books.

Bachman, R. and Zaheer, A. (2008) *Landmark Papers on Trust*, Cheltenham, UK: Edward Elgar Publishers.

Baier, A. (1986) "Trust and Antitrust," *Ethics* 96: 231–260.

Cohen, M.A. (2014) "Genuine, Non-Calculative Trust with Calculative Antecedents: Reconsidering Williamson on Trust," *Journal of Trust Research* 4: 44–56.

Cohen, M.A. (2015) "Alternative Conceptions of Generalized Trust (and the Foundations of the Social Order," *Journal of Social Philosophy* 46: 463–478.

Cohen, M.A. (2020) "Generalized Trust in Taiwan and (as Evidence for) Hirschman's doux commerce Thesis," *Social Theory and Practice*. doi:10.5840/soctheorpract202021477

Cohen, M.A. and Dienhart, J. (2013) "Moral and Amoral Conceptions of Trust, with an Application in Organizational Ethics," *Journal of Business Ethics* 112: 1–13.

Coleman, J.S. (1990) *The Foundations of Social Theory*, Cambridge, MA: Harvard University Press.

Cook, K.S., Hardin, R. and Levi, M. (2005) *Cooperation without Trust?* Volume 9 in the Russell Sage Foundation Series on Trust, New York: Russell Sage Foundation.

Craswell, R. (1993) "On the Use of 'Trust': Comment on Williamson, 'Calculativeness, Trust, and Economic Organization,'" *The Journal of Law and Economics* 36: 486–500.

Delhey, J., Newton, K. and Welzel, C. (2011) "How General Is Trust in 'Most People'? Solving the Radius of Trust Problem," *American Sociological Review* 76: 786–807.

Fukuyama, F. (1995) *Trust: The Social Virtues and the Creation of Prosperity*, New York: The Free Press.

Gambetta, D. (1988) "Can We Trust Trust?" in D. Gambetta (ed.), *Trust: Making and Breaking Cooperative Relations*, New York: Basil Blackwell.

Gilbert, M. (2013) *Joint Commitment: How We Make the Social World*, Oxford: Oxford University Press.

Hawley, K. (2014) "Trust, Distrust, and Commitment," *Nous* 48: 1–20.

Hayek, F. (1973) *Law, Legislation and Liberty, Volume 1: Rules and Order*, Chicago: University of Chicago Press.

Kramer, R.M. and Lewicki, R.J. (2010) "Repairing and Enhancing Trust: Approaches to Reducing Organizational Trust Deficits," *The Academy of Management Annals* 4: 245–277.

Mayer, R.C., Davis, J.H. and Schoorman, F.D. (1995) "An Integrative Model of Organizational Trust," *Academy of Management Review* 20: 709–734.

Moellering, G. (2014) "Trust, Calculativeness, and Relationships: A Special Issue 20 Years after Williamson's Warning," *Journal of Trust Research* 4: 1–21.

Nannested, P. (2008) "What Have We Learned About Generalized Trust, If Anything?" *Annual Review of Political Science* 11: 413–436.

Pillutla, M.M., Malhotra, D. and Murnighan, K. (2003) "Attributions of Trust and the Calculus of Reciprocity," *Journal of Experimental Social Psychology* 39: 448–455.
Shook, J. (2010) "How to Change a Culture: Lessons from NUMMI," *MIT Sloan Management Review* (Winter): 63–68.
Wechsberg, J. (1966) *The Merchant Bankers*, Boston, MA: Little, Brown and Company.
Williamson, O.E. (1993) "Calculativeness, Trust, and Economic Organization," *Journal of Law and Economics* 36: 453–486.
Zucker, L.G. (1986) "Production of Trust: Institutional Sources of Economic Structure, 1840–1920," *Research into Organizational Behavior* 8: 53–111.

Further Reading

Axelrod, R. (2006[1984]). *The Evolution of Cooperation*, revised edition, Cambridge, MA: Basic Books. (Classic game theoretic study of human society.)
Cohen, M.A. and Dienhart, J. (2013). "Moral and Amoral Conceptions of Trust, with an Application in Organizational Ethics," *Journal of Business Ethics* 112: 1–13. (Distinguishes between moral and amoral approaches, aims to recover the moral dimension of trust in human relationships.)
Fukuyama, F. (1995) *Trust: The Social Virtues and the Creation of Prosperity*, New York: The Free Press. (Very influential work on the role of trust in economic activity.)
Gambetta, D. (1988) "Can We Trust Trust?" in D. Gambetta (ed.), *Trust: Making and Breaking Cooperative Relations*, New York: Basil Blackwell.
Shook, J. (2010) "How to Change a Culture: Lessons from NUMMI," *MIT Sloan Management Review* (Winter): 63–68. (Perhaps the best example of the positive effects of trust in business.)
Williamson, O.E. (1993) "Calculativeness, Trust, and Economic Organization," *Journal of Law and Economics* 36: 453–486. (Williamson's distinction between economic and trust-based explanations for economic activity.)

23

TRUST IN ARTIFICIAL AGENTS

Frances Grodzinsky, Keith Miller and Marty J. Wolf

23.1 Introduction

Work on trust and artificial agents done in the last 20 years offers us some interesting perspectives that we will explore in this chapter. Is trust likely – or even possible – when discussing interactions between a human (H) and an artificial agent (AA)? Is trust an issue among AAs themselves? Many of the earlier chapters highlight facets of trust such as intentionality, belief, hope and reliance, facets that come into to play when the trustor and the trustee are both humans, or in trust relationships that involve at least one person.

Some readers may object that trust involving AAs is not possible, since the aforementioned facets are (currently) not thought to be characteristics possessed by AAs. We take a different approach. The advent of the potential of something akin to human trust, if not human trust itself, arising with AAs, leads to deeper questions of how trust should be understood, modeled and perceived. In addition to AAs not possessing many of the traits that are often associated with traditional notions of trust in humans, AAs have qualities (such as quick, barely noticeable software updates) that are not present in humans. These can potentially influence any notion of trust involving AAs, especially as they pertain to interactions in cyberspace.

In this chapter, we briefly discuss important features of AAs and then highlight questions raised in Taddeo's (2009) paper "Defining Trust and E-trust: From Old Theories to New Problems." Next we outline developments in trust involving AAs starting with our object – oriented model of trust (Grodzinsky et al. 2010), Tavani's (2015) concept of diffuse trust, de Laat's (2016) co-active trust, and finally a phenomenological-social approach from Coeckelbergh (2014) that attends to the possibility that we do not always and perhaps not usually have full control over trusting or not trusting.

23.2 Artificial Agents

In the literature on AAs and trust, there is no standard definition of an AA. For the most part, this is not a problem. However, there is an important feature that one needs to bear in mind when considering trust and AAs. In general, an AA is a machine entity designed and constructed by people to run without direct human intervention for long periods (days, not seconds). Its design and construction allow an AA to change its internal state based on its interaction with the environment over time. When we talk about an AA changing its internal state, we are talking about changing the information it has recorded in its table (T) and that it is going to use to direct its next decision. This basic AA has the feature that if at some point in the future the AA has the same internal state, its next decision will be exactly the same as it was the last time it was in this internal state. Similarly, if we take a second copy of the AA and imbue it with the same internal state, it, too, will make the same next decision. A more advanced AA has a significant additional capability. It has the ability to change its own programming. One might suggest that it exhibits what we will call learning* (Grodzinsky et al. 2008).

23.3 Learning* in Artificial Agents

An exact definition of "learning" is controversial in several different disciplines, even when applied only to humans. We will define a new term, learning* to apply to AAs and demonstrate how it affects trust relationships.

The first type of AA learning uses the static-table model of the artificial agent as described in (Grodzinsky et al. 2008). We represent as T the table holding information that controls the AA. A new fact comes to the agent in the form of the input. The input, in combination with the current state of the AA, causes the agent to enter a new state. If the input is not represented in T, it is not integrated into T, though it may be communicated to the AA's owners or operators.

If a new fact is worth permanently noting (a decision made by the designer), the new state represents an entry point to an entire collection of states that represent, among other things, having learned the new fact. Information then gets added to the table T, which is reloaded into the AA. Subsequent behavior may be changed; however, the basic programming model, the code of the AA, does not change. Essentially the designer has included in the program a statement of the form "if you learn X, then produce this collection of outputs." Note that in this case, the designer[1] anticipates the entire universe of learnable facts for the agent (or adds them in updates). The careful designer, we assume, will never be surprised by what the agent learns. So in this case, the AA does *not* learn on its own.

A second type of learning is possible in a modifiable-table model. In this case, the AA is given the ability to modify the table T without direct intervention from a human developer, operator or owner. Instead, the AA "decides," on its own volition, to add information into T about an unanticipated input, and also generates an output. It is a crucial difference that the AA can do this change in real time, changing its future behavior.

The special case of neural net computing is illustrative here. Neural net computers are modeled loosely on a simplified conception of interconnected neurons in the human brain. A network of these simplified artificial neurons is given an initial set of weights for each neuron and an initial set of connections between the neurons. A process called "training" during which inputs are presented to the neural net adjusts the weights and connections, and the resulting outputs from the neural net are examined. Either a human or an algorithm including a function of merit is used to distinguish "better" outputs from "worse" outputs, and the weights and connections are adjusted to favor "better" outcomes. This process is repeated often, and the aim is for the neural net to converge to a configuration that gives "good" outputs for future, perhaps unanticipated sets of inputs.

If an artificial agent includes a neural net, and if the net's training is done algorithmically (that is, no human judgment is required once the training begins), this training process can continue after the artificial agent no longer is under control of the designer. In our model, a neural net has a fully modifiable table. This type of agent exhibits learning* that may continue in ways that the designer is unlikely to predict.

The possibility of emergent behaviors increases the probability that the artificial agent (or agents in a group) will eventually exhibit behaviors that the designer did not directly program into the agent(s). Furthermore, these behaviors could very well be behaviors the designer did not anticipate. How would we recognize such an AA, and more specifically, how could we trust its behaviors? In the case of an agent with an unmodifiable transition table, however, we might expect a responsible designer to anticipate all behaviors. If we trust the designer and his/her process, chances are, we will trust the AA and its behaviors.

Even in a complex system, the designer who is responsible for the complexity is responsible for the resulting system. However, mitigation of responsibility could be possible if, for example, the system is used in an environment that was explicitly prohibited by the designer. Some may counter that the designer of such an agent or agents would become *less* responsible for the agent behavior as the agent becomes less directly controlled by the designer's original plans and implementation. We strongly disagree. The designer is in some sense responsible for *all* subsequent behaviors, whether or not they were planned or anticipated. We fully realize that this places a heavy burden on a designer of an artificial agent. In order to fulfill this responsibility, the designer should endeavor to carefully constrain the possibilities of learning* in the agent, and to precisely define constraints on the changes that can take place in T. Without these constraints, any confidence the designer has that the artificial agent will not develop into an artifact that produces serious harm is unjustified. Trust in such an artifact would be misplaced.

Some may insist that imposing such limits significantly reduces the possibility of important benefits that could result from unexpected learning* that emerges from artificial agents. While it is true that some immediate benefits could be lost, we contend that the designer can carefully balance the capabilities and limits in order to maximize benefits while limiting possible risks. An analogy to this strategy is the extraordinary precautions taken when scientists study dangerous, disease-inducing microbes or unknown samples brought back by space travelers. We do not seek to discourage the progress that may come from artificial agents, but we seek to minimize the perhaps catastrophic harms that may occur if artificial agents are not carefully constrained. We can imagine a design where an agent records new entries in T, but requires some sort of human intervention before it can access them. Work on constraining artificial agents appropriately would increase trust in these artifacts and could be patterned on the considerable theoretical and practical work accomplished in the study of software safety.

In his attempt to describe machine ethics, James Moor (2006) has classified AAs according to their levels of ethical agency. Several of the papers we cite in this chapter have found these levels helpful in exploring AA trust. Moor characterizes the four levels as:

1 Ethical Impact Agents (AAs whose acts have ethical consequences);
2 Implicit Ethical Agents (AAs that have some ethical considerations built into their design in prescribed ways);

3 Explicit Ethical Agents (AAs that have representations for "ethical categories and perform analysis" based on context);
4 Full Ethical Agents (AAs that can make "explicit ethical judgments and generally [are] competent to reasonably justify them").

Moor contended (in 2006) that we were still at levels 1 and 2 in our development of AAs. According to Tavani (2015:77), Moor subscribes to the claim that "an AA qualifies as a normative agent simply in virtue of whether it can be evaluated in terms of how well or how poorly it performs the task(s) it was designed to do." An AA performing at any of these levels seems to lack the more advanced capability noted in the previous paragraph, i.e. the ability to change its own programming. In light of that, it may be that we add an additional level to Moor's hierarchy, one in which the AA can, after reasoning, change its ethical categories, i.e. the way in which it performs analysis, or the way in which it provides explanations. Unless otherwise noted, our discussion surrounding AAs focuses on the basic type of AA (Levels 1 and 2). The reader should also be aware that others have used "autonomous agent" or "intelligent agent" to refer to these AAs, but for now, we will avoid making any claims about the autonomy or intelligence of these entities.

23.4 From Trust to E-Trust: Theories about Trust and AAS

How do we define trust when talking about a human trusting an AA (H→AA)? If we consider AAs to be computer artifacts, we might treat them as mere objects, and therefore assign to any kind of human trust for the artifact the definition of "trust as reliance." However, because of their logical complexity, their capacity to store and manipulate data, and their potential for sophisticated interaction with humans, most scholarship that addresses trust and AAs treats them as more than simple artifacts. There are significant differences between trusting that a boat will stay afloat and trusting that an AA will give appropriate advice on medicine interactions. A useful description of H→AA trust must account for these significant differences, yet still capture their similarities.

"Trust as reliance" in computer artifacts means that we expect an object to do something to help us attain our goals (see Goldberg, this volume, and Coeckelbergh 2012). We rely on our GPS or thesaurus and "trust" them to do the job they were designed to do. However, as Buechner and Tavani (2011) point out, we do not hold the GPS itself or the thesaurus responsible if they do not work correctly; instead, we assign responsibility to the human developer of the artifact (see Grodzinsky et al. 2011). People, both consciously and unconsciously, transfer responsibility from machine to human because they cannot envision AAs as "fully moral agents." The argument put forth by Moor (2006) and Johnson (2006) is that because AAs are not fully moral agents, it is difficult (and arguably inappropriate) to assign responsibility to them.

Trust in AAs, it seems, lands somewhere in between trust for humans and, for example, trust in boats. These distinctions have led scholars to approach the problem of the possibility of trust with AAs differently. One of the first strategies was to identify trust in digital contexts as e-trust. E-trust is, at least potentially, different from trust based on face-to-face encounters.

Numerous scholars have argued that e-trust cannot emerge in digital environments. According to Taddeo (2009), this is due to three conditions of traditional trust not being met: "direct interaction between agents … the presence of shared norms and ethical values that regulate the interaction in the environment"; and "the identification of the parties involved in the interactions." She addresses these conditions in the digital domain and identifies "a major problem with e-trust. If e-trust does not rest on direct physical interaction, it must rest on some other grounds" and demands that any "theory of e-trust must explain what these grounds are."

Taddeo goes on to analyze a proposal by Weckert (2005) to ground e-trust on "[human] agents' attitudes to trust." While she finds Weckert's approach largely sound, she concludes that Weckert must accept that if an agent is acting as if she trusts, then the trustor "actually *does trust* another agent" (emphasis in the original). She finds it unsettling because it does not explain, "why an agent should decide to engage in the very dangerous behaviour of unjustified trust."

Taddeo also considers an AA trusting an AA (AA→AA) and critiques work by Castelfranchi and Falcone (1998), who "take e-trust to be a threshold value that is the result of a function of the subjective certainty of the beliefs held by an AA." It is easy to see that their notion of e-trust stems from traditional notions of human trust. Further, Castelfranchi and Falcone must be considering AAs that are significantly advanced from AAs we have today, some 20 years later, for as far as we know, AAs do not hold beliefs in the same way that humans hold beliefs. According to Taddeo, even if we accept some interpretation of "belief" in an AA to be a combination of software and data, the Castelfranchi and Falcone belief-based model of trust is still unsatisfactory.

Ultimately, Taddeo does not find any existing model of trust or e-trust satisfactory to explain the trust-like phenomena present and emerging on the Internet in the mid-2000s. In response, we developed an object-oriented model of trust.

23.5 An Object-Oriented Model of Trust

In building on our previous work, and reviewing the literature, we have found that there is a problematic, ambiguous nomenclature around trust and e-trust that confuses the discussion of trust and AAs; this is detrimental to a dialogue about important issues involving these terms. The purpose of our object-oriented model is to offer software developers, who are responsible for building AAs, and others who analyze AA's behavior, a way to describe more precisely and to analyze more carefully scenarios involving trust, especially when AAs are involved. This model is based on the premise that there is an overarching notion of trust with attributes of trust found in both face-to-face and electronic environments. We build our classes with the attributes: predictability, identity, transparency, reliability, and the behaviors necessary to implement these in AAs. In our model, we use H to designate Humans and AAs for artificial agents.

For the sake of brevity, we use an arrow (→) to denote one entity (the source of the arrow) trusting another entity (the point of the arrow) and the double headed arrow (←→) to designate reciprocity. As noted above, we are primarily interested in understanding trust in the following contexts: a human trusts an artificial agent (H→AA), an artificial agent trusts a human (AA→H), and an artificial agent trusts an artificial agent (AA→AA). These types of interactions, plus H←→AA, and AA ←→AA interactions, present different challenges as we are faced with the question "What does it mean to trust when one or both of the agents is not human?" Trust will be an increasingly important issue as interactions between humans and AAs increase in frequency and significance. The relevance of an extensible model-based approach to trust can help organize discussions about different aspects of this complex subject.

Object-orientation is a powerful software design technique that has many applications and useful nuances in software design. Briefly, object-orientation is a hierarchical relationship among classes, each representing a concept that describes a particular system. The classes at the top contain the most general features and capabilities of the system under consideration; these classes are the most abstract and, as such, cannot (and are not) instantiated in the real world. Classes at the bottom are more concrete and may exist in the real world. The classes at the middle layers gather common features of the classes below to allow for grouping of lower-level classes. This model is helpful in exploring issues of trust as they relate to AAs.

According to the model, we hypothesize an abstract concept of trust in a class called TRUST*.[2] TRUST* captures common characteristics of trust found both in electronic and physical (face-to-face) encounters (Figure 23.1). Using the model requires asking where we ought to place characteristics of trust relationships such as normativity, reliance, risk, accountability and responsibility. For example, where does normativity belong? Is it a trait found only in physical trust situations, or is it also found in electronic encounters? If we find it in both, then normativity properly belongs in TRUST*; otherwise, it belongs only in one of the subclasses. Both humans and AAs can be involved in electronic trust (E-TRUST) and physical trust (P-TRUST) as trustors and trustees. Using TRUST* instead of trust allows us to move beyond bickering about whether AAs and humans are identical when it comes to trust (we are convinced that they are not identical, but do not make that case here); and instead to engage with questions about how AAs and humans are alike and different with respect to issues of trust.

We have identified eight subclasses of E-TRUST and P-TRUST (Table 23.1), which classify the trustor (either human or artificial), the trustee (either human or artificial) and a mode of communication (either physical or electronically mediated). This organization aids analysis when an instance of a subclass is paired with a socio-technical context. The classes in the left column are subclasses of P-TRUST and the classes in the right column are subclasses of E-TRUST. This conceptual model of trust and AAs is a starting point to explore how we should adjust our understanding of trust as AAs become more common and more complex in diverse socio-technical environments. Again, consider the characteristic of normativity. If normativity exists only in HHP and not any of the other P-TRUST subclasses, then the characteristic moves down to HHP and cannot be part of TRUST*. Should normativity (or any other characteristic of any form of TRUST*) occur in more than one of the subclasses found in Table 23.1, the model is flexible in that it does not preclude the introduction of additional higher-level classes that capture those shared characteristics.

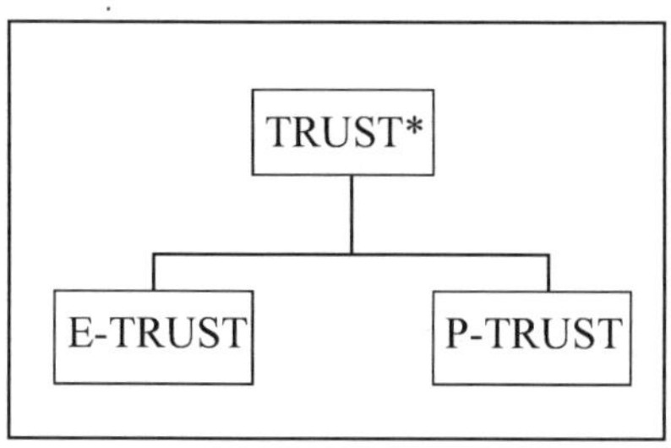

Figure 23.1 Object-Oriented Model of Trust Class Diagram

Table 23.1 Eight subclasses of E-TRUST and P-TRUST

Human→Human Physical: HHP	*Human→Human Electronic: HHE*
Human→AA Physical: HAP	Human→AA Electronic: HAE
AA→Human Physical: AHP	AA→Human Electronic: AHE
AA→AA Physical: AAP	AA→AA Electronic: AAE

The kind of trust we are most familiar with is HHP, a human trusting a human where the humans communicate face-to-face (physically). It is the type of trust that most of this volume is dedicated to and is most commonly associated with the word "trust." HHE describes a human trusting another human, but communication between the humans is electronic. For example, when someone gets an email from family or friends, he/she trusts that the electronic media has faithfully reproduced the message as it was sent. The two HH subclasses and their differences are worthy of study, but in this chapter, we will instead focus on the six other subclasses, each of which involves at least one AA.

The HA subclasses (HAP and HAE) refer to a human trusting an AA, either after face-to-face encounters (for example, a human encountering a robot receptionist) or electronic encounters (for example, a human interacting with a Web-based shopping bot). Although HAP trust encounters are still relatively rare, we are seeing more of them. For example, seven humans and several robots run the Henna Hotel in Nagasaki, Japan. Humans trust the robots (they rely on them) to check customers in, deliver their baggage, and clean their rooms (CBS News 2017). (See more on robots in Chapter 24 by John Sullins, this volume.) However, we will focus on non-robot HAE encounters that are becoming more common worldwide. Indeed, some have made extravagant claims about the importance of some HAE encounters, such as a magazine article entitled "IBM's Watson Supercomputer May Soon Be the Best Doctor in the World" (Friedman 2014). Accepting medical or financial advice from an AA surely requires significant confidence in the AA and some risk-taking by the human, essential elements of TRUST*. Presumably, humans who come to rely on AAs for advice and information are adapting their well-developed sense of HH trust to the newer phenomenon, HA trust.

The AH subclasses (AHP and AHE) are TRUST* classes that require an AA to take a risk based on confidence in a human. Although we are early in the development of AH trust, some examples are now commonplace. For example, the Captcha (2017) system is a method for an AA to determine automatically if a website visitor is a human. That distinction may seem trivial compared to more complex conceptions of trust, but we contend that it is appropriately classified as part of TRUST* because we are expecting the AA to act predictably according to its role in a context.

AAP and AAE are instances of AAs establishing some form of a TRUST* relationship with each other. One early example of an issue we include in AAE is the "robots exclusion standard" also known as "robots.txt" (Sun et al. 2007). The robots.txt protocol has web developers include a text file in their web site information that details which parts of the website the developer wishes to block from AAs acting as search engine "crawlers." This is not a legally enforced standard, but instead is a voluntary protocol.

If we do not claim intentionality in AAs (and for the purposes of this chapter, we do not make that claim), we contend that manifestations of trust from AA to AA are instances of direct trust as reliance. In the case of the Henna Hotel in Japan, the robot desk clerks rely on the electronic check-in system to accomplish the task of checking in the client. In an airport, the sensor systems rely on the barcode system to route bags; in a car, component systems communicate with each other and rely on each other to provide a safe vehicle to drive. We see this even more in autonomous vehicles. We might consider these AAs to be ethical impact agents or implicit ethical agents, depending on their individual designs (Moor 2006). Will we ever reach the point when trust can be more than reliance in AA-to-AA relationships? Probably not until AAs have reached the level of full ethical agents in Moor's hierarchy.

In establishing the model, we have identified three attributes of the TRUST* class: transparency, identity and predictability and that make trust relationships involving AAs distinct from those that only involve humans. We identify all three as attributes of trust when the trustee is human, providing an argument that trusting a human is different than trusting an AA.

The first attribute is that of transparency. The ubiquity of mobile phones has turned many of us into multi-taskers, yet it remains mostly transparent to others when someone gives at least some attention to his/her mobile device rather than to them. In contrast, AAs often are not only multi-taskers by design, but this multiprocessing is also not transparent to the user. The interaction it is having with the human may very well not be the only interaction it is having with another agent at the same time. Yet most people are not sensitive to the fact that multiprocessing is the default mode for most AAs and many of them are intentionally opaque to the user.[3] This opacity, while helpful in some situations (assessing your location while assembling directions for your GPS) can be detrimental when trying to ascertain whether to trust an AA that is learning*[4] is a socio-technical environment.

Strategies for ascertaining the identity, a second attribute, of an AA are likely to be different from those we use to ascertain the identity of a person. This is certainly true in an electronic environment. In a physical context, we typically use visual cues or things such as tone of voice. In trying to identify a physical AA, these cues are likely insufficient. As its software is updated, either through maintenance or through changes due to learning, an AA's identity may change. Further, it is possible that two AAs that look and sound alike (either in physical space or online) in fact have very different identities – that is, the code that they are running is distinct.

A third feature that influences the trust relationship with AAs is predictability. This attribute also allows us to briefly introduce a feature of the object-oriented model. Our assumption to this point is that the AA under consideration does not have the ability to modify its table. If an AA is not modifying T, then its actions are predictable given a state and a set of inputs. If, however, an AA is modifying its table, and exhibiting learning*, there is the potential for it to be less predictable. For example, the Twitterbot Tay adopted racist and sexist attitudes based on unanticipated input; this seemed to catch its developers off guard (see Wolf et al. 2017). Unlike Tavani's (2015) model of trust, in which the trustor has the disposition to expect normatively that the trustee will perform an action responsibly, in this case, the trustee (Tay the AA) did not exhibit predictable behavior. There is a subtle distinction here between predictably and performing an action responsibly (the role of the designer to insure the proper constraints). At the very least, predictability is part of performing an action responsibly. It would have been more responsible to test this AA with a range of inputs in a closed environment, rather than on the open Internet. Modifications could have then been made, making the resulting artifact more predictable.

This example demonstrates that the classes we introduced initially may not be fine-grained enough to support analysis of different types of trust. A more thorough set of classes will include at least two types of AA classification: those that learn and those that do not. In general, the object-oriented model allows for complex relationships among the subclasses. Those relationships are themselves worthy of consideration and study.

23.6 Zones of Trust

Recent work by Buechner and Tavani (2011), Buechner, Simon and Tavani (2014), Tavani (2015) and de Laat (2016) explore trust interactions between humans and AAs. We will discuss these papers, looking at them through the perspective of the object-oriented model. All of these scholars claim that there can be some sort of trust relationships between humans and AAs, but they include different emphases on factors such as the sophistication of AA, and the AA's relationships with humans and other AAs. All of them point out ways in which H→AA trust is something that is different from H→H trust.

Buechner and Tavani (2011:42) ask us to consider if there are any conditions "under which the AAs are a functional part of an environment in which individual humans enter into trusting relationships with that environment?" They also write (p. 44):

> Among the properties generally attributed to an agent are the ability to: (1) act in an environment, (2) communicate with other agents, (3) have individual objectives (driving its behavior), (4) possess resources to perform actions, (5) perceive its environment (though it has only a partial representation of it), (6) possess skills needed to perform actions, and (7) offer services using those skills to other agents to satisfy certain goals. Simulating these seven properties or characteristics in a software system is the subject of multi-agent systems theory.

As we see from this description, we could straightforwardly attribute all but (3) to AAs alone. The individual objectives driving AA behavior would be in the form of program code. Depending on the type of AA, these objectives might be hard-coded or learned. If the objectives are coded directly into the AA, then it seems that they are objectives that might more properly belong to the developer and the AA considered an what Moor calls an implicit ethical agent. However, if the AA has the ability to learn and modify its own programming, it becomes increasingly difficult to justify attribution of the AAs objectives to the developer. As we relate to AAs in our environment, and they perform as expected, trust in them grows, and as the complexity of AAs grows, their capabilities grow and the expectations of those interacting with them grow as well.

This brings us back to questions of predictability and the current capabilities of AAs to exhibit learning*. Earlier, we examined the risks of AAs modifying their own future behaviors (fully modifiable tables, as described above). The ability of an AA to change its future behaviors seems to undermine the kind of trust Buechner and Tavani envision.

Moreover, Buechner and Tavani (2011) analyzed multi-agent systems instead of only studying single AAs. The "multi-agents" could include AAs and humans. This "team approach" to analyzing trust that includes AAs has proven helpful. Our object-oriented model is well suited to take on this additional complexity. A major adjustment to the model as originally proposed is to allow TRUST* to include descriptions of trust among multi-agent systems that include both AAs and humans. We still hypothesize that TRUST* for multi-agent systems should include trust characteristics that all such multi-agent systems share. Then we can isolate, for example, characteristics of systems that include only humans, another set of characteristics of systems that include only AAs, and a third set of characteristics for systems that include both AAs and humans. In addition to the TRUST* characteristics that they share, there are characteristics that distinguish each of those three groups. For example, a system of only AAs is capable of communicating wirelessly not only among themselves but also with entities on the Internet.

Buechner and Tavani adopt the idea of "zones of default trust" from Walker (2006). Adapted to our object-oriented model and to a multi-agent system that may include AAs, a zone of default trust occurs when an agent in a system knows what to expect and that other agents in the system can be assumed to be trustworthy in the sense of TRUST*.

One interesting idea from Buechner and Tavani (2011) is their contention that scholars interested in studying trust interactions should exploit the possibilities of experiments with AAs. Such experiments avoid the inconvenience and expense of experiments involving only humans. Moreover, experiments involving AAs can proceed with more repetitions than would be practical with human agents as part of the protocol. Such experiments are potentially interesting for exploring characteristics of TRUST* in general and of AA trust in particular. The more characteristics shared by AAs and humans with respect to trust, the more applicable to humans are insights gained by studying experiments only involving AAs.

Buechner, Simon and Tavani (2014) share many of the assumptions in Buechner and Tavani (2011). But the 2014 paper explores trustworthiness in addition to trust, especially as those terms apply to multi-agent systems that include AAs and humans. Again, the relationship between the agents (AA or human) is center stage in this paper. Buechner et al. (2014) claim that both parties in a trust relationship (both trustor and trustee) participate in any establishment of trustworthiness.[5] In this chapter, we will not explore trustworthiness, except to note that the emphasis in Buechner et al. (2014) on shared trust and trustworthy relationships is consistent with the theme of shared aspects of TRUST*.[6] Emphasis on groups of agents, rather than only on isolated agents, increases the potential breadth of characteristics that belong in TRUST*.

Tavani (2015) notes that there are three "key" variables necessary to determine the appropriate level of trust between a person and an AA: autonomy, risk/vulnerability and interactions (direct vs indirect). His claim that the more autonomous an AA, the less we should trust it, corresponds to our claim that a fully modifiable AA is more unpredictable. This level of unpredictability also increases the risk for the trustor (see Grodzinsky et al. 2011:21–22). The variable of direct vs indirect trust speaks to the claim of whether the human involved in the H→AA relationship trusts the AA itself (direct) or trusts the AA only because he/she trusts the people or institution that developed the AA (indirect). In an HAP or HAE trust instance, agents know what to expect in certain contexts or environments. In these zones of trust, AAs are considered part of the functional environment and therefore trusted as such (Buechner et al. 2014). Agents in these zones can be individual or collective (like organizations) and trust can be direct or indirect.[7]

23.7 Trust through Co-Active Teams

de Laat (2016) also considers the issue of trusting AAs, yet introduces a slightly different perspective on multi-agent systems. At first, de Laat applies the terms "trusting as-if" to H→AA situations. Trust "as-if" happens when a person enters a potential trusting situation and behaves as if the other person is trustworthy, essentially creating "a normative claim on the trustee to respond in a like fashion" (2016:256). de Laat quickly rejects trust "as-if" for H→AA, claiming that human "expectations are not of the normative kind" since we "do not hold the bot responsible ..." (2016:256). He holds open the possibility that future AAs may have the sort of sophistication necessary for trust "as-if" relationships.

de Laat goes on to consider zones of trust for humans interacting with AAs. This leads him to consider the developmental history of AAs. Many of these devices, de Laat asserts, are developed and tested within a closed environment within a research institution. Only after the institution has some confidence in the system do they release the device outside the institution. The "zone of trust" is built up during this development (de Laat 2016: 259).

Unlike Tavani, however, de Laat believes that trust with AAs can only be non-normative, "since they harbour no intentions, but just embody those of their designers" (2016:259). He limits the trust interaction to "indirect trust."

> If people "happen to trust the institution, they are going to assume that all actors inside contribute to an overall trustworthy performance ... Notice that the normative claim of trust no longer attaches to individuals but to the institution as a whole; accountability is the central concept. Although this is not – and obviously cannot be – an issue of humans resorting to blank trust, their relying on institutional trust is an important option towards developing full-blown trust towards artificial agents in a fashion."
>
> *(de Laat 2016:259)*

Yet, de Laat notes that this raises a question as to "how mutual trust between human and artificial agents has been established within the institution in the first place" (2016:257).

In response, de Laat calls on the notion of co-active teams for establishing this sort of H→AA trust and possibly AA→H trust.[8] A co-active team consists of an AA and a human operator working collaboratively for the same purpose, each given part of the task according to ability. For a co-active team to form, it is necessary for the human to have direct access to the state of the AA. According to de Laat, one challenge is to enable the human "to actively probe the machine to test whether specific hypotheses about trust are warranted" (2016:258).

de Laat sees the trust situation with co-active teams as being more complicated but "the prospects for trust to emerge and grow have become better" (2016:258). Co-active teams of people and machines could help mitigate trust issues in H→AA interactions, especially in HAP instances, but also possibly in HAE instances. In these instances, a person manages the trust relationship between people who use the system and the AAs in the system because they serve as the interface between users and the system. de Laat argues that the normative features of "as-if" trust may come to bear on the situation since those involved in managing the trust relationship should be "fully functioning members taking part in the operations themselves" (2016:258). As a result, he claims, "users may more easily approach the system as anthropomorphic. The process of mentally modelling the ensemble involved transforms potentially from mere (non-normative) TRUST to (normative) trust. If this transformation takes place, the option for human users to take a chance and just assume that trust obtains becomes more realistic" (2016:259). At least in an initial encounter, for a person encountering a co-active team, the risk level goes down relative to an encounter with an AA that is not part of a co-active team.

One consideration not addressed by de Laat (2016) is how the co-active team might open up the opportunity for the transference of trust (from indirect to direct), or at least some attributes of trust, and how that might come to bear on the model of trust. As a user continues to engage with a co-active team, a user may come to trust the AA directly in a manner similar to the human operator, even though the user does not have the same direct access to the state of the AA. Analysis of such a trust relationship may better illuminate the nature of both HAP and AHP trust.

Contrary to de Laat, we do not see support for the claim that the trust relationship has to be limited to indirect trust. Instead, we continue to emphasize that the ethical significance both of direct trust (to AAs) and of indirect trust (to the humans responsible for the institutions and AAs) lies in the hands of AA developers. They honor that giving of trust by making their AAs worthy of trust – through transparency about the limitations of the AA, and through thorough testing and safety analysis of any AA before it is deployed.

23.8 A Social-Phenomenological Approach to Trust

In the previous approaches, AAs assume the roles as agents who represent either a trustor or trustee. It is the agents that create a social relationship in which trust can develop. Our object-oriented model adopted this approach from Taddeo (2009). The AA in our model, however, was always situated in a socio-technical context. It is, therefore, interesting to apply our model to Mark Coeckelbergh's approach where trust is already in this context and AAs are part of this environment. Our attributes of predictability, identity, and transparency applied to social relations involving AAs can help assess if the social relationship is viable as one of trust.

According to Mark Coeckelbergh (2012) most accounts of trust, e.g., Taddeo (2009), are based on a contractarian-individualist model: a relationship between a trustor and a trustee. In his paper on robot trust, Coeckelbergh puts forth a phenomenological-social approach to trust and contrasts it to the contractarian-individualist model. He states,

> In the former approach, there are 'first' individuals who 'then' create a social relation (in particular social expectations) and hence trust between them. In the latter approach, the social or the community is prior to the individual, which means that when we talk about trust in the context of a given relation between humans, it is presupposed rather than created. Here trust cannot be captured in a formula and is something given, not entirely within anyone's control.
>
> *(Coeckelbergh 2012:54)*

In other words, "the social-phenomenological … defines trust not as something that needs to be 'produced' but that is already there, in the social" (Coeckelbergh 2012:55).

In the phenomenological-social approach to trusting technology, trust is less about a decision to trust, and more about adapting to environments. Because AAs are part of a constructed digital environment, they are an integral part of that environment. Trust is already part of the social context and less under control of the agent. Therefore, trust emerges from social relations (Coeckelbergh 2012). He indicates that if there is a problem about trust, it is probably because there is a problem with the social relationship itself. In this regard, Coeckelbergh aligns himself with the views of Charles Ess (see Ess, this volume).

If humans perceive an AA as trustworthy, we move from the cognitive to the emotive and have a feeling of trust. Causes for this perception of trustworthiness might include: recognition of the properties of the AA (identity) including its competence to do its task (predictability), the familiar context or recognition of the trustworthiness of the developer or institution as pointed out by de Laat (2016).

Coeckelbergh has argued that

> robots may appear as more than machines and that this has consequences for the ethics of robotics … Here the question is not whether or not robots are agents (individual-ontological approach) but how they appear and how that appearance is shaped by and shapes the social (social-relational approach).
>
> *(Coeckelbergh 2012: 57)*[9]

Coeckelbergh contends that robots, although they may not be able to use language and make free choices (two of his preconditions for human trust), "… may contribute to the establishment of 'virtual trust' or 'quasi-trust' in so far that they appear as quasi others or social others … we trust robots if they appear trustworthy and they appear trustworthy if they are good players in the social game" (Coeckelbergh 2012:58). For example, our immersion in our devices such as phones and technological environments such as smart homes is testimony to the idea that "they are part of our 'existential and social' fabric from which we emerge as individuals" (Coeckelbergh 2012:58).

Coeckelbergh's emphasis is distinct from the other scholars cited in this chapter because Coeckelbergh focuses on the environment rather than on the agents themselves and because he focuses on the affective domain instead of on conscious, rational choices.

A strength of Coeckelbergh's approach is that is invites a broader focus than AAs and the people interacting with the AAs. Consider the AAs that people interact with in numerous and sometimes intimate ways on a daily basis: voice-based virtual assistants such as Siri or Alexa are common examples. These close interactions may encourage people to unconsciously trust their phones; that trust, in turn, leads people not to consider rationally how much private information about them is being collected and communicated by their phones. The socio-technical system of phones, networks, and corporations collects and exploits enormous amounts of data from individuals, and the individuals either do not pay attention to this transfer, or trust that the information will be used appropriately. Coeckelbergh's explanation makes this seemingly irrational behavior more understandable.

The diffuse-default zones of trust discussed by Buechner, Simon, and Tavani (2014) seem compatible with Coeckelbergh's emphasis; de Laat's human-AA teams co-active teams are another expression of a certain kind of environment. All of these emphases are important ways to look at how humans and AAs interact with each other when involved in TRUST* relationships.

23.9 Conclusion

The work on trust between humans and AAs is progressing both normatively and empirically. Each has the potential to inform the other, yet many questions remain. Are there additional abstract classes to be added to the object-oriented model that might better refine our understanding of trust? What are the further attributes of TRUST* that might be applied to the social relations specified by Coeckelbergh? Are there alternate groupings of trust properties that would better serve our understanding of trust as it applies to relationships where both agents are AAs who learn? Should we be moving towards a more phenomenological model as we become more immersed in digital environments? We have described the significance of recent scholarship that emphasizes the importance of considering the collective nature of humans and AAs in TRUST* relationships, and we are confident that future research exploring the ways in which TRUST* is both similar to and different from human trust will continue to inform and refine our understanding.

Notes

1 We are referring to the perfect designer. In practice, no such designer exists. However, a designer with high moral values will take care to constrain and understand this universe as completely as possible.
2 At this point the classes in model are insufficient to capture any notion of trust, broadly construed, present in the world. It is important to remember that TRUST* here refers to the top-layer class of our model, i.e. it is a container that holds properties that are identified as being part of any trust relationship regardless of the nature of its participants. The asterisk is not meant to indicate a fake or artificial trust; it is meant to represent a set of characteristics related to our notions of trust.
3 Thanks to John Sullins for this helpful clarification.
4 See the following example of Tay, the learning* Twitterbot.
5 This is contrary to a more traditional approach in which trustworthiness is only a characteristic of the trustee, the entity being trusted.
6 Please refer to the chapters by Scheman (Trust and Trustworthiness, Chapter 2) and Potter (Interpersonal Trust, Chapter 19) in this volume.
7 See Tavani (2015) for an interesting discussion on levels of trust that correspond to Moor's (2006) levels of ethical agency.
8 de Laat uses the term "mutual trust" which presumably involves both directions. However, he does not address AA→H trust in the co-active teams.
9 It is beyond the scope of this chapter to explore deception, but Grodzinsky et al. (2015) explore it in detail.

References

Buechner, J. and Tavani, H.T. (2011) "Trust and Multi-Agent Systems: Applying the "Diffuse, Default Model" of Trust to Experiments Involving Artificial Agents," *Ethics and Information Technology* 13(1): 39–51.

Buechner, J., Simon, J. and Tavani, H.T. (2014) "Re-Thinking Trust and Trustworthiness in Digital Environments," in *Ambiguous Technologies: Philosophical Issues, Practical Solutions, Human Nature: Proceedings of the Tenth International Conference on Computer Ethics*, Menomonie, WI: INSEIT.

Captcha (2017) "CAPTCHA: Telling Humans and Computers Apart Automatically." www.captcha.net/

Castelfranchi, C. and Falcone, R. (1998) "Principles of Trust for MAS: Cognitive Anatomy, Social Importance, and Quantification," Paper presented at the Proceedings of the Third International Conference on Multi-Agent Systems. www.csee.umbc.edu/~msmith27/readings/public/castelfranchi-1998a.pdf

CBS News (2017) “Japan Battles Population Decline with Robots,” www.cbsnews.com/news/japan-battles-population-decline-with-robots/

Coeckelbergh, M. (2012) “Can We Trust Robots?” *Ethics Information Technology* 14:53–60. doi:10.1007/s10676-10011-9279-9271

Coeckelbergh, M. (2014) “Moral Standing of Machines: Towards a Relational and Non-Cartesian Moral Hermeneutics,” *Philosophy and Technology* 27: 61–77. doi:10.1007/s13347-13013-0133-0138

de Laat, P.B. (2016) “Trusting the (Ro)botic Other: By Assumption?” *ACM SIGCAS Computers and Society* 45(3): 255–260.

Friedman, L.F. (2014) “IBM’s Watson Supercomputer May Soon Be the Best Doctor in the World,” *Business Insider*. www.businessinsider.com/ibms-watson-may-soon-be-the-best-doctor-in-the-world-2014-4

Grodzinsky, F.S., Miller, K.W. and Wolf, M.J. (2008) “The Ethics of Designing Artificial Agents,” *Ethics and Information Technology* 10(2): 115–121.

Grodzinsky, F.S., Miller, K.W. and Wolf, M.J. (2010) “Toward a Model of Trust and E-trust Processes Using Object-oriented Methodologies,” ETHICOMP 2010 Proceedings, Universitat Rovira i Virgili, Tarragona, Spain, April, 14–16. https://www.researchgate.net/profile/Simon_Rogerson/publication/296976124_Proceedings_of_ETHICOMP_2010_The_backwards_forwards_and_sideways_changes_of_ICT/links/56dc2ef808aebabdb4141e0c/Proceedings-of-ETHICOMP-2010-The-backwards-forwards-and-sideways-changes-of-ICT.pdf#page=275

Grodzinsky, F.S., Miller, K.W. and Wolf, M.J. (2011) “Developing Artificial Agents Worthy of Trust: ‘Would You Buy a Used Car from this Artificial Agent?’” *Ethics and Information Technology* 13(1):17–27.

Grodzinsky, F.S., Miller, K.W. and Wolf, M.J. (2015) “Developing Automated Deceptions and the Impact on Trust,” *Philosophy & Technology* 28(1): 91–105.

Johnson, D. (2006) “Computer Systems: Moral Entities but Not Moral Agents,” *Ethics and Information Technology* 8(4): 195–204.

Moor, J. (2006) “The Nature, Difficulty and Importance of Machine Ethics,” *IEEE Intelligent Systems* 21(4): 18–21.

Sun, Y., Zhuang, Z. and Giles C.L. (2007) “A Large-scale Study of robots.txt,” *Proceedings of the 16th International Conference on World Wide Web*, ACM.

Taddeo, M. (2009) “Defining Trust and E-trust: From Old Theories to New Problems,” *International Journal of Technology and Human Interaction* 5(2): 23–35.

Tavani, H. (2015) “Levels of Trust in the Context of Machine Ethics,” *Philosophy and Technology* 28: 75–90. doi:10.1007/s13347-13014-0165-0168

Walker, M.U. (2006) *Moral Repair: Reconstructing Moral Relations after Wrongdoing*. Cambridge: Cambridge University Press.

Weckert, J. (2005) “Trust in Cyberspace,” in R.J. Cavalier (ed.), *The Impact of the Internet on Our Moral Lives*, Albany: University of New York Press.

Wolf, M.J., Grodzinsky, F.S. and Miller, K.W. (2017) “Why We Should Have Seen that Coming: Comments on Microsoft’s Tay ‘Experiment’ and Wider Implications.” https://digitalcommons.sacredheart.edu/cgi/viewcontent.cgi?article=1104&context=computersci_fac

24
TRUST IN ROBOTS

John P. Sullins

24.1 Introduction

It had seemed like the right thing to do at the time, but now Lin was regretting storming out of the club. Lin had shared her feelings with Crystal but then Crystal went and posted them all over social media and now she just needed her space. Unfortunately, now that her anger had come down a bit, she realized that she was now walking in an area of the city that she had never been before. She quickly got out her phone and looked at her Lyfter rideshare app and saw that there was an autonomous car nearby that could pick her up. Just as she was about to tap the screen and call the car to her location, another taxi pulled up and the driver called out from the vehicle. "Hey, it looks like you need a ride. I can take you just about anywhere in town and I will do it cheaper than Lyfter." "No thanks," she replied as she tapped the screen. "Human drivers are just too sketchy," she thought. Within a few moments, the autonomous car arrived, and its door swung open and Lin slid into the comfortable seat. On the ride back to her apartment she tapped furiously on the screen of her phone trying to limit the damage Crystal had done to her.

What kind of trust might evolve between humans and robotic agents? Are we rapidly approaching a time when we are more likely to trust machines than fellow human beings? Since trust involves vulnerability, are we opening up a new troubling susceptibility to our technologies? In this chapter, we will refer to definitions of trust, trustworthiness, reliance, and epistemic responsibility that have been discussed in detail in other chapters of this volume and discuss how they can be applied to the technology of robotics. We will look at how robotic technologies are affecting trust and how the designers of robotics technologies create systems that use human psychology to cause those who use or interact with robots to place their trust in them, whether that trust is warranted or not. We will seek to determine when it might, or might not, be ethical to place our trust in robots and we will be introduced to a term herein called "ethical trust" that refers to how acts of trust can affect the growth of human virtuous character.

24.2 Trust, Trustworthiness, Reliance and Epistemic Responsibility

Each of these topics has been thoroughly discussed in this volume (see Scheman; Goldberg; Frost-Arnold, this volume). In later sections, we will look at trust as it is mediated by technology in general and then more specifically as it relates to robotics.

When we are referring to trust in this chapter, we are primarily concerned with the role that trust plays in building character in virtuous agents. Others have argued that trust is an important character trait that is under some stress given the impacts of modern information technologies (See Coeckelbergh 2012; Ess 2014a,b, and this volume; Vallor 2016; Weckert 2005, 2011, and this volume). Trust and reliance are closely related terms and much of the philosophical debate – also in this volume – revolves around whether to keep them distinct or perhaps reduce trust to reliance. In this chapter, we will assume that there are important distinctions but with some conceptual overlap as well. It is useful to look at the work of Shannon Vallor who conceives of trust and reliance as being related to each other in what she calls "Technomoral Honesty" (Vallor 2016:120–122). Technomoral honesty is a character trait that she argues must be developed by those that use information technologies to mediate their communications, given that these technologies have been shown in recent history to erode trust in "… traditional notions of expertise and authority" (ibid.:122). Robots might be an additional vector in this process of the erosion of trust, this means that honesty is going to be a concern we will have in talking about both trust and reliance in robotics. We will discuss this in more detail later but it must be acknowledged in this section that it is very natural to be skeptical that robots can be trusted given that they are very much lacking in any of the human qualities and character traits that are prerequisite for being an agent capable and worthy of trust (see Coeckelbergh 2012). In this chapter, we will take the stance that it will always be better to look at each robotic system on its own and determine if it is reliable first, then ask if it mediates trust relationships between humans and then finally, if we might have reached the point where we can even conceive a trust relationship between the machine and humans. The answer to that last question may remain forever negative, but we cannot judge it a priori. It is best to remain open but skeptical to the eventuality of robust human machine trust. In this chapter, we will focus on a more realistic scenario, namely on the development of robotic systems that act as if they deserve trust or appear as trustworthy fellow agents, when in fact they are nothing other than semi-autonomous machines acting in the interests of their makers and not their owners.

Following Weckert (in this volume) we will treat trust as existing on a continuum of reasons to trust an agent one is interacting with as cognitive (evidence-based) to non-cognitive (attitudes/feelings-based). We also agree that most simple machines are things we can only rely on but not trust. For instance, I merely rely on the rope to hold me as I climb it. But what if a rescue robot says to me in a language I understand and with feeling in its voice; "Please trust me, I can take to you to safety," does this open the possibility of *trusting* the robot?

Weckert (2005, and this volume) reminds us that while we can choose not to trust, we mostly trust unconsciously and by default. This default trust is great news for the designers of robots, given that all they have to do is make their machines provide the social cues we are pre-programmed by evolution to unconsciously accept. It might be bad news for us the users of these systems because fooling us in this way makes it harder for us to use conscious choices in our reactions to these machines. In these situations it is helpful to consult theories of virtue ethics which provide us with centuries of advice on how to live a more aware and purposeful existence and how to modify our own habits to better achieve a good and meaningful life. What follows is a meditation on how to properly confront the problem of trusting cleverly designed and programmed robots. We have an epistemic responsibility (See Frost-Arnold, this volume) to gather the needed evidence to determine whether or not a robot is reliable and trustworthy. This responsibility will be ever-present while we exist in the company of robots. Unfortunately, it is also likely that the designers and builders of these machines will try to circumvent this process so that the user just acquiesces to a trusting attitude to facilitate nudging, economic behavior or just increased engagement and ease of use with the technology.[1]

In the context of socio-technical systems like robots, it may be useful to distinguish between two types of trust which we will call thin and thick trust. *Thin trust* refers to trusting behavior that is not well justified, possibly manipulated, and leads to potentially unethical or undesirable outcomes for the user. *Thick trust*, in contrast, is epistemically justified trust and more likely to lead to ethical outcomes that align with the interests of the user.[2]

The central concern of this chapter is the possible misperception of thin trust as thick trust in the interaction with robots as well as the resulting preference of such thin trust relations by users given that thin trust is less demanding as it obscures the epistemic responsibility of the user. Primarily, we will track the central role that trust plays in the development of human character, both as trustors and trustees (see Goldberg and Frost-Arnold, this volume), and how the growing preference for thin trust that robots provide will outcompete thick trust that develops in good human relations. The result will be less opportunity to develop one's character as a trustworthy, honest and reliable person meaning that we are possibly building a world where ethical trust – the process of building one's character through trusting and being trusted, becomes more difficult. Let us now look at this problem in more detail.

24.3 Robotic Systems and Trust

Robots are a subcategory of information technologies that share some similarities with other technological agents such as software bots and artificially intelligent assistants.[3] Robots interact in our environments and can sense that environment and through their programming, they can determine a course of action and effect change in that environment. This can result in a feedback loop, where the changes the robot makes in the environment cause it to make other changes, and so on. Given that loop, robots working in complex environments can sometimes become difficult to predict. In particular, the actions and reactions of robots and humans working together on a shared problem can result in a complex set of difficult to predict behaviors. Some of these behaviors, when accomplished by a complex enough robotics system interacting with a complex environment, can result in situations that require behaviors or attitudes from the human agents towards the robotics system that resembles the way humans have to trust one another in order to work successfully together. There are five significant sectors where robotic applications are starting to emerge. These sectors are work, transportation, security, health, and entertainment. We are most familiar with robots in the work setting where these systems have been a major part of automated manufacturing for a while already. However, a new kind of workplace automation is on the way involving robots that can move around a workspace and even interact with human workers.[4] Transportation is a new area of use for robotics that has people excited that in the near future we might be using autonomous vehicles. Automatic pilot features on aircraft are well known, but automated driving technologies for the cars and trucks driving on our highways are a radically new step. Drones may soon be delivering packages and companies like Uber have plans to use them to move people around cities as well in autonomous flying taxis. Drones and robots have revolutionized the security sector. They are now a common tool used in warfare, surveillance, policing, and workplace security. In the health industry, we have seen robotic assistance in surgery as well as systems that support nursing staff in moving items from one place to another in hospitals. In entertainment, robotic systems play an increasing role not only in amusement parks but also at home through toys and various companion robots. All of these systems have commercial, public, and home applications and range from small, cheap, and somewhat trivial systems to large, complex, and expensive machines. Given this, the range of situations that involve robotic trust will occur on a spectrum from the mundane to critical situations where lives may be at stake.

Safety is a major concern because these systems will be operating in close proximity to people and animals. When these systems are used in security applications such as in warfare, or in policing, their actions have to be safe, justified, and proportionate. There are also questions of loyalty, such as when a robotic system might be purchased by a person to help care for their elderly parent. Will the system be one that the elderly patient can trust to work for their own interests, or will the robot default to the interests of those who bought it, or might its true allegiances be only to the company that designed, built, and sold the system? These issues also include a concern for privacy at various levels given that robots can and will collect a lot of information about their users that is likely to be shared with the companies that manufacture these machines. Users will be trusting robotic systems, and the companies that build them, to not misuse the information they are bound to collect.

Finally, these systems are not to be thought of as replacement or surrogate persons that will fulfill standard roles in society without altering those roles. A robotic system used to care for the elderly in their home is not a mechanical nurse that acts in every way like a human nurse would. Designing and deploying such a system will present us with a new way of caring for the elderly that will be unlike anything we have seen before and will afford us access to new forms of technologically mediated relationships between caregivers, robotics, and those needing care. We will find that wherever we use robotic technologies they will alter our society. A great deal of trust will have to be placed in these systems in the hope that those changes will be mostly for the better.

Before we look at the specific negative and positive ways that robotics will effect trust, we will first look at how technological systems in general require a certain amount of trust from their users and from there we can see how robotics systems add to already existing areas of technological trust and distrust.

24.4 Trusting Technologies

Technologists typically hold an optimistic view of science and technology and naturally place a great deal of reliance on technology and tend to celebrate the world that we have created through technologies. On the other hand, if one holds a pessimistic view of technology, then the opposite holds and it is logical to worry about our growing reliance on technologies and to be deeply skeptical of believing that the changes they bring to our lives will prove to be beneficial.

One solution to the dichotomy of uncritical optimism and impotent pessimism is provided by Asle Kiran and Peter-Paul Verbeek (2010) who argue that both the optimistic and pessimistic responses are due to a philosophical mistake in our assumptions that technology is something non-human and deeply separate from us as a kind of inhuman savior or villain. Kiran and Verbeek argue that if we think of our relationship to technology as external and instrumental, then this will obscure how closely we are connected to our technologies (Kiran and Verbeek 2010). We will refer to this argument as the technological essentialist position. This position is important in considering trust and robots, since it means that instead of having to trust or fear some external force that controls our lives, we have to confront the reality that technologies are just another aspect of humanity. Following this argument, when we trust some particular technology, we are actually engaged in another social relation where we are trusting (or not trusting) ourselves through the technologies we build and use. If we follow Kiran and Verbeek's logic, when we trust some technological system, it is not only a passive kind of trust where we might simply trust that the system we are using is safe and reliable: instead, they argue that we are also engaging in a more active trust where we use the technologies to shape ourselves and our society. This kind of trust made possible by the technological essentialist position is philosophically interesting, since a major thesis of philosophy is the search for a good and meaningful life and trust will play an important role in achieving such a life. Technological optimists will tend to argue that advances in technologies increase human access to better and more meaningful lives. Predictably, technological pessimists tend to argue that technologies inhibit humans in their pursuit of good and meaningful lives. The technological essentialist perspective acknowledges that every technology brings to light new possibilities while at the same time pushing other possibilities into the background. Every device gives us new actions we can do in the world and causes us to see the world differently than we did before. Those of us who lived prior to 1993 when the World Wide Web started bringing Internet technologies to the general population, really lived in a different world that is hard to imagine now that so much of our lives are conducted online. Looking back, we can see that these world-changing technologies did not deliver either a utopia or a dystopia – instead, we have a mixed bag of devices and systems. From the standpoint of virtue ethics, we have to take collective responsibility for our decisions to trust that each new technology we adopt will actually make not only our lives better but our character as well.

It might sound odd to bring up human character in a discussion about robots and trust, but it is actually a central issue in this discussion. If we ignore it, we might conclude that as long as no one is physically harmed through trust in a robot, then that act is ethical or at least not something an ethicist has to think about. As Shannon Vallor argues in her book *Technology and the Virtues*, only from the standpoint of an ethics that takes seriously human virtue, or character, can we ask important questions such as:

> How are advances in robotics shaping human habits, skills, and traits of character for the better, or for the worse? How can the odds of our flourishing with robotic technologies be increased by collectively investing in the global cultivation of the technomoral virtues? How can these virtues help us improve upon the robotic designs and practices that already emerging?
>
> *(Vallor 2017:211)*

We can see that if we divorce discussions of virtue and character from our discussions of the ethics of trust in robotics, we will only have a partial view of how to design these machines in the most ethical way possible. Trust is part of our character and this trait extends to various aspects of our surroundings, even our technological creations.

> From this manifestation of trust, human beings deliberately and actively trust themselves to technology. Rather than being risky or useful, technology is approached here as trustworthy. While recognizing the technological condition of human existence – and, therefore, thinking in terms of 'internal' relations between human beings and technologies – caring for one's existence does not imply a blind surrender to technology; instead, it comes down to taking responsibility for the ways in which one's existence is impacted by technology.
> *(Kiran and Verbeek 2010)*

To put this simply, technology is an essential part of what it means to be human, which further implies that human nature is not set but can be shaped by changing technologies. Realizing this essential fact of humanity gives us the power to make better decisions as to which technologies we chose to design, adopt, and use.

One final complication that needs to be considered when we are deciding on which specific technologies are worthy of our trust is to realize that they are designed in complex ways where it may be difficult to ascertain the motives of those who have designed and deployed them. Companies, where technological optimism is the dominant corporate philosophy, will design devices that they believe will extend human power. On the surface, this is largely admirable. Think of the motives for building personal computers that the young technologists in Silicon Valley had. They wanted to give computing power to the individual that had, up to that point, been only available to large corporate and government powers. The computer revolution was seen as part of a social revolution, the goal of which was to increase the access individuals had to information and thereby enhance democracy. A very fine sentiment indeed, but when these technologies have been trusted uncritically and, as we can see in current events, then these same information technologies that were designed to extend democracy have proven instead to be a threat to democracy. This threat has come in the form of filtering information to match people's preconceived opinions and giving undue outside influence to nefarious agencies that produce biased ersatz news reports designed to eroded people's trust in news of any kind. It is still unclear if this was an unintended consequence of the design of social media or if it was something these companies knew about but tolerated as it was making them lots of money. Either way, it is a very good example of how we can place too much trust in the designers of information technologies. Technologists have employed the technological optimism of their customers to foster trust that the great economic and political power these companies have acquired will be used in the public interest. The technological optimism of both the customers and the designers interacts to blind both parties of potential problems and abuse that this concentration of power will lead to.

Companies that might hold to the technological essentialist viewpoint in the design of their technologies are much more likely to take an honest and ethical look at how their products might change the world. These companies will take their ethical responsibilities seriously by attempting to foresee and avoid any possible negative consequences of their products already, during the design phase, thereby mitigating unforeseen consequences that often emerge only after the technology has been released to the public. This design philosophy realizes that they are in a reciprocal relationship with their customers and together they will work to build a world where there is ethical trust, trust that helps builds the character of both the customers as well as the companies building and using these technologies. These situations are admittedly rare, but it is our job as professionals to make this a more normal occurrence.

Throughout the following discussion, we will be adopting a technologically essentialist position, since we have shown above that technological optimists replace or prefer reliability to trust and technological pessimists would not believe that any occurrence of trust between a human and a robot would be ethical and might be skeptical of even reliance on robotic technologies. Technological essentialism gives us room to continue the discussion. Now we will see how ethical trust in technology plays out more specifically in robotics technologies.

24.5 Robotic Systems and Trust

The robotics ecosystem is vast and expanding. Some robotic systems are androids designed to look and act like humans or animals, while still others look like machines but still have human-like actions, while others look and act mechanical. To simplify this complexity for the purposes of our discussion here, it will be convenient to separate all these various systems into two general categories. The first will be Robotic Systems (RS), which will contain all the more mechanical systems such as autonomous cars, autonomous weapons systems, rescue robots, workplace robots, etc. These systems are classified based on the fact that they are designed to look and act like machines. These systems may include voice commands and some simple language interactions, but they are not meant to insinuate themselves into human social relations. The second category will be Affective Robotic Systems (ARS). This category contains both android systems that are designed to look and act like humans and animals as well as some of the more mechanical looking systems: the primary distinction between AR and ARS robots is that ARS machines are designed to detect, motivate, and simulate human affective emotions in order to interact more naturally with humans.

Mark Coeckelbergh (2012) argues that there are two ways of looking at trust and robotics. The first is what he calls a "contractarian-individualistic" approach and the second is a "phenomenological-social" approach. In the contractarian-individualistic approach, human and artificial agents interact in operationally autonomous ways, some of which may require trust from either the human to artificial agents or even the artificial agents to the human agents in the system. This "contractarian-individualistic" approach has been well explained by Mariarosaria Taddeo and Luciano Floridi in the development of their theories of trust (e-trust) in software agents (Taddeo 2009, 2010; Taddeo and Floridi 2011).[5] For our discussion here it is sufficient to just note that e-trust is an attempt to formalize the new social contract that will need to be constructed around interactions with all kinds of artificial agents, include those of the robotic kind.

In contrast to contractarian-individualistic accounts, Coeckelbergh argues that in the phenomenological-social approach, robots are not considered full agents, and this means that robots cannot enter into the same kinds of trust relationships that humans can enter into with other humans. But when it comes to certain well-designed robots, Coeckelbergh acknowledges that:

> ... they may nevertheless contribute to the establishment of 'virtual trust' or 'quasi-trust' in so far that they *appear* as quasi-others or social others, as

> language users, and as free agents. We trust robots if they appear trustworthy and they appear trustworthy if they are good players in the social game.
>
> *(Coeckelbergh 2012)*

Thus, depending on the theory you accept, either robots can be fellow agents that can operationally act as trustees or trustors, or robots are not capable of that but we humans can nevertheless act as if they were fellow social agents and interact with them in false, but possibly economically or emotionally useful, trusting relationships.

24.5.1 Verification, trust and robotics

Whether we are talking about RS or ARS – given that these agents are programmed – we are talking about systems whose behavior can, at least in principle, be verified. From the technological optimist position, the more that a system's behavior can be verified, the less one has to trust that system and the relationship becomes fully one of verified reliability. If we hold this view, we might think that in the near future, getting into a robotic cab will require less trust than getting into a human operated cab does today. Humans are complex agents with many conflicting goals and desires and human cab drivers have been known to take advantage of their riders. Robotic cabs can have their routes verified and have no real personal desires or motives that the customer has to worry about. Therefore, in some ways this points to a future where the relevance of trust when getting into a cab will become less important. A technological optimist will find this very comforting given that we will seem to have removed human vulnerability. We place ourselves in a vulnerable position when we have to trust someone, but in a future where one might assume that their interactions with robotic systems can be fully verified, it might be assumed that humans have become much less vulnerable. What we give up here is that this will come at the cost of losing the skill and interest in building trusting human relationships.

We also need to acknowledge that this kind of techno-optimism can be very misplaced. While some simple programs can be perfectly verified, once one places a robot into a complex physical environment, many unexpected outcomes can occur. Part of what caused the high-profile fatal accident where an autonomous Uber test car killed a jay walker was that on later analysis we found that the system had no conception that jaywalking was a possibility and was unable to effectively process the situation it found itself in (Marshall and Davies 2019). The Uber engineers felt the system was reliable and was running verified programming but they were tragically wrong. While it is true that a robotic cab is not going to harbor ill will towards its users or other human agents around it, its sensors and programming may yet interact with a situation and environment causing dangerous and even fatal accidents that impact the lives of the humans that encounter the autonomous vehicle. Thus, the behavior of the robotic system may be impossible to fully predict even if the programming is verified. If we were then to give the system the ability to learn and self-modify its programming, we have ratcheted up the complexity of predicting the behavior of the robotic system even more.

Also, we need to note that while the user of the robotic taxi can rest easy in the assumption that they are safe from the real, but extremely unlikely, danger of violence from the cab driver, the users are still placing a great deal of trust in the company that operates the robotic cab in regards to operational safety, information privacy, and pricing policies. All of these arguments tend to weaken the technological optimist position and it seems that old fashioned human trust is not going to disappear in a world with robotic systems, but that it will just shift the location of who and where we human agents are entering trust relationships. We will discuss this further in the following section.

We should now consider the question of whom, or what, do we trust when we trust robots? Here we need to look at this question from the technological essentialist position. All robotic systems obscure underlying trust relationships. On the surface it might look simple – the human user instructs the robot to do some action(s). For instance, the passenger orders the robot cab to take her to her home address. But there are some hidden layers of implicit or explicit trust. The user is trusting, whether she realizes it or not, that the system is well designed and programmed and will work efficiently and safely. Additionally, the user is trusting that the machine will advance her interests and not just the interests of the owners or manufactures of the robotic system. For instance, robotics may give the manufacturing companies an intimate access point into the lives and personal data of their customers. These systems can also be hacked or infected with computer viruses that would make the system untrustworthy. Robots, therefore, have hidden layers of trustworthiness that are difficult or impossible for the casual user to recognize. As such, users may develop a false sense of invulnerability, when in fact they have entered relationships with hidden human trustees whose motives they may not be fully aware of.

24.5.2 Robots and the Manipulation of Trust

The manipulation of trust is nothing new, and has arguably been a component of the human condition since the start of our species. When it comes to information technologies, nefarious actors have been able to find many ingenious new ways to manipulate trust. In his analysis of trust online, John Weckert (2005) suggested that trust comes easy for human beings even in the realm of online interactions. We trust first and only modify that default stance when there is a problem. This tendency is probably due to some pro-social artifact of our biological and social evolution but it does leave us vulnerable to those that might want to take advantage of it.

Important debates in ethics and robotics involve the nature and value of relationships between robots and humans involving the following: friendship (Sullins 2008), companionship (Coeckelbergh 2011; Sparrow 2002), love (Sullins 2012), sexual intimacy (Sullins 2012; Sharkey et al. 2017) and care (Sharkey and Sharkey 2012; Van Wynsberghe 2013, 2016). Given that trust plays a role in all of these different modes of human relationships, roboticists will need to invoke human trust in their machines in order to successfully simulate these various types of relationships. When it comes to ARS that are designed to engage in simulated social relations with their users, there is the real possibility that robots will be designed to manipulate users into trusting these machines, which will be necessary in order to facilitate the affective relationships that they are trying to create. The roboticist and philosopher Matthias Scheutz explains that

> ... the rule-governed mobility of social robots allows for, and ultimately prompts, humans to ascribe intentions to social robots in order to be able to make sense of their behaviors (e.g., the robot did not clean in the corner because it thought it could not get there). The claim is that the autonomy of social robots is among the critical properties that cause people to view robots differently from other artifacts such as computers or cars.
>
> *(Scheutz 2012)*

Scheutz finds evidence in studies of human-robot interaction that show that humans form these bonds with machines quickly and easily in much the same way we personify pets (ibid). The problem here is that this bond we form with the machine is unidirectional, we have feelings for the machine but it cannot have any for us. "It is interesting to note how little these robots have to contribute on their end to any relationship, in other words, how inept and unable they are to partake as a genuine partner …" (ibid.:214). Even so, there is a great deal of interest amongst designers in the field of social robotics to use this psychological tendency in humans to help bootstrap the acceptance of robots into the social world of their users (Sullins 2008).

In this way, humans who interact with robots, especially robots that they have brought into their homes, will naturally form strong emotional bonds with the machines like those that have been reported between soldiers and their bomb disposal robots (Carpenter 2016). These bonds can cause humans to construct relationships where they may like and trust the machine. But as we have seen, this bond only goes one way. The users may think they have a faithful robot friend, but this hides the real trustee in the relationship, which is the company or entity that built the machine, or even possibly a hacker that has accessed the system without the owner noticing. Machines like this could be used to subtly nudge consumer behavior in ways that benefit the company that made the robot and may or may not be of benefit to the user/owner of the robot.

Thus, the primary distinctions between trust in robots and trust in technology, in general, is that the robot can so easily tap into the deep psychology of the humans it interacts with in such a way that it obscures the trusting relationships the user is engaging in. In the case of social robots, they can manipulate users to enter into unidirectional trusting relationships that they ought to be skeptical of since robots can become a surrogate of trust between the designers/manufacturer and their customers in ways that users might not be fully aware of.[6]

24.6 Ethical Trust in the Age of Robotics

We have seen that robotics is an emerging field that will have an interesting impact on how humans trust each other through, and with, the use of robotics. It will be easy for those who design and produce robots to build machines that we will instinctively trust. Given that earlier we defined ethical trust as the process of building one's character through trusting and being trusted, we have to spend some time thinking about when it is ethical for us to trust robotic systems. There are more than just our own interests at stake, given that any mistakes in ascribing trust may involve others, such as our families or coworkers, so we have a good deal of epistemic responsibility to make responsible decisions. For instance, one's elderly parent may trust us to provide due diligence in choosing to engage home care services providers for them than may include robotics systems.

There are at least three distinct situations of robotic trust and each has a different set of ethical considerations that must be attended to.

The first situation is personal trust in robots. This occurs when a user trusts a robot (or robots) to accomplish a task that only effects the user herself. In this case, the user and robot form a distributed agent. If the robot is a simple system that is not connected to the Web in any way, then the ethical responsibility of these actions is entirely borne by the user and since, by definition, no other person is involved in this situation the only ethically troublesome action imaginable is perhaps the machine is used to commit self-harm in some way. Ethically, we would just need to make sure that machines that could potentially harm their users were only used by adults with no history of mental illness.

Secondly, we have interpersonal trust in robotics. This situation arises when a user (or users) trust(s) a robot to accomplish a task that has an effect on multiple humans. This includes robots that may be accessing the Web and are possibly passing information back to the company that built the robotic system. This is a much more ethically important situation and it includes some serious issues such as robots used to harm or kill other humans. The process of properly assessing the potential ethical impacts of these kinds of systems can get quite complex and would include evaluating the intended uses of the system, and whether or not it was designed to harm humans or not or could be easily converted from a benign to a harmful system. The physical and computational capacities of the system will matter such as the types of sensors, computing power, specific types of effectors and types of communication must all be accounted for. The level of autonomy that the robot has will also be a factor. This includes its ability to find and use its own energy in the environment, its control independence, its capacity to learn and change its programming, and its mobility. All these factors must be assessed before a system can be confidently released onto an unsuspecting public and it is the primary duty of the designers to assure that all of this has been properly audited, though the user should take some personal responsibility in this area as well. We should also add a concern for animals, and the environment in general, in our analysis of the operations of these systems.[7]

Finally, there is inter-systemic trust in robotics. This occurs when user(s) (which potentially also includes additional artificial systems such as AI programs or other robots) trust a robotic system to accomplish a task that has ethical impact on humans, on one or more artificial systems, and/or on one or more natural systems such as animals and/or the environment. Here an ethical analysis such as the one described above must be done but it needs to also include the cascading effects that will occur to the additional artificial agents involved.

In all of these situations described above, if the relationship of trust that develops between the various human and artificial agents involved leads to the further development of human character in a virtuous and beneficial way, then we have an instance of ethically justified trust in robotics. This would result due to the fact that we had successfully avoided the trap of preferring the easy cognitive load provided by the low epistemic responsibility involved in thin robot trust. Instead we confront our responsibility and analyze the permutations of the various robot trust scenarios outlined above. This gives us a chance to grow as moral agents. Possibly even one day our robots will use a similar process to grow as moral agents through a practice that might be called "artificial phronesis" but that is a topic for another paper (see Sullins 2014).

24.7 Conclusion

We have seen that robots share in many of the concerns that we have in trusting technologies in general, but that they also include an interesting new problem. Robots can be designed to exploit the deep pro-social capacities human naturally have to trust other humans. Since robots can move around our shared environment and seem to be autonomous like animals or other human agents, we tend to treat them in similar ways to animals and other humans; we learn to "trust" them. There are numerous potential ethical impacts that come out of our use of these new technologies and we have outlined many of them here. To ethically trust these technologies, it is important for those building and using robotic systems to thoroughly audit the potential ethical impacts of trusting robots. By adopting a technological essentialist position and by carefully assessing the robots we build and deploy, we may have a better chance of realizing a future with robots that includes an ethically justified level of trust in these technologies.

Notes

1 This process is found in AI as well as robotics but the embodiment of robots makes it much easier to achieve than with any other technology. Designers already know how to manipulate our prosocial psychology in ways that can manipulate users in this way (Sullins 2008).

2 Please note, however, that the relation between the epistemology and ethics of trust is not as straightforward as suggested above: robots might actually ethically nudge users who are operating on thin trust, to nevertheless produce ethical outcomes; thick trust in contrast could possibly result in unethical outcomes, such as when a trustworthy robot is used as a henchman to help a human agent obtain unethical goals.

3 We can distinguish robots from these other artificial agents because robots interact in physical space along with human and other biological agents. While your AI assistant on your phone may be able to accomplish certain tasks for you in cyberspace such as calling for a car on a rideshare app, robots can do real work in the real world, such as when an autonomous car might drive you from one place to another. Every robot has to have sensors that give it ways to sense the world around it, be that through touch, vision, sonar, temperature sensors, radar, and, LIDAR (LIDAR stands for – Light Detection and Ranging). LIDAR is a method that uses pulsed lasers that bounce off the local environment and measure ranges to objects. These have revolutionized autonomous vehicles and give them a way to build 3D representations of their local environment through which the autonomous vehicle can navigate.). In addition, the robotic system needs a way to interact with the environment it senses. This is done through actuators. Actuators are systems such as arms, manipulators, wheels, propeller blades, probes, and projectiles. To control its sensors and actuators the robotic system has to have some form of central processor that is located on the robot. This processor may, or may not, be connected to more powerful computers through the internet or the machine might simply rely on its own self-contained computing power.

4 An example is the highly automated warehouses used by companies like Amazon where robots help move goods from storage to shipping.

5 Another interesting theory of trust in regards to artificial agents developed by Grodzinsky, Miller and Wolf is based on the concepts of object-oriented programming methodologies (see also Grodzinsky, Wolf and Miller, Chapter 23 in this volume). The key notion from this work is that since traditional notions of trust focus on interactions between humans only, it is not going to be easy to just fit artificial agents into those traditional understandings. What is needed is a new category for e-trust that would exist at the same theoretical level as human-to-human trust and that both of these make reference to a much more broad and abstract notion of trust that they call "TRUST."

6 An example of a design stance for robotic systems where the designers are self-consciously aware of the problems described above and provide ways of mitigating it can be found in Seibt and Vestergaard (2018). They use a process they call "Fair Proxy Communication," that is designed to remove all implicit bias and perceptual cues in order to make a more fair communications platform that might be mediated through a robotic system, "that social robotics applications should be developed with the goal of preserving or enhancing a value that has top rank in a given axiological system (ethical or sociocultural values are typically top rank values)" (ibid.:3). This is a very interesting option as it causes us to think about robots not as fellow agents in the world but separate means of mediating communications between humans and machines that will require new behaviors and social cues to ensure fair, reliable, and trustworthy communications.

7 An example set of criteria and a process for accomplishing such an audit can be found in Christen et al. (2017) which is accessible here: https://ssrn.com/abstract=3063617

References

Carpenter, J. (2016) *Culture and Human-Robot Interaction in Militarized Spaces: A War Story*, Abingdon: Routledge.

Christen, M., Burri, T., Chapa, J.O., Salvi, R., Santoni de Sio, F. and Sullins, J. (2017, November 1) "An Evaluation Schema for the Ethical Use of Autonomous Robotic Systems in Security Applications." https://ssrn.com/abstract=3063617

Coeckelbergh, M. (2011) "Humans, Animals, and Robots: A Phenomenological Approach to Human-Robot Relations," *International Journal of Social Robotics* 3(2): 197–204.

Coeckelbergh, M. (2012) "Can We Trust Robots?" *Ethics and Information Technology* 14: 53–60.

Ess, C. (2013) *Digital Media Ethics*, 2nd edition, Oxford: Polity Press.
Ess, C. (2014a) "Selfhood, Moral Agency, and the Good Life in Mediatized Worlds? Perspectives from Medium Theory and Philosophy," in K. Lundby (ed.), *Mediatizattion of Communication* (Handbook of Communication Science, vol. 21), Berlin: De Gruyter Mouton.
Ess, C. (2014b) "Trust, Social Identity, and Computation," in R. Harper (ed.), *The Complexity of Trust, Computing, and Society*, Cambridge: Cambridge University Press.
Gerdes, A. (2015) "The Issue of Moral Consideration in Robot Ethics," *Computers and Society* 45 (3): 274–280.
Grodzinsky, F., Miller, K. and Wolf, M. (2011). "Developing Artificial Agents Worthy of Trust: 'Would You Buy a Used Car from This Artificial Agent?'" *Ethics and Information Technology* 13 (1): 17–27.
Horsburgh, H.J.N. (1960). "The Ethics of Trust," *Philosophical Quarterly* 10: 343–354.
Kiran, A. and Verbeek, P.-P. (2010) "Trusting Our Selves to Technology," *Knowledge, Technology & Policy* 23(3): 409–427.
Marshall, A. and Davies, A. (2019). "Uber's Self-Driving Car Didn't Know Pedestrians Could Jaywalk: The National Transportation Safety Board Releases Hundreds of Pages Related to the (2018) Crash in Tempe, Arizona, that Killed Elaine Herzberg," *Wired*, November 11. www.wired.com/story/ubers-self-driving-car-didnt-know-pedestrians-could-jaywalk/
Sarmah, D.D. (2016) "Trust in Technology," *Auto Tech Review* 5(7): 1.
Scharff, R.C. and Dusek, V. (eds.) (2014) *Philosophy of Technology: The Technological Condition an Anthology*, Malden, MA: Wiley-Blackwell.
Scheutz, M. (2012) "The Inherent Dangers of Unidirectional Emotional Bonds between Humans and Social Robots," in P. Lin, K. Abney and G. Beekey (eds.), *Robot Ethics*, Cambridge, MA: MIT Press.
Seibt, J. and Vestergaard, C. (2018) "Fair Proxy Communication: Using Social Robots to Modify the Mechanisms of Implicit Social Cognition," *Research Ideas and Outcomes* 4: e31827. https://doi.org/10.3897/rio.4.e31827
Sharkey, A. and Sharkey, N. (2012) "Granny and the Robots: Ethical Issues in Robot Care for the Elderly," *Ethics and Information Technology* 14(1):27–40.
Sharkey, N., van Wynsberghe, A., Robbins, S. and Hancock, E. (2017) "Our Sexual Future with Robots: A Foundation for Responsible Robotics Consultation Report." https://responsible-robotics-myxf6pn3xr.netdna-ssl.com/wp-content/uploads/2017/11/FRR-Consultation-Report-Our-Sexual-Future-with-robots-1-1.pdf
Sparrow, R. (2002) "The March of the Robot Dogs," *Ethics and Information Technology* 4(4): 305–318.
Sullins, J.P. (2008) "Friends by Design: A Design Philosophy for Personal Robotics Technology," in *Philosophy and Design*, Dordrecht: Springer.
Sullins, J.P. (2012) "Robots, Love, and Sex: The Ethics of Building a Love Machine October," *IEEE Transactions on Affective Computing* 3(4): 398–409.
Sullins, J.P. (2014) "Machine Morality Operationalized," in J. Seibt, R. Hakli, and M. Nørskov (eds.), *Sociable Robots and the Future of Social Relations: Proceedings of Robo-Philosophy (2014)*. Berlin: IOS Press.
Taddeo, M. (2009) "Defining Trust and E-trust: From Old Theories to New Problems," *International Journal of Technology and Human Interaction (IJTHI)* 5(2): 23–35.
Taddeo, M. (2010) "Modelling Trust in Artificial Agents: A First Step toward the Analysis of E-Trust," *Minds & Machines* 20(2): 243–257.
Taddeo, M. and Floridi, L. (2011) "The Case for E-Trust," *Ethics and Information Technology*, 13: 1–3.
Vallor, S. (2016) *Technology and the Virtues: A Philosophical Guide to a Future Worth Wanting*, Oxford: Oxford University Press.
Van Wynsberghe, A. (2013) "Designing Robots for Care: Care Centered Value-Sensitive Design," *Science and Engineering Ethics* 19(2), 407–433.
Van Wynsberghe, A. (2016) "Service Robots, Care Ethics, and Design," *Ethics and Information Technology* 18(4), 311–321.
Weckert, J. (2005) "Trust in Cyberspace," in R. Cavalier (ed.), *The Impact of the Internet on our Moral Lives*, Albany: State University of New York Press.
Weckert, J. (2011) "Trusting Software Agents," in C. Ess and M. Thorseth (eds.), *Trust in Virtual Worlds: Contemporary Perspectives*, New York: Peter Lang.

PART III

Trust in Knowledge, Science and Technology

25
TRUST AND TESTIMONY

Paul Faulkner

This entry discusses how issues to do with trust engage with the epistemology of testimony. The entry is structured as follows. It starts, in section 25.1, with a discussion of the epistemology of testimony, and argues that trust only matters to the assurance theory of testimony. Section 25.2 outlines the assurance theory of testimony and shows how trust figures in it. Section 25.3 raises some problems for the assurance theory and points to an incompleteness in it: some further account is needed as to how trust can provide an epistemic reason for belief. Section 25.4 introduces the distinction between doxastic and non-doxastic conceptions of trust, where this distinction determines the kind of account that can be provided of how trust provides an epistemic reason for belief. Section 25.5 discusses what conception of trust best fits the testimonial context and argues that there is no decisive consideration. Sections 25.6 and 25.7 then respectively show how the assurance theory might be coupled with doxastic and non-doxastic views of trust; these sections present accounts of how each conception of trust allows an answer to the question of how trust provides an epistemic reason for belief. The balance of argument is presented as favoring the non-doxastic view.

25.1 The Epistemology of Testimony

The epistemology of testimony aims to explain how it is that we learn facts through communication. I see that it snowed last night by looking out the window; you get to know this by my telling you. Focusing on such paradigmatic cases, the question is: how is it that you can get to know that it snowed last night by my telling you this? This question should be broken in two. What justifies your believing me, or accepting that it snowed when this what I tell you? And if you do believe me, what determines that you know it snowed rather than merely believe this? Trust is relevant to the discussion of the first of these two questions: it is relevant to the question of our justification for accepting what others tell us. Put simply: when asked why you accepted what I told you, a natural and straightforward answer is that you trusted me. How this natural and straightforward answer is theoretically elaborated then depends on the epistemology of testimony given and the way trust is conceived. With respect to the former, there are, broadly speaking three, possibly four, positions one might take, but while all these positions could employ talk of "trust," trust is only theoretically significant for the *assurance theory of testimony.* Since it is only the assurance position that needs to be considered properly, I run through the other three positions quickly.

According to the *reductive theory* of testimony, testimonial justification reduces to justification from other sources of belief. Given that human testimony is overly fallible, because too partial, mendacious and questionably competent, credulity is an epistemic failing and we must always support testimonial belief. Focusing on the paradigmatic case of a speaker S telling an audience A that p, A is thereby justified in believing that p if and only if other things that A believes allow A to justifiably judge that this is a good instance of testimony, or that p is probably true given S's testimony (Hume 1740; Fricker 1987). This position could be put in terms of trust, thus: A is justified in believing that p if and only if A is justified in trusting that S's testimony is true. This is an accepted use of "trust": we similarly speak of trusting that our car will start, or trusting that the ice will hold our weight. Or arriving at work without my keys, I might trust that you will be there to let me in, given that you always come in early. This is the *predictive* sense of trust (Hollis 1998:10; Faulkner 2011:145); it does no more than conjoin reliance with a positive belief about outcome: it is to say, for instance, that I rely on the ice holding my weight and believe that it will do so. Trust, so understood could be disappointed but not betrayed. I could not feel betrayed by you if I found that this morning, exceptionally, you are not at work. I trust that you are at work, I do not trust you to be at work; my expectation is a belief, it is not an expectation *of you*, which you might then let down. However, trust identifies a unique and philosophically interesting notion only insofar as it is understood as the kind of thing that can be let down or betrayed; that is, only insofar as it is understood *affectively* or *second-personally* (Faulkner 2011:146; McMyler 2011:122). Since trust figures in the reductive theory only if it is conceived predictively, this theory can be put aside for the present discussion.

According to the *non-reductive theory*, testimony is an epistemically distinctive source of knowledge and warrant. It follows that we possess a general entitlement, or epistemic right, to believe testimony, other things being equal (Reid 1764; Burge 1993). In terms of the paradigmatic case, when S tells A that p, A is justified in believing that p – in the sense that A is entitled to this belief – other things being equal. A thereby does not need to justifiably judge that this is a good instance of testimony but need only not judge that it is a bad instance. This position could equally be put in terms of trust because trust, in its affective sense – and I will only be using it in this sense henceforth – is characterized by both an absence of doubt (Horsburgh 1960; Möllering 2009) and an absence of rational assessment (Jones 1998; Løgstrup 1997). So the claim that we do not need to base acceptance on judgement and that we are entitled to it without supporting reasons could be presented as the claim that we possess an epistemic right to trust testimony. However, as with the reductive theory, talk of trust is playing no substantial theoretical role, it is merely serving as shorthand for this pair of claims. As such, this theory of testimony can equally be put aside in the present discussion.

The final position to be put aside is the *reliabilist theory* of testimony. According to this theory, A is justified in believing that p on the basis of S's testimony to p if and only if forming belief on this basis is reliable. The locus of reliability might then be identified as S's testimony, or words (Lackey 2006); A's understanding (Graham 2000); or the conjunction of these (Goldberg 2010). A reliabilist might then acknowledge that trust is the vehicle by means of which A comes to believe that p, but would give no significance to this fact since what matters are facts about reliability. Since trust is given no epistemological role, this theory, again, is not relevant to the present discussion.

25.2 The Assurance Theory of Testimony

What reason does A have for believing that p when S tells A that p? According to an assurance theory (Moran 2005; Hinchman 2005; Faulkner 2007a; McMyler 2011; Fricker 2012), A can have two different reasons for believing that p. First, A has that reason described by the reductive theory, which comes from S's telling reliably indicating that p and being judged to do so. This is the reason that S's telling provides as a piece of evidence for p, where to view S's telling as evidence is to view it in the same way that one views the readings of a thermometer. It is to take an "objectifying" (Strawson 1974) attitude to testimony – an attitude that is liable to provoke S's resentment. It would do so because in treating S's testimony as a piece of evidence, A comes to believe that p *because of her judgement*; but in telling A that p, S expects A to defer to his, S's, authority and believe that p *because of his telling*. The possibility of this reactive attitude then matters to the epistemology of testimony, per the assurance theory, because it reveals that there is a second reason that A can have for believing that p. This reason follows from A taking a "participant stance" (Holton 1994) and believing that p on S's authority.[1]

To elaborate this reason for belief, Moran (2005) appeals to Grice's (1957) distinction between "telling" and "letting know" where Grice (1957:218) illustrates this with the following two cases: "(1) I show Mr. X a photograph of Mr. Y displaying undue familiarity to Mrs. X. (2) I draw a picture of Mr. Y behaving in this manner and show it to Mr. X." The photograph lets Mr. X know the facts. And I could let Mr. X know the same facts simply by leaving the photograph around for him to find. The photograph is evidence; the drawing is not. The drawing does not let Mr. X know anything unless he can work out what I am trying to tell him with it. But if Mr. X can recognize what I intend to convey, then he can learn the facts *insofar as* he regards my intention that he come to believe them as a reason for belief. It is, Grice claimed, because I have this intention to convey these facts and intend that Mr. X regard this intention as a reason for belief that my drawing is a telling and not a mere doodle. This is then the basic mechanism by means of which A gains a non-evidential reason to believe that p: in telling A that p, S intends that A regard his intention that A believe that p as a reason for belief.

Two layers then need to be added to this basic mechanism: *assurance* and *trust*. First, in general, we do not regard another's desire that we do something as "any reason at all for complying" (Moran 2005:14). So why should S's intention that A believe that p suffice to give A reason for belief? To answer this question, Moran adds to Grice's basic mechanism the idea that S intends that A regard his intention that A believe that p as a reason for belief because in intending this S *assumes responsibility* for A believing truly, and thereby "presents himself as *accountable* for the truth of what he says" (Moran 2005:11). In this way, in telling A that p, S offers A his *assurance* that p.

To clarify this, consider practical reasons. Suppose I decide to φ, and so form the intention to φ. My intention to φ is evidence that I will φ, but my belief that I will φ is not based on the evidence my intention provides but on the decision this intention embodies. Suppose, now, that S tells me that he will φ and I thereby know that S intends to φ. S's intention to φ is equally evidence that S will φ, but (assuming I take participant stance) my belief that S will φ will not be based on the evidence that S's intention provides but on the recognition that S's intention embodies the decision to φ (Marušić 2015). Moran's claim is then that something similar holds when S's testimony is fact-stating. When S tells me that p (and I take the participant stance) my belief that p is not based on the evidence of S's telling but on the recognition that S's intention in telling me that p embodies S's decision to take responsibility for my believing truly.

Trust is then the second layer that needs to be added to this mechanism. It is implicit in talk of *seeing-as*, specifically: *seeing a telling as an assumption of responsibility*, but it needs to be made explicit. The issue is that while we tell one another what we know, we also tell lies. Moreover, were S lying to A, S would equally intend A to believe that p because A recognizes that this is what he, S, intends; and S would equally purport to assume responsibility for A believing truly – only in this case S would not in fact assume this responsibility (Faulkner 2007b; Simpson 1992). Once lies are introduced, it then seems, again, that S's intentions in telling A that p do not suffice to give A reason for belief. What follows is that the assurance theory seems to face a dilemma: either what is needed is a belief to the effect that this is a good case of testimony – the belief that S does, in fact, assume the responsibilities that he purports to assume; or what is needed is an epistemic right not to worry about lies, other things being equal. The dilemma is that insofar as these are the only options, there ceases to be a distinctive assurance position: the epistemology of testimony becomes either reductive or non-reductive.

This dilemma can be seen to be a false one, once trust is fully integrated into the assurance account. Trusting is something we do and an attitude that we can have and take. The *act of trusting* is one of relying on someone doing something, and thus the general form of trust is three-place: A trusts S to φ. In the testimonial context, the action is that of testimonial uptake: A's believing S or accepting S's testimony to p. But acts of trusting crucially differ from acts of reliance in that trusting is necessarily willing. Although reliance can be voluntary – one can be confident that someone or thing will prove reliable – it can also be forced: one might have no choice but to take the least bad option. The *attitude of trust* is then characterized as that attitude towards reliance that explains why reliance is willing; and when trust is conceived affectively, as it is here, also explains the susceptibility to feelings of betrayal were the trusted party to prove unreliable. It is only when the reliance is governed by this attitude of trust, that it is an act of trusting.[2] Thus, in the testimonial context the act of trust is properly described as A's believing S, or accepting S's testimony to p, because A trusts S for the truth as to whether p. And this involves more than relying on S for truth because if A found out that S made a wild guess but luckily got it right, A would still feel let down by S, would feel that her trust was betrayed, even if no other harm was done. *Telling the truth* involves a commitment on S's behalf to getting it right, which in turn presupposes that the capacity to take on this responsibility and discharge it. Telling the truth, in short, requires being trustworthy, and this is what A trusts S to be. This is why the dilemma is a false one: in trusting S for the truth, A will thereby not worry about the possibility of S lying or not paying proper care and attention. Insofar as A trusts, A will *see* S's telling *as* the assumption of responsibility is purports to be and for this reason believe that p.[3] This attitude of trust is thereby an essential part of the specification of A's reason for belief – it is the inward facing or internal part of this reason.

25.3 Criticism of the Assurance Theory

Lackey (2008) raises two problems for the assurance theory. First, suppose that S tells A that p but A has reason to reject what S says in believing that S does not know whether p. Then suppose that T tells A that S is "one of the best in his field": insofar as T's telling A this provides A with a reason for belief "it should be capable of functioning as a defeater-defeater for the original counter-evidence" (Lackey 2008:225).

And the problem is that "it is entirely unclear how a purely non-evidential reason could defeat counter-evidence" (Lackey 2008:225). The simple response here is to assert the assurance theory's contention that the class of *epistemic reasons* is broader than the class of evidential reasons. It includes the reason provided by a speaker's assurance. Insofar as A's trusting T yields the (non-evidentially) justified testimonial belief that S is one of the best in his field, then the issue of defeat is entirely clear: there is no problem with a justified belief functioning as a defeater-defeater.

Lackey's second objection starts with the observation that we do not trust everyone. Rather, we discriminate in whom we trust. Specifically, we trust only those we believe to be either antecedently trustworthy or likely to be moved to trustworthiness by our trust. If one trusted in the absence of these beliefs "it will simply be a matter of luck" if the speaker turns out to be trustworthy; and such luck "is incompatible with the hearer forming epistemically justified beliefs solely on the basis of the speaker's testimony" (Lackey 2006:246). But in this case, it is this background of belief, which informs our discriminations, that matters epistemically. It is this background of belief that grounds any reason for belief that trust ostensibly supports. In response, suppose it is allowed that our background of belief is sufficient to justify every actual case of testimonial belief. This is a presupposition of a reductive theory, and it is plausible (Faulkner 2002). Given this supposition, it follows that in every case of actual trust, we could argue for the truth of what is said. But allowing so much is no criticism of the assurance theory. Its starting point is that confronted by a piece of testimony, we have two categorically different kinds of reasons for belief: (third-personal) reasons of evidence, and (second-personal) reasons of trust-cum-assurance. This allows for the possibility that we *could* go out on a limb and trust in the absence of evidence, and even in the face of counter-evidence. And it allows that our grounds for belief can be second-personal even when we have plenty of evidence that would allow us to argue for the truth of what is said. That is, even if A has ample evidence to believe that p, when this is what S tells her, in trusting S for the truth, A will base her belief on S's assurance (defer to S's authority) rather than this evidence.

However, both these responses to Lackey's criticism assume that the assurance theory has some account of how trust-cum-assurance provides an epistemic reason for belief. The external aspect of this reason has been characterized: assurance provides a reason insofar as it embodies the decision to assume responsibility. But some account is yet to be given of the internal aspect; that is, of how the attitude of trust rationalizes testimonial uptake. To elaborate this point, suppose that A trusts and, as such, bases her belief on S's ostensible assurances rather than the evidence. This supposition is compatible with two possibilities, which are the good and bad cases familiar to epistemology. In the good case, S knows that p, and genuinely assumes responsibility for A's believing truly. The assurance, one might say, is *genuine*. In the bad case, either S lies, and so does not assume responsibility for A believing truly, or S does not know whether p, and so cannot discharge the responsibility assumed. The assurance one might say is *empty*. From A's perspective, these good and bad cases can be subjectively indistinguishable: in both cases, uptake might proceed from A's trusting S for the truth. As such, it is natural to assume that the reason for belief provided by trust will be essentially the same in both cases. Objectively, this reason for belief will be better in the good case since it then it is coupled with a genuine assurance: things are the way that A takes them to be in trust. But in both cases, A has that reason for belief that comes from trusting S for the truth. The further account needed is then one of this subjective or rationalizing reason for belief; specifically, some answer is needed to the question of *how is it that trust makes testimonial uptake epistemically reasonable?*

25.4 Our Trust in Testimony: Doxastic and Non-Doxastic Conceptions

According to doxastic views of trust, A's trusting S to φ either involves or entails the belief that S will φ. It is this belief that explains the willingness of A to rely on S φ-ing. Thus, in the testimonial context, trusting S for the truth involves believing that S is telling the truth (Adler 1994; Hieronymi 2008; McMyler 2011; Keren 2014; Marušić 2015).[4] On this conception, the answer to the question of how trust provides reason for belief is straightforward. If A's trusting S to tell the truth involves believing that S will tell the truth, then conjoining this belief with the fact that S tells A that p gives A reason to believe that p. Trust gives a reason for belief because belief can provide reason for belief

According to non-doxastic views of trust, A's trusting S to φ neither involves nor entails the belief that S will φ. Thus, and for instance, for Holton (1994:66) trusting S to φ is a matter of reliance from within the "participant stance"; for Hawley (2014:10) it is a matter of relying on S φ-ing when believing that S has a commitment to φ-ing; for myself, Faulkner (2011:146), and Jones (1996:8) it is a matter of relying on S φ-ing and expecting S to be moved by this fact to φ. None of these further conditions – operating within the participant stance, believing the trusted to have a commitment, and expecting something of the trusted – involve or entail the belief that trusted will act in the way one relies on them acting. On this conception, there is no simple answer as to how trust provides a reason for belief.

Before considering how these views of trust might each be added to an assurance theory to complete it, let me consider which view of trust best fits the testimonial context.

25.5 Metaphysical Issues: Trust as It Is Found in Testimony

While the doxastic theory of trust promises to make the epistemology simpler it confronts various metaphysical worries (see also Keren, this volume). These are threefold, with each worry being a fact that seems to motivate a non-doxastic conception of trust. First, it seems that in some circumstances *one can decide to trust*. For example, Holton (1994:63) gives the example of a drama class where you are spun around until you lose your bearings and are then encouraged to fall with your hands at your side and let the other class members catch you. If you let yourself fall, then you rely on the others catching you. And it seems that one can choose to so rely with a positive attitude that makes this reliance an act of trust. Equally, one can rely on someone again after being let down, choosing to give them the benefit of the doubt and continuing to trust, where Løgstrup (2007:78) talks about this choice involving "the renunciation of attitudes or movements of thought and feeling that are incompatible with trust." However, one cannot decide to believe something, so if trust involves belief, one could not decide to trust either. Second, it seems that up to a point trust has a certain *immunity to doubt*. In trusting someone to do something, one will not worry about them not doing it and will demonstrate a certain insensitivity to the evidence that they will not. In this respect, Jones (1996:11–12) compares trust to emotions in that it blinkers vision through making the positive salient and the obscuring the negative. But beliefs are not, or should not be, similarly insensitive to evidence. Third, *too much reflection can undermine trust*. "Trust is a fragile plant," Baier (1986:260) says, "which may not endure inspection of its roots, even when they were, before inspection, quite healthy." But reflection on whether the trusted is trustworthy should be able to consolidate one's belief that they are so.

These metaphysical considerations are not decisive: advocates of a doxastic conception of trust can say something to each of them. Hieronymi (2008), for instance, draws a distinction between trust and *entrusting*. In the drama case, either one trusts because, after deliberation, one reaches the conclusion that one's class members are trustworthy; or, if one cannot make this judgement, one merely entrusts them with one's safety: choosing to rely on them and being disposed to resent them if one is not caught. Cases where one gives others the benefit of the doubt are equally cases of entrusting, not trust. That one demonstrates a certain immunity to doubt when one trusts, Keren (2014) argues, can then be explained by the fact that in trusting someone to do something one has a *pre-emptive reason* not to take precautions against the possibility of their not doing that thing. This idea fits the testimonial case well: in trusting S for the truth as to whether p, A thereby has a pre-emptive reason not to consider evidence that not-p. The idea that trust gives one pre-emptive reasons is then compatible with both doxastic and non-doxastic conceptions of trust. And it provides grounds for a further response to Lackey's question about defeat: insofar as in trusting T, A gains a pre-emptive reason to ignore evidence that S is not one of the best in his field, A thereby gains a reason to ignore her original counter-evidence. The mechanism of defeat is that of pre-emption. The fact that reflection undermines trust can then be explained if, following Hieronymi (2008) and McMyler (2017), it is held that the belief that the trusted is trustworthy is itself a *trusting belief* or one that must be held on second-personal grounds, and not third-personal grounds. Reflection undermines trust because it seeks a third-personal, or evidential, grounds for the belief in trustworthiness, but grounded in this way, the belief in trustworthiness ceases to be trusting – it ceases to be a *trusting* belief.

On the other side, Hieronymi (2008:219) and McMyler (2011:132) have argued that non-doxastic conceptions of trust get its metaphysics wrong. Their argument starts from cases where S tells A something out of the ordinary or something that matters much to A, and then asks to be trusted. For instance, Hieronymi (2008:219) imagines an accused friend asking you to trust her when she tells you that she is innocent. In this case, the demand to be trusted is the demand to be believed. This is captured by doxastic theories: to trust your friend for the truth is to trustingly believe that she is telling the truth when she tells you that she is innocent, and so to believe that she is innocent. But it is not so obvious that non-doxastic accounts give this result; thus Hieronymi (2008:219) quips "[y]our friend does not want you merely to rely on her claim from a participant stance"; nor, one might add does your friend merely demand that you rely on her believing her to have committed to the truth; or rely on her expecting this to motivate her to tell you the truth; since it seems that you can do all these things and still believe your friend is guilty.

The short response here is that any account of trust, be it doxastic or not, should hold that trusting a telling involves believing a speaker, which entails believing what is told. When S tells A that p, then A will believe S and so believe that p insofar as A trusts S for the truth. This should be a datum that any view of trust must accommodate; thus, and for instance, Holton (1994) argues that, while trust does not involve belief, in trusting one *comes to believe*. So Hieronymi's (2008:221) developed criticism is that there is something unstable about beliefs based on trust insofar as trust does not involve a belief in trustworthiness. The instability is that reflection on these beliefs should prompt their suspension because, unless it involves belief in trustworthiness, trust is not a truth-conducive process of belief-formation. Whether this further claim is true depends on what account is given by the non-doxastic theorist of how trust provides a reason for belief. On the account outlined in section 25.8 below, this further claim is false: a belief in trustworthiness turns out *not to be necessary* for conceiving of trust as a truth-conducive process.

But before turning to the epistemological question of how the trust supplies a reason for belief, it is worth noting that cases like the accused friend are also difficult for a doxastic view of trust. Since if trust involves belief, one could trust only for reasons that one could believe.[5] But then it follows that one should not be able to imagine a case where the balance of evidence points to your friend's guilt, but where you can still trust your friend when he tells you that he is innocent. However, it seems that in imagining the case of the accused friend, it is easy to imagine the case takes this form, since this is a staple of Hollywood plots. But insofar as this can be imagined, one allows that trust can be demanded and given even when the evidence would otherwise make belief impossible (see Faulkner 2018). The difficulty for doxastic accounts of trust is how this could be possible. And here the strategy that Hieronymi (2008) proposed in response to Holton's (1994) drama case is inadequate: entrusting is not enough since the demand for trust is the demand to be believed.

25.6 The Assurance Theory Combined with a Doxastic View of Trust

The doxastic view of trust can be combined with an assurance theory of testimony (Hieronymi 2008; McMyler 2011; Marušić 2015). Doing so promises to make the epistemology very simple: the explanation of A's being assured by S's telling her that p. is that in trusting S for the truth, A believes that S is trustworthy.

However, there is a challenge associated with this combination of views. Recall that trust was introduced in response to the recognition that the duplicitous and the incompetent equally proffer assurance. This recognition entails that being an assurance is not sufficient for being a reason for belief. What is needed for sufficiency is the further claim that A sees the telling as a genuine assurance – as opposed to an empty one – where this seeing-as follows from A's attitude being one of trust. However, if trust involves or entails the belief that the trustee is trustworthy, the question is raised as to what grounds we have for this belief. And here, again, the options can seem to be: either this belief is justified on the basis of our background belief, which is to say the evidence (and the epistemology becomes reductive); or we have an epistemic right to presume that others are trustworthy (and the epistemology becomes non-reductive). Either way, the problem re-emerges that there ceases to be a distinctive assurance position.

The response to this epistemological challenge is given by the idea that a belief in trustworthiness is itself a *trusting belief*, and so grounded on second-personal rather than third-personal considerations. That is, in believing p on the basis of trusting S, when S tells her that p, A believes that p on the basis of recognizing S's utterance embodies a decision to take responsibility for her, A, believing truly. But in recognizing this A equally has a basis for believing that S is telling her the truth, or is trustworthy. Thus, A's testimonial belief that p *and* A's belief that S is trustworthy are justified *on the same second-personal basis*. Here is McMyler (2011:137, n.15): "[t]he attitude of trusting a person to φ itself involves believing that the person will φ, where this belief is justified by an irreducibly second-personal reason for belief. This is what makes this trusting belief different from other forms of belief – this is what makes it the case that this belief doesn't involve the truster's coming to her own conclusion about things." Otherwise put: this is why the doxastic conception of trust does not introduce evidential considerations, and insinuate a reductive theory of testimony; it is why it does not, as Moran (2005:24) says, create "disharmony" in the testimonial relationship.

The problem with this strategy, however, is that the fact that trust involves a belief in trustworthiness was meant to explain how it is that trust makes it epistemically reasonable to accept an ostensible offer of assurance, and so form a testimonial belief. However, on the proposed account the belief in trustworthiness is grounded on the second-personal facts, which is to say the ostensible assurance given. But if the belief in trustworthiness has this ground, it cannot itself offer rationalizing grounds for taking an ostensible assurance to be genuine. What follows is that the doxastic view of trust cannot explain how it is that trust makes testimonial belief epistemically reasonable; it cannot explain why we take assurances to be genuine when we know they are often offered by the duplicitous and incompetent, and so are often empty. It cannot explain this given that it rightly rejects all attempts to ground this belief in the evidence as being untrusting.[6]

The non-doxastic view of trust, in my opinion, fares better here. It can explain how trust can provide a reason for belief that is grounded in something other than second-personal considerations, but which is nevertheless not evidence. I turn to this view of trust now.

25.7 The Assurance View Combined with a Non-Doxastic View of Trust

The principle challenge to combining the non-doxastic view of trust with an assurance theory of testimony is epistemological: explaining how trust so conceived could supply a reason for belief. The nature of this challenge might be put like this: one can have practical reasons for trusting, which would be considerations that "show trust useful, valuable, important, or required" (Hieronymi 2008:213). In the drama case, for instance, one is encouraged to let oneself fall in order to cultivate trusting relations with other class members. However, these practical reasons for trusting do not support the belief that the trustee is trustworthy. So in the testimonial case, these practical reasons do not support the belief that the speaker is telling the truth. As such, if it is also the case that the attitude of trust itself neither involves nor entails this belief, it becomes problematic how trust could make testimonial belief epistemically reasonable. Certainly, this is a challenge that non-doxastic views of trust have to address; I describe the account I have outlined elsewhere (Faulkner 2011).

The starting point is the observation made by Jones (1996:8), amongst others, that "trust essentially involves an attitude of optimism that the goodwill and competence of another will extend to the domain of our interaction with her." So considering A's trusting S to φ, which in the testimonial case is A's trusting S to tell the truth, A's willingness to rely on S φ-ing or telling the truth is an expression of this positive and optimistic attitude (Faulkner 2017 and Løgstrup 1997). In trusting S to φ, or to tell the truth, A takes an optimistic view of S's motivations and competencies. The expectation constitutive of trust follows: it is that A expects it *of* S that were A to rely on S φ-ing, or telling the truth, S would view A's reliance *as a reason* to φ, or tell the truth (Faulkner 2007a:882). Insofar as holding S to this expectation is a way of thinking well of S, in trusting S, A will then presume that S would be sensitive to this reason, and give it due deliberative weight. It follows that, other things being equal, A will presume that S will be moved by this reason and so φ, or tell the truth, because of it. But to presume that S will φ, or tell the truth, for this reason is just to presume that S is trustworthy. Thus, in trusting S to φ, or tell the truth, A thinks well of S and thereby presumes that S is trustworthy and so will φ, or tell the truth.

A presumption is not a belief; this is a non-doxastic view of trust. A presumption is not evidentially constrained in the way a belief is constrained. Thus, A can continue, up to a point, to think well of S even in the absence of evidence, or even in the face of counter-evidence – as the accused friend case illustrates. Equally, a presumption cannot justify belief in the way that belief can justify belief. However, it can play the epistemic role demanded: the presumption that S is trustworthy, and so telling the truth, makes it epistemically reasonable for A to take S's telling at face value as the assumption of responsibility that it purports to be. This reason is not grounded on those second-personal facts that justify A's resulting testimonial belief, as is proposed by the doxastic view; rather, it is grounded, ultimately, on A's "optimistic world-view" (Uslaner 2002:25) or A's "zest for life" (Løgstrup 1997:13 and 36).

This account of the epistemic reason that trust provides then fits into an assurance account of the reason A has for accepting S's testimony to p in the following way; and here I return to the good and bad cases described above. In the good case, S tells A that p knowing that p and recognizing A's need to know whether p. Moreover, it is because he, S, knows that p and recognizes A's need to know whether p, that S tells A that p – thereby intending A to believe that p on his authority. In trusting S for the truth as to whether p, A expects S to be trustworthy – or tell her, A, that p just because he knows that p and recognizes her need to know whether p. Moreover, trusting S for the truth, A not only expects this of S, A presumes this of S. In presuming that S is trustworthy, A will then take S's intention that she, A, believe that p as a reason to believe that p. In so doing, she will believe that p on S's authority, and thereby regard S's telling as the assurance it purports to be. And things will be as they purport. Since S knows that p, S can genuinely offer his assurance, and A thereby gains a *justifying reason for belief* – a reason based, by way of A's trust, on S's decision to tell A what he knows to be the case. By contrast, in the bad case, in trusting S for the truth, A expects and presumes various things about S's position and motivation which turn out to be false. There is no actual desire to inform or credible assumption of responsibility for A's trust to latch onto; S's assurance is empty. It follows that A's testimonial belief, *while epistemically reasonable, is unjustified.* This description of the good and bad cases then explains why it is that trust renders A's testimonial belief *epistemically* reasonable: it does so, even in the bad case, because there is a route to the truth of A's belief from the presumptions constitutive of trust in the good case.[7]

Set up this way the assurance theory has a significant epistemological advantage over reductive, non-reductive and reliabilist theories: its account of how testimonial beliefs are justified is explanatory, which is to say, *it can explain why it is that these beliefs are true*. Normally, the advantage of the assurance theory is stated to be phenomenological: the other theories do not get the facts about our testimonial relationships right; hence, for instance, Moran's (2005:24) claim that reductive theories put speaker and audience into "disharmony" with one another. While this phenomenological advantage should not be understated, the epistemological advantage is too often missed. This point might be made by comparison with reliabilist theories; consider, for instance, Lackey (2008)'s view that, when A acquires the testimonial belief that p on the basis of S telling A that p, the justification this testimonial belief possesses is fundamentally determined by the reliability of S's utterance. On this account, statements "are the central bearers of epistemic significance" (Lackey 2008:72); and their significance is that they are reliable, or not. Here facts about reliability are taken to be epistemologically basic. There is no discussion as to why a given statement might or might not be reliable. But were an explanation of the reliability facts sought, it would be delivered by reference to the facts that an assurance theory takes to ground testimonial justification, namely facts to do with speakers' attitudes towards utterance and how these engage with audiences' expectations of speakers. That is, if the statement S produces in telling A that p is reliable, it will be so, in normal conditions, because S has decided to tell A what he knows to be the case, and thereby has taken responsibility for A believing truly.[8]

Related Topics

In this volume:

Trust and Reliance
Trust and Belief
Trust and Emotion
Trust and Will
Trust and Epistemic Responsibility
Trust and Trustworthiness

Notes

1 Reasoning about whether to accept what S says is compatible with deferring to S's authority. The claim that there are two kinds of reason for belief is the claim that there are two kinds of grounds for belief; and A could reason about whether to accept what S says and on this basis decide to believe that p on S's authority.
2 Marušić (2015:186–187) sharply distinguishes trust and reliance: reliance is an action, trust is an attitude. Conceiving of trust in solely attitudinal terms pulls one away from the three-place predicate, see Faulkner (2015) and Domenicucci and Holton (2016).
3 Thus, in telling A that p, S thereby invites trust (Hinchman 2005).
4 Hinchman (2005:578) says, "[t]rust is not belief, although it may give rise to belief."
5 This is something Hieronymi (2008) argues at length.
6 Of course, it is possible to say that in trusting one takes a view of the situation wherein one accepts the offer of assurance and thereby gains a reason for accepting this offer of assurance; it is possible to claim that trust bootstraps a reason for itself. The problem is then the plausibility of this claim compared to non-doxastic accounts of a trusting party's reason.
7 By analogy: the hallucinatory perceptual appearance of p renders the percipient's perceptual belief that p epistemically reasonable because and insofar as there is a route to the truth of this belief from the perceptual appearance of p in the veridical case.
8 I develop this criticism in Faulkner (2013); and develop a parallel criticism of non-reductive theory in Faulkner (forthcoming).

References

Adler, J.E. (1994) "Testimony, Trust, Knowing," *Journal of Philosophy* 91(5): 264–275.
Baier, A. (1986) "Trust and Antitrust," *Ethics* 96(2): 231–260.
Burge, T. (1993) "Content Preservation," *Philosophical Review* 102(4): 457–488.
Domenicucci, J. and Holton, R. (2016) "Trust as a Two-Place Relation," in P. Faulkner and T. Simpson (eds.), *The Philosophy of Trust*, Oxford: Oxford University Press.
Faulkner, P. (2002) "On the Rationality of Our Response to Testimony," *Synthese* 131(3): 353–370.
Faulkner, P. (2007a) "On Telling and Trusting," *Mind* 116(464): 875–902.
Faulkner, P. (2007b) "What is Wrong with Lying?" *Philosophy and Phenomenological Research* 75 (3): 535–558.
Faulkner, P. (2011) *Knowledge on Trust*, Oxford: Oxford University Press.

Faulkner, P. (2013) "Two-Stage Reliabilism, Virtue Reliabilism, Dualism and the Problem of Sufficiency," *Social Epistemology and Reply Collective* 2(8):121–138.
Faulkner, P. (2015) "The Attitude of Trust is Basic," *Analysis* 75(3): 424–429.
Faulkner, P. (2017) "The Problem of Trust," in P. Faulkner and T. Simpson (eds.), *The Philosophy of Trust*, Oxford: Oxford University Press.
Faulkner, P. (2018) "Giving the Benefit of the Doubt" *International Journal of Philosophical Studies* 26(2): 139–155.
Faulkner, P. (Forthcoming) "The Testimonial Preservation of Warrant," in S. Wright and S. Goldberg (eds.), *Testimony and Memory: New Essays in Epistemology*, Oxford: Oxford University Press.
Fricker, E. (1987) "The Epistemology of Testimony." *Proceedings of the Aristotelian Society* Suppl. 61:57–83.
Fricker, M. (2012) "Group Testimony? The Making of a Collective Good Informant," *Philosophy and Phenomenological Research* 84(2): 249–276.
Goldberg, S. (2010) *Relying on Others*, Oxford: Oxford University Press.
Graham, P.J. (2000) "The Reliability of Testimony," *Philosophy and Phenomenological Research* 61 (3): 695–709.
Grice, P. (1957) "Meaning," reprinted in P. Grice (ed.), *Studies in the Way of Words*, Cambridge, MA: Harvard University Press.
Hawley, K. (2014) "Trust, Distrust and Commitment," *Noûs* 48(1):1–20.
Hieronymi, P. (2008) "The Reasons of Trust," *Australasian Journal of Philosophy* 86(2): 213–236.
Hinchman, E. (2005) "Telling as Inviting to Trust," *Philosophy and Phenomenological Research* 70 (3): 562–587.
Hollis, M. (1998) *Trust within Reason*, Cambridge: Cambridge University Press.
Holton, R. (1994) "Deciding to Trust, Coming to Believe," *Australasian Journal of Philosophy* 72 (1): 63–76.
Horsburgh, H.J.N. (1960) "The Ethics of Trust," *Philosophical Quarterly* 10(41): 343–354.
Hume, D. (1740) *A Treatise of Human Nature*, Oxford: Clarendon Press.
Jones, K. (1996) "Trust as an Affective Attitude," *Ethics* 107(1): 4–25.
Jones, K. (1998) *Trust*, in *Routledge Encyclopedia of Philosophy*, London: Taylor & Francis.
Keren, A. (2014) "Trust and Belief: A Preemptive Reasons Account," *Synthese* 191(12): 2593–2615.
Lackey, J. (2006) "Learning from Words," *Philosophy and Phenomenological Research* 73(1): 77–101.
Lackey, J. (2008) *Learning from Words – Testimony as a Source of Knowledge*, Oxford: Oxford University Press.
Løgstrup, K.E. (1997) *The Ethical Demand*, Notre Dame, IN: University of Notre Dame Press.
Løgstrup, K.E. (2007) *Beyond the Ethical Demand*, Notre Dame, IN: University of Notre Dame Press.
Marušić, B. (2015) *Evidence and Agency: Norms of Belief for Promising and Resolving*, Oxford: Oxford University Press.
McDowell, J. (1994) "Knowledge by Hearsay," in J. McDowell (ed.), *Meaning, Knowledge and Reality*, Cambridge, MA: Harvard University Press.
McMyler, B. (2011) *Testimony, Trust and Authority*, Oxford: Oxford University Press.
McMyler, B. (2017) "Deciding to Trust," in P. Faulkner and T. Simpson (eds.), *The Philosophy of Trust*, Oxford: Oxford University Press.
Möllering, G. (2009) "Leaps and Lapses of Faith: Exploring the Relationship between Trust and Deception," in B. Harrington (ed.), *Deception: From Ancient Empires to Internet Dating*, Stanford: Stanford University Press.
Moran, R. (2001) *Authority and Estrangement: An Essay on Self-Knowledge*, Princeton: Princeton University Press.
Moran, R. (2005) "Getting Told and Being Believed," *Philosophers' Imprint* 5(5): 1–29.
Reid, T. (1764) "An Inquiry into the Mind on the Principles of Common Sense" in W.H. Bart (ed.) *The Works of Thomas Reid*, Edinburgh: MacLachlan & Stewart.
Simpson, D. (1992) "Lying, Liars and Language," *Philosophy and Phenomenological Research* 52 (3): 623–639.
Strawson, P.F. (1974) "Freedom and Resentment" in P.F. Strawson (ed.) *Freedom and Resentment and Other Essays*, London: Methuen & Co.
Uslaner, E.M. (2002) *The Moral Foundations of Trust*, Cambridge: Cambridge University Press.
Zagzebski, L. (2012) *Epistemic Authority: A Theory of Trust, Authority, and Autonomy in Belief*, Oxford: Oxford University Press.

26

TRUST AND DISTRIBUTED EPISTEMIC LABOR

Boaz Miller and Ori Freiman

26.1 Introduction: Trust – The Glue That Binds the Products of Distributed Research into Knowledge

In a seminal paper "Epistemic dependence," Hardwig (1985) observes that he has acquired many of his true beliefs that are commonly regarded as knowledge from testimonial sources, such as experts and the media. These include beliefs about the causes of lung cancer or economic inflation. He claims that he does not personally possess evidence for the truth of these claims, or at most only weak evidence. This is because he, qua an individual, lacks and is realistically unable to gain the necessary expertise to evaluate the evidence supporting all these beliefs. Even if he had the required expertise, it would take him more than his lifetime to acquire the relevant evidence to justify all his beliefs. This evidence is dispersed among many members of his epistemic community. Rather than basing such beliefs on evidence, so Hardwig argues, he must form them on trust in the testimonies of other people who he believes possess the required evidence.

Hardwig stresses that the asymmetry he identifies does not only characterize expert-lay relationships but also expert-expert relationships. Due to the increased specialization in modern science, even in their own field, experts do not always have the knowledge and abilities for evaluating their peers' claims, and even when they do, they do not have enough time and resources to evaluate them in practice (see also Rolin, this volume).

Consequently, Hardwig poses a dilemma to the traditional analysis of knowledge: if we want to maintain that such propositions are known, then either only an epistemic community and none of its members individually knows them, because the community is the only body that possesses the evidence required to justify them (Hardwig 1985), or individuals know these propositions vicariously, i.e., without possessing justification for them (Hardwig 1991).

If we follow Hardwig's lead, trust is as fundamental to knowledge as epistemic justification, e.g. evidence. Trust is the glue that binds researchers' testimonies about products of their distributed epistemic labor into collective knowledge. Trust, in lieu or in addition to epistemic justification, is the element that grants the status of knowledge to individuals' true beliefs about the products of epistemic labor of other members of their epistemic community.

Hardwig's argument, or something like it, has been accepted by many social epistemologists who study distributed scientific research, and they have explored its complications and ramifications, which will be reviewed in this chapter. Other social epistemologists, however, especially those who do not focus on scientific knowledge, have resisted Hardwig's argument. Their grounds for resisting Hardwig's argument are based on the claim that an individual subject typically possesses sufficient justification for her testimonially obtained beliefs to reach the status of knowledge. They acknowledge that an individual may lack *direct* evidence for these beliefs, but they insist that she normally possesses *indirect* evidence for these beliefs in the form of multiple testimonial confirmations of the same report, evidence about her informants' sincerity and competence, and evidence about experts' success rate in making true predictions (Adler 1994; Fricker 2002:374; Goldman 2001:106–107). Therefore, an individual need not normally base her beliefs on blind or partly blind trust, and Hardwig's dilemma is avoided.

Miller (2015) defends Hardwig's claims against these objections. By drawing on examples from the practice of science, Miller argues that there are sufficiently prevalent cases in which the evidence that an individual scientist possesses is insufficient to grant her knowledge according to standard theories of knowledge. Nevertheless, such scientists often offer testimony based on their insufficient evidence, and it is trusted by their peers and the lay public. For example, scientists often make discovery claims although the evidence they have for their claims are defective. Such cases, so Miller argues, are indistinguishable from the point of view of the recipients of the testimony from cases in which the testifying scientist possesses sufficient evidence for her claims. If we want to explain, why a scientist does not acquire knowledge when he trusts a colleague whose evidence is defective, but does acquire knowledge when the colleague possesses the required evidence, even if in both cases the scientist personally possesses the exact same evidence about his colleague's trustworthiness, then we must acknowledge that the evidence that justifies the scientist's belief is possessed by another person, rather than located solely in his own mind. Hence, Hardwig's challenge stands.

If we accept Hardwig's argument, or something similar to it, many questions arise. These questions are both conceptual and empirical, and they pertain to the nature of the trust that binds individuals' testimonies into collective knowledge. This paper thematically surveys these questions. In the next section we explore what grounds trust. We first sketch what trust is, and ask what factors are involved in granting it. We then ask how trust in distributed research is established and maintained. Possible answers ranging from ethnographic field studies, game-theory considerations and problems, and a moral (rather than epistemic) approach to trust are discussed.

26.2 What Grounds Trust? How Trust is Built, Given and Maintained?

In the last section, we saw that researchers must extend trust to each other beyond the evidence they can personally possess for the truth of each other's claims. But researchers neither indiscriminately trust each other nor should they. Rather, they distinguish between different people and different circumstances, and use a variety of strategies for deciding whom to trust on what issues and to what extent. This section reviews research on trust in social epistemology as well as science and technology studies that addresses the question of the grounds on which researchers trust each other. This question has both empirical and philosophical dimensions, and the answers to it depend inter alia on the disciplinary background of those who study it.

Before we review the different answers to this question, we should first note that trust is not an all-or-nothing stance. That is, it is not the case that a person either categorically trusts or distrusts another person or institution. Rather, trust may be preferential, selective, and come in degrees: a person may trust another person on some matter to some extent, but distrust her on another issue (Miller 2014:71–73). In addition, trust may be either rational or irrational. Trust is rational when the trustor has evidence about the trustworthiness of the trustee on a given mater, or at least when the trustor does not have evidence that the trustee is untrustworthy; trust is irrational when she does not. But even when rational, the evidence a person has for trusting another person does not conclusively rule out the possibility that the trustee will violate the trustor's trust (Simpson 2011:30).

What factors determine, then, whom, to what extent, and on which issues researchers involved in distributed research trust? Let us start with ethnographic field studies of distributed scientific research, which answer this question empirically. Such studies reveal several possible answers. Based on a field research of an interdisciplinary collaborative research team, Wagenknecht (2015) identifies two strategies that scientists use to assess their collaborators' testimonies and credibility over time. While Wagenknecht calls them "strategies alternative to trust" (2015:164), these practices are better construed as strategies *for* giving trust.[1] One such strategy is assessing a collaborator's explanatory responsiveness. Wagenknecht depicts various practices of cross-examination in which researchers evaluate their collaborators' responses to clarification questions about their work, which are in turn used to establish their trustworthiness. The second strategy is appealing to formal indicators, such as affiliation with prestigious research institutions or publication in high-ranking journals, which are regarded as gate-keepers for credibility. In particular, a researcher affiliated with a prestigious institution may be accorded more trust for a prima facie suspect claim than a researcher affiliated with a less prestigious institution.

Origgi (2018: chapter 4) notes an inherent problem with such trustworthiness indicators, both for people who use them to evaluate others, as well as for people who try to accumulate them to build their own reputation. This problem stems from two uncertainties: an uncertainty about the value of these indicators, namely, how much they are actually correlated with reliability, and a second-order uncertainty about what value other people give them. Origgi (2018: chapter 9) further notes specific problems with their values in science, which stem from systematic distortions, such as administrators' preference for quantified indicators such as journals' impact factors, which do not necessarily best indicate a researcher's real trustworthiness (see also Origgi, this volume).

The problem of whom to trust is aggravated in interdisciplinary collaborations, when experts from different fields may work under different, possibly incompatible background assumptions and professional standards. By analyzing cooperative activities, Andersen and Wagenknecht (2013) note several ways in which researchers overcome this barrier: (1) one person (a leader) is typically responsible for the integration of research from different fields; (2) researchers gradually learn each other's' background assumptions; (3) researchers negotiate background assumptions with their collaborators from other fields.

Drawing also on an empirical field study of the laboratory, Collins (2001) argues that trust between collaborating experimenters is grounded in their appreciation of their peers' tacit knowledge. According to Collins, when in doubt, only when researchers are persuaded through personal observation and interaction that their peers have the tacit knowledge required to successfully carry out the experiments they describe in their published papers, do they trust their experimental results.

Another approach to answer the question of the grounds for trust in distributed research does not appeal to empirical research, but to game-theoretical considerations (see also Tutić and Voss as well as Dimock, this volume). Blais (1987) models a researcher's decision to testify truly to another researcher as an iterated prisoner-dilemma game, where testifying truly is analogous to cooperating. He argues that a simple "tit for tat" tactic of rewarding reliable researchers and punishing unreliable ones is a stable strategy that may explain how scientific collaboration is possible.[2] There are, however, problems with this approach. Frost-Arnold (2013) argues that scientific collaboration does not always fit this model. Some requests for information sharing occur only once, hence do not correspond to an iterated game; some researchers cannot know when their trust is violated; others, especially junior researchers and graduate students, are not in a position to retaliate to trust violations. But they nevertheless do extend trust. Hardwig (1991) argues that in reality, institutional sanctions for fraud or trust violation are often absent or ineffective, and therefore cannot account for researchers' trustworthiness.

As an alternative to this approach, Frost-Arnold (2013) argues that moral trust, rather than self-interested (i.e. game-theoretical) trust or epistemic trust, enables scientific collaboration. This is because scientists not only trust others when they receive others' work, but also when share their work with others. When they share their work, they trust their colleagues not to plagiarize it or steal their credit for it. When they do so, they trust their peers' moral character, rather than merely the truth of their claims. She argues that such trust is grounded in their evaluation of their peers' moral character.

Another account of the grounds for trust is given by Rolin (2004), who claims that trust in another person's testimony is prone to the influence of social biases, especially sexist biases, which may cause women's claims and research outputs to be unjustly distrusted. She stresses that when such biases operate systematically, the body of knowledge produced and accepted by an entire research community may become accordingly biased as well (see also Medina; Potter; and Scheman, this volume). Miller (2014) expands on Rolin's argument and claims that the influence of social values on trust in testimony is not just another aspect of the familiar claim that values fill the logical gap of underdetermination between theory and evidence (Longino 2002: chapter 5), which some philosophers find unconvincing (Laudan and Leplin 1991; Norton 2008). Miller argues that values affect trust in testimony not only by filling the gap between theory and evidence, but by adjusting the weight a person gives to other people's testimonies qua evidence. Miller argues that the same mechanism operates not only with respect to testimony, but with respect to evidence in general, including evidence produced by non-humans. This may indirectly support the claim that non-humans are genuine objects of trust (see Section 26.5 below).

26.3 Inductive Risk and Calibration of Reliability Standards

When scientists report information to each other, there is always a possibility of error. Merely reporting an error does not necessarily amount to a breach of trust, since researchers take into consideration the possibility that the reports they receive are inaccurate. But how are error-rate and reliability standards established to begin with, and what constitutes breaching them? This question arises with respect to communication between researchers in the same discipline, cross-disciplinary communication and communication of scientists with the public. This section reviews answers given to these questions.

Gerken (2015) argues that there are reliability standards that are shared by all sciences. Within collaborative research, he distinguishes a testimony that constitutes input to mono-disciplinary research from a testimony that constitutes input to an interdisciplinary research. Gerken argues that a general scientific norm of assertion is that it is appropriate to offer testimony only if it is possible to discursively justify it in the context in which it is given. He further argues that the scientific discursive standards of justification associated with this norm are closely connected with scientific virtues such as replicability, revisability and accountability.

Gerken's account, however, is at most partial, because scientists make reports under different implicit or explicit weightings of inductive risks against each other. There is still the question of how these weightings arise, and how scientists recognize them, particularly as these weightings may differ between individual researchers and between fields. Inductive risk is the risk that stems from making a wrong epistemic judgment, such as rejecting a true hypothesis or accepting a false hypothesis (Douglas 2000; 2009: chapter 5). Wilholt (2009) argues that shared epistemic norms and standards by researchers in a field are *social conventions* that are defined in terms of an accepted weighting of different inductive risks, where the weights are determined by competing social values, such as environmental protection versus economic innovation. As such, Wilholt *defines* trustworthiness as adherence to these conventions, and violating trust is as infringing them, either by fraudulent or sloppy research.

Miller (2014) argues that the epistemic mechanism by which values affect epistemic standards according to Wilholt's model is assigning different evidential weights to different types of evidence, for example, assigning more evidential weight to epidemiological studies than toxicology studies when determining a substance's harmfulness. While Wilholt (2009:98) argues that epistemic norms are merely conventional, and that any convention can establish justified trust between researchers as long as it is shared and followed by all of them, Miller (2014:75) argues that only conventions that do not allow for too high or too low rates of errors can effectively be adopted in a well-functioning research community.

Wilholt (2013) further analyzes the weighting of inductive risks that underpins these conventions, and argues that it consists of a complex trade-off between three salient values: the reliability of positive results, the reliability of negative results, and the investigation's rate of delivering definitive results (its power). Reliably trusting another researcher involves correctly assessing the trade-offs she makes between these values, hence affording trust in distributed research is inherently value-laden.[3]

With respect to the role inductive risks ought to play in public trust in science, a possible view is that inductive risk considerations should affect the level of certainty scientists need to meet in order to give testimony to the public. Franco (2017) argues that inductive risks should affect public scientific assertion. Suppose, for example, that scientists deem the potential negative health consequences to babies that are not breastfed as more severe than the inconvenience and career impediment from which some mothers suffer due to prolonged breastfeeding. In such a case, scientists should lower the level of certainty required to report to the public the health benefits of breastfeeding. In particular when the risks are severe, e.g. the catastrophes that may be caused by the public not accepting the theory of global climate change, scientists should express their public claims with more certainty. Steel (2016) stresses that the values that should govern such scientific testimony are not the scientists' individual values, but publicly accepted values, democratically decided upon. By contrast, John (2015) argues that inductive risks should *not* affect the testimony of scientists to audiences outside the scientific community. Rather, scientists should transparently explain the relevant inductive risks and the dependency of the scientific results on them. He sees the communication of inductive risks as part of scientists' obligations to the public and to public-policy makers.

26.4 Trust Transforms Individuals into a Collective

So far we discussed trust between individual members of a distributed research community, that is, trust between individual researchers who rely on others' testimonies about the methods and products of their research. We may also ask what the status is of the community itself. Can distributed epistemic labor turn the individuals who pursue it together into a group that can be accorded trust as a collective? In other words, can the fact that people divide research tasks between them and rely on each other's results turn them into a collective that may be trusted over and above the trust that is given to its individual members?

Bird answers this question in the positive. He writes, "individuals can compose a social unity when they cohere because of the mutual interdependence that arises from the division of labor" (2015:54). Bird argues that such groups can be trusted as collectives because they have what Durkheim ([1893] 1984) calls "organic solidarity." While in societies characterized by mechanical solidarity, social cohesion is achieved because individual members have similar thoughts and attitudes, such as a shared religion, in organic solidarity, individual members do *not* necessarily share the same beliefs and attitudes. Organic solidarity is characterized by division of epistemic labor and mutual dependence of members on each other. In organic solidarity, so Bird argues, a scientist deeply epistemically depends on the products of other scientists' epistemic labor, such as background theories, experimental equipment, statistical tools and computer software, to the extent that her epistemic products can be seen as collectively produced by the scientific community as a whole. Bird draws on Ed Hutchins's famous examples of the USS Palau (1995a), and the airplane (1995b), in which the social organization and individuals' various distinct roles on the ship or airplane closely match the functions needed to perform a knowledge generating process in organic solidarity.

Wray (2007) also adopts Durkheim's distinction between organic and mechanical solidarity and argues that the division of labor characterizing research teams enables the group, as a whole, to know things that individual members cannot know. This is since individual members of research teams contribute their own pieces of puzzle, the outcome of their epistemic labor, to the big picture. Wray shares Bird view that having organic solidarity is necessary for a society to constitute a collective object of trust, but unlike Bird, Wray thinks that the scientific community as a whole does *not* have organic solidarity, because individuals' epistemic dependence on each other is not that great. Only smaller research teams in which there is high epistemic dependence between members have such solidarity. Hence only smaller teams, rather than a scientific community as a whole, can be a collective object of trust, or so Wary argues.

Knorr-Cetina (1999: chapter 3) also relates the social organization of distributed research with the question of whether groups can be trusted as collectives. She analyzes the High Energy Physics (HEP) experiments at CERN. Scientists who work at CERN have distinct roles, with their own special areas of expertise. Each individual epistemically contributes to the general outcome. In addition to correspondence between the organizational structure of the experimental team and the elements of a knowledge generating process, Knorr-Cetina argues that the epistemic culture of the HEP experiments erodes individuals' sense of self and enhances their sense of collectivity. The epistemic culture makes "the experiment," with "experiment" referring to the people, equipment and process, the object of trust rather than the individual experimenters. Knorr-Cetina contrasts the HEP experiments with laboratory experiments in molecular biology, which do *not* turn the individuals who participate in them into a knowing collective because of their small scale and hierarchical social structure.

Against the views reviewed so far, Giere (2007) argues that distributed cognitive labor does *not* turn those who pursue it into a collective that can be trusted on its own. According to Giere, Knorr-Cetina's argument, and by extension others like it, rest on a mistaken assumption:

> Knorr-Cetina seems to be assuming that, if knowledge is being produced, there must be an epistemic subject, the thing that knows what comes to be known. Moreover, knowing requires a subject with a mind, where minds are typically conscious. Being unable to find a traditional individual or even collective epistemic subject within the organization of experiments in HEP, she feels herself forced to find another epistemic subject, settling eventually on the experiment itself.
>
> *(Giere 2007:316)*

But, so Giere argues, as a collective entity, the experiment lacks features that make up genuine epistemic agents, such as self-consciousness, consciousness of others and intentionality. Hence it does not constitute a genuine agent. Distributed cognition does not entail distributed knowing.

So far in this section, it was assumed that for an epistemic community or a research group to be trusted as a collective, it must possess agency, which minimally includes having collective representations of reality, collective goals, and the ability to rationally collectively act to achieve these goals (List and Pettit 2011). Both Giere and his opponents make this assumption. They only differ on whether such an agent exists, hence their different answers to the question of trust in a collective. Wilholt (2016) denies this assumption, but argues that a community that divides epistemic labor among its members can be a collective object of trust regardless of whether it has agency. He argues that research groups indeed usually do not form agents because they exist only for the publication, the experiment or the study, spread spatially, and involve many institutions. However, to answer whether, and how, the entire community can be an object of trust, he advocates a position according to which individual scientists trust the *conventions of a community*. These conventions, which affect the methodological standards of collaborative research groups, are not reducible to the beliefs of any individual; hence the entire community is an object of trust. In other words, the trustworthiness of research groups cannot be reduced to the trustworthiness of the group's members.

When a group is regarded as a collective entity that produces results together, a problem arises with respect to who is responsible and accountable for the claims made by the group. Traditionally, lead authors are the locus of responsibility for a paper. Wagenknecht (2015:178) recognizes that under hierarchical authorship of multi-author papers, the lead author has various roles such as responsibility for the composition of the paper, providing the main argument and evidential basis, making adjustments, additions and criticism on the various parts added to the paper, and its submission. In a way, the lead author serves as the central knot in the trust relations of the authorship group. The lead/first author is also, most of the times, the most recognized person by which other researchers trust the results of a collaborative research paper.

However, as highly distributed research becomes more and more common, it becomes increasingly unclear that lead authors have this role, as other members make vital contributions that may be outside the lead author's expertise. The scientific literature is experiencing a continuous increase in co-authored papers in almost all scientific disciplines, especially in the natural sciences (for statistics, see references within Wagenknecht 2016:21, and within Wray 2006:507).

Moreover, due to the globalization and commercialization of research, especially pharmaceutical research, it become increasingly impossible to identify a lead author or a person who can assume epistemic responsibility for a trial's outcomes (Kukla 2012). How, then, can trust be established? What is the collective character of an author and who is accountable for scientific papers written by a group?

In current scientific practice, these questions are still open, and are highly relevant for both scientists and social epistemologists who study them (Kukla 2012; Huebner, Kukla and Weinsberg 2017). Clement (2014) suggests a method for addressing who deserves to be an author of a scientific article, by mentioning who are behind the ideas, the work, the writing and the stewardship. Wray (2006) argues that authors of collaborative papers be conceptualized as plural subjects and not as groups of individuals. The realistic prospects of these proposals remain to be seen in particular given the different disciplinary norms in deciding about authorship orders.

The problem of holding authors accountable in highly collaborative research is aggravated by the phenomena of ghost writing – when lead authors are a rubber stamp for other people's work (Sismondo 2004, 2007, 2009; Sismondo and Doucet 2010); by sponsorships influencing published results (see meta-analysis by Sismondo 2008); and problems associated with publication practices such as gift-authorship and conflicts of interest (Smith and Williams-Jones 2012).

26.5 Technological Instruments as Objects of Trust

When distributed research is conducted, cognitive tasks are delegated to non-humans, such as instruments and computers, which manufacture, represent and disseminate data. Wagenknecht (2014:477–478) notes that researchers need not only extend trust to other researchers' testimonies but also to epistemic artifacts. For example, they must trust a dataset to be accurate and complete, an instrument to be properly calibrated, etc. But are such non-humans entities objects of genuine trust, or are they merely relied upon? Trust is distinguishable from mere reliance in that reliance is merely an expectation of a certain regularity to happen, whereas trust is a normative attitude. When trust, as opposed to mere reliance, is breached, the trustor feels let down and betrayed (Baier 1986).

The premise of this chapter is that trust binds the products of distributed epistemic labor into collective knowledge. We saw that trust can also transform an ensemble of individuals into a collective body worthy of trust on its own. The significance of the question of whether instruments are objects of genuine trust is therefore twofold. First, can unmediated instrumental outputs constitute part of this collective knowledge, or do they first need to be testified by a human researcher? Second, do instruments constitute part of a collective body worthy of trust, or do only humans take part in it?

Within analytic epistemology and philosophy of technology, Freiman (2014) identifies two extreme sides in the debate about whether it is categorically possible to genuinely trust technological artifacts, the orthodox camp and non-orthodox camp. The orthodox camp represents the common and traditional views of mainstream epistemology, and holds that genuine trust is based on a human quality, such as intentionality, consciousness, free will or even good will (for a survey of reasons, see Nickel et al. 2010:432), and therefore cannot be directed at artifacts. Unlike mere reliance, trust is "inherently subject to the risk that the other will abuse the power of discretion" (Hardin 1993:507; for more about the distinction between trust and mere reliance, see references within Hawley 2014:1 as well as Goldberg, this volume). According to the orthodox view, I rely on my computer to work, but I do not trust it. When it malfunctions, I might be disappointed, but not betrayed.

The current accepted view of trust can hold that "trusting is not an attitude that we can adopt toward machinery" (Jones 1996:14). As such, inquiries about trust and technologies commonly bypass the technologies as objects of trust and point to the humans who are behind the technologies – such as engineers, designers, etc., as the objects of trust. For example, when a person trusts a bridge not to collapse while crossing it, she actually trusts the people who designed and built the bridge and those who are responsible for its maintenance (Origgi 2008; Pitt 2010). Freiman and Miller (2019) offer a middle ground position, according to which instruments may be subject of "quasi-trust," which is distinguishable both from mere reliance, and from full-fledged normative trust.

Nickel (2013) argues that trust regarding technologies means not only trusting the people who are behind the technologies but also social institutions, as entities. According to his entitlement account of trust in technological artifacts and socio-technological systems, an trustor has evidences that indicates to her the trustworthiness of the humans behind the technologies and their interests in serving the interests of the users. In such a way, for example, a technology failure to perform will lead to an effective sanction by institutional structures; and others are willing to stake their reputations on the technologies' performances.

The question of whether instruments that are involved in distributed research are genuine objects of trust is relevant also to the issue of trust in groups. Assuming that collectives can be genuine objects of trust, do they consist of only humans or also non-humans? As we saw, Knorr-Cetina (1999) argues that in the case of the HEP experiments, the experiment as a whole, both the humans who perform it and the instruments they use, is an collective entity. Against this, Giere (2007) argues that this claim is metaphysically extravagant, and raises principled ontological problems about setting the boundaries of the alleged collective agent.

Assuming, however, that humans and non-humans can constitute an extended cognitive system, under which conditions can this happen, and what role does trust play in them? In a famous paper, Clark and Chalmers (1998:17) describe four conditions, known as the "trust and glue" conditions, for a person and external artifacts to be part of one extended cognitive systems. One of these criteria is that the person automatically trusts the outputs of the artifact, e.g. measurement results. It is unclear whether Clark and Chalmers use "trust" to denote genuine trust, or understand it only as a form of reliance, but however understood, relations of trust must exist between a human and an artifact for them to be part of an extended cognitive system.

When Clark explains how he wishes to apply the trust criterion, he acknowledges that if a person becomes suspicious of his artifact, it "would at that point cease to unproblematically count as a proper part of his individual cognitive economy" (2011:104). This is in striking contrast to our treatment of dubious brain-bound recollection, whose status as mental does not waver. Externally stored information is part of a subject's cognitive system and may thus realize a subject's mental states only insofar as it is implicitly trusted, and ceases to be so when it is not, while internal information sources, such as memory or perception, remain part of the subject's cognition regardless. Clark argues that this distinction between external and internal information sources makes no difference in practice, because occasions of doubt are rare and responsibilities for checking are rare. By contrast, Record and Miller (2018) argue that responsible instrument users should sometimes doubt the epistemic output of external artifacts on which they rely, rather than trust them implicitly. They illustrate their argument with the use of a GPS app on a smartphone, and argue that a responsible driver should not blindly follow the GPS instructions, lest she endangers herself. It therefore seems that the existence of trust relations between a user and an instrument is too strong a condition for them to constitute together an extended cognitive system. The issue of the conditions under which humans and technological artifacts constitute an extended cognitive system, and what role trust plays in them, remains underexplored in the philosophical literature.

26.6 Conclusion

To sum up, the introductory section of this paper presented Hardwig's argument from trust in the testimonies of others, which entails that trust is the glue that binds researchers' distributed labor products into communal knowledge. In order for trust, whatever it is, to work well, it must have certain properties. Additionally, different kinds of tasks require different kinds of glue. The social epistemology of trust studies these properties as well as the ways in which they bind individuals, knowledge and communities together.

The second section explored what grounds trust. We reviewed research on trust from the fields of science and technology studies and social epistemology. Answers included appeals to assessing collaborators' explanatory responsiveness and appealing to formal indicators such as affiliation and credibility. Other answers ground trust in the appreciation of peers' tacit knowledge. We then considered a self-interest account of trust, which is embedded in game-theoretical considerations. The section ended with exploring the role of the moral character of peers, social biases, and social values, in the formation of trust relations.

The third section turned to questions concerning establishing communal reliability standards, which are required for the formation of justified trust, and no less important – breaching them. These issues were dealt in respect to researchers communicating within the same discipline, across to other disciplines, and outside science – to the public and decision makers. Each communication route involves different epistemic considerations and its own underpinning inductive risks.

In the fourth section, we raised the question of whether distributed epistemic labor can turn individuals into a group that can be accorded trust as a collective entity; that is, whether a group can be trusted over and above the trust that is given to its individual members. The question surveyed several relevant debates within group ontology about correctly characterizing the division of labor and the collective objects of trust.

The last section raised the issue of technological artifacts in distributed research and collective knowledge. It began by raising the fundamental question of whether technological artifacts can categorically be considered as trustworthy. The common view within epistemology regards apparent trust in technologies as ultimately appealing to the humans who are behind the technologies, rather than the technological artifacts as objects of genuine trust. We then turned to present some existing accounts of trust that do take technological artifacts into consideration. These accounts consider technologies as well as social institutions as entities. We showed that the answer to the question of whether technological artifacts are genuine objects of trust is relevant to the issue of trust in groups. Last, we turned to the role trust plays in extended cognitive systems, where its existence it is considered a criterion for constituting such a system. We ended by noting that the roles trust plays in constituting a cognitive system of humans and technological artifacts are still largely underexplored.

Notes

1 For Wagenknecht, trust is an indiscriminating stance toward a particular person's credibility, which does not differentiate between different testimonies this person may give, whereas we construe trust as an attitude that differentiates both between people and testimonies, possibility from the same person.

2 Game theorists tend to see trust as mere reliance in a game. But there is still the possibility of being betrayed by an irrational actor, which a game-theoretical model does not account for.

3 Freedman (2015) argues that inductive risks set norms of testimony in general, not just in science. She argues that interests are involved in the assessment of the normative status of beliefs because evidence, on its own, does not set the bar of how much certainty is needed in any given case. The amount of evidence needed depends on the hearer and the hearer's inductive risk of believing what has been told.

References

Adler, J.E. (1994) "Testimony, Trust, Knowing," *The Journal of Philosophy* 91(5): 264–275.

Andersen, H. and Wagenknecht, S. (2013) "Epistemic Dependence in Interdisciplinary Groups," *Synthese* 190(11): 1881–1898.

Baier A. (1986) "Trust and Antitrust," *Ethics* 96(2): 231–260.

Beatty, J. (2006) "Masking Disagreement among Experts," *Episteme* 3(1): 52–67.

Bird, A. (2015) "When is There a Group that Knows? Distributed Cognition, Scientific Knowledge, and the Social Epistemic Subject," in J. Lackey (ed.), *Essays in Collective Epistemology*, Oxford: Oxford University Press.

Blais, M. (1987) "Epistemic Tit for Tat," *The Journal of Philosophy* 84: 363–375.

Clark, A. (2011) *Supersizing the Mind: Embodiment, Action, and Cognitive Extension*, Oxford: Oxford University Press.

Clark, A. and Chalmers D. (1998) "The Extended Mind," *Analysis* 58(1): 7–19.

Clement, T.P. (2014) "Authorship Matrix: A Rational Approach to Quantify Individual Contributions and Responsibilities in Multi-Author Scientific Articles," *Science and Engineering Ethics* 20 (2): 345–361.

Collins, H.M. (2001) "Tacit Knowledge, Trust and the Q of Sapphire," *Social Studies of Science* 31 (1): 71–85.

Douglas, H. (2000) "Inductive Risk and Values in Science," *Philosophy of Science* 67(4): 559–579.

Douglas, H. (2009) *Science, Policy, and the Value-Free Ideal*, Pittsburgh, PA: University of Pittsburgh Press.

Durkheim, E. ([1893] 1984) *The Division of Labor in Society*, W.D. Halls (trans.), New York: The Free Press.

Franco, P.L. (2017) "Assertion, Nonepistemic Values, and Scientific Practice," *Philosophy of Science* 84(1): 160–180.

Freedman, K.L. (2015) "Testimony and Epistemic Risk: The Dependence Account," *Social Epistemology* 29(3): 251–269.

Freiman, O. (2014) "Towards the Epistemology of the Internet of Things: Techno-epistemology and Ethical Considerations through the Prism of Trust," *International Review of Information Ethics* 22(2): 6–22.

Freiman O. and Miller B. (2019) "Can Artificial Entities Assert?," in S. Goldberg (ed.), *The Oxford Handbook of Assertion*, Oxford: Oxford University Press.
Fricker, E. (2002) "Trusting Others in the Sciences: a priori or Empirical Warrant?," *Studies in History and Philosophy of Science* 33(2): 373–383.
Frost-Arnold, K. (2013) "Moral Trust and Scientific Collaboration," *Studies in History and Philosophy of Science* 44: 301–310.
Gerken, M. (2015) "The Epistemic Norms of Intra-Scientific Testimony," *Philosophy of the Social Sciences* 45(6): 568–595.
Giere, R.N. (2007) "Distributed Cognition without Distributed Knowing," *Social Epistemology* 21 (3): 313–320.
Goldman, A.I. (2001) "Experts: Which Ones Should You Trust?" *Philosophy and Phenomenological Research* 63(1): 85–110.
Hardin, R. (1993) "The Street-Level Epistemology of Trust," *Politics & Society* 21(4): 505–529.
Hardwig, J. (1985) "Epistemic Dependence," *The Journal of Philosophy* 82(7): 335–349.
Hardwig, J. (1991) "The Role of Trust in Knowledge," *The Journal of Philosophy* 88(12): 693–708.
Hawley, K. (2014) "Trust, Distrust and Commitment," *Noûs* 48: 1–20.
Huebner, B., Kukla, R. and Winsberg, E. (2017) "Making an Author in Radically Collaborative Research," in M. Strevens, S. Angere, E.J. Olsson, K. Zollman and D. Bonnay, (eds.), *Scientific Collaboration and Collective Knowledge*, Oxford: Oxford University Press.
Hutchins, E. (1995a) *Cognition in the Wild*, Cambridge MA: MIT Press.
Hutchins, E. (1995b) "How a Cockpit Remembers its Speeds," *Cognitive Science* 19: 265–288.
John, S. (2015) "Inductive Risk and the Contexts of Communication," *Synthese* 192(1): 79–96.
Jones, K. (1996) "Trust as an Affective Attitude," *Ethics* 107(1): 4–25.
Knorr-Cetina, K. (1999) *Epistemic Cultures: How the Sciences Make Knowledge*, Cambridge, MA: Harvard University Press.
Kukla, R. (2012) "'Author TBD': Radical Collaboration in Contemporary Biomedical Research," *Philosophy of Science* 79(5): 845–858.
Laudan, L. and Leplin, J. (1991) "Empirical Equivalence and Underdetermination," *The Journal of Philosophy* 88(9): 449–472.
List C. and Pettit P. (2011) *Group Agency: The Possibility, Design, and Status of Corporate Agents*, Oxford: Oxford University Press.
Longino, H. (2002) *The Fate of Knowledge*, Princeton, NJ: Princeton University Press.
Miller, B. (2014) "Catching the WAVE: The Weight-Adjusting Account of Values and Evidence," *Studies in History and Philosophy of Science* 47: 69–80.
Miller, B. (2015) "Why (some) Knowledge is the Property of a Community and Possibly None of its Members," *The Philosophical Quarterly* 65(260): 417–441.
Nickel, P.J. (2013) "Trust in Technological Systems," in M.J. Vries, A.W.M. Meijers and S.O. Hansson (eds.), *Norms in Technology*, Dordrecht: Springer.
Nickel, P.J., Franssen, M. and Kroes, P. (2010) "Can We Make Sense of the Notion of Trustworthy Technology?" *Knowledge, Technology & Policy* 23(3–4): 429–444.
Norton, J. (2008) "Must Evidence Underdetermine Theory?," in M. Carrier, D.A. Howard and J. Kourany (Eds.), *The Challenge of the Social and the Pressure of Practice: Science and Values Revisited*, Pittsburgh: University of Pittsburgh Press.
Origgi, G. (2008) *Qu'est-ce que la confiance?*Paris: Vrin.
Origgi, G. (2018) *Reputation: What It Is and What It Matters*, Princeton, NJ: Princeton University Press.
Pitt, J.C. (2010) "It's Not about Technology," *Knowledge, Technology and Policy* 23(3–4): 445–454.
Record, I. and Miller B. (2018) "Taking iPhone Seriously: Epistemic Technologies and the Extended Mind," in D. Pritchard, A. Clark, J. Kallestrup, O.S. Palermos and J.A. Carter (eds.), *Extended Epistemology*, Oxford: Oxford University Press.
Rolin, K. (2004) "Why Gender Is a Relevant Factor in the Social Epistemology of Scientific Inquiry," *Philosophy of Science* 71(5): 880–891.
Simpson, T.W. (2011) "e-Trust and Reputation," *Ethics and Information Technology* 13(1): 29–38.
Sismondo, S. (2004) "Pharmaceutical Maneuvers," *Social Studies of Science* 34(2): 149–159.
Sismondo, S. (2007) "Ghost Management: How Much of the Medical Literature is Shaped behind the Scenes by the Pharmaceutical Industry?" *PLoS medicine* 4(9): e286.
Sismondo, S. (2008) "Pharmaceutical Company Funding and Its Consequences: A Qualitative Systematic Review," *Contemporary Clinical Trials* 29(2): 109–113.

Sismondo, S. (2009) "Ghosts in the Machine: Publication Planning in the Medical Sciences," *Social Studies of Science* 39(2): 171–198.

Sismondo, S. and Doucet, M. (2010) "Publication Ethics and the Ghost Management of Medical Publication," *Bioethics* 24(6): 273–283.

Smith, E. and Williams-Jones, B. (2012) "Authorship and Responsibility in Health Sciences Research: A Review of Procedures for Fairly Allocating Authorship in Multi-Author Studies," *Science and Engineering Ethics* 18(2): 199–212.

Steel, D. (2016) "Climate Change and Second-Order Uncertainty: Defending a Generalized, Normative, and Structural Argument from Inductive Risk," *Perspectives on Science* 24(6): 696–721.

Wagenknecht, S. (2014) "Opaque and Translucent Epistemic Dependence in Collaborative Scientific Practice," *Episteme* 11(4): 475–492.

Wagenknecht, S. (2015) "Facing the Incompleteness of Epistemic Trust: Managing Dependence in Scientific Practice," *Social Epistemology* 29(2): 160–184.

Wagenknecht, S. (2016) *A Social Epistemology of Research Groups: Collaboration in Scientific Practice*, London: Palgrave Macmillan.

Wilholt, T. (2009) "Bias and Values in Scientific Research," *Studies in History and Philosophy of Science* 40(1): 92–101.

Wilholt, T. (2013) "Epistemic Trust in Science," *The British Journal for the Philosophy of Science* 64 (2): 233–253.

Wilholt, T. (2016) "Collaborative Research, Scientific Communities, and the Social Diffusion of Trustworthiness," in M.S. Brady and M. Fricker (eds.), *The Epistemic Life of Groups: Essays in the Epistemology of Collectives*, Oxford: Oxford University Press.

Wray, K.B. (2006) "Scientific Authorship in the Age of Collaborative Research," *Studies in History and Philosophy of Science* 37(3): 505–514.

Wray, K.B. (2007) "Who Has Scientific Knowledge?" *Social Epistemology* 21(3): 337–347.

27
TRUST IN SCIENCE

Kristina Rolin

27.1 Introduction

Trust plays an important role in research groups, scientific communities, and the relations these communities have with the society. Much of present-day scientific knowledge is possible only by means of teamwork because the process of gathering and analyzing empirical evidence is too time-consuming or expensive for any individual scientist to accomplish independently (Hardwig 1991). Sometimes collaboration is a necessity because a research project requires expertise from different specialties or disciplines (Andersen and Wagenknecht 2013). A research group with a division of labor is capable of carrying out a project that no individual scientist could do on their own. In research groups, trust makes it possible for an individual scientist to rely on other group members, and to have good reasons to believe in the group's joint conclusion (de Ridder 2013). Trust is also needed in scientific communities that control the quality of research by means of training, peer review, and criticism (Longino 1990). While experimental and observational findings are sometimes reproduced or replicated successfully, not all research results are double-checked because excessive reviewing is costly and likely to delay other research projects (Kitcher 1992). Also, scientists may lack incentives to make effort to replicate research results because novelty is valued more than replication. Instead of questioning their colleagues' findings, scientists often refer to them as indirect support for their own results. One could even argue that trust makes it possible for individual scientists and science students to have good reasons to believe in scientific theories that are an outcome of the epistemic activities of an entire scientific community over a long period of time. Moreover, if scientific research is to provide public benefits, scientific communities must be trustworthy in the eyes of lay people (Grasswick 2010; Scheman 2001; Whyte and Crease 2010).

In this chapter, I focus on the question of what can ground rational epistemic trust within and in science. Trust is epistemic when it provides epistemic justification for one's beliefs, and epistemic trust is rational when it is based on evidence of the right kind and amount. I approach the question by dividing it into two sub-questions: (i) What can ground rational epistemic trust in an individual scientist? (ii) What can ground rational trust in (or reliance on) the social practices of scientific communities and the institutions of science?

Before moving on to discuss these questions, I explain how trust and epistemic trust are conceptualized in philosophy of science. The paradigmatic case of trust is a three-place relation involving two persons and a particular action or type of action. In a relation of trust, a person A trusts another person B to perform an action x (or A trusts B with valued good y). When A trusts B to do x, A takes the proposition that B will do x as a premise in her practical reasoning, or A works it into her plans that B will do x (Frost-Arnold 2013:302). Drawing on Annette Baier's seminal analysis of trust (1986), many philosophers stress that trust involves more than A's reliance on B to perform an action x (or to take care of valued good y). It involves an assumption of the goodwill of B towards A (Almassi 2012; Frost-Arnold 2013; Wilholt 2013). If B lets A down, then A is justified in feeling betrayed, and not merely disappointed (Baier 1986:235). Some philosophers extend this analysis of trust to cover relations that involve collective epistemic agents, such as research groups (Wilholt 2016), or impersonal elements, such as the social practices of scientific communities and the institutions of science (Wagenknecht 2015). Some others think that "reliance" is a more appropriate term than "trust" to characterize relations we can have with groups and organizations (Hawley 2017).

Epistemic trust is often distinguished from social trust. In a relation of social trust, a person A trusts another person B to act co-operatively or with A's best interests in mind, and in accordance with the social mores and norms of the society or the situation in which A and B find themselves (McDowell 2002:54). In a relation of epistemic trust, a person A trusts another person B to have good reasons to believe that p, and this is a reason for A to believe that p (Hardwig 1991:697). Many philosophers of science assume a doxastic account of epistemic trust and reductionism about testimony. A doxastic account is the view that A's epistemic trust in B involves A's having beliefs about B, for example, the belief that B is competent in the relevant domain and honest in rendering her testimony (Keren 2014:2593; see also Keren, this volume). Reductionism is the view that A's entitlement to place epistemic trust in B must be earned by her possession of enough evidence to ground the belief that B is a trustworthy testifier (Fricker 2002:379; see also Faulkner, this volume). Given these two assumptions, epistemic trust involves beliefs, and for these beliefs to be rational, they need to be grounded on evidence. Consequently, much of the debate on trust within and in science is concerned with the question: What kind of evidence can ground rational epistemic trust?

In section 27.2, I discuss the view that rational epistemic trust can be grounded on evidence concerning the epistemic and moral character of B. In section 27.3, I discuss the view that rational epistemic trust can also be grounded on evidence of the social practices of the scientific community that B belongs to and the relevant institutions of science. In section 27.4, I discuss rational epistemic trust from the perspective of citizens (including scientists who are lay people with respect to other scientists' expertise).

Throughout the discussion, it should be kept in mind that the question of what can ground rational epistemic trust arises only in a relation of epistemic dependence (see also Miller and Freiman, this volume). A person A is epistemically dependent on another person B when, for example, B possesses the evidence A is interested in, and it is more rational for A to rely on B than to rely on herself, or to spend a significant amount of time and effort to acquire and to fully understand the evidence B has (Hardwig 1985, 1991; Kitcher 1992). Unless A wishes to stay ignorant, she can try to manage the relation of epistemic dependence by considering whether epistemic trust in B is a rational way of grounding her belief. A relation of epistemic dependence can be opaque, translucent or a combination of both. A's epistemic dependence on B is opaque when A does not possess the expertise necessary to independently gather and analyze the evidence B has. A's epistemic dependence on B is translucent when A possesses the necessary expertise but, due to a division of labor, does not participate in the gathering and analyzing of the evidence (Wagenknecht 2014:483). If A has access to the evidence that B possesses and the expertise necessary for analyzing the evidence on her own, she does not need to rely on B. But when A does not have first-order reasons for believing what B tells her (e.g. A does not understand the evidence or its analysis), she can still have second-order reasons, that is, reasons other than the evidence and its analysis. What these reasons are is the topic of the first section.

27.2 Trust in the Moral and Epistemic Character of the Scientist

John Hardwig (1991:697) argues that when scientists find themselves in a relation of epistemic dependence, they can legitimately appeal to the principle of testimony: If A has good reasons to believe that B has good reasons to believe that p, then A has good reasons to believe that p. The principle of testimony makes it possible for an individual scientist to have knowledge of p even when she is in a relation of epistemic dependence. Thus, the principle of testimony is an alternative to the suspension of judgment concerning p (Hardwig 1991:699). In Hardwig's view, it is needed also to supplement scientific knowledge that is attributed to collective epistemic agents, such as research groups (Hardwig 1991:699).

Having defended the principle of testimony, Hardwig poses the following question: when is it rational for A to believe that B has good reasons to believe that p? In his view, A's belief can be rational when A trusts B in matters concerning p. Also, A's epistemic trust in B can be rational when A has evidence of the intellectual character of B. As Hardwig explains: "The reliability of A's belief depends on the reliability of B's character," which involves "moral and epistemic qualities" (Hardwig 1991:700). According to Hardwig, B is a trustworthy testifier to the extent that B is (i) honest (that is, truthful in claiming both that she believes that p and that she has good reasons to believe that p); (ii) competent in the domain to which p belongs (that is, knowledgeable about what constitutes good reasons for believing that p); (iii) conscientious; and (iv) capable of epistemic self-assessment. Even though competence is not a character trait per se, it depends upon character. As Hardwig explains, "becoming knowledgeable and then remaining current almost always requires habits of self-discipline, focus, and persistence" (Hardwig 1991:700).

Hardwig acknowledges that there is another possible answer to the question of when it is rational for A to believe that B has good reasons to believe that p (Hardwig 1991:702). The alternative answer is that A's epistemic reliance on B can be rational when A has evidence of the incentives and disincentives that guide B's behavior. A does not need to have evidence of B's moral and epistemic character; it is enough for A to assume that B is a self-interested agent. This account is often called a self-interest account of trust because trust is seen merely as a matter of reliance on the self-interests of scientists (Frost-Arnold 2013:302). A self-interest account of trust shifts the focus away from an individual scientist's moral and epistemic character to the social practices of scientific communities and the institutions of science. When the social practices and institutions of science are well-designed, there are incentives for scientists to behave in a trustworthy way, and prudential considerations are likely to ensure that they will actually do so. Also, sanctions for betraying trust are so serious that it is in scientists' self-interest to be trustworthy. In this account, trust is placed in the scientific community's ability (i) to detect not merely honest bias and error but also intentional attempts to distort the research process (or gross negligence leading to such distortions), and (ii) to effectively impose sanctions on fraudulent scientists.

A self-interest account of trust can be seen as either a replacement or a supplement to Hardwig's moral account of trust. Many philosophers are skeptical of the view that a self-interest account can fully replace a moral account of trust. For example, in Hardwig's view, prudential considerations alone are not sufficient to guarantee that scientists will be trustworthy. As he explains it: "Institutional reforms of science may diminish but cannot obviate the need for reliance upon the character of testifiers" (Hardwig 1991:707). "There are no 'people-proof' institutions" (Hardwig 1991:707).

Torsten Wilholt (2013) advances another argument against the view that a self-interest account of trust can eliminate the need for a moral account of trust. In his view, epistemic trust involves more than mere reliance on the testifier. It involves trust in the testifier's ability to understand her moral responsibility for inductive risks involved in scientific reasoning and make sound moral value judgments concerning these risks. Wilholt appeals to the inductive risk argument according to which accepting or rejecting a hypothesis involves uncertainties, and a moral value judgment is necessary in decisions concerning an acceptable level of uncertainty. When scientists accept or reject hypotheses, they make moral value judgments, either implicitly or explicitly, concerning the potential consequences of errors (e.g. of accepting a false hypothesis or rejecting a true one). According to Wilholt (2013:250), this means that epistemic trust in scientists has to be understood as "trust in the moral sense."

Karen Frost-Arnold (2013) argues that a self-interest account of trust is incomplete because it is based on two idealized assumptions, (i) that untrustworthy behavior will always be detected, and (ii) that untrustworthy behavior will always be punished with effective retaliation. The first assumption is unrealistic because the social practices that are meant to control the quality of research (e.g. peer review) are meant to ensure that published research is, among other things, significant, original, well-argued and clearly presented; they are not designed to audit every stage in the research process. Also, it is not self-evident that detection mechanisms for fraud can be made more effective. Excessive monitoring of scientists' behavior may be counter-productive because some scientists interpret it as a sign of distrust and disrespect, and they do not try to live up to the expectation of those who do not respect them (Frost-Arnold 2013:307; see also Frost-Arnold, this volume). The second assumption is problematic because scientists, university administrators and journal editors are not always in a position to impose sanctions; at best, they can enforce discipline locally. This means that untrustworthy behavior is seldom punished with effective retaliation. Frost-Arnold (2013:302) concludes that the incentives and disincentives recommended by a self-interest account of trust cannot protect scientists from risks involved in collaborations, including the risk that one's collaborators waste valuable time, work in a sloppy way, produce fraudulent data, or take credit for others' ideas and work. For this reason, many scientists, especially junior scientists, attempt to reduce the risks of collaboration by looking for evidence of the moral character of their potential collaborators (Frost-Arnold 2013:306).

Given the criticism of the view that a self-interest account of trust can replace a moral account of trust, a more plausible view is that a self-interest account of trust is needed to supplement a moral account of trust (or vice versa). If a self-interest and a moral account are seen as mutually supplementing each other, then rational epistemic trust can be grounded on evidence of the moral and epistemic character of the testifier, or the social practices of scientific communities and the institutions of science, or both.

This view is supported by empirical findings concerning scientists' behavior in collaborations. Based on her empirical study of research groups, Susann Wagenknecht argues that personal epistemic trust (that is, A's epistemic trust in B with respect to a particular domain) is often supplemented with impersonal trust, that is, A's reliance on the practices and institutions of science (Wagenknecht 2015:174). Moreover, personal epistemic trust is rarely a stand-alone reason for A to believe B's testimony that p. More often it is the case that A's epistemic trust in B comes in degrees, and it is enhanced with strategies that are an alternative to epistemic trust. These strategies aim at understanding the first-order reasons B has for believing that p, for example, by engaging B in question-and-answer type of interactions, or by checking the coherence of B's testimony against background information. Thus, even when A trusts B to have good reasons to believe that p, A's reasons for believing that p are likely to be a mixture of first-order reasons (that is, A has a partial understanding of evidence and its analysis) and second-order reasons (that is, A has reasons to believe that B is trustworthy).

In the next section, I review debates on impersonal trust within and in science. By impersonal trust is meant trust in or reliance on impersonal elements, such as the social practices of scientific communities and the institutions of science. If rational epistemic trust in scientists can be based on evidence of the social practices and institutions of science, then the question is: What aspects in these practices and institutions are of interest and why?

27.3 Social Practices and Institutions as Background Conditions of Trust

The philosophical literature on impersonal trust within and in science is focused on three questions, (i) which social practices of scientific communities are needed to support rational epistemic trust besides formal peer review processes, (ii) which institutional arrangements are needed to ensure that the evaluation of scientists is fair and reliable, and (iii) how scientific communities should interact with lay communities to earn their rational epistemic trust.

As to the first question, I have argued that epistemic trust in scientists involves more than reliance on the scientific community's ability to detect careless, sloppy or fraudulent research; it involves also reliance on the community's ability to facilitate inclusive and responsive dialogue based on shared standards of argumentation (Rolin 2002:100). The requirement for inclusive and responsible dialogue goes beyond the demand for formal peer review processes. What is needed are venues and incentives for criticism and response to criticism taking place after scientific research has passed a formal peer review process. The social practices of scientific communities are of epistemic interest because a relatively high degree of epistemic trust is often placed in scientists' consensus views (Anderson 2011; Goldman 2006). A consensus may not guarantee truth, but it can be seen as the best approximation to objectively justified belief in science. However, not just any consensus will deserve to be called objective. A consensus may be spurious if, for example, the community ignores the scientific work of some of its members. As Helen Longino (1990:76) argues, scientists (as well as non-scientists) should be able to trust that a consensus in the community has been achieved by means of inclusive and responsive dialogue based on shared standards of argumentation. Boaz Miller (2013:1294) argues that a consensus is likely to be knowledge-based when it is supported by varied lines of evidence that all seem to agree with each other, and the parties to the consensus are socially diverse, but nevertheless, committed to using the same evidential standards, formalism and ontological schemes. Much work remains to be done to understand which consensus formation practices can support rational epistemic trust within and in science. How reliable are such practices as meta-analyses, systematic reviews, expert committees, and the common practice of trusting individual scientists who are in leadership positions in their field?

Epistemic trust in scientists involves also reliance on the institutions' ability to evaluate scientists in a fair and reliable way (Rolin 2002; see also Wray 2007). As to the second question, which institutional arrangements are needed to ensure that the evaluation of scientists is fair and reliable, Stephen Turner (2014:187) suggests that the evaluation of scientists and scientific research can be understood as a kind of market. In the market of evaluations, there is a demand for certifications for both scientists (e.g. degrees and awards) and scientific research (e.g. publications in high profile journals) because certifications, if reliable, reduce the risk of relying on an untrustworthy source. There is a supply for evaluators (e.g. high education institutions, journals, and grant awarding agencies) because reliable certifications are likely to increase the evaluators' credibility. In a well-functioning market, no agent has a monopoly over certifications, and there is a legitimate concern about ranking systems (e.g. of universities, departments and journals) that authorize some agents as dominant players in the market of evaluations, thereby having a significant impact on the standards of evaluation. Also, a well-functioning market for certifications and evaluators is not closed; the rise of new forms of scientific activity may make previously important certifications peripheral or worthless (Turner 2014:192).

Elizabeth Anderson (2012) argues that epistemic trust in scientists involves reliance on the scientific institutions' ability to prevent and counter epistemic injustice. According to one definition of epistemic injustice, it is a wrong done to someone specifically in their capacity as a knower (Fricker 2007:44). While epistemic injustice may come in many forms, one much discussed form is testimonial injustice which occurs when "prejudice causes a hearer to give a deflated level of credibility to a speaker's word" (Fricker 2007:1). An example of testimonial injustice is a situation in which a hearer finds a person's testimony suspicious due to the hearer's racist and/or sexist perception of the testifier. Testimonial injustice is of concern to any theory of rational epistemic trust because it can generate a systematic mismatch between trustworthiness and credibility (that is, perceived trustworthiness). When there is such a mismatch, some people are assigned credibility in spite of the lack of trustworthiness, and some others are denied credibility in spite of trustworthiness (Fricker 1998; Rolin 2002; see also D'Cruz as well as Scheman, this volume). Epistemic trust can hardly be rational under social conditions in which the institutional markers of credibility (e.g. titles and positions in formal organizations) fail to track trustworthiness (see also Medina, this volume). For this reason, Anderson (2012) argues, the institutions of science have an obligation to advance epistemic justice. When epistemic justice is realized, the institutional markers of credibility can function as proxies for trustworthiness. While Anderson acknowledges that individual remedies are needed to combat testimonial injustice (e.g. attempts to identify and correct one's cognitive biases), she emphasizes that such remedies are insufficient. In her view, testimonial injustice calls for structural remedies. The institutions of science are responsible for designing peer review and other gate keeping practices so that they prevent cognitive biases from being triggered and facilitate the conscious exercise of counteracting procedures to ensure a fair assessment of scientists (Anderson 2012:168).

Let me turn to the third question, how scientific communities ought to interact with lay communities to earn their rational epistemic trust. Naomi Scheman (2001) argues that epistemic trust in scientists involves reliance on the scientific institutions' ability to take responsibility not merely for epistemic justice but more broadly for social justice. When the trustworthiness of scientists is understood to require goodwill towards those who are epistemically dependent on the scientists, scientists may lack trustworthiness in the eyes of marginal social groups even when they are honest and competent. The lack of trustworthiness may be due to historical connections between science and social injustices (e.g. past uses of science against the interests of particular social groups, the unjust underrepresentation of particular social groups within the ranks of scientists, and the abuse of members of particular social groups in scientific research). As Scheman (2001:43) argues: "It is, in short, irrational to expect people to place their trust in the results of practices about which they know little and that emerge from institutions – universities, corporations, government agencies – which they know to be inequitable."

Scheman's argument gives rise to the question of what scientific communities and institutions need to do to earn the rational epistemic trust of citizens, and especially marginal social groups (e.g. indigenous communities). In response to this question, Heidi Grasswick argues that rational epistemic trust in scientists requires more than good scientific practices as philosophers of science often understand them; it requires sharing significant knowledge with lay communities (Grasswick 2010:401). Failures of knowledge sharing with lay communities can legitimately erode epistemic trust in scientific communities. As Grasswick (2010:392) explains: "If we want scientific practices to be epistemically praiseworthy, scientific communities will need the rationally grounded trust of lay communities, unless it can be shown that such rationally grounded trust of a particular community is unnecessary."

To summarize, impersonal trust is often seen as a supplement to personal epistemic trust (that is, the epistemic trust one person places in another person), because impersonal trust functions as a background condition that makes it more rational to place epistemic trust in a person than otherwise. Without impersonal trust in the social practices and institutions of science, in every knowledge transaction between scientists (or between scientists and non-scientists), each party would have to spend a significant amount of time and effort to scan the trustworthiness of the other party. But when impersonal trust functions as a background condition supporting personal epistemic trust, the cost of examining the trustworthiness of the other party is reduced, and knowledge transactions between individuals are smoothened.

Thus far we have seen that rational epistemic trust can be based on evidence concerning the epistemic and moral character of the testifier, the social practices of the scientific community the testifier belongs to, or the relevant institutions of science. While this seems to be a plausible view, it gives rise to yet another problem. If rational epistemic trust needs to be grounded on evidence of individual scientists or the social practices and institutions of science, the task of gathering and synthesizing such evidence is likely to be demanding. The requirement for evidence seems to undermine the very idea of why epistemic trust has been introduced into the social epistemology of scientific knowledge in the first place. The idea is that epistemic trust makes it possible for individual scientists (as well as non-scientists) to know more than they could know otherwise. Epistemic trust broadens the category of good reasons so that even those persons who do not have first-order reasons for believing in the results of scientific research, can still have second-order reasons for doing so. However, if rational epistemic trust requires gathering and synthesizing a wide range of evidence, then it seems to be no less demanding than the task of acquiring and understanding the first-order reasons.

Thus, the challenge is to strike a balance between the demand for evidence and the feasibility of rational epistemic trust. In response to the challenge, I suggest that the requirement for evidence is modified so that rational epistemic trust does not always need to be grounded on evidence. Sometimes it can be grounded on default assumptions concerning the trustworthiness of testifiers or the reliability of social practices and institutions. That default assumptions can legitimately ground rational epistemic trust is easy to see especially in the case of personal epistemic trust. As we have seen in section 27.2, trustworthy character is thought to include two major components: competence and honesty. However, there is an asymmetry between these two components (Andersen 2014; Rolin 2014). While scientists can examine their collaborator's track record for evidence of the collaborator's competence in a particular domain, the moral character of the collaborator is to a large extent taken for granted. This is because evidence of moral character is necessarily incomplete. When group leaders recruit scientists into their teams, they may seek evidence of the moral character of the candidate in letters of recommendation. Or when scientists work in relatively small teams, they are likely to gain some evidence of the moral character of other team members by means of an extended experience of collaboration. But even when there is evidence of good moral character, trust in the moral character of other team members is underdetermined by evidence. This is because the notion of character refers to a disposition to behave in certain ways across a range of social situations. Consequently, trust in the moral character of other scientists is based at least partly on a principle of charity (Rolin 2015:171).

The example of trust in the moral character of a scientist is meant to illustrate a more general position concerning rational epistemic trust. In order to ensure that rational epistemic trust is feasible for scientists and non-scientists, we can weaken the demand for evidence by allowing that trustworthiness can sometimes be treated as a default entitlement. This view is consistent with a position Martin Kusch (2002) calls quietism and contextualism about testimony. Quietism means that we give up the search for global justifications of testimony, and contextualism means that we accept local and contextual justifications of testimony as the best we can have (Kusch 2002:37). Quietism combined with contextualism is an alternative to both reductionism and irreductionism about testimony. Reductionism is the view that A's entitlement to trust B must always be based on evidence. Irreductionism is the view that A enjoys an a priori epistemic right to believe what B tells her (an a priori right to trust is defeated only when A possesses evidence of B's untrustworthiness) (Fricker 2002:379, see also Faulkner, this volume). Quietism combined with contextualism gives rise to the alternative view that sometimes epistemic trust needs to be based on evidence for it to be rational; at other times it is rational to treat trustworthiness as a default assumption. When trustworthiness is treated as a default assumption, a testifier is assumed to be trustworthy unless one has a reason to doubt it. By relaxing the demand for evidence, quietism and contextualism pave the way for a discussion of citizens' ability to assess the trustworthiness of scientists. This is the topic of the next section.

27.4 The Trustworthiness of Scientists with Respect to Lay People

In technologically complex and interdependent societies, responsible public policy making needs to make use of scientific knowledge. But due to the unequal distribution of expertise in society, the majority of citizens cannot directly assess the trustworthiness of scientists. The relation of epistemic dependence between citizens and scientists gives rise to the question of how citizens can make reliable second-order assessments of the trustworthiness of scientists. The question is especially pressing when citizens are faced with disagreement among scientists. The challenge is to understand what kind of evidence citizens with ordinary education and access to the Internet and the library can obtain, at relatively low cost, so that they will be able to make informed decisions regarding whom to trust. In what follows, I will use the term "expert" rather than the term "scientist" to indicate that the challenge arises when scientists act as experts in the society. In the role of an expert, a scientist is expected to speak as an expert rather than as an interested party in a social or political controversy (Turner 2014:9). While the term "expert" can be understood in many ways (Collins and Evans 2007), I take an expert to be a person who has a relatively high level of knowledge in a particular domain, an ability to deploy her knowledge in answering questions, and an ability to generate new knowledge (Goldman 2006:19–20).

According to Alvin Goldman (2006), citizens can use five kinds of evidence when they assess the trustworthiness of competing experts. Each of these five types of evidence gives rise to further problems waiting for solutions. First, citizens can attempt to ground their epistemic trust on arguments the contending experts present in support of their own views and in criticism of their rivals' views (Goldman 2006:21). Even when citizens are not in a position to evaluate the arguments directly, they can evaluate them indirectly by focusing on the experts' dialectical performance. Assessing a (putative) expert's dialectical performance includes such things as assessing how well she responds to criticism coming from the competing expert. When an expert fails to offer a rebuttal or a defeater to the evidence advanced by the other expert, she has to concede the other expert's dialectical superiority (Goldman 2006:22–23). Thus, the first strategy for assessing experts is based on the assumption that dialectical performance is a reliable indicator of expertise. However, this assumption can be questioned on grounds that dialectical performance can easily be manipulated with the intention of misleading citizens. As Ben Almassi (2012:35) argues, when there is a market for certain kinds of rhetoric in business, law and politics, it is not self-evident that the supposed expert's ability to respond to counterarguments quickly and smoothly is an indicator of her expertise.

Second, Goldman (2006:24) suggests that citizens can attempt to ground their epistemic trust on the relative numbers of (putative) experts on each side of the dispute. This strategy faces two challenges. For one thing, it is not self-evident that citizens are capable of delineating the relevant pool of experts in which the numbers of experts are counted. For another, it is far from obvious that citizens are capable of understanding how the experts have achieved a consensus. As Goldman himself admits, the simple idea of "using the numbers" to judge experts fails if the presumed experts form a community in which a guru's views are slavishly accepted by followers (Goldman 2006:25). Thus, the second strategy will take us back to the question raised in the last section: Under what conditions is consensus likely to be knowledge-based?

Goldman's third suggestion is an extension of the second one. The third proposal is that citizens can attempt to ground their epistemic trust on the appraisals by "meta-experts" of the experts' expertise (Goldman 2006:21). Whereas the second strategy involves finding evidence about agreement among experts, the third strategy involves finding evidence about other experts' evaluations of the competing experts, including their academic merits (e.g. degrees, positions, awards and high profile publications). The third strategy gives rise to the question of how citizens can identify "meta-experts." Against Goldman's view, one could argue that the appeal to "meta-experts" does not solve the problem of assessing the trustworthiness of experts; instead, it merely moves the problem from one citizen-expert relation to another citizen-expert relation.

Fourth, Goldman (2006:30) suggests that citizens can attempt to take into account the competing experts' interests and biases. However, it is not clear that citizens are capable of doing so. Identifying interests and biases in scientific research is a demanding task requiring a high degree of expertise. Goldman's proposal may be interpreted as a recommendation to seek evidence of the experts' financial ties. Given this interpretation, the fourth strategy relies on the assumption that a funding source is potentially also a source of interests and biases in scientific research. Kevin Elliott (2014) examines further the question of whether the presence of financial conflicts of interest should count as a reason for treating experts with suspicion. By a financial conflict of interest is meant a set of conditions in which professional judgment concerning a primary interest (the epistemic interests of science) tends to be unduly influenced by a secondary interest (the financial interests of scientists and their paymasters). In Elliott's view, citizens should take financial ties into account when they attempt to assess the trustworthiness of experts. The funding sources of scientific research are relevant especially when scientific findings are ambiguous, or require a good deal of interpretation, or are difficult to establish in an obvious and straightforward manner (Elliott 2014:935). There is a reason to be suspicious of experts also when funding agencies have strong incentives to influence research findings in ways that damage the credibility of research, and they have also opportunities to do so (Elliott 2014:935).

Fifth, Goldman (2006:31) suggests that citizens can attempt to ground their judgments on the competing experts' past track records. By track record Goldman refers to the experts' past rate of success in various epistemic tasks. Again, it is not easy to see how citizens can obtain evidence of the experts' past success rate if they are not in a position to judge directly what counts as an epistemic success. Also, citizens can be misled by an expert's strong track record in one domain to trust the expert in matters that lie outside that domain (Martini 2014:13). Goldman's fifth proposal may be interpreted as an advice to seek evidence of the experts' curriculum vitae and list of publications. This is precisely what is recommended by Anderson (2011). She claims that ordinary citizens who have access to the Internet should be capable of assessing the competing experts' expertise on the basis of the biographical and bibliographical information available online. Laypersons can weigh various experts depending on their education, specialization, number and quality of publications, citations, awards, and leadership positions in the field (Anderson 2011:146–147).

None of the five criteria introduced by Goldman mentions explicitly what many other philosophers see as an irreducible component of trustworthiness: the moral integrity of the expert. In Anderson's (2011) view, honesty is one of the main criteria citizens should use when they judge the trustworthiness of experts. Citizens can look for evidence of factors that may cast doubt on experts' honesty, including conflicts of interest, previous scientific dishonesty (such as plagiarism), misleading statements, and misrepresenting the arguments and the evidence of the rival experts (2011:147). Drawing on Karen Jones's (2012) analysis of trustworthiness, Almassi (2012) argues that trustworthiness requires not merely honesty but also goodwill towards those people who are epistemically dependent on experts. This means that trustworthiness is a relational property. An expert is trustworthy with respect to citizens only when the expert recognizes the citizens' epistemic dependence on her and takes the fact that they count on her as a compelling reason for striving to be trustworthy (Almassi 2012:46). Given this analysis of trustworthiness, citizens should look for evidence of the goodwill of experts toward them.

Anderson (2011) argues that citizens can also search for evidence of the competing experts' epistemic responsibility. An expert is epistemically responsible for her knowledge claims when she is responsive to evidence, reasoning and arguments others raise against her view. As Anderson explains (2011:146):

> To persist in making certain claims, while ignoring counterevidence and counterarguments raised by others with relevant expertise, is to be dogmatic. To advance those claims as things others should believe on one's say-so, while refusing accountability, is to be arrogant. Dogmatists are not trustworthy, because there is no reason to believe that their claims are based on a rational assessment of evidence and arguments. The arrogant are not trustworthy, because there is reason to believe they are usurping claims to epistemic authority.

In Anderson's view, the crucial question is whether experts are epistemically responsible for their claims toward their own scientific communities (2011:146). Thus, the criterion of epistemic responsibility is different from the criterion of dialectical performance since the latter applies merely to the performance of experts in confrontations with rival experts. Regarding epistemic responsibility, Anderson suggests that citizens look for evidence of the evasion of peer review, refusal to share data, and dialogic irrationality (e.g. continuing to repeat claims even after others have refuted the claims) (2011:147). All of these factors can discredit an expert by suggesting that she is not epistemically responsible.

In sum, there is no algorithm citizens can use when they attempt to assess the trustworthiness of experts. Yet, the philosophical literature offers tools that can be used to probe the trustworthiness of experts. The literature suggests also topics that are in need of further exploration. Instead of discussing trust in experts in general, the analysis of rational epistemic trust would benefit from studies that focus more specifically on particular sciences. For example, trust in the experts of the social sciences (e.g. economics) may be different from trust in the experts of the natural sciences. In the former case, citizens' epistemic trust is weakened by failures to predict financial crises, whereas in the latter case, citizens' epistemic trust is bolstered by technologies on which they rely in their everyday lives. Also, analyses of rational epistemic trust in experts would benefit from case studies aiming to understand why citizens sometimes distrust science or fail to defer to scientific experts (see e.g. de Melo-Martín and Intemann 2018; Goldenberg 2016; Grasswick 2014; John 2011; Whyte and Crease 2010).

27.5 Conclusion

When we rely on the results of scientific research, our epistemic trust is directed not only to individual scientists and research groups but also to the social practices and institutions of science. While epistemic trust in collective epistemic agents is an understudied topic in philosophy of science (Wilholt 2016), there is a significant amount of literature on epistemic trust in individual epistemic agents. Rational epistemic trust in an individual epistemic agent can be based on evidence of the agent's competence, honesty, goodwill and epistemic responsibility. Reliance on the social practices and institutions of science is thought to be a background condition that makes it more rational to place epistemic trust in an individual epistemic agent than otherwise. Ideally, the social practices and institutions of science are designed so that they are capable of exposing scientific misconduct and imposing retribution for it. Moreover, the social practices of scientific communities should ensure that scientific consensus is formed in an appropriate way, and the institutions of science should ensure that scientists are evaluated in a fair and reliable manner. Both scientists and citizens are expected to demonstrate goodwill to support relations of trust between scientific communities and lay communities.

Acknowledgments

I am grateful to Ori Freiman, Gernot Rieder and Judith Simon for their comments on earlier versions of the manuscript. I also wish to thank the participants of the workshop on Trust and Disagreement at the University of Copenhagen in November 24–25, 2016, and the workshop on Current Trends in the Philosophy of the Social Sciences at the University of Helsinki in December 15, 2017.

References

Almassi, B. (2012) "Climate Change, Epistemic Trust, and Expert Trustworthiness," *Ethics and the Environment* 17(2): 29–49.

Andersen, H. (2014) "Co-Author Responsibility: Distinguishing between the Moral and Epistemic Aspects of Trust," *EMBO Reports* 15(9): 914–918.

Andersen, H. and Wagenknecht, S. (2013) "Epistemic Dependence in Interdisciplinary Groups," *Synthese* 190(11): 1881–1898.

Anderson, E. (2011) "Democracy, Public Policy, and Lay Assessment of Scientific Testimony," *Episteme* 8(2): 144–164.

Anderson, E. (2012) "Epistemic Justice as a Virtue of Social Institutions," *Social Epistemology* 26 (2): 163–173.

Baier, A. (1986) "Trust and Antitrust," *Ethics* 96(2): 231–260.

Collins, H. and Evans, R. (2007) *Rethinking Expertise*, Chicago and London: The University of Chicago Press.

de Melo-Martín, I. and Intemann, K. (2018) *The Fight against Doubt: How to Bridge the Gap Between Scientists and the Public*, New York: Oxford University Press.

de Ridder, J. (2013) "Epistemic Dependence and Collective Scientific Knowledge," *Synthese* 191: 37–53.

Elliott, K. (2014) "Financial Conflicts of Interest and Criteria for Research Credibility," *Erkenntnis* 79: 917–937.

Fricker, E. (2002) "Trusting Others in the Sciences: A Priori or Empirical Warrant?" *Studies in History and Philosophy of Science* 33: 373–383.

Fricker, M. (1998) "Rational Authority and Social Power: Towards a Truly Social Epistemology," *Proceedings of the Aristotelian Society* 98(1): 156–177.

Fricker, M. (2007) *Epistemic Injustice: Power & the Ethics of Knowing*, New York and Oxford: Oxford University Press.

Frost-Arnold, K. (2013) "Moral Trust & Scientific Collaboration," *Studies in History and Philosophy of Science Part A* 44: 301–310.

Goldenberg, M.J. (2016) "Public Misunderstanding of Science? Reframing the Problem of Vaccine Hesitancy," *Perspectives on Science* 24(5): 552–581.

Goldman, A. (2006) "Experts: Which Ones Should You Trust?" in E. Selinger and R.P. Crease (eds.), *The Philosophy of Expertise*, New York: Columbia University Press.

Grasswick, H. (2010) "Scientific and Lay Communities: Earning Epistemic Trust through Knowledge Sharing," *Synthese* 177: 387–409.

Grasswick, H. (2014) "Climate Change Science and Responsible Trust: A Situated Approach," *Hypatia* 29(3): 541–557.

Hardwig, J. (1985) "Epistemic Dependence," *Journal of Philosophy* 82(7): 335–349.

Hardwig, J. (1991) "The Role of Trust in Knowledge," *Journal of Philosophy* 88(12): 693–708.

Hawley, K. (2017) "Trustworthy Groups and Organizations," in P. Faulkner and T. Simpson (eds.), *The Philosophy of Trust*, Oxford: Oxford University Press.
John, S. (2011) "Expert Testimony and Epistemological Free-Riding: The MMR Controversy," *The Philosophical Quarterly* 61(244): 498–517.
Jones, K. (2012) "Trustworthiness," *Ethics* 123(1): 61–85.
Keren, A. (2014) "Trust and Belief: A Preemptive Reasons Account," *Synthese* 191: 2593–2615.
Kitcher, P. (1992) "Authority, Deference, and the Role of Individual Reasoning in Science," in E. McMullin (ed.), *The Social Dimensions of Science*, Notre Dame, IN: University of Notre Dame Press.
Kusch, M. (2002) *Knowledge by Agreement*, Oxford and New York: Oxford University Press.
Longino, H.E. (1990) *Science as Social Knowledge: Values and Objectivity in Scientific Inquiry*, Princeton, NJ: Princeton University Press.
Martini, C. (2014) "Experts in Science: A View from the Trenches," *Synthese* 191: 3–15.
McDowell, A. (2002) "Trust and Information: The Role of Trust in the Social Epistemology of Information Science," *Social Epistemology* 16(1): 51–63.
Miller, B. (2013) "When Is Consensus Knowledge Based? Distinguishing Shared Knowledge from Mere Agreement," *Synthese* 190: 1293–1316.
Rolin, K. (2002) "Gender and Trust in Science," *Hypatia* 17(4): 95–118.
Rolin, K. (2014) "'Facing the Incompleteness of Epistemic Trust': A Critical Reply," *Social Epistemology Review and Reply Collective* 3(5): 74–78.
Rolin, K. (2015) "Values in Science: The Case of Scientific Collaboration," *Philosophy of Science* 82 (2): 157–177.
Scheman, N. (2001) "Epistemology Resuscitated: Objectivity as Trustworthiness," in N. Tuana and S. Morgen (eds.), *Engendering rationalities*, Albany: State University of New York Press.
Turner, S. (2014) *The Politics of Expertise*, New York and London: Routledge.
Wagenknecht, S. (2014) "Opaque and Translucent Epistemic Dependence in Collaborative Scientific Practice," *Episteme* 11(4): 475–492.
Wagenknecht, S. (2015) "Facing the Incompleteness of Epistemic Trust: Managing Dependence in Scientific Practice," *Social Epistemology* 29(2): 160–184.
Whyte, K.P. and Crease, R.P. (2010) "Trust, Expertise, and the Philosophy of Science," *Synthese* 177: 411–425.
Wilholt, T. (2013) "Epistemic Trust in Science," *British Journal for Philosophy of Science* 64: 233–253.
Wilholt, T. (2016) "Collaborative Research, Scientific Communities, and the Social Diffusion of Trustworthiness," in M.S. Brady and M. Fricker (eds.), *The Epistemic Life of Groups: Essays in the Epistemology of Collectives*, New York and Oxford: Oxford University Press.
Wray, K.B. (2007) "Evaluating Scientists: Examining the Effects of Sexism and Nepotism," in H. Kincaid*et al.* (eds.), *Value-Free Science? Ideals and Illusions*, Oxford and New York: Oxford University Press.

28
TRUST IN MEDICINE

Philip J. Nickel and Lily Frank[1]

28.1 Introduction

In this chapter, we consider ethical and philosophical aspects of trust in the practice of medicine. We focus on trust within the patient–physician relationship, trust and professionalism, and trust in Western (allopathic) institutions of medicine and medical research. Philosophical approaches to trust contain important insights into medicine as an ethical and social practice. In what follows we explain several philosophical approaches and discuss their strengths and weaknesses in this context. We also highlight some relevant empirical work in the section on trust in the institutions of medicine (cf. Ozawa and Sripad 2013). It is hoped that the approaches discussed here can be extended to nursing and other topics in the philosophy of medicine (see Dinç and Gastmans 2013).

28.2 Trust and the Physician–Patient Relationship

The idea of the trusting physician–patient relationship is important to medical ethics, and is thought by some to be foundational (Beauchamp and Childress 2013; Pellegrino 1999; Zaner 1991; Rhodes and Strain 2000). The physician–patient relationship contains inherent inequalities of knowledge, skills and control of resources, and it treats matters both intimate and potentially of great importance to the patient. In these matters the patient often needs confidentiality and discretion. Because of these factors, the idea that trust is necessary for the relationship to be healthy is plausible, and it has been remarkably resilient even while the technological and institutional complexity of medical practice has vastly increased, and even while the basic norms of the practice have shifted from a paternalistic model to one of information-sharing and participatory decision-making. The resilience of the idea may also be linked to trust's utility in reducing complexity through such transitions: if one trusts one's physician, the resulting division of epistemic labor allows the patient to divert scarce attentional resources elsewhere (see Miller and Freiman, this volume). One could even go so far as to assert that without the existence of some level of trust in physicians' competence and good will, the practice of medicine would not be possible because patients would be unwilling to seek medical care.[2]

Medical ethics, in keeping with this picture, often models the trusting physician–patient relationship as one in which the physician (the GP, in particular) serves as the trusted gatekeeper for other practices such as delivery of diagnostic and prognostic information, prescription medication, referral to specialists and the use of technologies for self-care (Voerman and Nickel 2017). Much less frequently studied is physicians' trust in patients, e.g. to deliver accurate information and to follow through on care routines (Entwistle and Quick 2006). Physicians' trust in patients is a natural counterpart to patients' trust in physicians if we consider the trusting patient–physician relationship as mutual or reciprocal; however, asymmetries of expertise and control have often led medical ethicists to neglect it. The physician–patient relationship, like relationships between other sorts of professionals and their clients, is an asymmetrical fiduciary relationship in which one person is given control over an aspect of another person in some domain, and is obligated to act for the good of the other, putting their own interests second (Rodwin 1995).

In medical ethics, the interest in deriving ethical conclusions from reflection about the nature of the physician–patient relationship has led to a particular focus on the values and normativity associated with trust. Philosophically there is more than one way of trying to analyze this normativity. In order to clarify some promising lines of inquiry, we draw a distinction between three types of theories: *supporting-relations accounts, grounded-expectation accounts* and *moral-adequacy accounts.*

The supporting-relations account starts with the assumption that a trusting relationship is good and tries instrumentally to derive the value of other practices supporting trust. For example, Zaner (1991) argues that a trusting patient–physician relationship is a basic good, and that empathy and perspective-taking are required to support it, and are therefore important ethical capacities for physicians.

Trusting relationships, indeed, *are* often goods to be strived for. However, for reasons put forward by Baier (1986) and more recently for the medical context by Hawley (2015), it must be admitted that they are not always beneficial. Trust can provide a fertile ground for exploitation and manipulation, it can be epistemically poorly grounded, and it can lead to unreasonable demands by those who trust, along with unreasonable efforts to meet these demands by those who are trusted. For these reasons, any account needs to take a stand on what makes some instances of trust good or justified, and others bad or unjustified. That task is addressed by the second and third accounts we consider.

Grounded-expectation accounts hold that whether trust is good or justified depends on whether the expectations implicit in one's trust – for example, the expectation that my physician will prescribe me the best medicine for treating my illness – are based on sound or unsound reasons. Such an account emphasizes that people take on moral responsibilities by creating expectations in others. Tim Scanlon (1998:300) expresses the relevant moral principle as follows: "One must exercise due care not to lead others to form reasonable but false expectations about what one will do when one has good reason to believe that they would suffer significant loss as a result of relying on these expectations." Scanlon's principle is about reliance rather than trust, but it can be extended to trust because it is even more exploitative or manipulative to create false expectations in another person when they are relying on one *trustingly*, than when they are relying on one strategically or reluctantly (see Goldberg, this volume). On a grounded-expectation account, physicians take on responsibilities by creating expectations of professionalism, expertise and commitment to promoting the health and wellbeing of the patient. They must then exercise due care to live up to the expectations they have created.

A grounded-expectations account can also add the claim, put forward by Manson and O'Neill (2007), that patients can and should place their trust intelligently, by making sure that their expectations are well-informed: "Trust is well placed when it is given to trustworthy claims and commitments, and ill placed when it is given to untrustworthy claims and commitments" (160). This implies that intelligent trust is based on cues that are reliably or rationally linked with trustworthiness: "Anyone who seeks to place and refuse trust intelligently must try to discriminate the various claims and commitments that agents make. I may trust a genetic diagnosis if it is based on reputable tests … but not if it is based on quirky views of heredity" (ibid.:165). Implicit in Manson and O'Neill's example are two importantly different kinds of objects of trust within the patient–physician relationship: one is the physician herself, and the other is the medical care that she mediates and for which she is the gatekeeper, including such items as genetic tests. Other versions of the grounded-expectations account stress the importance of social context, including institutions and technology, in grounding people's trusting expectations. Rather than focusing primarily on the agency and intelligence of the patient in placing trust, the focus is on the broader idea of "sound" or "healthy" trust, in which the patient's environment guides and provides epistemic grounding for her expectations. By providing institutions and informational cues that reliably "track" trustworthiness, policymakers and designers facilitate sound trust (Voerman and Nickel 2017). (See O'Neill on "Questioning Trust" and Scheman on trust and trustworthiness, this volume.)

A positive feature of grounded-expectation accounts is that they derive conclusions in medical ethics from the normativity of commitments and expectations, not directly from controversial ethical theories or domain-specific medical ethics principles. However, it is doubtful whether such accounts are sufficient to include all the moral features that contribute to a healthy trust relationship. According to Annette Baier (1992) the idea of reasonable expectation-formation cannot distinguish between healthy and unhealthy trust relationships because one person can trust another reasonably as the result of unfair power relationships that give her few other options. In this way, a person's reasonable expectations can be exploited or rendered fragile in ways that do not actually render the expectations themselves unreasonable or unjustified. Baier (1992) also holds that the expectations-based view is too *rigid* to account for what matters to trusting relationships. A physician who faultlessly lives up to a list of expectations but fails to *care* for the patient in a broader sense is less trustworthy than a physician who uses her discretion wisely to promote the well-being of the patient but fails to perform exactly as expected along the way.

That is where moral-adequacy accounts exhibit their strength. They hold that there are norms for the moral decency of trusting relationships that do not derive from expectations. Baier's view, for example, proposes a transparency test of the moral decency of trust, meant to distinguish between exploitative and non-exploitative trust. According to this test, "trust is morally decent only if, in addition to whatever else is entrusted, knowledge of each party's reasons for confident reliance on the other to continue the relationship could in principle also be entrusted" (Baier 1986:128). Other versions of the moral-adequacy account focus on other adequacy tests of trust. For example, Carolyn McLeod's (2002) theory of trust, developed in part to analyze trust in medicine, holds that trust is morally adequate when it is based on shared values and moral integrity. We may need to tweak these accounts when applying them to trust in the *institutions* of medicine rather than in individuals (a kind of trust we discuss in section 28.4). However, the argument stands that an individual could sometimes have good pragmatic and epistemic reasons to trust the institution of medicine as well as to trust individual physicians, even if both the institution and the physicians within it were exploitative in their motives. We therefore need a further moral test to determine morally sound trust in both kinds of entities.

We advocate a hybrid account that sees both grounded expectations and moral adequacy as part of sound, healthy trust in medicine. Developing a moral-adequacy test in more detail and applying it to this context is a task for future research. Yet, a moral-adequacy account centered on a narrow conception of the patient–physician relationship may not be the best approach for accommodating the technological and institutional transformations of the practice of medicine in the long term, which may depart substantially from this conception. For example, Baier's theory, by focusing on a mutual awareness test of the moral decency of trust, presupposes that trust obtains between two agents who are each able to form an explicit awareness of the expectations and motivations of the other. In the future it may increasingly be the case that there is no such relationship at the heart of the institution of medicine, and that a relationship-based test is therefore inapplicable to trust in medicine. We return to this scenario at the end of the chapter.

28.3 Trustworthiness and Professionalism

Professionalism is a phenomenon in which a group of experts who engage in some field of practical activity (education and research, law, medicine, engineering, etc.) develop a shared identity with official standards for membership and a measure of exclusiveness in having the right to evaluate one another's work. Often, professions adopt internal codes of ethical principles (Davis 1991). One line of research in medical ethics has linked professionalism and professional ethics to the trustworthiness of physicians and by extension, trust in them (Pellegrino and Thomasma 1993; Manson and O'Neill 2007; Banks and Gallagher 2008; Kelly 2018). The underlying idea is that the development and continuing identity of professions has, as one of its main purposes, to signal trustworthiness to those who turn to the profession in a situation of need.

Traditionally, the professional ideals of medicine were uniquely paternalistic among the professions. Yet when the paternalistic ideal of the practice of medicine was superseded by an ideal of shared decision-making and respect for patient autonomy, trust did not become less important to the practice of medicine. This seems to suggest, perhaps surprisingly, that while trust is essentially bound up with professionalism, it is not strongly affected by the balance of decision-making and openness between the professional and the one seeking the professional's services.

These normative ideals of professionalism suggest that the appropriate default attitude towards the medical profession is one of trust. Kelly (2018) presents a systematic theory of the ethics of trust and professionalism, arguing that medicine has an internal functional end or *telos*, relating to a basic human need (health care) in which people have to rely on others' expertise, and that as a consequence, trust and trustworthiness are constitutive goods linked to the medical profession. For Kelly, professions are required, first, to sustain internal standards of behavior and expertise; and second, to guard the reputation of qualified professionals. Both conditions are essential in the long run for maintaining widespread trustworthiness in individual physicians (2018:63). For Kelly, it is therefore insufficient to focus on the doctor–patient relationship alone as the principal source of the normativity of trust and trustworthiness.

However, the normative ideals of professions themselves bear scrutiny. Critics argue that a more realistic view of the relationship between patient and physician is that between customer and supplier. Since the 1970s medical professionals, historians, sociologists and ethicists have observed and sometimes lamented a shift, spurred by changes in the structure of health care delivery, towards rising costs, increased specialization, an expanding role for technology in medical care, and an increasing presence of direct-to-consumer marketing of pharmaceuticals (cf. Reeder 1972 and Friedler 1997). On this view, not trust, but contractual obligations, oversight and enforceable regulations should guarantee the customer-patient a high quality of care.[3]

One may thus argue that taking a selective and strategic attitude toward reliance, or even taking a default attitude of distrust, might be more rational than taking a default attitude of trust. Recent philosophical work provides a substantive account of distrust that distinguishes it from mere lack of trust. On Hawley's (2014) view, distrust is a matter of regarding the distrusted party as being committed to meet certain standards, while also finding that this party fails to meet those standards. (See D'Cruz, this volume.) Such a default attitude of distrust could be justified on a variety of grounds. Worries about meeting a commitment to competence and due care, for example, may be bolstered by the prevalence of medical errors. In the United States alone, medical errors have been estimated in the past to be responsible for between 44,000 and 98,000 unnecessary deaths each year (Weingart et al. 2000). Distrust could also be justified if the general public has reasons to believe physicians fail to meet commitments to ethical impartiality, by being biased in their prescription of certain pharmaceuticals or having financial interests in performing certain kinds of procedures. For comparison, it is useful to consider the financial professions, where widespread misconduct has made it plausible to claim that a default attitude of distrust in banking and investment firms is warranted. If this were to happen in the field of medicine, then distrust in the profession could threaten trust in individual physicians.[4]

28.4 Trust in the Institutions of Medicine

The institutions of medicine include pharmaceutical companies, public health agencies, health insurers and other managed care providers, as well as hospitals, physician professional organizations like the American Pediatric Association, etc. Hall et al. (2001:620) point out that people's trust or distrust in one of these entities can impact their trust or distrust in the others in a wide range of ways. Although there is a large empirical literature aimed at measuring and understanding patients' levels of trust in individual care providers, like their primary care doctor or their nurse, there has been less empirical research on trust in medical institutions or the medical profession as a whole.

There is a sharp difference between trust in the institutions of medicine and trust in particular physicians. This is due to two key features of institutions: unspecificity and impersonality. There is broad consensus on the kinds of things patients expect their physicians to do and be, including but not limited to acting beneficently, maintaining their knowledge and skills; protecting patient confidentiality; respecting patient autonomy, etc. (Mechanic 1996, Rhodes 2007). These expectations may arise from both personal knowledge of the physician, as well as an awareness of what they stand for as medical professionals. For institutions of medicine, these expectations and the obligations they ascribe to different actors become more unspecific, since we are discussing a wide variety of roles and groups, governed by varying interests, institutional norms and legislation.

In addition to being unspecific, trust in institutions is impersonal. Like interpersonal trust (see Potter, this volume), it involves a complex of expectations based on the perceived interests, motives and past behavior of the institution. However, it is also based on the norms and functional aims that govern and define institutions and the roles within them, rather than on personal characteristics of goodwill or responsiveness to the trustor's reliance. An institution is not capable of having personal motives and characteristics in a literal sense. For that reason, the interaction of social, legal, technological and political forces, rather than good will and individual intentions, governs the effect of the institutions of medicine on individuals.

For some theorists, these reflections provide reason to doubt whether institutions are genuine objects of trust, either because they wish to reserve the concept of trust for explaining cooperation in terms of the individual motives of two or more interacting agents (Hardin 2006), or because they think that genuine trust conceptually requires affective or reactive attitudes that are out of place when extended beyond individuals (e.g. Faulkner 2011). For our purposes here, we do not wish to claim that trust in institutions is "genuine" or is the same as trust in individuals, but we do assume that there is an important normative phenomenon here: the functions and norms that govern institutions provide a reason for reliance that is not merely strategic or predictive. To put it in Hawley's (2014) terminology, institutions can have normative commitments that are either met or unmet in one's reliance on them. This makes the language of trust and distrust fitting.

Even if we did reserve the notion of genuine trust for relationships between individuals, institutions would be important to trust because they frame these relationships (Mechanic and Schlesinger 1996). Particular ways of organizing and institutionalizing the delivery of medical care can promote or undermine patient's trust in individual physicians, as Brown and Calnan (2012) have shown in the case of mental health care institutions. Davies and Rundall (2000) argue that *managed care*, in particular – defined as the effort to control cost, quality and access to care through principles of management (Kongstvedt 2009) – has the potential to undermine patient's belief that physicians can be trusted. Furthermore, they argue that the extent to which patients *should* trust their physicians is partially dependent on "the organizational, financial and legal situation within which their health care is delivered" (Davies and Rundall 2000:613). They point to several ways in which managed care undermines the trust between patient and physician, through what can be labeled a reverse halo-effect. They cite research showing that patients in managed care see their physicians as having divided loyalties between patient needs and interests and the demands of other institutions with economic motivations.

Reflecting on these points, Goold (2001) emphasizes that the ethics of trust in health care institutions goes beyond the need to support healthy trust in clinicians working within those institutions. She argues that health care organizations are ethically bound to be trustworthy actors in ways that extend beyond the obligations of individual physicians. For example, such institutions may be obligated to safeguard an individual's "financial well-being in the case of catastrophic illness," as well as to protect "the health of the community," not just of the individual (Goold 2001:29). In terms of the normative accounts of trust presented earlier, such proposals could be seen as part of the moral adequacy of trusted institutions, and therefore as part of healthy trust in medicine. In what follows we zoom in on two specific challenges to meeting this test of moral adequacy for institutions.

28.4.1 Discrimination and Distrust

One challenge is that some groups have reason to distrust the institutions of medicine. A well-studied example is African Americans in the United States, who have expressed lower levels of trust in medical institutions, clinical care and medical research (Shavers et al. 2002; Corbie-Smith et al. 1999; Ebony Boulware et al. 2003), and in their physicians (Kao et al.1998), compared with other groups. Distrust also seems to have played a role in the reluctance of African Americans to become organ donors (Davidson and Devney 1991).

High levels of distrust in medical institutions are thought to contribute to, and be a result of, systematic health and health care inequalities between African Americans and whites in the United States (Ebony Boulware et al. 2003). This distrust has been attributed to medicine's historic and ongoing racist practices and attitudes (Krakauer, Crenner and Fox 2002). Historically this included the infamous Tuskegee syphilis study, and the forced sterilization of persons deemed "feeble minded" or "promiscuous" as part of a pseudo-scientific practice of eugenics that disproportionately affected minority women in the US until the 1970s. More recently, it has been found that physicians discriminate on the basis of race in their prescribing behavior, being less likely to prescribe opioid pain medication to black patients, potentially based on the assumption that they are more likely to be drug-seeking than whites (Tamayo-Sarver et al., 2003).

Many other groups also experience distrust in medicine because of a history of being stigmatized or shown a lack of respect by health care providers. For example, Underhill et al. (2015) describes such a pattern in the case of male sex workers, and Bradford et al. (2013) describes a pattern of discrimination in the health care of transgendered persons. Such studies emphasize the role that experience plays in one's pattern of trust, and they make it plausible that historical discrimination makes it, in some sense, *reasonable* to take a default attitude of distrust toward the institutions of medicine. This is a challenge that would take years of reconciliation and engagement to overcome.

28.4.2 Trust in Medical Research

A rather different challenge, specific to the institution of medical *research*, is that medical research does not aim at providing direct clinical benefit to each individual patient. Unlike physicians, researchers aim to produce generalizable knowledge, not to provide a direct benefit to individual research participants. Because of the very nature of scientific research, it is impossible to know in advance all of the possible complications and harms that the participant might experience while participating in a study. In addition, some essential elements of scientific research, such as randomization or the use of placebos, imply that individual research participants may receive differential benefits or no benefits at all through participation. When the researcher is also a care provider, the double identity that results implies an essential conflict of loyalty that can threaten trust. The recent trend toward developing so-called *learning health care systems*, in which scientific and knowledge-generation goals are fully integrated into everyday clinical practice, implies that this double identity has potential ethical implications for medical practice as a whole (Faden et al. 2013). If such systems were widely adopted, the double identity might complicate trust within individual physician–patient relationships, threatening the idea that the *telos* of medicine aligns with the interests of each individual patient.[5]

The phenomenon of therapeutic misconception further complicates trust in medical research. In many cases, people have a natural bias toward thinking that new interventions being studied by science will benefit them. de Melo-Martin and Ho (2008) argue that this is a phenomenon of "misplaced trust." Individuals may have reason to distrust medical research if their trust depends on the natural expectation that medical decisions, even those in the context of research, should always provide individual clinical benefit to them.

In response to this challenge, research institutions and academic medical centers have made efforts specifically aimed at building trust between the medical research community and the general public. This is reflected in large part in research institutions' insistence on adhering to strict research regulations involving human participants (Yarborough and Sharp 2002). Efforts at establishing trust may also need to take additional measures beyond mere compliance to convince the public that researchers are trustworthy and to obtain greater participation in and support for biomedical research. For example, in research with samples stored in biobanks, transparency and communication with research participants is a strategy to build trust. Communicating with donors about the kind of research being performed (and by whom), and about results that may affect or interest them, may help to foster good will and make participant expectations more realistic, by better communicating the aims, intentions and interests of those maintaining the biobank.

Greater community participation in research is another means of fostering trust, especially among communities that may be vulnerable or wary of the presence of researchers, such as indigenous populations. Yarborough and Sharp (2002:9) suggest that the general public should have a greater role in determining the priorities and goals of biomedical research that relies on shared resources and widespread participation. One way of doing this, they suggest, is through the creation of community advisory councils which would include members of the general public as well as representatives from research institutions, to debate, critically reflect on, and generate consensus on research priorities and tradeoffs (ibid.:10).

In sum, then, it is useful to talk about trust in the institution of medicine for two reasons. First, different groups' historical experiences with the institutions of medicine strongly affect the trust or distrust that they (reasonably) have towards particular actors such as physicians and medical researchers who operate in the context of those institutions. Second, trust in medicine seems to be well grounded in the underlying purpose of this institution to improve health, but this purpose is complicated and sometimes even called into question by the changing nature of the institution itself. This can have powerful effects on trust within the doctor–patient relationship.

28.5 Trust through Institutional and Technological Change?

In this chapter we have explored trust within the physician–patient relationship, professionalism and trust, and trust in the institution of medicine. We conclude by reflecting briefly on the future of trust in medicine. As indicated above, the idea of a trusting patient–physician relationship has remained important to how people think about medical practice through a wide range of institutional, scientific and technical, and value changes to the practice of medicine. However, some recent and anticipated future changes in the practice of medicine might be so fundamental that they make interpersonal trust in this relationship less central. Some relevant changes are:

- the practice of fully institutionalized care, in which no one physician is in regular contact with a given patient;
- the use of expert and automated systems in which the individual expertise and ability of a given physician is replaced by artificial intelligence; and
- the practice of technologically mediated care, in which the patient does not directly interact with human individuals in order to receive care.

These changes would imply, to varying degrees, that there is no suitable individual human object of trust in the practice of medicine. Although trust in the institution of medicine might remain, trust within the physician–patient relationship would not. There would no longer be a single type of professional or group of professionals (physician, nurse, pharmacist, etc.) with fundamental roles as individuals in the delivery of care. As a consequence, there would need to be more focus on other roles and entities, currently peripheral but already important for the delivery of health care, such as eHealth and mHealth companies, engineers and software designers, and electronic health records companies.

Theorists of trust would then need to rethink the ways in which the value of trust is still salient to the practice of medicine or whether its focus and nature has simply changed. As indicated earlier, for some scholars, trust is fundamentally interpersonal and these changes would so "depersonalize" medicine as to render genuine trust irrelevant. However, in our view it would still be useful to think about trust in the practice of medicine in such a scenario, because the notion of trust helps bring forward useful questions about the normative and predictive expectations that people have about the technologically and institutionally complex systems that deliver our health care. Human reliance on medicine can be expected to remain constant. Hence our need and desire for such reliance on medicine to be well grounded and morally satisfactory will also persist, no matter what form the practice of medicine may take.

Notes

1 This research is affiliated with the Netherlands Organization for Scientific Research Responsible Innovation (NWO-MVI) project "Mobile Support Systems for Behaviour Change," project number 100-23-616.

2 Brown and Calnan (2012), in their fascinating study, discuss the particular case of mental health patients who in some cases manage to form fragile trust relationships with professionals within a system under strain.

3 For a critique of this view see Pellegrino (1999).

4 While Kelly (2018:101ff.) is well aware of the conflicts of interest that threaten the trustworthiness of the medical profession, he does not see this as changing the internal *telos* of the profession itself or as giving reason to adopt a different basic stance (e.g. strategic reliance or distrust) toward the medical profession.

5 This double identity seems to go beyond the "limits to professional trustworthiness" discussed by Kelly (2018:125ff.).

References

Baier, A. (1986) "Trust and Antitrust," *Ethics* 96(2): 231–260.

Baier, A. (1992) *Tanner Lectures on Human Values* 13: 107–174.

Banks, S. and Gallagher, A. (2008) *Ethics in Professional Life: Virtues for Health and Social Care*, Basingstoke: Palgrave Macmillan.

Beauchamp, T.L. and Childress, J.F. (2013) *Principles of Biomedical Ethics*, 7th edition, New York: Oxford University Press.

Bradford, J., Reisner, S.L., Honnold, J.A. and Xavier, J. (2013) "Experiences of Transgender-Related Discrimination and Implications for Health: Results from the Virginia Transgender Health Initiative Study," *American Journal of Public Health* 103(10): 1820–1829.

Brown, P. and Calnan, M. (2012) *Trusting on the Edge: Managing Uncertainty in the Midst of Serious Mental Health Problems*, Bristol: The Policy Press.

Corbie-Smith, G., Thomas, S.B., Williams, M.V. and Moody-Ayers, S. (1999) "Attitudes and Beliefs of African Americans Toward Participation in Medical Research," *J Gen Intern Med* 14: 537–546.

Davidson, M.N. and Devney, P. (1991) "Attitudinal Barriers to Organ Donation among Black Americans," *Transplant Proc* 23: 2531–2532.

Davies, H.T.O. and Rundall, T.G. (2000) "Managing Patient Trust in Managed Care," *Milbank Quarterly* 78(4): 609–624.

Davis, M. (1991) "Thinking like an Engineer: The Place of a Code of Ethics in the Practice of a Profession," *Philosophy & Public Affairs* 20(2): 150–167.

de Melo Martin, I. and Ho, A. (2008) "Beyond Informed Consent: The Therapeutic Misconception and Trust," *Journal of Medical Ethics* 34(4): 202–205.

Dinç, L. and Gastmans, C. (2013) "Trust in Nurse-Patient Relationships: A Literature Review," *Nursing Ethics* 20(5): 501–516.

Ebony Boulware, L., Cooper, L.A., Ratner, L.E., LaVeist, T.A. and Powe, N.R. (2003) "Race and Trust in the Health Care System," *Public Health Reports* 118: 358–365.

Entwistle, V.A. and Quick, O. (2006) "Trust in the Context of Patient Safety Problems," *Journal of Health Organization and Management* 20: 397–416.

Faden, R.R., Kass, N.E., Goodman, S.N., Pronovost, P., Tunis, S. and Beauchamp, T.L. (2013) "An Ethics Framework for a Learning Health Care System: A Departure from Traditional Research Ethics and Clinical Ethics," *Ethical Oversight of Learning Health Care Systems, Hastings Center Report Special Report* 43(1): S16–S27. doi:10.1002/hast.134

Faulkner, P. (2011) *Knowledge on Trust*, Oxford: Oxford University Press.

Friedler, E. (1997) "The Evolving Doctor-Patient to Provider-Consumer Relationship," *Journal of Family Practice* 45(6): 485–486.

Goold, S.D. (2001) "Trust and the Ethics of Health Care Institutions," *Hastings Center Report* 31: 26–33.

Hall, M.A., Dugan, E., Zheng, B. and Mishra, A.K. (2001) "Trust in Physicians and Medical Institutions: What Is It, Can it be Measured, and Does It Matter?," *Milbank Quarterly* 79(4): 613–639.

Hardin, R. (2006) *Trust*, Cambridge: Polity.

Hawley, K. (2014) "Trust, Distrust and Commitment," *Nous* 48(1): 1–20.

Hawley, K. (2015) "Trust and Distrust between Patient and Doctor," *Journal of Evaluation in Clinical Practice* 21(5): 798–801.

Kao, A.C.*et al.* (1998) "The Relationship between Method of Physician Payment and Patient Trust," *JAMA* 280: 1708–1714.

Kelly, T.M. (2018) *Professional Ethics: A Trust-Based Approach*, Lexington, KY: Lexington Books.

Kongstvedt, P.R. (2009) *Managed Care: What It Is and How It Works*, Burlington, MA: Jones and Bartlett Publishers.

Krakauer, E.L., Crenner, C. and Fox, K. (2002) "Barriers to Optimum End-of-Life Care for Minority Patients," *Journal of the American Geriatrics Society* 50(1): 182–190.

Manson, N.C. and O'Neill, O. (2007) *Rethinking Informed Consent in Bioethics*, Cambridge: Cambridge University Press.

McLeod, C. (2002) *Self-Trust and Reproductive Autonomy*, Cambridge, MA: MIT Press.

Mechanic, D. (1996) "Changing Medical Organization and the Erosion of Trust," *Milbank Quarterly* 74: 171–189.

Mechanic, D. and Schlesinger, M. (1996) "The Impact of Managed Care on Patients' Trust in Medical Care and Their Physicians," *Journal of the American Medical Association* 275: 1693–1697.

Ozawa, S. and Sripad, P. (2013) "How Do You Measure Trust in the Health System? A Systematic Review of the Literature," *Social Science & Medicine* 91: 10–14.

Pellegrino, E.D. (1999) "The Commodification of Medical and Health Care: The Moral Consequences of a Paradigm Shift from a Professional to a Market Ethic," *Journal of Medicine and Philosophy*, 24(3): 243–266.

Pellegrino, E.D. and Thomasma, D.C. (1993) *The Virtues in Medical Practice*, New York: Oxford University Press.
Reeder, L.G. (1972) "The Patient-Client as a Consumer: Some Observations on the Changing Professional-Client Relationship," *Journal of Health and Social Behavior* 13(4): 406–412.
Rhodes, R. (2007) "The Professional Responsibilities of Medicine," in R. Rhodes, L.P. Francis and A. Silvers (eds.), *The Blackwell Guide to Medical Ethics*, Oxford: John Wiley & Sons.
Rhodes, R. and Strain, J.J. (2000) "Trust and Transforming Medical Institutions," *Cambridge Quarterly of Healthcare Ethics* 9(2): 205–217.
Rodwin, M.A. (1995) "Strains in the Fiduciary Metaphor: Divided Physician Loyalties and Obligations in a Changing Health Care System," *American Journal of Law and Medicine* 21: 241–257.
Scanlon, T.M. (1998) *What We Owe to Each Other*, Cambridge, MA: Harvard Belknap.
Shavers, V.L., Lynch, C.F., Burmeister, L.F. (2002) "Racial Differences in Factors that Influence the Willingness to Participate in Medical Research Studies," *Annals of Epidemiology* 12: 248–256.
Tamayo-Sarver, J.H., Hinze, S.W., Cydulka, R.K. and Baker, D.W. (2003) "Racial and Ethnic Disparities in Emergency Department Analgesic Prescription," *American Journal of Public Health*, 93(12): 2067–2073.
Underhill, K.*et al.* (2015) "A Qualitative Study of Medical Mistrust, Perceived Discrimination, and Risk Behavior Disclosure to Clinicians by US Male Sex Workers and Other Men Who Have Sex with Men: Implications for Biomedical HIV Prevention," *Journal of Urban Health* 92 (4): 667–686.
Voerman, S.A. and Nickel, P.J. (2017) "Sound Trust and the Ethics of Telecare," *Journal of Medicine and Philosophy* 42: 33–49.
Weingart, S.N., Wilson, R.M., Gibberd, R.W. and Harrison, B. (2000) "Epidemiology of Medical Error," *Western Journal of Medicine* 172(6): 390–393.
Yarborough, M. and Sharp, R.R. (2002) "Restoring and Preserving Trust in Biomedical Research," *Academic Medicine* 77(1): 8–14.
Zaner, R.M. (1991) "The Phenomenon of Trust and the Patient-Physician Relationship," in E.D. Pellegrino, R.M. Veatch and J.P. Langan (eds.), *Ethics, Trust and the Professions: Philosophical and Cultural Aspects*, Washington DC: Georgetown University Press.

29

TRUST AND FOOD BIOTECHNOLOGY

Franck L.B. Meijboom

29.1 Introduction

Food biotechnology is a broad field in which technologies are developed by making use of biological processes, organisms, cells or cellular components. The technology is used in many contexts and in the production process of many food and feed products. Sometimes the food product itself is modified, like in the case of genetically modified (GM) corn or soy. In other cases, the role of biotechnology is less obvious for the end-user, e.g. when it is used in the brewing process of beer. Despite these differences, in all situations food biotechnology is complex. Individuals cannot fully control or have full knowledge of all human activities related to food biotechnology. Consequently, everyone has to rely on others, both individuals and institutions. As for technology in general, the exact nature of the relation between trust and food biotechnology is not directly clear. Sometimes technology is portrayed as an element that causes or intensifies a lack of trust or even distrust in science or private companies. In other cases, technology is proposed as a way to deal with risks and uncertainties and therefore is considered as a way to reduce the need to trust (cf. Levidow and Marris 2001; Hsiao 2003).

This general picture of the relation between technology and trust is even further complicated in the case of food biotechnology. Food biotechnology combines the discussion on changing basic elements of life and flourishing with an essential element in human life: food consumption. As a consequence, trust in food biotechnology is often framed as a problematic relation (Marques et al. 2015; Lucht 2015; Master and Resnik 2013). While I will adopt this framing of a "trust problem" for my analysis of the role of trust in food biotechnology, I will in the end challenge this framing and suggest a focus on trustworthiness instead of trust. In the following, I first analyze the dual relation between trust and technology. Second, I discuss the question whether it is possible to trust food biotechnology before, third, elaborating on the question how to address low trust or distrust in food biotechnology. Finally, I argue that trustworthiness is an indispensable prerequisite for trust in food biotechnology.

29.2 Trust, Food and Biotechnology: A Complex Relation

Trust and the lack thereof is often discussed explicitly in the context of technology (cf. Drees 2009; Myskja 2008; Master and Resnik 2013). This especially holds for food biotechnology. Since the debate on genetically modified (GM) food at the end of the last century, consumer trust in biotechnology has received a lot of attention. Trust is often considered as a pivotal, but problematic element for any use of biotechnology. Right from the start of the GM-food debate, the reluctance of consumers to buy and consume GM-products was considered to be related to an issue of low consumer trust. Therefore, it has been stated repeatedly that there is a clear need for rebuilding and maintaining public trust. For instance, in 2000 the OECD reported after a meeting on GM-food that "a strong sense emerged that there was a need to take steps to rebuild trust among the various actors, particularly governments, industry, scientists, regulatory agencies and the public" (OECD 2000). Two years later, the FAO stated that "the food safety system … must be able to both manage risks and create trust" (FAO 2003). More recently, Frewer emphasizes that "[s]ocietal trust … is an important factor in determining societal acceptance of agrifood technologies" (Frewer 2017:4). Also, Runge et al. (2017) stress the importance of trust when they claim that "[a]wareness of food-related biotechnology, and a decrease in trust that institutions within the food system can keep food safe, work concurrently to prompt the public to reconsider its way of thinking about food" (Runge et al. 2017:590). While a decline or lack of trust is lamented in regards to many institutions and technologies, the intensity of these debates in the context of food biotechnology is and remains remarkably high.

29.2.1 Defining Trust

Following Baier, who compares trust to an atmosphere, explicit attention to trust is an important sign. She argues, "we notice trust as we notice air only when it becomes scarce or polluted" (1994:98). From this perspective, discussing trust in the context of food biotechnology implies that trust apparently has become "scarce or polluted." However, before jumping to an analysis of whether this metaphor is apt, it is important to start with the question what we mean with the concept of trust. This conceptual clarity is important, because Hardin accurately noticed that, "the notion of trust in the vernacular is often vaguely warm and fuzzy" (1999:429). This vagueness is not restricted to the vernacular. Also at the level of academic analysis there is a "conceptual jungle" (Lindenberg 2000) and a lack of conceptual clarity (Gambetta 1988).

Some philosophers of trust define trust as a form of belief (see also Keren, this volume). However, conceiving trust as a form of belief raises some questions. While such belief-based definitions clearly have some plausibility, they appear unable to account for the so-called leap element of trust, indicating that trusting includes more than a belief that is exclusively based on evidence. Information facilitates trust, but it is impossible to define a sufficient level of evidence to arrive at trust. There is an element in trust that "happens to us," rather than that we decide to adopt a stance of trust. Secondly, the dynamic relation between trust and evidence remains unanswered if we consider trust as a cognitive belief. Evidence is not the only input in the process of coming to trust. The direction is also the other way around: trust appears to be a precondition to obtain knowledge (see also, Miller and Freiman, this volume).

This illustrates that trust has an ability that beliefs normally do not have: it can color the value we attach to certain beliefs, make them resistant to change or exclude other beliefs from deliberation. To deal with these features of trust the emotional element of this concept has to be taken seriously (see also Lahno, this volume). Explicating the emotional element shows that emotional judgments steer the perception of the available evidence. This is not to say that trust is only a feeling that appears fully independent of evidence. The emotional component quite often refers to an implicit assessment of the competence or motivation of the trustee rather than to pure irrationality or ignorance.

Based upon these considerations, I propose the following working definition of trust: Trust is an attitude towards individual or collective human agents that enables an agent to cope with situations of uncertainty and lack of control, by formulating a positive expectation towards another agent, based on the assessment of the trustworthiness of the trusted agent (Meijboom 2008).

29.2.2 Biotechnology and the Relevance of Trust

Trust as an attitude that enables us to cope with situations of uncertainty and lack of control seems especially relevant in late modern society. Many sociologists have shown that the complexity of social life has led to increased levels of risk and uncertainty (Giddens 1990; 1991; Luhmann 1988). This has changed the character and scope of the need to rely on others. Furthermore, scandals and affairs have affected trust in a range of institutions, such as food-related animal diseases, but also the impact of the recent financial crisis in 2008–2010 on the banking system (e.g. Van Esterik-Plasmeijer and Van Raay 2017).

From this perspective, the relation between trust and biotechnology is ambivalent. When we define trust as a way to deal with uncertainty and lack of personal control, biotechnology can be considered both as source of and a remedy for low trust or even distrust. On the one hand, technology can provide tools that enable us to have control over situations. On the other hand, technologies such as modern biotechnology intensify the dependency of individual agents because of the complicated nature of the topics involved in dealing with issues such as food safety, quality and health. These call for abilities that most of us do not have. Consequently, we cannot but rely on others. This dual effect of biotechnology on trust can be recognized with respect to the impact of this technology on (a) risks and uncertainties and (b) predictable patterns on which one can anticipate.

First, the dual effect of technology can be recognized at the level of risk and uncertainties. On the one hand, technologies are often introduced to address uncertainties and risks. With the help of modern biotechnology, it is possible to get a grip on a situation. For instance, in the past one could only hope that a breeding process would result in the preferred outcome, e.g. a plant that is better resistant to a virus. Nowadays, biotechnology makes it possible to select target genes to make the breeding process of plants more specific. Consequently, we are in a less dependent and less vulnerable position when confronted with the outbreak of a plant disease that in the past would have destroyed the harvest. From this perspective, biotechnology provides us with more control and thus can reduce the need to trust on others or to rely on natural processes.

Nevertheless, the use of biotechnology also raises new uncertainties and risks. When we define risks in terms of chance and hazard, technology can affect both levels. Food biotechnology has an impact on the element on chance due to its influence on the structure of the food chain. It contributes to longer and more complex production chains that are interrelated with many other systems, such as transportation and global trade. Due to this complexity, minor effects of a technology can have consequences with a major impact for the society. For instance, if there was a problem in the production of one batch of genetically modified soy bean that remains unnoticed, it may affect the safety and quality of hundreds of products all over the world.

Furthermore, uncertainties arise along with the introduction of new technologies. This is the case when the probability and the nature of the hazard are not yet well defined. The debate on food biotechnology is an interesting case, because discussions regarding both the probability that something goes wrong and the precise hazard have been ongoing since the first introduction of genetically modified food in Europe in 1996 (cf. Gaskell et al. 2003; OECD 2000). Such discussions show that the use of biotechnology entails risks and uncertainties which are often difficult to assess, especially because of complicating factors like unknown carry-over effects, possible long-term effects, but also because the consequences are mostly invisible without advanced instruments. Therefore, assessing issues like safety, quality and health are tasks that require powers that most of us do not have. Since only few have the expertise and can assess and evaluate these problems, all others cannot but rely on these experts (see also Rolin, this volume).

This shows a shift in focus. The problem is not merely the dimension and acceptability of the risk at stake, but also one of the reliability of the experts. The experts, not the consumer, make an assessment. Consequently, problems not only occur at the level of the risk itself but also with respect to the trust in the experts on whom one has to rely. The debate on the safety of genetically modified food, however, shows striking tensions amongst experts in their assessment of the risks of modern biotechnology for humans, animals and the environment (e.g. Hilbeck et al. 2015; Meyer 2016). Hence, even though more knowledge and information are available, it is difficult for an individual to decide whom to trust. This shows that even if food biotechnology reduces the need to trust others or rely on natural processes, the implementation and use of this technology is only possible if there is some level of trust.

Second, one could question the importance of trust in the case of food biotechnology by referring to the effects of technology on predictable patterns. Regularly, technology results in procedures that make a situation more predictable. For instance, the use of biotechnology can standardize a food production method so that one can anticipate that the quality of the product is similar at any time and any place. As a consequence, a consumer can anticipate these patterns and, for instance, can buy a food product in a country that one has never visited before. This seems to reduce the need to trust. However, the picture is more complicated. The introduction of new technologies also can thwart existing predictability and familiarity in the food sector. When a technology is introduced, there is often no predictability that can serve as a basis for trust. The example of the introduction of food products with a health claim is an interesting case (Meijboom 2007). Although the relation between food and health is not new, lowering one's blood cholesterol with the help of a margarine or using prebiotics in yoghurt for the maintenance of gut microbiota are still new. Both for drugs and for dairy products there are rather clear conventions and traditions that provide a certain predictability explicating what one can expect regarding issues of safety and justice. This predictability helps individuals to make choices about both food and pharmaceutical products even if they do not fully understand or control the production process. However, since a food product with a real health claim can be categorized in both groups, we lack such predictability. Thus, the introduction of this type of dairy product complicates the possibility to rely on existing roles and patterns. Hence, once more trust in experts, companies or governments becomes essential.

29.3 Is Trust in Biotechnology Possible?

If biotechnology results in an increased need to trust, it raises the question of what it implies to speak about trust in this technology. To answer that question, it is important to look at the three dimensions of a trusting relationship: a trustor (A) entrusts something (x) to a trustee (B).

If we focus on public trust or consumer trust, the trustor commonly is a citizen or a consumer. Mostly these persons are capable of trusting, i.e. they have a certain level of freedom and competence to consider and evaluate situations to assess whether trust is applicable.

With regard to the object of trust, the discussion is more complicated. First, in comparison to other technologies, biotechnology is special because it is changing basic elements of life and flourishing. Consequently, biotechnology links to fundamental views on the value of life and human responsibility. Additionally, more than once the discussion starts with biotechnology, but turns out not be about the technology as such, but (also) about what is modified with the help of biotechnology. For instance, food biotechnology resulted in fierce public discussion also due to the fact that food is special. Food is not merely the combination of all the nutritional ingredients one needs to stay alive, but has strong social, cultural, religious and emotional aspects too (e.g. Gofton 1996). This makes the lack of personal control that come with biotechnology even more problematic. Furthermore, debates regarding food biotechnology are related to broader concerns about food, such as the tensions between industrial food production, cultural and historical perspectives on food or views on sustainable farming. Consequently, what is at stake in the trust relation with regard to biotechnology has a multifaceted character and is not about risks only (Sandin and Moula 2015).

The third element of the trusting relationship is the object of trust. In the daily practice of trusting we can speak about trust in biotechnology. However, the question is whether the object of trust is the technology. In my definition of trust this is not possible. Trust presupposes both the ability and the freedom to choose a goal and to choose it among alternatives. If a trustee lacks freedom there is no need to trust and no possibility to act trustworthily. There is no need to trust if we know that external forces coerce an individual to act in one specific way. Then we know or can calculate based on the available information how someone will act if he is compelled to do so. This is why one need not, in fact cannot, trust the operation of a machine or other inanimate objects. A bridge can perform in a way that is counter to what is expected, but it does not choose to adopt this alternative. It does not have the ability to choose at all. As a result, the bridge can neither trust nor be trusted. This equally holds for other types of technologies. Consequently, trust in biotechnology can only refer to trust in human agents involved in biotechnology, but not the technology itself.

However, even if we focus on human agents, it still is not clear whom to trust. Given the complexity of food biotechnology and the practices in which it is applied, there are multiple agents on whom one has to rely. For instance, a consumer is confronted with a wide range of individual and collective human agents, including researchers, food industry, retailers, governmental agencies and non-governmental organizations (NGOs). This is an important characteristic for trust: the wide range of involved parties is not a sign of inefficient ways of organizing the food chain or the research and development. It is a direct result of the complexity of biotechnology and food production in a globalized world. Due to this complexity not only the consumers but also those involved in food biotechnology need to trust other actors. Suppose one institutional trustee has a clear competence in assessing the safety of biotech products, we still need another that has an expertise in evaluating the health claims of genetically modified products. Even if both competence fields are combined in one organization, it is most likely that this organization cannot be entrusted with the question whether a GM-food product or biotechnology as such fits to my core values. For that question, I may need to rely on an organization that represents my lifestyle, e.g. an animal welfare organization or a church. This picture is further complicated by the fact that biotechnology is a global issue. Biotech companies often are multinationals and also critical NGOs often operate on a global level. This implies that a trustor is not only confronted with a local retailer or a national food safety agency but with a wide variety of local, national and multinational trustees.

The question at the start of this section was whether trust in biotechnology is possible. The short answer is that (a) trust in biotechnology is related to a broad range of objects of trust rather than only focused on the technology as such, and (b) the technology and the practice of application have a high level of complexity that entails that trust in biotechnology cannot be reduced to trust in one party. This has direct implications for the question how to deal with trust and biotechnology in practice.

29.4 How to Deal with Issues of Trust Related to Food Biotechnology?

In situations of low public trust in technologies, three strategies can be distinguished that aim at increasing trust: empowering people, increasing predictable patterns and improving trustworthiness. While all three strategies are being employed, I conclude from my analyses that especially the third approach is the most promising if confronted with issues of trust in the context of food biotechnology.

The first route to approach problems of trust starts in the vulnerability of the trustor. He or she is confronted with a lack of control and an asymmetry in knowledge and power. Consequently, empowering people in a way that makes them less vulnerable or provides them with more control seems a promising start to address problem with biotechnology. This approach often focuses on two aspects: risks and information. The risk and safety aspects of biotechnology have dominated the public debate (Gaskell et al. 2004; Eiser et al. 2002), and since trust is relevant in situations of uncertainty, enabling consumers to deal with risks is regularly seen as an effective answer to questions of trust. The idea is that if individuals are able to assess a danger as a risk, they have the opportunity to decide how to deal with the situation rather than the restricted choice to take or leave the danger (cf. Luhmann, 1988). This approach seems promising. If the danger that the use of gene editing in cow breeding may have adverse effects on animal welfare or food safety can be translated into a matter of risk, it becomes an object of action, because a risk can be assessed, analyzed and managed. Therefore, providing information on risks and the enhancement of transparency is often proposed as the most efficient (regulatory) approach to low trust related to biotechnology (cf. Barbero et al. 2017; White House 2017). Despite the importance of both transparency and risk communication the approach has two genuine limitations.

First, the relationship between information, communication and trust is highly complex and remains unclear (cf. Rose et al. 2019). If one does not share any information, it is hard to trust another. At the same time, we lack criteria to determine the minimum level of information that is sufficient to start trusting. Furthermore, communication already presumes some levels of trust. Only if one already considers the provider of information reliable, the information becomes useful. For instance, someone who trusts a biotech company will probably perceive an open communication strategy on possible risks as a confirmation of his trust. Someone who lacks such trust may well have the idea that this communication on potential risks is another proof that biotechnology should be banned. The same situation with the same level of available information is perceived completely differently.

Second, empowering people to take risk is something fundamentally different from building trust relationships. In trusting you always run a risk: your trust can be harmed. Accordingly, trust is referred to as a risky matter (Gambetta 1988: 235) and as a venture (Luhmann 2000: 31). Nonetheless, trust is fundamentally different from taking risks, even though they can be relevant in the same situation. Trust is not the outcome of an assessment of the risks and benefits of trusting in the light of the aims and goals one pursues. In contrast to someone who takes a risk, a trustor is not calculating risks, but coping with complexity and the uncertainty he is faced with. Therefore, better risk assessment and more risk information do not necessarily lead to more trust. Trust has a different focus. It starts where a risk focus ends. It arises in situations that remain uncertain despite the attempts to turn the uncertain aspects into risk factors. Therefore, a risk-focused approach mainly helps to reduce the need to trust, because it enables a person to assess and control the situation oneself. However, given the complexity of the discussions about food biotechnology, not all problems can be reduced to risks. There remain situations in which we are confronted with uncertainty because "the system behaviour is basically well known," but not the probability distributions (Wynne 1992:114). In these situations one has to rely on others and trust can play a central role.

A more fruitful response to low trust focuses on the relevance of predictable patterns. Trust needs certain levels of predictability regarding its subject or object. This is what is meant by "anticipatory trust" (Sztompka 1999) or "predictive trust" (Hollis 1998). This type of trust is based upon the expectation that the other party will act according to normal patterns and routines. If clear patterns and routines are available, it is often easier to predict how the person who is being trusted will react and what one can expect. For instance, if you have bought a product for many years, you will expect that its safety and quality remain unchanged the next time you buy the product. Hence you rely on this being so even though there is always a risk that this may be the first time the product is unsafe. Unfortunately, biotechnology lacks such clear patterns and thus routine-based trust appears problematic. Since biotechnology is a relatively new technology and has a broad range of applications, we still lack a normal pattern, a history upon which we can rely and in which the trustee can show his reliability. In regulatory frameworks this lack has been recognized and translated into a strong focus on providing information on underlying standard procedures and routines, either regarding the products themselves or the actors involved. However, information on the level of predictability provides some control in cases of uncertainty but does not necessarily tell us whether and why the other person would act along the normal pattern in a specific case. Since we have the freedom to act, we have the freedom to leave normal patterns and act against predictability. This means we are confronted with new uncertainties: even if there are predictable patterns regarding biotechnology in food, one is still uncertain whether the other party will act according to expectations. Recent food scandals all over the world show that in most cases the problem was not the lack of procedures or regulations, but individuals or organizations who deliberately acted against what has been agreed on (e.g. Fuseini et al. 2017; Mol 2014). These problems suggest that we need additional procedures and regulation that serve as a foundation for our trust which could result in an endless regression, because we can only rely on patterns if we have sound indications that the other party is reliable.

Responses to low trust in food biotechnology focusing on empowerment and predictable patterns have severe limitations due to the complexity of food biotechnology and the resulting uncertainty and lack of control. As a consequence, a focus on risk, information and transparency will only be fruitful if the "problem of trust" is rather addressed as a "problems of trustworthiness."

29.5 The Importance of Trustworthiness

My working definition of trust entails an assessment of someone's competence and motivation, otherwise we talk about other mechanisms to cope with lack of control or uncertainty, such as hope or coercion. The central role of making an assessment of the trustee is a clear indication that most issues of trust about food biotechnology are not so much about trust but about trustworthiness. More specific, if a lack of trust is approached as a failure of the trustor, the issue is defined wrongly and remains intangible for three reasons.

First, there is an argument from strategy: trust as an attitude is difficult to change. As we have seen at the start of this chapter a trustor cannot decide to trust. Trust results in beliefs and expectations but is not a belief itself. One can want to trust, but one cannot trust at will (see also Hinchman, this volume). For the same reason, you cannot make others trust you. Therefore (policy) measures that aim to improve trust in food biotechnology should start from another perspective. The question should not be "How to increase trust?," but rather "Why would an individual agent trust the other agent?" and "Is this agent actually worth being trusted?" Thus, we need to move from a "problem of trust" to a "problem of trustworthiness." Biotech companies or governments cannot change individuals in a way that they adopt a trustful attitude. Nevertheless, they can show themselves to be trustworthy. Accordingly, for pragmatic and strategic reasons, enhancing trustworthiness seems a more promising starting point in the process of regaining public trust.

The second argument starts in the trustee's assessment of the lack of trust as problematic. For instance, if a governmental agency considers a lack of trust as problematic, this implies an implicit claim about their own trustworthiness. Unless, a trustee hopes that someone trusts him blindly, he believes that trust is based on an assessment of his competence and motivation. Thus, if he considers the lack of trust problematic, he implicitly argues that, according to him, the trustor has very good reasons to trust him, i.e. that he is trustworthy. From this perspective, it would be too easy to define a lack of trust as a problem of the individual trustor only. The trustee has a problem too. Even if he is competent and adequately motivated to do what is entrusted, he obviously failed to signal this sufficiently to the trustor.

Finally, the importance of the shift from trust to trustworthiness does not merely have a practical or strategic background. There is also a strong moral reason: the autonomy of the consumer. We have already mentioned that a trusting relationship is by definition asymmetric and marked by differences in knowledge and power. This vulnerable status of the trustor is constitutive for trust. Without this vulnerable position, there would be no need to trust. Nonetheless, this is no permit for the trustee to make use of this vulnerability. Despite the vulnerable status, the trustor should be treated as a person who is capable of autonomous agency, i.e. as a person who has the capacity to choose one's goals and values personally. This makes the trustor and the trustee equals on a moral level. Despite the vulnerable and depending position of the trustor and his imperfect knowledge about – in our case biotechnology and food – he still is an autonomous agent. This makes him worthy of respect and has direct implications for the trustworthiness of the trustee. If one takes this moral attitude of respect as a start, a lack of or hesitance to trust cannot longer be defined as failure of the trustor only. Such a view disregards the autonomy of the trustor in two ways. First, it does not take the assessment of an autonomous agent seriously. From the moral attitude of respect, a lack of or hesitance to trust should be acknowledged as a legitimate point of view, rather than as failure only. This does not imply that the trustor cannot be wrong but shows that the burden of the proof also lies on the side of the trustee. The vulnerability of an autonomous agent comes with a moral reason for the trustee to take additional care in being trustworthy and signaling this appropriately. Consequently, the main question is not how the individual can be changed so that he will trust, but what conditions the trustee has to fulfill to be worthy of such trust.

29.6 Challenges for Trustworthy Food Biotechnology

With trustworthiness as the answer to the question of how to deal with issues of trust related to food biotechnology, we are confronted with the question of what trustworthiness implies in the context of biotechnology. At face value the answer seems easy: to be trustworthy one must be competent in the relevant matter and has the motivation to respond adequately to what one is entrusted. In practice, however, acting in a trustworthy way in the context of biotechnology is not that easy. This has its origin in (a) the broad scope of what is entrusted in the context of biotechnology, (b) the complexity of food biotechnology and the impact on the number of trustees and (c) the lack of consensus on societal values related to biotechnology.

As mentioned before, food biotechnology is related to an impressive list of issues that can entrusted, such as food safety, cultural and historical traditions of food production, animal welfare, biodiversity, justice, freedom of choice, and privacy. Therefore, clarity regarding both one's competence and motivation as well as the limits of both are essential. For instance, when an international biotech company only communicates about its competence in scientific progress although it has equally strong competence and motivation regarding responsible research and innovation, it should not come as a surprise that trustors will perceive the company only competent in a technical way and will not entrust it with questions of societal implementation. Suppose conversely, the explicit commitment of a local governmental body to improve animal welfare results in the expectation of a trustor that this government will only license biotech applications that improve animal welfare in food production. Even if this organization is genuinely committed to improving animal welfare standards, to be entrusted with this idea of regulating food biotechnology is problematic. Due to international trade regulations it is very unlikely that a local governmental body is capable to allow animal friendly biotech applications only (cf. Meijboom and Brom 2003; De Simone and Serratosa 2005). Therefore, to be trustworthy, a trustee has to be clear on its commitments, but also on the limits of what can be entrusted.

A second hurdle in dealing with trustworthiness is related to the complexity of food biotechnology and the related distribution of responsibilities. Food biotechnology covers a wide range of products, tasks and actors. Consequently, a division of labor and responsibilities is already in place to guide and regulate this technology. For instance, product development is the responsibility of companies, whereas licensing and regulation is the task of governments. However, such as division of responsibility and related ideas of what one can reasonably expect of this organization is not always that well defined. Small startups in biotechnology next to multinational companies, lobby organizations for biotechnology next to critical NGOs and local governmental bodies next to global trade agreements all play a central role in food biotechnology. Because of this broad spectrum of relevant actors, it is not directly clear who is trustworthy and should be trusted, when I – as a citizen and consumer – am concerned about the effects of food biotechnology on the position of farmers in developing countries. This shows that biotechnology raises questions of trust without a well-defined set of trustees nor consensus on what one can reasonable expect from whom. This issues touches on a more fundamental debate on how a global society should be arranged in way that do justice to the complexity at stake. It is unlikely that one super-national organization, either governmental, non-governmental or commercial can deal with all trust issues. As a consequence, cooperation among the trustees is essential as well as clarity in the communication amongst the trustors on the content and limits of a trustee's competence and motivation.

Finally, biotechnology confronts us with the fact that many societies harbor a striking plurality of moral views. We lack consensus on the importance and relative weight of moral notions such as animal welfare, the value of nature, biodiversity or duties towards future generations. Although we have tools and ways to address this plurality, e.g. by improving communication, increasing transparency or enhancing the level of reflection, the problem or moral pluralism remains.

Trust and trustworthiness can be complicated by this moral pluralism because of conflicting moral views, but also because of doubts about whether a trustee is competent and motivated to deal with individual concerns. For both challenges there is no easy solution and they show that trustworthiness in the context of food biotechnology requires a competence to deal with ethical concerns and conflicts. This implies that trustees can benefit from awareness of their own normative presuppositions and from identifying potential ethical issues early on.

Moreover, trustees need to reflect upon the fundamental context-specific commitments and concepts relevant for trust. In the context of food biotechnology, for instance, freedom of choice appears to be crucial. Being trustworthy therefore requires reflecting upon this freedom and guaranteeing consumer choice as a translation of this basic commitment. Finally, a trustee can deal with the challenges of the plurality of moral views by participating in or initiating public debates. These debates help to explore the nature of moral concerns and clarify the mutual expectations between trustor and trustee.

29.7 Conclusion

From the perspective of trust, food biotechnology is a special case. It has two sources from which trust questions can occur: the technology and food. As a technology biotechnology is special because it is changing basic elements of life and flourishing, because of its many fields of application and the related range of potential impact, and because the results are mostly invisible for the end-user. As a result, biotechnology leads to situations of uncertainty and lack of control, i.e. to situations in which trust is essential. The application of biotechnology to food makes it even more distinctive, since food is linked to personal values and people's identity. Therefore, what needs to be entrusted to others is special and important to trustors.

Neglecting this special and multifaceted character of food biotechnology, we run the risk of paying simultaneously too much and too little attention to trust and biotechnology. On the one hand, it may result in paying too much attention to, and even overload biotechnology with all kind of trust problems that are not specific to this technology, e.g. debates on the freedom of farmers, food security or animal welfare. On the other hand, we run the risk of paying not enough attention to the special character of food biotechnology if we strip the debate to the technology part only. In that case issues of trust can easily, but mistakenly be restricted to a matter of risk and safety only.

The special character of food biotechnology also becomes explicit in dealing with the question how to deal with the lack of or hesitance to trust. Next to strategies to empower consumers/ citizens that reduce the need to trust in the context of biotechnology, approaches that start in trustworthiness are most promising. This holds for individuals as well as institutions. In the context of food biotechnology, showing oneself worthy of trust implies awareness of and clear communication about one's competence and motivation. Given the wide range of goods being entrusted and the complexity of issues at stake, four steps are essential for trustworthiness.

First, acknowledging individual or intuitional limits and clear communication about trust expectations that one cannot fulfill. Second, it is important that trustees in the field of biotechnology bring their own ideas about mutual responsibility more closely into line with each other. Since no trustee can be trustworthy in regards to all relevant issues related to food biotechnology it must be clarified who is responsible for what. For instance, food safety may be primarily entrusted to the government. However, both for the trustors and for the government it is essential to be aware whether the relevant private companies also recognize this as a shared responsibility. If this were not the case, the government may not be even competent enough to act trustworthy or at least has to rearrange its organization, e.g. by installing a stronger food safety authority. This shows the relevance of third step. Trustworthiness in food biotechnology asks for systematic attention to a renewed institutional infrastructure that can deal with questions of trust related to a technology that is researched and developed in a global setting and traded on a global market, but at the same time implemented in specific and local contexts and used by individuals. This asks for both cooperation among trustees and innovation in institutional structures. Finally, the combination of food and biotechnology shows that trustworthiness requires attention to the ethical and socio-cultural dimensions. The debates in food biotechnology on issues such as farmers' autonomy, just distribution of benefits and animal welfare show that these topics are not just an addendum to the debate on risk and uncertainty. They are a core element of food biotechnology and need to be addressed if one aims to be worthy of trust

This proposal to focus on trustworthiness in food biotechnology will not solve all problems related to trust but is an essential step to address the relation between trust and food biotechnology.

Acknowledgments

Thanks are due to the reviewers and Judith Simon for their valuable comments on an earlier version of the manuscript.

References

Baier, A.C. (1994) *Moral Prejudices, Essays on Ethics*, Cambridge: Harvard University Press.

Barbero, R., Kim, J., Boling, T. and Doherty, J. (2017) "Increasing the Transparency, Coordination, and Predictability of the Biotechnology Regulatory System," The White House, Obama Administration. https://obamawhitehouse.archives.gov/blog/2017/01/04/increasing- transparency-coordination-and-predictability-biotechnology-regulatory

De Simone, F. and Serratosa, J. (2005) "Biotechnology, Animal Health and Animal Welfare within the Framework of European Union Legislation," *Rev. Sci. Tech. Off. Int. Epiz.* 24(1): 89–99.

Drees, W.B. (ed.) (2009) *Technology, Trust, and Religion*, Leiden: Leiden University Press.

Eiser, J.R., Miles, S. and Frewer, L.J. (2002) "Trust, Perceived Risk and Attitudes towards Food Technologies," *Journal of Applied Social Psychology* 32: 2423–2433.

FAO(2003) "Expert Consultation on Food Safety: Science and Ethics,"September 3–5, 2002, Rome. http://www.fao.org/3/j0776e/j0776e00.htm

Frewer, L.J. (2017) "Consumer Acceptance and Rejection of Emerging Agrifood Technologies and Their Applications," *European Review of Agricultural Economics* 1–22. doi:10.1093/erae/jbx007

Frewer, L.J. and Salter, B. (2003) "The Changing Governance of Biotechnology: The Politics of Public Trust in the Agri-Food Sector," *Applied Biotechnology, Food Science and Policy* 1(4): 199–211.

Fuseini, A., Wotton, S.B., Knowles, T.G. and Hadley, P.J. (2017) "Halal Meat Fraud and Safety Issues in the UK: A Review in the Context of the European Union," *Food Ethics* 3, doi:10.1007/s41055-41017-0009-0001

Gambetta, D. (ed.) (1988) *Trust: Making and Breaking Cooperative Relations*, Oxford: Basil Blackwell.

Gaskell, G., Allum, N., Wagner, W., Kronberger, N., Torgersen, H., Hampel, J. and Bardes, J. (2004) "GM Foods and the Misperception of Risk Perception," *Risk Analysis* 24: 185–194.

Gaskell, G., Allum, N. and Stares, S. (2003) *Europeans and Biotechnology in 2002; Eurobarometer 58.0*, 2nd edition. A Report to the EC Directorate General for Research from the Project "Life Sciences in European Society" QLG7-CT-1999–00286.

Giddens, A. (1990) *The Consequences of Modernity*, Cambridge: Polity Press.

Giddens, A. (1991) *Modernity and Self-Identity: Self and Society in the Late Modern Age*, Cambridge: Polity Press.

Gofton, L. (1996) "Bread to Biotechnology: Cultural Aspects of Food Ethics," in B. Mepham (ed.), *Food Ethics*, London: Routledge.

Hardin, R. (1999) "Book Review, Trudy Govier, Social Trust and Human Communities," *The Journal of Value Inquiry* 33: 429–433.

Hilbeck, A., Binimelis, R., Defarge, N., Steinbrecher, R., Székács, A., Wickson, F., Antoniou, M., Bereano, P.L., Clark, E.A., Hansen, M., Novotny, E., Heinemann, J., Meyer, H., Shiva, V. and Wynne, B. (2015) "No Scientific Consensus on GMO Safety," *Environmental Sciences Europe* 27 (4), doi:10.1186/s12302-12014-0034-0031

Hobbes, T. (1651) *Leviathan or the Matter, Forme, & Power of a Common-wealth, Ecclesiasticall and Civill*, London: Andrew Crooke. http://socserv2.socsci.mcmaster.ca/~econ/ugcm/3ll3/hobbes/Leviathan.pdf

Hollis, M. (1998) *Trust within Reason*, Cambridge: Cambridge University Press.

Hsiao, R.-L. (2003) "Technology Fears: Distrust and Cultural Persistence in Electronic Marketplace Adoption," *The Journal of Strategic Information Systems* 12(3): 169–199. https://doi.org/10.1016/S0963-8687(03)00034-9

Levidow, L. and Marris, C.C. (2001) "Science and Governance in Europe: Lessons from the Case of Agricultural Biotechnology," *Science and Public Policy* 28(5), 345–360.

Lindenberg, S. (2000) "It Takes Both Trust and Lack of Mistrust: The Workings of Cooperation and Relational Signalling in Contractual Relationships," *Journal of Management and Governance* 4: 11–33.

Lucht, J.M. (2015) "Public Acceptance of Plant Biotechnology and GM Crops," *Viruses* 7(8): 4254–4281. doi:10.3390/v7082819

Luhmann, N. (1988) "Familiarity, Confidence, Trust: Problems and Alternatives," in D. Gambetta (ed.), *Trust: Making and Breaking Cooperative Relations*, Oxford: Basil Blackwell: 94–107.

Luhmann, N. (2000) *Vertrauen, ein Mechanismus der Reduktion der sozialer Komplexität*, 4. Auflag, Stuttgart: Lucius & Lucius.

Marques, M.D., Critchley, C.R. and Walshe, J. (2015) "Attitudes to Genetically Modified Food over Time: How Trust in Organizations and the Media Cycle Predict Support," *Public Understanding of Science* 24(5): 601–618. doi:10.1177/0963662514542372

Master, Z. and Resnik, D.B. (2013) "Hype and Public Trust in Science," *Science and Engineering Ethics* 19(2): 321–335.

Meijboom, F. (2007) "Trust, Food and Health, Questions of Trust at the Interface between Food and Health," *Journal of Agricultural and Environmental Ethics* 20(3): 231–245.

Meijboom, F.L.B. (2008) "A Proposal to Broaden the Analysis of Problems of Trust Regarding Food and Biotechnology," in R.J. Busch and G. Prütz (eds.), *Biotechnologie in Gesellschaftlicher Deutung*, München: Herbert Utz Verlag.

Meijboom, F.L.B. and Brom, F.W.A. (2003) "Intransigent or Reconcilable: The Complex Relation between Public Morals, the WTO and Consumers," in A. Vedder (ed.), *The WTO and Concerns Regarding Animals and Nature*, Nijmegen: Wolf Legal Productions.

Meyer, G. (2016) "In Science Communication, Why Does the Idea of a Public Deficit Always Return?" *Public Understanding of Science* 25: 433–446.

Mol, A.P.J. (2014) "Governing China's Food Quality through Transparency: A Review," *Food Control* 43: 49–56.

Myskja, B.K. (2008) "The Categorical Imperative and the Ethics of Trust," *Ethics and Information Technology* 10(4): 213–220.

OECD (2000) "Genetically Modified Foods, Widening the Debate on Health and Safety," The OECD Edinburgh Conference on the Scientific and Health Aspects of Genetically Modified Foods. www.oecd.org/sti/emerging-tech/2097312.pdf

Rose, K.M., Howell, E.L., Su, L.Y.-F., Xenos, M.A., Brossard, D. and Scheufele, D.A. (2019) "Distinguishing Scientific Knowledge: The Impact of Different Measures of Knowledge on Genetically Modified Food Attitudes," *Public Understanding of Science*. doi:10.1177/0963662518824837

Runge, K.K., Brossard, D., Scheufele, D.A., Rose, K.M. and Larson, B.J. (2017) "Attitudes about Food and Food-Related Biotechnology," *Public Opinion Quarterly* 81(2): 577–596.

Sandin, P. and Moula, P. (2015) "Modern Biotechnology, Agriculture, and Ethics" *Journal of Agricultural Environmental Ethics* 28: 803–806. doi:10.1007/s10806-10015-9567-9566

Sztompka, P. (1999) *Trust: A Sociological Theory*, Cambridge: Cambridge University Press.

Van Esterik-Plasmeijer, P.W.J. and van Raaij, W.F. (2017) "Banking System Trust, Bank Trust, and Bank Loyalty," *International Journal of Bank Marketing* 35(1): 97–111.

White House (2017) "Modernizing the Regulatory System for Biotechnology Products: Final Version of the 2017 Update to the Coordinated Framework for the Regulation of Biotechnology," The Obama Administration. https://obamawhitehouse.archives.gov/sites/default/files/microsites/ostp/2017_coordinate d_framework_update.pdf

Wynne, B. (1992) "Uncertainty and Environmental Learning: Reconceiving Science and Policy in the Preventive Paradigm," *Global Environmental Change* 2(2): 111–127.

Further Reading

Bovenkerk, B. (2012) *The Biotechnology Debate: Democracy in the Face of Intractable Disagreement*, Library of Ethics and Applied Philosophy, Dordrecht: Springer.

Korthals, M. (2004) *Before Dinner: Philosophy and Ethics of Food*, The International Library of Environmental, Agricultural and Food Ethics book series (LEAF), volume 5, Dordrecht: Springer.

Thompson, P. and Kaplan, D. (eds.) (2014/ 2019), *Encyclopedia of Food and Agricultural Ethics*, 1st and 2nd edition, Dordrecht: Springer. (Includes section with entries on (bio)technology.)

30
TRUST IN NANOTECHNOLOGY

John Weckert and Sadjad Soltanzadeh

30.1 Introduction

Why do we want to talk about trusting nanotechnology? It is, after all, just another technology, yet one that has generated some heated public debates. There have even been calls for a moratorium on its development (see for example ETC 2006).[1] Apart from an apparent lack of trust suggested by this debate, there are two main reasons why examining trust in this context is useful. First, nanotechnology is still relatively new so we do not really know what its potentials are. Second, nanotechnology is an enabling technology, that is, it can be used to improve other technologies. One example is the use of nanotechnology in electronics which can, amongst other things, improve the performance of computers. Another is its use in sunscreens and cosmetics. Because it can be used to enhance many different technologies, its consequences are even more uncertain than the consequences of many other technologies. Some of these consequences are intrinsic to nanotechnology while others are more instrumental, but this will be discussed later.

In order to make clear what trust in nanotechnology is, the chapter will attempt to answer two related questions: (1) Does it make sense to talk of trust in nanotechnology? And if it does, (2) What do we trust if we trust nanotechnology? The answer to the first question relates to risk. All technologies have risks but because nanotechnology is, in a sense, many technologies, its risks are spread over a wide area. Risk here refers both to the risk of not doing what it is supposed to do as well as the risk of causing harm. Risk is a prerequisite for trust (another is autonomy but more on that later). Where there is no risk, trust is not required. There is no space for it. Because of its risks, there is plenty of space with respect to nanotechnology, so in that sense, talk of trusting nanotechnology does make sense.

What do we trust if we trust nanotechnology? If we trust a person we know the object of our trust (see chapter by Potter, this volume), and the same is true if we trust an organization (although that may reduce to trusting individual people) (see chapter by Alfano and Hujits, this volume). But trusting nanotechnology is not so straightforward. It might be trust in nanotechnology in general, trusting a type of product that contains nanotechnology, or trusting a particular product of that type. It may even be trust in those who develop it or those who say that it is safe or reliable.

The chapter will begin with a general account of trust, which will be followed by an outline of an account of technology. It will then turn to nanotechnology by first giving a brief description of that technology including some of its uses and risks. The account of trust in nanotechnology focusing on the two questions above will then be developed based on these three sections.

30.2 Trust[2]

Trust has been categorized in various ways, but most accounts are either cognitive or non-cognitive or something in between. An account is cognitive if it is based primarily on belief and evidence, and non-cognitive if attitudes are most important (see Keren, this volume). At the simplest level, if I trust someone to do some particular thing, then on a cognitive view, this means that I believe that I have good evidence that that person will do that particular thing (Coleman 1990 is a good example). On a non-cognitive account, it is rather that I have a particular attitude towards that person (Jones 1996, Govier 1997 and Holton 1994 tend towards this type of account). The account to be outlined here is somewhere in between the cognitive and the non-cognitive, but first we need to look at the difference between trust and reliance (see Goldberg, this volume).

30.2.1 Trust, Reliance and Autonomy

If I am rock climbing, I rely on a rope to stop me falling. If the rope is defective, I am disadvantaged, perhaps seriously. But in no interesting sense do I trust the rope. On the other hand, when I rely on my friend to belay me, I do trust him. The main difference between these cases is that my friend can choose to keep the rope relatively tight or not; he can choose to help or harm me. In an obvious sense, the rope can also either help or harm me, but it does not choose to. So, trust involves making certain choices. While it makes sense in English to say that I trust the rope, that is a very different sense of trust, and a much thinner one, than the sense in which I trust my friend. Trust involves the trustee having the ability and opportunity to make a choice. But the trustor must also be in a position to choose to trust or not to trust. The trustor choses to rely on the trustee making a particular choice. More specifically, the trustor must rely on the trustee choosing to act favorably toward him. Reliance, on the other hand, might or might not involve choice (see Baier 1986, Holton 1994 and Weckert 2005 for more detail on this point). We now elaborate trust as "seeing as."

30.2.2 Trust as "Seeing As"

Ambiguous pictures, that is, pictures that can be seen in a variety of ways, are common. Two well-known examples are the Jastrow duck-rabbit and the Necker cube. The former can be seen as either a picture of a duck or of a rabbit, while the latter can be seen as a cube viewed from above or from below. The argument here is that this is a useful way of explaining trust. If a person A trusts another person B then A sees B as someone who will, typically, do as he or she says, who is reliable, who will act with the interests of A in mind, and so on. That is, A sees B as trustworthy. Consider the ambiguous Jastrow duck-rabbit drawing which can be seen as a duck or as a rabbit. I can actually *see* it as a duck or as a rabbit. "I see a duck (or rabbit)" is a truthful description of what I see (see Wittgenstein 1986:193–195). "A sees B as trustworthy" can also be explained like this. If I see my friend as trustworthy, I could say "He is trustworthy" or "He is reliable, will do as he says, he has my interests in mind, and so on." Beliefs and expectations are in some way involved, but they are not normally in the forefront of my mind. Rather, most of the time they are implicit.

Looking at trust in this way makes it resemble a Kuhnian paradigm (Kuhn 1970). Thomas Kuhn argued that much of the time scientists undertake their research within a fixed and assumed framework or paradigm. "Normal science," as he called it, operates within a generally accepted paradigm, and it is this that enables the puzzle-solving activity of normal science. The underlying basic theories or the frameworks within which the scientist are working are not usually questioned. These are held constant in order to solve the problems that arise within those paradigms. They tend to be questioned only when there are repeated failures in puzzle-solving. This may eventually lead to a scientific revolution. The claim here is that trust is very much the same. In the case of scientific theories, we take the whole paradigm and our general attitude towards the theory for granted, while the rational puzzle-solving happens at the forefront of normal scientists' activities. In the case of interpersonal trust relations, in most cases when A trusts B to do X, A does not go through some rational decision procedure, weighing up the options and examining the evidence before deciding to trust or not to trust. Person A just trusts person B to do X (or just does not trust, as the case may be). Trust can be seen as a paradigm for puzzle-solving, the puzzle to be solved being how to achieve X. The background condition is that A can rely on B to do X because of the trust paradigm within which A is operating, just as our general attitude towards a scientific theory creates an atmosphere for puzzle-solving within that theory. Where there is trust, that is, where the potential trustor is operating within a trusting paradigm, there will not be, in most cases, any conscious thought. Person A will just trust as a matter of course.

This is not a complete account of trust, but it is sufficient to provide a basis for an examination of trust in nanotechnology (see Weckert 2005, 2011 and 2013 for more detail). We turn now to technology.

30.3 Technology and Nanotechnology[3]

According to Karl Popper (1963) and Larry Laudan (1977 and 1981), scientific research can be seen as epistemic problem solving, while technology, Sadjad Soltanzadeh (2015, 2016) argues, can be defined as practical problem solving. The former increases the stock of knowledge while the latter attempts to solve or alleviate practical problems. Science and technology, of course, are not always independently achievable, each dealing with its own set of problems. Perhaps they never are completely independent, just more or less so, depending on the particular science and technology. They often rely on each other. For example, a part of our devised solution to a practical problem may require epistemic problem solving. Almost all modern technologies are built on the basis of empirical theories. Aeroplanes are designed by applying the laws of aerodynamics, and electric devices are designed by applying the laws of electromagnetics and so on. Similarly, part of our solutions to epistemic problems may require some practical problem solving. Most achievements of modern sciences have been made possible as a result of the experiments done by laboratory instruments. To know whether an elementary particle is real or not, we need to first build a particle accelerator; to test the reaction of different molecules at certain temperatures, we need to first build a technology that keeps the temperature within the acceptable range; and research into nanotechnology only really advanced with the development of the Scanning Tunneling Microscope.

The problem-solving properties of objects, and more generally the technological functionality of objects, is defined in relation to the activities in which they are used (Soltanzadeh 2016). A hammer (or a rock) used to hit tent pegs can also be used as a paperweight. A lighter used to start fires can also be used to open drink bottles, and so on. Depending on the problem they are used to solve, objects would be identified by different problem-solving properties and by different functions. Choosing, designing and applying technological objects, therefore, are linked to the problems that we want to solve, the way we want to solve those problems, and what roles we want material objects to play in the process of solving the problems. Trust in technology then is trusting in the problem-solving properties of an object or trusting that an object can help us to solve a particular problem. Trusting an aeroplane is trusting that it will help us to solve the problem of getting from one particular place to another.

While technology can be explained in terms of problem solving, there is a close relationship between technologies and problems to be solved. Technologies to a large extent determine the problems themselves. Seeing the degree to which technologies have shaped our interactions and have helped us fulfil our basic needs, we realize that the role of technologies in our individual and social lives is broader than helping us satisfy our momentary goals. We do not apply technologies to fulfil our "pre-technological" expectations; rather, most of the time our desires and expectations have emerged out of the technologically conditioned lifestyle we have adopted (Soltanzadeh 2015): our need to use cars and public transport systems is rooted in the way we have designed our cities; beauty products have changed our aesthetic norms and desires; many people use computers for hours every day, and to solve the ergonomic problems that this lifestyle causes, we design software to remind us once in an hour that we should get up, stretch and give a few minutes of rest to our eyes. We might even install certain software on our computers to block our access to the Internet at intervals in order to prevent us getting distracted by it.

We not only *use* technologies, we have accepted a technological lifestyle. This acceptance is so deep that most of the time we are not consciously aware of the influences technologies have had and are still making on our cultures. Technologies are not always thoughtfully used to fulfil our pre-defined goals, rather we set our goals and the problems to be solved on the basis of our technological resources. Our technologies affect the way that we see the world.

We turn now to nanotechnology. What kind of technologies are nanotechnologies, and does being made of nanomaterials make nanotechnologies functionally and normatively special?

Technologies can be categorized by different criteria: what designers want them to be, the way they are historically used, their physical properties and structure, the manufacturing techniques used to build them, and so on. Although each of these categorizations can be useful for some purposes, not all categorizations are functionally or normatively relevant. We believe that a pragmatic categorization of technologies should not be based on what goes on inside them. What technologies carry along with them to all contexts, independently of their interactions with the users or other contextual elements is not important in how we pragmatically categorize technologies. Rather, a pragmatic categorization of technologies should be in relation to what technologies bring to the outside world and the intended consequences of their usage (Soltanzadeh 2019).

Nanotechnologies make up a category of technologies that share similar production techniques. We argue that the presence of nanoparticles in nanotechnologies and the very production techniques that nanomaterials share can make them functionally and normatively special. This is because nanotechnologies can bring two distinct changes to the outside world that deserve our attention. Some of these changes are intrinsic to nanotechnologies and some others are related to the enabling aspect of nanotechnologies and hence are instrumental. The intrinsic risks and trust associated with using nanotechnologies pertain to the very materials that constitute nanotechnologies, namely different forms of nanoparticles. However, at the functional level, the risks and trust associated with nanotechnology are all instrumental. They pertain to the type of technology whose function is enhanced via nanomaterials. We will come back to these points later.

As mentioned earlier, nanotechnology is a relatively new technology that aims to manipulate matter at the nanoscale. Its beginnings are often traced back to a talk by Richard Feynman in 1959, "There is plenty of room at the bottom," where he discussed "the problem of manipulating and controlling things on a small scale" (Feynman 1960:22). The manipulation of matter at the nanoscale in the manner envisaged by Feynman, however, really only began in 1981 with the development of the Scanning Tunneling Microscope.

A nanometer is 10^{-9} of a meter, that is, one billionth of a meter (a typical sheet of paper is about 100,000 nanometers thick). So nanotechnology is often said to be engineering at a very small scale. It is most often explained in terms of size and is concerned with matter in the 1–100 nanometer range where new properties emerge. The science.org.au website explains it like this:

> Materials behave very differently at scales below about 100 nanometers … Desirable properties of nanomaterials can be exploited for exciting applications such as improved chemical reactivity, ability to absorb or reflect light, and differences in material strength, flexibility or response to rises in temperature or pressure. In addition, we can engineer or pattern materials at the nanoscale, such as in advanced silicon chips or nanosensors, to gain amazing enhancements in desired properties.
>
> (*National Nanotechnology Research Strategy 2012:2*)

Nanotechnology is commonly seen as an enabling technology, that is, it is used to enhance other technologies. One example is its role in the development of computer technology in recent years through advances in nanoelectronics. This has contributed to the greater processing speed and particularly the expansion of memory capacity of current computers, and to the development of much smaller devices.

Much of the research and development in nanotechnology has concerned manufactured nanoparticles, particles that have a variety of shapes with at least one dimension of 100nm or less. These particles have a variety of uses and have been the subject of most of the discussions of risk and ethical concerns in nanotechnology.

Because nanotechnology is an enabling technology it has applications in a wide variety of fields. The Consumer Products Inventory lists the following categories of products, with some examples in parentheses: Appliances (batteries, washing machines), Automotive (rain repellents, green engine oil), Cross-Cutting (antibacterial pet products), Electronics and Computers (memory, processors), Food and Beverage (nano-silver cutting board, nanotea, food containers), Goods for Children (toys, nano-silver teeth developer), Health and Fitness (cosmetics, sunscreens, tennis rackets), and Home and Garden (antirust spray, antibacterial chopsticks) (Consumer Products Inventory 2017).

This is just a sample of the various types of products that are listed as containing nanotechnology. Research is underway in many other areas, particular in drug delivery sensing devices (see Maynard 2016).

Before proceeding, it is worth mentioning another view of nanotechnology. When Eric Drexler published his book, *Engines of Creation: The Coming Era of Nanotechnology* (Drexler 1986), he envisaged a rather different kind of nanotechnology from that outlined above. His vision was that just about anything could be manufactured by the manipulation of atoms or by their self-assembly. This much more radical view became sidelined but his recent book, *Radical Abundance: How a Revolution in Nanotechnology will Change Civilization*, can be seen as an attempt to resurrect it (Drexler 2013). Sometimes called molecular manufacturing, he now calls it Atomically Precise Manufacturing (APM). Perhaps a move in this direction is current research into molecular machines (Nobel Prize 2016). While the focus here will be on the mainstream version outlined earlier, we will also briefly consider molecular machines.

30.4 Trust in Nanotechnology

We said earlier that trust and risk are related, so before considering trust in nanotechnology in more depth, we will outline some of the risks and uncertainties.

30.4.1 Some Risks of Nanotechnology

Not much can be done in life without taking risks. Living is risky. Science and technology in general are risky enterprises and consequences often are difficult to predict while unintended consequences and dual use make the uncertainties even greater. Worries are particularly prevalent in new and emerging technologies, and nanotechnology is no exception. In this section, a number of different kinds of risks of nanotechnologies will be considered.

Earlier we mentioned the distinction between intrinsic and instrumentalist consequences of nanotechnology. The intrinsic consequences are things that a nanotechnology product brings simply because it is a nanotechnology product, not because of what it does. The risks associated with sunscreens or cosmetics are a good example here. These risks are perceived not because of what the sunscreens or the cosmetics do, but because they are made of nanoparticles. These are intrinsic risks of nanotechnology. Another example is molecular machines. Because they involve the manipulation of atoms and molecules, any perceived risks are intrinsic to nanotechnology.

However, given that nanotechnology is an enabling technology, some of the consequences emerge from the functional aspects of the product itself. For example, suppose that nanoelectronics enable the development of nano-robots that possess a high level of intelligence, equal to or even greater than that of humans. Any risks would be instrumental. The same consequence would occur if the same functionality were achieved using a different technology. The same is true for dangers arising for privacy due to greater monitoring and surveillance enabled by nano-enhanced electronics. Any harmful consequences in both cases are not intrinsic to the nanotechnology. Rather, they can be referred to as instrumental consequences of nanotechnology.

30.4.1.1 Intrinsic Risks

Nanoparticles

Most discussions of the risks of nanotechnology concern manufactured nanoparticles (for an overview see Seaton et al. 2010). In most cases the issue is not that it is known that particular nanoparticles are health or environmental risks, but rather that not enough is known yet to properly understand their effects. Nanoscale particles, those in the 1–100 nanometer range, have properties different from larger particles of the same material, due at least partly to their greater surface area relative to size. According to Seaton and co-authors "surface area is the metric driving the pro-inflammatory effects," and "in cells, high surface area doses appear to initiate inflammation through a number of pathways but oxidative stress-responsive gene transcription is one of the most important" (Seaton et al. 2010:123). However, their effects in the body are not yet completely understood. One concern is the use of these particles in food and food packaging. Examples include nano-clay for enhancement of barriers, nano-silver to increase the shelf-life of food, and nano-titanium dioxide and titanium nitride for more durable packaging. While a recent report prepared for Food Standards Australia New Zealand concluded that the health risks were low, it also stated that research in the area was meager (Drew and Hagen 2016). This paucity of research was taken to justify the claim of low health risks, a claim challenged by Friends of the Earth. After examining what research there is, they suggest that on the available evidence it is reasonable to assume serious health risks and that therefore pre-cautionary actions should be taken (FOE 2016). The US Environmental Protection Agency also seems more worried than the Australian and New Zealand body, agreeing to review the use of nano-silver in response to concerns raised about its safety (EPA 2015). Another concern is with products such as cosmetics and sunscreens that are applied to the skin. Some worry that the nanoparticles could pass through the skin and lodge in various parts of the body where they could cause harm. Faunce and co-authors, for example, suggest that the evidence so far is inconclusive whether or not titanium dioxide and zinc oxide, both used in sunscreens and known to be harmful to cells, can penetrate the skin (Faunce et al. 2008). A 2013 Australian Government report however claims that sunscreens containing these particles do not pose a risk, although admitting that the current evidence is inconclusive (TGA 2013).

Nanomachines

The 2016 Nobel Prize for Chemistry was awarded to three scientists for what have been called molecular machines:

> Operating on a scale a thousand times as small as the width of a human hair, these "machines" are specially designed molecules with movable parts that produce controlled movements when energy is added. They may one day be used to build new materials, operate microscopic sensors and create energy-storage mechanisms too tiny to be seen with the naked eye.
>
> *(Kaplan 2016)*

Uncertainty regarding the benefits and risks of these machines is extremely high. While we are familiar with machines at the macro level, we have no experience of manufactured machines at the molecular level and can only speculate on their uses. The new materials mentioned above could be smart materials that adapt to their environment or repair themselves when damaged. Other suggestions include the development of tiny robots inserted into the body that hunt cancer cells and tiny energy-storage devices to power computers (Fischman 2016). The following quotation sums up the situation well:

> Compared with the machines that changed our world following the industrial revolution of the nineteenth century, molecular machinery is still in a phase of growth. However, just as the world stood perplexed before the early machines, such as the first electric motors and steam engines, there is the potential for a similar explosive development of molecular machines. In a sense, we are at the dawn of a new industrial revolution of the twenty-first century, and the future will show how molecular machinery can become an integral part of our lives.
>
> *(Drahl 2016)*

For the purposes here, the important point is that very little can yet be said about potential benefits and risks.

30.4.1.2 Instrumental Risks

Privacy, autonomy and the Internet of Nano Things (IoNT)

New monitoring and surveillance technologies are not always classified as risks, but they do pose threats to personal privacy and autonomy, so it is not unreasonable to classify them in this way. There is the potential for harm through loss of autonomy and increased vulnerability to control. Moreover, just as manufactured nanoparticles are already in use and some evidence exists, as seen earlier, of dangers, so technologies such as certain computer technologies are already threatening privacy. These new monitoring and surveillance technologies therefore do pose risks. The problem is that the more that is known about a person, the greater the ability of those with the information to harm that person and to restrict his or her autonomy. One relevant technology here is the Internet of Things Nano (IoNT).

The Internet of Things (IoT) is already with us. According to the Internet Society,

> The term Internet of Things generally refers to scenarios where network connectivity and computing capability extends to objects, sensors and everyday items not normally considered computers, allowing these devices to generate, exchange and consume data with minimal human intervention.
>
> *(Internet Society 2015)*

The IoNT is listed in the World Economic Forum's top ten emerging technologies of 2016 and is being enabled by the developments in nanotechnology, particularly of nanoscale sensors (World Economic Forum 2016). According to Javier Garcia-Martinez (2016) these sensors will be "small enough to circulate within living bodies and to mix directly into construction materials." If and when the IoNT becomes a reality, vast amounts of information not readily available now will become accessible not only to humans but to other devices that will be able to use it without much or any human intervention.

The IoNT has the potential to improve our lives, but concerns have been expressed. "Being infused with Internet nano-sensors that reveal your most intimate biological details to the world could present social and psychological risks ..." (Maynard 2016), and these nanodevices could "be toxic or provoke immune reactions" as well as causing problems for privacy and surveillance (Garcia-Martinez 2016).

30.5 Returning to Trust

The account of trust outlined earlier was an account based on trust between people. Trusting a technology (any technology, not just nanotechnology) seems not to fit well here, given that it is trust between a person and a thing. We will see that some sense can be made of the claim that trust is appropriate here, but this trust is not the thick kind that can exist between people, albeit not as thin as reliance.

30.5.1 Trusting Technology

As just mentioned, that earlier account of trust is a trust relation between people. If A trusts B, A and B are both people. Two core features of this account are that trust is "seeing as" and that A and B are both autonomous. A third, although not emphasized as much, was good will (or at least a lack of ill will). A can choose to trust or not trust B, and B can choose to do or not do what A trusts him/her to. Is this account applicable to A trusts T where A is a human but T is a technology? Can sense be made here of the claim that A trusts T? Seeing as, autonomy, and good will are considered in turn.

First, *seeing as*. If A trusts B then A sees B as trustworthy so if A trusts T then A must see T as trustworthy. *Seeing as* seems not to be a problem here but suggesting that a technology can be trustworthy is more problematic. Seeing someone as trustworthy was spelt out in terms of seeing that person as having good will towards one or at least having no ill will. A sees T as reliable is unproblematic. I can see my car as reliable; it has a long history of always starting and never breaking down. Calling it trustworthy, though, seems a little unreasonable, but we will get to this shortly. The important point here is that the *seeing as* element in itself is not a problem. In fact, if what was said earlier is right, seeing technology as reliable and seeing people as trustworthy are very similar. We operate within a technological framework without giving it much thought, and it was argued previously that this is the way in which we work much of the time with other people. We just assume that they are trustworthy and likewise we just assume that technology is reliable unless we have reason to assume otherwise.

Second, *autonomy*. This is more problematic. In the earlier account, if A trusts B, A and B must both be autonomous in the sense that A can choose to rely on or not rely on B and B can choose to do or not do what A relies on B to do. If A trusts T, then A must be able to choose to rely on T and T choose to do what A relies on it to do. But technologies do not choose to do anything (except perhaps some autonomous technologies but we will exclude them here because they are discussed in the chapters by Sullins and by Grodzinsky et al., this volume). While A trusts T may be not as rich a sense of trust as A trusts B, it is not unreasonable to call it trust. The situation in which A can choose to rely on T is different from that in which A cannot choose but must rely anyway. If I choose a sunscreen containing nanoparticles when others containing no such particles are readily available, and assuming that I am aware of the controversy surrounding their safety, then that situation is closer to trust than the one in which no other choices are available. I can choose to use none, of course, but in the longer term that could be a death sentence in a country like Australia where deaths from melanoma are relatively common.

Third, a favorable attitude or *good will*. If A trusts B then A chooses to rely on B's favorable attitude towards him, or at least on B's lack of ill will. Sunscreens or cars are not the sorts of things that have any kind of attitude or will, favorable or unfavorable, good or ill. In this case then A can see T as reliable, can choose to rely on T, but cannot choose to rely on T's good will.

Given then that A can see T as reliable and can choose to rely on T, it is not completely out of place to call this trust, even if it is a poor relation of interpersonal trust. It can be more than mere reliance. In the sunscreen case it is more than *mere* reliance if A can choose a product with nanoparticles or one without those particles. If A has no choice because all available sunscreens contain nanoparticles, then it is mere reliance.

While this trust might not be very rich, more can be said about trusting in technologies. Considering technologies in terms of problem solving, something that we did in an earlier section, changes things a little. We turn our attention now to nanotechnology specifically in order to see what more can be said. First, what exactly is trusted when nanotechnology is trusted?

30.5.2 Trusting Nanotechnology

As suggested at the beginning of the chapter, trust might relate to nanotechnology in general, to a type of product, to a particular product or perhaps to those who undertake the research and development.

30.5.2.1 Nanotechnology in General

Trusting nanotechnology in general might mean that we trust that it is safe, that it will be able to do the things that it is claimed that it will be able to, or perhaps something else. The safety issue is the most discussed and probably the most important. It is claimed by some that sunscreens containing nanoparticles are safe and by others that they are not or at least that we as yet do not know. Saying then that we trust these sunscreens is really saying that we trust the claims of those who maintain that they are safe and that they do protect against skin cancers. It is not a matter of trusting the sunscreens themselves, it is a matter of trusting the word of the scientists. Compare this with the Genetically Modified Organisms (GMO) case. Many people did not believe that GMOs were safe for human consumption. They did not trust the word of the scientists and others who claimed that they were safe. The object of the trust or distrust was not an object but a person or group of people.

30.5.2.2 A Type of Product

As already noted, nanotechnology is an enabling technology that can be used in many different technologies and products, from sunscreens to computers. Trusting nanotechnology then is not like trusting cars or aeroplanes. We might trust sunscreens but not computers, both of which use nanotechnology. Trusting a type of product is like believing that, say, cars in general are reliable. Even if we trust nanotechnology in the sense of trusting the word of the nano-scientists, it is another matter to trust all *uses* of nanotechnology. We might believe that sunscreens that contain nanoparticles are safe but worry that computers that are much more powerful because of nanotechnology will pose a threat to privacy, autonomy or employment. We might trust that they work, that is, that they solve the problems that they are supposed to, based on the word of others and our own experience, but not trust that my privacy will not be compromised.

30.5.2.3 A Product

Trusting a particular product can mean different things in different situations. Suppose that I am making a long-haul flight, say from Sydney to Dubai. Do I trust the pilot, the plane or something else? Trusting that the plane is safe amounts to trusting at least the manufacturers and the maintenance engineers. Trusting the flight itself involves these together with the pilots and navigators, the security officers and so on. The situation of trusting a particular bottle of sunscreen containing nanoparticles is similar. It involves at least trusting the manufacturers, those in charge of safety checks as well as the nano-scientists and –technologists who developed the product and vouch for its safety. Regarding its efficacy, however, I might base my trust primarily on my own experience.

Many cases of trusting nanotechnology, as we have seen, seem to reduce to trusting people, so the account of trust with which this chapter began, which focused on people, is appropriate. However, we do often speak about trusting a particular kind of technology or a particular piece of technology. I might trust my four-wheel drive SUV to get me along a dirt road, but not your sports car. I might trust this nano product, but not that standard one. Can this reasonably be called trust given the earlier account of trust? We have seen that talk of trust is not completely out of place, but it is a thinner trust than the more robust version between people. However, even here there can be an element of trust in people. Technologies are developed to solve problems, so trust in a product is at least partly trust in those who developed this product to solve this particular problem.

Trusting nanotechnology as a technology in the abstract seems to be, as was said previously, a matter of trusting the scientists who researched it (see Rolin, this volume). This is so because, at least initially, we have not experienced it, so we are relying on the testimony of scientists and perhaps others who know something about it. We see the scientists as trustworthy. They might not have any positive attitude or good will towards me, but at least I assume that they don't have ill will towards me or any of those who might use technologies based on their research. But perhaps it is not only a matter of seeing the scientists as trustworthy (or not, as the case may be). Consider the much discussed use of nanoparticles in sunscreens. Is this safe? We might believe that it is, based on the word of the scientists, but we do not trust the sunscreen in the way that we trust the scientists. We see it as reliable in the sense of safe and efficacious. It solves the problem of sunburn.

In summary, trust in nanotechnology can be trust in the effectiveness in solving a problem or trust in safety. The former can be thin trust in a technology (although trust in those who vouch for its effectiveness can play a role too), while the latter is more trust in the scientists, developers, etc., who say that it is safe. The main example used so far has been that of sunscreens containing nanoparticles. These sunscreens are already on the market and thus are a concrete example of a nanoproduct. We will now briefly consider two futuristic examples because much of the discussion around nanotechnology is about its potential. First we will look at the Internet of Nano Things and then at molecular machines.

30.5.2.4 Cases

The Internet of Nano Things (IoNT)

Trust will be considered here in relation to whether or not it will work and the two issues of risk, that is, with respect to human health and privacy. Given that the IoNT has not yet eventuated, we cannot trust or rely on its reliability or its ability to solve problems for us. If trust applies here, it is trust in those who predict its coming and its value. This is not irrational given that the IoT is already here, at least to some extent, and research in nanotechnology is producing results. Our trust can fit into a paradigm of trusting new technologies. We see them as being developed by people of good will or at least not of ill will, and developed in a way that has the potential to solve problems in a way that will improve life.

Trust in the safety of the nanodevices that could be inserted into our bodies will be trust in those who say that they are or will be safe. But it is more than this. It is trust in a whole system, where if some devices are not safe, this will be discovered and regulations will be put in place to ensure that nobody is harmed. Privacy, too, is a potential problem because so much personal information will be available regarding the state of our bodies, about where we are and who we meet and communicate with, what we do and so on. This opens the way for surveillance on an unprecedented scale. If we are to trust here, it will not only be in the nano-scientists and developers, but in the computing professionals maintaining the computer systems, in the users of the systems, in the regulators and those enforcing the regulations and so on. In this case, just as in that of safety, trust in the IoNT is trust in a whole system comprising many people with many different roles. While it is trust in a system, this can be spelt out in terms of trust in individuals. It is trust that the individuals of good will – or at least no ill will – will perform their respective roles in the system. The system comprises at least regulations developed and enforced by individuals, other individuals who monitor the activity in the system and modify it where necessary, and those who undertake the research into safety, privacy and other problematic issues.

When the IoNT becomes a reality, however, even there it may not merely be a matter of trusting the people behind the IoNT. Perhaps people will see the IoNT as reliable and choose to rely on it, thereby trusting it in the thin sense.

Molecular Machines

As noted previously, molecular machines are in the very early stage of development, and as yet there are no practical applications and, it seems, few clear ideas of what such applications will be. One suggestion is that "possible applications range from robots that hunt cancer cells to tiny energy-storage devices to power computers" (Fischman 2016:4) and another is smart materials (Ritter 2016). One of the Nobel Prize recipients said that it was difficult to predict where his innovations might lead, but that he was not too worried because safeguards will be built in (Kaplan 2016).

If trust applies to these machines, it must be trust in those researching and developing the technology, and perhaps trust that future developers of this technology will put it to uses that will benefit people. At this stage there is nothing else to trust with respect to molecular machines. It is unclear, in fact, given the amount of uncertainty regarding applications and uses – even on the part of the scientists themselves – whether trust is appropriate at all.

30.6 Conclusion

Nanotechnology is an enabling technology and is still largely in its infancy. Because of these two factors, uncertainty is high regarding its risks. This is true whether we are talking of the technology in general, types of products or individual products. Given the account of trust outlined at the beginning of this chapter, some sense can be given to the claim that nanotechnology itself can be trusted. It can be trusted in a thin sense if we choose to trust the technology itself and in a thick sense if the trust is directed to the scientists and technologists who develop it or the regulators who regulate it. Where the technology is still so underdeveloped that very little can be known about where it will lead in the future, perhaps trust does not yet apply at all.

Notes

1 These calls seem to have abated more recently although there are still concerns particularly about health issues which are discussed in a later section.
2 Excerpts of this section are taken from Weckert (2005).
3 Excerpts of this section are taken from Weckert et al. (2016).

References

Baier, A.C. (1986) "Trust and Antitrust," *Ethics* 96: 231–260.

Coleman, J.S. (1990) *Foundations of Social Theory*, Cambridge, MA: Harvard University Press.

Consumer Products Inventory (2017) "The Project on Nanotechnologies." www.nanotechproject.org/cpi/

Drahl, C. (2016) "What's Next for Molecular Machines and the 2016 Nobel Prize in Chemistry?" *Forbes*, October 5. www.forbes.com/sites/carmendrahl/2016/10/05/whats-next-for-molecular-machines-and-the-2016-nobel-prize-in-chemistry/#35367f.0e214d

Drew, R. and Hagen, T. (2016) "Nanotechnologies in Food Packaging: An Exploratory Appraisal of Safety and Regulation." A report prepared by ToxConsultant Pty Ltd for Food Standards Australia New Zealand. www.foodstandards.gov.au/publications/Documents/Nanotech%20in%20f.ood%20packaging.pdf

Drexler, E. (1986) *Engines of Creation: the Coming Era of Nanotechnology*, New York: Anchor Books.

Drexler, E. (2013) *Radical Abundance: How a Revolution in Nanotechnology Will Change Civilization*, New York: PublicAffairs.

EPA (2015) "EPA Response to 'Petition for Rulemaking Requesting EPA Regulate Nano-Silver Products as Pesticides'" United States Environmental Protection Agency, Washington, DC 20460, March, The International Center for Technology Assessment, Washington, DC 20003. www.centerforfoodsafety.org/files/epa_nanosilver_2015_03_19_icta_petition_response_10041.pdf

ETC (2006) "Nanotech Product Recall Underscores Need for Nanotech Moratorium: Is the Magic Gone?" www.etcgroup.org/content/nanotech-product-recall-underscores-need-nanotech-moratorium-magic-gone

Faunce, T., Murray, K., Hitoshi, N. and Bowman, D. (2008) "Sunscreen Safety: The Precautionary Principle, the Australian Therapeutic Goods Administration and Nanoparticles in Sunscreens," *NanoEthics: Ethics for Technologies that Converge at the Nanoscale* 2: 231–240.

Feynman, R.P. (1960, February) "There's Plenty of Room at the Bottom," *Engineering and Science* 23(5): 22–36. http://calteches.library.caltech.edu/1976/1/1960Bottom.pdf

Fischman, J. (2016) "Molecular Machine-Makers Grab the 2016 Nobel Prize in Chemistry," *Scientific American*, October 5. www.scientificamerican.com/article/molecular-machine-makers-grab-the-2016-nobel-prize-in-chemistry1/

FOE (2016) "FRANZ Misleads the Public on the Risks of Nano-Ingredients in Food Friends of the Earth," Friends of the Earth. https://emergingtech.foe.org.au/wp-content/uploads/2016/06/FSANZ-reports-summary-FINAL.pdf

Garcia-Martinez, J. (2016) "Here's What Will Happen when 30 Billion Devices are Connected to the Internet," World Economic Forum. www.weforum.org/agenda/2016/06/nanosensors-and-the-Internet-of-nano-things/

Govier, T. (1997) *Social Trust and Human Communities*, Montreal: McGill-Queen's University Press.

Holton, R. (1994) "Deciding to Trust, Coming to Believe," *Australasian Journal of Philosophy* 72: 63–76.

Internet Society (2015) "Internet of Things." www.Internetsociety.org/iot

Jones, K. (1996) "Trust as an Affective Attitude ," *Ethics* 107: 4–25.

Kaplan, S. (2016) "Nobel Prize for Chemistry Is Awarded for Molecular Machines," *Washington Post*, October 5. www.washingtonpost.com/news/speaking-of-science/wp/2016/10/05/2016-nobel-prize-in-chemistry-awarded-for-molecular-machines/?utm_term=.8cdef96d7eb0

Kuhn, T.S. (1970) *The Structure of Scientific Revolutions*, 2nd edition, Chicago: University of Chicago Press.

Laudan, L. (1977) *Progress and its Problems: Towards a Theory of Scientific Growth*, Berkeley: University of California Press.

Laudan, L. (1981) "A Problem-Solving Approach to Scientific Progress," in I. Hacking (ed.), *Scientific Revolutions*, Oxford: Oxford University Press.

Maynard, A. (2016) "Edge of Innovation: Risks, Rewards and Emerging Technologies: How Risky are the World Economic Forum's Top 10 Emerging Technologies for 2016?" *The Conversation*, June 23. www.theconversation.com/how-risky-are-the-world-economic-forums-top-10-emerging-technologies-for-2016-61349

National Nanotechnology Research Strategy (2012) Australian Academy of Science. www.science.org.au/files/userfiles/support/reports-and-plans/2015/nanotech-research-strategy.pdf

Nobelprize (2016) Nobelprize.org, the official site of the Nobel Prize. www.nobelprize.org/nobel_prizes/chemistry/laureates/2016/

Popper, K. (1963) *Conjectures and Refutations*, London: Routledge.

Ritter, K. (2016) "Three Win Nobel Chemistry Prize for World's Tiniest Machines." https://phys.org/news/2016-10-nobel-chemistry-prize-world-tiniest.html#jCp

Seaton, A., Tran, L., Aitken, R. and Donaldson, K. (2010) "Nanoparticles, Human Health Hazard and Regulation," *Journal of the Royal Society Interface* 7: S119–S129.

Soltanzadeh, S. (2015) "Humanist and Nonhumanist Aspects of Technologies as Problem Solving Physical Instruments," *Philosophy and Technology* 28(1): 139–156. https://link.springer.com/article/10.1007%2Fs13347-013-0145-4

Soltanzadeh, S. (2016) "Questioning Two Assumptions in the Metaphysics of Technological Objects," *Philosophy and Technology* 29: 127–135. http://link.springer.com/article/10.1007%2Fs13347-015-0198-7

Soltanzadeh S. (2019) "A Practically Useful Metaphysics of Technology," Techné: Research in Philosophy and Technology 23(2): 232-250. https://www.pdcnet.org/techne/content/techne_2019_0999_9_24_103

TGA (2013) "Literature Review on the Safety of Titanium Dioxide and Zinc Oxide Nanoparticles in Sunscreens," Scientific Review Report, Version 1.0 August, Australian Government Department of Health and Ageing, Therapeutic Goods Administration.

Weckert, J. (2005) "On-Line Trust," in R. Cavalier (ed.), *The Impact of the Internet on Our Moral Lives*, New York: SUNY Press.

Weckert, J. (2011) "Trusting Software Agents," in C. Ess and M. Thorseth (eds.), *Trust and Virtual Worlds: Contemporary Perspectives*, New York: Peter Lang.

Weckert, J. (2013) "Workplace Monitoring and Surveillance: The Problem of Trust," in M. Boylan (ed.), *Business Ethics*, 2nd edition, Hoboken, NJ: John Wiley & Sons.

Weckert, J., Rodriguez Valdes, H. and Soltanzadeh, S. (2016) "A Problem with Societal Desirability as a Component of Responsible Research and Innovation: The 'If we don't somebody else will'-Argument," *NanoEthics* 10(2): 215–225.

Wittgenstein, L. (1986) *Philosophical Investigations*, G.E.M. Anscombe (trans.), Oxford: Basil Blackwell.

World Economic Forum (2016) "These are the Top 10 Emerging Technologies of 2016." www.weforum.org/agenda/2016/06/top-10-emerging-technologies-2016/

31

TRUST AND INFORMATION AND COMMUNICATION TECHNOLOGIES

Charles M. Ess

31.1 Introduction

Trust has long been explored as a central component of human society and interaction. The Danish philosopher and theologian, K.E. Løgstrup ([1956] 1971), argues specifically that our judgments, assumptions and experiences of trust are entangled in nothing less than foundational markers of our human condition as grounded in *embodiment*. Quite simply, as embodied creatures we are at once utterly vulnerable and absolutely dependent upon one another for our very survival – much less, I will add, for our thriving and flourishing as both individuals and larger communities.

We will see – and as multiple contributions to this volume exemplify – that the conditions and characteristics of trust are yet more complex and that trust for human beings is further complicated within and centrally challenged by our ever increasing interactions with one another – and with machines – in online communication environments. I approach these challenges by first building on Løgstrup to develop a broader philosophical anthropology, one emphasizing human beings as both rational and affective, and as relational autonomies. This anthropology grounds virtue ethics and (Kantian) deontology, leads to a robust account of human-to-human trust and helps identify and clarify general challenges to trust in online environments. I then take up two critical examples of such challenges – namely, pre-emptive policing and loss of trust in (public) media – to show how these standpoints indicate possible remedies to these critical problems. I close by conjoining this philosophical anthropology with larger contemporary developments – primarily the increasing role of virtue ethics in ICT design and emerging existentialism – that likewise offer grounds for overcoming some of these challenges.

31.2 Trust: Requirements and Challenges Online

As Bjørn Myskja (2008) points out, Løgstrup's phenomenological account of trust begins with our fundamental condition as *embodied* human beings – namely, we are thereby both vulnerable and absolutely dependent on one another for our very survival, much less our well-being. This initial condition can also be characterized in terms of *risk*: however else we can (and will) characterize trust, it entails the absence of certain knowledge that the Other[1] will indeed respond to my vulnerability with the care and respect that I hope for and require. To trust is hence to *risk* – a risk that often cannot be avoided, especially for embodied and vulnerable human beings who are interdependent with one another in the innumerable ways that constitute familial, social, civil and political life (Clark 2014; Keymolen 2016).

As several scholars have pointed out in connection with especially *affective* accounts of trust – as exemplified in the trust a small child may express within family contexts – trust is thereby something of a default starting point for human beings and society at large (so Annette Baier (1994:132), cited in Weckert (2005:102); see Lahno, this volume). But of course, relationships of trust can be easily broken – or simply not presumed in the first place. Løgstrup points out a painfully obvious fact about us humans: in the absence of first-hand, embodied encounters with the Other, we are inclined to accept the multiple prejudices built up around our apparently primal "us" vs. "them" schema for understanding the larger world. Racism, xenophobia and sexism are but the most dramatic – and, apparently, most stubborn – examples of such prejudgments.

For Løgstrup, embodiment as our defining status is further at work in what is required to overcome these primary obstacles to trust – namely, "the personal meeting," the experience of one another in an embodied, co-present way: "These judgments will normally break down in the presence of the other, and this proximity is essential for the eradication of these preconceptions" (Myskja 2008:214, with reference to Løgstrup 1971:22f.; Ess 2014b:214).[2]

31.2.1 Anthropology, Trust and Ethics

Løgstrup thus foregrounds embodiment and vulnerability, coupled with the central importance of the rational and the affective, as core components of the sorts of communicative co-presence required for trust as foundational to human sociality. These starting points ground a philosophical anthropology initially developed in collaboration with the Norwegian applied ethicist May Thorseth (Ess, 2010a,b; Ess and Thorseth 2011). I begin here with key elements of this anthropology, followed by later enhancements, in order to approach core issues of trust online. As we will see by way of conclusion, this account coheres with an especially *existential* emphasis on our taking our mortality seriously, where mortality stands among the ultimate expressions of human vulnerability.

To begin with, Kantian understandings of being human are centrally useful. First, Annamaria Carusi has foregrounded the role of the Kantian *sensus communis* as an intersubjective aesthetic framework that grounds a shared epistemic universe that is at once both affective and rational (2008; Ess 2014b:208). This framework, as thereby in play prior to our communicative engagements with one another, thus helps to "bootstrap trust" – in Carusi's example, among biologists, computer scientists and mathematicians who collaborated with one another online, specifically through the use of visualizations (2008:243; Ess, 2014b:208; see Rolin, this volume).

A Kantian understanding of the human being is further at work in Mariarosaria Taddeo's *rationalistic* account of trust (2009; see also Grodzinsky et al., this volume). Taddeo finds this rationalistic account useful for machines – namely, Artificial Agents (AAs) and Multi-Agent Systems (MASs). At the same time, Taddeo recognizes that rationalistic trust among machines is a limited sense of trust as compared with trust among human beings – most importantly, as we have seen, precisely because human trust implicates the affective as well (2010).

A starting point in Kantian rationality further foregrounds the human being as an *autonomous* rationality, i.e. a freedom capable of rationally establishing his or her moral principles as well as more particular goals and aims. Such a freedom anchors Kantian ethics – namely, Kant's *deontology* and his *virtue ethics*. Deontology is critical for grounding duties of respect between human beings precisely as autonomies, as freedoms who must thereby always be treated as "ends only, never as means in themselves" (Kant, [1785] 1959:47). As a dramatic example: I violate this respect when I treat another human being as a slave, as only a means to my own goals and ends. This is to override the central reality of human beings as freedoms who thereby determine their own ends and goals, turning them instead into instruments and objects.

I have built upon this initial framework first of all by incorporating the work of virtue ethicist Shannon Vallor. To begin with, Vallor has demonstrated how trust counts among the primary *virtues* – i.e. capacities and excellences of habit that must be practiced and cultivated. Trust *qua* virtue is central, along with the virtues of patience, honesty and empathy, first of all to friendship, and thereby for a good life of contentment (*eudaimonia*) and flourishing (2010:165–167; 2016:120).

Moreover, prevailing readings of Kantian rationality presume that individuals exist as discrete and isolated atoms: this assumption is rooted in Thomas Hobbes and is in play in contemporary Rational Choice theory, for example (see Tutić and Voss, as well as Dimock, this volume). In sharp contrast, I take the rational-affective self as simultaneously *relational*. This relational self is intimated in Jürgen Habermas's expansion on Kant in his notion of "communicative reason" (McCarthy 1978:47; Ess 2014b:217). Relationality as intrinsic to our rational-affective selfhood is further developed in more recent feminist accounts of human being as *relational autonomy*, i.e. as conjoining Kantian autonomy with relationality (e.g. Veltman and Piper 2014; Ess 2014a). Expanding on Kantian ethics, the relational-autonomous self undergirds both traditional and contemporary systems of virtue ethics. As Shannon Vallor expresses it, virtue ethics traditions presume that we are "… beings whose actions are always informed by a particular social context of concrete roles, relationships, and responsibilities to others": virtue ethics is thereby especially well-suited to our contemporary context, as it expands upon "traditional understandings of the ways in which our moral choices and obligations bind and connect us to one another, as the [technologically-mediated] networks of relationships upon which we depend for our personal and collective flourishing continue to grow in scale and complexity" (2016:33; cf. Ess 2014a).

This relationality, we will see, renders online communicative environments very much a two-edged sword. On the one hand, such a relational self is dramatically enhanced and literally embodied in the extensive communicative networks contemporary ICTs make possible – especially those categorized as social media. At the same time, our entanglement in these networked webs of relationships – especially as constrained by the effects and affordances of algorithms, artificial agents, and so on – may entail severe limits on the possibility of establishing and sustaining trust.

A last feature of this philosophical anthropology – one foregrounded especially by virtue ethics – likewise presents a critical condition for trust relationships among humans that thereby may be challenged by online affordances and conditions. In more recent work, several philosophers and computer scientists (among others) have examined *phronēsis* – typically translated as practical wisdom or prudential judgment – as, first of all, a critical, indeed, overarching virtue (e.g. Vallor 2016:37 and 105). Secondly, a number of scholars and researchers have argued that as context-based, reflective *judgment, phronēsis* is (likely) not computationally tractable, i.e. it cannot be fully reproduced by computational devices (Gerdes 2014; Ess 2016, 2019: Cantwell Smith 2019). More specifically, I have argued that *phronēsis*, as a kind of judgment that does not proceed deductively or algorithmically, is thereby affiliated with a foundational human freedom – specifically, the freedom to choose which specific norms, principles, etc. may apply in a given context or case (Ess 2014b:211f.; Ess 2016). If I have this right, then both *phronēsis* and autonomy function more broadly as conditions for human trust. That is, in these terms, in the face of risk and uncertainty, I may nonetheless *choose* to trust a specific person in a given context; this in part further means that I *judge* that the trustee is trustworthy – a judgment that is always context-dependent, open to error, as well as open to correction (cf. Ess 2014b:211–213).[3]

31.3 Trust and Reliance amongst and between Humans and ICTs

Various philosophical analyses of trust suggest that there are differing degrees, if not kinds, of trust (e.g. Lanho, this volume; Potter, this volume). In these directions, the conditions and criteria for human-to-human trust marked out in this philosophical anthropology set a very high bar for trust. This is in keeping with the role of *phronēsis* in moments of maximum freedom and humanity, such as in loving itself as a virtue (Ess 2016). *Phronēsis* is likewise central to critical movements beyond prevailing norms and practices – such as the establishment of democratic polity and rights, the abolition of slavery, the struggles for civil and women's rights and other forms of emancipation (Ess 2019). This robust set of conditions is further useful as it illuminates the sharpest possible contrasts between human-to-human trust and the possibilities of trust vis-à-vis machines and ICTs.

Here we will first take up some general consequences of this anthropology for trust online, as a prelude to a more detailed focus on two primary cases in which challenges to trust online are severely, perhaps fatally problematic.

To begin with, the final two components of autonomy and *phronēsis* condition a critical distinction between *trust*, on the one hand, and *reliance* on the other. As Sanford C. Goldberg (this volume) explains, most philosophers approach trust "as a species of reliance" (page reference to be given in proof). These approaches begin with Annette Baier's foundational paper (1986) that emphasizes strongly moral characteristics of trust that thereby restrict trust to human interrelationships, in contrast with reliance more generally (cf. Potter, this volume). Also drawing on Baier, John Weckert has pointed out that trust entails *choice* on the part of both trustor and trustee. Very simply: the trustor is free to choose whether or not to trust the trustee – and the trustee in turn is free to choose whether to honor and/or break that trust. *Reliance*, on the other hand, characterizes our relationships with objects and machines – i.e. entities that lack human-style capacities for choice. For example, if I choose to put my weight on a ladder, it is more accurate to say that I rely on, not choose to trust, the ladder. Very simply, either the ladder will hold my weight or not. Whether or not it succeeds or fails in doing so is not a matter of choice on the part of the ladder, but a matter of my specific weight vis-à-vis its specific design, materials, quality of construction, and current conditions (e.g. a fresh wooden rung vs. one worn or damaged, possibly rotting, etc.). For his part, Weckert argues that some devices are – or eventually will be – capable of sufficiently human-like autonomy that it is accurate to describe our relationships with such devices as trust relationships. Unlike the simply material ladder, that is, a sufficiently autonomous system can thereby choose whether or not to return my choice to trust it (Weckert 2011).

Whatever the future may hold for machine-based autonomous systems, many contemporary philosophers distinguish between a complete human autonomy – for example, of the Sartrean sort (Sullins 2014) – and a more limited, "artificial autonomy." Moreover, human autonomy is coupled with our experience of a first-person phenomenal consciousness – an awareness of being a self distinct from others, of having specific emotional states, along with choice and needing to reflect on our choices in both rational and affective ways, and so on. There is considerable skepticism that such first-person phenomenal consciousness can be replicated with computational techniques (e.g. Searle 2014; Bringsjord et al. 2015). I am specifically skeptical regarding the possibility of replicating human *phronēsis* with machine techniques (cf. Weizenbaum 1976; Gerdes 2014; Cantwell Smith 2019). If I am correct about this, then an artificially autonomous algorithm, AI, etc., is again incapable of choosing to trust me and/or to fulfill the trust I place in it – because such choice includes the critical function of *phronēsis* in *judging* whether or not I am trustworthy. Insofar as this holds, then it remains more correct to say that I can choose and judge to *rely* on such devices – but not *trust* in such devices. (Cf. the related topic of trusting human developers of such devices in Grodzinsky et al. this volume.)

A second obstacle to trust online follows from similar comments regarding the crucial role of emotion in conjunction with the affective dimensions of trust. As we have seen, important sources on trust emphasize the role of the affective along with the rational (Baier 1994; Lanho, this volume). There is, however, widespread pessimism with regard to the possibility of replicating genuine emotions or affect with computational techniques (Sullins 2012). Rather, especially in the field of social robotics, the field of *artificial emotions* focuses on developing robots capable of mimicking the human vocabulary of affective communication, from nod and gesture to gaze, tone of voice, etc. We are thereby susceptible to what Sullins identifies as a profoundly unethical trick – namely, as we can be easily fooled through such displays into believing, indeed, *feeling* on our part that the machine somehow has emotion and so responding in kind with emotions of our own (2012:408). Building AIs and social robots that seek to evoke our trust in part by mimicking the relevant emotive signals of trust is certainly possible, but given that these signals derive from solely *artificial* emotions, such "design for affective trust" (my phrase) would be the height of deception and so a complete violation of any extant trust relationship.

A third key obstacle to trust online is grounded in Løgstrup's account of human beings as embodied, vulnerable and given to prejudgments that preclude trusting the Other – such that embodied co-presence is often the requisite condition for overcoming such prejudgments and coming to trust the Other. Manifestly, however, the vast majority of our communicative engagements with one another in online environments are predominantly, if not fully *disembodied*. Certainly, online videos or video calls can give us voices and images of the Other as embodied. In these and other ways, we all but inevitably "bring our body with us"[4] into cyberspace.[5] But these are more than offset by online engagements that are predominantly textual and comparatively distant from the embodied Other. Especially in the examples of anonymous or pseudonymous comments, chats, and so on, the Other remains conspicuously hidden. Indeed, a particular problem in the contemporary media landscape is the rise of communicative bots (robots), whether in the form of "robot journalism" or, more darkly, trolls and fake news sites (e.g. Tam 2017).

Such bots point to a large family of computational relatives – namely, the increasingly predominant role of algorithms, artificial agents and multi-agent systems in shaping and controlling our communicative media (Taddeo 2010; Mittelstadt et al. 2016). But such agents are the disembodied other *par excellence*. Not only do these lack key components of affect, judgment (including *phronēsis*), and autonomy that define human selfhood: they further lack the embodiment required of the human Others we may learn to trust through embodied co-presence.

This absence of an autonomous, affective, *phronetic*, embodied Other in the complex machineries of online communication then leads to a significant array of problems for trust. Here I take up two of the most severe – namely, pre-emptive policing and the rule of law, and then the collapse of trust in news media and online public spheres.

31.4 Case 1: Trust, Pre-emptive Policing and the End(s) of Law?

The philosopher of law Mireille Hildebrandt takes up a series of problems and challenges to both the practices and the very foundations of modern law as posed by the rise of "smart technologies" (2016). A primary example is the increasing practice of "pre-emptive policing." Most briefly, police departments use Big Data techniques and AI to scrape personal profile data from social media and relevant databases, in order to analyze individual and larger crime patterns. The ultimate aim is to predict ahead of time which individual or group of individuals are likely to commit a specific crime, in order to intercept those suspected and thus preempt a crime.

Broadly, Hildebrandt traces out the emergence of modern law as a set of institutions and practices, including specific sorts of *media literacies*. Such literacies foreground two specific conditions for the legitimacy and practice of modern law. The first condition is medium-specific: the rise of the printing press and thereby what Medium theorists categorize as the communication modality of *literacy-print* from the Reformation forward make possible a new level of authority for the book and text. The Bible and the Lutheran principle of *sola scriptura* – "only the Scripture" – are the prime exemplars (Ong 1988; Ess 2010a; Ess 2014a). Over the following three centuries of what Elizabeth Eisenstein (1983) documents as "the printing revolution," these developments helped establish the modern legal system and notions of the Rule of Law. Most simply, in modern liberal democracies, the Rule of Law means that ultimate authority and legitimacy cluster about articulated laws as accessible in fixed texts and thereby open to study, critical interpretation and revision (see Hildebrandt 2016:173–183, for more detailed discussion). Secondly, the Rule of Law intersects with democratic norms of equality and respect for persons. This is in part, as we have seen, correlative with the emergence of strongly *individual* conceptions of the self as a rational autonomy (Ess 2010a, 2014a). Here again, both within Medium Theory and, for example, the last work of Foucault, such a self is dependent first of all upon *literacy* as allowing us, in effect, to "freeze" oral expression in writing – self-expression that in turn becomes the object of self-reflection and issues in the *virtue* of self-care (Foucault 1988:19; Bakardjieva and Gaden 2012:400–403; cf. Ess 2010a, 2014a; Vallor 2016:196–198). Again, such autonomies further require basic rights, including rights to privacy and, we can now add, *due process*.

Due process specifically includes the possibility of our *contesting* how we are "read" by others. Hildebrandt argues that the shift from print to digital media, coupled with the increasingly central role of algorithms and related "smart technologies," directly threatens to undermine not only basic rights to privacy and due process, but, more fundamentally, the very existence and practices of modern law as such. Specifically, where surveillance, Big Data scraping techniques, and algorithmic analyses are directed against citizens – as in the practice of pre-emptive policing – a body of evidence can be quickly accumulated about us in ways that are entirely hidden and opaque. These processes directly short-circuit due process – specifically in terms of our ability to contest how we are read or *interpreted* by others in a court of law. In human-to-human interaction, accusations and evidence are brought forward through protocols of *rational* defense and critical interrogation aimed towards maximum fairness and equality. But in the case of pre-emptive policing, the evidence presented against me is the result of machine techniques, including algorithmic analysis that is not fully understood even by its own creators. The result is an opaque "reading" of me and my actions that cannot be critically interrogated, much less contested (Hildebrandt 2016: esp. 191–199).

We can amplify this critique by way of the distinction between reliance and trust. In these terms, we may be forced to rely on such systems – ideally, under well understood and tightly constrained circumstances. But such systems are not machineries that we can somehow choose to trust, nor are such systems capable of choosing to engage in or sustain trusting relationships with human beings. Whatever else they entail, legal processes of gathering evidence, building cases, critically evaluating evidence and accusations against one another, and drawing *judgments* (precisely of the *phronetic* sort) are hermeneutical processes that are inextricably bound up with relationships of trust (and mistrust) among human beings. As we have seen, Weckert is optimistic that trust relationships can emerge between autonomous humans and (approximately or analogously) autonomous AIs. I have argued, by contrast, that such systems lack intentionality, genuine emotion, judgment, human-level autonomy and embodiment – all required for the sort of embodied co-presence highlighted by Løgstrup as necessary for establishing and sustaining relationships of trust. In these ways, then, a further critique of the machineries of pre-emptive policing is that they are incapable of the trust (and mistrust: see D'Cruz, this volume) relationships foundational to the human processes of reading and contesting our readings of one another in a court of law (cf. Vallor 2016:193).

31.5 Case 2: Fake News and Social Media: The Collapse of Trust Online

Both popular and more scholarly literatures are awash with debate and discussion of "fake news" and related social media phenomena in which online information, discussion – and, most specifically, election campaigns and results – have been both intentionally and inadvertently manipulated in ways largely opaque to most readers (e.g. Stothard 2017). As with Hildebrandt's analysis concerning the Rule of Law, there is here again every good reason for deepest concern. A prime example is the role of these practices and phenomena in the 2016 U.S. elections and the resulting threats to American democratic norms and polity. More fundamentally, these and related phenomena – including algorithmic processes for pre-emptively censoring what are clearly legitimate political and cultural debates – open up deeply serious challenges to the possibilities of free expression online and a possible electronic public sphere. Thereby, especially as our communication and engagement with one another are increasingly all but exclusively "digital," the core norms and processes of democratic polity as such are radically under threat (Ess 2017a)

Manifestly, a core component in these developments is precisely the complex issues surrounding trust online. As Shannon Vallor (2016:187) succinctly observes: "Today, radical changes in the economic model of the industry have led to widespread collapse of public trust in the media, and in our age of increasing information-dependence, it is difficult to overstate the global social price of this collapse."[6] As we have seen, Vallor (2010) highlights trust as a primary virtue – one that, alongside affiliated virtues such as empathy, patience, perseverance, and so on, is essential to communication per se, and thereby to especially human relationships, beginning with friendship and family that are essential to our flourishing and good lives. More recently, Vallor (2016) includes attention to the virtue of trust – one deeply threatened not only by the profit-driven media landscapes generated by especially U.S.-based companies: trust is further threatened by the rise of Big Data and the mantras of "transparency" that its proponents blandish. Vallor uses the example of a Monsanto-owned Big Data analytics firm, whose CEO endorses the new technologies as "the empowerment of more truth, and fewer things taken on faith" (Hardy 2014, cited in Vallor 2016:192).

Such defenses of the urge for transparency via technology go back much further. Vallor gives the additional example of Eric Schmidt, then CEO of Google, who defended Google glass with the argument: "If you have something that you don't want anyone to know, maybe you shouldn't be doing it in the first place" (cited in Vallor 2016:191; cf. Streitfeld 2013). Unbeknownst, to Mr. Schmidt, he was repeating the political and social views of both contemporary dictators and traditional authoritarians. In particular, in traditional societies that presume purely *relational* selves – in contrast with purely autonomous or relational-autonomous selves – individual privacy does not exist as a positive good or concept, much less as a civic right foundational for democratic societies. On the contrary, for such a purely relational self – one whose entire sense of identity, meaning, status and power in a family and larger social group completely depends on the complex web of relationships that defines these – any effort to disconnect, to turn away from those relationships can only be motivated by something suspect, if not simply wrong. As but one example, the traditional Chinese analogue to "privacy" denotes something shameful or dirty (Lü 2005; cf. Ess 2020:65–71). Total transparency, in short, is not simply the mantra of Eric Schmidt and Mark Zuckerberg: It is at the same time the mantra of traditional authoritarian regimes and, specifically, the emerging Chinese Social Credit System (Ess 2020:57f.).

Unhappily, these claims and arguments are consistent with an increasing shift in Western societies from more individual to more relational senses of selfhood, and thereby towards more relational conceptions of privacy, such as Helen Nissenbaum's account of privacy as "contextual integrity," in which "privacy" is defined not in terms of a bit of information itself, but what that information means in the context of specific relationships (Nissenbaum 2010). Along these lines, media scholars such as Patricia Lange (2007) and philosophers have developed increasingly sophisticated notions of group privacy (e.g. Taylor, Floridi and van der Sloot 2017). This is precisely why notions of *relational autonomy* are so critical as these sustain modern notions of autonomy as grounding modern concepts of privacy rights and democratic polity (Veltman and Piper 2014). Without such relational *autonomy*, it seems that a (re)turn to a purely relational self would thereby revert "privacy" to a negative rather than a positive good. Even more dire, the loss of autonomy would thereby eliminate the primary ground and justification for democratic norms, rights, and polity as such (Ess 2010a, 2014a).

For her part, Vallor is quite clear that the consequences of the drive towards total transparency are extreme, and include precisely the virtue of trust as a target:

> … one might conclude that the technologies driving this phenomenon [of a global sousveillance culture] promise only to magnify asymmetries of political and economic power; to diminish the space of moral play and authentic development; to render *trust* in human relations superfluous; to reduced embodied moral truth to decontextualized information; and to replace examined lives with datasets.
>
> *(2016:204; emphasis added)*

31.6 What Can Be Done?

31.6.1 Care-giving and the Virtue of Trust

Vallor provides two primary counter-responses to these attacks, as part of her larger program of our cultivating what she identifies as 12 "Technomoral virtues" necessary for good lives in the contemporary world. These are: honesty, self-control, humility, justice, courage, empathy, care, civility, flexibility, perspective, magnanimity and technomoral wisdom – the last of which incorporates *phronēsis* (Vallor 2016:120).

The first counter-response is in the context of *care-giving* – e.g. caring for elderly parents, in contrast with "offloading" the chores and obligations of such caring to carebots. Specifically, the reciprocity of our becoming the care-givers to those who once cared for us entails our development of trust:

> We learn in a time of need that others are there for us *now*, and just as importantly, we learn *through being there for others* to **trust** that someday someone will be there for us once again. For once I perceive that I, who am *not* a moral saint but an often selfish and profoundly imperfect creature, can reliably give care to others, then I can more easily believe and **trust** that equally imperfect humans can and will care for me when the time comes.
>
> *(2016:223; bold emphasis added)*

This development of trust, moreover, collates with the necessary cultivation of courage as a virtue likewise requisite for care-giving:

> Caring requires courage because care will likely bring *precisely* those pains and losses the carer fears most – grief, longing, anger, exhaustion. But when these pains are incorporated into lives sustained by loving and reciprocal relations of selfless service and empathic concern, our character is open to being shaped not only fear and anxiety, but also by gratitude, love, hope, **trust**, humor, compassion and mercy.
>
> *(2016:226; bold emphasis added)*

To return to our philosophical anthropology, Vallor intersects here with Løgstrup's starting point in our vulnerability as embodied and, ultimately mortal human beings. In terms that we will return to shortly, the cultivation of courage is requisite not only in the context of care-giving, but to the larger *existential* recognition of precisely our mortality:

> Caring practices also foster fuller and more honest moral perspectives on the meaning and value of life itself, perspectives that acknowledge the finitude and fragility of our existence rather than hide it.
>
> *(2016:226)*

31.6.2 Virtue Ethics and Ethics of Care in Design

More broadly, especially as we are increasingly and ever-more inextricably entangled in contemporary webs of digital communication, the preservation and fostering of trust, along with the other requisite virtues, requires nothing less than going to the heart of the technologies themselves – i.e. not simply their use, but more foundationally, their design (Vallor 2010, 2016:206f.) Happily, while she was among the first to call for this sort of turn, Vallor is by no means alone. On the contrary, recent years have witnessed a remarkable rise in the application of virtue ethics and care ethics both in philosophy of technology broadly (e.g. Puech 2016) and specifically in guiding the design and implementation of ICTs. For example, Bendert Zevenbergen and colleagues at the Oxford Internet Institute, following a two-year project of gathering the ethical insights and practical experiences of computer scientists and engineers around the world, concluded that "… virtue ethics should be applied to Internet research and *engineering* – where the technical persons must fulfill the character traits of the 'virtuous agent'" (Zevenbergen et al. 2015:31: emphasis added). Most dramatically, the IEEE (International Electrical and Electronic Engineers) is setting the standards for "ethically-aligned design" for Artificial / Independent Systems (IEEE 2019). This project draws on both Vallor's work and Sarah Spiekermann's *eudaimonic* approach to ICT design, i. e. design for human contentment and flourishing (2016), as primary sources for its ethical orientation and development. Certainly, the first edition of the IEEE guidelines incorporates diverse global ethical traditions – as it must for such globally distributed technologies. But the document centers on Aristotle's understanding of *eudaimonia* and thereby virtue ethics more broadly as the primary ground of ethically-aligned design. *Eudaimonia* is defined here as "human well-being, both at the individual and collective level, as the highest virtue for a society. Translated roughly as 'flourishing,' the benefits of eudaimonia begin with conscious contemplation, where ethical considerations help us define how we wish to live" (IEEE 2019:4).

31.6.3 (Re)Turn to the Existential – and the Enlightenment?

We began with a philosophical anthropology that emphasizes our condition *qua* embodied human beings as thereby vulnerable and dependent on others. In Karl Jasper's existential terms, as foregrounded by Amanda Lagerkvist (2019), we are thereby *thrown* into having to take up relationships of trust. More broadly, our vulnerability as ultimately mortal human beings is driving a relatively recent phenomenon in social media. The past seven years or so have witnessed a rapidly developing set of practices of grieving death and memorializing life online. Such online practices often offer striking new forms of healing and comfort: on occasion, at least, they also inspire young people to abandon social media in favor of grief – and joy – in "real life," i.e. in the offline world of embodied co-presence (Hovde, 2016).

These link with still larger developments. To begin with, in both religious and philosophical traditions – specifically those collected under the umbrella of existentialism – recognition of our mortality is an essential moment in growing up, where maturity is marked by taking responsibility for our existence, including our identity, our relationships with and responsibilities to Others, and, perhaps most significantly, our sense of meaning. Such existential themes and approaches are coming more and more to the fore in recent years (Lagerkvist 2019).

This (re)turn to the existential is likewise central to Shannon Vallor's "technosocial virtue ethics" aimed at helping us better realize lives of meaning and flourishing in the contemporary world. Specifically, Vallor invokes José Ortega y Gasset's 1939 essay, "Meditación de la Técnica," which she characterizes as an

> ... existentialist conception of human life as autofabrication: a project of self-realization, bringing into being "the aspiration we are." For Ortega y Gasset as for later existentialists, the freedom of human choice means that a human person is not a thing, natural or otherwise, but "a project as such, something which is not yet but aspires to be" ... "in the very root of his essence man finds himself called upon to be an engineer. Life means to him at once and primarily the effort to bring into existence what does not exist offhand, to wit: himself."
>
> *(Ortega y Gasset 2002:116; in Vallor 2016:246)*

Vallor further comments that

> The unresolved crisis of the 20th century, still with us in the 21st, is a crisis of meaning – the meaning of human excellence, of flourishing, of the good life ... Ortega y Gasset tells us that our humanity rests entirely upon the "to do" of projected action, and hence "the mission of technology consists in releasing man for *the task of being himself*."
>
> *(Ortega y Gasset 2002:118, in Vallor 2016:247)*

The primary problem, however, is that in the contemporary world, we do not know how to proceed with such a task. As Vallor convincingly portrays it, the contemporary world offers us an all-but-paralyzing array of choices of what to consume – amplified all the more precisely by an Internet driven primarily by commercialism and the pursuit of material profit. But we do not know "what to wish for" when it comes to being and becoming human – what Vallor characterizes as a "crisis of wishing" brought on by "a culturally-induced deficiency of practical wisdom, the absence of authentically motivating visions of the appropriate ends of a human life" (2016:248). She goes on to warn that

> If Ortega y Gasset was right, then in the absence of some deliberate intervention, contemporary technosocial life is likely to be marked by a progressive paralysis of practical wisdom, in which our expanding technical knowledge of effective means receives less and less direction by meaningful desires and moral ends.
>
> *(2016:248)*

Part and parcel of our seeking to revive and cultivate such practical wisdom, as we have seen, is to acquire and cultivate the requisite virtues – including the virtue of trust.

Additional considerations might be brought to bear here. For example, I and others have argued that it is more accurate and helpful to think about our contemporary world as post-digital, rather than digital. The post-digital does not discard the digital, but seeks to rebalance our understanding of human existence as incorporating both analogue and digital dimensions, beginning precisely with our prime status as embodied beings (Ess 2017b; cf. Lindgren 2017). Taking up the phrase post-digital thereby reinforces our philosophical anthropology and its beginnings in embodiment.

Taken together, these potential remedies to the crises of trust online begin precisely with Løgstrup's and later feminist emphases on human embodiment and its correlative vulnerability as the foundations of trust among human beings as rational-affective relational autonomies. In particular, cultivating trust among the other virtues practiced in the context of embodied care-giving not only enhances our capacity for trust: it further heightens our awareness of what trust entails, and so helps sharpen our sense and understanding of what "virtuous design" should design *for* – i.e. creating environments and affordances that avoid, e.g. the trickery of an emotive "design for trust," and instead foster honesty and clarity about the possibilities and limits of trust in such online environments, at least as between human beings engaging through these environments. Still more broadly, the affiliated themes of an existential (re)turn in media practices and media studies, coupled with an increasing recognition of our living in a post-digital era, would thereby reinforce and amplify our sense of vulnerability and dependency, and thereby the inescapable requirements of learning to cultivate trust and its affiliated virtues.

Most broadly, such a post-digital (re)turn to the existential is nothing less than to recover an especially Kantian understanding of the Enlightenment – namely, to have the (virtue of) courage to think for ourselves: *sapere aude* – have the courage to think (and act) for yourself (Kant [1784], 1991). Kant's predecessors here reach back to the beginnings of the virtue ethics traditions in Western philosophy (Antigone, Socrates, Plato and Aristotle). Successors include Nietzsche (e.g. [1882] 1974) as well as the later existentialists. In all cases, responding to this call to think for ourselves means to cultivate the virtues, beginning with the virtue of the courage needed to confront rather than deny our foremost reality as embodied and thereby mortal beings – and from there, to undertake the arduous tasks of cultivating a human(e) selfhood. To be sure, such cultivation is hard work and not always satisfying or rewarded – a fact partially grounding the ancients' insistence that such cultivation would always be restricted to the few, not the many. The Enlightenment bets, to the contrary, that the many can likewise take up this call and cultivation, precisely in order to generate the rational-affective relational autonomies that ground and legitimate democratic norms and processes (Ess 2014a).

However this bet ultimately turns out: as Vallor has made especially clear, our failure to take existential responsibility for cultivating such virtues – ultimately, for cultivating our selves – seems all but certain to condemn us to a feudal enslavement in systems and machineries designed for others pecuniary interests and power, not our own human flourishing and meaning.

Acknowledgments

I am deeply grateful to Judith Simon, Mariarosaria Taddeo and Marty Wolf for extensive criticisms and suggestions which have much improved this chapter.

Notes

1 Other (i.e. as capitalized) denotes recognition of the Other as fully equal, fully human, while simultaneously irreducibly different from us. This draws from Levinas's analysis of "the Other as Other," as a positive "alterity" (Levinas 1987; Ess 2020:74, ftn 5.)

2 This emphasis on embodied co-presence – and, as we will see, the role of *affect* in trust and human-to-human communication more broadly – immediately means that our analyses and understanding of trust entails culturally-variable dimensions. This is apparent in the fact that levels of trust vary dramatically across the globe. As measured in the World Values & European Values Surveys, trust levels in the Scandinavian countries are the highest in the world: 76% of Danes and 75.1% of Norwegians agree that "most people can be trusted," in contrast with, e.g. 35.1% for the United States (thus ranking the U.S. as 23rd in the list of nations surveyed: Robinson 2014). In terms we will take up below, we can say that trust in the Scandinavian countries is largely already "bootstrapped" or in place: the problem of bootstrapping trust in other contexts – whether online (so Carusi 2008) or offline, as in countries with lower levels of trust – is, by contrast, formidable. Attention to the culturally variable aspects of the problem of trust thus seems critical, but apart from note 6, below, here I can only point to their importance.

3 While Norbert Wiener (among others) used the term "cybernetics" to denote self-correcting systems ([1950] 1954) – he did not point out that the κυβερνήτης (*cybernetes*), a steersman or a pilot, is used in Plato as a primary exemplar of *phronēsis*, of *ethical* judgment that is capable of self-correction, i.e. of learning from mistakes: see Plato, *Republic* 360e–361a; Ess (2020:262f).

4 The phrase is intended to echo Sidney Morgenbesser's proverbial refutation of Cartesian dualism. We do not say when entering a room, "Hi, I'm here, and I've brought my body with me."

5 One of the earliest analyses of the role of gender in shaping online writing style (Herring 1996) already showed the difficulty of masking gender in (even) purely textual online writing environments. Subsequent research has reiterated both the difficulty of disguising one's gender textually – along with the importance of being honest in one's self-representation as an embodied being, precisely for the sake of establishing and building trust in online communities: see Kendall (2011), Bromseth and Sundén (2011), (Ess 2014a:204f.).

6 This is, however, a somewhat culturally variable assessment. As noted above (endnote 2), trust levels vary widely from country to country. Correlative with the highest levels of trust in the world, the Nordic models for media – with an emphasis on public media as public goods – retain much higher levels of trust than elsewhere (Robinson 2014). This is not to say that the threats to trust posed by fake news, etc., are of no concern. Because these threats directly attack institutions central to trust and democracy in these regions, they are taken very seriously indeed. It may be, then, that trust in public media may well survive these threats more robustly in Scandinavia than, say, in the U.S. where, as Vallor emphasizes, a market-oriented media model indeed seems less likely to sustain trust against such threats.

References

Baier, A. (1994) "Trust and Its Vulnerabilities," in A. Baier (ed.), *Moral Prejudices: Essays on Ethics*, Cambridge, MA: Harvard University Press.

Bakardjieva, M. and Gaden, G. (2012) "Web 2.0: Technologies of the Self," *Philosophy of Technology* 25: 399–413. doi:10.1007/s13347-13011-0032-0039

Bringsjord, S., Licato, J., Govindarajulu, N.S., Ghosh, R. and Sen, A. (2015) "Real Robots that Pass Human Tests of Self-Consciousness," in Proceedings of RO-MAN 2015, The 24th International Symposium on Robot and Human Interactive Communication, August 31–September 4, 2015, Kobe, Japan. www.kokdemir.info/courses/psk423/docs/RealRobots.pdf

Bromseth, J. and Sundén, J. (2011) "Queering Internet Studies: Intersections of Gender and Sexuality," in M. Consalvo and C. Ess (eds.), *The Blackwell Handbook of Internet Studies*, Oxford: Wiley-Blackwell.

Cantwell Smith, B. (2019) *The Promise of AI: Reckoning and Judgment* Cambridge, MA: MIT Press.

Carusi, A. (2008) "Scientific Visualisations and Aesthetic Grounds for Trust," *Ethics and Information Technology* 10: 243–254.

Clark, D. (2014) "The Role of Trust in Cyberspace," in R. Harper (ed.), *The Complexity of Trust, Computing, and Society*, Cambridge: Cambridge University Press.

Eisenstein, E.L. (1983) *The Printing Revolution in Early Modern Europe*, Cambridge: Cambridge University Press.
Ess, C. (2010a) "The Embodied Self in a Digital Age: Possibilities, Risks, and Prospects for a Pluralistic (democratic/liberal) Future?" *Nordicom Information* 32(2): 105–118.
Ess, C. (2010b) "Trust and New Communication Technologies: Vicious Circles, Virtuous Circles, Possible Futures," *Knowledge, Technology, and Policy* 23: 287–305. doi:10.1007/s12130-12010-9114-9118
Ess, C. (2014a) "Selfhood, Moral Agency, and the Good Life in Mediatized Worlds? Perspectives from Medium Theory and Philosophy," in K. Lundby (ed.), *Mediatization of Communication*, Handbooks of Communication Science, vol. 21, Berlin: De Gruyter Mouton.
Ess, C. (2014b) "Trust, Social Identity, and Computation," in R. Harper (ed.), *The Complexity of Trust, Computing, and Society*, Cambridge: Cambridge University Press.
Ess, C. (2016) "'What's Love Got to Do with It?' Robots, Sexuality, and the Arts of Being Human," in M. Nørskov (ed.), *Social Robots: Boundaries, Potential, Challenges*, Farnham: Ashgate.
Ess, C. (2017a) "God Out of the Machine?" in A. Beavers (ed.), *Macmillan Interdisciplinary Handbooks: Philosophy (MIHP)* 10, New York: Macmillan.
Ess, C. (2017b) "Digital Media Ethics," in D. Cloud (ed.), *Oxford Encyclopedia of Communication and Critical Studies*. doi:10.1093/acrefore/9780190228613.013.50
Ess, C. (2019) "Ethics and Mediatization: Subjectivity, Judgment (phronēsis) and Meta-Theoretical Coherence?" in T. Eberwein, M. Karmasin, F. Krotz and M. Rath (eds.), *Responsibility and Resistance: Ethics in Mediatized Worlds*, Berlin: Springer. doi:10.1007/978-3-658-26212-9_5
Ess, C. (2020) *Digital Media Ethics*, 3rd edition, Cambridge: Polity.
Ess, C. and Thorseth, M. (2011) "Introduction," in C. Ess and M. Thorseth (eds.), *Trust and Virtual Worlds: Contemporary Perspectives*, New York: Peter Lang.
Foucault, M. (1988) "Technologies of the Self," in L.H. Martin, H. Gutman and P. Hutton (eds.), *Technologies of the Self: A Seminar with Michel Foucault*, Amherst: University of Massachusetts Press.
Gerdes, A. (2014) "Ethical Issues Concerning Lethal Autonomous Robots in Warfare," in J. Seibt, R. Hakli and M. Nørskov (eds.), *Sociable Robots and the Future of Social Relations: Proceedings of Robo-Philosophy 2014*, Berlin: IOS Press.
Hardy, Q. (2014) "How Urban Anonymity Disappears When All Data is Tracked," *New York Times*, Bits, April 19. http://bits.blogs.nytimes.com/2014/04/19/how-urban-anonymity-disappears-when-all-data-is-tracked/?_php=true&_type=blogs&_r=0
Herring, S. (1996) "Posting in a Different Voice: Gender and Ethics in Computer-Mediated Communication," in C. Ess (ed.), *Philosophical Perspectives on Computer-Mediated Communication*, Albany, NY: SUNY Press.
Hildebrandt, M. (2016) *Smart Technologies and the End(s) of Law: Novel Entanglements of Law and Technology*, Cheltenham: Edward Elgar.
Hovde, A.L.L. (2016) "Grief 2.0: Grieving in an Online World." MA thesis, Department of Media and Communication, University of Oslo. www.duo.uio.no/bitstream/handle/10852/52544/Hovde-Master-2016.pdf?sequence=5&isallowed=y
IEEE (2019) "The IEEE Global Initiative on Ethics of Autonomous and Intelligent Systems. Ethically Aligned Design: A Vision for Prioritizing Human Well-being with Autonomous and Intelligent Systems, First Edition." https://standards.ieee.org/content/ieee-standards/en/industry-connections/ec/autonomous-systems.html
Kant, I. ([1785] 1959) *Foundations of the Metaphysics of Morals*, L.W. Beck (trans.), Indianapolis, IN: Bobbs-Merrill.
Kant, I. ([1784] 1991) "An Answer to the Question: 'What is Enlightenment?,'" H.B. Nisbet (trans.), in H. Reiss (ed.), *Kant: Political Writings*, Cambridge: Cambridge University Press.
Kendall, L. (2011) "Community and the Internet," in M. Consalvo and C. Ess (eds.), *The Blackwell Handbook of Internet Studies*, Oxford: Wiley-Blackwell.
Keymolen, E. (2016) *Trust on the Line: A Philosophical Exploration of Trust in the Networked Era*, Oisterwijk, the Netherlands: Wolf Legal Publishers.
Lagerkvist, A. (2019) "Digital Existence: An Introduction," in A. Lagerkvist (ed.), *Digital Existence: Ontology, Ethics and Transcendence in Digital Culture*, London: Routledge.
Lange, P.G. (2007) "Publicly Private and Privately Public: Social Networking on YouTube," *Journal of Computer-Mediated Communication* 13(1). https://doi.org/10.1111/j.1083-6101.2007.00400.x

Levinas, E. (1987) *Time and the Other and Additional Essays*, R.A.Cohen (trans.), Pittsburgh, PA: Duquesne University Press.
Lindgren, S. (2017) *Digital Media and Society: Theories, Topics and Tools*, London: Sage.
Løgstrup, K.E. ([1956] 1971) *The Ethical Demand*, Philadelphia, PA: Fortress Press. [Originally published as *Den Etiske Fordring*, Copenhagen: Gyldendal.]
Lü, Y.H. (2005) "Privacy and Data Privacy Issues in Contemporary China," *Ethics and Information Technology* 7(1):7–15.
McCarthy, T. (1978) *The Critical Theory of Jürgen Habermas*, Cambridge, MA: MIT Press.
Mittelstadt, B.D., Allo, P., Taddeo, M., Wachter, S. and Floridi, L. (2016) "The Ethics of Algorithms: Mapping the Debate," *Big Data & Society* 3(2). https://doi.org/10.1177/2053951716679679
Myskja, B. (2008) "The Categorical Imperative and the Ethics of Trust," *Ethics and Information Technology* 10: 213–220.
Nietzsche, F. ([1882] 1974) *The Gay Science: With a Prelude in Rhymes and an Appendix of Songs*, W. Kaufmann (trans.), New York: Vintage Books.
Nissenbaum, H. (2010) *Privacy in Context: Technology, Policy, and the Integrity of Social Life*, Stanford, CA: Stanford Law Books.
Ong, W. (1988) *Orality and Literacy: The Technologizing of the Word*, London: Routledge.
Ortega y Gasset, J. ([1939] 2002) *Toward a Philosophy of History*, H. Weyl (trans.), Urbana and Chicago: University of Illinois Press.
Puech, M. (2016) *The Ethics of Ordinary Technology*, New York: Routledge.
Robinson, J. (2014) "Statistical Appendix," in T. Syvertsen, G. Enli, O.J. Mjøs and H. Moe (eds.), *The Media Welfare State: Nordic Media in the Digital Era*, Ann Arbor, MI: University of Michigan Press. doi:10.3998/nmw.12367206.0001.001
Searle, J. (2014) "What Your Computer Can't Know," *New York Review of Books*, www.nybooks.com/articles/archives/2014/oct/09/what-yourcomputer-cant-know/
Spiekermann, S. (2016) *Ethical IT Innovation: A Value-Based System Design Approach*, New York: Taylor & Francis.
Stothard, M. (2017) "Le Pen's Online Army Leads Far-Right Fight for French Presidency: Social Media Unit and Shadowy Networks Use Shock Tactics to Push National Front Agenda," *Financial Times*, February 26. www.ft.com/content/b65f.9a50-f8d2-11e6-9516-2d969e0d3b65
Streitfeld, D. (2013) "Google Glass Picks Up Early Signal: Keep Out," *New York Times*, May 6. www.nytimes.com/2013/05/07/technology/personaltech/google-glass-picks-up-early-signal-keep-out.html?nl=todaysheadlines&emc=edit_th_20130507&_r=2&
Sullins, J. (2012) "Robots, Love, and Sex: The Ethics of Building a Love Machine," *IEEE Transactions on Affective Computing* 3(4): 398–409.
Sullins, J. (2014) "Machine Morality Operationalized," in J. Seibt, R. Hakli and M. Nørskov (eds), *Sociable Robots and the Future of Social Relations: Proceedings of Robo-Philosophy 2014*, Berlin: IOS Press.
Taddeo, M. (2009) "Defining Trust and E-trust: Old Theories and New Problems," *International Journal of Technology and Human Interaction* 5(2): 23–35.
Taddeo, M. (2010) "Modelling Trust in Artificial Agents: A First Step toward the Analysis of e-Trust," *Minds and Machines* 20(2): 243–257.
Tam, P.W. (2017) "Daily Report: The Continued Creation and Dissemination of Fake News," *New York Times*, Bits, January 19. www.nytimes.com/2017/01/19/technology/daily-report-the-continued-creation-and-dissemination-of-fake-news.html?_r=0
Taylor, L., Floridi, L. and van der Sloot, B. (eds.) (2017) *Group Privacy: New Challenges of Data Technologies*, Dordrecht: Springer.
Vallor, S. (2010) "Social Networking Technology and the Virtues," *Ethics and Information Technology* 12: 157–170. doi:10.1007/s10676-10009-9202-9201
Vallor, S. (2016) *Technology and the Virtues: A Philosophical Guide to a Future Worth Wanting*, Oxford: Oxford University Press.
Veltman, A. and Piper, M. (eds.) (2014) *Autonomy, Oppression and Gender*, Oxford: Oxford University Press.
Weckert, J. (2005) "Trust in Cyberspace," in R. Cavalier (ed.), *The Impact of the Internet on Our Moral Lives*, Albany: State University of New York Press.
Weckert, J. (2011) "Trusting Software Agents," in C. Ess and M. Thorseth (eds.), *Trust and Virtual Worlds: Contemporary Perspectives*, New York: Peter Lang.

Weizenbaum, J. (1976) *Computer Power and Human Reason: From Judgment to Calculation*, New York: W.H. Freeman.

Wiener, N. ([1950] 1954) *The Human Use of Human Beings: Cybernetics and Society*, Garden City, NY: Doubleday Anchor.

Zevenbergen, B., Mittelstadt, B., Véliz, C., Detweiler, C., Cath, C., Savulescu, J. and Whittaker, M. (2015) *Philosophy Meets Internet Engineering: Ethics in Networked Systems Research* (GTC workshop outcomes paper), Oxford: Oxford Internet Institute.

INDEX

Note: Since the major subject of this title is trust, entries under this heading have been kept to a minimum, and readers are advised to seek more specific references.
Page numbers in italic type refer to Figures; those in bold type refer to Tables.

Made in the USA
Monee, IL
13 September 2026

62977686R10249